DETROIT PUBLIC LIBRARY
3 5674 00182066 2
D1161611
HUBBARD BRANCH LIBRARY
12929 W. McNICHOLS
DETROIT, MI 48235
313-481-1752

DETROIT
PUBLIC
LIBRARY

MICHIGAN IN FOUR CENTURIES

MICHIGAN

IN FOUR CENTURIES

BY F. CLEVER BALD

LINE DRAWINGS BY WILLIAM THOMAS WOODWARD

REVISED AND ENLARGED EDITION

HARPER & BROTHERS, PUBLISHERS
NEW YORK

L-L

LIBRARY OF CONGRESS CATALOG CARD NUMBER: 61-17179

CONTENTS

PART IV

EXPLOITING NATURAL RESOURCES 1837–1860

PART V

BEGINNINGS OF INDUSTRIAL DEVELOPMENT 1860–1890

PART VI

CHALLENGE TO DEMOCRACY 1890–1920

PART VII

ECONOMIC ACHIEVEMENT AND SOCIAL PROGRESS 1920–1950

List of Illustrations

List of Maps

FOREWORD

Michigan In Four Centuries is a legacy of Dr. John M. Munson to the people of Michigan. Dr. Munson was proud of the history of Michigan. He often deplored the neglect of state history in the teaching programs of Michigan schools. It was no surprise to those who knew him best, therefore, that he left the residue of his estate to be expended under the direction of the Michigan Historical Commission in having written and published a history of the state, and a history of education in Michigan.

Dr. Munson devoted his life to public education in Michigan. His life history is an inspiring one. It is the history of the son of a poor Swedish immigrant, who, by sheer determination, hard work, and a compelling love of learning, advanced from lowly beginnings to high positions in public education. Dr. Munson began his educational career in the rural schools of Menominee County, went on to the Deputy State Superintendency of Public Instruction, and ended with the Presidency of Michigan State Normal College.

Michigan In Four Centuries is the first result of Dr. Munson's bequest. It is directed to the adult as well as to the youthful resident of the state. In a state which has so large a proportion of residents who were born elsewhere, such a general history as this is an essential for good citizenship.

The responsibility offered it by Dr. Munson was accepted by the Michigan Historical Commission with the determination to produce as sound a history of Michigan as possible. The members of the Commission have given much time and thought to the publication of a history which would be as sound, complete, and unbiased as human nature will permit. They selected the author with care and gave him a free hand to write.

In Dr. F. Clever Bald, the Historical Commission has as the author a fully competent historian. He is a member of the faculty of the Department of History at the University of Michigan. Dr. Bald has spent, as the preface indicates, over 21 years in the study of the history of this state. MICHIGAN IN FOUR CENTURIES is Dr. Bald's book—it is his judgments or conclusions that are expressed, not necessarily those of the members of the Commission.

The Michigan Historical Commission presents MICHIGAN IN FOUR CENTURIES to the public with the expectation that it will fulfill Dr. Munson's intent that a knowledge of this State's history be increased, and in the hope that, through that knowledge, all of us will become better citizens.

PRENTISS M. BROWN
President
Michigan Historical Commission

June 1, 1954

PREFACE

Michigan has had a long and colorful history. During more than three centuries it has been inhabited by men and women from beyond the seas. All of them brought something of their cultures to furnish their new home.

Before history began to be recorded, Indians lived in the deep forests, and navigated streams and lakes. They, too, contributed much to the way of life in the land now known as Michigan. The explorer, the missionary, and the fur hunter would have made slow progress without canoes, and the first settlers might have starved if they had not learned how to grow Indian corn.

Complacent Indians, restless Frenchmen, conservative Britons, and ambitious Americans—all had a share in the beginnings of Michigan. Then came new peoples: Germans, Irish, Dutch, Finns, and Scandinavians. Mines, forests, and fields absorbed their strength, and they laid firm foundations for the future.

Later, other nationalities settled in the state: Italians, Poles, Greeks, Hungarians, and others. Most of them became city dwellers, seeking employment in the fast growing industries. All brought new customs which became to some extent threads in the culture pattern of the state. These peoples did not remain foreigners. By the transmutation characteristic of the New World, they became Americans and Michiganians, if not in the first generation, then in the second through the medium of the public schools.

Michigan today is a composite formed of innumerable elements. Blessed by nature with rich and varied resources, it has been developed by people with courage, ambition, and skill. If the early exploitation of resources was wasteful, in recent years the state legislature has provided agencies to protect the interests of present and future residents. If in "the good old days" widows, orphans, the unemployed, the crippled, and the blind were considered subjects for private charity, today both the state and the nation treat them as members of the community entitled to assistance for the general welfare.

The history of Michigan is a record of the way of life of its people. It is a story of men and women striving for better things for themselves and their children, of sacrifice in the present for benefits in the future, of steady faith and splendid achievement. Failures there were, of course, crimes public and private were committed; and villains have ever been present; but successful labors, devoted public service, and honorable men and women have always predominated.

It is hoped that this book will provide both information and inspiration for those who read it. True patriotism is based on knowledge and understanding rather than on ignorant prejudice. By learning how far we have come during preceding centuries, we should be able better to chart our course for the future. Recognition of past mistakes ought to help us avoid making the same ones a second or a third time. Acquaintance with great men and women who have gone before should instill pride in our hearts and determination to accomplish something worth while.

The arrangement of materials in the book is fundamentally chronological. As far as space would permit, some background of significant national and world events has been included in order to place the history of Michigan in its proper setting.

This book is the result of many years of research. Twenty-one years ago I began the systematic study of Michigan history under Dr. Milo M. Quaife, dean of historians of Michigan and the Old Northwest. At that time he was secretary and editor of the Burton Historical Collection, Detroit Public Library, and lecturer in history at Wayne University. Ever since, he has been my mentor and good friend.

For immediate assistance in writing this book, I owe gratitude to many persons. To Mrs. Elleine H. Stones, chief of the Burton Historical Collection and members of her staff, who have been ungrudging of their time; to Miss Louise Rau, former curator of manuscripts in the Burton Collection, for reading my manuscript and making helpful suggestions; to Miss Marcillene Barnes, director of curriculum, Grand Rapids Schools, for aid in adjusting the vocabulary to the high school level; to Professor James B. Griffin, director of the University of Michigan Museum of Archaeology, for comments on the first two chapters; to Professor Claude W. Hibbard, curator of the Museum of Paleontology, for information about prehistoric Michigan; to Mrs. Carroll Paul, curator of the Marquette County Historical Society Museum and her assistant Miss Ruth C. Schoonover, for information about the Upper Peninsula; to Alexis A. Praus, director of the Kalamazoo Museum and Dr. Edward Palmer, pastor of the People's Church, for information about the Reverend Caroline Bartlett Crane; to W. F. Foshag of the Smithsonian Institution for accurate details about the Ontonagon Boulder; to the late Ernest Chapelle, superintendent of Ypsilanti schools, for arranging to have a chapter of the manuscript read by classes in the schools and to Miss Bernice Davis, who conducted the experiment; to Karl Karsian of the Ann Arbor High School faculty, who also tested a chapter in his classes; to Roy Overpack of Manistee for a detailed description of the "big wheels"; to William T. Woodward, artist, for his cheerful co-operation in turning my ideas into lively drawings; to Philip P. Mason, records administrator of the Historical Commission, for gathering and arranging photographs for the half-tone illustrations; to the administrative officers of the University of Michigan for giving me leave of absence on two occasions so that I might work on the book; to the Houghton Mifflin Company for permission to quote from *The Private Papers of Senator Vandenberg* (Boston, 1952) by Arthur H. Vandenberg, Jr.; to William V. O'Connor for permission to quote from *The Banking Crisis and Recovery Under the Roosevelt Administration* (Chicago, 1938); and to all the members of the Michigan Historical Collections staff for assistance in research and for their interest in my work.

I take this opportunity to thank all the members of the Michigan Historical Commission for their fine co-operation. Whenever I called upon them, they were always ready with helpful advice and assistance. Above all, I am grateful that they gave me a free hand to write as I pleased. I, alone, am responsible for the interpretations implied or expressed in the text.

This book could not have been written without the devoted services of my wife, Laura McGrath Bald, who did not live to see it in print. During two years and a half she typed and retyped the manuscript, made helpful suggestions as to form and content, and cheerfully assumed many extra duties so that I might have more time for research and writing.

F. C. B.

PART I

IN THE BEGINNING
Prehistoric Michigan

— 1 —

When Elephants Walked in Michigan

If you had lived in Michigan eight or ten thousand years ago, you would very likely have seen mammoths in the upland regions. In the lower-lying land, you certainly would have seen mastodons, which looked much like mammoths and were more numerous. Perhaps you would have gone hunting for these animals or for the musk ox, giant beavers, and big wild hogs. You might even have seen a whale or two if you had happened to be at the right place. It is not likely that anyone actually saw these creatures, for, as far as we know, they existed before man came to Michigan; but they were really here, because fossil remains of all of them have been unearthed within the area of the state.

Although ten thousand years seem like a long time, they are really only a few seconds by geological reckoning. The record of the rocks, the means by which geologists discover the facts about prehistoric times, shows that Michigan has been two billion years in the making.

During that period the surface was frequently changed. Sometimes the land was nearly covered with water. Vast beds of salt were deposited in places to a thickness of a thousand feet. Billions of minute coral animals and small shellfish provided material for limestone. Sand and clay produced by erosion of the rocks settled in the deep water and became sandstone and shale. For a long period of years tropical forests grew luxuriantly in warm, shallow seas of fresh water. Reptiles and amphibians crawled on the shores, and huge scorpions and dragonflies flitted about under the fronds of giant fern trees. The

Michigan coal beds were formed from the remains of these tropical forests covered deep with mud. Iron minerals also accumulated in the shallow sea of the Upper Peninsula, forming through northern Michigan, Wisconsin, and Minnesota the richest iron deposits in the world.

Upheavals from inside the earth have caused great changes in the surface of Michigan. Millions of years ago hot, molten rock forced up by internal pressure formed high, rugged mountains. Worn down by erosion, only bare, rounded granite knobs of these mountains now remain in the Porcupines of Ontonagon County. They were long considered the highest spot in Michigan, but a recent survey shows that the highest is actually a 1,980 foot elevation in Baraga County. Volcanic eruptions poured lava over the western part of the Upper Peninsula. Later, into cracks, crevices, and gas blisters of the lava, pure copper was deposited, providing one of Michigan's most valuable natural resources.

The record of the rocks shows that plant and animal life increased in number and variety. After animals developed shells or bones, the remains of some of them were preserved in mud or sand that turned to stone. Today fossils of prehistoric plants and animals, or at least impressions of their shapes, are found in quarries and gravel pits. Plant and animal life gradually evolved from the original single-celled creatures into complex organisms—trees, fish, birds, and mammals.

More than a million years ago many species of dinosaurs roamed over North America. They were probably numerous in Michigan, but no remains of them or of other animals common at the time have been uncovered within the state. The reason must be that they were destroyed by the great glaciers which advanced and retreated over the land during a period of about a million years.

2

A marked change in climate from temperate to frigid caused a massive ice cap to be formed in the north. After sufficient ice had accumulated, it began moving south. Slowly but relentlessly it crept along, destroying or driving before it all life in its path. Great forests were uprooted, and the trees were crushed to pulp. Animals retreated before the advancing ice mountain. Breaking chunks off bare rocks, gathering stones and boulders, using them as tools for grinding rocky surfaces and gouging out sand and earth, the glaciers continued southward to the line of the Ohio and the Missouri rivers.

Then came another change in climate. Continuous warm weather melted the ice, and the glaciers gradually retired. Plants and fish and animals moved north in the wake of the vanishing ice, until another frigid period caused a southern movement of the ice mountains again.

Four times the glaciers advanced, and four times they retreated during the span of about a million years. The fourth glacier crunched along like a giant bulldozer, in some places covering Michigan with ice, rocks, pebbles, earth, and sand to a depth of two or three miles. Each of the previous glaciers had changed the face of Michigan, and this one changed it again. When its forward movement ceased, and warmer weather forced it to retire, about twelve thousand years ago, it melted back gradually, leaving behind huge heaps of rock debris—boulders, gravel, sand, and earth. In some places this glacial deposit is a thousand feet deep. The numerous accumulations of gravel—one of Michigan's important natural resources—are a gift of the glaciers.

The bare rocks in the western part of the Upper Peninsula were broken, scoured, and smoothed by the gigantic glacial tools that passed over and around them. Large pieces which were split off were rolled and rounded into boulders which may still be seen in southern Michigan fields.

The rolling countryside which is characteristic of most of the state was sculptured by the glaciers. Rock debris and earth from many regions far to the north were deposited over the face of the state, giving Michigan a great variety of soils. These are important for agriculture, making possible a diversity of crops.

Another service performed by the retreating glacier was the formation of the Great Lakes—the largest bodies of fresh water in the world. For Michigan they are invaluable. They temper the winds that blow over them, giving Michigan a climate more moderate than that of other states in the same latitude; they provide broad highways for ships carrying cargoes to and from the ports of the state; and they support a valuable fishing industry. The thousands of beautiful inland lakes are also the gift of the glacier. Lakes great and small attract thousands of tourists to Michigan every year.

In its retreat the glacier determined the flow of creeks and rivers. Through the Lower Peninsula it made a low divide extending in a general north and south direction. As a result, the streams flow either into Lake Michigan or Lake Huron. Sometimes there is only a short distance between the sources of rivers flowing in opposite directions. This condition made it easy for the Indians, the early explorers, and the fur traders to reach the interior of the land and made possible, with short portages, the crossing of the state in canoes. The arrangement of the streams also aided the early farmers, for small steamers could ascend some of the rivers for many miles, carrying merchandise up and farm produce down.

The lumber industry, too, profited greatly by the pattern of the rivers. Logs were floated many miles to sawmill towns near the mouth of streams—Menominee, Manistique, Saginaw, Alpena, Muskegon, Manistee, and others. There lumber from the mills was loaded on ships and carried cheaply to Milwaukee, Chicago, Detroit, Cleveland, and Buffalo. Today the streams are smaller than they once were, and they carry no logs, but they are used for fishing and for other recreational purposes. Surely the glaciers performed invaluable services in providing the Great Lakes and in molding the surface of Michigan in so favorable a fashion.

3

When the last glacier retreated, there were no human beings to appreciate the work that it had done. Man did not come into Michigan for several thousand years. Meanwhile, plants, fish, and animals gradually moved in behind the withdrawing ice. Mammoths, mastodons, giant beavers, caribou, musk oxen, and big wild hogs roamed over the countryside eight or ten thousand years ago. All of them are now extinct. They are known only by the fossilized skeletons which are found from time to time under the ground.

The mammoth was a kind of elephant. Its body was covered with long, coarse hair. The ivory tusks had an outward and upward sweep different from those of the elephant, and it was somewhat larger than the elephants in today's circuses and zoos. Because mammoths lived in the uplands, few of their remains have been found. When they died their skeletons were destroyed by action of the weather.

Fossilized remains of mastodons are much more numerous, for they lived in the lowlands, and when they died their skeletons were preserved in beds of marl and peat in swamps or shallow lakes. About one hundred and fifty whole or partial fossilized skeletons of mastodons have been found in Michigan, most of them in the southern half of the Lower Peninsula. Mastodons resembled the elephant and the mammoth. Like the latter, they were covered with coarse hair. Their tusks, however, curved upward only slightly, and their teeth were quite different from those of the mammoth. It is possible that both the mammoth and the mastodon lived in Michigan until the advent of man, about 6000 B.C.; but no human remains have ever been discovered with the fossils of these extinct mammals in Michigan.

The strangest fossils found in Michigan are well-preserved parts of the skeletons of three whales. One of them was dug up near Tecumseh, another near Flint, and the third near Oscoda. How ocean-going whales reached Michigan, no one knows. It is probable, however, that the first two swam up the Mississippi River into Lake Chicago, which was much larger than Lake Michigan, through the Grand River into Lake Saginaw and Lake Whittlesey. These prehistoric lakes have now vanished, and the fossilized bones of the whales were found buried in the sand of Lake Whittlesey's beach.

The third whale, whose bones were found near Oscoda, could have swum up the Saint Lawrence River and the Ottawa River into prehistoric Lake Nipissing; for the remains were discovered in the sand on the shore of that vanished lake. The three of them apparently became stranded in shallow waters, died, were covered with sand, and their bones were fossilized.

Other animals, ancestors of those which exist wild in Michigan today, gradually appeared on the scene; and they have remained as residents of the state. After plants, fish, and animals became abundant, there were means of subsistence for man. When he first came into Michigan is not known exactly, but it may have been as long ago as 6000 B.C.

2

The First People

THE FIRST PEOPLE of Michigan were Indians. No one can say exactly when they arrived, but they had been occupying the land for several thousand years before the coming of the white man. Tribes drifted into Michigan and out again, sometimes in search of better hunting grounds and sometimes fleeing from enemies who were stronger than they. Considerable evidence has been found of these early inhabitants, especially the copper miners of the Upper Peninsula, the designers of the garden beds in the southwestern counties, and the late agricultural prehistoric Indians of the Lower Peninsula.

During the historic period the principal tribes in Michigan were the Chippewa, the Ottawa, the Potawatomi, the Miami, the Menominee, and the Wyandots. The last belonged to the Iroquoian language group, but all the others were Algonquian. The Chippewa, Ottawa, and Potawatomi were closely related; perhaps in very early times they had been a single tribe. Recognizing this relationship, they called themselves the Three Fires, and the Chippewa were known as the Elder Brothers.

Because the tribes changed their positions from time to time and because no definite boundary lines were marked off, it is possible to give only the approximate region occupied by each. The Wyandots, or Hurons, who were few in number, lived near Georgian Bay and Lake Simcoe until they were driven away by the Iroquois. For a time they lived near the western end of Lake Superior; then they moved to St.

Ignace, and later to the region of the Detroit River. The Chippewa, also known as Ojibwa, occupied most of the Upper Peninsula. As neighbors they had the Menominee, whose hunting grounds extended across the Menominee River and into Wisconsin.

The home of the Ottawa was the upper two thirds of the Lower Peninsula. The Miami for many years lived in the southwestern part of Michigan, especially along the St. Joseph River. Gradually the Potawatomi pushed most of them out of this region, and they moved down into Indiana, the Potawatomi becoming the dominant tribe in the south from Lake Michigan to Detroit.

There were differences among these tribes in language and in certain customs. For example, the Algonquian group usually lived in wigwams, low dome-shaped huts made of saplings bent over and covered with bark or with mats woven from reeds. But the Wyandots, like the Iroquois to whom they were related, built for themselves long houses sometimes more than one hundred feet in length. Constructed of two rows of heavy poles set in the ground, bent over and tied at the top, the houses had a rounded roof and were completely covered with elm, spruce, or cedar bark except for an opening about two feet wide along the center of the roof, extending from one end to the other. The long house was usually about twenty-four feet wide and twenty feet high.

Inside, the building was divided into compartments with a middle passage running from the front to the rear. A family occupied a compartment on each side of the passage, and a fire was built in the center, on which the two opposite families cooked their meals or warmed themselves in the winter. The smoke was supposed to find its way out through the opening in the roof, but much of it remained inside, to the great discomfort of the tenants. A raised platform in each compartment served as the family bed.

There were, of course, other differences besides housing among the customs of the various tribes; but there were so many similarities that it is possible to deal with all of them in general.

2

Wampum and the calumet were important to all the Indian tribes in the making of treaties and other solemn agreements. Belts or strings of wampum made of beads strung on deerskin thongs took the place of written documents. The pattern of white and black beads in the belt spelled out a story that was perfectly understood by the Indians. If ambassadors from one tribe brought to another a belt into which the crude figures of two men clasping hands had been woven, everyone recognized it as a symbol of peace.

Two black lines running lengthwise of the belt signified an open trail. They meant that neither tribe, agreeing to receive such a belt, would put any obstacles in the way to hinder travel and trade between them. When one tribe wanted another to join it in a war against its enemies, it sent a belt painted red.

Indians Smoking the Calumet

When a wampum belt was brought to a village, a council of the chiefs and the principal men of the tribe was held. If they decided to accept the proposal of the visitors, they invited them to the council house; the red stone calumet with its symbolically decorated pipe stem was brought in, filled with tobacco, and lighted. Then it was passed from hand to hand, each man smoking briefly in silence. The promise to observe faithfully the terms of the treaty was pledged in the smoke of the sacred calumet. Both the pipe and the belt were carefully preserved by a trusted member of the tribe.

Government of villages or tribes was under the direction of chiefs who were chosen by a sort of election. They owed their position to their intelligence and ability rather than to their relationship to a former chief. Because the Indians disliked being ruled, the chiefs often had little power; but if they looked to the old men of the tribe for advice, and if they used their authority wisely, they might have great influence.

Other chiefs were the leaders in war. They were chosen because of their experience and success in battle. No one was compelled to follow them when they called upon the young men to go to war against the enemy, but the braves went gladly if they trusted the chief.

Indian warfare usually consisted of quick, stealthy expeditions. The purpose might be to drive invaders from their own hunting grounds, or to avenge the death of members of their tribe. An attempt was always made to surprise the foe, capture and kill as many as possible, take some scalps for trophies, and retire quickly to their own villages. After a successful raid, the victors were welcomed home by a great celebration. Young men who had taken scalps were proclaimed seasoned warriors, and many of the prisoners were tortured to death. The Indians were not cannibals in the sense that they ate human flesh for food. They did, however, practice a sort of ceremonial cannibalism, eating the heart or other parts of a brave enemy killed in battle or after torture. By this means they hoped to acquire some of his warlike spirit.

Sometimes prisoners were adopted into families which had lost their own children, and they were treated with the greatest kindness, for the Indians were not always cruel. Their actions, however, were largely unpredictable. At the last minute a prisoner might escape death simply because an influential Indian changed his mind. Some prisoners were kept as slaves.

If a raiding party found itself outnumbered and threatened with defeat, the warriors took to their heels and retired as rapidly as possible. They were not charged with cowardice, for the Indians believed that it was foolish to fight against overwhelming odds. To their way of thinking it was much more sensible to run away and try again when conditions were favorable. Indians were brave enough according to their own code, for they frequently ran great risks to bring away with them their wounded comrades or even the bodies of the dead.

Indians going on a hostile raid wore as little clothing as possible, but their faces and their whole bodies were smeared with paint. The juices of plants or colored clays mixed with bear's grease were used to cover them from head to foot with fantastic designs which were supposed to frighten the enemy. Frequently the eyes were circled with bands of white clay, and each cheek was painted with stripes of various colors—red, yellow, green, and blue.

In summer, when they were in their villages or hunting game, the Indian men wore only moccasins and breechcloth. On special occasions or when it was cold, they wore deerskin leggings reaching to the hips, and an animal skin for a coat. Their blankets were the skins of bears or of smaller animals sewed together. The men pierced their ears and noses so that bits of shell or beads could be suspended from them as ornaments, and a band around the head held two or three feathers upright at the back.

Michigan Indians in the early days never wore the tall feather bonnets seen in the movies and at northern Michigan summer resorts. Those were the ceremonial headdress of the Sioux and other plains tribes. Because the Indians in the moving pictures wear such bonnets, the idea has become prevalent that all Indians wore them. Tourists probably would be disappointed if they saw only two or three feathers, and Michigan Indians today go to the movies and imitate the styles they see on the screen just as their white brothers and sisters do.

3

Indian women wore a loose-fitting waist and a skirt reaching to the knees. Both were made of soft deerskin, fringed and painted to make them attractive. Like the men, they frequently wore leggings, and their moccasins were embroidered with brightly dyed porcupine quills. Necklaces and earbobs of beads or shells, and amulets of copper, were the jewelry of the first women of Michigan.

The women were the homemakers. They were the tenders of the fires, and wherever the fires were, inside the smoky wigwam or under the open sky, each one was the family center. Here the mother prepared *sagamité*—cornmeal mixed with bits of meat or fish, cooked in an earthen pot—the principal food of Michigan Indians. Here the children gathered for their meals, and here the father brought game which he had killed in the forest and fish which he had caught in his net. Nearby, swinging gently in the breeze, a papoose strapped to his *tickenagun* suspended from a low-hanging branch watched with round, black eyes his mother's various activities.

Seamstress, potter, cook, weaver, tanner, moccasin maker, miller, gardener—these were some of the roles of the women. They tanned the skins of animals, cut and sewed them into garments, made clay pots for cooking, pounded corn in a hollow stump with a post for a pestle until it was crushed into meal. The women also tilled the soil and harvested the crops.

All the Indians in Michigan depended to a great extent on fruit and vegetables for their food. In the woods they found blueberries, strawberries, raspberries, blackberries, grapes, acorns, and a variety of nuts. In the Upper Peninsula the Menominee and the Chippewa harvested the wild rice which grew abundantly along the streams.

But the Indians did not depend entirely on nature's bounty. All of them were farmers, to some extent at least, cultivating corn, beans, squash, and tobacco. Each family had a plot large enough for its needs, assigned by the chief or occupied by common consent, for the Indians had no idea of private property in land. To them it was a good thing to be used, not a tract to be fenced in and posted with no-trespassing signs. There was enough for all, and when the soil was worn out, they moved their village to a more fertile place.

Corn requires a great deal of sunshine. To prepare a patch of woodland for planting, the Indians simply cut a ring of bark from each tree, so that it would die—a much easier task than felling the great oaks with stone implements. Then the women with their wooden hoes scraped the earth into hills about four feet apart, and into each hill they put a few grains of corn.

Green corn was roasted in hot ashes, and the kernels of ripe corn were pounded into meal. Some of the ears were hung in the wigwams where they were convenient for use, but the bulk of the crop was stored in bark-lined pits dug in the ground. There it was safe during the winter when the villagers went away for the great hunt.

4

In the fall of each year the Indians left their villages near the corn fields and set up winter camps for hunting. Only the old men and women remained at home. Although hunting was a man's work, the women were needed as cooks, and the children could help around the camp. Besides, they could learn by example the things they would have to know when they had grown up. Some of the older boys were permitted to accompany the men on their shorter trips into the woods. They might even have a chance to try for a squirrel or a rabbit with their small bows and arrows. If one of them actually brought down an animal, he was hailed as a coming huntsman, the envy of all of his young comrades.

Indians killed game with bow and arrow before they acquired guns from the white men. They also set snares and deadfalls. In order to catch beavers in the winter when their furs were in the best condition, they cut holes in the ice on a beaver dam and lowered traps near the entrance to their houses. If that method failed, a sure way to bring them out was to break the dam. When the beavers came out as the falling water warned them that there was work to be done, they easily fell a prey to the waiting Indians. The Indians never killed a whole colony, however, but left several families so that there would be some animals the next year. Only after the white men demanded more and more furs did the Indians kill indiscriminately.

Beaver skins were much sought after for trade and for clothing, and the meat was used for food. Front paws and tail were considered special delicacies.

Bears were fat in the fall before they went into hibernation for the winter. Indians used their pelts for robes and blankets, and bear's grease served both as an ingredient of *sagamité* and as a cosmetic. Mixed with berry juices or colored clay, it became war paint, and generous handfuls spread over a warrior's body helped keep out the cold of winter.

Deer were caught by snares, stalked and shot with arrows, or driven by a line of beaters into a lake or stream where hunters waiting in canoes easily killed them with ax or spear. Deerskins well tanned and pliable as cloth were made into clothing for both men and women.

Although the Indians often suffered for lack of food, they were very hospitable, sharing gladly whatever they had with a visitor. There were always dogs in the village, and one of them might be prepared for the guest. Dog meat was greatly relished by the Indians.

In the winter camp there was plenty of work for the women to do. They must skin the animals, prepare the meat for the day's meals, smoke some for later use, and tan the skins. The children helped with these important tasks.

Fish as well as game were sought by the Indians for food. To catch them they used hooks made of bone. They also used spears and nets. Into Saginaw Bay every spring the sturgeon swam in great schools to lay their eggs in the shallow water near the shore. The huge fish, sometimes weighing a hundred pounds, then were easy prey for the Indians. Wading into the water, the fishermen speared them, stunned them with clubs, or, picking them up in their arms, threw them upon the shore where the women and children attacked them with knives. It was great sport. In keeping with the spirit of fun, a small Indian might straddle a great sturgeon and, cheered on by cries of his comrades, ride him to the beach.

The favorite fishing place of the Chippewa was Sault Sainte Marie. In the autumn, before going on the winter hunt, they gathered near the foot of the rapids. The water there was full of whitefish trying to swim up to Lake Superior. To catch them, two men paddled out into the swift current swirling among the rocks. While the one in the stern held the fragile craft in position, the one in the prow stood upright grasping a long pole with a net at the end. Balancing himself skillfully in the bobbing canoe, he selected a fish which he could see plainly in the clear, cold water. A quick thrust of the pole and a sweep of the net invariably brought up a fish, which he tossed into the canoe. The action was repeated until he had caught enough, or until the canoe had been carried by the current beyond the best fishing ground.

The canoe was a valuable invention of the Indians, and in the region of the Great Lakes they developed it into its finest form. The best were made by the Chippewa. Essentially, the craft was a light frame of side rails, keel, and ribs covered with bark of the white birch. The bottom was made of one or two pieces of bark stretched over the frame, and the sides consisted of pieces stitched to the edges of the bottom and to each other with spruce roots called *wattap*. Smearing the seams generously with pine pitch kept out the water. To strengthen the bark bottom so that the occupants would not break through, thin strips of cedar were laid lengthwise and crosswise.

The canoe was the perfect vehicle for early Michigan. Drawing only a few inches of water, it could be paddled upstream to the headwaters of a river, picked up and carried over a portage to another stream, and paddled down to its mouth. With it, Indians could cross both peninsulas easily. It was even sturdy enough for travel on the lakes if the navigator skirted the shore. At the first sign of a storm he would seek a sandy beach where he could camp and wait for calm weather.

5

Indians were very indulgent with their children. Small boys and girls were permitted to do just about as they pleased, and their parents never whipped nor cuffed them. Villages were usually near a stream where they could swim and fish, and the boys had small bows and arrows made by their fathers with which they could shoot birds or squirrels or rabbits. They also played games—shooting arrows through a rolling hoop and in winter launching snowsnakes, rods turned up at one end which were slid along a packed or crusted course of snow. Each Indian boy tried to send his snake farther than the others.

There were no schools, but Indian children learned by watching their parents and by helping them with their work. The girls assisted their mothers in the many tasks in the wigwam and in the fields. The boys learned to hunt and fish, to make canoes, bows, arrows, snowshoes, and animal traps. Before they were grown up they knew the habits of the animals, and all the lore of the lakes, streams, and forests. At night in the wigwam or sitting in the flickering shadows round the campfire, they listened with close attention to the stories of their ancestors, of spirits good and evil, of the exploits of tribal heroes from the lips of the old men. Much of this they committed to memory so that they in turn could transmit to their children the annals and the folklore of the tribe. This was their literature and their history. Although their education was informal, it was practical. Indian boys and girls learned what they needed to know to live successfully in their own environment; and there was a stern incentive to learn the lessons well, since nature provided few accommodations for men or women ignorant of her secrets. Painful death might be the penalty for failure to master the subjects required for graduation from childhood into youth and adulthood.

At the age of thirteen or fourteen, a boy was sent by his parents into the woods alone without food or shelter. Stopping some distance from the village, he made for himself a little bower of branches and lay down to await the visit of a spirit. Hungry and alone, he had time to recall the stories of his elders and the experiences of other youngsters who had undergone the same ordeal.

When night fell, all the little noises of the forest caught his ear—the rustling of leaves, the distant howling of a wolf pack, the cry of a whippoorwill. He was not alarmed, for these were common sounds, and soon he fell asleep, hoping for a favorable dream. Perhaps it would come the first night; perhaps he would have to stay longer; but when it came, he could go back to his village happy in the knowledge that he was no longer alone.

In the dream an animal appeared to him. It might be a lumbering bear or only a timid chipmunk; but whatever it was, he believed that it had been chosen for him by supernatural means and that his spirit and its were closely allied forever. He returned to his father's wigwam joyfully, told of his dream, and was assured that he had a guardian spirit which would always be with him. Ever afterward he showed great respect to that animal, and if ever he had to kill one of the species for food or fur, he made a sacrifice of tobacco to its spirit and humbly begged its pardon.

6

Among the Indians, religion, magic, and medicine were closely related. To them spirits were very real. Spirits inhabited the bodies of men and animals, and they were also present in trees, rocks, and streams. There were spirits in the sun, rain, thunder, lightning, and wind. A man's health or sickness and his good or bad luck in hunting, fishing, planting, or war were dependent on the favor of spirits.

Religion was of the utmost importance to the Indian. Believing as he did in the existence of spirits, he felt the constant necessity of communicating with them. The Indian had no conception of one supreme God. He believed that there were many powerful spirits, some good, others evil. Nanabozho of the Ottawa was one of the great spirits. He was of gigantic size and lived in the sky, but occasionally he descended to Mackinac Island, his earthly home. Creator of the earth, man, and animals, Nanabozho was considered a benefactor of the race. According to tradition, it was he who had invented nets and taught the Ottawa how to catch fish. The aid of this deity was invoked by casting tobacco on the water to assure good fishing.

An Indian offered gifts to the gods, not in gratitude for favors already received, but as presents for benefits which he expected. If they were not forthcoming, he was very angry with the spirit who had taken a gift and given nothing in return.

If an individual found that his offerings were not effective in bringing him good luck, he might engage a medicine man to act for him. Believed to be possessed himself by a powerful spirit and thought to have knowledge of how to control other spirits, the medicine men were expected to gain for others what they were unable to obtain for themselves. Although there were some specialists among them who practiced in one field alone, in most cases a medicine man was priest, sorcerer, or physician as the occasion demanded.

Whole villages or tribes, as well as individuals, appealed to the spirits for aid. Ceremonial dances were performed in the hope of being rewarded by a bountiful crop of corn, a plentiful supply of fish and game, protection against disease, or success in war. Medicine men and chiefs were the leaders in these acts of worship.

The Indian had no church in which to call upon his gods, but he did recognize certain places as sacred. Strangely shaped rocks, especially near the shore of a lake, were considered dwelling places of powerful spirits, and he usually left a gift for them when he passed that way. The Chippewa, for example, always made an offering of tobacco at the Portal Rock on the south shore of Lake Superior.

The Indians believed that after death the spirit left the body and traveled to a pleasant country far in the West. The way was beset with hardships and perils, especially for the spirits of little children and feeble old folk; but if they were brave and persevering, they would eventually reach the spirit land. In order to assist them on the way, Indians buried bows and arrows and household utensils with the bodies. They usually broke them or pierced them with holes so that the spirits of the objects could escape and accompany the spirit of the deceased. Every spirit went to the pleasant country in the West, for the Indian had no belief in a place of eternal punishment.

Medicine and magic were closely related to religion. Some medicine men were supposed to be sorcerers. It was believed that they had the power to bewitch persons and to remove spells which had been cast upon individuals by other sorcerers. Certain diseases were thought to be caused by spells, and medicine men were paid to use their knowledge of magic to free the patients of the evil influence.

One might decide that the evil spirit could be frightened out of the patient. To the beating of drums and the shaking of rattles, the medicine man would dance and shout at the top of his voice. The patient suffered through this confusion in silence, and if he died it was believed that the evil spirit which possessed him was too strong for the medicine man. If he recovered the medicine man got the credit.

The practitioner might also dose his patient with medicines made from roots, seeds, barks, and gums. Perhaps he hoped by this means to sicken the evil spirit and cause him to depart. Some of the medicines used by the Indians, however, were found by the white men to be effective for treating certain diseases.

One practice of the medicine men in treating disease required skill in sleight of hand. After telling the patient that he had discovered the cause of his pain, the medicine man applied a hollow reed or bone to the affected part. Then he sucked hard on the tube and, by a bit of jugglery, produced a seed, a pebble, or, perhaps, a worm, which he declared he had withdrawn from the sufferer's body. If the patient believed him, it may be that the psychological effect was great enough to help him get well.

In spite of the ministrations of medicine men, disease took a heavy toll of Indians. The death rate of infants and young children, as among all primitive peoples, was especially high. Starvation also claimed its share from time to time. Seldom having a surplus of food, the Indians depended on each season's production for their living. Failure of crops or scarcity of game frequently took so many lives that a tribe was seriously weakened. Conditions under which the Indians lived were so severe that only the strongest survived.

7

Although the Indian was a savage, he developed skills and inventions which the white man found very useful, and it is only fair to acknowledge the debt we owe to the first people of Michigan.

The early explorer and fur trader found the canoe the perfect vehicle for his travels, and today it is used as a pleasure craft. Indian snowshoes also were adopted by the white man. Without them in the wintertime he would have been unable to walk far from his cabin, and he might have starved for lack of game.

The white man used the narrow trails that had been marked out through the forests by the tread of innumerable moccasined feet during many centuries. So well did the Indian choose his route that today our principal roads and railroads follow the path he once trod.

The Indian showed the white man which of the plants and fruits were good for food, and the herbs which could be used for medicine. He also taught him how to cultivate corn, a grain which was not known in Europe. Easy to grow and very productive, corn became the staple food of hunter and frontier farmer alike. He would scarcely have been able to live without corn in its various forms: hominy, johnnycake, and mush.

One game, lacrosse, has been borrowed from the Indians, and today many hunters use bow and arrows for shooting at targets, or even for hunting deer.

Americans have taken many Indian words and made them part of the English language. Canoe, succotash, hominy, wigwam, maize, and mugwump are a few of them.

Although few Indians remain in Michigan, we have many reminders of their former occupation of the land in the name of the state itself, and in the names of rivers, lakes, counties, and towns. Shiawassee, Escanaba, Mackinac, and Ishpeming—there is music in those words, and whenever we hear them we should remember the first Michiganians who prepared the way for our ancestors.

PART II

UNDER FLEUR-DE-LIS AND UNION JACK 1622–1796

— 3 —

The Upper Peninsula Is Michigan

Two HARDY young Frenchmen were the first Europeans to visit Michigan. Searching for a water route to the Pacific, Étienne Brulé and a companion named Grenoble reached the Upper Peninsula, probably in 1622.

Sent by Governor Samuel de Champlain in 1610 to live with the Hurons in their villages between Georgian Bay and Lake Simcoe, Brulé had learned the language and the ways of the Indians and had pushed farther and farther toward the West. The Governor urged him to explore the lakes in the hope of finding a waterway through the continent.

Starting from the eastern end of Georgian Bay, Brulé and Grenoble paddled their canoe along the rocky north shore until they entered the island-strewn St. Mary's River. Pushing on against the current, they finally reached the rapids where the waters of Lake Superior tumble down over the rocks on their way to Lake Huron.

Brulé and his companion discovered Lake Superior, and they may even have paddled cautiously along its lonely shore. At any rate, they were on Michigan soil, and on his way back in 1623 to report to Governor Champlain at Quebec, Brulé told the story of his exploration to Gabriel Sagard, a lay brother of the Franciscan missionaries who were living with the Hurons. Sagard mentioned Brulé's discoveries in his *Histoire du Canada*, published in 1636.

Jean Nicolet in His Damask Robe

A glance at a map of North America will show how far this daring young man had penetrated into the continent. At the time the English had only two settlements in America, Jamestown and Plymouth, both on the shore of the Atlantic Ocean.

Governor Champlain had other young men also searching for a route to the Pacific. One of them was Jean Nicolet. In 1634, the Governor sent him on what turned out to be a wild-goose chase. So eager was Champlain to believe Asia was not beyond his reach that he interpreted vague reports of the Indians to mean that they could lead him to China. Outfitting Nicolet with a gorgeous silken robe so that he would be appropriately dressed to meet the Great Khan of Tartary, Champlain in high hope sent him away with the Indians.

Although their exact route is not known, they probably took Brulé's course to the Sault, then followed the shore through the Straits of Mackinac and on to Green Bay. There Nicolet found not civilized Chinese but only naked savages. Never before having seen a white man, they were deeply impressed by his arrival among them, by his colorful robe, and by his pistols which he fired into the air. This creature who "carried thunder in both hands" appeared to them like a god. They entertained him as best they could, but he took no pleasure in their hospitality; for he knew that Champlain would be sorely disappointed with his report. Nevertheless, Nicolet had pushed back a little farther the curtain of ignorance which shrouded the West. He had discovered the northern expanse of Lake Michigan, and he had touched parts of the Upper Peninsula not visited by Brulé.

2

Only the Upper Peninsula of Michigan was known at this time, and it was to be thirty-five years before Frenchmen visited the Lower Peninsula. The reason was the hostility of the Iroquois to the French. Controlling Lake Ontario, the Iroquois prevented the French from following the chain of the lower lakes toward the West. The only route open to explorers was pointed out by the friendly Hurons.

From Quebec these brave men paddled up the broad St. Lawrence and entered the turbulent Ottawa, where rapids compelled them to take their canoes out of the water thirty-six times before they reached the portage to Lake Nipissing. From that lake they floated down the French River into Georgian Bay. If they turned to the left, they would come to the Huron villages at the eastern extremity of the bay; if they turned to the right, they would traverse the North Channel between rugged Manitoulin Island and the north shore, reaching eventually the St. Mary's River, or, turning to the west, as Nicolet had done, enter Lake Michigan and Green Bay. Because furs purchased from the Indians defrayed the expense of exploring expeditions, and this was rich fur-producing country, they were satisfied with the north country.

The next French visitors to Michigan were two Jesuit missionaries from the Huron villages who went to the foot of Lake Superior in 1641. Fathers Isaac Jogues and Charles Raymbault preached to the Chippewa who were there catching whitefish. Before returning to their mission, the priests named the foaming torrent the Sault de Sainte Marie. Later the French called the Chippewa Saulteurs because they frequented the Sault.

There were several reasons why the French penetrated deep into the continent. Champlain, the first governor of Canada, wanted to extend the territory of the king of France and to find a water route to Asia. The missionaries, Franciscan and Jesuit, were eager to save the souls of the savages, and merchants wanted furs. The search for a way to Asia was abandoned after the extent of the continent came to be better understood, but the other motives continued to urge men farther and farther from Quebec. Many of them came into Michigan.

The quest for more and finer furs led to the discovery of new regions. One of the most adventurous of the traders was Médard Chouart, Sieur des Groseilliers. As early as 1654 he was on Lake Superior, and he brought down to Quebec in 1656 canoes loaded with rich furs. Setting out again in 1658, he was accompanied by his brother-in-law, Pierre Esprit Radisson. Because he hoped to keep for himself a monopoly of the trade in the north, Groseilliers refused to take with him either agents of the governor or missionaries to the Indians. He and Radisson left secretly without permission of the governor.

When they returned in 1660 with cargoes of the finest furs, the governor punished them for ignoring his authority. Besides, he paid no attention to their suggestion that the best furs could be obtained north of Lake Superior, and that the most convenient approach to that region would be through Hudson Bay. Angered by their punishment, Groseilliers and Radisson went to England with their information, and as a result the Hudson's Bay Company was organized in 1670. It is still in business today.

Radisson wrote an account of the journey which is difficult to follow. Perhaps he was intentionally vague at times to prevent those who might read his story from knowing exactly where he had been. The wild beauty of the Lake Superior scenery, however, so impressed him that some of the places he mentioned are easily identified. He described in glowing terms the turbulent charm of the Sault de Sainte Marie, the majestic splendor of the Pictured Rocks, and the deep gloom of the virgin forests. He was the first to write enthusiastically about the scenic attractions of the Upper Peninsula.

3

It was not primarily the beautiful scenery that lured men to the upper country. They did, indeed, like living in the woods, free from the restraint of royal officers and the routine of the settlements. They gloried in their hardihood—their ability to overcome the dangers of streams and lakes, of winter storms, and of hostile savages, and they enjoyed the lazy life in villages of friendly Indians who received them hospitably.

Perhaps these were reasons enough to draw some young men into the woods, but the desire for furs was for most of them the strongest motive. Sometimes the profits were fabulous, as much as 1,000 per cent on the investment in trade goods. In other years so many skins were taken to Quebec that the prices were ruinous; yet the search for furs continued, and more and more of upper Michigan was traversed by the traders.

In Canada the fur trade was the monopoly of a company chartered by the king. To regulate the gathering of furs, traders going out into the West were required to purchase a license from the governor. Hundreds, however, went without a license and sold their furs to the Dutch or English in New York, or they disposed of them to corrupt officials in Quebec who divided the profits with them.

Two groups of men were indispensable to their employers in carrying on the fur trade. The first, called *coureurs de bois,* or woods rangers, went out into the lake country, hunted and trapped, lived with the Indians, and bargained with them for furs. Sturdy, rough, and independent, they could endure unbelievable hardships. Frequently their only food was hominy and bear's grease cooked together, and their only protection from the weather a rude bower of evergreen branches. Leaving Montreal in the fall, they spent the winter in the woods, then came down again in the spring with canoe loads of furs. Some of the *coureurs de bois* operated legally with licenses or worked for men who had them. A great number, however, were outlaws, spending nearly their whole lives in the woods, and becoming almost like Indians.

The other group, the *voyageurs,* were the boatmen. Seemingly tireless at the paddles of a canoe, they would drive the frail craft upstream for hours on end, keeping time with their strokes to the lilt of a lively song. When a rocky reach of water blocked their way, they unloaded the canoe, swung a hundred-pound pack of furs or merchandise onto their backs, and trotted along the portage path to a place where the canoe could be launched again. Both *coureurs de bois* and *voyageurs* were essential to the fur trade, but they were frightful nuisances in the settlements. Drinking, brawling, swaggering along the streets, always ready for a fight, they frightened the peaceful *habitants,* who were greatly relieved when they set out again for the north country in the fall.

The Indians, of course, were the most successful gatherers of furs. White men carried great quantities of merchandise to their villages—knives, hatchets, axes, guns, bright-colored cloth, ribbons, blankets, cheap silver jewelry—articles which the Indians greatly desired. When they learned that the white men wanted only furs, the Indians abandoned every other activity to slaughter animals for their skins. Previously the Indians had killed only for their immediate needs. Now they killed wholesale so that they might exchange the pelts for the attractive goods which the traders brought. Unfortunately for the Indians, the Frenchmen also carried brandy to the villages. Many became so addicted to drink that they gave their whole winter's catch of furs for liquor. Debauched and cheated by unscrupulous traders, the Indians gradually became dependent upon the white men even for their food.

The fur trade was very important for Canada, which, of course, included what is now Michigan. During the whole period of French occupation, furs were almost the only valuable export to the mother country. Besides, the never-ceasing quest for new hunting grounds enlarged the territory of the king. But the trade had disastrous effects also. It drew vigorous young men away from the settlements. Instead of taking a farm, marrying, having families, tilling the soil, and increasing the production of food in the colony, they spent most of their lives in the woods living with the Indians, marrying squaws, and leaving half-breed children to grow up as savages. This was one of the reasons for the slow growth of population in Canada. It will appear later that the search for furs led to wars with the Iroquois, the Fox, and finally with the British. The trade which seemed to be the principal support of the colony contributed largely to its downfall.

4

The willingness of the *coureurs de bois* to undergo great hardships to obtain furs was surpassed only by the eagerness of the missionaries to carry Christianity to the Indians, regardless of the cost to themselves. They too suffered from hunger and cold; they risked the dangers of the rivers and lakes; and, in addition, they had to endure the mockery of many of the savages. Some of them were brutally murdered by those for whom they were trying to do good.

The first missionaries to the Indians in Canada were the Recollects, a branch of the Franciscan Order. Father Joseph Le Caron went out to live with the Hurons near Georgian Bay in 1615. Others followed him, but the order was too small to carry on the work, and the Jesuits replaced them. Thereafter, the Recollects served as parish priests and as chaplains with the troops in Canada. The Sulpicians, with headquarters in Montreal, also provided village priests and chaplains.

The first missionaries in Michigan were the Jesuits Jogues and Raymbault who have already been mentioned as having preached to the Chippewa at the Sault in 1641. They returned to the Huron villages near the eastern end of Georgian Bay, and it was nearly twenty years before another missionary went to Michigan.

Meanwhile the ferocious Iroquois, after many murderous attacks, finally destroyed the Huron settlements near Georgian Bay and tortured to death five of the missionaries. The surviving Hurons fled to the western end of Lake Superior in terror for their lives.

After the return of Groseilliers and Radisson from the northwest in 1660, many traders set out for that rich fur-producing country. The superior of the Jesuits at Quebec sent Father René Ménard with them to search for the Christian Hurons and establish a mission among them. Traveling by the Ottawa River route, Lake Huron, the St. Mary's River, and Lake Superior, he finally reached the head of Keweenaw Bay late in the autumn of 1660. There he remained during the winter, near the site of the present town of L'Anse, Michigan. In the spring he resumed his journey, portaging across the Keweenaw Peninsula and skirting the south shore of Lake Superior until he came to Chequamegon Bay, where Ashland, Wisconsin, today is situated. There he established the mission of the Holy Spirit for the Hurons and the Ottawa, but his period of service was short; on a missionary journey into northern Wisconsin, he was lost in the woods and perished.

The Iroquois, not satisfied with the dispersal of the Hurons, carried their war of extermination into Michigan, determined to destroy all Indians friendly with the French. In 1662 a war party of Iroquois reached the Sault and embarked on Lake Superior. Met by a band of warriors, most of whom were Chippewa and Ottawa, they were defeated and put to flight. The name Iroquois Point today marks the place where the invasion of Michigan by the fierce tribesmen was turned back.

Father Claude Allouez went out to Michigan in 1665 on his way to re-establish the mission of the Holy Spirit at the western end of Lake Superior, and others soon followed him. The first mission in Michigan was founded in 1668 by Father Jacques Marquette and Father Claude Dablon at Sault Sainte Marie. Near the foot of the rapids they built a chapel and a house with a palisade around them. This was a strategic point. Chippewa and Ottawa lived roundabout, and the fur traders made it a stopping place on their way up and down the lakes.

In 1669, Father Marquette was sent to Chequamegon Bay. There he heard from visiting Illinois Indians of the great river Mississippi. He eagerly gathered all the information he could about this stream which he believed flowed into the Gulf of California, and determined that he would some day go in search of it and carry the gospel to the savages living along its course.

The Hurons and the Ottawa who had fled to Chequamegon Bay to escape the Iroquois soon found themselves threatened by a new enemy. In the summer of 1670, Indians from the mission on the bay murdered several Sioux. Fearing destruction at the hands of the fierce warriors of the plains, the Hurons and Ottawa fled in terror eastward along the Michigan shore of Lake Superior. There was nothing for Father Marquette to do but to abandon the mission and follow his parishioners. They erected their wigwams and long houses on the peninsula jutting down from the north into the Straits of Mackinac. The Indians called the place Michilimackinac.[1] There Marquette in the summer of 1671 established the mission of St. Ignace. In addition to the Indians and the missionaries, traders also settled there, and officers of the king frequently stopped at this important crossroads of the lakes.

Other missionaries, besides those who have been mentioned, labored in Michigan or passed through on their way to the former station at Chequamegon Bay or to the one on Green Bay. The only missions in Michigan, however, were at Sault Sainte Marie and St. Ignace, both on the Upper Peninsula.

For all their courage, persistence and earnest endeavor, the missionaries accomplished little in Christianizing the Indians. Only the Hurons had shown real interest in their teachings, and they had been nearly exterminated by the Iroquois.

The missionaries had met obstacles that would have discouraged

[1] The name Michilimackinac was used by the Indians to mean all the region around the Straits of Mackinac, including Mackinac Island.

men less devoted to duty. They had to undergo the hardships and dangers of the long journey to the West and the unfriendliness of *coureurs de bois*, who disliked taking them to the Indians. If the missionaries had not had the support of the king, they would have had to remain in lower Canada.

When they tried to establish a mission they often found the Indians unfriendly. The medicine men particularly feared them, believing that they were competitors. If the God whom the missionaries served turned out to be as powerful as they said he was, He would defeat the spirits over which the medicine men claimed to have control. If that happened, they would lose their influence in the tribe.

It was to be expected that they would use all their efforts to arouse suspicion of the missionaries' motives. Sometimes a missionary was permitted to baptize sick babies or feeble old men and women. If one of them died, the medicine man spread the word that the rite of baptism was a spell which the priest as a sorcerer had cast upon the victims. If smallpox or some other epidemic appeared among the Indians, the medicine man could easily persuade his people that the missionary was responsible. The missionaries regarded the medicine men as agents of the devil.

The fickleness of the Indians made any continuous program of teaching impossible. One day they would be attentive, and the next, for no apparent reason, they would avoid the missionaries. Their unsettled way of life, the frequent moving of their villages, and their absence during the winter, when they went to hunt, made the missionaries' work very difficult.

Besides, the Indians were attached to their own way of life, and they were proud of their ancestors who had handed down to them their religion. They resented being told that their beliefs were false. On several occasions chiefs frankly told missionaries that they would retain the ways of their fathers. One of them declared, "If the Great Spirit had wanted the Indians to be like the white men, he would have made them that way in the beginning." This was an argument difficult to answer. When Indians accepted Christianity, it was frequently because they were afraid not to do so. If the God whom the missionaries preached really was a powerful spirit, it would be safer to have Him on their side than to oppose Him.

The *coureurs de bois* and the *voyageurs* also made the task of the missionaries more difficult. The brandy they carried to the villages turned hospitable Indians into murderous savages. The missionaries protested repeatedly against the practice of furnishing liquor to the

Indians, but the feeble efforts of the authorities to regulate the trade were of slight avail.

Although they had made little impression on the Indians before 1671, the missionaries had performed some very valuable services of another kind. These men were well educated, and they were encouraged to take notes of the regions through which they passed and where they lived. Every year each of them wrote a report of his labors and included in it information about the lakes and rivers, the forests, the animals, the plants, and the customs of the Indians. These reports were edited and published in France. Known as the *Jesuit Relations,* they are the most important early source of information about Michigan and the other land around the lakes. The most accurate map of the period was published in 1672 in the *Relation* of 1670–1671. On it appear all of Lake Superior, the Sault, and the northern part of Lake Michigan and Lake Huron. The missions of Sault Sainte Marie and St. Ignace are shown. This map was drawn by Father Allouez and Father Dablon as a result of their own travels and observations. The remarkably exact outline of the north shore of Lake Superior was based on the notes of Father Allouez, who had coasted along it in 1667. To the missionaries we owe a debt of gratitude for their services in making known the new regions into which they carried the gospel.

— 4 —

The Lower Peninsula Takes Shape

BEFORE 1669, no white man had ever visited the Lower Peninsula of Michigan; at least no one had ever reported having been there. It is entirely possible, of course, that some *coureurs de bois* in search of new hunting grounds had passed through; but if they had, they kept the knowledge to themselves. Anyone who ventured into that region would have run a great risk, for Iroquois war parties ranged along the lower lakes, and they would have tortured any Frenchman they caught.

So dangerous were the Iroquois to the people of Canada that in 1665 King Louis XIV sent out the famous Carignan-Sallières Regiment. Led by General de Tracy, these soldiers decisively defeated the Iroquois, who in 1667 agreed to a treaty of peace which permitted the French to travel on the lower lakes.

The first white man to take this route was Adrien Jolliet, a seasoned trader and explorer. In the spring of 1669 he had been sent out by the great Intendant Jean Talon[1] to find a copper mine which the Indians

[1] The intendant was next in authority to the governor in Canada. He was in charge of commerce, finance, and the courts.

had reported in the Upper Peninsula. Unsuccessful in his search, in the fall he was at the Sault preparing to return to Quebec by the Ottawa River route which he had taken on his way to the west. An Iroquois prisoner, who had been released by the terms of the recent treaty and was going to rejoin his tribe, offered to guide him home through the lower lakes.

Jolliet accepted the offer, and they paddled their canoe south along the Michigan shore of Lake Huron, through the St. Clair River, Lake St. Clair, the Detroit River, and the north shore of Lake Erie—a much easier route, unless there were storms on the lakes, than down the turbulent Ottawa River. Jolliet and his guide traveled overland from Lake Erie to the western extremity of Lake Ontario.

Near the site of Hamilton, Ontario, on September 24, 1669, they met a party of Frenchmen and Indians going west. The leader was Robert Cavelier, Sieur de la Salle, who had set out to discover the Ohio River, of which he had heard the Indians speak. Accompanying him were two Sulpician priests, Father François Dollier de Casson and Father René de Brehan de Galinée. Eager to establish a mission among distant tribes, they were going with La Salle to the Ohio.

Jolliet drew a map of the lakes he had just traversed and urged them to take the route to the north country, assuring them that there were many tribes still not served by the Jesuits. They enthusiastically adopted his proposal and separated from La Salle, who would not be turned from his purpose.

The two priests, after spending the winter on the north shore of Lake Erie, set out in the spring of 1670 for the upper lakes. Father Galinée kept a journal which contains the first description of the Detroit River, Lake St. Clair, and the St. Clair River. He also drew a rather crude map of the voyage. Somewhere on the Michigan side of the Detroit River, perhaps within the limits of the present city of Detroit, the priests discovered a peculiarly shaped rock, on which the Indians had crudely painted a red face. To them the rock was sacred, and they made offerings of furs, food, and tobacco to it, hoping thereby to insure for themselves a safe passage across Lake Erie.

To fathers Dollier and Galinée the rock was an idol. Determined that the Indians should no longer worship a false god, Galinée smashed it in pieces with his ax. Then in order to leave no trace of the image, they loaded the fragments into their canoes, carried them out into the stream, and threw them overboard. In his journal, Father Galinée wrote that God rewarded them for their righteous act by sending that same day a buck and a bear which they shot for food.

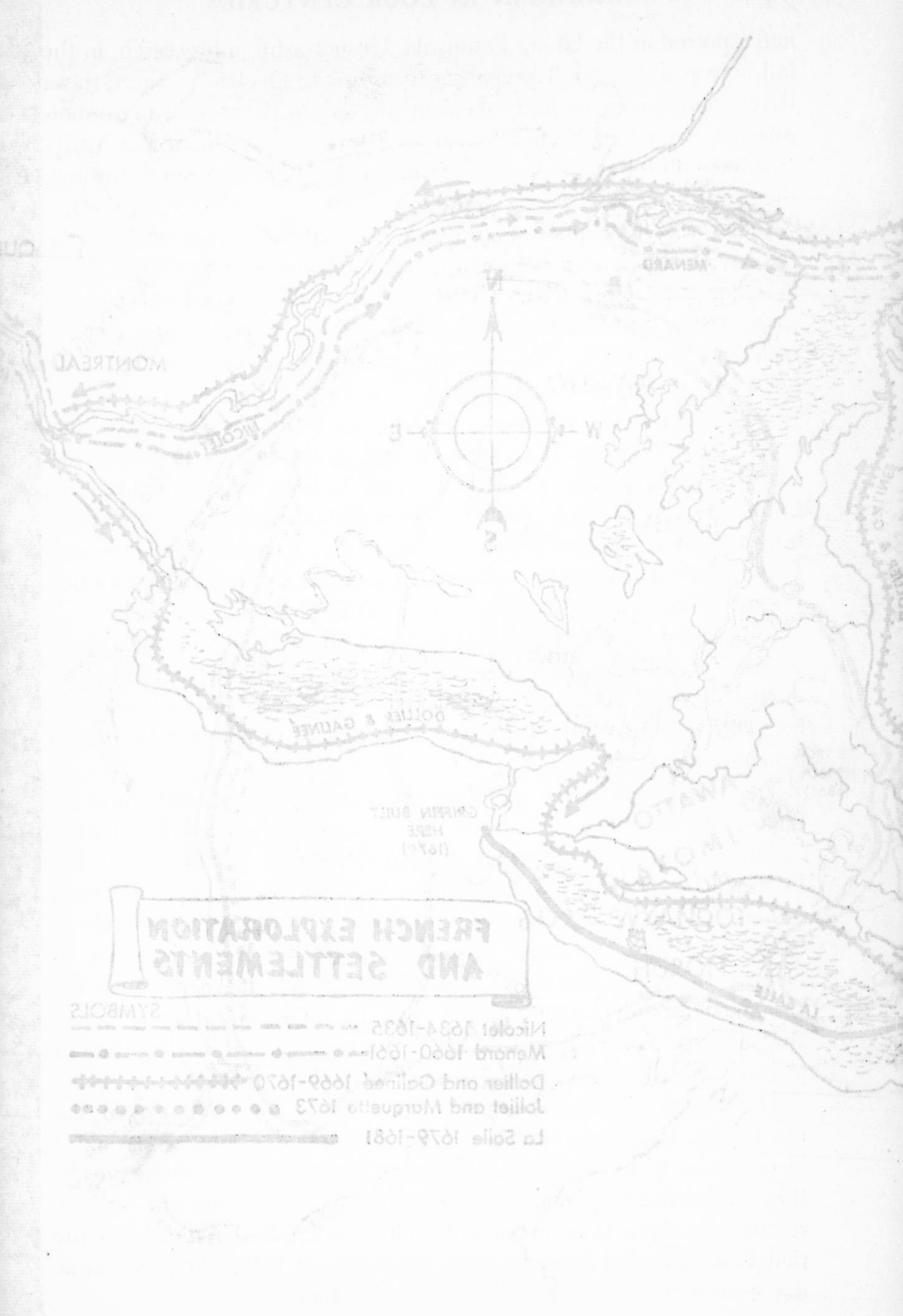

The priests paddled through Lake St. Clair and the St. Clair River, well pleased with the country. Proceeding north along the eastern shore of Lake Huron, they finally reached Sault Sainte Marie. There they found the Jesuit mission consisting of a house and a chapel surrounded by a high stockade. Nearby was a large vegetable garden.

Fathers Dablon and Marquette received the travelers courteously, and entertained them in their house; but they made it clear that there was no place in the West for any but Jesuit missionaries. The two Sulpicians in turn were somewhat critical of their hosts. Father Galinée wrote that they had accomplished little in Christianizing the savages. Although they had baptized a few, not one Indian was permitted to attend the Mass, which was celebrated only for the twenty or twenty-five Frenchmen who were there at the time. After a three-day visit, Fathers Dollier and Galinée returned to Montreal by the old Ottawa River route.

2

Jean Talon, the intendant, was determined to expand the territory of Louis XIV. He realized that immediate action was necessary in the northwest because the Hudson's Bay Company was likely to send its agents down from the north toward Lake Superior. In order to forestall them, late in 1670 he sent Nicolas Perrot, an intrepid explorer familiar with the languages of the natives, to assemble all the tribes of the northern lakes at Sault Sainte Marie the following spring. As the representative of the king, Talon sent François Daumont, Sieur de St. Lusson.

On June 14, 1671, beside the rapids of the St. Mary's River, was enacted a ceremony which has been called the Pageant of the Sault. A great crowd of Indians were waiting expectantly on a little hill where a large wooden cross had been laid upon the ground. Soon they saw the gates of the mission open and a procession emerge, moving toward the hill.

At the head were four missionaries—Claude Dablon, Louis André, Claude Allouez, and Gabriel Dreuillettes in their somber black robes—then came Nicolas Perrot, the interpreter, and St. Lusson, the latter wearing the blue uniform of an army officer. They were followed by the traders and *voyageurs* with bright colored sashes about their waists.

The procession halted before the cross, and Perrot read aloud St. Lusson's commission and translated it for the Indians. The cross was then set up and the little band of Frenchmen removed their hats and sang an ancient hymn. Beside the cross, a cedar post was planted bearing a metal plate inscribed with the royal arms of France. The Frenchmen sang a psalm, and after one of the priests had offered a prayer for the king, St. Lusson stepped forward.

Raising his sword in his right hand and a piece of sod in his left, in a loud voice he took possession, for Louis XIV, of the Great Lakes, Manitoulin Island, "and of all other countries, rivers, lakes, and tribu-

St. Lusson at Sault Sainte Marie Claiming the Region for King Louis XIV, 1671

taries contiguous and adjacent thereunto, as well discovered as to be discovered, which are bounden on the one side by the Northern and Western seas and on the other side by the South Sea including all its length and breadth." This formula he repeated three times.

The Frenchmen discharged their muskets and shouted *vive le roi*, while the Indians, pleased with the pageantry, whooped their approval. Then Father Allouez spoke at length on the glory of God and the power of Louis XIV, and St. Lusson delivered an oration "in eloquent and martial language."

The ceremony ended with a great bonfire, around which the Frenchmen gathered and sang the *Te Deum* "to thank God on behalf of these poor peoples [the Indians], that they were now the subjects of so great and powerful a monarch." Then chiefs, priests, and traders signed the official report. Among the signers was Louis Jolliet, a young brother of Adrien.

After St. Lusson and his band left the little hill, the Indians ripped the royal coat of arms from the cedar post, believing it to be strong medicine which would bring them good luck. They had only the faintest notion of what the ceremony meant. St. Lusson himself did not know how much territory he had claimed for his king. The language of the proclamation was vague enough to include the whole interior of the continent. Eventual ownership, however, and the fate of the Indians too, would be determined by the test of war.

3

Jean Talon hoped to find a water route to the Pacific, and so in 1672 he commissioned Louis Jolliet to go in search of "the great river which [the Indians] call Michissipi and which, it is believed, discharges itself into the Sea of California." Before the young explorer was ready to leave in the fall of the year, a new governor arrived, Louis de Buade, Count Frontenac. Destined to become the greatest governor of Canada during the French regime, Frontenac knew nothing of the country or the people at this time, and so he simply seconded Talon's appointment of Jolliet.

Louis Jolliet was a native of Canada, born in Quebec in 1645. Educated in the Jesuit Seminary, he had given up the idea of becoming a priest and had gone to France in 1667 for about a year. Returning to Canada, he accompanied St. Lusson to Sault Sainte Marie in 1671 and afterward engaged in the fur trade. Intelligent, educated, hardy, and courageous, he was well fitted to be the leader of a dangerous expedition.

Before Jolliet left Quebec, Father Claude Dablon, now superior-general of the Jesuits in Canada, gave him a message for Father Jacques Marquette. It was an order to accompany Jolliet as missionary to the Indians whom they might meet on the journey. Dablon had good reasons for naming Marquette for this difficult task. He knew that while the latter was at the mission of the Holy Spirit he had heard of the Mississippi River from Illinois Indians who had invited him to come and preach to them. In fact, Dablon had given him permission to go to the Illinois in 1671. The flight of the Hurons and Ottawa to St. Ignace in that year, however, had made the journey impossible; but Dablon knew that Marquette still hoped to see the Mississippi and to visit the Illinois.

Jolliet arrived at St. Ignace early in the spring of 1673. Father Marquette was delighted with the order to accompany him. Their preparations were soon made, and they set off toward the middle of May with five men in two birchbark canoes. From St. Ignace they paddled west along the north shore of Lake Michigan and to the mission at the head of Green Bay. Their route then was by the Fox and the Wisconsin rivers to the Mississippi. The explorers were overjoyed when their canoes floated at last in the current of the great river of which they had heard so often.

They continued downstream, stopping from time to time to visit Indian villages on the banks. By the middle of July they had reached a village a short distance above the mouth of the Arkansas River. Certain now that the Mississippi flowed into the Gulf of Mexico, they began their weary return voyage against the current. Marquette became seriously ill, but they continued until they entered the Illinois River, and stopped in the principal village of the Illinois Indians. Remaining there a short time, Jolliet and Marquette set out for Lake Michigan after the priest had promised the Indians that he would return.

By way of the Des Plaines and Chicago rivers, they reached Lake Michigan and finally came to the mission at the head of Green Bay. Marquette remained there to recover from his illness, but Jolliet went on to Sault Sainte Marie, where he spent the winter. In the spring of 1674 he returned to Quebec to report to Count Frontenac the success of his expedition.

Marquette's illness kept him at Green Bay until the fall of 1674. Then, having received permission to return to the Illinois, he set out with two of the men who had accompanied the Mississippi expedition, Pierre Porteret and Jacques Largilier. A recurrence of his illness compelled Marquette and his companions to spend the winter in a cabin beside the Chicago River. In April they reached the Illinois town, and Father Marquette, in spite of his weakened condition, preached to the Indians.

Believing that he had only a little while to live and hoping to see again his mission of St. Ignace, Marquette set out with his two companions shortly after Easter. Having reached Lake Michigan, they skirted the eastern shore until they reached the mouth of a river now called the Pere Marquette. There the missionary asked to be taken ashore, and there he died on May 18, 1675, and was buried near the present city of Ludington. He was only thirty-eight years old. Two years later a party of Ottawa came upon the grave. Opening it, they cleaned the bones and packed them in a box of birchbark. Then they carried them to St. Ignace, where they were buried beneath the altar of the mission chapel.

Louis Jolliet, on his return journey to Quebec, had the misfortune to lose his map and the journal of his expedition when his canoe capsized in the rapids above Montreal, and so he drew a map from memory which he presented to Governor Frontenac. The governor was well satisfied with his conduct of the exploration, but he never sent Jolliet on another trip to the West. Frontenac became involved in quarrels with the Jesuits, and he believed that Jolliet was too friendly with them to serve the governor faithfully.

4

The first expedition to discover the Mississippi River, that of Jolliet and Marquette, set out from Michigan; the second, which completed the task by following the stream to its outlet, also began its journey from a base in Michigan. The man who led the second party was Robert Cavelier, Sieur de la Salle.

After Dollier and Galinée left La Salle on Lake Ontario, he set out to discover the Ohio River. Whether he did or not is a question that has never been answered. Wherever he went at that time, he retained a strong determination to make certain once and for all into what sea the Mississippi flowed.

La Salle was a well-educated man of good family who arrived in Canada in 1666 when he was twenty-three years old. Going to Montreal, where his brother Jean was a priest in the Order of St. Sulpice, he obtained from the order a large tract of land on the Saint Lawrence River. Farming, however, was too monotonous an occupation for the adventurous young man, and so he sold the land to provide funds for the explorations which he was eager to begin.

His great plan was to explore the Mississippi River to its mouth and to erect a chain of forts which would prevent the English from settling in the middle of the continent. With the support of Governor Frontenac he gained from Louis XIV permission to explore the West, build forts, and carry on the fur trade. Proceeds of the trade would have to pay the expense of the expedition, for the king made it clear that La Salle would receive no financial aid from him.

To provide transportation for the great number of furs La Salle expected to gather in the West, he had a little sailing vessel built on the bank of the Niagara River above the falls. At the prow was a carved figurehead representing the griffin, a monster of ancient fables. It was a fearsome-looking creature with an eagle's head and the body of a lion. La Salle had it copied from Frontenac's coat of arms. Five small cannon were mounted on the deck. Named for the figurehead, the *Griffin*, it was the first ship on the upper lakes.

On August 7, 1679, the *Griffin* set sail across Lake Erie and entered the Detroit River. Game was plentiful, and the scenery was beautiful to the eyes of the travelers. Father Louis Hennepin, a Recollect priest who accompanied La Salle, declared that "Those who will one day have the happiness to possess this fertile and pleasant strait, will be much obliged to those who have shown them the way."

Leaving the river, the *Griffin* entered the lake, which Hennepin named Sainte Claire. Finally, after weathering a severe storm on Lake Huron, the sturdy little ship reached St. Ignace, or Michilimackinac, as the Indians called it. There La Salle and his party rested for several days; then they sailed to the entrance of Green Bay. After loading the ship with furs which had been collected there for him, La Salle ordered the captain to carry the cargo to the Niagara and to return at once to the St. Joseph River.

In four canoes La Salle and his men made their way along the west coast of Lake Michigan and around the head of the lake to the mouth of the St. Joseph River. There in November, 1679, La Salle built Fort Miami on the site of the present city of St. Joseph, Michigan. He was joined by his faithful lieutenant, Henri de Tonty, called "the man with the iron hand" because he wore a metal hand to replace the one he had lost in battle.

La Salle was disappointed when the *Griffin* did not arrive. Instead of waiting for her, he pushed on to the Illinois River, where he built another fort. Returning to Fort Miami, where there was still no news of the *Griffin*, he decided that she was lost. To this day no one knows what happened to the ship, but it seems likely that she sank in a storm.

At various times, claims have been made that the wreck of the *Griffin* has been discovered at one place or another. The most likely story is that it was driven on the rocks about two miles from Mississagi Lighthouse at the western end of Manitoulin Island. Part of an ancient hull was found there years ago, and in 1890 the lighthouse keeper found four skeletons in a cave and two others nearby. He also uncovered a watch, a chain, and seventeenth-century coins. The number of skeletons is the same as the number of the crew, and analysis of a bolt taken from the wreck showed that it was like those of La Salle's day. It is probable that a storm from the west drove the ship before it until it struck the rocks of Manitoulin Island, and the crew, escaping from the wreck, died of starvation.

The loss of the *Griffin* with her cargo of furs made necessary a trip to lower Canada to make new arrangements. From Fort Miami La Salle set out on the thousand-mile journey in March, 1680, and crossed Michigan on foot. Only a man of indomitable spirit and with an iron constitution could have endured the hardships of this trip through wild country with no provisions except the game he and his companions killed. His exact route is not known, but he probably passed through the second tier of counties above the Ohio and Indiana boundaries, and it is possible that somewhere near Ann Arbor he struck the Huron River and followed it to Lake Erie.

Enemies tried their best to prevent La Salle from carrying out his great plan, but he vigorously overcame all opposition and was back again in November, 1681, at Fort Miami. During Christmas week he and Tonty set out from there with twenty-three Frenchmen and thirty-one Indians on the journey that took them to the Gulf of Mexico in 1682.

When La Salle returned to Quebec to make his report, he found that his good friend Frontenac had been recalled. Because the new governor, La Barre, was hostile to him, he sailed for France to obtain permission from the king to establish a colony at the mouth of the Mississippi to keep the English out of that region, and to plant forts along the upper reaches of the river to hold it for France.

He was successful in his quest at court. Sailing with a small fleet to the Gulf of Mexico, he was unable to find the mouth of the Mississippi. He landed on the coast of Texas, and there he was killed by some of his disaffected followers on March 19, 1687. La Salle had not completed the task which he had set for himself, but he had showed how the English might be excluded from the heart of the continent.

5

Another great explorer who spent some time in Michigan was Daniel Greysolon, Sieur Duluth. Like La Salle, a friend of Governor Frontenac engaged in the fur trade on a large scale, he made peace between the Michigan Indians and the fierce Sioux, thus opening the West beyond Lake Superior to the French. On numerous occasions he was at the Sault or at Michilimackinac (St. Ignace) on his journeys to and from Quebec.

In 1686 Governor Denonville ordered him to build a fort between Lake Huron and Lake Erie to prevent English traders from reaching the upper lakes. Leaving Michilimackinac with fifty *coureurs de bois,* he chose a spot at the head of the St. Clair River, on the site of the present city of Port Huron for his stockade, which he named Fort St. Joseph. Such a post was necessary if the French were to retain their monopoly of the fur trade in the North and West, for in 1685 eleven canoes filled with merchandise had reached Michilimackinac from Albany. The leader, a merchant named Roseboom, found the Indians eager to exchange furs for English goods, which were cheaper than the French, and he promised them that he would return to trade the next summer.

Governor Denonville planned a great campaign against the Iroquois, the allies of the English, to punish them for guiding English traders into French territory. To augment his force of French regulars and Canadian militia, he ordered the leaders in the region of the upper lakes to meet him on Lake Ontario in the summer of 1687. They were to assemble at Fort St. Joseph and descend by water in a great flotilla of canoes.

Fort St. Joseph became the mobilization center of nearly two hundred *coureurs de bois* and about five hundred Indians—Chippewa, Hurons, Menominee, Winnebago, Potawatomi, Illinois, Fox, Kickapoo, and Mascouten. Henry de Tonty, Nicolas Perrot, and La Forest each brought in a contingent, and La Durantaye arrived with English and Iroquois prisoners, the trader Roseboom and his party, whom he had caught while they were on their way a second time to Michilimackinac.

There was great rejoicing at Fort St. Joseph. The savage Indians and the half-savage *coureurs de bois* celebrated the capture with great enthusiasm. Near distraction because of their wild demonstration, Duluth and the other leaders hurried them away for the rendezvous with Governor Denonville. On Lake Erie the French and Indians met another party of English traders led by Major Patrick McGregory and easily captured them.

Governor Denonville's expedition did not accomplish a great deal, but the force which went from the West at his order showed how large a body of hardy *coureurs de bois* and Indians could be raised for the defense of Canada.

Duluth returned to the far West, and, as the new commandant of Fort St. Joseph, Governor Denonville sent Louis Armand de Lom d'Arce, Baron de Lahontan. This young nobleman had a keen sense of humor and unusual ability as a writer. Although he sometimes exaggerated the conditions which he observed, he wrote very interestingly of the people, the resources, and the happenings in Canada, or New France, as it was also called.

Lahontan was an ardent sportsman, and he described with enthusiasm the Indian chase of the deer on the islands in the St. Clair River. He arrived at his post on September 14, 1687. Hunting was good in the surrounding country, and the commandant was very happy during the autumn. The long winter, however, without occupation and without boon companions to help pass agreeably the tedious days, caused Lahontan to wish for more populous places. Being short of supplies and deciding that the fort was not worth maintaining, he burned it and set out on August 27, 1688, for Michilimackinac. Fort St. Joseph had a brief existence, but its location is certain, for in his book *New Voyages to North America*, Lahontan marked it clearly at the head of the St. Clair River.

Governor Denonville was unable to cope with the growing influence of the English and the increasing hostility of the Indians. In 1689 the Iroquois massacred Frenchmen on the outskirts of Montreal, and the western Indians were planning to receive the English at Michilimackinac. In that year France and England began war against each other, the first of a series that extended over more than a century. Louis XIV sorely needed a new governor for Canada, and he appointed Frontenac, whom he had recalled in 1682. Although he was now seventy, the former governor was active, experienced, and feared by the Indians. He returned to Quebec in the dangerous year of 1690.

Immediately he went into action. To Michilimackinac he despatched Louis de la Porte, Sieur de Louvigny, with one hundred and fifty Canadians. There he built Fort de Buade, named for Count Frontenac, near the mission of St. Ignace and the villages of the Hurons and the Ottawa. English traders would receive a warm welcome if they dared come to trade.

Frontenac himself invaded the Iroquois country, and he beat off a dangerous attack on Quebec by an English squadron in 1690. The next year he sent Augustin le Gardeur, Sieur de Courtemanche, to build a fort on the St. Joseph River. Choosing a spot about twenty-five miles up from the mouth where La Salle had established Fort Miami in 1679, the Commandant erected a palisade and a few buildings, which he called Fort St. Joseph. The site of the fort is just outside the present city of Niles.

This was a strategic position. Situated where the trail from Detroit to the southern bend of Lake Michigan met one coming up from Indiana, and not far from the portage to the Kankakee River which led to the Mississippi by way of the Illinois, the fort was astride the principal trade and war routes in the southern part of Michigan. It was in a pleasant and fruitful country. The woods were teeming with animals, wild fruits abounded, and the rich soil produced an ample supply of corn, beans, and squash. Archaeological investigations show that the region was heavily populated by Indians from the earliest days of human occupation of Michigan.

Courtemanche had for a neighbor Father Claude Aveneau, who was in charge of the St. Joseph Mission. The date of founding is not certainly known. Perhaps Father Claude Allouez began the work before he died in 1689 somewhere in that region. Father Aveneau was there in 1690 and missions for both the Miami and the Potawatomi were maintained on the river for many years.

For three years the life of the garrison at Fort St. Joseph was peaceful enough, but in the spring of 1694 a large war party of Iroquois suddenly attacked the fort. Courtemanche and his men defended themselves so vigorously that the savages withdrew and gave up their purpose of carrying war to the Illinois Indians, allies of the French.

6

In 1694 Louvigny obtained permission to return to France, and Frontenac appointed as his successor at Fort de Buade Antoine de la Mothe Cadillac, a captain in the troops of the colony. In reporting the change in command, the Governor praised Cadillac for his valor, wisdom, experience, and good conduct.

Born in the province of Gascony on March 5, 1658, Cadillac went out to Canada probably in 1683. He spent some time in Nova Scotia, and in 1687 he married in Quebec Marie-Thérèse Guyon, daughter of a sea captain with whom he had explored the coast of New England. For a time he and his wife lived on a seigniory at Bar Harbor, Maine, which had been granted to him by the king.

After the outbreak of the war with England in 1689, Cadillac was recalled to France because of his expert knowledge of the New England coast, for Louis XIV was contemplating an expedition against Boston and New York. When he returned to Canada, the king directed Frontenac to reward him for his services. The governor soon discovered that this man had great capabilities.

Cadillac was a true Gascon—proud, energetic, sharp of tongue, quick to draw his sword, and facile with a pen. His letters are lively and interesting. Sometimes he exaggerated the benefits to be derived from plans which he made, but his vigorous administration of his post, his ability to control the Indians, and his loyalty to his superiors won him the support of Count Frontenac; of Count Pontchartrain, the minister of colonies; and of Louis XIV, himself.

Michilimackinac was the most important place in the West. The commandant of Fort de Buade had supervision over all the other forts, and Father Henri Nouvel, superior of all the western missions, had his headquarters there in the mission of St. Ignace. A French village of sixty houses was nearby, and the Hurons and the Ottawa each had a large town close to the mission. During the trading season more than five thousand Indians camped in the neighborhood, and the settlement was crowded with several hundred *coureurs de bois*.

At Fort de Buade, Cadillac was soon embroiled with the missionaries over the sale of brandy to the Indians. Although Frontenac defended his actions and praised his conduct in his report to the minister in Paris, this was the beginning of a feud between Cadillac and the Jesuits which had disastrous consequences for him.

In spite of his heavy duties, at Michilimackinac Cadillac had time to make observations and to do some writing. His long *Memoir* of the lake region contains a great deal of useful information about the country and many details of Indian life and customs.

Governor Frontenac by his energetic action had made the lake region again safe for Frenchmen, but now so many furs were carried to Montreal that the merchants complained about the low prices, and the Jesuit missionaries redoubled their demands that the Indians be protected from the traders who went to their villages. As a result, in 1696, Louis XIV issued a decree closing the West to all Frenchmen except the missionaries. The Indians henceforth would have to carry their furs to Montreal.

7

Much blood and treasure had been spent to develop Canada as a prosperous colony of France. Unlike the kings of England, who had permitted the colonies on the Atlantic coast to stand or fall by their own efforts, the kings of France had lavished attention on Canada. Money had been poured into the colony, regular troops had been sent to protect the *habitants* from the Indians, and the king had even provided wives for Canadian bachelors.

Still the population remained small. In 1689 when England and France went to war, only about thirty thousand men, women, and children lived in Canada, while in the English colonies the total was approximately three hundred thousand.

There were several reasons for the great disparity in numbers. In the first place, religious groups in England which were persecuted fled to America, where they could worship as they pleased. Pilgrims, Puritans, Quakers, and Roman Catholics found refuge in one colony or another. Besides, foreigners were welcome in some, notably the Germans in Pennsylvania.

The French king, on the other hand, permitted only Frenchmen who were Roman Catholics to enter Canada. Thousands of French Protestants, known as Huguenots, would have been glad to settle in a French colony if they could have had freedom of worship. Because they were persecuted by the French government and denied entrance into Canada, many of them fled to Germany, England, and the English colonies in America, where they became valuable members of their communities.

Another reason for the slow growth of Canada was the northern location. Living conditions were harsh there, especially in the winter, and furs were almost the only product which could be exported. It was the eager search for furs which drew off from the settled parts of the colony many of the most vigorous of the young men. Instead of remaining along the Saint Lawrence, developing farms, and rearing families, they took to the woods, lived with Indian squaws, and were fathers of half-breed children who remained in the wilderness. They could be relied on to come to the defense of the colony when either the Iroquois or the English threatened to attack, but they made slight contributions to the peacetime development of Canada.

The English colonies, by contrast, extending along the Atlantic coast from north to south, had a great diversity of soils, climate, and natural resources. The people became largely self-sufficient, and they had a variety of products to send back to the mother country. Because it was easy to acquire land in America, thousands came to make their homes in this land of opportunity.

The decree of King Louis XIV issued in 1696 was displeasing to Frontenac and others who had interests in the West. Nevertheless, the governor had to obey, and so, reluctantly and tardily, Fort de Buade and Fort St. Joseph were abandoned in 1698.

8

Cadillac went down to Quebec with a heavy heart. He had made a great deal of money at Michilimackinac in the fur trade, and he had been able to hold the unstable Indians faithful to the French. Commanding an important military post and making his fortune at the same time suited him exactly. Now that all the posts were closed, such an opportunity would not come again. If he wanted another chance, he would have to make it for himself.

Cadillac's active mind soon formulated a daring plan. He would ask the king to permit him to establish a post on the strait between Lake St. Clair and Lake Erie. It would cost the king nothing to maintain, for Cadillac would offer to pay all the expense from profits of the fur trade. In view of Louis XIV's recent order closing all the posts, how could Cadillac induce him to permit a new one to be built? He would call his attention to the growing danger from the British, and the strategic position of a fort on the strait, much superior to that of Michilimackinac.

In addition to maintaining the fort, Cadillac would ask that the king grant him a seigniory. Cadillac would encourage settlers to come and settle on his land. Farmers would raise crops, and a self-supporting town would rise in the wilderness.

Cadillac took his plan to Frontenac, who was easily convinced of the necessity for such an establishment. He chafed at the restrictions on the fur trade and the closing of the West, and hoped that this plan might make possible a return of more prosperous days. Frontenac was well satisfied with Cadillac's behavior at Michilimackinac. He knew that this officer was capable of commanding the proposed post, and he was certain that no one could present the proposal more attractively to the minister of colonies. And so he gave Cadillac permission to go to France, providing him with a letter of recommendation to aid his cause. He sailed from Quebec in October, 1698.

— 5 —

France Bows to Britain

In Paris, Cadillac convinced Count Pontchartrain, minister of colonies, that a fort should be built on the strait between Lake St. Clair and Lake Erie, and Louis XIV sent him back to Quebec bearing orders to the governor and the intendant to assist him in carrying out his plans. Count Frontenac had died in 1698, shortly after Cadillac sailed for France. His successor, Governor Callières, was hostile to Cadillac, but he had to obey the order of the king.

Early in June, 1701, Cadillac set out from Montreal with fifty soldiers, fifty *coureurs de bois,* and one hundred Indians in twenty-five canoes. His son, Antoine, nine years old, accompanied him. Alphonse de Tonty, brother of La Salle's loyal lieutenant, was second in command. Two priests, Father François Vaillant, a Jesuit, and a Recollect, whose name is not known, accompanied the expedition. Because a treaty of peace made with the Iroquois had not yet been signed, Cadillac was ordered to follow the old route by way of the Ottawa River, Georgian Bay, and Lake Huron so as not to irritate the Iroquois by passing through their country.

The flotilla finally reached the Detroit River, and on July 24 Cadillac's experienced eye picked out a perfect spot for his fort. The canoes swung in to a narrow sandy beach at the foot of a high clay bank. At the top of the bank the ground was level, and a swift-flowing creek ran parallel to the river, then turned and joined with it. On this high ground protected by water on three sides, Cadillac built Fort Pontchartrain du Detroit, that is, Fort Pontchartrain on the Strait. The river was narrow enough there so that his cannon could destroy any hostile fleet moving up or down the strait.

In the dense forest Cadillac's men felled trees and made a palisade twelve feet high and two hundred feet square, with bastions at the corners. Inside they built houses of logs set upright like the palisade and covered the roofs with grass. They also constructed a church, which they called St. Anne's.[1] If the little fort were set down in Detroit today, it would lie between Griswold and Shelby streets on the east and west and between Larned and Woodbridge on the north and south. The palisades were later extended toward the west, reaching nearly to Wayne Street.

In order to discourage Indians and settlers from going to Detroit, Cadillac's enemies spread the word that Fort Pontchartrain was only a temporary post. To counteract this propaganda, Cadillac asked his wife and Madame Tonty to come, believing that other families would make their homes on the strait if he set them an example.

The two ladies traveled by canoe, Madame Cadillac taking her son Jacques, who was six years old. They went by way of the lower lakes, and the Iroquois were greatly surprised to see them passing through their country. When they landed at Detroit in the fall of 1701, the Indians fired their guns in welcoming salute. They had doubted that women would come to this distant post, but now that they had arrived, the Indians were sure that it would be a permanent settlement.

Madame Cadillac and Madame Tonty were Michigan's pioneer women. In spite of the dangers along the way, and the difficulties of life in the wilderness, they were ready to leave the comforts of civilization to make new homes for their families. To friends at Fort Frontenac who tried to dissuade Madame Cadillac from going farther she replied: "Do not waste your pity on me, dear friends. I know the hardships, the perils of the journey, the isolation of the life to which I am going; yet I am eager to go. For a woman who truly loves her husband has no stronger attachment than his company, wherever he may be."

[1] Father Vaillant left shortly after arriving, and although Cadillac asked for a Jesuit missionary for the Indians, none ever went to Fort Pontchartrain. Father Constantin Delhalle, a Recollect, probably reached Detroit in June, 1702.

Mme. Cadillac and Mme. Tonty Arriving at Detroit, 1701

2

Cadillac praised the region along the strait extravagantly in his first report to Count Pontchartrain. "The banks [of the river]," he wrote, "are so many vast meadows where the freshness of these beautiful streams keeps the grass always green. These same meadows are fringed with long and broad avenues of fruit trees which have never felt the careful hand of the watchful gardener; and fruit trees, young and old, droop under the weight and multitude of their fruit, and bend their branches toward the fertile soil which has produced them." He described the neighborhood as "so temperate, so fertile, and so beautiful that it may justly be called the earthly paradise of North America," and he informed the count that "Winter (according to what the savages say) lasts only six weeks at most."

Many Indians accepted Cadillac's invitation to settle on the strait. The Hurons and the Miami built their villages a short distance below the fort; the Ottawa and Chippewa built theirs above. So many Indians left Michilimackinac that Father Carheil in 1705 burned the chapel of St. Ignace and withdrew to Quebec.

Cadillac had hoped to civilize the Indians and enlist them as soldiers. Although he repeatedly requested the establishment of a school, none was ever opened, and the king forbade him to give the Indians military training for fear that they would be dangerous to the French.

At first the Company of the Colony at Quebec had a monopoly of trade with the Indians, but Cadillac bought them out in 1705 and got complete control of the post. The Indians of numerous tribes who came to trade were constantly quarreling with one another, but Cadillac was able to prevent any serious outbreak.

In 1706, while Cadillac was in Quebec, the Sieur de Bourgmont, whom he had left in command, supported the Miami in a quarrel with the Ottawa. The latter for revenge killed a French soldier and Father Delhalle, who happened to be outside the fort. Cadillac had to hurry back and settle the trouble. Since there was war again with the British, it was very important to keep the Indians loyal to the French.

Cadillac, like the commandants of the other posts and the governor himself, always received visiting Indian chiefs with great courtesy. He invited them to dine with him at his table, and he gave them presents that pleased their savage fancy—vermilion to paint their faces, red coats trimmed with gold lace, white shirts with ruffles, silver bangles, tobacco, and brandy. The Indians, in turn, presented fine furs as gifts to him.

In council, Cadillac addressed the chiefs as "My Children," and they called him "Our Father." Understanding their manner of speech, he used the figurative language which they always employed in diplomatic negotiations. Speaking to the Ottawa in August, 1707, he described his post in the following words: "I had lighted a great fire here, I had planted four great trees near this beautiful fire, two on my right hand and two on my left." The trees, of course, were the villages of Ottawa, Huron, Chippewa, and Miami which were near the fort. When he offered a slave to the Miami chief, he said: ". . . there is a little meat which I give you to revive your dead a little."

Cadillac always had on hand wampum, which he used in the Indian fashion to serve as a record of the articles of agreement, and he gravely smoked the red calumet when it was passed from hand to hand. Because the French respected the customs of the Indians, they were able to live together for the most part on friendly terms.

3

Besides being commandant of the fort and having the trade monopoly, Cadillac wanted to be the seignior of the region; that is, the feudal landowner. Noblemen or other prominent colonists in Canada received large estates called seigniories. In return the seignior had to perform the ceremony of pledging fealty and homage to the king. Appearing at the Château St. Louis in Quebec before the governor as His Majesty's royal representative, a seignior removed his hat and on his knees swore to be the king's loyal vassal. In addition, he was required to deposit at Quebec a description and a map of the seigniory, to grant land to tenants, to build a mill for their use, and to perform military service. The seignior was the judge in his seigniory.

The people to whom land was granted were called *habitants*. They owed the seignior the ceremony of fealty and homage; they must raise their hats to him and stand in his presence; they had to take their grain to his mill and pay one fourteenth of it for the grinding; they must agree to work a certain number of days each year on the seignior's farm and they were charged rent, which they usually paid in produce because coins were very scarce in New France.

Although Cadillac never received a seigniory, he was permitted to grant land along the Detroit River and to collect rent. During the years 1707–1711, he distributed to settlers sixty-eight small lots within the stockade and seventy-five farms nearby. So long and narrow that they are often called ribbon farms, they varied in width from one arpent[2] to five, and in length from one and a half to three miles. The longest reached back into the woods as far as the present line of Harper Avenue. Many of the north and south streets of Detroit bear the names of French *habitants* who owned ribbon farms: Beaubien, St. Aubin, Chêne, Dequindre, for example.

The ribbon farms at Detroit were like those which earlier had been granted along the Saint Lawrence. Because there were no roads, the river was the highway and a canoe was the *habitant's* runabout. In it he could easily carry his grain and his vegetables to the fort, or he could set out on a journey to the farthest reaches of Lake Superior.

Cadillac required his tenants to pay rent either in furs or in cash, and to pay him for the privilege of trading or working as skilled craftsmen. Besides, it was their duty each year on the first of May to erect a maypole in front of his residence. This last was not a heavy burden, for a general celebration, in which the commandant and his family joined, followed the raising of the pole. Cadillac built a windmill on the river bank. Sometime later, after complaint had been made to the governor that he charged one eighth instead of one fourteenth for grinding, the king ordered him to reduce the price to the usual rate.

Cadillac had cattle and horses sent overland from Montreal. The cattle throve and multiplied, but two of his three horses died, leaving only one, which he called Colin. Many pigs were brought to the settlement. Because they were kept on Belle Isle where they were safe from marauding wolves, the island was at first called Isle aux Cochons, Hog Island.

4

Detroit did not grow rapidly. Frenchmen were more interested in the fur trade than in settling down as farmers, and Cadillac's enemies used their influence against him. The merchants in Montreal feared that his post would injure their trade, and the missionaries opposed the gathering of Indians about a frontier fort where brandy and rough *coureurs de bois* soon debauched them. Even Alphonse de Tonty, he learned, was in league with his opponents.

In spite of attempts to have him dismissed, Cadillac retained the

[2] An arpent was 192.25 feet long.

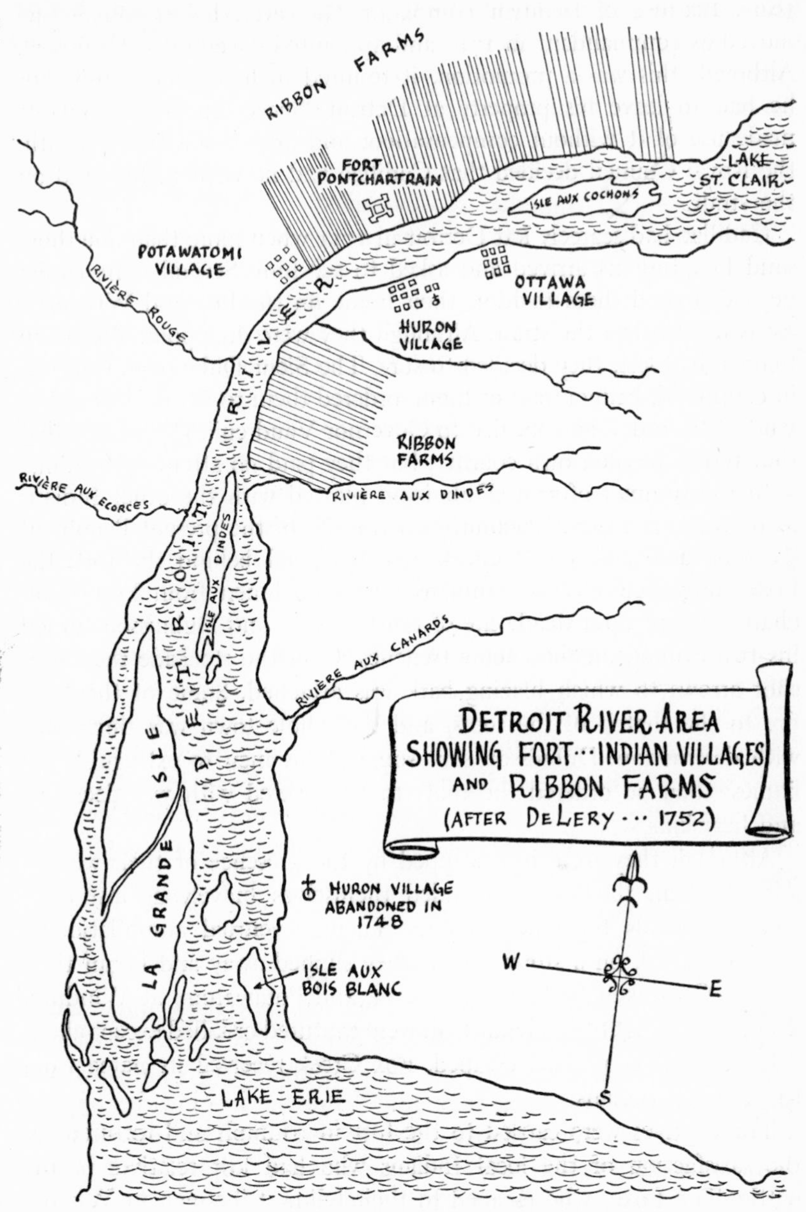

RIBBON FARMS
FORT PONTCHARTRAIN
LAKE ST. CLAIR
ISLE AUX COCHONS
POTAWATOMI VILLAGE
OTTAWA VILLAGE
HURON VILLAGE
RIVIÈRE ROUGE
DETROIT RIVER
RIBBON FARMS
RIVIÈRE AUX DINDES
RIVIÈRE AUX ECORCES
ISLE AUX DINDES
RIVIÈRE AUX CANARDS
DETROIT RIVER AREA
SHOWING FORT... INDIAN VILLAGES
AND RIBBON FARMS
(AFTER DeLERY ... 1752)
LA GRANDE ISLE
HURON VILLAGE ABANDONED IN 1748
ISLE AUX BOIS BLANC
W
E
S
LAKE ERIE

favor of Count Pontchartrain, and of Louis XIV himself, for some years. Because of frequent complaints, however, he was finally removed as commandant in 1710 and appointed governor of Louisiana. Although this was a promotion, it resulted in his financial ruin, for he had to leave his property at Detroit. Succeeding commandants made use of it without compensation, and after Louis XIV's death, the Royal Council decided that Cadillac had no right to the land on the strait.

Cadillac had scarcely left Detroit in 1711 when more than one thousand Fox Indians arrived and asked to see him. Several years earlier he had invited them to leave their home on the Fox and Wisconsin rivers to settle on the strait. Although they were disappointed to learn that he had left, they decided to stay. The Sieur Dubuisson, who was in command, being afraid of them, ordered them to leave. When they ignored his order, he appealed to Governor Vaudreuil. He insisted that they return to their own country, but they paid no attention to him.

In the summer of 1712 Dubuisson plotted with the other Indians to destroy the Foxes. Encamped on the site of the present Penobscot Building across Savoyard Creek, which flowed behind the fort, the Foxes dug themselves in. Indians and Frenchmen from Fort Pontchartrain kept up a steady fire of musket balls, and Dubuisson turned his two cannon on the enemy trenches. Over the stockade the Foxes shot arrows to which blazing bark was attached. Some of them set fire to the thatch of the roofs, and the whole town was threatened with destruction. Dubuisson sent some of his men to extinguish the flames; then he ordered the roofs to be covered with wet deerskins and bearskins.

Although they were handicapped by the presence of their women and children, the Foxes defended themselves bravely against overwhelming odds for nineteen days. Facing eventual annihilation if they remained, on a stormy night they slipped away and began their retreat. Overtaken by Hurons, Ottawa, and Potawatomi at Windmill Point, they fought bravely until all were captured or killed except about a hundred warriors who escaped. Fox Creek received its name from these brave Indians.

The captives were carried to the fort in triumph and tortured for the satisfaction of the local Indians who had lost relatives in the battle. The Foxes who escaped to their fellow tribesmen in Wisconsin imparted to them their bitter hatred of the French. For many years they blocked the Fox-Wisconsin water route to the West, and it was only in 1734 that they were finally forced to remove to Iowa after having defeated several expeditions which had been sent to destroy them.

5

Between the years 1689 and 1763, Britain and France were engaged in four wars on both sides of the Atlantic. In America they were called King William's War (1689-1697), Queen Anne's War (1702-1713), King George's War (1744-1748), and the French and Indian War (1754-1760). Although no battles were fought in Michigan, it was essential to French security to keep the western Indians loyal. And so in 1715 a new fort was built to control the upper lakes, this time near the tip of the southern peninsula where Mackinaw City now stands. It was called Michilimackinac. Fort St. Joseph on the St. Joseph River was reoccupied at about the same time, and Fort Pontchartrain, of course, was maintained.

From 1748 until 1756 Britain and France were officially at peace, but border raids continued in the East, and traders from the colonies along the Atlantic seaboard crossed the Allegheny Mountains into the Ohio country. Determined to maintain French dominion there, Governor La Galissonière in 1749 sent Pierre-Joseph Céloron de Blainville to traverse the region with a force of two hundred men. From Lake Erie Céloron reached the headwaters of the Allegheny River and floated down to the Ohio. From time to time he landed, urged the Indians to remain loyal to France, and planted in the river bank lead plates proclaiming the sovereignty of the French king.

Céloron continued down the Ohio and up the Great Miami. Everywhere he found traces of English traders, and he discovered that the Indians were lukewarm in their attachment to France, preferring the cheaper English merchandise. At Pickawillany, a great village of the Miami, now Piqua, Ohio, the chief known as La Demoiselle, or Old Britain, received him coldly. The Indian favored the English traders, and he refused to obey Céloron's order to remove to the Maumee River, where he would be under close supervision of the French. After gaining only a vague promise to move later, Céloron made his way to the Maumee and to Detroit, where he had been commandant from 1742 until 1744. Then he had to return to Quebec to report the dangerous situation in the Ohio country.

Céloron was sent back to Detroit as commandant with orders to punish La Demoiselle and drive the English out of the region. Probably because he believed it was impossible, Céloron did nothing. Nevertheless, La Demoiselle was not to remain long undisturbed. Early in June, 1752, a great flotilla of canoes carrying two hundred and fifty Ottawa and Chippewa warriors appeared at Detroit. The commander was Charles-Michel Mouet, Sieur de Langlade, a half-breed from the north who had gathered his war party at Sault Sainte Marie and Michilimackinac for the purpose of destroying Pickawillany. Taking some reinforcements from Detroit, Langlade hastened to the Miami town.

His fierce attack was successful. Six English traders were captured, and La Demoiselle was killed. His body was boiled and eaten with relish by the savage warriors from the North.

6

A new post established at Sault Sainte Marie had made the Indians aware of the determination of the French to maintain their ascendancy and had made easier Langlade's task of enlisting his punitive force. In 1750, Governor La Jonquière, alarmed by reports that traders and Indians were avoiding Michilimackinac and carrying furs to the English, ordered Louis le Gardeur de Repentigny to build a fort at the Sault.

Lacking a permanent settlement since the missionaries had left in 1689, the Sault was still a resting place for Indians and traders going up or down the lakes. A fort there might serve as the nucleus for a settlement, and the commandant would be expected to direct all trade to the French. In order to make the post self-supporting, the king granted a seigniory to Repentigny and to Captain Louis de Bonne on what is now the Michigan side of the St. Mary's River, extending eighteen miles along the river and eighteen miles back into the forest.

Louis le Gardeur de Repentigny was a descendant of one of the old Canadian families. Entering the military service in 1739, he had been actively engaged ever since that year. For a time he was stationed at Michilimackinac, and in June, 1748, he had gone down to Montreal with eighteen canoes of Indians. A raid into New York under his leadership produced eleven prisoners and twenty-five scalps. Repentigny was a capable partisan captain.

De Bonne, on the other hand, had only recently come to Canada with his uncle, Governor La Jonquière, as captain of the guard. Apparently the nephew was made co-owner of the seigniory simply because he was a relative of the governor, for there is no record that he ever visited the property.

Repentigny erected three buildings, which he enclosed in a stockade one hundred and ten feet square, established Jean Baptiste Cadotte and his Indian wife on the estate as tenants, and had cattle and horses sent from Michilimackinac for their use. According to the terms of the grant, the land was to be cleared and cultivated, but because Repentigny and De Bonne were given the right to trade, it is likely that Cadotte busied himself more with the fur business than with farming.

Repentigny called the Chippewa together, gave them a belt of wampum from the governor, and compelled them to deliver to him a belt which had been sent by the English. The fort was useful for keeping the local Indians loyal to the king.

Although Britain and France were officially at peace, events west of the Alleghenies were rapidly moving toward an eventual collision. Langlade's attack on Pickawillany aroused the wrath of the English, and the large number of English traders beyond the mountains moved the French to act.

A new governor, the Marquis Duquesne, ordered a line of posts built from Lake Erie to the forks of the Ohio to exclude the English from the West. During 1753 forts were erected at Presque Isle (Erie, Pennsylvania), on French Creek (Waterford), and at the junction of French Creek with the Allegheny River (Franklin).

Determined to maintain Virginia's claim to the country, Governor Robert Dinwiddie sent Major George Washington during the winter of 1753–1754 to warn the French to leave. The commandants of Fort Venango, at the junction of French Creek and the Allegheny River, and of Fort Le Boeuf on French Creek received Washington with great courtesy. They informed him, however, that they would not leave their posts, and that they intended to take control of the Ohio River.

Now it was a question which nation could first seize and fortify the forks of the Ohio. Washington was sent to build a fort there, but the French drove off his advance detachment and compelled him to surrender his whole force on July 4, 1754. This action was the beginning of the French and Indian War. Then the French erected a fort, which they named Duquesne (now Pittsburgh), at the forks of the Ohio.

The next year General Edward Braddock marched across the mountains to capture Fort Duquesne. In the attack, which cost Braddock his life and hurled his army back in panic retreat, Charles Langlade and Indians from Michigan played an important part; and in 1756 Repentigny and Langlade, with seven hundred Indians and *coureurs de bois* from Michilimackinac and the Sault, ravaged the western settlements of Pennsylvania, Maryland, and Virginia.

7

The war which had begun in America broke out in Europe in 1756. Known as the Seven Years' War, it was fought by Britain and Prussia against France, Austria, and Spain.

In America, Great Britain appeared to have the advantage because of the larger population. Practically ignored by the mother country, the thirteen colonies had grown until at that time they had a million and a quarter men, women, and children; while Canada, including Michigan, of course, had only about eighty thousand. Too few Frenchmen found Canada attractive enough to go there and remain, and except for the *coureurs de bois,* the western country was practically without settlers.

Attempts had been made to induce families to go to Detroit. In 1749, for example, Governor La Galissonière promised farm tools, chickens, a sow, powder, and lead to those who would occupy a farm there, but only forty-six people took advantage of the offer. The next year fifty-seven went to Detroit. This official encouragement of migration failed of its purpose. Some shiftless persons accepted the benefits, but drifted away after they had consumed the supplies. The total population of the fort and the neighboring farms was only about nine hundred, and, except for soldiers, there were probably not more than one hundred additional permanent residents in Michigan.

Detroit was primarily a military post ruled by a commandant. The only civil officer was Robert Navarre, subintendant and royal notary. He collected the rents due to the king from those who occupied land within the stockade or along the river, served as a judge in minor cases, and drew up all sorts of contracts.

The people were satisfied to be ruled by appointed officers. They had never known any other system, and it relieved them of responsibility. The *habitants* were lighthearted, sociable, and hospitable to a fault. Having little concern about the future, they were satisfied if they produced the bare necessities of life. There was no school at Detroit, and many of the people were illiterate. Some, however, sent sons and daughters to Montreal or Quebec to be educated by the priests or the nuns.

The *habitants* were devoted to their church and gladly celebrated the numerous holidays on her calendar. After the Sunday morning Mass at St. Anne's, they gathered outside to hear the sexton read announcements of sales or other notices; then, unloading their carts, the farmers set up the weekly market. Young fellows raced their horses on the Common, and in the evening everyone danced to the music of fiddles.

Life in Detroit was pleasant, but there was little progress. Everyone looked to the priest, the commandant, or to the royal notary for instruction or advice; and the officers, in turn, received their orders from Quebec after they had been issued in Paris.

8

At first the French in America had the advantage over the British because they had unity of command. The regular troops, the Canadian militia, and the *coureurs de bois* were under the control of the governor. Having no elected assembly to consult, he could move swiftly with his whole force. The British colonies, on the other hand, were jealous of each other. When the French and Indians threatened New England, the colonies farther south usually felt no responsibility to come to her aid; and colonial governors lost precious weeks pleading with assemblies to vote men and money for defense.

France also had the advantage of a capable military leader, the Marquis de Montcalm. Brilliantly directing his forces, he easily defeated the British until 1758. Then the tide began to turn. All Montcalm's ability could not save Canada from the weakness which had been steadily creeping upon her as a result of the graft and corruption practiced by Governor Vaudreuil and Intendant Bigot. In addition, the British fleet cut off supplies and reinforcements for Canada.

In 1758 new and capable generals chosen by William Pitt, prime minister of Great Britain, were commanding the troops in America. General John Forbes in that year took Fort Duquesne. In 1759, General Jeffrey Amherst captured Ticonderoga and Crown Point, and Sir William Johnson compelled the surrender of Fort Niagara. In the great battle for Quebec, Langlade, Repentigny, De Bonne, *coureurs de bois,* and Indians from the West fought bravely; but on the Plains of Abraham the British under General James Wolfe won the victory which cost him his life and also that of the Marquis de Montcalm, commanding the French. Captain de Bonne was killed in the fighting around Quebec, and Repentigny, sick at heart, soon abandoned his seigniory and went to France.

Montreal alone remained to be taken. Attacked from three sides, Governor Vaudreuil capitulated to General Amherst on September 8, 1760. Four days later Amherst ordered Major Robert Rogers with about two hundred Royal Rangers to go to Detroit by way of the lakes and take over the French posts in the northwest.

Major Rogers was a New Hampshire man who had distinguished himself during the war as leader of the Rangers. Used to living and fighting in the woods, he was well chosen to make the difficult and dangerous journey from Montreal to Detroit. Traveling by whaleboat and bateau, at Presque Isle he was joined by a company of Royal Americans from Fort Pitt under the command of Captain Donald Campbell.

When Major Rogers reached the mouth of the Detroit River, he sent Captain Campbell ahead to inform Captain François-Marie Picoté, Sieur de Belèstre, commandant of Fort Pontchartrain, that he was approaching. Belèstre, who had received no instructions from Montreal, at first refused to believe that Canada had fallen; but when Captain Campbell showed him the capitulation and a letter from Governor Vaudreuil, he prepared to receive the British troops politely.

It was on November 29, 1760, that Major Rogers and his troops occupied Detroit. The white flag bearing the lilies of France was hauled down, and the red banner of Britain was raised in its place. The French regulars stacked their arms and were sent down the lakes. The local militia was disarmed, and all the *habitants* took an oath of allegiance to King George II of England.

Learning that it was too late in the season to send garrisons to Michilimackinac, the Sault, St. Joseph, and Green Bay, Major Rogers left Captain Campbell in command at Detroit and returned to the East.

Captain Campbell reported that the *habitants* were friendly to the occupying troops and that Robert Navarre, the notary, was arranging to supply them with provisions. He decided that Navarre should continue to act as civil officer among the people on the strait. The transfer from French to British sovereignty was made with no apparent difficulty.

— 6 —

Michigan Becomes British

CAPTAIN DONALD CAMPBELL liked Detroit. His Royal Americans in their green uniforms behaved well, and the *habitants* were friendly. Because he spoke French, they felt that he was almost one of them. During the winter the merchants invited him and his officers to their dances, and he had a party for them every Sunday evening in his quarters. In June he gave a ball for the merchants, their wives, and their daughters to celebrate King George's birthday.

When they attended such a party, the men wore brocaded waistcoats, lace jabots, long-tailed coats, and breeches with buckles at the knee. Their hair was powdered and done up in a queue. The ladies dressed in the styles of Paris or London, a little behind the times, for news traveled slowly in those days.

These were the party clothes of the well-to-do merchants. The poorer people—*coureurs de bois,* farmers, artisans—dressed more simply. The men wore brightly colored shirts, trousers supported by a leather belt or a cloth sash, and straw hats or colored kerchiefs on their heads. Most of them preferred moccasins to shoes, and some went barefoot in the summer. The women wore short gowns reaching only to their knees, with petticoats falling to their ankles. Broad-brimmed straw hats protected their faces from the sun.

There were always Indians inside the stockade in the daytime—visiting their friends, bargaining with the merchants, or quarreling with each other when they got a little brandy or rum to drink. In the evening, before the gates were closed for the night, they had to go outside. The only Indians who remained were slaves who had been purchased by the French from the Indians. Some belonged to farmers, others to merchants. The women were house servants. From whatever tribe they had come, the French called them Panis.

2

Captain Campbell got along with the Indians as well as he did with the French. When in the early summer of 1761 two Iroquois chiefs of the Seneca tribe came bearing a blood red wampum belt to the Ottawa, Potawatomi, and Hurons, urging them to join in an attack on all the British forts, the local chiefs refused. They were satisfied with their treatment at Detroit. Captain Campbell reported the affair, and in September Sir William Johnson, British Indian superintendent, went to Detroit to hold a council with the Indians.

The discussion lasted many days. Johnson urged the Indians to be loyal to their new British father, King George III. In the figurative language of the savages, he said that he had come to brighten the chain of friendship and that he hoped they would hold fast to it. He promised that the king would look after their welfare. To emphasize each point of the speech, he gave the chiefs belts of wampum.

Indian chiefs spoke in reply, also giving belts of wampum. One expressed the pleasure of his tribe in the peace which existed, saying that the British had made the roads and the lakes smooth and passable. He also declared that his people would be friendly and would pay no attention to such "bad birds" as those which had come last spring to make trouble. After the council was completed, Sir William distributed presents and had an ox roasted for a feast. The Indians seemed to be completely satisfied.

Sir William was entertained at a ball given by Captain Campbell, and he gave one for the officers and the merchants. He found the ladies very attractive, especially Mademoiselle Angélique Cuillerier *dit* Beaubien, with whom he danced at both affairs. Detroiters and their visitors in those days had great endurance. Sir William noted in his diary that they "danced the whole night until 7 o'clock in the morning, when all parted very much pleased and happy."

Sir William Johnson Dancing with Angélique Cuillerier, 1761

At this time garrisons were sent to the forts in the north and west. Lieutenant William Leslye reached Michilimackinac on September 28 with twenty-eight men. There he learned that the French garrison under Captain Louis de Beaujeu had retired to Fort Chartres, a French post in southern Illinois. Charles Langlade, the partisan leader, had been left to deliver the fort. Lieutenant Leslye found a few daring British traders already at Michilimackinac.

Ensign Francis Schlosser was sent to Fort St. Joseph, where he arrived on November 19 and took possession with his detachment of fifteen men. These were the only forts immediately occupied in Michigan, but garrisons were placed at Green Bay, Fort Miamis (Fort Wayne, Indiana), Ouiatenon (Lafayette, Indiana), and in a new fort at Sandusky, Ohio. These stockades and blockhouses in the wilderness with their tiny garrisons were expected to keep the Indians in check.

In August, 1762, a new commandant arrived at Detroit, Major Henry Gladwin. He had come to America as an officer with General Edward Braddock in 1755, and had been wounded in the battle which had cost the general his life. With him came reinforcements for the western posts. He sent Captain George Etherington to take command of Michilimackinac and Lieutenant John Jamet to occupy Repentigny's fort at Sault Sainte Marie.

Jamet found Repentigny's man Jean Baptiste Cadotte, with his Chippewa wife and their half-breed children, living in one of the houses inside the stockade. He and his small detachment took over the others.

There is a legend in Lower Canada that Cadotte defied the British troops and, all alone, defended the fort until he was shot down. Then wrapping the flag of France about him for a shroud, he died gloriously. This is an interesting story, but there is no truth in it. Cadotte was not a romantic Gascon but a shrewd businessman. The very next year he entered a partnership with a British trader, Alexander Henry, and lived to a great age.

Perhaps he did find a way to clear the fort of British troops. On the night of December 10, 1762, a fire of uncertain origin broke out. All the houses except Cadotte's burned to the ground. Having no shelter, Lieutenant Jamet was forced to remove his detachment to Michilimackinac. There was very likely a smile of satisfaction on the weather-beaten face of Jean Baptiste Cadotte as he watched the soldiers depart.

3

During 1762 the Indians began to become restless because they were thoroughly dissatisfied with the treatment they were receiving from the British. The traders, many of them conscienceless ruffians, swarmed through the country cheating the Indians and robbing them of their furs. Many of the commandants received delegations of chiefs coldly, telling them to state their business and be on their way. Besides, obeying the orders of General Jeffrey Amherst that presents must be given sparingly to the Indians, they seldom gave them anything.

This treatment was very different from that which the Indians had received from the French, who had entertained them as friends. Among other gifts the French commandant had always included some powder for hunting. Amherst's orders forbade the giving of ammunition, and so the Indians easily believed the rumor that the British were trying to starve them to death.

Sir William Johnson urged Amherst to change his orders, warning that the Indians might cause trouble if they were not treated according to the French custom. The general, who despised Indians, believing them a sort of vermin which should be exterminated, replied that he would not purchase their good behavior. If they misbehaved, they must be punished, not bribed. This haughty attitude turned the Indians even more against the British.

The appearance of settlers on Indian lands in western New York and western Pennsylvania aroused the hostility of the Seneca, the Delawares, and the Shawnee. Because the Indian never understood private ownership of land, he was puzzled by the statement that the king of France had given the region to the king of Great Britain. To the Indian way of thinking, he had simply permitted the French to use the land. There had seldom been any conflict, for the *habitants* received the Indians into their houses and shared their food with them. The British had a different idea. When they purchased land from the Indians, it was theirs exclusively, and an Indian or anyone else might be punished for trespassing on it.

The French very naturally encouraged the Indians in their developing hatred of the British. They disliked the competition of the traders, their aggressiveness, and the superior attitude of the British toward them. Hoping to arouse the Indians to expel the intruders, they whispered that their French Father would soon return with new armies against the British. Then he would reward the Indians for their part in helping to destroy them.

There were three Indian villages near Detroit. The Potawatomi lived about two miles below the fort near the Ambassador Bridge approach. Almost directly across the river, in the present city of Windsor, Ontario, was the Huron village, and the Ottawa were on the same side farther up opposite the lower end of Belle Isle. The war chief of the Ottawa was Pontiac, a proud man, easily offended.

Although he had at first welcomed the British to Detroit, he soon began to brood over the changed situation since the French had surrendered the post. Unlike Captain Campbell, Major Gladwin was haughty in his treatment of the chiefs. Gradually Pontiac's resentment was fanned into intense hatred by the urging of the Seneca and the local Frenchmen. The British garrison at Detroit, he decided, must be destroyed.

To gain the support of the other tribes, he sent messengers to the Hurons and Potawatomi, asking them to attend a secret council on the Ecorse River, about ten miles below the fort. When they gathered there on April 27, 1763, he recited the wrongs which they had suffered at the hands of the British and won their support for a concerted attack whenever he should give the command.

Pontiac's plan for capturing the fort was simple. With a band of Ottawa braves he would go to meet Major Gladwin in council. Under their blankets the warriors would carry knives, tomahawks, and guns with shortened barrels. Other Ottawa, including the women, would also enter the fort with concealed weapons. While speaking to the major, Pontiac would hold in his hand a wampum belt, white on one side and green on the other. If he turned the green side up when he gave it to the commandant, the Indians were to attack the British.

Pontiac reserved the most dangerous part of the plot for himself and his Ottawa. The Potawatomi and the Hurons were to lie in wait outside the fort to capture persons in the vicinity. Pontiac hoped assistance would come from the Chippewa of Saginaw and the Ottawa of L'Arbre Croche, a village on Lake Michigan about twenty miles from Michilimackinac, to whom he had sent invitations to come to Detroit.

May 7 was the day set by Pontiac for the attack. Fortunately for the British, Gladwin learned of the plot the night before. Who warned him, the major never told. Probably he wanted to protect the person or persons from death at the hands of the Indians. Many interesting stories have been written about how he obtained the information.

One is about the Indian squaw named Catherine. When the story was first told, she was old and ugly; but gradually in the telling, the story was changed until she finally became a beautiful young Indian maiden in love with Major Gladwin.

On the evening of May 6, so the legend goes, Catherine brought to Gladwin's quarters a handsome pair of deerskin moccasins. He was so pleased with them that he asked her to make him another pair.

When she told him that she feared she would not be able to bring them to him, he asked why. After some hesitation, she told him of the plot.

An artist, J. M. Stanley, painted a picture of this scene in Major Gladwin's quarters. It has been frequently published, and many persons have accepted it as the portrayal of an actual event. There is little foundation in fact for this local myth.

Because the Indians had to borrow files from the French blacksmith and other artisans to cut off the barrels of their guns, it is likely that a number of persons knew that some sort of conspiracy was afoot. Who told, or how many, will never be known. A Madame St. Aubin is said to have reported the shortening of the guns, and William Tucker, a soldier in the fort, who had been captured as a child by the Chippewa and had grown up among them, is reputed to have learned of the plot from his Indian sister. If this is true, he certainly informed Major Gladwin.

The most interesting story of all, and one for which there is some basis of fact, has for its heroine Angélique Cuillerier *dit* Beaubien, the Detroit girl who had danced with Sir William Johnson. In 1763, she was engaged to James Sterling, a young merchant of Detroit. Her father, Antoine Cuillerier *dit* Beaubien, was a friend of Pontiac, and he had good reasons for wanting the British destroyed.[1] He was a Frenchman, and the last French commandant, Captain Belèstre, was his half brother. Pontiac is known to have visited in his home, and it is possible that Angélique overheard their discussion of the plan. If she did, she surely warned her lover, so that he might escape death at the hands of the Indians.

There is no absolute proof that Angélique and James were the only informants or even the principal ones, but ten years later, Major Henry Bassett, commandant of Detroit, wrote that Sterling, "through a lady that he then courted, from whom he had the best information, was in part a means to save this garrison." Angélique and James were married in 1765.

4

In accordance with his plan, Pontiac with ten chiefs and sixty warriors met Major Gladwin on May 7. The rest of the Ottawa, men and women, followed them into the fort. When they passed through

[1] Beaubien's farm was the second one east of the fort. Beaubien Street in Detroit occupies a part of his farm which reached north to Harper Avenue.

the gates, they were surprised to see the garrison under arms as if expecting an attack. Pontiac realized at once that the British had been warned. Nevertheless he went through with the ceremony of the council, but he was careful to keep the white side of the wampum belt uppermost.

Major Gladwin gave the Indians some presents which they asked for, and they retired to the Ottawa village, furious because of the failure of the plot. Seeking to find the person who had warned the major, the Indians seized a squaw named Catherine. They carried her to the fort, where Gladwin was asked if she had told lies about them. He denied that she had spoken with him, but he said that it was an Indian who had brought the warning. In spite of his denial, Catherine was taken before Pontiac, who ordered that she be beaten. This affair is seemingly the basis for the story of Catherine, the beautiful Indian maiden.

Still hoping to take Major Gladwin off guard, Pontiac and three of his chiefs entered the fort the next morning. He asked that the commandant receive him and all his warriors the next day so that the British and the Indians could smoke the peace pipe together. Gladwin coolly told him that only chiefs would be admitted to the council. Pontiac withdrew, but the next morning, May 9, all the Ottawa crossed the river to the fort. When Gladwin refused to admit them, Pontiac rejected the invitation to enter with a few of the chiefs. Taking to their canoes, they returned to their village.

Pontiac's plot had failed, but he was determined to destroy the British even if he had to starve them out by a long siege. Ordering his village moved across the river to a spot about two miles above the fort, a short distance beyond Parent's Creek, he dispatched his warriors to begin the attack.

Thirsting for British blood, the braves hastened toward the stockade. One band began the slaughter by killing a woman and her two sons on a farm some distance back of the fort. Another band landed on Isle aux Cochons and murdered five people there. The main body of savages stealthily approached the stockade and began firing at it. This was the beginning of a siege which lasted one hundred and fifty-three days, the longest in the history of Indian warfare.

Major Gladwin was determined to hold the fort at all costs. To defend it he had about one hundred soldiers and twenty merchants, a wholly inadequate force if the Indians attacked continuously for several days and nights. He had a few small cannon in the fort, and his two ships, the schooner *Huron* and the sloop *Michigan*, moored in front of the stockade would have the Indians in a cross fire if they were foolish enough to show themselves there. Provisions were scarce, but Gladwin was expecting a shipment from Fort Niagara which would relieve his wants. On the return trip the supply boats could carry his request for reinforcements.

Pontiac's resources appeared to be sufficient to accomplish his purpose. Under his command were more than eight hundred warriors from the local villages, from Saginaw Bay, and from the Thames River. Pontiac could count also on some of the Frenchmen for aid. The most influential among them were Antoine Cuillerier *dit* Beaubien, whom the chief had promised to put in command of the fort after he had captured it, and Jacques Godfroy. Others helped with advice and food for the warriors, even though all of them had taken the oath of allegiance to King George. Major Gladwin believed that more than half of the *habitants* were guilty of treason.

A few Frenchmen were loyal to the British. Robert Navarre, François and Jacques Duperon Baby, and the two interpreters, Pierre La Butte and Jacques St. Martin, performed valuable services. The two Babys, particularly, at great risk of their lives, secretly carried provisions to the fort at night.

5

The Indian war of 1763 spread over the whole region west of the Allegheny Mountains, and eventually every fort except Niagara, Pitt, and Detroit was captured. Pontiac did not plan all the attacks in advance, as was once believed, nor was he the supreme commander in the war. His authority, in the beginning, reached no farther than the Detroit River region. Even there the Hurons who were under the influence of Father Pierre Potier at the Jesuit mission in Windsor refused to follow him, and the Ottawa of L'Arbre Croche ignored the invitation to come to his assistance.

Several forts were taken by local Indians who were induced to make the attacks by Indians sent by Pontiac after he had begun the siege of Detroit: Sandusky on May 16, St. Joseph on May 25, Miamis on May 27, and Ouiatenon on June 1.

The forts in Pennsylvania were captured by Seneca, Delawares, and Shawnee after they had received word of the attack on Detroit. Although Pontiac had not planned the widespread campaign in advance, his example set off the uprising which raged throughout the western country.

The little stockade on the St. Joseph River was occupied by Ensign Francis Schlosser and fifteen men. When word was brought to him on May 25 that Potawatomi from Detroit had arrived and wanted to talk with him, he had no suspicion of danger. The chiefs had scarcely entered his quarters when he heard a warwhoop and shots in the direction of the barracks. The chiefs seized the ensign, and the warriors killed nine of the soldiers. Schlosser and the other survivors later were exchanged at Detroit for Indian prisoners.

The remaining fort in Michigan, Michilimackinac, was destined also to fall into the hands of the Indians. On June 1, Wawatam, a Chippewa chief who had adopted Alexander Henry, the English trader, as a brother, urged him to go along on a journey. When Henry declined the invitation, Wawatam went away very sad. Although Henry warned the commandant, Captain George Etherington, that trouble was brewing, and Charles Langlade hinted that the Indians were planning mischief, he refused to believe them. He had no suspicion that Chief Minavavana, the Grand Saulteur, had set a trap for the garrison. And so on June 2, when the Chippewa and some visiting Sauk began a game of lacrosse beside the fort, Captain Etherington, Lieutenant Leslye, and some of the traders and soldiers went out through the gate to watch.

They paid no attention to squaws who entered the enclosure or to others near the gate wrapped in blankets which concealed knives and tomahawks. Suddenly the ball was thrown wide and fell almost beside the gate. The players dashed after it. Dropping their crosses, they snatched knives and tomahawks from the squaws and dashed through the gate. Captain Etherington and Lieutenant Leslye were overpowered and carried away into the woods.

Inside the stockade Lieutenant Jamet tried in vain to rally the soldiers. Alone, he fought off the savages with his sword until he was struck down. Twenty of the garrison of thirty-five and one of the four English traders were killed.

Alexander Henry was writing letters when the attack began. Looking out the window, he saw the handful of Englishmen being overwhelmed and scalped by the ferocious Chippewa, while the French coolly looked on. They neither assisted in the slaughter nor tried to stop it.

Hoping to save his life, Henry ran next door to the house of Charles Langlade. There the whole family was at a window, calmly watching the massacre. Langlade was unmoved by Henry's plea for protection, but the Pani slave woman took pity on him and hid him in the attic. Lying terror-stricken under a pile of birchbark, he watched the Indians search for him; then, after they had gone, managed to sleep until morning.

Another party of savages came and carried Henry away. A huge Indian named Wenniway, painted black from head to heel except for a white band around each eye, seized him and raised a knife to plunge it into his breast. Instead of killing Henry, Wenniway changed his mind and adopted him. Henry narrowly escaped death several times afterward. He was finally ransomed by his Indian brother Wawatam. After peace was restored, Henry became one of the most successful Canadian fur merchants, and years later he wrote an account of his experiences at Michilimackinac.

Lieutenant Jamet, twenty-four soldiers, and one trader were killed at Michilimackinac. Captain Etherington, Lieutenant Leslye, eleven soldiers, and three traders, including Henry, were held prisoners. The Chippewa were jubilant over the success of their ruse and delighted with the great haul of traders' goods which they had taken. Because they had wanted to keep all the loot themselves, they had not notified the Ottawa at L'Arbre Croche of their plan to take the fort.

When the Ottawa learned what had happened, they descended upon Michilimackinac in an angry swarm led by Chief Okinochumake. At their demand, Chief Minavavana gave up the two officers, two traders, eleven soldiers, and some of the merchandise they had taken. Going back to L'Arbre Croche, the Ottawa permitted Captain Etherington to send an order to Lieutenant James Gorrell at Green Bay to abandon the fort and join him. Some friendly Menominee and Winnebago accompanied him and his men to L'Arbre Croche. Wishing to be at peace with the British, the Ottawa decided to take their prisoners to Montreal. In spite of opposition from the Chippewa, they set out and delivered them safely to the commanding officer there.

6

Major Gladwin first learned of the massacre at Michilimackinac on June 18 when Father Pierre du Jaunay, the missionary at that post, arrived with a letter from Captain Etherington asking for assistance. The major, of course, could do nothing. A reinforcement of nearly a hundred men sent from Fort Niagara under the command of Lieutenant Abraham Cuyler had been ambushed at Point Pelee in Lake

Erie, and the Indians had rowed the eight bateaux which they captured past the fort on May 30 with loud howls of triumph.

Finally, on July 29, twenty-two bateaux carrying a reinforcement of two hundred and sixty men arrived from Fort Niagara under the command of Captain James Dalyell. Major Robert Rogers accompanied the expedition.

Eager to strike a telling blow against the Indians, whom he despised, Dalyell induced Major Gladwin to sanction a night attack on the Ottawa village. His force of two hundred and fifty officers and men filed silently out of the Pontiac Gate along the River Road (Jefferson Avenue) toward the east at two o'clock on the morning of July 31.

Dalyell's purpose was to fall upon the Ottawa by surprise, but that was impossible. Frenchmen inside the fort had sent out a warning, and Pontiac's braves were waiting in the darkness.

A mile and a half from the fort, the advance detachment reached the bridge over Parent's Creek, a stream which flowed into the river along the present Adair Street. A few of the men were already across when a burst of fire from invisible enemies struck down the leaders. Others were ordered up and across the bridge. They dispersed the Indians in front of them, but bullets came now from the left flank where the Indians had taken shelter behind the *habitants'* picket fences. Captain Dalyell himself was wounded, and when he heard heavy firing toward his rear, he realized that Pontiac was trying to cut off his column. At once he ordered a retreat.

Bravely leading a detachment in a charge against a party of Indians protected by an excavation, Dalyell was killed. Then Captain James Grant and Major Robert Rogers by their shrewd tactics held off the savages until the column had withdrawn into the fort.

Although he had failed to destroy the expeditionary force, Pontiac had thoroughly defeated it. Besides Dalyell, fifty-eight officers and men were killed or wounded, and the little stream where the fighting began was afterward called Bloody Run.

The success of Pontiac against Dalyell was the high point in his siege of Detroit. As time wore on, he found it more and more difficult to keep his followers interested in the war. In July some Hurons and Potawatomi made peace with Major Gladwin, and early in October some Chippewa chiefs did likewise. As cold weather approached, many of the Ottawa left for the winter hunt. Pontiac stubbornly held on until he received a message on October 29 from Major Neyon de Villiers, commandant of Fort Chartres in Illinois. Notifying him that peace had finally been signed between France and Great Britain,

Villiers warned the chief that he must no longer continue the siege. Another letter to the local *habitants* urged them to live peaceably with the British.

As a result of these messages, on the last day of October, 1763, Pontiac sent a note to Major Gladwin offering to make peace. The major replied that he must send the request to General Amherst. Not waiting for a reply, Pontiac retired to the Maumee River for the winter, then moved to the Illinois country, where he continued to stir up hostility against the British.

In August, 1764, Colonel John Bradstreet, under orders to destroy the Indians or make peace, reached Detroit with a force of twelve hundred men. Tired of the long useless war, the local chiefs appeared at a council early in September and promised to cause no more trouble; but it was not until July, 1766, that Pontiac went down to Fort Ontario at Oswego, New York, to make his submission to Sir William Johnson. There he and the other western chiefs agreed to a treaty. They acknowledged King George III as their father; they promised to deliver all white captives and to make war on Indians who violated the peace. The British pardoned Pontiac and the other chiefs who had participated in the uprising, and they promised to remove white settlers from Indian lands.

Pontiac went to live in the Illinois country. There he was unpopular with many Indians, apparently because he was now a loyal supporter of the British. On that account, or more likely because of a local feud, Pontiac was killed by a Peoria Indian in Cahokia on April 20, 1769. His body is said to have been carried across the Mississippi to St. Louis for burial. The exact location of his grave is not known.

With the end of the French and Indian War in America in 1760, and of the Seven Years' War in Europe in 1763, Great Britain became the principal colonial power in North America. By the Treaty of Paris, France gave up Canada and the region east of the Mississippi to the British, and Louisiana west of the river to Spain. Not an acre of land on the continent of North America remained to France. Great Britain also acquired Florida from Spain, the ally of France in the recent war.

— 7 —

The Americans Take Over

THE TREATY OF PARIS, signed on February 20, 1763, seemingly had freed the British from the French and Indian menace, but other problems appeared immediately. The fur merchants wanted the West to remain uninhabited, except by Indians and traders, while farmers and speculators demanded that the newly acquired lands be opened to settlement. There were also the problems of how best to govern the eighty thousand new French subjects and how to manage the Indians of the West.

Before any steps had been taken, news of the Pontiac uprising reached London. An attempt was made to devise a solution for the pressing problems, but it was not until October 7, 1763, that a plan was announced. Known as the Proclamation of 1763, its provisions affecting the northern part of the continent were as follows: (1) The Colony of Quebec was created extending from the Atlantic Ocean up the Saint Lawrence to the Ottawa River. A governor and a council were to be appointed by the king, and an elected assembly was promised in the future. English law was to be introduced, and English courts were to be established. The question of religion was ignored. (2) To protect the Indians from the intrusion of settlers, a line was drawn along the crest of the Appalachian Mountains beyond which, for the present, settlers were forbidden to go. (3) Trade and other relations with the Indians were to be carried on through superintendents responsible to the Crown rather than by agents of the colonies.

The Proclamation of 1763 was the constitution of Quebec until 1774. Devised with the best of intent, it caused dissatisfaction among both the Canadians and the English-speaking colonists. The French resented the imposition of a new legal system upon them, they had no desire for an elected assembly, and they feared that the practice of the Roman Catholic religion might be prohibited.

To the English colonists, the line drawn along the ridge of mountains seemed to be an attempt to cancel their claims to western land and to prevent them from seeking new homes simply for the benefit of lazy and worthless savages. Land speculators, among whom were many influential persons, felt that they were being cheated of a favorable opportunity to make their fortunes now that the Indians were pacified.

The situation west of the Ottawa River was curious. Although there were about two thousand men, women, and children at Detroit and in the Illinois country, as far as the Proclamation was concerned, they were completely ignored. No government was provided for them except the authority of the commandants of the military posts. That condition did not disturb the *habitants,* who were accustomed to being ruled by a commandant, but the English traders who took up residence wanted civil law.

2

At Detroit Lieutenant Colonel John Campbell was put in command in August, 1764, and Gladwin was permitted to sail for England, having been promoted to lieutenant colonel for his valiant defense of the fort. No troops were sent to Fort St. Joseph, which became simply a headquarters for traders.

Fort Michilimackinac was reoccupied, and in August, 1766, Major Robert Rogers, accompanied by his wife and his secretary, Nathaniel Potter, became commandant. As commander of the troops and Indian agent, Rogers held complete sway in the northwest, subject only to the orders of General Thomas Gage and Sir William Johnson; but they were far away, and Rogers began to rule as if he were completely independent in his vast inland empire.

Disregarding Johnson's instructions to be economical and to limit trade to the vicinity of his post, he lavished gifts on the Indians and permitted the traders to visit distant tribes. In the spring of 1767 he assembled a great Indian council at Michilimackinac and induced the chiefs to cease their intertribal forays and to invite traders to their villages. This policy he defended as necessary to prevent French and Spanish traders across the Mississippi from monopolizing the fur trade.

While in England in 1765, Rogers had asked permission to lead an expedition to search for a northwest passage to the Pacific. Although his request was denied, he believed that he was now in a position where he could direct such a project. And so he sent out from Michilimackinac Captain James Tute, formerly an officer in the Rangers, Captain Jonathan Carver, and others to find a route to the west coast. They reached the western extremity of Lake Superior, but could go no farther because Rogers failed to send them the supplies which he had promised.

Desiring to put his rule on a firmer basis, Rogers petitioned the British government to erect a new colony in the northwest with himself as governor, responsible only to the authorities in London. Sir William Johnson denounced this scheme as impractical, refused to sanction Rogers' exorbitant expenditures, and censured him for disobeying orders.

Rogers was now in the complete disfavor of the Indian superintendent, and he was soon to be in the bad graces of the military authorities as well. After a violent quarrel, his secretary, Potter, fled to Quebec, where he charged Rogers with treasonable negotiations with the Spaniards beyond the Mississippi. General Gage ordered him under arrest. On November 6, 1767, he was put in confinement in the fort and held prisoner until navigation opened in the spring.

At his trial, no evidence of treason was produced, but he had conducted himself in so highhanded a manner at Michilimackinac that he was dismissed from the service. During the Revolution Rogers was a Loyalist. He went to England and died there in obscurity.

3

Many persons believed that the Treaty of Paris in 1763, by removing the French threat in America, promised a prosperous future for the empire. There were others, however, who feared that elimination of the French would cause the colonists to feel less dependent on the mother country. So it turned out, but the rift between mother and daughters also was widened by mismanagement in London.

Before 1763 the colonies had been largely neglected by the British government. Left to their own devices, the people had become accustomed to managing their own affairs. As a result, when the authorities in London decided to maintain garrisons in America and to levy taxes on the people to defray part of the expense, there was strong opposition. Ignorant of the conditions in America and of the temper of the colonists, the Cabinet devised one tax after another, trying in vain to find one which would be acceptable. After Parliament had repealed all of them, retaining only a small tax on tea in order to show its authority, resentment over this subterfuge aroused resistance in several seaports when ships bearing the tea cast anchor. In Boston on December 16, 1773, a band of men disguised as Indians broke open the chests of tea and dumped them into the harbor.

In retaliation Parliament in 1774 passed four acts reducing the political power of the people and closing the port of Boston. These laws were called the Intolerable Acts, and another, which actually had no bearing on the matter, was added to the list by American patriot leaders.

This fifth law of 1774 was the Quebec Act. Intended to allay the discontent of the French Canadians, who had never become reconciled to living under the Proclamation of 1763, it contained provisions which the seaboard colonists believed were meant as a threat to their liberties.

In brief the Quebec Act provided (1) that all the Indian country extending to the Ohio and the Mississippi rivers be annexed to the province of Quebec, and that a lieutenant governor be stationed at each important post; (2) that English criminal law be continued in force, but that French civil law be re-established, thus permitting the maintenance of the feudal system; (3) that an appointed legislative council be provided for Quebec instead of an elected assembly; and (4) that the Roman Catholic religion be protected.

The *habitants* were entirely satisfied with these provisions, but the colonists along the coast found cause for complaint. The extension of Quebec west of the mountains put an end to the claims of certain colonies to western lands, and speculators saw their schemes defeated. Some leaders, either ignorant of the preference of the French to be ruled or reading more into the law than met the eye, declared that Britain would soon abolish assemblies in the seaboard colonies; and the wise provision by which the Roman Catholic Church was recognized in Quebec was denounced by some as showing the intent of the British government to interfere with religion in her old colonies.

The Quebec Act had one important result for Michigan. Under this law for the first time civil government was established within its borders. Colonel Arent Schuyler de Peyster was sent to Michilimackinac as commandant and lieutenant governor in 1774, and in 1775 Lieutenant Governor Henry Hamilton arrived at Detroit. As a matter of fact, in spite of the law there was very little difference for many years, because the Revolutionary War kept the military authority predominant at both posts.

4

Michigan did not play a decisive part in the war, but Detroit was the base of operations for murderous raids into the western country. On July 27, 1777, Hamilton reported that he had sent fifteen war parties of whites and Indians into Kentucky. They attacked frontier settlements; killed and scalped men, women, and children; and brought many miserable captives to Detroit. At one time nearly five hundred prisoners of war, including Negro slaves, were in the town or the vicinity. Hamilton's purpose was to destroy the settlements, and he almost succeeded. Many survivors of his attacks recrossed the mountains to their former homes, but the hardiest remained in spite of danger.

So bitterly was Hamilton hated by the Kentuckians that they called him the "Hair Buyer" because he paid the Indians for scalps. They ignored the fact that he was obeying orders from higher authorities, that other officers were doing the same thing, and that he paid more for prisoners than for scalps. Singling him out for special attention was simply a measure of the Kentuckians' fear and hatred of the man.

In the spring of 1778 a party of Shawnee captured and brought to Detroit the most famous of Kentucky's pioneers, Daniel Boone. Hamilton offered £100 for him, but the Indians were so proud of their illustrious prisoner that they rejected the offer. Taking him to their town at Chillicothe, Ohio, they adopted him into the tribe.

When Boone heard that the Indians were planning to attack Boonesboro, he escaped and reached home in time to warn his friends. The invading force under the command of Captain Antoine Dequindre of Detroit was beaten off.

Colonel George Rogers Clark was commandant in Kentucky under the authority of Virginia. In 1777 he boldly decided to prevent further raids by a counterattack. At his request, Governor Patrick Henry of Virginia authorized an expedition against the Illinois towns and Detroit, which were in territory claimed by Virginia under her colonial charter.

Moving rapidly with his small army, Clark entered Kaskaskia without opposition on July 5, 1778, and occupied Cahokia and Fort Chartres. France was now in the war as an ally of the United States, and the *habitants* willingly gave up their British allegiance. Emissaries sent by Clark to Vincennes easily won the support of the *habitants* there to the American cause, and Captain Leonard Helm with a small detachment occupied Fort Sackville.

When Lieutenant Governor Hamilton at Detroit learned of Clark's coup, he raised an expeditionary force to retake Vincennes. Leaving on October 7, 1778, with thirty-three soldiers and two officers of the regular army, one hundred and twenty volunteers, including officers and interpreters, and seventy Indians, he arrived at Vincennes on December 17. Captain Helm surrendered Fort Sackville, and the *habitants* were required to take a new oath of allegiance to Great Britain. Believing himself safe from attack during the winter, Hamilton permitted the Indians and most of the volunteers to go home until spring.

In a surprise movement, Clark marched his men across country covered with water from swollen streams and forced Hamilton to surrender on February 25, 1779. He and his officers were sent to Williamsburg, Virginia, where they were confined in the prison.[1]

Clark now planned to attack Detroit. To be prepared for the bold leader and his "long knives," as the Indians called the Kentuckians, Captain Richard B. Lernoult in 1779 built a fort back of the town, about where the Federal Building now stands. It had a high earthen rampart with half-bastions so that fire could be directed against enemy soldiers who might penetrate the outer defenses. In front of the rampart was a ditch with a palisade in the middle, then the glacis, a low rampart of earth. Outside the glacis an abatis of felled trees, with the branches cut short and sharpened, served the purpose of a present-day barbed-wire entanglement. The stockade of the town was extended back to the forward extremities of Fort Lernoult. Detroit was well protected.

At Michilimackinac, the commandant, Major Patrick Sinclair, also feared an attack by Clark. For greater safety he moved from the main-

[1] A replica of the prison, and even of the cell in which Hamilton was confined, may be seen in Williamsburg.

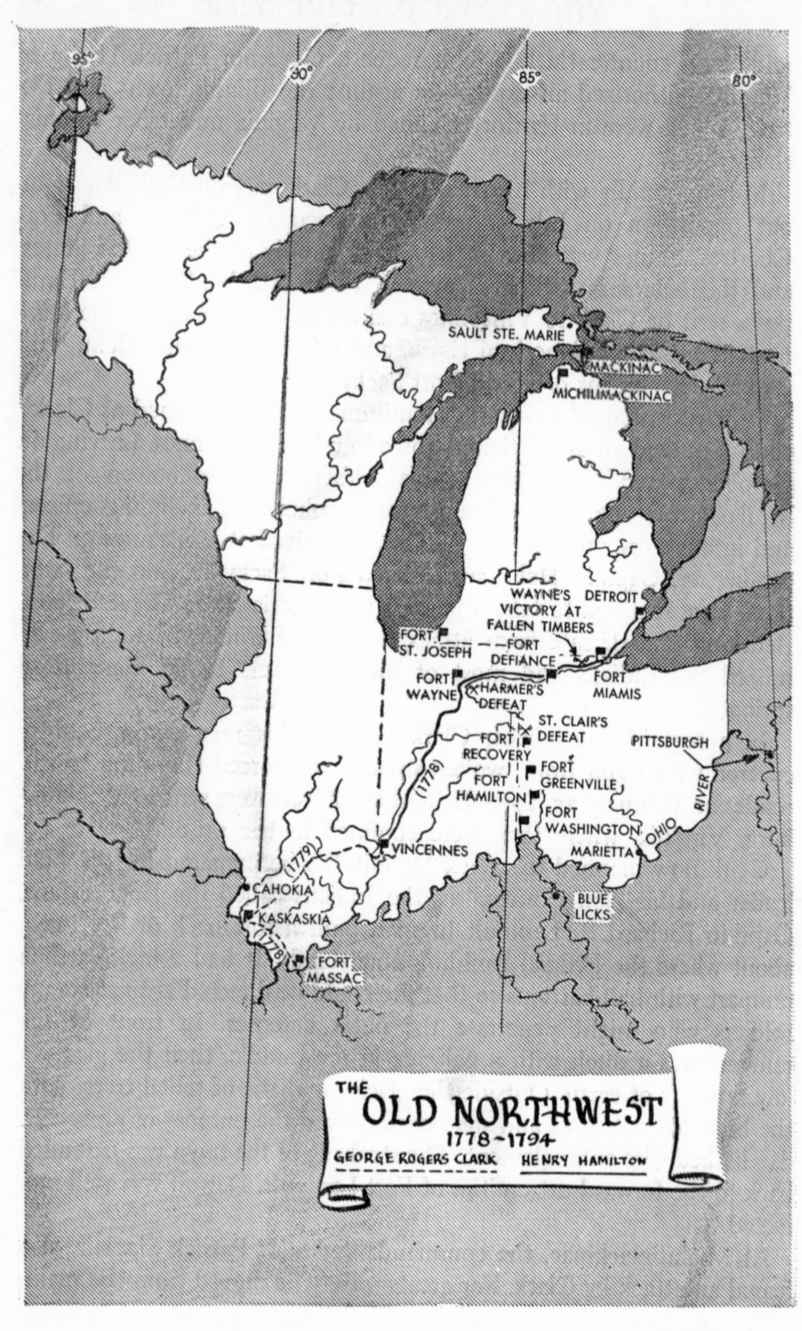

95°
90°
85°
80°
SAULT STE. MARIE
MACKINAC
MICHILIMACKINAC
WAYNE'S VICTORY AT FALLEN TIMBERS
DETROIT
FORT ST. JOSEPH
FORT DEFIANCE
FORT WAYNE
HARMER'S DEFEAT
FORT MIAMIS
ST. CLAIR'S DEFEAT
FORT RECOVERY
PITTSBURGH
FORT GREENVILLE
FORT HAMILTON
FORT WASHINGTON
OHIO RIVER
(1778)
VINCENNES
MARIETTA
(1779)
CAHOKIA
KASKASKIA
(1778)
BLUE LICKS
FORT MASSAC
THE OLD NORTHWEST
1778–1794
GEORGE ROGERS CLARK
HENRY HAMILTON

land to Mackinac Island, where, during the years 1779 to 1781, he constructed a fort on the hill overlooking the harbor. These precautions turned out to be unnecessary, for Clark never was able to gather sufficient men or supplies for an expedition against Detroit, much less against Michilimackinac.

Colonel Arent Schuyler de Peyster was transferred from Michilimackinac to Detroit as Hamilton's successor in 1779. At both places, the Colonel amused himself by writing verses. They are not very good poetry, but they contain some interesting information about life at these posts. At Michilimackinac he had as pets a spaniel and a swan, and Mrs. de Peyster had a striped squirrel named Tim.

At Detroit the colonel wrote verses about the pleasure of sleighing on the Detroit River and of a winter picnic on the bank of the River Rouge, which he called "sweet River Red." These poems, with numerous others which he wrote, were published in a book entitled *Miscellanies by an Officer*.

De Peyster continued Hamilton's practice of sending war parties into Kentucky. In April, 1780, he dispatched an expedition of twelve hundred whites and Indians under Captain Henry Bird to attack Clark at the Rapids of the Ohio (Louisville). Fearful of the bloody reception which would surely be given them there, the Indians refused to go. Instead they crossed into Kentucky, captured Ruddle's Station, and massacred men, women, and children. Captain Bird was thoroughly disgusted with the savagery of his Indian allies, but they paid no heed to his pleas for humanity. Continuing farther, the Indians took also Martin's Station and another small place. They returned to Detroit with about three hundred and fifty prisoners.

5

Major Sinclair in 1780 sent Charles Langlade with seven hundred and fifty men from Fort Michilimackinac to attack the Spaniards in St. Louis. Spain was not an ally of the United States, but she had declared war on England. Langlade's force was defeated by the Spaniards and compelled to retreat.

Old Fort St. Joseph, which had not been garrisoned after it had fallen to the Indians during Pontiac's War, was suddenly occupied by a band of *habitant* militia from the Illinois country in December, 1780. Learning that a party of British traders was returning to the post, the French retreated. Pursued and overtaken, most of them were killed or captured.

In order to avenge the victims of this disaster, a force of Spaniards from St. Louis, French from Cahokia, and Indians marched on Fort St. Joseph, where they arrived on February 12, 1781. Finding it again vacant, they occupied it for a day and raised the Spanish flag over the stockade. Because of this exploit, Niles is known as the city of four flags—French, British, Spanish, and American. The invaders retired before the British learned of their presence, and they returned safely to their homes.

In spite of George Rogers Clark's valiant efforts, parties of whites and Indians from Detroit continued to invade Kentucky. Bryan's Station was besieged in August, 1782, by a force of Hurons and other lake Indians. Their leaders were Captain William Caldwell, Alexander McKee, Matthew Elliot, and Simon Girty, all Loyalists who had been driven from their homes in western Pennsylvania. After having fled to Detroit, they became skillful partisan fighters.

Failing to take the station, Caldwell on August 17 decided to return to Detroit. The next day nearly two hundred mounted Kentuckians, summoned by messengers, set out in pursuit. In the expectation that he would be followed, Caldwell retired deliberately, keeping on the alert. On the night of August 18 he camped in a strong position where the enemy would have to cross the Licking River to attack him. He had about two hundred Indians under his command.

On the morning of August 19 the pursuers appeared, among them some of the best known men of Kentucky: Colonel John Todd, the commander, Daniel Boone, Silas Harlan, Levi Todd, and Stephen Trigg. Against the advice of Daniel Boone, Colonel Todd led his men across the river directly against the lurking enemy. A sudden blast of musket fire cut down the advance detachment. Indians broke through the right wing and flanked the rest of the line. Then ensued a bloody hand-to-hand engagement with knife and tomahawk. Leaving sixty-six dead on the field and four of their comrades prisoners in the hands of the savages, the Kentuckians fled. Among those killed in this Battle of the Blue Licks were Colonel Todd and Colonel Trigg. The force from Detroit had decisively defeated a party almost as large as their own, consisting of the most seasoned frontier fighters. Caldwell lost only ten Indians and one white man.

During the war, a small colony of refugees from Ohio settled in Michigan. Some years earlier Moravian missionaries had established settlements of Delaware Indians on the Muskingum River. Becoming Christians and learning agriculture from their teachers, these Indians were prospering. Like the Quakers, the Moravians were opposed to violence, and their Indians refused to take part with either of the warring nations. Suspected of treachery by both British and Americans, they were first ordered to Sandusky by the British so that they could be kept under supervision. In 1782, some returned to their town of Gnadenhutten, near the present Tuscarawas, Ohio, to collect supplies. There a party of American frontiersmen fell upon the unarmed Indians and murdered ninety of them in cold blood.

To protect the remainder, Colonel Arent Schuyler de Peyster called them to Detroit and found a place for them on the Clinton River, then called the Huron. There, under the leadership of the missionaries David Zeisberger, John Gottlieb Heckewelder, Gottlob Senseman, and others, the Christian Delawares built a village of twenty-seven log cabins and a meetinghouse, cleared the land, and raised crops from 1782 until 1786. A road which they opened to a mill on Connor's Creek, now in Detroit, was the first inland road in Michigan. In the spring of 1786 they sold their improvements and left, some returning to the Muskingum and others settling on the Thames River in Ontario. A small monument near Moravian Drive just west of Mount Clemens marks the site of the village.

Although the people of Michigan were on the British side during the Revolutionary War, a native son of the French period fought in the American Army. Captain Paul Louis Céloron de Blainville was an officer in Count Casimir Pulaski's Cavalry Legion. Born in Detroit on March 2, 1753, Paul Louis was a son of the commandant, Major Pierre Joseph Céloron de Blainville, who had made the tour of western Pennsylvania and Ohio in 1749, asserting the claim of France to that region.

Major Céloron died in Montreal in 1759. After Canada became a British province, Paul Louis Céloron went to France. In 1777, he was an officer of the garrison in Martinique, a French colony in the West Indies. Desiring to engage in the war against Great Britain, he took ship for the United States and obtained from Congress a captain's commission. As an officer in Pulaski's Legion, Captain Céloron fought in Georgia and South Carolina. When Charleston was taken by the British in 1780, he became a prisoner of war.

Captain Céloron was exchanged and rejoined the American Army, continuing in the service until 1782, when the fighting was done. Having helped to win independence for the new nation, he resigned his commission and returned to Martinique.

6

The Revolutionary War was officially ended by the Treaty of Paris in 1783. Just twenty years after she had taken the land east of the Mississippi from France, Britain gave it to the United States of America. Apparently the British authorities were glad to be rid of it. The support of garrisons in the western country had been expensive, and settlers moving West had caused trouble. Besides, Britain was tired of the war and willing to make concessions for peace. Nevertheless, on the pretext that the United States had not fulfilled the terms of the treaty, British garrisons were retained in the western forts, including Detroit and Mackinac. The real reason seems to have been to protect the trade of the London and Montreal fur merchants as long as possible.

Although civil government for Michigan had been promised in the Quebec Act, the war had kept the military authority supreme. After the end of hostilities, an insistent demand from Loyalists who had left the colonies and settled on land granted to them by the British government along Lake Ontario, Lake Erie, and the Detroit River produced results. In 1787 four administrative districts were established in the region inhabited by English-speaking people. Detroit was in the district of Hesse. A court of common pleas, a county lieutenant, a sheriff, and justices of the peace were provided for each district. Judge William D. Powell held court in Sandwich (1789–1794) rather than in Detroit because it was not known how soon Detroit would be delivered to the Americans. This was the real beginning of civil government for Michigan.

The next step was taken after the passage of the Constitutional Act in 1791 by the British Parliament. Recognizing the fact that the French were predominant in the East and the British in the West, Parliament divided Quebec into the two provinces of Upper Canada and Lower Canada. The boundary line between them was the Ottawa River. Each province was provided with an appointed council, an elected assembly, and a lieutenant governor under the governor general.

The first lieutenant governor of Upper Canada, which included Michigan, was Colonel John Graves Simcoe, a veteran of the Revolutionary War. Like most of the inhabitants of the province, he was hostile to the American government. Being a military man, Simcoe was impatient with the delays of democratic institutions.

Under the Constitutional Act, the first election in Michigan was held in the summer of 1792. From the Detroit River area William Macomb, François Baby, and David W. Smith were elected to sit in the Assembly at Niagara, and Alexander Grant was appointed to the Council. At last representative government had come to Michigan.

7

If anyone in the thirteen colonies had believed that winning independence from Great Britain would solve the problems that had caused revolt, he soon learned how wrong he had been. All the problems remained: taxation, land policy, Indian policy, settlement of the West, and protection of the frontier. Now, however, Americans had to try to find practical solutions. An unpopular tax caused the Whiskey Rebellion in western Pennsylvania (1794), and President George Washington had to send militia to enforce the law.

The Ordinance of 1785 was passed by the Congress of the Confederation to provide for the orderly sale of the national domain with fair treatment of the Indians, and to bring money into the empty treasury of the United States. According to the terms of the ordinance, large areas could be purchased only by government agents meeting with chiefs and making treaties. Then surveyors were to run lines dividing the land into townships six miles square, and each township into thirty-six sections one mile square. Section Sixteen in each township was reserved for the support of schools.

After the land was surveyed it was to be sold at auction to the highest bidder. At first a section, 640 acres, was the smallest quantity that could be purchased, and the minimum price was a dollar an acre. Later, in order to give poorer people an opportunity to own a farm, the amount was reduced to eighty acres.

By treaties with the Indians at Fort Stanwix (1784) and at Fort McIntosh (1785) the government acquired a tract of land immediately west of the upper Ohio River, and surveyors began running township and section lines. Land-hungry settlers would not wait until the land was offered for sale. They swarmed into the treaty area and beyond along the Ohio. Indians, resenting this intrusion, began to take scalps, encouraged and assisted by British agents at Detroit, who provided them with arms and ammunition. Colonel Josiah Harmar was ordered to detail soldiers to protect the surveyors and remove squatters. It was an unpleasant task, and an impossible one; for settlers continued to enter the West regardless of the Indian menace and government orders.

The Ordinance of 1787 provided a government for the Northwest

Territory, the region between Pennsylvania and the Mississippi River and from the Ohio River north to the international boundary. Michigan was included in the Territory, or would be, as soon as the British decided to give it up.

According to the Ordinance, there were to be three stages in the progress of the Territory toward statehood. At first there were a governor, a secretary, and three judges, appointed by the President. The governor and judges sitting as a body were the legislature, and the judges constituted the supreme court. In the absence of the governor, the secretary acted in his place.

The second stage was reached when the Territory had five thousand free male inhabitants. Then the property owners would be permitted to choose an assembly and nominate ten men, from whom the President would choose five to sit as a legislative council. The legislature was permitted to elect a delegate to Congress with the right to speak for his territory but not to vote.

The ordinance provided that three or five states should eventually be formed from the Northwest Territory. This would be the third stage. When a part of the Territory contained sixty thousand free inhabitants, it might make a constitution and be admitted by Congress to the Union as a state equal in rights to the original thirteen.

Besides providing a framework of government, the ordinance contained six articles of compact between the original states and the people of the Territory. These articles guaranteed freedom of religion, the benefits of the writ of habeas corpus, and trial by jury; declared that states formed from the Territory should forever remain a part of the United States; prohibited slavery; provided that the navigable waters of the West were open to the use of all United States citizens; urged considerate treatment of the Indians; and declared that "Religion, morality, and knowledge, being necessary to good government and the happiness of mankind, schools and the means of education shall forever be encouraged."

This ordinance, passed by the Congress of the Confederation sitting in New York City at the same time the Constitutional Convention was meeting in Philadelphia, had liberal features, such as freedom of religion and trial by jury, which were lacking in the original Constitution. These two, with others, were added in the first ten amendments; but the prohibition of slavery throughout the nation came only with the Thirteenth Amendment after four bloody years of war, and education was not considered by the Constitution makers a responsibility of the national government.

8

Marietta was founded in the spring of 1788 at the junction of the Muskingum River with the Ohio by settlers from New England, and it became the capital of the Northwest Territory when Governor Arthur St. Clair, the secretary, and the judges arrived in July of the same year. The coming of more settlers caused further Indian depredations. With the purpose of punishing the savages, President Washington sent General Josiah Harmar in 1790 with an expeditionary force of fifteen hundred men, mostly raw recruits, into the Indian country. At the Miami towns, where Fort Wayne, Indiana, now stands, his little army was defeated and forced to retire.

The next year, 1791, Washington ordered Governor St. Clair, a Revolutionary War general, to march against the Indians. Attacked by a horde of savages in western Ohio, his army of two thousand men was nearly destroyed. Determined to remove the Indian menace, the President chose General Anthony Wayne to command a new western army. Called "Mad Anthony" because of his impulsiveness during the Revolution, he was believed by many persons to be the wrong man for the task.

This time, however, Wayne was coolly deliberate. Knowing that lack of training had been largely responsible for the two previous disasters, he drilled his men thoroughly and taught them to shoot. Setting out from Pittsburgh in 1792, he moved slowly down the Ohio, literally whipping his men into shape. His orderly books are filled with court-martial sentences of lashings on the bare back, ranging from twenty-five to one hundred strokes, for breaches of discipline.

During 1793 he had to wait at Cincinnati while President Washington sent commissioners in a final effort to make peace with the Indians. Lieutenant Governor Simcoe detained the commissioners until Colonel Alexander McKee and other British agents had induced the chiefs to ignore the American proposals. Permitted to advance after the negotiations had failed, Wayne proceeded north and built Fort Greenville[2] for his winter quarters.

Setting out in the spring of 1794, he marched to the Maumee River and descended it almost to the point where Lieutenant Governor Simcoe had built Fort Miamis, just outside the present town of Maumee, Ohio. There he expected to stop Wayne, who, he believed, was intending to attack Detroit. On August 20, 1794, at the Fallen

[2] Now Greenville, Ohio.

Timbers, Wayne met the enemy under Chief Blue Jacket: Shawnee, Delawares, Hurons, Ottawa, Potawatomi, Chippewa, Miami, and about fifty British volunteers from the Detroit area. Colonel McKee, Matthew Elliot, and Simon Girty were with the savages on that day.

Dragoons, infantry, and mounted Kentucky riflemen advanced like veterans. Dragoons with flashing sabers cut down the savages, the infantry flushed them out of the tangled timbers with bayonets, and the mounted men drove them to Fort Miamis and beyond. Defeated and despondent when Major William Campbell, obeying his orders, refused to receive them into the fort, the Indians lost faith in their British Father.

Wayne was not so rash as to attack Fort Miamis, which mounted a number of cannon, nor to try to reach Detroit. Instead, satisfied with his victory, he moved up the Maumee and built Fort Wayne (Indiana); then he returned to Fort Greenville, to which he invited the Indians for a parley. They went to meet him there in the summer of 1795, and by the Treaty of Greenville ceded nearly all of Ohio to the United States and put an end to forty years of warfare in the valley of the Ohio.

The time had now come for Great Britain to relinquish the western posts. The United States was much stronger than it had been, and Wayne's campaign had showed that the Americans could take Detroit if they made a determined effort. The British wanted no war with the United States, for in 1793 they had become involved in a war with France. And so, in the fall of 1794, the British agreed in an article of the Jay Treaty to evacuate the forts in the West on or before June 1, 1796.

True to their word, the British were ready to withdraw their garrisons by June 1, but the Americans asked for time to advance their troops. Lieutenant Colonel John Francis Hamtramck with the First Sub-legion[3] reached Camp Deposit on the Maumee above Fort Miamis on June 6 and remained there awaiting orders. Captain Henry De Butts, General Wayne's chief aide, sent to arrange for the transfer of sovereignty, arrived at Detroit on June 30. Colonel Richard England, the British commandant of Fort Lernoult, received him courteously and helped him procure three ships to bring the American troops forward.

When the ships reached Camp Deposit, Colonel Hamtramck ordered Captain Moses Porter and sixty-five men to sail for Detroit. There

[3] Wayne's army was called the Legion of the United States. It consisted of four sub-legions, each composed of infantry, cavalry, and artillery. In 1796 a reorganization was carried out and the First Sub-legion became the First Infantry Regiment.

Raising the Flag of the United States at Ft. Lernoult, 1796

on July 11, 1796, at about noon, the British hauled down the Union Jack and embarked for Lower Canada. Captain Porter and his men marched into Fort Lernoult and raised the flag of the United States. Captain De Butts, who was present at the ceremony, reported that "the exchange was effected with much propriety and harmony on both sides," and that "every attention was paid by the British and [the] inhabitants to our troops."

On September 1, Major Henry Burbeck with a force of one hundred and ten men occupied Fort Mackinac after Lieutenant Andrew Foster withdrew the British garrison. At last, thirteen years after the Treaty of Paris was ratified, Michigan became a part of the United States.

PART III

FROM TERRITORY INTO STATEHOOD 1796–1837

— 8 —

American Beginnings, 1796–1812

LIEUTENANT COLONEL HAMTRAMCK with the remainder of the First Sub-legion arrived at Detroit on July 13, 1796, and took command. The garrison then numbered about four hundred officers and men. Some of them were quartered in Fort Lernoult, and the others in the Citadel, a palisaded enclosure inside the west wall and just north of St. Anne Street.

Since no civil government had yet been provided, Colonel Hamtramck had authority over the inhabitants as well as over the soldiers. He was well qualified for his position because he was a native of Quebec and, of course, spoke French, as did most of the people at Detroit. His military experience had been ample. When only nineteen years of age he had left Canada for the United States, and joined the army in 1775. Serving throughout the Revolutionary War, he had twice won the commendation of General George Washington.

After the war Hamtramck had served in the West under General Josiah Harmar and General Arthur St. Clair; then he had fought under

Wayne at the Battle of Fallen Timbers, winning a citation for his gallantry on that day. He was small in stature, only five feet five inches tall, but a peppery temper and a stern manner kept his subordinates attentive to their duty.

Detroit was still a small town. Enclosed on three sides by the palisade, and with Fort Lernoult behind it, there was no room for expansion. If it were set down in the present city, it would fill the space between Griswold Street on the east and Cass Avenue on the west, and between Larned Street on the north and Woodbridge Street on the south. At that time the river reached almost to Woodbridge Street. The space between that and the river at present was made by leveling the high bank of the river and dumping the earth from Fort Lernoult into the water after the garrison was withdrawn in 1826.

Four narrow streets ran north and south, and four others crossed them running east and west. The widest was St. Anne Street, now Jefferson Avenue, which extended from the West Gate to the Pontiac Gate in the east wall. It was only twenty feet wide.

Near the Pontiac Gate, St. Anne's Church faced on St. Anne Street, and Joseph Campau's store was just opposite. Other merchants who had stores on this street were William Robertson, James Abbott, and Angus Mackintosh. John Harvey's bakery was on the north side of St. Anne Street near the Citadel, and John Dodemead's tavern was on the south side, just opposite.

Outside the stockade, the ribbon farms reached up to the St. Clair River and down to the River Rouge. There were farms also along that stream, and another cluster of them along the River Raisin.

The number of people living in the town was not more than five hundred, and twenty-one hundred were living on the farms. Counting the permanent inhabitants on Mackinac Island, the traders living on the St. Joseph River, and the handful at Sault Sainte Marie, the population of Michigan was certainly less than three thousand.

2

Detroit today is a city of many nationalities. Even in 1796 it contained a great variety of inhabitants. Among them were several Dutch merchants from New York: John Visger, Gerrit Graverat, William Groesbeck, and Jacob Visger.

A number of Germans also were living in Detroit when the Americans came: Jonathan Schieffelin, merchant; Israel Ruland, silversmith; Conrad Seek, tailor; Conrad Showalter; and Dr. Hermann M. Eberts.

There was also the numerous family of Michel Yax. He and his wife, who were the first German settlers in Michigan, had been brought to Detroit from Kentucky as Indian captives in 1747. Ransomed by sympathetic townspeople, they had acquired a farm and spent the remainder of their lives in the neighborhood.

The English and the Scottish merchants who had come to Detroit after the British occupation in 1760 were now the leading businessmen of the region. Some, disliking the new American regime, moved across the river to British territory. Most of them, however, continued to live in Detroit, although some retained their allegiance to Great Britain. Nearly all married French girls.

John Askin, besides engaging in the fur trade, occupied the first farm east of the town, which had belonged to the family of his wife, Marie Archange Barthe. An American, Elijah Brush, married one of his daughters and bought the farm from Askin. Brush Street occupies a strip of that farm.

The wealthiest merchant at Detroit during the British regime was William Macomb. He and his brother Alexander had been in business together until after the Revolutionary War, when Alexander moved to New York. William owned Belle Isle, Grosse Ile, and other property, including the first farm west of the town. There, besides the big house, there were a barn, a sheep shed, a cider press, a root cellar, and a bakehouse. Part of the farm had been made into a deer park with a pavilion in it.

William Macomb, although he was a British subject, had taken an active part in preparing for the occupation by the Americans. Using his great influence with the Indians, he had induced some of them to go to Greenville to make a treaty with General Wayne. Macomb died three months before Colonel Hamtramck reached Detroit.

James Abbott, in partnership with his sons Robert and James, was a leading merchant in the town. James May, another merchant, owned a ship and kept a boardinghouse.

Living on his farm at Grosse Pointe, Commodore Alexander Grant was in command of the Royal Navy of the Upper Lakes. His wife was Thérèse Barthe, sister of John Askin's wife. They had twelve children, ten girls and two boys. The commodore talked about moving across the river after the Americans came, but he never did. A loyal Briton, he retained command of the British fleet, going down to the navy yard at Amherstburg when his presence was required. After his death in 1813, his body was carried to Sandwich and buried in British soil.

The French-speaking inhabitants of the Detroit area were, of course, the most numerous. Under British rule they had retained their language and their customs. Although they were not entirely happy as British subjects, they were grateful that they were permitted to practice their religion. When Colonel Hamtramck arrived, they were temporarily without a pastor, for Father Pierre Frechette had left for Quebec on July 6, 1796, and the people were awaiting a priest to be sent by Bishop John Carroll, head of the Roman Catholic Church in the United States.

In addition to the Dutch, Germans, Scots, English, and French, there were also Negroes and Indians at Detroit. Nearly all of them were slaves. The Indian slaves were the Panis who have previously been mentioned. Most of the Negroes had been brought as captives from Kentucky or were children of those captives. There were, besides, a few free Negroes.

Even after the American government began to function in Michigan, slavery continued to exist in spite of the Ordinance of 1787. British subjects who had owned slaves before the transfer of sovereignty on July 11, 1796, were permitted to keep them under the clause of Jay's Treaty which protected their property. Americans, however, could not own slaves in Michigan.

Numerous Indians lived in the vicinity of Detroit. During the day they were permitted within the palisades, but they were required to leave before the gates were closed in the evening. Colonel Hamtramck had to feed many of these Indians to retain their friendship for the United States. Soon he found his supplies were running low, for Indians from the lakes and the Ohio country flocked to Detroit to see General Wayne, whom they expected to find there. In a short while twelve hundred Indians had assembled to welcome the commander in chief, and Hamtramck had to feed all of them.

3

General Anthony Wayne reached Detroit on August 13, 1796. With him came Winthrop Sargent, acting governor of the Northwest Territory, and Peter Audrain, a Frenchman who had become an American citizen. As the general with his bodyguard of dragoons rode up toward the West Gate of the town, a horde of whooping Indians raced out to meet him. Little Turtle, the Miami chief, was among the first to shake the hand of the "Chief-who-never-sleeps," as he called him; and Blue Jacket, chief of the Shawnee, who had been in command at Fallen Timbers, was not far behind. The Indians respected this soldier who had defeated them in battle, and who had dealt with them fairly in council. By the Miami he had been nicknamed the "Blacksnake" because of his deceptive advance through the forest; and the Potawatomi, mindful of his crushing cavalry charge at Fallen Timbers, called him the "Tornado."

Wayne was pleased with his reception by the Indians, and by the preparations which Colonel Hamtramck had made to honor him. A national salute was fired by the cannon of the fort, and the soldiers of the First Sub-legion passed in review before the commander in chief.

The general was delighted with the location of the town. To his son he wrote: "Detroit is beautifully situate upon the west bank of the river of the same name. . . ." And he expressed his amazement at the heavy waterborne traffic of the strait: "Here in the center of a Wilderness you see Ships or large vessels of War & Merchantmen laying at the Wharf or sailing up & down a pleasant river of about one mile wide as if passing & repassing to & from the Ocean."

The town and the people also impressed him favorably. He described the houses as "generally from One story to two stories & a half high—many of them well finished & furnished, & inhabited by people from almost all nations, among whom are a number of wealthy & well informed Merchants & Gentlemen & fashionable well bred Women."

Because he knew Philadelphia and other eastern cities, General Wayne's opinion of the people of Detroit is interesting. He was apparently surprised to find evidences of culture in the wilderness. Many of the leading inhabitants had rather large collections of books. William Macomb, for example, had nearly two hundred. There were several teachers in Detroit, and the well-to-do inhabitants sent their children to them for instruction.

Two pupils at this time were James and John Burnett, sons of William Burnett and his Indian wife Kakima, daughter of the Potawatomi chief Aniquiba and sister of Topinabee. Burnett was a trader on the St. Joseph River. Wanting his sons to be educated, he sent them to live in Detroit with his friend James May, who put them in John Burrell's school.

Another of Burrell's pupils was John Williams. He was the son of Thomas Williams, who had died in 1785, and Marie Cecile Campau, sister of Joseph Campau. After her husband's death, Mrs. Williams had married again and had gone to live on the Clinton River near the present city of Mt. Clemens.

In 1796, when John was fourteen, he wrote to his Uncle Joseph, asking for a job in his store and promising to do whatever might be required of him. In return he wanted only his board and lodging, and schooling in the evening with a good schoolmaster. The letter was written in French, the only language the boy knew.

Joseph Campau gave John a job in his store and sent him to John Burrell to learn English and mathematics. Joseph also had Burrell come to the store to teach him English, for he realized the importance of knowing that language if he wanted to be successful in business.

Later, in order to avoid confusion with another John Williams, Campau's nephew inserted the letter R in his name. John R. Street in Detroit is named for him. He and his uncle Joseph became wealthy and distinguished citizens of Michigan.

There was no post office nor newspaper in Michigan when the Americans took over. Newspapers from Europe and the eastern cities came usually with shipments of merchandise, weeks late but welcome just the same. Letters were carried by travelers and delivered personally. Government officials and some of the merchants sent letters and orders by "expresses"—men engaged to carry them as rapidly as possible to their destination. Two men were paid thirty dollars a month and rations to carry government dispatches on horseback between Detroit and Pittsburgh. During the winter they were given a bonus of ten dollars if they could get to Detroit in twenty days.

There was no Protestant church in Detroit, but while General Wayne was there, the Reverend David Jones, chaplain of the United States Army, came and preached several times. A Baptist minister and an ardent patriot, he had first become a chaplain in 1777. During the Revolutionary War he had served with Wayne, and they had become fast friends. It was through the influence of the general that Dr. Jones had been appointed chaplain to the Legion. After he left, the Protestants of Detroit had religious services only when traveling preachers, called circuit riders, came to town.

Father Michel Levadoux, the new priest of St. Anne's, arrived a day later than Wayne. A member of the Sulpician Order, he had fled to America because of the French Revolution. Bishop John Carroll had first sent him to Cahokia in Illinois, and now he had transferred him to Detroit. Father Levadoux was grateful for the religious freedom permitted by the United States government, and he wanted to make his new parishioners loyal American citizens. As a beginning, he invited Wayne, Hamtramck, and the other officers to a special service in the church, where he sang a *Te Deum*, praising God for bringing the Americans to Detroit and asking His blessing on President Washington and General Wayne.

4

On August 15, Acting Governor Winthrop Sargent organized Wayne County, Northwest Territory. Within its boundaries lay all of the present state of Michigan except the western extremity of the Upper Peninsula, with the addition of northern Ohio and Indiana, and a strip of eastern Illinois and Wisconsin bordering on Lake Michigan. Today Cleveland, Toledo, Detroit, Chicago, and Milwaukee are within the limits of that immense county.

Sargent had difficulty in finding men able and willing to fill the various county offices. The only American civilian in town was Peter Audrain. Some of the British decided to retain their allegiance to the king, and many of the French were illiterate or had no interest in self-government. They were so accustomed to being ruled that they preferred to be treated as subjects rather than as citizens. A few, however, had held office under the British, and Sargent appointed them to office.

Because of the scarcity of eligible men, two or more offices were conferred on the same person; but Peter Audrain had more than anyone else. His perfect knowledge of both French and English made him indispensable, and so he was appointed clerk of the court of quarter sessions, judge of probate, prothonotary of the court of common pleas, and recorder of land titles. Although Audrain was seventy years old in 1796, he continued to hold public office until 1819, when he was removed because of his advanced age. He died on October 6, 1820.

After civil and military affairs were arranged at Detroit, Wayne and Sargent turned their attention to Mackinac. There alone, of all the forts in the northwest, a British garrison remained. On August 19 the sloop *Detroit,* carrying Acting Governor Sargent, Major Henry Burbeck, and one hundred and ten officers and men, set sail for the island fortress.

When they landed on September 1, Lieutenant Andrew Foster, the British commandant, after exchanging civilities with the American officers, had the Union Jack hauled down and marched his men aboard a transport. Major Burbeck occupied the fort with his detachment, and the flag of the United States was hoisted on the flagstaff. The only two forts in Michigan were now garrisoned by American troops.

Major Burbeck was pleased with the situation of the fort on a high rock commanding the village and the harbor below. In front it extended in a straight line for 160 yards along the brow of the hill. Behind, it had an irregular shape with four projecting points. Part of the defensive wall was built of stone, and part of timbers and pickets. The stonework was in good condition, but the wood was badly decayed. Burbeck estimated that 1,420 logs twenty feet long, 4,000 cedar pickets twelve feet long, 6,000 smaller pickets, and several thousand feet of planks and boards would be necessary to make the fortification defensible.

Inside the walls were a storehouse, a barrack built of logs, a half-finished stone barrack, a guardhouse, and a stone magazine which could hold a thousand barrels of powder. The wooden barrack needed repairs, and the one of stone would have to be completed; but the other buildings were in good condition. Major Burbeck set his men to work, and near the end of October he reported to General Wayne that all the troops were comfortably quartered, provisions were stored, and plenty of firewood had been stacked up for the winter.

The United States acquired also some buildings and cultivated land outside the fort. Major Burbeck mentioned the government house, the council house, the bakehouse, the engineer's storehouse, the barrack-master's house, and stables. All were built of wood, and all were in poor condition. The bake oven, however, was usable.

In addition to the buildings there were the commandant's garden, which was "filled with vegetables," and the subaltern's garden "filled with potatoes." Besides these two gardens there was the Government Park, a large irregular tract surrounded by a fence.

In early summer Mackinac was a lively place. Then hundreds of Indians, traders, and boatmen swarmed over the island bartering furs, drinking, and quarreling. When Burbeck and Sargent arrived, the island was almost deserted. Few except the children, the women, and the older men remained. All the rest had set out for their hunting grounds or trading posts, some beyond the Mississippi, others far north of Lake Superior, and still others in Michigan, Wisconsin, Indiana, and Illinois.

The population was so small and willingness to serve as United States officers was so slight that the acting governor had difficulty in filling the few civil posts which he believed were essential. As justices of the peace, he appointed Toussaint Antoine Adhémar *dit* St. Martin and George Young. For lack of a third civilian, he named Major Burbeck. As officers of a local militia company that was to be organized, Sargent chose Alexis Laframboise as captain, George Young as lieutenant, and George Shindler as ensign.

General Wayne gave orders for the repair of the fort and the Citadel at Detroit, and he made Colonel Hamtramck the commandant. Then he prepared to leave for home. A very flattering farewell message signed by Father Levadoux and a number of the inhabitants was delivered to him in his quarters. The general wrote a gracious reply which ended with the following sentence: "I cannot permit myself to depart from hence without assuring you that I shall always take a peculiar interest in whatever may contribute to promote the happiness & prosperity of this County, to which my name has the honor to be attached." Then on November 15 he sailed away to Presque Isle (Erie, Pennsylvania), and died there on December 15, 1796.

5

During the first ten years of the American regime, only a few Americans came to live in Michigan. Some of them deserve to be mentioned. James Henry of Lancaster, Pennsylvania, opened a store in Detroit, and Frederick Bates of Virginia had a position in the quartermaster's department. He was a lively young fellow, but he spent some of his spare time studying law, and in 1802 he became the first postmaster of Detroit. From Massachusetts came Solomon Sibley, a lawyer, who was a graduate of Brown University. Elijah Brush of Connecticut was also a lawyer, and a graduate of Dartmouth.

During the summer of 1798 Father Gabriel Richard was sent to Detroit to assist Father Levadoux. Father Richard, like Father Levadoux, was a Sulpician who had fled from France because of the Revolution. They had been sent to the Illinois country, where the two had labored together, and it was at the request of Father Levadoux that Bishop Carroll had sent his friend to be his assistant. Father Richard helped by visiting the River Raisin settlement and Mackinac, where there was no resident priest; and, after Father Levadoux left in 1802, he had charge of the parish.

Until 1799, the Northwest Territory was under the rule of the governor and judges. When a census taken in 1798 showed that there were more than five thousand free white males in the territory, Governor Arthur St. Clair ordered elections to be held for representatives to an assembly, in accordance with the provisions of the Ordinance of 1787. Because the census returns from Wayne County were slow in reaching the capital, Governor St. Clair allotted one representative to the county until the total population should be known.

The election was held in John Dodemead's tavern, which also served as the courthouse, on December 17, 18, and 19, 1798. The candidates were James May, formerly a British subject, who was supported by Peter Audrain and the British residents, and Solomon Sibley, who had been urged to run by the Americans and by many of the French-speaking inhabitants. Two judges sat at a table in the polling place and each voter appeared before them and announced for whom he cast his vote. Detroit was the only polling place in the whole county.

According to James May, Sibley's friends supplied liquor to the voters, and discharged soldiers armed with clubs stood by and threatened men who wanted to vote for May.[1] Sibley won the election, and early in January he set out on horseback to ride to Cincinnati, the capital, for the meeting of the legislature. It was a three-hundred-mile trip over rough trails through the woods.

After the census returns were in, Governor St. Clair assigned two additional representatives to Wayne County and ordered a second election to be held on January 14 and 15, 1799. James May ran again, but again he was defeated, this time by François Joncaire de Chabert and Jacob Visger. Peter Audrain, who supported May, asserted that votes for his opponents were purchased with cash at the polls. This time some men from the River Rouge came to vote, but there were no votes from the River Raisin nor from Mackinac Island.

There was really no party politics in Michigan at first, for everyone, at least nominally, was a Federalist. Neither President Washington nor President John Adams appointed Democrats to office if he could help it. Frederick Bates, a Democrat in Virginia and a friend of Thomas Jefferson, pretended to be a Federalist in order to hold his job. He explained to his brother that "A young fellow in this Country [Michigan] whose principles are democratic could scarcely find employment as a Shoeblack." Bates declared himself a Democrat after Jefferson became President, and from that time on, for many years, Michigan was solidly Democratic.[2]

6

Michigan remained in the Northwest Territory until 1800, when it was divided by a line running north to the international boundary. It was approximately an extension of the present Ohio-Indiana boundary. The land to the east of it remained in the Northwest Territory; the

[1] These charges are probably false. May contested the election, but the legislature, after hearing testimony, awarded the seat to Sibley.

[2] Followers of Jefferson were called Antifederalists, Republicans, Democratic-Republicans, or simply Democrats. Later the name Democrats was used exclusively.

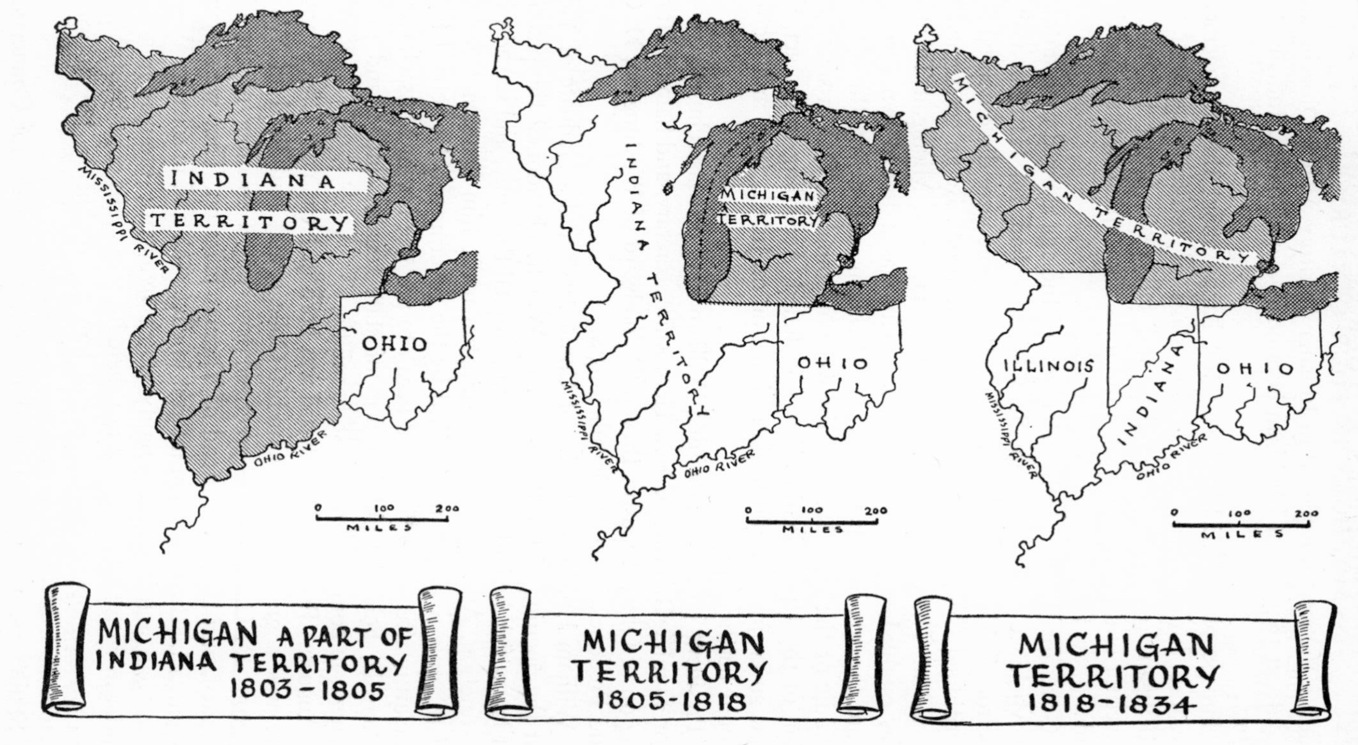
INDIANA
TERRITORY
MISSISSIPPI RIVER
OHIO
OHIO RIVER
0 100 200
MILES
MICHIGAN A PART OF
INDIANA TERRITORY
1803-1805
INDIANA TERRITORY
MICHIGAN
TERRITORY
MISSISSIPPI RIVER
OHIO
OHIO RIVER
0 100 200
MILES
MICHIGAN
TERRITORY
1805-1818
MICHIGAN TERRITORY
ILLINOIS
INDIANA
OHIO
MISSISSIPPI RIVER
OHIO RIVER
0 100 200
MILES
MICHIGAN
TERRITORY
1818-1834

land to the west was placed in Indiana Territory. When Ohio became a state in 1803, all of Michigan became Wayne County, Indiana Territory.

The people of Michigan were not happy about this arrangement. Because Indiana was in the first stage of territorial government, Michigan lost its representatives and fell again under the rule of governor and judges. Besides, Vincennes, the capital, was six hundred miles away, twice as far as Cincinnati.

Governor William Henry Harrison of Indiana showed more interest in Michigan than Governor St. Clair ever had, for Harrison visited Detroit in May, 1803. Nevertheless, the people were discontented and petitioned Congress to organize a new territory. By an act signed by President Thomas Jefferson on January 11, 1805, Michigan Territory was established. The southern boundary was a line drawn eastward from the southern bend of Lake Michigan, and a line through the middle of the same lake was the western boundary. Only a small portion of the Upper Peninsula was included. According to the act, the new government would begin to function on July 1, 1805, and Detroit would be the capital.

President Jefferson appointed William Hull of Massachusetts governor; Stanley Griswold of New Hampshire secretary; and Samuel Huntington of Ohio, Augustus Brevoort Woodward of Washington, D. C., and Frederick Bates of Detroit judges.

William Hull was a native of Connecticut and a graduate of Yale. At the opening of the Revolutionary War he abandoned the practice of law which he had recently begun, entered the army, and served with distinction. After the war, Washington made him lieutenant colonel of the only regiment maintained by the government. He retired from the army after a few years and began to practice law in Massachusetts. There he held the public offices of state senator, judge, and major general in command of the state militia.

Augustus Brevoort Woodward was born in New York City in 1774. He was a graduate of Columbia College and had lived in Washington, D. C., where he practiced law, was a member of the city council, and became a friend of Thomas Jefferson. They were drawn together by their common interest in education and in science. Woodward had a forceful personality which frequently brought him into collision with those who did not share his views. His eccentricities gave his enemies opportunities to hold him up to ridicule, but he was a genius with ideas far in advance of his time.

Stanley Griswold, like Governor Hull, was a native of Connecticut and a graduate of Yale. For a time he was a minister, then a newspaper editor. He was a contentious person with a talent for getting himself into trouble.

Samuel Huntington, also a Connecticut man and a Yale graduate, was chief justice of the Ohio supreme court when President Jefferson offered him a judgeship in Michigan Territory. He declined the appointment, and Michigan had only two judges at first.

Destruction of Detroit by Fire, June 11, 1805

The people of Michigan looked forward eagerly to the day when they would have their own government. Before the time came, however, Detroit suffered a great catastrophe. On June 11, 1805, about nine o'clock in the morning, a fire started in the stable behind John Harvey's bakery. Local legend has it that one of Harvey's employes knocked the ashes out of his pipe, and a breeze blew the live coal into a pile of hay, which blazed up and set the stable afire.

A brisk wind from the southwest fanned the flames, which spread to neighboring buildings. At the first alarm men snatched up buckets, ran to the river, and formed a line to the town's little fire engine, which was simply a tank on wheels with a pump operated by six or eight men.

The bucket brigade and the volunteer firemen labored valiantly, but the engine was too small to quench such a fire as this.

Soon the flames were leaping across the narrow streets. Soldiers from the fort attacked buildings, tearing them down to stop the progress of the fire; but their efforts were in vain. Women and children fled from their homes, carrying as many of their possessions as they could. Some of them embarked in canoes or bateaux and pushed out into the river to escape the intense heat. Others hastened to the open Common east of the town and watched the progress of the flames.

The old town was doomed. By three o'clock in the afternoon all that remained of Detroit was a deep bed of hot embers with naked chimneys of brick or stone standing as monuments to the stricken village. Houses, stores, barns, St. Anne's Church, the Citadel, and the stockade, all had been consumed. Only the old blockhouse, near the river, and the fort remained intact.

Families assembled on the Common, and it was soon determined that no one had been killed by the conflagration. The immediate necessities were food and shelter. Some of the homeless went to stay with friends or relatives in farmhouses up or down the river; others made bowers of branches cut from the forest trees. Farmers of the neighborhood brought provisions and those across the river on the Canadian side also contributed supplies.

Many of the residents wanted to begin to rebuild their houses at once. Others suggested extending the town to include the Common and laying it out with wider streets. Like the walled cities of Europe, Detroit had been unable to expand because of the stockade. Here was an opportunity for planning a better town. At a meeting in Macomb's orchard, the leaders of the various groups appealed to Judge Frederick Bates for advice. He urged them to await the arrival of the governor before doing anything, and they decided to accept his counsel. Judge Augustus Brevoort Woodward arrived on June 30, and he gave them the same advice.

7

Governor William Hull reached Detroit on July 1, 1805. With the governor came his wife, two daughters Ann and Maria, and Stanley Griswold, secretary of the territory. The governor was shocked to find only ashes where he expected the capital to be, and he was glad to take temporary lodging in the house of a farmer about a mile upstream. Wasting no time, Hull administered oaths of office to the secretary and the judges on July 2. A large crowd gathered to see the ceremony, and Captain Samuel T. Dyson fired a salute from the cannon of the fort to announce the birth of Michigan Territory.

Governor Hull had a difficult position to fill. As a matter of fact, he had four positions. He was the chief executive officer of the territory; with the judges, he was a member of the legislature; he was commander in chief of the territorial militia; and he was superintendent of Indian affairs. Local conditions made his task even more difficult. Before he left for Michigan, Secretary of War Henry Dearborn had warned him that he might have trouble. "You will find a heterogeneous mass of materials to govern," Dearborn wrote, "which will call for the exertions of your whole mass of skill, judgment, prudence and firmness. . . ." Nevertheless, Hull seems to have entered upon his manifold duties with entire confidence in himself.

The governor met with the judges in legislative session to arrange for rebuilding the town. Judge Woodward presented a plan said to be like that of Washington, D.C., but it was an even better one. Major Pierre Charles L'Enfant had laid out the capital city with streets crossing at right angles and with some avenues running diagonally across them. Woodward's basic plan was a regular hexagon with a circular park in the center and streets radiating out from it. As the town grew, additional hexagons could be laid out adjoining the original, thus providing for regular symmetrical expansion. Principal avenues would be two hundred feet wide; intermediate ones, one hundred and twenty; and the narrowest, sixty.

At first the people accepted the plan. In time, opposition arose, especially among the French-speaking element. To them the scheme seemed fantastic. Living as they did close together on their narrow farms, streets two hundred feet wide were unthinkable. Most of the plan was eventually abandoned. Today, what remains can be seen below Adams Avenue centering about Grand Circus Park, which is only half of one of the circles. Judge Woodward had faith in the future of Detroit, but his opponents could see only the little backwoods village. As a result, the city has spent millions of dollars widening narrow streets and opening new ones.

Governor Hull, too, had faith in Detroit. In an address he predicted that if the inhabitants would make the best use of the favorable location of the town and of the natural resources of the territory, "the most sanguine imagination could form no conception of the number of human beings whose happy destination will be here fixed or of the useful and magnificent scenes which will here be displayed."

For a time there was harmony in Detroit. The officers labored for the general welfare, and the people were satisfied. Lots were distributed on the new plan, and houses were rapidly erected. Truly, in the words of the official seal of the city, there was hope for better days, and Detroit was arising from the ashes.[3]

Woodward's plan and the granting of lots by the governor and judges required the sanction of Congress, and so Governor Hull and Judge Woodward went to Washington in the fall and induced Congress to pass a law with very generous provisions. A lot in the new town was to be given free to every person who had owned or occupied land in the old town and to each inhabitant seventeen years of age or older. The remaining lots were to be sold. In addition, Congress granted a ten-thousand-acre tract north of Adams Avenue which could be laid out into lots and sold, the income to be used for defraying the cost of erecting public buildings.

The distribution of lots to inhabitants was slow and aroused much bitter feeling against the officials. Many persons complained that the lots they received were not as favorably situated as those which they had had. In spite of delays on the part of officials and grumbling of the inhabitants, the task was finally completed.

8

The population of Michigan increased slowly. In 1800 it was only 3,106, and in 1805 it was not much larger. Aside from the opportunities for officeholders, a few lawyers, merchants, and artisans, there was slight attraction in the Territory for Americans. Nearly all who went west wanted land, and there was practically none available in Michigan. Only a strip six miles wide from the River Raisin to the St. Clair River, and a small area at Detroit, Mackinac, and Sault Sainte Marie, had been ceded by the Indians in the Treaty of Greenville in 1795, and even that had not been surveyed and offered for sale.

Americans hesitated to buy farms from the French and British inhabitants because the titles to their land were not recognized by the United States. In 1804 Frederick Bates and George Hoffman, acting in accordance with a law of Congress, had begun to take evidence of ownership from the inhabitants up and down the river. When they discovered that few persons had deeds to their farms, Congress required

[3] The official seal of Detroit, adopted in 1827, bears the inscription in Latin: *Speramus Meliora. Resurget Cineribus.* "We hope for better days. It will arise from the ashes."

them to show only that they had possessed improved land before July 1, 1796. Finally, in 1807, Congress confirmed the decisions of Bates and Hoffman by granting titles to six claimants. Others were granted during the succeeding years in the present Wayne County, Monroe County, Washtenaw County, on Mackinac Island, and at Sault Sainte Marie. They are called private claims.

At Sault Sainte Marie, because of the strong pro-British sentiment, claimants were denied titles until 1855. Meanwhile, heirs of Louis le Gardeur de Repentigny and Louis de Bonne had filed with the commissioner of the General Land Office in Washington claims to the seigniory granted by Louis XV in 1751. Congress rejected their plea but in 1860 passed a law giving them the privilege of suing for the land in the United States courts.

Suit was begun in the United States District Court in Detroit in 1863, and on April 5, 1864, Judge Ross Wilkins handed down a decree granting the seigniory or a similar area elsewhere in the public lands, if the original tract had already been granted. The United States District Attorney appealed the case to the Supreme Court. On May 6, 1867, in a unanimous opinion, the Justices reversed the decision of the District Court, thus legally terminating the existence of the only French seigniory on Michigan soil.

To procure land for settlers, Governor Hull was instructed in 1806 to assemble the Indians and negotiate a treaty with them. This he found difficult to do. Tecumseh's brother, the Shawnee Prophet, was busily at work in Ohio and Indiana urging the Indians to have nothing to do with the whites. He exhorted them to give up the liquor, weapons, and clothing of the white men, to refuse to sell their land, and to return to the ways of their fathers.

At L'Arbre Croche, a chief who had probably visited the Prophet was teaching these doctrines to Michigan Indians. He was especially hostile to Americans. The Great Spirit had told him, he said: "I am the Father of the English, of the French, of the Spaniards, and of the Indians. . . . But the Americans I did not make. They are not my children but the children of the Evil Spirit. They grew from the scum of the great water when it was troubled by the Evil Spirit, and the froth was driven into the woods by a strong east wind. . . . They have taken away your lands which were not made for them." Besides the teachings of this chief, the Indians were under the influence of British agents at Fort Malden and on St. Joseph Island in the St. Mary's River, where the garrison of Mackinac had built a fort after leaving the island in 1796.

The murderous attack of the British man-of-war *Leopard* on the United States frigate *Chesapeake* in June, 1807, caused talk of a war with Great Britain. If it came, of course, the Indians would be her allies. Under these circumstances it was scarcely expected that Governor Hull would be able to assemble the chiefs, much less induce them to sell their land. In fact the rumors of an Indian attack were so persistent in the summer of 1807 that Hull called out the militia and set some of the men at work repairing the stockade.

After some delay, the governor finally assembled chiefs of the Ottawa, Chippewa, Potawatomi, and Huron nations at Detroit. There in the new stone Council House on the southwest corner of Jefferson and Randolph on November 17, 1807, they signed a treaty, ceding to the United States a large area in southeastern Michigan. It was bounded on the west by a line drawn due north from Fort Defiance, Ohio, to a point opposite the outlet of Lake Huron; from there on the northwest by a line slanting in a northeasterly direction to the White Rock in Lake Huron, near the present town of Harbor Beach; on the east by the international water boundary; and on the south by a line running due east from the southern tip of Lake Michigan (see map, p. 149). In return for this grant, the Indians received $10,000 in cash and merchandise on the spot, and the promise of $2,400 annually. This land would not be ready for sale and settlement until after it had been surveyed. Not even a beginning was made before 1815.

9

Governor Hull was not so successful in dealing with the white inhabitants of the territory as he had been with the red. An Easterner, he did not understand either the frontier people or their needs. The large alien population also made his position very difficult. Of all the territorial officers, Judge Bates alone knew the people, and it was unfortunate that he left Michigan in November, 1806, to become secretary of Louisiana Territory. Before he went, John Griffin, who had been a judge in Indiana Territory, became the third judge. Then there were only two again until James Witherell of Vermont was appointed on April 23, 1808.

Judge Griffin was undistinguished, but Judge Witherell soon became and remained a leader in the territory. Born in Massachusetts, he had served in the Revolutionary War and then settled in Vermont, where he practiced law. His experience in a frontier community fitted him for the post in Michigan.

Perhaps the most notable instance of Governor Hull's lack of understanding was his attempt to dress the militia in fancy uniforms. Specifications were drawn up in detail for each rank and each branch of the service. Riflemen, for example, were to wear "short green coats, turned up with buff, buff capes, round hats, black cockades and green feathers; in the warm season white vest and pantaloons with black gaiters; in the cold season green pantaloons edged with buff."

The commander in chief wanted his militiamen to look smart, but he entirely ignored the poverty of the people. As each man would have had to pay for his own uniform, an expense far beyond the means of most, they simply disobeyed the order. To make the matter worse, because Hull had ordered cloth for the uniforms sent to Detroit, he was accused of expecting to make a profit for himself.

There was also much hostile criticism of the legislature composed of the governor and the judges. Forbidden by the Ordinance of 1787 to enact laws, they were required to adopt laws already in force in the original states. Because conditions in Michigan were unlike those in the East, the legislature frequently selected parts of laws of several states and combined them into a law for the territory. This was, of course, a clumsy procedure, but one which they could scarcely avoid. On occasion they enacted laws when no satisfactory models could be found.

One law especially caused bitter attacks on the governor and judges. Led to believe by some Boston speculators that a bank would facilitate the carrying on of the fur trade and aid in the development of the territory, the legislature on September 19, 1806, issued a charter. Although a capitalization of $400,000 was requested, Judge Woodward, in his enthusiasm for the project, induced his colleagues to make it $1,000,000, and he became president of the bank.

The Boston men erected a brick building and sent a cashier to Detroit with a supply of bank notes. Signed by the officers, at least $165,000 worth of them were carried to Boston and circulated. When some were brought to Detroit and presented for payment, the cashier refused to receive them. Then Governor Hull realized that he and the others had been duped.

Congress in 1807 annulled the bank law, and the legislature, when Judge Woodward was absent, passed an act prohibiting the circulation of notes of a private bank. The fraudulent institution was closed, but the territorial officers were held responsible by the people for having permitted it to exist.

Quarrels among the officers tended to bring their regime into disrepute with the citizens, and sometimes even brought the wheels of government to a standstill. While Judge Bates remained, there was comparative harmony; but after he left, the legislature was divided. Young and aggressive, Judge Woodward attempted to seize the leadership from the governor, and Judge Griffin supported him. The count was two against one, and sometimes Woodward withdrew to his farm on the River Raisin, refusing either to sit on the bench or meet with the legislature. Then nothing could be done. The arrival of Judge Witherell gave Hull an ally, and the two, when Woodward was absent, controlled the government.

Certain British subjects made a great deal of trouble. One of them, John Gentle, wrote articles, which were published in eastern newspapers, ridiculing Judge Woodward in particular, and attacking the whole governing body of the territory. There were, indeed, reasons for complaint, but Gentle's charges were greatly exaggerated.

Secretary Griswold was a special problem. Quarreling with everyone, he attacked both Governor Hull and Judge Woodward, circulating rumors and falsehoods. Finally, in 1808, he was found guilty of inciting militiamen to desert, apparently with the intention of injuring the governor. To assure future good conduct, he was compelled to post a bond. Later in the same year President Jefferson removed him from office and sent in his place Reuben Atwater of Vermont.

10

During the years 1804 to 1812, Father Gabriel Richard was busily engaged in establishing schools for children. In 1804 and 1805, he and his assistant, Father John Dilhet, conducted a preparatory school for a few boys whom he hoped to send to St. Mary's Seminary in Baltimore. The fire put an end to that project.

In 1806 he trained four young women as teachers—Angélique Campau, Elizabeth Williams, Monique Labadie, and Elizabeth Lyons—and opened schools in Detroit and the vicinity. These schools were supported by payment of tuition.

Father Richard was eager to help improve the condition of the Indians. Believing that they should be trained in the ways of the white men, he established a school at Springwells below Detroit for both Indian and white children. In 1808 he went to Washington with a letter of introduction from Judge Woodward to President Jefferson and laid his plan before him.

His idea was to give manual training as well as a common school education. The girls would learn carding, spinning, weaving, and sewing; the boys, farming, printing, weaving, bookbinding, and carpentry. In order that the Indians might become self-supporting, he asked that each be given a farm.

President Jefferson was greatly interested in Father Richard's plan, and he asked the secretary of war, who was in charge of Indian affairs, to contribute to the support of the school. He promised $400 a year, which was to be paid on the recommendation of Governor Hull.

While he was in the East, Father Richard bought a printing press, looms, spinning wheels, electrical apparatus, and surveying instruments. He sent them to the school at Springwells, where they were used to instruct the pupils, both white and Indian. The priest continued to conduct this unusual school, but he was disappointed in the support that he had hoped to receive from the national government. In 1811 he wrote to Jefferson complaining that the promises which had been made to him were not being kept. It is likely, too, that he was disappointed in the small number of Indians who attended, for in 1809 Governor Hull reported that there were only twelve. The school was discontinued when the War of 1812 began.

Father Richard's press was the first in Michigan on which a large quantity of printing was done.[4] The first product was *The Child's Spelling Book and Michigan Instructor*, issued in 1809. The printer, James M. Miller, hopefully put out a newspaper on August 31, 1809. Entitled *The Michigan Essay; Or, The Impartial Observer*, it was a four-page sheet of news, essays, and advertisements. Abstracts in French of the important articles filled a column and a half on the last page. Probably because insufficient interest was shown, no more numbers of the paper were printed, but books came from the press for a number of years.

Additional schools and the printing press were making available for the people of Michigan a larger measure of culture than they had previously had within her borders, but the calamities of war for a time would reduce many of the inhabitants almost to the condition of savages.

[4] In 1796 John McCall printed an act of Congress and some legal forms used by court officers. The press he used seems to have been sold and removed from Detroit in 1800.

— 9 —

The War of 1812

To some extent, Michigan had been involved in all the wars between France and Great Britain during the eighteenth century; she had been the base of operations for murderous raiding parties of British troops and Indians against the Americans during the Revolutionary War; and now her soil became a battleground in another war between Britain and the United States. This time the people of Michigan were in the midst of the conflict.

War came as a result of the grim struggle for existence between Great Britain and France which continued from 1793 until 1815. Each nation, trying to starve the other by cutting off foreign trade, greatly injured the seaborne commerce of the United States. Protests to Napoleon and to the British government were ignored.

Because she had command of the seas, Britain caused more damage than Napoleon. Besides taking ships and cargoes, British naval officers took sailors from American ships, on the pretext that they were British subjects, and forced them to serve on British men-of-war. Finally, in 1807, after the *Leopard* fired on the United States frigate *Chesapeake* and carried away four seamen, President Thomas Jefferson induced Congress to pass the Embargo Act, prohibiting American ships from sailing to any foreign port.

The people would have supported the President in a request for war, but he preferred to try starving Great Britain instead. His successor, President James Madison, followed his example, and Congress passed several other laws intended to punish both the British and Napoleon for interference with our trade. The embargo was injurious to Americans, because they could not sell their products, and the other laws were difficult to enforce.

An act passed in 1810 reopened trade with France and Great Britain. It promised that if one of those nations would withdraw its rectrictions, the United States would refuse to trade with the other. Napoleon soon informed Madison that his decrees would be withdrawn, and the President proclaimed nonintercourse with Great Britain.

Besides interfering with our commerce and impressing our seamen, the British continued to nourish the hostile feelings of the Indians for the Americans. In truth, Americans hungry for land gave the Indians cause for hostility. Ignoring treaties made by the government, squatters swarmed over Indian lands. In addition, Governor William Henry Harrison of Indiana and other officials purchased millions of acres for the government at treaties attended by only a few irresponsible Indians.

Stirred by the unhappy plight of his people, the Shawnee Prophet preached a revival of Indian virtues and the abandonment of the white man's vices. His brother Tecumseh warned Harrison to stop his illegal purchases and organized a confederacy to resist the further advance of settlers.

In November, 1811, Harrison marched to the Prophet's headquarters on Tippecanoe Creek, Indiana, put the Indians to flight after a sharp encounter, and destroyed the town. Although he lost nearly two hundred killed and wounded, Harrison was hailed as the hero of Tippecanoe. His report that he had found guns and ammunition in the original British wrappings convinced Westerners that their old enemy was still active against them.

The truth was that now, as in the days before Wayne's victory, it was not the British government but traders and Indian agents who provided arms and incited the savages. The Indians visited Fort Malden at the mouth of the Detroit River and Fort St. Joseph in St. Mary's River to receive presents from their British Father. Traders and agents gladly exchanged weapons for furs, hoping to check the advance of Americans who were ruining hunting and excluding them from some of the best fur-producing regions.

The Westerners were land hungry. Those in the northern area were eager to invade Canada and seize the Ontario peninsula. Besides acquiring additional territory, they would be able to remove the Indians and their British protectors. Farther south the Westerners looked upon the Spaniards in Florida as their enemies and as inciters of the Indians. Because Spain was now an ally of Great Britain, war with the latter would make possible an attack on the former. North and south, beyond the mountains, there was a warm enthusiasm for war that had little to do with the freedom of the seas.

The elections of 1810 had sent to the Congress which met in December, 1811, a number of bellicose young men from the western country. One of them, Henry Clay of Kentucky, was elected Speaker of the House. So eagerly did they press for war with Great Britain that they were nicknamed the "War Hawks."

The policy of economic pressure originated by Jefferson finally was successful. British manufacturers urged that trade with America was necessary if they were not to be ruined, and the people were in dire need of food. As a result, on June 16, 1812, the British government announced that the Orders in Council were revoked. Unfortunately, His Majesty's ministers had delayed too long. Before the news could reach Washington, Congress declared war on June 18.

The United States was wholly unprepared. The regular army consisted of only about seven thousand officers and men dispersed as garrisons at distant posts, and the general officers were too old and too long out of touch with military matters to be capable of carrying on offensive operations.

The navy was insignificant compared with Great Britain's. To oppose her more than a thousand ships, the United States had only sixteen frigates and some brigs and sloops. Although American ships won some brilliant victories in the early months of the war, by the spring of 1813 a tight British blockade had swept from the seas all our men-of-war except the *Constitution* and a few others. Privateers, however, continued to prey successfully on British commerce until the end.

In addition to military feebleness there were other unfavorable conditions. Transportation was difficult and slow, especially beyond the Appalachian Mountains. Sectional jealousies and partisan bitterness divided the nation at a time when co-operation was most necessary. The Federalists of New England were opposed to the war, and the governors of Connecticut and Massachusetts refused to order out their militia when the President called for them. It was fortunate for the United States that the enemy was almost completely occupied in fighting Napoleon and that the Atlantic Ocean made invasion difficult.

2

Governor William Hull, who had made an excellent record in the Revolutionary War, was asked to take command on the Detroit front. Refusing at first because he believed that Detroit could not be held unless the United States controlled Lake Erie, he finally accepted the appointment.

At Dayton, Ohio, he joined the troops which had been ordered to Detroit—three regiments of Ohio volunteer militiamen under Colonel James Findlay, Colonel Duncan McArthur, and Colonel Lewis Cass. Each had been elected by the men of his regiment, although of the three only McArthur had had any military experience—in 1790 with General Josiah Harmar. The strength of the three regiments was nearly fifteen hundred.

On June 7, General Hull marched his force to Urbana. The next day he was joined by Lieutenant Colonel James Miller with the Fourth United States Infantry, composed of about five hundred officers and men.

On June 15 Hull began his advance to Detroit. Because they had not been paid, the Ohio volunteers refused to move until Hull sent a company of regulars to start them on the way. Even though it was necessary to cut a road through the woods and to build blockhouses at strategic points, the army reached the mouth of the Maumee River in two weeks. Officers and men were unaware that the war had begun.

General Hull loaded two small ships with baggage, including his military correspondence, some sick soldiers, and wives of officers, and ordered them to sail to Detroit. When the larger of the two, the *Cuyahoga* under Captain Chapin, was off Fort Malden, the British captured her, thus gaining possession of Hull's orders and other military papers. News of the declaration of war had reached Fort Malden on June 28.

After leaving the Maumee, the army still had sixty miles ahead with only a trail to follow. Again a road had to be made. While the army was moving slowly forward on July 2, a dispatch from the War Department finally arrived with the news that war had been declared two weeks previously. Instead of sending the information by special courier, the Secretary of War had simply put it in the mail. General Hull and his army reached Detroit on July 8.

The people of the town and the vicinity must have felt pretty secure with the comparatively large military force at hand. Before General Hull arrived, there had been only one company of the First United States Infantry in garrison, and a detachment of volunteer Michigan militia to protect the settlements. Now Hull had under his command about twenty-two hundred officers and men.

General Hull had many responsibilities. As general in command of the North Western Army, he had authority over Fort Detroit, Fort Mackinac, Fort Dearborn at Chicago, and Fort Wayne, Indiana. It was his duty to hold those posts against any British or Indian attack. The lack of roads, and British control of the Lakes, made it almost impossible for him even to keep in communication with them. Sending them reinforcements and supplies was beyond his power.

Hull, of course, was still governor of Michigan Territory. He was the chief executive charged with enforcing the laws, and he was also a member of the territorial legislature. As the principal civil officer, he was responsible for the welfare of the people.

In addition to these heavy military and civil burdens, the governor also had charge of Indian affairs. Because it was the policy of the United States Government to try to maintain the neutrality of the Indians rather than to enlist their services against the enemy, Governor Hull called together the chiefs of the Wyandots living below Detroit and urged them to remain aloof from the impending conflict. They agreed to do so. Although they soon went over to the British, for the moment the safety of Detroit seemed assured.

3

Shortly after General Hull's arrival, he received from Secretary of War William Eustis an order to take Fort Malden if he could do it without endangering the safety of Detroit. Believing that he should make the attempt, he began preparations at once for crossing the river. Muskets and rifles were repaired, and carpenters were set at work making field carriages for some of the heavy cannon in the fort.

When the order to cross the river was read, about one hundred and eighty of the Ohioans refused to obey, on the ground that they could not be compelled to serve outside the country. Shamed into compliance by the taunts of their comrades, some of them changed their minds, and the invasion began early on the morning of July 12. The troops crossed just below the foot of Belle Isle and landed without opposition.

General Hull established his headquarters in a new house that belonged to François Baby, who, as a militia colonel, was with his regiment at Fort Malden.[1] He issued a bombastic proclamation to the people of Canada, announcing that he had come to free them from the tyranny of Great Britain, and urging them to go about their usual business. Although he did not encourage them to enlist under his flag, he promised that volunteers would be accepted. Anyone who took up arms against the United States, he declared, would be treated as an enemy; and if the Indians were let loose upon the American people, the general warned that no man found fighting beside the savages would be taken prisoner—"instant destruction will be his lot." For a while, some deserters from the army and some civilians joined the Americans, but the proclamation had slight effect on the people.

Governor Hull treated the civilian population courteously. Necessary supplies for his army were purchased, and he did his best to prevent looting and pillaging by his soldiers. John Askin, a loyal British subject, in his home on the Canadian shore, was little disturbed by the army of occupation. In his diary he praised Hull for protecting private property. Friends in Detroit were permitted to cross the river to Askin's house to take tea.

The war, however, as it continued, caused John Askin many worries. To him and to many other persons on both sides of the river, the conflict was really a civil war. Askin, for instance, had four sons, ten grandsons, and three sons-in-law in the British service. Another son-in-law, Elijah Brush, was colonel of the First Regiment of Michigan Volunteers. Brush's wife, the former Alice Askin, and their three sons were in Detroit. The boys were too young to fight, but they were exposed to the dangers of war.

There were other divided families, too. James Abbott was a wealthy merchant and the postmaster of Detroit. His wife, Sarah Whistler, was a daughter of Captain John Whistler, an officer in the garrison of the fort. Two of her brothers were officers also. Abbott's three sisters, however, had married Canadians and were living across the river. Mary was the wife of William Hands, sheriff of Essex County; Frances was the wife of François Baby; and Elizabeth was the wife of his brother Jacques. The two Babys were colonels in the Canadian militia. Because he had relatives in Canada, James Abbott was unjustly accused of

[1] The house, which is in Windsor, has recently been made into a historical museum.

being disloyal to the United States. The war along the Detroit River caused many a heartache on both shores.

If Hull had attacked at once, it is possible that he might have taken Fort Malden, for the garrison was small. The Ohio colonels were eager to advance, but Hull believed that he would need artillery to reduce the fort. He had no faith in the willingness of undisciplined militia to storm a position defended by palisades and earthworks mounting cannon. Their own officers refused to guarantee their dependability when the general asked them point-blank about it.[2]

In addition to the protection of the fort, the British had three ships based on Amherstburg—the *Lady Prevost*, the *Hunter*, and the *Queen Charlotte*. In case of attack, they could have blasted away at the besieging force with their cannon. Complete control of the Upper Lakes was in the hands of the British, for Hull had only the brig *Adams*, which was in the shipyard on the River Rouge undergoing repairs.

On July 16, General Hull sent Colonel Cass with about three hundred men to reconnoiter the bridge over the Canard River, or the Ta-ron-tee, as the Indians called it, about six miles from Fort Malden. He ordered Cass not to fight if the enemy offered opposition. Eager for action, Cass ignored his orders, attacked the detachment holding the bridge, and forced it to retreat, leaving two men wounded. In this skirmish occurred the first bloodshed of the War of 1812, and Colonel Cass was hailed throughout the country as the hero of the Ta-ron-tee. The Colonel asked permission to hold the bridge, and he was angry when Hull ordered him back to Sandwich.

4

On July 28, General Hull received the discouraging news that Fort Mackinac had been captured. He could scarcely have been surprised, for he had not sent reinforcements, nor even the news that war had been declared.

Lieutenant Porter Hanks was in command at Mackinac with fifty-seven officers and men. Completely isolated, he knew only that relations between the United States and Great Britain were strained, and that war might come. Hoping to find out what was the current state of affairs, on the evening of July 16 he sent Michael Dousman, a

[2] Although Cass denounced Hull at the time for not moving immediately on Fort Malden, some months after the surrender of Detroit he wrote: ". . . the militia are not to be depended on for an offensive campaign."

trader, to St. Joseph Island in the St. Mary's River to visit his friends among the British traders who lived near the fort. Dousman set out in his canoe. Night came on, and he continued his voyage. Suddenly there were canoes all about him, and he saw the dark shape of a small sailing vessel. All were headed toward Mackinac Island.

There was no chance to escape. Dousman was captured and told that the flotilla, which included the brig *Caledonia,* was on its way to attack the fort. Captain Charles Roberts, who was in command at Fort St. Joseph, had received news of the declaration of war on July 15. Immediately assembling *voyageurs,* Indians, and his small garrison of regulars, between five hundred and six hundred men, he set out the next day.

Early on the morning of July 17 the invaders landed behind the fort, where they were hidden from view by the dense woods. Captain Roberts ordered Dousman to go warn the civilians on the island to leave their houses quietly and seek places of safety. Then, occupying a hill which overlooked the fort and mounting a cannon on it, Captain Roberts called upon Lieutenant Hanks to surrender. Realizing that resistance was useless, Hanks agreed to give up the fort without firing a shot.

Captain Roberts permitted the little garrison to march out with the honors of war and lay down their arms. As prisoners of war they gave their word that they would not fight until regularly exchanged, and Captain Roberts sent them by ship to Detroit, where they arrived on August 2. Now that Mackinac had fallen, General Hull expected that swarms of Indians, *voyageurs,* and *coureurs de bois* would descend upon Detroit from the north.

5

General Hull had received word from Captain Henry Brush that he had reached the River Raisin with supplies for the army and that he needed an escort to Detroit. Hull ordered Major Thomas B. Van Horne with two hundred militia to march to the River Raisin. Setting out in the afternoon of August 4, he stopped for the night on the River Ecorse. The next day he continued the march as far as Brownstown Creek.

Suddenly, from the bushes to the left of the trail and beyond the stream, a hail of bullets struck down the men in front. Terror-stricken, the militia broke and ran. Officers who tried in vain to rally them paid for their bravery with their lives. Only at the River Ecorse was it possible to halt the flight. Then it was learned that eighteen had been killed and twelve wounded. Among the dead were six officers. Major Van Horne's force had been defeated by Tecumseh and twenty-four Indians and one white man who had crossed over from Fort Malden. General Hull's dispatches to the secretary of war, in which he described his precarious situation, were captured and carried to Colonel Henry Procter, commandant at Fort Malden.

When General Hull learned of Van Horne's defeat, he gave up the idea of attacking Fort Malden. Captain Samuel T. Dyson, in command of the artillery had informed him that heavy guns could not be moved over the marshy ground below Sandwich, and he expected a horde of savages to sweep down from the north. In addition, he had received dispatches from Niagara notifying him that no attack against the British would be made there and that reinforcements were being sent to Fort Malden. His most important concern now was to open the road for supplies from Ohio. On August 7 he began withdrawing the army from Canada to Detroit while the militia colonels protested vigorously. The next day he ordered Lieutenant Colonel James Miller with his regulars to march to the River Raisin.

In addition to the regulars of the Fourth Infantry, General Hull put under the Colonel's command about 250 Ohio militia, a company of Michigan militia under Captain Antoine Dequindre, and some artillerymen with a six-pounder and a howitzer. Altogether, he had about six hundred men, approximately one third of Hull's army. After crossing the River Rouge, the force camped for the night and resumed the march early on the morning of August 9.

When British Indians prowling through the woods on the American side of the river brought Colonel Procter word of Colonel Miller's march, he sent a force of about two hundred regulars and militia under Major Adam C. Muir and several hundred Indians led by Tecumseh to contest his passage. Landing at Brownstown, the British moved up the road to a ravine that lay like a gash across it at the little Indian village of Monguagon, now within the city of Trenton. Taking position there behind trees and fallen timbers, they awaited the approach of the American column.

As Captain Josiah Snelling with the vanguard of regulars neared the ravine, a single shot was heard from the woods ahead of them. It was the signal for attack, and firing became general. Snelling's men held their ground until Colonel Miller brought up the main body of troops. The British behind the fallen timbers were well protected, and the naked savages, clothed only in breechcloth and war paint, were elusive targets as they flitted from tree to tree, like evil spirits in the semigloom of the dense forest.

Colonel Miller brought the six-pounder into action, but it was ineffective in the woods. As a last resort he ordered a charge. Yelling like wild Indians, his men advanced with fixed bayonets. Captain Dequindre was the first into the enemy line. Taken by surprise, the British turned and fled. Tecumseh and his savages held on a little longer, then took to the woods away from the river. Driving onward until he feared the Indians might return and take him in the rear, Colonel Miller halted the pursuit and led his men back to the field of battle. The British stopped at Brownstown only long enough to launch their boats and retire to Fort Malden.

In this victory the Americans lost eighteen killed and fifty-seven wounded. According to Colonel Procter, the British loss was only four soldiers killed and fifteen wounded. If he may be believed, the Indians lost only two killed and six wounded.

Colonel Miller sent a runner to Detroit asking for boats to bring him supplies and to carry back the wounded. He also reported that he was ill. The boats finally arrived, but without sufficient supplies. When a second messenger was sent for provisions, General Hull ordered the force to return to Detroit. Although he had completely routed the enemy and marched nearly halfway to the River Raisin, where reinforcements and supplies were waiting, Colonel Miller retired to the fort without having accomplished his mission.

It is useless to try to fix the responsibility for the failure of this expedition. Even if Colonel Miller had reached the River Raisin, he would have had the British and their Indian allies between him and Detroit. General Hull's position at Detroit was wholly untenable as long as the British controlled the lakes and could cross the river at will.

Colonel Miller and his men reached Detroit on August 12. On the same day Colonel Cass wrote to Governor R. J. Meigs of Ohio, expressing lack of confidence in General Hull and begging the governor to come to Detroit with supplies and a force of at least two thousand men to escort them. A postscript to the letter, apparently written a day or two later, added: "The British force is opposite, and our situation has nearly reached its crisis. Believe all the bearer will tell you. . . . Even a C______ is talked of by the ______ ______! The bearer will supply the vacancy." It was later explained that the words to be supplied were "Capitulation" and "Commanding General." The postscript was signed by Colonel Cass, Colonel Findlay, Colonel

McArthur, Quartermaster James Taylor, and Colonel Elijah Brush of the Detroit militia. General Hull's officers had almost reached the point of open mutiny.

6

On August 13, General Isaac Brock arrived at Fort Malden with a reinforcement of regulars and militia. An alert and energetic officer, he had decided that there was little likelihood of an American attack on the Niagara frontier where he was in command. Accordingly, he had hastened westward. At Fort Malden, after reading General Hull's captured dispatches, he at once prepared to take the offensive. By his order a battery of artillery was erected opposite Detroit.

General Hull now made a last attempt to bring in the supplies from the River Raisin. On August 14, he ordered Colonel McArthur and Colonel Cass to take four hundred men and march by a back trail. Hull had no idea that the British intended to attack Detroit, and the need for provisions was great. Perhaps he also wanted to be rid for a time of two ringleaders of the opposition to him. Colonel Cass later declared that only the absence of McArthur and himself prevented the militia officers from divesting General Hull of his command.

On August 15, General Brock sent to General Hull a demand that he surrender Detroit. Saying that he wanted to "conclude any arrangement that may lead to stop the unnecessary effusion of blood," he warned that "the numerous body of Indians who have attached themselves to my Troops will be beyond my Controul the moment the contest commences." This was more than a hint that the women and children on the farms along the river would fall victims to the scalping knives if General Hull dared to fire on the British forces.

Without delay, General Hull replied: "I am ready to meet any force which may be at your disposal, and any consequences which may result from any exertion of it you may think proper to make." After General Brock had received this answer, he ordered his cannon to open fire on Detroit. Shore batteries in front of the town replied, and a lively artillery duel across the river ensued. The town was quickly emptied of civilians, some taking refuge in the fort, others fleeing to a ravine on the Macomb farm just west of the stockade. The firing continued until ten o'clock that night.

7

Fort Dearborn, on Lake Michigan at the mouth of the Chicago River, was under General Hull's command. Fearing that the little garrison there would be overwhelmed by hostile Indians, he sent orders to Captain Nathan Heald to retire to Fort Wayne, Indiana. On August 15, the day of the opening bombardment of Detroit, Captain Heald marched out with his sixty-four men, accompanied by twenty-seven women and children.

The little column had marched only a short distance from the fort when it was attacked by a horde of Indians. Although the men fought bravely, they were soon killed or captured. Only twenty-seven, including Captain Heald and his wife, survived the battle.

8

At his headquarters in Sandwich, General Brock made preparations to invade Michigan. During the night of August 15, several hundred Indians crossed the river to Springwells as an advance force. Early the next morning, while the *Queen Charlotte* stood by to cover the movement, the British regulars, militia, and the remainder of the Indians crossed over, landed without opposition, and began marching up the River Road. General Brock's force consisted of about 1,350 men, nearly half of them Indians. To oppose them General Hull had 1,060 fit for duty besides the 400 who were absent with Colonels McArthur and Cass. Hull, of course, had the advantages of the stockade, the fort, and numerous cannon.

While Brock was crossing the river, his cannon opposite Detroit resumed their bombardment. Women and children crowded into the fort seeking safety. None of them was hit, but one shell killed Lieutenant Porter Hanks and Dr. James Reynolds, and wounded Dr. Hosea Blood. American shore batteries returned the fire, but they were unable to silence the enemy's guns.

In spite of the danger from this bombardment, General Hull's situation appeared to be favorable. Two twenty-four-pounders loaded with grapeshot were aimed down the River Road up which the British were approaching; Colonel Findlay's regiment was deployed along the western stockade; the fort was garrisoned by the regulars; and Colonel Elijah Brush's Michigan militia was posted above the town to prevent an assault on the settlement from that direction.

Hull could have beaten off an attack, but Indians would surely have been killed, and their kinsmen would have wreaked vengeance on the farmers' families up and down the river bank. Besides, Hull's provisions would not last long with women and children to feed. There was no hope of supplies from the River Raisin. Since Colonel

McArthur had set out on August 14, Hull had had no word from him, and messengers whom he had dispatched had been unable to find him and his men.

Suddenly General Hull decided to surrender without firing a shot. Sending an officer to General Brock under a flag of truce to ask for a cessation of hostilities, he ordered the gunners to leave their posts and withdrew Colonel Findley's regiment into the fort. At the same time he learned that two companies of Michigan militia had deserted to the enemy.

Two British officers sent by General Brock arrived to arrange the terms for surrender. In spite of the bitter jeers of officers and soldiers, the capitulation was soon drawn up and signed. Shortly after noon on August 16, the Americans stacked their arms and marched out of the fort, prisoners of war. The British marched in, and again, after sixteen years, the Union Jack floated over the ramparts.

The articles signed by General Hull included the troops under Colonels McArthur and Cass. After leaving Detroit, these officers had wandered aimlessly in the woods. On the morning of August 16, having approached to within a mile of the fort, they heard of the surrender. Immediately falling back to the River Rouge, they sent an officer with a flag of truce to report their whereabouts. Ordered to come in, they reached the fort that evening. Officers and men were loud in their denunciation of General Hull for his cowardly surrender, Colonel Cass taking the lead in condemning him.

Captain Henry Brush and his detachment at the River Raisin also were included in the surrender. Brush ignored the order and withdrew his men safely to Ohio.

General Brock embarked General Hull, the other officers of the regular army, and the enlisted regulars, and shipped them to Quebec as prisoners of war. Officers and men of the Ohio and Michigan militia were permitted to go home on parole, promising not to serve in the war until they had been exchanged. General Brock, leaving Colonel Henry Procter in command at Detroit, returned to the Niagara River front.

Colonel Cass at once set out for Washington, where he preferred charges against General Hull. The court-martial which General Hull demanded was not convened until January 3, 1814. General Henry Dearborn was president of the court. By some the opinion was expressed that Dearborn himself should have been tried, for it was his dallying at the eastern end of the line that had permitted General

Brock to move west and take Detroit. Dearborn, however, had not surrendered a fort and a town to the British.

Hull's former subordinates were the witnesses against him. Among the most hostile were Cass and McArthur, now generals. Charged with treason, cowardice, neglect of duty, and unofficerlike conduct, Hull was acquitted of the first, but he was held guilty of the other three. The court sentenced him to be shot but, because of his service in the Revolutionary War and his advanced age, recommended mercy. President James Madison approved the sentence of the court, but he remitted the execution of it, and General Hull retired to his home in Massachusetts.

Although he was condemned by most of his contemporaries, many believed that he was made the scapegoat by the administration to relieve itself of criticism for the inept management of the war. Hull's surrender did save the civilians from massacre, and General William Henry Harrison, with an army larger than Hull's, was unable to retake Detroit while the British kept control of the lakes.

Farther east, the generals and their armies were accomplishing nothing. General Stephen Van Rensselaer was in command at Lewiston and Fort Niagara, New York. On October 13 he sent Captain John E. Wool with a force of regulars to take Queenston Heights. The first attack was successful, but General Brock brought up reinforcements, and the New York militia, refusing to cross the river, watched the British kill or capture their comrades on the other side. In the fight Brock was killed.

Van Rensselaer resigned his command in disgust and was succeeded by General Alexander Smyth. He ordered an attack above the falls with no better results than Van Rensselaer's. Following his example, Smyth also resigned.

General Henry Dearborn, senior major general, wasted valuable time at Plattsburg on Lake Champlain. Finally on November 20 he began his advance toward Canada. At the border, the militia refused to cross, and so he marched them back to Plattsburg.

9

After General Brock left Detroit, Colonel Procter assumed the office of governor of Michigan Territory. To Judge Augustus B. Woodward, the only American official who remained, he offered the position of secretary. The judge accepted the post on an unofficial basis and remained in Detroit for a time, laboring as best he could to protect the interests of the conquered people.

There was plenty for him to do. Colonel Procter induced bands of Shawnee, Ottawa, and Potawatomi to establish villages along the river below Detroit in order to close the route to Ohio. These savages ranged over the farms, stole horses and cattle, and ransacked the homes of the Americans. Judge Woodward, by constant vigilance, was able to obtain some protection for their lives and property.

10

After General Hull's surrender, General William Henry Harrison was appointed commander of the North Western Army. He gathered troops in Ohio, planning to recapture Detroit. Progress, however, was slow, and by January, 1813, only an advance detachment of Kentuckians under General James Winchester had got as far as the rapids of the Maumee River, a little above the present city of Toledo, Ohio. To Winchester came an appeal from the people of the River Raisin Settlement,[3] now Monroe, to send troops to protect them from the ravages of British soldiers and Indians.

On January 17, 1813, General Winchester ordered Colonel William Lewis with nearly seven hundred men to march for the River Raisin. Because the margin of the lake was frozen, the troops were able to move rapidly over the ice and, after a march of forty miles, on the next day reached the vicinity of the town. Informed by scouts that about six hundred British militia and Indians were in Frenchtown, Colonel Lewis moved forward resolutely and crossed the frozen Raisin River in the face of heavy enemy fire. A spirited charge by the Kentuckians drove the British and the savages out of the settlement. After making a stand in the woods, they retired toward Fort Malden, while the Americans occupied the town.

Colonel Lewis sent a dispatch to General Winchester with news of his victory and a request for reinforcements. Since Fort Malden was only twenty miles away, he expected that Colonel Procter would soon be upon him with a large force. When he received the message, General Winchester set out from the Maumee River with about three hundred men. Arriving on January 20, he conferred with Colonel Lewis, who was with his men on the left bank of the river where most of the houses were situated. Winchester then crossed to the right

[3] The River Raisin Settlement was also known as Frenchtown because most of the inhabitants were French.

bank and made his headquarters in the home of Colonel François Navarre, principal citizen of the place.

Navarre's house was so comfortable that Winchester preferred to stay there rather than venture out into the bitter January cold, although he was half a mile from his little army. Even a report that the British had been seen on their way to Frenchtown failed to arouse him, and he remained by the fire without giving any orders to prepare for battle.

Early on the morning of January 22, before daylight, a sudden burst of fire from muskets and light artillery aroused the sleepy sentinels. Before the Kentuckians had time to form, the British and Indians were upon them. The soldiers who were encamped on open ground to the right of the town were soon dispersed and driven across the river. General Winchester, arriving tardily on the scene, tried in vain to rally them. Pursued by Indians, many were struck down and scalped. Winchester himself was captured.

The soldiers under Major George Madison, who were protected by the houses and a stockade, gave a good account of themselves. So deadly was the fire of the Kentuckians that Colonel Procter ordered his men to retire into the woods. Then he induced General Winchester to sign an order to Major Madison to surrender, warning him that, if he did not, the Indians could not be restrained from massacring the prisoners. Reluctantly Major Madison complied with the order, after having been assured that his men would be protected against the bloodthirsty Indians.

Fearing that General Harrison might arrive with reinforcements, Colonel Procter left for Malden with his troops and the American prisoners who were able to walk. The wounded were left behind to be cared for by the people of Frenchtown and two army surgeons. Early on the morning of January 23, about two hundred drink-crazed Indians dashed into the village. Seeking out the wounded, they murdered and scalped without hindrance; then, setting on fire the two houses in which most of the Americans lay, they threw into the flames any of the prisoners who tried to escape.

When news of this fiendish butchery spread, the whole country was aroused. The people of Kentucky were especially bitter, for many of their brave sons had perished in the battle and massacre. During the rest of the war, "Remember the River Raisin" was the battle cry of the Kentuckians.

The massacre caused so much hostile comment in Detroit that Colonel Procter, stung by the criticism of his conduct, declared martial law on February 4, 1813, and ordered a number of leading citizens to leave the territory. Against this decree, Judge Woodward protested in vain. Finding that he was powerless to prevent injustice, he left Detroit and went to Washington.

Later, on May 21, 1813, Procter ordered Father Gabriel Richard to Sandwich, where he was to remain under arrest in the house of Father Jean Baptiste Marchand. His offense was expressing frankly his opinion of Procter's rule. About a month later he was released after signing a promise to refrain from publicly criticizing the British commandant.

Because Colonel Procter made no attempt to check the excesses of his Indian allies, after the River Raisin massacre they became more insolent and dangerous than ever. They looted the houses of the inhabitants in the Detroit region, stole or killed horses and cattle, and carried off men, women, and children as prisoners. Herding their captives into Detroit, they beat them to excite the sympathy of onlookers and threatened to kill all who were not ransomed. Although the people of Detroit had already suffered seriously from the war, they gave the Indians anything they would accept to free the poor wretches. Some of the Canadians, too, among them François Baby and Matthew Elliot, purchased American prisoners to save them from torture and death.

After the defeat of General Winchester at Frenchtown, General William Henry Harrison moved to the foot of the rapids of the Maumee and built Fort Meigs on the right bank of the river in February, 1813. With this as his base, he intended to move on Detroit and Fort Malden as soon as he had sufficient troops. Unfortunately for Harrison's plans, General Procter,[4] assembling regulars, militia, and Indians, besieged him in Fort Meigs for a time and otherwise kept him so occupied that he was unable to do more than take measures to protect northern and western Ohio from the enemy.

II

Meanwhile important activities were in progress near the eastern end of Lake Erie. Finally convinced that control of the upper lakes was essential for the taking and holding of Detroit, the national government had ordered the building of a fleet. At Presque Isle, now Erie, Pennsylvania, several warships were under construction. In spite of the best efforts of Sailing Master Daniel Dobbins and Master Ship-

[4] Procter was promoted after the Battle of the River Raisin.

wright Noah Brown, progress was slow. Near the end of March, 1813, Captain Oliver Hazard Perry arrived and took command. Under his energetic direction two brigs and three schooners were hurried to completion.

Building ships of war in a frontier village out of planks sawed from trees just felled in the neighboring forest was a tremendous achievement, but equipping and arming them was an even more difficult feat. Rigging, anchors, chain, and cannon all had to be transported through the wilderness. In spite of delays, Perry had his five ships in the water by the end of May. The two brigs were named the *Niagara* and the *Lawrence*, the latter for Captain James Lawrence of the *Chesapeake*, who had been killed in a battle with the *Shannon*.

The British naval base was at Amherstburg. There Captain Robert H. Barclay, commander of the warships on Lake Erie, was having built a brig named *Detroit*, and from there he sailed out to watch Captain Perry's little fleet nearing completion. A sandbar prevented the British ships from entering the harbor of Presque Isle, and so Captain Barclay hovered off shore. The bar also prevented Perry from sailing his two brigs out to meet the enemy. With their guns mounted they drew too much water, and with the guns removed they would be harmless targets for the British gunners.

Captain Perry waited for an opportunity to reach the open lake. On August 1 it came when Captain Barclay left and sailed back to his base to replenish his supplies. Perry at once put his plans into operation. After all her guns had been removed, the *Lawrence* was towed to the sandbar. Scows were sunk on each side of her; timbers were thrust into open gunports and laid across the scows. Then water was pumped out of the scows. As they became lighter, they rose under the timbers, lifting the brig higher in the water. Finally she cleared the bar and was anchored while the *Niagara* was helped across. The cannon were again put on board.

Captain Perry now had under his command the two brigs, *Lawrence* and *Niagara*, which he had built, and the brig *Caledonia*[5] which had been captured from the British; the three schooners built at Presque Isle, *Ariel*, *Scorpion*, and *Porcupine*; two schooners which had been purchased, *Somers* and *Tigress*; and a sloop, *Trippe*. As soon as he had men enough to man the vessels—a motley crew of sailors, soldiers, and frontiersmen—he sailed out in search of the British fleet. Not finding it, he put into Sandusky Bay.

5 This is the same ship that carried some of Captain Charles Roberts' men from St. Joseph Island to attack Mackinac in July, 1812.

General William Henry Harrison with his army was encamped upon the Sandusky River. He and Perry had been in communication with each other, planning for the invasion of Canada; and so, when Perry anchored his little fleet in the bay, he invited Harrison to come aboard his flagship for a conference. The general came, bringing with him General Lewis Cass, General Duncan McArthur, and twenty-six chiefs of friendly Ohio tribes. After making plans for transporting the troops across the lake, Harrison returned to his headquarters and sent Perry nearly one hundred Kentucky riflemen to serve aboard his ships.

12

Perry selected Put in Bay, a small island near the western end of Lake Erie, for his base. Here in a spacious harbor his fleet had safe anchorage, and he was not far either from the Ohio shore or from the British fleet at Amherstburg.

Hoping to draw Captain Barclay out to fight, Perry sailed for the British base. There he found the enemy ships moored under the guns of Fort Malden. To attack them in that position would put his ships at a great disadvantage, subjected to the fire of both the fleet and the fort. Finding Barclay unwilling to meet him in the open lake, Perry returned to Put in Bay to wait impatiently for a chance to fight.

It came on September 10, 1813. Early that morning a lookout on the masthead of the *Lawrence* sang out: "Sail ho!" Others took up the cry, and soon the British fleet was seen approaching in the distance. The crews were called to quarters, anchors were weighed, and the American ships with all their canvas spread filed out of the harbor. Although each commander could see the other's ships, so light was the breeze and so slowly did they approach that it was nearly noon before the first shot was fired.

Captain Barclay was forced to fight. Supplies at Amherstburg were almost exhausted, and none could be obtained as long as Perry's fleet was on the alert. Unless he defeated the Americans, the British would have to abandon Fort Malden and Amherstburg. Barclay's fleet consisted of the *Detroit*, a new ship built at Amherstburg; the *Queen Charlotte*; the brig *Hunter*; the schooners *Lady Prevost* and *Chippeway*; and the sloop *Little Belt*. Perry had three brigs, five schooners, and one sloop, nine ships to Barclay's six. Besides being more numerous, the American ships were able to throw a much heavier broadside; but the British had more long-range guns. In this respect

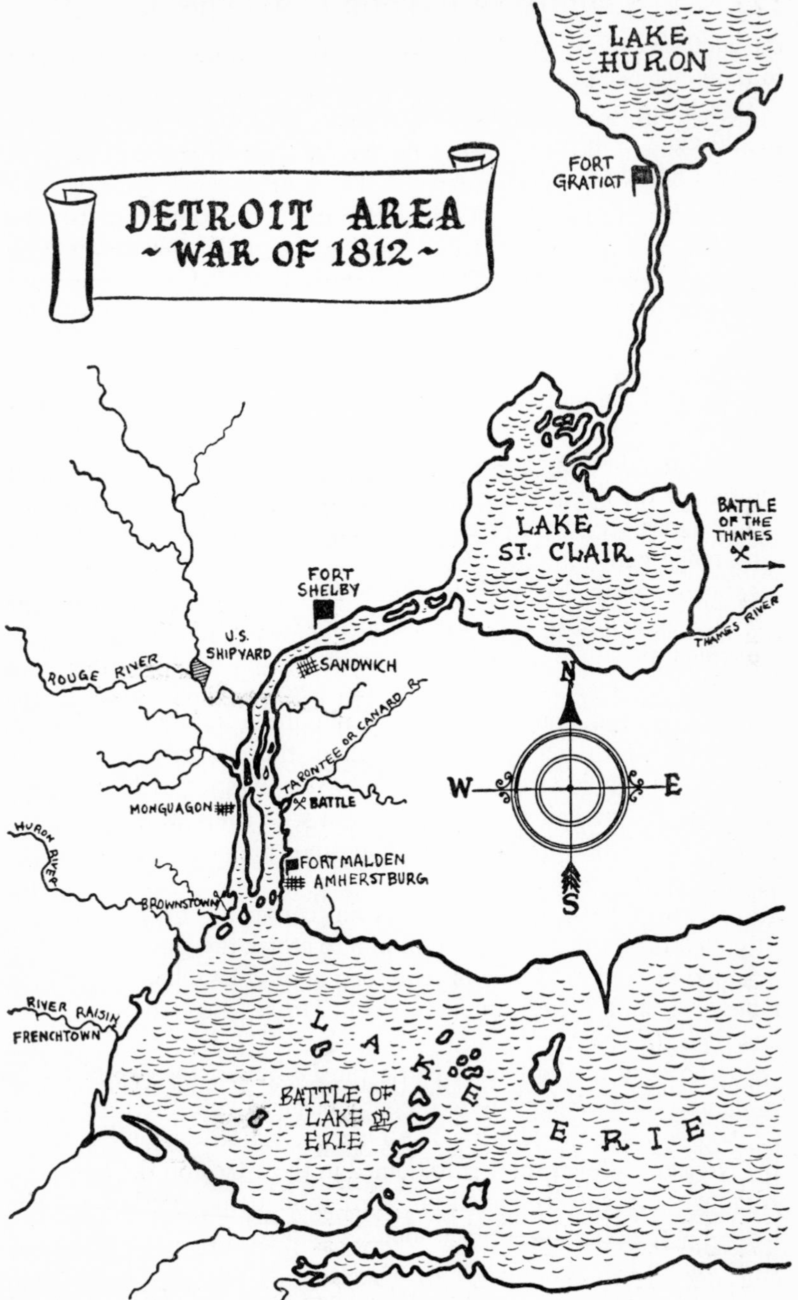
DETROIT AREA
~WAR OF 1812~
LAKE HURON
FORT GRATIOT
LAKE ST. CLAIR
BATTLE OF THE THAMES
THAMES RIVER
FORT SHELBY
U.S. SHIPYARD
ROUGE RIVER
SANDWICH
TARONTEE OR CANARD R.
BATTLE
MONGUAGON
HURON RIVER
FORT MALDEN
AMHERSTBURG
BROWNSTOWN
N
W
E
S
RIVER RAISIN
FRENCHTOWN
LAKE ERIE
BATTLE OF LAKE ERIE

the *Detroit* far outclassed the *Lawrence,* with seventeen long guns to the *Lawrence's* two.

This being the case, Captain Perry had given orders that the ships should close with the enemy as quickly as possible to make the best use of their short guns. While the fleets were still beyond cannon range, Perry had hoisted to the mast of his ship a blue flag on which appeared in white letters the dying words of Captain James Lawrence, "Don't give up the ship." Cheers greeted the sight of the flag, for it was the signal to attack.

Perry steered for Barclay's ship, but before the *Lawrence* could get within range, the *Detroit* let go with one of her long guns. It was just 11:45 in the morning. The ball plunged into the lake, sending up a shower of spray short of the *Lawrence.* Perry continued on his course, and five minutes later a second ball from the *Detroit* crashed through the side of the flagship and killed one of the crew.

The *Lawrence* was still unable to reply effectively because of her short-range guns but the little schooner *Scorpion* opened the battle for the American fleet with two shots from her long thirty-two. The schooner *Ariel* and the brig *Caledonia* also supported the *Lawrence* as she sailed slowly toward her antagonist, taking a terrific pounding from the *Detroit's* long guns. The *Lawrence* soon opened with her two long twelves, but it was twenty minutes before she could lash the *Detroit* with her broadside of short thirty-twos. By 12:30 the principal antagonists were almost side by side, blasting each other with solid shot and sweeping each other's decks with canister. In the rigging Kentucky riflemen calmly took aim and picked off officers and gunners at their posts.

Lieutenant Jesse D. Elliott was in command of the *Niagara.* Although the battle plan called for him to attack the *Queen Charlotte,* he stood off and fired only his two long guns. The schooners *Somers, Porcupine,* and *Tigress,* and the sloop *Trippe,* engaged the *Prevost* and the *Little Belt.*

At the head of the line of battle the *Lawrence,* the *Scorpion,* the *Ariel,* and the *Caledonia* were furiously engaged with the *Detroit,* the *Chippeway,* and the *Hunter.* The *Queen Charlotte,* unable to reach the *Niagara* with her short guns, joined in the attack on the *Lawrence.* Although the smaller American ships were doing good work with their long guns, the British almost ignored them, concentrating their fire on Perry's flagship.

The British ships suffered severely. The *Queen Charlotte* was badly battered and lost both her commander and the second in command early in the fight. The *Detroit* also was nearly a wreck. Captain Barclay was seriously wounded, and the second in command was killed. The *Lawrence,* however, was in worse straits. The rigging had been shot to pieces, the sails were hanging in shreds, the bulwarks had been shattered, and the rudder controls shot away. By 2:30 every gun had been knocked out of action and 83 of the crew of 103 had been killed or wounded. Of all the officers, Perry alone, as if by a miracle, was unwounded by the storm of shot and shell. His younger brother, thirteen-year-old Alexander Perry, a midshipman, also was unscathed.

The Battle of Lake Erie

The *Lawrence,* without a single cannon, was unable to continue the battle; but the *Niagara,* still too far away to take an effective part in the fight, was practically untouched. Perry now made a daring decision. Hauling down his personal pennant and the "Don't give up the ship" flag, he embarked in a rowboat with four sailor oarsmen, determined to transfer his flag to the *Niagara.* Although solid shot struck the boat and splashed beside it in the water, he safely reached the deck of the laggard ship. Ordering Lieutenant Elliott to row back to the small schooners and bring them into the battle, he ran up his flags, gave the signal for close-order action, and bore down again on the larger enemy ships.

Perry's maneuver now was to break the British line. Steering between the *Lady Prevost*, the *Little Belt*, and *Chippeway* on his port side, and the *Detroit*, the *Queen Charlotte*, and the *Hunter* on his starboard, he let go with both broadsides of solid shot and canister at close quarters. Already badly shattered, the British ships could weather the storm of iron no longer. At 3 o'clock, Barclay ordered his colors struck, and the entire fleet surrendered. To General Harrison, who was impatiently awaiting news of the battle, Perry wrote the famous message: "We have met the enemy, and they are ours: two ships, two brigs, one schooner, and one sloop."

Brave and daring in battle, Perry was magnanimous in victory. When the officers of the captured British ships came aboard the shattered *Lawrence* and offered their swords to him in token of surrender, the victor courteously refused to take them, and he took special pains to see that Captain Barclay's wounds were promptly attended to.

Perry's victory of September 10, 1813, was decisive. The destruction of the British fleet gave the Americans control of the upper lakes. Now General Henry Procter at Fort Malden was in the same difficult position that General Hull had occupied at Detroit. Procter's case was even worse than Hull's, for not only were his supplies cut off but also he was in danger of attack by an overwhelming force. Just across the lake General William Henry Harrison was ready to invade Canada with an army of 7,000 men. Among them were several regiments of mounted Kentucky riflemen who arrived a few days after the Battle of Lake Erie. Led by their doughty old Governor Isaac Shelby, who had distinguished himself in the Battle of King's Mountain during the Revolutionary War, those men were eager to avenge the massacre of their fellow Kentuckians at the River Raisin.

13

Knowing that he could not withstand Harrison's army, General Procter decided to abandon Fort Malden and retreat to Toronto, then called York. When Tecumseh learned of this plan, he begged the general to stay and defend his post. Failing to change Procter's mind, the chief angrily denounced him for a coward.

The public buildings at Amherstburg, Fort Malden, and Detroit were burned, surplus supplies were destroyed, and on September 26 the British and Indian force began their retreat to Lake St. Clair and the Thames River. General Harrison's army was carried across Lake Erie by Captain Perry's ships and landed without opposition near Amherstburg on September 27, 1813. Two days later General Duncan McArthur entered Detroit at the head of an American force. The inhabitants were happy to be relieved from the rule of a foreign military governor and to be free from Indian attacks. The fort, which had first been called Lernoult and then Detroit, was now named Shelby in honor of the gallant governor of Kentucky.

General Harrison pursued Procter up the Thames River and overtook his little army near the present city of Thamesville. There on October 5 was fought the Battle of the Thames. Harrison found Procter's force of about 850 whites and 800 Indians drawn up between a large marsh on its right and the river on its left. Between river and marsh lay a small swamp. The British occupied the space between the river and the swamp; the Indians were between the swamp and the marsh.

General Harrison had about 2,500 men, among them Colonel Richard W. Johnson's regiment of mounted Kentucky riflemen. General Lewis Cass, Governor Isaac Shelby, and Captain Oliver H. Perry were with General Harrison.

The general ordered Colonel Johnson to open the battle. He divided his regiment. To the right of the swamp Lieutenant Colonel James Johnson, brother of the Colonel, formed his battalion into four columns of twos. Colonel Richard Johnson took position on the left of the swamp facing the Indians. When the bugle gave the signal, both battalions set spurs to their horses. In spite of a fusillade from the regulars and militiamen, James Johnson's men broke through the two thin lines, wheeled, and rode them down from the rear. Terrified by this whirlwind attack, the British threw down their arms and surrendered.

Colonel Richard Johnson's battalion met more serious resistance. After the first charge against the Indians, finding that his horses were impeded by the trees and undergrowth, he dismounted his men and continued the battle. Johnson was wounded, and an Indian sprang forward to dispatch him with a tomahawk. The Colonel killed him with a shot from his pistol. Infantrymen were ordered to support the Kentuckians, and soon the Indians were put to flight. About 600 British were captured, but Procter eluded his pursuers and escaped. Tecumseh was killed, some said, by Colonel Richard Johnson.

14

Harrison's victorious army returned to Detroit, and General Lewis Cass was put in command. On October 29, 1813, President Madison appointed him governor of Michigan Territory. Before winter set in, Cass left for his home in Ohio, after naming Colonel Anthony H. Butler as commandant.

Because General Procter had had the barracks destroyed, the soldiers built huts to shelter them during the winter. For firewood they chopped down the fences of the *habitants* and even demolished buildings on the Macomb farm.

Colonel Butler had to feed both the soldiers and the civilians from his scanty stores. Cholera appeared among the troops, and so many died that they were buried in a common grave. Civilians also took sick, and, as if there were not already sufficient misery, Indians ranged the countryside, frightening farmers so that they were unable to plant their crops. The savages became so bold that they carried on their depredations even in the vicinity of Fort Shelby. On September 15, 1814, a marauding band killed Ananias McMillan, near the corner of the present State and Griswold streets, and carried his son Archie into captivity.

During the summer of 1814, a fleet under the command of Captain Arthur Sinclair, consisting of Perry's ships *Niagara, Lawrence, Caledonia, Scorpion,* and *Tigress,* sailed from Detroit to attack the northern British posts. Colonel George Croghan was in command of the troops aboard the ships. Additional men joined the force at Fort Gratiot, a new post which had recently been built by Captain Charles Gratiot just below the outlet of Lake Huron. The site is now in the city of Port Huron and is about the same as that occupied by Duluth's Fort St. Joseph from 1686 to 1688.

The expedition first landed on St. Joseph Island in the lower St. Mary's River. Finding the British fort deserted, they set the buildings afire. A detachment under Major Andrew H. Holmes was sent to Saulte Sainte Marie to destroy any property of the North West Company which it could find there. The company was British, and its agents influenced the Indians in favor of the king. Besides, North West fur traders and employes had assisted Captain Charles Roberts in the taking of Mackinac in 1812.

Arriving at the Sault on July 21, Major Holmes destroyed all the company property he found and also that of John Johnston, the principal trader on the American side of the rapids. Even though he was living in Michigan, Johnston had led a company of militia to Mackinac at the call of Captain Roberts; and when Major Holmes destroyed his property, he was doing military duty on the island.

The commanders of the expedition now decided to make an attack on Mackinac. When they discovered that the cannon on the ships could not be elevated sufficiently to fire on the fort, a land attack from the rear of the island was attempted on August 4. Colonel Robert McDouall, the British commander, had built an outwork which he called Fort George behind the fort and on higher ground. The attack upon it was repulsed, and Major Holmes was among the killed. After this reverse, the commanders abandoned the attempt to take Mackinac and returned to Detroit.

15

After the abdication of Napoleon on April 11, 1814, had freed Great Britain from the need for troops in Europe, the government planned new offensives against the United States. The first, under General George Prevost, set out to cut off the New England states by way of Lake Champlain. The troops were supplied by ships which proceeded down the lake. On September 11, 1814, Captain Thomas Macdonough decisively defeated the British fleet, and General Alexander Macomb, a native of Detroit, turned back General Prevost in the Battle of Plattsburg. General Prevost, deprived of the support of his ships, retreated to Canada.

Another British expedition landed in Chesapeake Bay and captured Washington, but a fleet which sailed up to Baltimore and bombarded Fort McHenry was repulsed. During the attack on the fort, Francis Scott Key wrote "The Star Spangled Banner." An attempt to take Baltimore by land also was defeated.

The third expedition was sent against New Orleans. Under the command of General Edward Pakenham, an army aboard warships and transports sailed up the Mississippi. General Andrew Jackson was in command of the American forces, largely frontiersmen who were sharpshooters to a man. He had also about 800 regulars and the fierce followers of the pirate Jean Lafitte. His total force was about 5,500 officers and men.

The British had nearly 10,000, all veterans of the war against Napoleon. Pakenham himself had won victories against the Emperor's ablest marshals, and he had no doubt that he could easily defeat the Americans.

On the morning of January 8, 1815, General Pakenham led his army in a frontal attack against the breastwork General Jackson had constructed. Cannon from both sides opened fire, and American riflemen blazed away at the solid ranks of redcoats. Pakenham rode to the front to encourage his men. He was struck down by a hail of bullets. His men wavered, then fell back. Human flesh could not stand against hot lead from American rifles. The British retired and withdrew from the Mississippi. Their loss in the battle was more than two thousand, while Jackson lost only seventy.

Although neither General Jackson nor General Pakenham knew of it, a treaty of peace had been signed at Ghent, Belgium, on December 24, 1814, two weeks before the battle was fought. The victory at New Orleans had important results. Jubilation of the people over this decisive rout of the British was so great that it erased from their minds the humiliation of past defeats. The war had ended in victory. Throughout the country there was a surge of patriotic fervor and a strong sense of nationalism.

Wars always leave a heritage of bitterness to erstwhile enemies. Leading citizens of Detroit, after peace had returned, were determined to erase memories of the recent hostilities as quickly as possible. To effect their purpose, on March 29, 1815, they gave a "Pacification Dinner" at which former foes from across the river sat down amicably with Detroiters. The resumption of friendly intercourse between British and American neighbors was made easier by this gracious gesture.

Although the war was over, time was required to make necessary readjustments. As the treaty had provided for the return of all conquered territory, Fort Malden was delivered to the British on July 1, 1815, and American troops under Colonel Anthony H. Butler occupied Mackinac on the eighteenth of the same month. The Americans renamed Fort George Fort Holmes in honor of the major who had lost his life in the attack the previous year. The British garrison withdrew to Drummond Island, where they built a fort.[6] They remained until 1828, even after the island had been awarded to the United States in 1822 by the International Boundary Commission. Ironically enough, St. Joseph Island, which the British had formerly

[6] The fort was on the southwestern promontory of the island. Today, a few massive stone chimneys and fireplaces stand as reminders of the vanished post which at one time was intended to be the "Gibraltar of North America."

occupied, was placed on the British side of the international boundary line.

Neither Great Britain nor the United States wanted to engage in an expensive naval building program. To prevent it, Richard Rush, acting secretary of state, and Charles Bagot, British minister in Washington, signed a pact in 1817 by which each nation bound itself to operate no armed vessels on the Great Lakes except revenue cutters to enforce the customs laws.

The Rush-Bagot Agreement did not apply to land defenses, and a few forts were built on each side of the boundary line. Since they served no useful purpose, they were soon permitted to fall into decay. Canada and the United States have lived side by side for more than a century as friendly neighbors, proud of their unfortified frontier.

— 10 —

Governor Cass Explores the Territory

LEWIS CASS returned to Michigan in 1814 as governor of the territory. In the fall of that year, William Woodbridge of Ohio was appointed secretary. Because Governor Cass was temporarily absent, Woodbridge wrote to General Duncan McArthur at Detroit asking for information about conditions there before accepting the appointment. The general replied on November 14, advising Woodbridge that he had better visit Detroit and judge for himself whether or not he wanted to become an officer of the Territory.

McArthur had a poor opinion of the town and the territory of which it was the capital. To Woodbridge he wrote: "I have no hesitation to say that it would be to the advantage of Government to remove every inhabitant of the Territory, pay for the improvements and reduce them to ashes, leaving nothing but the Garrison posts. From my observation, the Territory appears to be not worth defending and merely a den for Indians and traitors. The banks of the Detroit River are handsome, but nine-tenths of the land in the Territory is unfit for cultivation."

Woodbridge, in spite of McArthur's adverse opinion, accepted the office of secretary and moved to Detroit. He found conditions bad enough. As acting governor in the absence of Cass, he wrote to Secretary of State James Monroe on April 8, 1815, explaining the condition of the people. "The pressure of the war," he asserted, "has been indeed severe upon them. While it is to be remarked that perhaps no section of the Union could have exhibited more indubitable evidence of a fervid attachment to their Government than the people of this Country have exhibited, no equal portion of the Community, I am confident, have been so greatly harassed or so greatly distressed." He declared that the inhabitants had been systematically plundered by the Indians during the whole course of the war.

Michigan Territory was indeed in a deplorable condition, and the task of improving it was the responsibility of the new officials. Both the governor and the secretary were New Englanders, but they had lived long enough in the West to understand the people and their needs. Both of them, too, were comparatively young, being in their thirties.

Woodbridge, born in Connecticut, had gone to Marietta, Ohio, with his parents when he was eleven years old and had grown up with the country. A man of scholarly tastes and a retiring manner, he was certainly not a typical politician; but he liked to hold office, and the people elected him to numerous positions because they trusted him.

Cass was a native of New Hampshire. After graduation from Exeter Academy, he went west and studied law in Marietta. Admitted to the bar in 1800, in 1804 he was elected to the legislature, and in 1807 President Jefferson appointed him United States marshal of Ohio. His service in the War of 1812 took him to Michigan and resulted in his appointment as governor.

Governor Cass was eager to promote the prosperity of the territory. The population was small, only four thousand in 1810, and he knew that settlers must be attracted to develop the natural resources. The War of 1812 had drawn attention to Michigan, and some soldiers who had served there returned after hostilities ceased.

Many more would have come if Edward Tiffin, surveyor general of the United States, had not given Michigan a bad reputation. Acting under a law of Congress which provided that two million acres of land were to be surveyed and given to soldiers for their service in the war, he sent surveyors into the southeastern part of the territory in 1815. Encountering lakes and swamps which made their task difficult, they wrote unfavorable reports to their superior.

Tiffin in turn reported that Michigan apparently consisted of swamps, lakes, and poor, sandy land which was not worth the cost of a survey. He declared that in his opinion "not more than one acre in a hundred, if there were one out of a thousand that would in any case admit of cultivation." This report, of course, was a libel against Michigan; but it caused Congress to designate land in Illinois and Missouri for the veterans of 1812, and it caused settlers to avoid the state for some years.

Governor Cass assailed Tiffin's report as untrue, and at his demand surveying was resumed in 1816. It was soon evident that in addition to some swamps and sandy patches there were magnificent forests and rich soil in Michigan. Only a small part, however, had been ceded by the Indians.

In September, 1817, Governor Cass negotiated a treaty with some chiefs at Fort Meigs by which the United States acquired a small tract along the southern boundary; and in 1819, at the Treaty of Saginaw, he bought for the government a large area west and north of Governor Hull's 1807 purchase. (See map, page 149.) Beginning at a point on the western boundary of that tract six miles below the base line, a line was run directly west almost to the Kalamazoo River. From the end of this line, another was extended in a northeasterly direction to the source of the Thunder Bay River and down the river to Lake Huron. (See map, page 149.) The land purchased by Governor Hull and the Saginaw Treaty purchase together comprised almost half the area of the Lower Peninsula.

To make it more convenient for settlers to acquire farms, the government in 1818 opened a land office in Detroit for the sale of tracts that had already been surveyed. Few persons took advantage of the opportunity for, under the existing law, the land was first offered to the highest bidder in parcels of not less than 320 acres. The individual of small means was unable to compete with speculators who intended to hold the land for a rise in price. After the auction, unsold land could be purchased in 320-acre lots for $2 an acre, with a down payment of $160. Even so, there were few sales to actual settlers in Michigan at this time.

2

Michigan acquired a great addition to its area in 1818. On the admission of Illinois to the Union in that year, Congress attached all the land remaining in the Northwest Territory north of the new state and west of Lake Michigan and Lake Superior to Michigan Territory.

Governor Cass was eager to explore the vast territory committed to his care. He had an urgent curiosity to see for himself its natural resources and to make them known as an attraction to settlers. Besides, as Indian superintendent, he wanted to meet the northern Indians, warn them to keep the peace, and make arrangements for further cessions. Cass realized that such a journey as he contemplated would be difficult and dangerous, but he was determined to go.

First he got permission from Secretary of War John C. Calhoun to explore the country south of Lake Superior and beyond. Then he organized his exploring party with great care. Captain David B. Douglass was detailed as geographer to make maps of the country through which they would pass, and Henry R. Schoolcraft as geologist to study the minerals along the way. In addition there were a journalist to write reports, a physician, two assistants for the geographer, and Cass's private secretary. A lieutenant and ten soldiers, two interpreters, nine Indians, and twelve *voyageurs* completed the party of forty-two men.

Setting out from Detroit on May 25, 1820, in three large canoes, the expedition reached Mackinac Island two weeks later, after having been roughly buffeted by a storm on Lake Huron. The next objective was Sault Sainte Marie. There Cass intended to assert the claim of the United States to a tract of land which the Indians had granted at the Treaty of Greenville in 1795 and to inform the savages that the government proposed to build a fort there. Knowing the influence exerted on the Indians by the British post at Drummond Island and by the traders, Cass took with him, when he left Mackinac, Lieutenant John S. Pierce and twenty-two soldiers as an additional escort. And it was well that he did so.

At the Sault, the governor found the Chippewa in an ugly mood. At a council of chiefs which he convened in his tent, he found himself confronted by hostile faces. After he had asked them to confirm the earlier grant so that the government could build a fort, Chief Sassaba, wearing the red coat of a British officer, loudly denounced the Americans, kicked away the presents Cass had brought, and stalked angrily out of the tent.

The parley broke up, and the Chippewa returned to their camp. Then Cass saw an act of defiance. The Indians were raising a British flag in front of Sassaba's wigwam. The governor acted decisively. Ordering his party to prepare for an attack, he strode boldly into the Indian camp, accompanied only by James Riley, his interpreter. Bluntly he informed Sassaba that no foreign flag might be raised over

American soil. Then he pulled down the Union Jack and carried it back to his tent.

The infuriated savages sent their women and children out of camp, and Cass expected momentarily to hear the war whoop. It never came, for Mrs. John Johnston, in the absence of her husband, called the chiefs together. Herself the daughter of a chief, she had great influence over them, and she knew better than they what would be the result of a fight. She convinced them that even though they might destroy the

Cass and the Chippewa, 1820, Sault Sainte Marie

governor's party, the government would loose upon them a war of extermination.

Realizing the foolishness of fighting, the chiefs met the governor again, recognized the authority of the United States, and acknowledged the claim to a tract of sixteen square miles on the river. They reserved to themselves the right to set up their wigwams and to fish.

Lieutenant Pierce and his men returned to Mackinac, and the expedition continued into Lake Superior and along the south shore. Henry Schoolcraft was greatly impressed by the Pictured Rocks, which he declared provided "some of the most sublime and commanding views

LAKE SUPERIOR
TREATY OF LA POINTE [1842]
TREATY OF WASHINGTON [1836]
CEDAR POINT [1836]
LAKE HURON
LAKE MICHIGAN
TREATY OF WASHINGTON [1836]
TREATY OF SAGINAW [1819]
TREATY OF DETROIT [1807]
TREATY OF CHICAGO [1821]
CAREY MISSION [1828]
CHICAGO [1833]
LAKE ERIE
FOOT OF THE RAPIDS [1817]
LAND ACQUIRED BY
INDIAN TREATY
1807 ~ 1842

in nature." While crossing the entrance to Keweenaw Bay, the party was caught in a storm which threatened to swamp their frail craft. Soon after escaping this danger they entered Portage River, passed through Portage Lake, and carried their canoes and supplies through a swamp to the western shore of Keweenaw Peninsula.

When they reached the mouth of the Ontonagon River, Schoolcraft and several others, guided by Indians, ascended the stream to look for a copper boulder of which they had heard. After traveling thirty miles they came upon it lying partly in the water. It was a huge nugget of pure copper encased in rock. Schoolcraft reported that it was a little more than three feet square, and from twelve to fourteen inches thick.[1] This Ontonagon boulder had been seen by Alexander Henry in 1766, and a company which he organized had begun mining in 1771. Finding no further masses of copper, they soon abandoned the project.

Continuing on to the western extremity of Lake Superior, the party ascended the St. Louis River, then, after a portage reached the Mississippi. Hoping to discover the source of the great stream, Cass ascended it for about 350 miles. Finding navigation more and more difficult and the summer nearly gone, he turned back and set out down the Mississippi, bound for Detroit. The party stopped briefly at Fort Snelling, now Minneapolis. At Prairie du Chien they took the Wisconsin River, portaged to the Fox, and arrived at Green Bay.

There several of the men were sent to examine the shore of Green Bay and of Lake Michigan as far as the Straits of Mackinac. Cass and the others proceeded by canoe along the western coast of Lake Michigan to Fort Dearborn (Chicago). Schoolcraft and Douglass continued around the southern bend of the lake and along the eastern shore by canoe to complete the topographical and geological survey. Governor Cass set out on horseback and returned from Fort Dearborn to Detroit over the old Sauk Trail, now U.S. Route 112. He was back at his starting place on September 13 after having traveled 4,200 miles. Ten days later Schoolcraft arrived with the others who had been detached from the party.

Although there had been perils and hardships enough, the long journey, most of it through the wilderness, had been completed without the loss of a man. The government published a report of the exploration which attracted much attention to Michigan. Cass had shown that the way was open, and Schoolcraft reported numerous traces of iron and copper in the Upper Peninsula.

[1] It is fifty inches long, forty-one inches wide, and eighteen inches thick.

3

One result of Cass's expedition was the building of Fort Brady at Sault Sainte Marie to hold the Indians in check. Colonel Hugh Brady and a body of troops arrived in July, 1822, and the next year they erected a stockade near the rapids. Henry R. Schoolcraft was sent to the Sault at the same time as Indian agent. The next year he married Jane Johnston, an educated half-Indian daughter of John Johnston.

Schoolcraft had become interested in the Indians during the journey of 1820, and now he began an intensive study of these people. With the intelligent assistance of his wife and her relatives, he acquired a vast collection of Indian lore, and he published numerous books on the Indians. It was from his writings that Henry Wadsworth Longfellow got both the inspiration and the material for his epic, *Hiawatha*. Schoolcraft remained at the Sault until 1833, when he was transferred to Mackinac Island. He left the Indian service in 1841.

With the purpose of controlling the dangerous Chippewa of the Saginaw Valley, the government in 1822 had a fort built on the west bank of the Saginaw River within the present city of Saginaw. Major Daniel Baker was in command. In 1823, nearly the whole garrison was disabled by malaria. Dr. Zina Pitcher, the post surgeon, was so ill that he had to be carried on a litter to visit his patients. In spite of his best efforts, many died. As a result, the fort was abandoned, and the troops were removed to Detroit. Major Baker declared that "Only Indians, muskrats, and bullfrogs can live in Michigan."

Although nearly all the eastern half of the Lower Peninsula had been purchased from the Indians, Governor Cass was eager to clear the title to additional land. In 1821 at Chicago he purchased for the United States the region south of the Grand River, excepting the extreme southwest triangle bounded on the east by the St. Joseph River. This triangle was acquired by treaties in 1828 and 1833. The remainder of the Lower Peninsula and the eastern part of the Upper, as far as the Chocolay and Escanaba rivers, were ceded by the Indians in the Treaty of Washington in 1836. (See map, page 149.) After the land acquired by these purchases had been surveyed, there would be plenty of room for settlers.

The slow growth of population in the Territory has been previously mentioned. In 1820 it was only 8,765. The stream of immigration to the West had flowed past Michigan into the new states of Ohio (1803), Indiana (1816), and Illinois (1818). Besides opening larger areas, means of transportation would have to be improved to attract more settlers. Most of them came from New York and New England along the Mohawk Trail to Buffalo. There they boarded sailing vessels for Detroit.

An improvement was made in 1818. On August 27 the first steamship on the upper lakes, the *Walk-in-the-Water*, reached Detroit from Buffalo. Everyone was excited by the appearance of this wonderful craft. A *habitant* declared it was a Yankee invention that got its smoke from the lower regions, and the Indians were convinced that it was pulled through the water by a gigantic sturgeon. Captain Job Fish proudly showed off his ship to visitors.

Regular trips from Buffalo continued, the ship making calls at towns along the Ohio shore. In 1819 the *Walk-in-the-Water* made a voyage to Mackinac and Green Bay. Two years later, the ship was wrecked in a storm. The machinery was salvaged and put into the *Superior*, which was immediately built. Soon other steamships made passage to Michigan faster and more comfortable.

Another aid to immigration was the Erie Canal. Completed in 1825 from Albany on the Hudson River to Buffalo on Lake Erie, it was a great convenience for people in New York and New England. Although the boats, drawn by horses, were slow and crowded, travelers preferred them to roads which were sometimes impassable.

Roads in Michigan were necessary for people who wanted to take up land in the interior. Nearly everyone came first to Detroit. From there ships sailed to Mackinac Island, Sault Sainte Marie, and up some of the rivers: for example, the Saginaw, the Grand, and the St. Joseph. But settlers with wagons, farm implements, and household goods needed roads to reach the land they had purchased.

Governor Cass induced Congress to appropriate money for roads, and several were begun during the 1820's. All of them followed Indian trails which had been in use for centuries. The first connected Detroit with Fort Meigs (Perrysburg) on the Maumee in Ohio. It is now U.S. Route 25.

While Father Gabriel Richard was a delegate in Congress, he succeeded in having a bill passed for the construction of a road from Detroit to Chicago. The survey was begun in 1825, and the road was completed ten years later. In 1835, two stage coaches a week made the round trip from Detroit to Chicago over the old Sauk Trail, now U.S. Route 112.

A road to Saginaw was started in 1829. Extensive swamps made

progress slow, and by 1835 it had been completed to a point only five miles beyond Flint. It is now U.S. Route 10.

The Fort Gratiot Road from Detroit to Port Huron, a continuation of U.S. 25, was built during the years 1830 to 1835. The Territorial Road, which branched off the Chicago Road at Dearborn, passed through Ann Arbor, Jackson, Battle Creek, and Kalamazoo to St. Joseph. Built at the same time as the Chicago Road, it gave settlers access to the rich land in the second tier of counties. It is now U.S. Route 12.

The last road begun during the territorial period was surveyed from Detroit to Grand Rapids in 1832. Five years later it had been completed as far as Howell. This is now U.S. Route 16.

4

The word "road" in the 1820's, and even in the 1830's and 1840's, meant something very different from what it does today. A road then was primarily a cleared strip through the woods. Stumps were cut as short as possible, and the undergrowth was chopped out. That was a road, at least before numerous wagons had passed over it. Ruts soon developed, and in wet seasons mudholes appeared. To make passage possible in such places and through swampy ground, small logs were laid side by side to form a corduroy road. Four to six horses or oxen were needed to draw heavy wagons, and they frequently bogged down. When this happened, extra horses from another team and the use of fence rails or saplings for levers were needed to get started again.

Travelers in stagecoaches were jostled together by the roughness of the road, and frequently they had to get out and walk to relieve the horses. Sometimes they had to push the coach or help pry it out of mudholes. They were fortunate if they could ride for a whole day without having a wheel or axle break. When that happened, they had to search for a tavern or the cabin of a settler where they might spend the night in crowded quarters. Roads, even as bad as they were, made it possible for settlers to reach lands in the interior of the Territory.

A tavern in the early days was likely to be no more than the cabin of a settler who was willing to feed and lodge travelers. Accommodations were few. The bill of fare usually consisted of salt pork, corn bread, and potatoes washed down with water or whisky. When it was time to go to bed, a blanket or two hung across the only room provided separate dormitories for the men and the women. Two or three women might sleep in the host's bed; the others, and the men, spent the night on the floor.

One traveler recalled stopping on a rainy night near Marshall in such a tavern, which was unfinished. A blanket served for a door, only half of the roof was on, and there was no floor. The host welcomed them in, provided dinner of pork and potatoes, and then assigned them to their sleeping quarters. Some of the women packed themselves into the only bed, and the others crawled under it. The men huddled together on the ground in the half of the building which was not exposed to the rain.

Soon buildings were erected expressly for receiving guests. Usually there were a large dining room with the bar at one end and a separate parlor for the ladies. Bedrooms were upstairs. Even in such a tavern there was overcrowding, and it was common for two or three to sleep in a single bed. Some of the taverns became regular stopping places for stagecoaches. The approach of the stage was heralded by the driver's horn, and the landlord came out ready to greet the travelers when the coach pulled up to his door.

Detroit had several first-class taverns and a number of ordinary ones. Among those preferred by discriminating travelers were the Mansion House and the Michigan Exchange on Jefferson Avenue, the Eagle Tavern and the Steamboat Hotel on Woodbridge. The last, kept by genial Uncle Ben Woodworth, was a popular hostelry for many years.

Improved transportation, extensive surveys, information about Michigan, new land offices, and a new land law were responsible for bringing more people into the Territory. Congress in 1820 repealed the previous land act and passed a new one which provided for auctions as before, but permitted individuals after the auction to purchase a minimum of eighty acres for cash at $1.25 an acre. At that rate a man with $100 could purchase a family-size farm.

Squatters were people who occupied land, cleared it, and erected a log cabin and perhaps a pole stable on a fertile spot before the land was officially offered for sale by the government. Speculators or wealthy farmers from the East usually hired land-lookers to select the best tracts so that they could bid on them at the auction. The squatter, of course, had no legal right to his land and buildings, and a speculator would be willing to bid high for a quarter section which had improvements on it. The money, of course, was paid to the government.

To protect themselves, squatters sometimes appeared at the land office when the auction began. Each carried his rifle under his arm, and some had ropes with a noose at the end, hints broad enough to discourage most speculators from bidding. After the auction was closed, the squatters could buy the land for $1.25 an acre.

As settlers moved farther inland, they found it inconvenient to return to the Detroit land office to make a purchase after having selected a tract. In response to their demands, new offices were opened—at Monroe in 1823, at White Pigeon in 1831, at Kalamazoo in 1834, at Flint and at Ionia in 1836. Sales at the Detroit office mounted during the 1820's to 92,332 acres in 1825. There was a recession until 1831, when 217,943 were sold. "Michigan fever," an overwhelming desire to settle in Michigan, had finally infected thousands of people in the East, and they moved westward in throngs.

Land sales continued to increase. In 1833 the quantity purchased in the whole Territory was 447,780 acres, and in 1836, more than four million, the largest amount in any state or territory in that year. Money was plentiful, and everyone expected to get rich. It was the high tide of a period of inflation which was soon to end in the Panic of 1837.

Although some of the land was bought by speculators, the millions of acres sold indicated a great increase in settlers. The United States census showed that the population of Michigan in 1830 was 31,640, and in 1840, 212,267, a gain of almost 700 per cent in ten years.

Prospective settlers looking for land to purchase had various ideas as to what was the most desirable kind. Some preferred a heavily wooded area, believing that the presence of great trees indicated fertility in the soil. Such land required much labor in clearing before crops could be raised.

Others preferred oak openings, areas in which large trees stood some distance apart, with little undergrowth between them. Travelers described such openings as looking like natural parks. A settler had wood enough for building and for fuel, and he let in enough sun for his crops simply by girdling the trees to kill them. Later, as he had time, he cleared the land.

The choicest spots in Michigan and those which were quickly purchased were the prairies. Scattered especially through the southwestern part of Michigan, these treeless areas were attractive because of natural beauty, fertility, and comparative ease of cultivation. They were covered with grass growing four or five feet high which was excellent pasturage for horses and cattle. In spring and early summer, wildflowers made spots of color on the prairies, and encircling the open plains stood great forest trees like a green-topped stockade.

There was timber enough beyond the edge of the prairie for buildings and for firewood. The soil was rich and deep, needing only to be plowed before putting in a crop. Breaking the tough sod of a prairie, however, was difficult. Sometimes six yoke of oxen were required to draw the clumsy bull plow through the matted grass roots. Once the ground was broken, the returns were unusually rewarding. Crops of fifty to eighty bushels of corn or forty bushels of wheat an acre were reported.

Largest and best known was Prairie Ronde, an area of 13,000 acres in Kalamazoo County. In the center of the grassy plain stood a large "island" of timber, and within the "island" a lake. Settlers and travelers alike praised it as the most beautiful spot in the world. On the edge of the "island" Lucius Lyon, the surveyor, platted the village of Schoolcraft, naming it for his good friend, the Indian agent. On Prairie Ronde the Big Island Hotel was a famous tavern for many years.

5

Although many settlers entered southern and western Michigan from Indiana and Ohio, Detroit was the principal point of entry for immigrants. During 1836, as many as two thousand arrived in a single day on steamships and sailing vessels. Most of them were from New York and the New England states. Hotels were crowded, stores were filled with customers purchasing supplies, and the streets were jammed with wagons drawn by horses or oxen.

When the wagons left town, each one was usually bound for a tract that had already been purchased. The father of the family had come to Michigan, selected the eighty or one hundred and sixty acres he wanted, and then paid for it at the nearest land office. In choosing a location, he had looked for a place with a stream running through it and, if possible, a spring near the spot where he intended to build his cabin.

If the farm was some distance inland, the family might be on the way for several weeks, especially when the roads were soft and muddy. The mother and the smaller children rode in the jolting, springless wagon, the father walked beside the team of horses or oxen, and the older children walked too, one of them, perhaps, leading a cow. At night, if they had sufficient money, they stayed at a tavern; but usually they camped in the wagon or beside it.

When they reached their destination, a temporary shelter was necessary. Perhaps they pitched a tent, or the father and the boys built a hut of saplings roofed with bark and open at the front where the fire was made. One pioneer mother in later years told of having lived for several weeks with her husband and their little daughter in a tent made of bed sheets. Whenever it rained, of course, the tent leaked. The parents got wet, but they put the baby under a washtub until the shower was over.

The first important task was to build the cabin. The father felled trees and cut them to the required length. When it was time to put the logs in place to form the walls, neighbors came to help. Before a log was laid, it was notched near each end by a skilled axman so that it would fit close to the one above and below it in line and be locked with those at right angles to it. After the wall was so high that logs could not be lifted into place, two or three small trees were laid with one end on the ground and the other on the top of the wall. Logs were then rolled up this incline until the wall was high enough. Spaces between the logs were filled with chips and mud.

An opening was made for a small window. Instead of glass, oiled paper or a piece of buckskin scraped thin and greased kept out the cold and admitted some light. A blanket usually served as a door until planks were split out of a log or until a trip was made to a sawmill. A wooden door was hung on handmade wooden hinges and fastened with a wooden latch. A string or thong, fastened inside above the latch, passed under it and to the outside through a hole just above it. To raise the latch from outside, one pulled the string. When the string was pulled in, there was no way to open the door from outside. Pioneer settlers were very hospitable, and at most houses during the daytime the latchstring was always out.

A ridgepole was fastened from the peak of the front wall to the peak of the back wall, and other poles were laid lengthwise and parallel with it on both sides down to the top of each side wall. The roof was made of bark or of long wide strips, called shakes, split from oak logs.

A chimney was built at one end of the cabin. Clay was packed tight and smooth to make a solid hearth. Using a great deal of wet clay as mortar, the fireplace and chimney were built with sticks of wood one upon another. The whole inside surface of the chimney was then plastered with a heavy coat of wet clay to keep the sticks from catching fire. The fireplace was big enough to take logs four or five feet long. It was the central heating plant in winter, and all year round it was used for cooking. Pots were suspended from an iron crane that could be swung over the fire.

For baking, a Dutch oven was commonly used. It was an iron kettle with a rimmed lid. Dough was placed in the kettle, the lid was put in place, and hot coals were heaped about the kettle and on top of the lid. Frying pans had short legs so that they would stand upon the hearth and above the coals.

The fire was carefully tended during the day and banked with ashes at night. If it went out, one of the boys had to run to the nearest neighbor, perhaps a mile away, to borrow some fire.

There was little furniture in a frontier cabin. A one-poster bed was made by driving a heavy two-crotched stake into the ground, fastening one end of two poles between the logs of the walls, and laying the other end of each one in a crotch. Strips of rope or rawhide run lengthwise and crosswise formed the spring. A tick filled with dry leaves, dry grass, hay, or straw was the mattress.

Wooden chests which the settlers brought with them were their first chairs. A stump outside near the door was the washstand. It held a tin basin, and a bucket with a tin dipper or a dried gourd floating in it was the water supply.

6

Except for the oak openings and the prairies, southern Michigan was covered with a heavy growth of hardwood trees: maple, oak, elm, hickory, ash, and beech. Growing close together, they formed a green leafy canopy so dense that the sun scarcely came through. Some of the settlers found this twilight in the woods depressing, and few had any love for trees. They were obstructions which had to be removed before crops could be grown.

The easiest and quickest way to let in the sun was to kill the trees by girdling them—cutting off a ring of bark with an ax. After clearing away underbrush, the settler planted his corn simply by scratching holes in the ground and dropping in a few grains. Corn was always the first crop because plowing was not necessary, and because corn would be eaten green, or it could be prepared for use by pounding it in a hollowed-out stump. After it was sifted, the meal was cooked into mush or baked into johnnycake. Corn was made also into hominy by soaking off the hard yellow husk in lye water.

The land had to be plowed before wheat could be sown. When it was ripe it was cut by hand with a scythe or a cradle. Threshing was done with a flail—a pole about four feet long to which a short chunk of wood was loosely attached with a thong. The thresher laid a loose bundle of wheat on a smooth, hard patch of ground and beat it with the flail. To separate the grain from the chaff he tossed the flailed straw into the air with a fork when a light wind was blowing. The heavy grain fell to the ground, and the wind blew the chaff and straw away.

After the wheat was threshed, it had to be carried to the mill, perhaps ten or fifteen miles away. That meant a ride on horseback for one of the boys with a bag in front and a bag behind him filled with wheat. At the mill he had to wait his turn, and he usually had plenty of time to investigate the power plant and the machinery.

Water from a dam was carried in a wooden sluice to the big water wheel which turned slowly on its thick wooden axle. Inside the mill, the axle transferred power to a shaft by sturdy wooden gears, and the shaft turned the upper millstone. Wheat was poured through the hole in the upper stone, and flour came out from between the stones. Then it was sifted by passing it over a slanted frame covered with fine cloth.

The pioneer mother usually had a garden in which she raised vegetables, and the father found plenty of game in the woods. There were bears, deer, rabbits, squirrels, pigeons, and wild turkeys which were good for food. The bears were hunted not only for food but because they preyed upon the farmers' livestock. They had a special liking for young pigs. Wolves were plentiful in the forests, usually appearing only at night. They, too, raided the farmers' pole stables. Although they were cowardly and rarely attacked a man, a howling pack following a solitary traveler in the dense woods at night was terrifying and dangerous. So destructive of farm animals were they that usually one of the first enactments of a township board provided a bounty of from two to five dollars for a wolf's head or scalp.

Although settlers from the East went into the woods with some fear of encountering Indians, they soon learned that they were harmless. As a matter of fact, an Indian might bring game to a farmer's cabin to trade for bread or pork. Although they were ordinarily friendly, when they were drunk they were dangerous. In some regions where Indians were numerous, they were nuisances, coming frequently to the houses to beg. By treaties between 1807 and 1836, all the land in the Lower Peninsula was acquired by the government and by 1840 most of the Indians were rounded up and moved across the Mississippi. Some hid in the woods and stayed behind when the soldiers herded the Indians away; others slipped away from the camps at night and returned to their old haunts in the state.

More dangerous than the wolves and the Indians were the mosquitoes. Day and night the woods were full of them, rising in clouds on the approach of a traveler or hunter and settling upon hands, face, and neck. Surveyors were sometimes driven from their work by mosquitoes, and everyone suffered from their attacks. A smudge fire near the cabin brought relief as long as one stayed to leeward of the fire. But the smoke was almost as irritating as the mosquitoes.

Although few even guessed at the connection, it was the mosquitoes which spread malaria, the greatest scourge of the early settlers. Called ague, it was believed to be caused by the exhalations of swamps and decaying vegetation. Night air was believed to be especially dangerous, and so windows and doors were closed to keep it out.

When a person had ague, he suffered alternately from chills and fever. He became cold and shook all over, and his teeth chattered violently. The chills were followed by burning fever, and finally by profuse perspiration which brought relief, but only for a time. Then the cycle began again. Although few died from ague, it so weakened its victims that they were unable to work. Every summer whole families were afflicted, and sometimes in a community there were not enough well persons to look after the sick. Quinine was known to be helpful, but it was scarce and expensive. In its place the settlers used various home-brewed decoctions. Barks of trees and roots of wild plants were the basic materials, and sometimes the remedy was so revolting that the patient declared he preferred the disease. The only certain cure was the coming of cold weather in the fall.

In spite of the many hardships, few who came to Michigan returned permanently to their former homes. If they went back for a visit, they quickly became aware of the advantages of their location in the West. Land was cheap and plentiful. An industrious man could acquire enough to provide a farm for each of his sons, and his daughters could easily find husbands with farms of their own. Michigan was a land of opportunity for courageous men and women.

— 11 —

Towns in the Woods

When Michigan became a territory in 1805, there were only four towns within its boundaries: Detroit, Sault Sainte Marie, Mackinac, and Monroe. Detroit, with a population of not more than one thousand, was the largest. It grew very slowly, the number of inhabitants decreasing for a time because of the War of 1812. Although ships brought throngs of immigrants to the Territory during the 1830's, in 1837, when Michigan became a state, the population of Detroit was only about eight thousand.

Detroit was a bustling port. Steamships and sailing vessels crowded its wharves, bringing merchandise and passengers and carrying away furs and farm produce. During the navigation season of 1836 it was estimated that two hundred thousand persons entered and left the town. There were warehouses on Woodbridge and Atwater streets, but most of the stores were on Jefferson. Lower Woodward Avenue, Griswold Street, and Randolph Street also had business establishments.

Exporting raw materials and importing merchandise to distribute to the interior and to the army posts on the lakes were the principal economic activities of Detroit. It was a commercial rather than an industrial town. In 1837 there were some sawmills and two iron foundries employing a few men. Attached to one of the foundries was a boiler and engine shop, but production was for local use rather than for export.

The two-wheeled carts of the French *habitants*, farm wagons, and wagons of the immigrants crowded the streets of the city. They were unpaved, dusty in dry weather and muddy in the spring or after a rain. Carts and wagons sometimes bogged down even on the main streets.

Dwelling houses of wood or of brick were intermingled with the stores and continued on beyond the business section. In 1826 the garrison was moved from Detroit, and Fort Shelby was given to the city by the United States Government. The ramparts were leveled, and buildings gradually occupied the site. Farther north in a small park near the upper extremity of Griswold Street, the territorial capitol was built. It was completed in 1828. At the time, many complained that it was too far from the center of the town.

In the middle of lower Woodward Avenue just below Jefferson was the market, and nearby stood the whipping post where petty criminals were flogged. North of Jefferson Avenue on Woodward between Larned and Congress streets stood the Presbyterian and Episcopal churches. The Methodist church also faced on Woodward Avenue across Congress Street from the Episcopal church. St. Anne's Roman Catholic Church faced on Larned just east of Bates Street. The Baptist church was on the northwest corner of Fort and Griswold streets.

Although there was no longer a stockade around the town, growth to the east was slow for a number of years because the French *habitants* refused to sell their farms or even to permit streets to be run across them. On the west side, the Cass farm, formerly the Macomb farm, extended three miles north into the woods. Lots were offered for sale from the river to Larned Street, but they were so far west of the center of town that they were not sold for a number of years. On the eastern edge of town the Brush farm, formerly the Askin farm, also was divided into lots, and purchasers were found for some of them.

Sault Sainte Marie, founded earlier than Detroit, had practically stood still. After the mission was closed in 1689, it continued to be an important stopping place for traders, and there were some houses near the portage. The arrival of the Indian agent, Henry R. Schoolcraft, and Colonel Hugh Brady with troops in 1822 and the building of the fort resulted in a slight growth of the civilian population. Permanent inhabitants were few, largely French, Indians, and half-bloods. In early summer, however, when the *voyageurs*, traders, and Indians came in from the wintering places, the town swarmed with people.

Because of the rapids, it was necessary to unload cargo either above or below and carry it over the portage to be reloaded. The principal article of commerce was furs, but whitefish and maple sugar were also valuable exports. There was an Indian agent, and the American Fur Company had a store there. Steamboats occasionally touched at the

Sault on pleasure voyages during the summer. From December until May the waterways were closed by ice, and the village was almost isolated.

Most of the people, except those in the garrison, were Catholics, but both the Baptists and the Presbyterians had missionaries at the Sault. Each had a school for white and Indian children. The Reverend Abel Bingham, a Baptist missionary, went there in 1828 and remained for many years.

2

On Mackinac Island the fort, on the high ground overlooking the spacious harbor, was the dominant feature. The village lay below near the water. Although the permanent population was only a few hundred whites, Indians, and half-bloods, Mackinac boats and canoes in the summer brought as many as two thousand Indians and fur traders from the north, west, and south. For the Indians there was a double attraction, the Indian agency where they received their treaty payments, and the store of the American Fur Company stocked with merchandise.

After the War of 1812, the Fur Company, which had been founded by John Jacob Astor in 1808, dominated the fur trade. Mackinac was its headquarters, where Robert Stuart managed the trade in the region of the Lakes and beyond. When the furs were brought in, the shore was covered with Indian wigwams, and noisy, brawling *voyageurs* filled the streets and the stores of the village.

By hiring or ruining independent traders, the American Fur Company obtained almost a monopoly of the trade in Michigan, and its agents encouraged Indian and white hunters to kill every fur-bearing animal they could find. By 1834 this destructive policy had reduced the annual catch of furs. Settlers also were beginning to occupy some of the hunting grounds. Astor, shrewdly observing that the business was on the decline, sold out and concentrated his efforts farther west.

Henry R. Schoolcraft, as Indian agent from 1833 until 1841, did his best to protect the Indians from the traders who supplied them with liquor and cheated them out of their furs. At Mackinac he continued his study of the Chippewa language and customs which he had begun at the Sault.

There was a Catholic church, St. Anne's, on the island, and in 1823 a Protestant church and school were established. The Reverend William M. Ferry, a Presbyterian minister, his wife, and several assistants conducted a school for more than ten years. Open to white and Indian children alike, it had at one time nearly one hundred boarding students and fifty day students. In 1834 the Rev. Mr. Ferry left and became a founder of Grand Haven on the Lake Michigan shore. The mission continued until 1837.

In 1822, an accident occurred on Mackinac Island which led to important scientific discoveries. On the morning of June 6, several men were in the store of the American Fur Company. While one of them was carelessly handling a shotgun, it discharged, the whole load entering the body of Alexis St. Martin. He fell to the floor, and his companions at first believed him dead. Noticing signs of life, one of them ran to the fort nearby for the army surgeon.

Dr. William Beaumont went at once to the store, treated the wounds, and nursed St. Martin back to health. A sturdy young fellow, his fine physique was not impaired, but a wound in his abdomen refused to heal. In fact, an opening remained through which the inside of his stomach could be seen.

Realizing that here was an unusual opportunity, Dr. Beaumont engaged St. Martin to work for him. His principal employment was to serve as a subject for the study of digestion, a process about which almost nothing was known. Over a period of years, Dr. Beaumont fed him various foods and, through the window into his stomach, watched the course of digestion. Being able to withdraw some of the contents at will, the doctor could examine the condition of partially digested food from time to time and thus discover the stages in the process. He also drew off gastric juice and analyzed it, something never done before.

Although Dr. Beaumont was transferred from Mackinac to various other army posts, he continued his study whenever he could induce St. Martin to co-operate. As can be imagined, the experiments were not entirely pleasant for the Frenchman, and, besides, his comrades teased him, calling him "the man with the lid on his stomach." Tiring of their ridicule, he would run away, and the doctor would have to coax him to return. In spite of the unhealed wound, he remained healthy, married, and lived to the age of seventy-six.

In 1833 Dr. Beaumont published *Experiments and Observations on the Gastric Juice and the Physiology of Digestion*. It was the first book on the subject, and physiologists the world over hailed the author as a benefactor of mankind. Inside the fort today stands a granite monument with an inscription honoring Dr. Beaumont for his contribution to the advancement of medical science.[1]

[1] The Michigan State Medical Society acquired the Fur Company store in 1947. The Society had it restored to its original form and in 1953 gave it to the state to be preserved as a memorial to Dr. Beaumont.

The fourth of the old towns in Michigan, Monroe, had its beginning about 1785 when François Navarre and a few other Frenchmen with their families settled on the Rivière aux Raisins about three miles above Lake Erie. The British and the Americans usually called the place Frenchtown or the River Raisin Settlement. It grew very slowly. The battle and the massacre in 1813 were a major disaster, but after the War of 1812 it took on new life. When President James Monroe visited Michigan in 1817, the village was named in his honor and made the seat of government of the new county of the same name. The opening of a land office in the town in 1823 attracted many people, and some remained.

Among them were several young men of unusual ability: Austin E. Wing; Warner Wing; Isaac P. Christiancy, who later became justice of the state supreme court and United States senator; Alpheus Felch, governor of Michigan, 1846–1847, and United States senator; and Robert McClelland, governor, 1852–1853, member of Congress, and Secretary of the Interior in the Cabinet of President Franklin K. Pierce.

These and other leaders were determined to make Monroe a great lake port. They induced Congress to open a channel connecting the town with Lake Erie, and the citizens themselves appropriated money to pay for part of it. In 1836 there were in Monroe three banks, six churches, a woolen mill, an iron foundry, a tannery, three sawmills, two flour mills, and two printing offices. Two warehouses and wharves had been erected for the use of shippers. In the population of about fifteen hundred there were thirty merchants, six physicians, and thirteen lawyers.

In spite of able and progressive leaders, Monroe did not become a lake port, except for a few years. Situated between Detroit and Toledo, it found most of the traffic it had hoped for going to those two towns.

3

New towns were founded on the old Indian trails leading from Detroit. Usually they sprang up along the roads which followed the trails, but sometimes they had their beginning before the roads were opened. Founders of a town chose a spot on a river or a creek where a dam could be built to provide power for mills, and the town became a center of trade and industry for the surrounding farms.

Pontiac, on the Saginaw Trail where it crossed the Clinton River, was one of these. Laid out in 1818 by a group of men from Detroit, it grew slowly but steadily. At first it was handicapped by the lack of a road and by the treacherous swamp on Woodward Avenue beyond the

Six Mile Road. Even after the road was built in the 1830's, the swamp made travel so uncertain that many preferred in the spring of the year to go to Pontiac by way of Mount Clemens rather than by the Saginaw Road.

By 1837 Pontiac was a flourishing town. It had a sawmill, a gristmill, and a woolen mill. So much grain was taken to the mill that large shipments of flour were sent to Detroit.

Farther along on the Saginaw Trail, Flint had its beginning in a fur post kept by Jacob Smith at a ford in the Flint River in 1819. After Smith's death, John Todd kept a tavern and operated a ferry at the same place. When the village was first platted in 1835, the settlers were largely from Genesee County, New York. At this time the Saginaw Road had been continued through the village to a point five miles beyond.

Saginaw had its beginning in a post of the American Fur Company on the Saginaw River. The treaty negotiated with the Chippewa by Governor Cass in 1819 and the erection of the fort in 1822 attracted attention to the locality. Although the garrison was soon removed from the fort, Louis Campau, an independent fur trader, platted the town of Saginaw in 1822. Ten years later Samuel W. Dexter of Washtenaw County purchased land on the river and laid out additional lots.

Two influential early residents were the brothers Ephraim S. and Gardner D. Williams, who began trading on the Saginaw as agents for the American Fur Company in 1828. In 1834 they built a sawmill, the beginning of what was later to become the great lumber industry of Saginaw.

The principal towns during the territorial period along the Military Road, or Fort Gratiot Road, were Mount Clemens and Port Huron. The former was near the site of the Moravian village on the Clinton River (1782–1786). Christian Clemens, from Pennsylvania, platted the town in 1818. Some ships were built there, and it served as an outlet for the farmers in the vicinity. In 1836 a glassworks was established.

Port Huron had its beginning in Fort Gratiot, built in 1814. A settlement which grew up where the Black River flowed into the St. Clair River became known as Desmond. The name was changed to Port Huron in 1837. It was a shipping center for lumber, and shipyards were early established.

4

The old Sauk Trail had for centuries been the route of Indians from Detroit to Chicago. White traders, soldiers, and settlers followed in the footsteps of the Indians. The beginning of the survey for a government road over the route in 1825 hastened the choosing of townsites. The importance of the road to new towns is shown by the abandonment after a few years of Woodruff's Grove, the first village in Washtenaw County, founded in 1823. The Huron River provided passage for small boats to Lake Erie, but when the Chicago Road was run through Ypsilanti, only a mile away, the Grove began to dwindle and was soon abandoned.

Ypsilanti was begun in 1824 by several land owners, the most prominent of whom was Judge Augustus B. Woodward. A classical scholar and, like many other Americans, intensely interested in the

An Early Michigan Town, 1832

Greek war for independence which was then raging, he named the town for two of the heroic Greek leaders, Demetrius and Alexander Ypsilanti.

The town grew steadily because of its strategic location on the Huron River and the Chicago Road. For a time large flatboats carried produce down the Huron to Lake Erie and up to Detroit. Although it was a long way round, it was better than going by road. A loaded wagon, because of the ruts and mudholes, required three days to reach Detroit.

Saline, Clinton, Jonesville, Coldwater, Sturgis, Niles, and New Buffalo, all were established along the Chicago Road before the end of the territorial period, and all were important centers of trade for the farmers in the vicinity. Although many settlers from the East reached these towns and the surrounding countryside by way of the Chicago

Road, many others came up through Ohio and Indiana. Some were originally from Virginia, Kentucky, and North Carolina.

Niles had the best location. Situated on the Chicago Road and on the St. Joseph River, which in the early days bore ships from Lake Michigan to its docks, it was bound to prosper.

Before the village of Niles was laid out in 1829, much of historic interest had already happened in the vicinity. La Salle had passed the site in 1679 and 1680. About ten years later a mission and a fort had been established beside the river. The British garrison had been overwhelmed by hostile Indians during the Pontiac War, and in 1781 the Spanish flag had briefly waved above the undefended stockade.

Although both the old mission and the fort were only memories, a new mission was established in 1822. At the request of Governor Cass, the Reverend Isaac McCoy, a Baptist minister, moved from Fort Wayne, Indiana, to build school, chapel, houses, and barns on the St. Joseph River about a mile west of where Niles was laid out seven years later.

Mr. McCoy, his wife, and other assistants labored to perform the services Governor Cass asked of them—to civilize the Indians and to protect them from the liquor of the traders. Under his guidance Carey Mission prospered. Several hundred acres of land were cleared and fenced, and the Indians raised corn, wheat, oats, and vegetables. Soon white settlers began to take up land near the mission. In spite of his best efforts, the Indians were demoralized. Mr. McCoy approved of the removal of the Indians beyond the Mississippi for their own good. He closed the mission in 1830 and went west to continue his services to the Indians.

By 1832 the Chicago Road was at least passable as far as Niles. Four-horse post coaches carried passengers and mail three times a week from Detroit, making the trip in three days if the road was dry. From Niles to Chicago one could sail down the St. Joseph River to St. Joseph and across Lake Michigan. In 1835 coaches from Detroit went through to Chicago.

Although they were off the line of the Chicago Road, two towns in Lenawee County, Tecumseh and Adrian, grew rapidly and prospered. Founded in 1824 by Austin E. Wing, Musgrove Evans, and Joseph W. Brown, Tecumseh soon had a sawmill, a gristmill, a tannery, and a furniture factory. Evans, Brown, and many of the early settlers were Quakers.

Adrian was founded in 1826 by Addison J. Comstock, a Quaker, at the confluence of two branches of the River Raisin which provided power for a sawmill and a gristmill. Numerous Quakers made their homes in Adrian. Comstock and other energetic residents were eager to bring a railroad to their town. Largely through their efforts and their subscriptions to stock in the enterprise, the Erie and Kalamazoo Railroad reached Adrian from Toledo in 1836. It never was extended farther.

Horses hauled the cars the first year, but in 1837 a steam locomotive was procured, and the first railroad west of Schenectady began to operate. In 1849 the directors of the Erie and Kalamazoo leased its right of way to the Michigan Southern Railroad, now a part of the New York Central System, for $30,000 a year, forever. Every year the stockholders of the Erie and Kalamazoo meet in Adrian, the directors declare a dividend, and the meeting adjourns—surely a pleasant way to run a railroad.

5

Before the Territorial Road was made, towns began to spring up along the route. The first was Ann Arbor, laid out in 1824. The founders were John Allen and Elisha Walker Rumsey, the former a Virginian, the latter a New Yorker. Traveling west from Detroit, they came upon a burr-oak opening where a creek flowed into the Huron. Sufficient water power was assured, and they laid out the town, which they called Ann Arbor in honor of their wives, both named Ann. It became the county seat in 1826, and ten years later it had a population of about two thousand.

Jackson, next west on the route of the proposed road, had its beginning in 1829. It also became a county seat.

Land purchased in 1831 at the forks of the Kalamazoo became the site of Albion. It was settled largely by people from New York.

Marshall, founded in 1831, where Rice Creek joins the Kalamazoo River, soon had a sawmill and a gristmill. Its early settlers were from the East. Among them were the Reverend John D. Pierce of New Hampshire, a Congregational missionary, Sidney Ketchum of New York, and Isaac E. Crary of Connecticut.

Battle Creek, next on the Territorial Road, had its beginning also in 1831 on the Kalamazoo River. Its progress was slow, only fifteen inhabitants being on the ground in 1835. By 1837, however, it had mills and a tavern.

Titus Bronson was the founder of Kalamazoo. Choosing a beautiful site on a burr-oak opening on the Kalamazoo River, in 1831 he platted the town, which he named Bronson. A native of Connecticut, he had come to Michigan by way of Ohio. He was a restless person, moving frequently, and always farther west. Bronson was rather eccentric in manner, but perfectly honest. By his frank denunciation of intemperance and trickery, he made numerous enemies.

In 1835, men who disliked him had the name of the town changed to Kalamazoo. Bronson sold his property and again moved west, this time to Illinois.

Kalamazoo had both water power and river transportation, besides being on the Territorial Road. In times of high water, ships came up the river from Lake Michigan with merchandise and carried away produce from the surrounding farms.

St. Joseph, the proposed terminus of the Territorial Road, had an excellent location at the mouth of the St. Joseph River. There La Salle in 1679 had built his little Fort Miami, and from there he had set out in 1681 to discover the mouth of the Mississippi. The river had been an important carrier for the fur traders, but the town of St. Joseph was not laid out until 1829. Steamboats sailed far up the river, and St. Joseph developed as a lake port.

Along the route of the Grand River Road also, villages sprang up: Farmington, a Quaker settlement, Brighton, Howell, Grand Rapids, and Grand Haven.[2] The founder of Grand Rapids was Louis Campau, a fur trader who removed from Saginaw in 1826 to the rapids of the Grand River. The town had its beginning in 1831, and it was platted two years later.

Even before Campau built his post, a Baptist mission for Indians was established at the Rapids in 1823. Known as the Thomas Mission, it had little success until 1827, when the Reverend Leonard Slater and his wife took charge. In 1833 the Reverend Frederick Baraga was transferred from L'Arbre Croche to the Rapids, where he opened a Catholic Mission for the Indians.

Grand Rapids developed slowly at first, but its location was excellent for future growth. There was abundant water power, and small steamships came up the river from Lake Michigan.

Grand Haven had its beginning as a headquarters of the American Fur Company with a store and a warehouse. Joseph La Framboise and his Ottawa wife wintered on the Grand River for many years collecting furs for the company. After Joseph was killed by an Indian, his widow continued until 1821 to carry on the trade in the region.

[2] Lansing, also on the Grand River Road, was founded in 1847, when the Capitol was built.

When she retired to Mackinac, Robert Stuart, manager of the company, engaged Rix Robinson to take her place.

Robinson, trained as a lawyer in the East, had given up his profession to enter the fur trade. As agent of the company he had charge of the gathering of furs in the Grand and Kalamazoo river basins. In 1834 the Reverend William M. Ferry, who had given up his mission at Mackinac, settled at the mouth of the Grand River. The next year he and Robinson laid out the town of Grand Haven. It soon had mills, and its location on Lake Michigan made its future as a port seem assured.

6

The towns which have been mentioned, of course, are only a few of those which were founded before Michigan became a state. Some have become large cities; others are still only villages. The founders of all of them expected great futures for their creations.

Some founders hoped to attract settlers by conferring names of famous foreign seaports on their villages—Singapore, Brest, and Gibraltar. Perhaps they believed that their towns would one day rival their namesakes. Today Singapore, which was near the mouth of the Kalamazoo River, lies buried deep beneath a dune. Brest is a village in Monroe County, and Gibraltar a village in Wayne.

Port Sheldon was the most spectacular of the boom towns. Planned by eastern capitalists as the great seaport of Lake Michigan, it was laid out on Pigeon Lake, ten miles south of the new village of Grand Haven. Having plenty of money to spend, the proprietors sent a shipload of workmen and materials in the fall of 1836 to this spot in the western wilderness.

Land was cleared, streets were laid out, and a handsome map of the proposed city was engraved to encourage investors to purchase lots. At the outlet of Pigeon Lake into Lake Michigan a lighthouse was erected. Stores, an office building, and a mill were constructed; but the crowning glory of the place was the Ottawa House, a luxury hotel in the woods.

It was a two-story frame building, eighty feet by one hundred and fifty, with six tall white columns across the front. No expense was spared in finishing and furnishing the hotel, which was said to have cost $200,000. During the few years of Port Sheldon's existence, the Ottawa House was the center of lavish entertainment for land speculators, politicians, sportsmen, and tourists.

The proprietors soon learned that they had chosen an unfavorable site for their projected metropolis. The outlet to Lake Michigan, which was to carry great ships to the docks of Port Sheldon, kept filling up with sand. Besides, the town was too far off the line of travel from east to west to attract commerce and industry. Then came the Panic of 1837.

Like other towns, Port Sheldon suffered from the shock; but, unlike some of them, it never recovered. Built from the top down, with a luxury hotel as the principal attraction instead of growing gradually by the labor of industrious inhabitants, Port Sheldon collapsed.

The promoters were bankrupt. In 1842 everything was sold at sheriff's sale. The hotel and the other buildings gradually fell into decay. Nothing remains except four columns of the Ottawa House, which were built into the mansion that is now the Grand Rapids Art Museum.

Another town begun in high hope of success was Pinckney. It is notable, not because of the founder's extravagant expenditures, but because it served as a setting for stories written by the founder's wife.

William Kirkland, the founder, was a teacher in New York. His wife, Caroline, was a writer of some reputation. Having caught the prevailing Michigan fever, they went West, hoping to make their fortune.

Kirkland became principal of the Detroit Female Seminary when it opened in 1836, and his wife taught in the school. Teaching, however, offering no quick road to riches, even in Michigan, Kirkland purchased some land in the southern part of Livingston County. He laid out lots, and he built a mill, a store, a tavern, and a house for his family. He named the budding village Pinckney.

Mrs. Kirkland accompanied her husband on his exploring expeditions through the back country, and she was delighted with the natural beauty of Michigan. There were also, she found, some discomforts. To a woman accustomed to the cities of the East, the bottomless mud-holes in the roads were appalling, the overcrowded taverns were disgusting, and the mosquitoes were ferocious.

Living in Pinckney and keeping house for her husband and children in a cabin which snakes and toads entered at will through cracks in the floor was a real hardship. Her neighbors were friendly and obliging, but careless in dress, crude in manner, and lacking in education—at least so they seemed to the lady from New York.

The beautiful country, the peculiar inhabitants, and life in the frontier community made a deep impression on Mrs. Kirkland. In spite of her manifold labors, she found time to write about the new environment in which she lived. Under the pseudonym Mrs. Mary Clavers, she published in 1839 a book entitled, *A New Home—Who'll Follow.* In it Pinckney was called Montacute.

In the East the book was highly praised by Edgar Allan Poe and other critics as an excellent portrayal of western life. The style is lively, and the character sketches are delightful. Undoubtedly Mrs. Kirkland painted some of her neighbors in unflattering colors. When, in spite of her pseudonym, her authorship became known, her popularity in the community declined.

Pinckney stagnated in the Panic of 1837. Becoming discouraged, the Kirklands in 1843 returned to New York. The years spent in Michigan, however, were not wasted, for Mrs. Kirkland used her experiences there as material for two additional books—*Forest Life* and *Western Clearings.*

Besides the kinds of villages which have been mentioned, there were also "paper cities"—purely imaginary developments except for colorful prints displayed by promoters trying to sell lots. One of these phantom towns was White Rock City. Allegedly located on the shore of Lake Huron, about ten miles south of the present site of Harbor Beach, this woodland metropolis, according to the elaborate pictorial map circulated by the founders, faced on a spacious harbor. Into it emptied a broad river up which steamships were sailing. A public square surrounded by churches, a courthouse, a bank, and other attractive buildings appeared in the center of the map. Wide streets reached away into the woods where sawmills were busily producing lumber for new houses. This was the picture.

The reality was quite different. In the fall of 1837, Bela Hubbard and Dr. Douglass Houghton were in the neighborhood engaged in a geological survey. Having seen pictures of the town, they were looking for it. Finally they found the river—a creek scarcely broad or deep enough to admit their canoe. There was neither harbor nor town, only dense woods. Three large beech trees stood where the city square should have been. Into the smooth bark of one of them, the members of the surveying party carved their names. According to Hubbard, they were the first guests to register in the White Rock City Hotel.

— 12 —

Teachers, Preachers, and Politicians

THE PRINCIPAL concern of the people who came to Michigan was to make a living, but many of them were not satisfied with that alone. Immigrants from New York and New England particularly had had some schooling, and a few were college graduates. As soon as possible after the first heavy labor of making new homes was finished, they turned their attention to providing schools, churches, literary societies, and other cultural organizations which had been a part of their lives in their old homes.

Settlers who had attended school themselves, and some who had not, were determined that their children should have some education. Means to support schools were meager in the sparsely settled Territory where nearly everyone was just getting started in farming or in business. Although the governor and judges adopted an act in 1809 to levy a tax for the support of schools, no attempt was made to enforce it.

In 1827 the Territorial Council passed a law which required every township with fifty inhabitants to employ a schoolmaster "of good morals" to teach children reading, writing, English, French, arithmetic, spelling, and "decent behavior." Schools were to be open for six months. According to the law, when there were two hundred inhabitants in a township, a school of higher grade in which Latin was to be taught should be established.

Although this law was not enforced, some schools were organized, but they were not supported by taxes. Instead, rate bills were issued by the school board to parents whose children received instruction, and they had to pay tuition. Besides, each parent was required to provide a proportion of the firewood necessary to heat the building. Usually, children of poor parents were permitted to attend free, but those who could not pay were frequently too proud to ask for free schooling. It was a long time before a free education was considered to be the right of every child. In Michigan there were no free schools until 1842, and then only in Detroit. Nearly thirty years passed before the system extended throughout the state.

The early schools were log buildings, sometimes with only one or two windows. The fireplace was usually in the wall opposite the door. Holes were bored in the logs of the side walls about three feet from the floor. Short stakes were driven into the holes and boards were fastened on them for desks. Homemade stools or benches served the pupils for seats.

The teacher's table stood at one end of the room. On it lay his birch rod and cherry rule. The rule he used to draw lines on slates and paper for writing practice and also to crack the knuckles of a laggard pupil. The birch rod went into action when harsher punishment was called for.

The teacher's inkwell, his quill pen, and some of the pupils' quills were always on his table, for he had to be skillful with a penknife so that he could repair the old quills or make new ones.

The teacher also had a record book in which he kept an exact account of attendance. Rate bills were made out according to the number of days pupils were in school, and the length of time the schoolmaster lived with each family also was determined by the record in the book; for the teacher boarded around the district, receiving part of his salary in meals and lodging.

The pupils ranged from beginners to boys and girls of sixteen or seventeen. In some districts it was the custom to keep school two or three months during the summer and two or three months during the winter. In that case a woman was engaged for the summer when only the children too small to work attended. A man was always hired for the winter term, for then the big boys who had been helping on the farms during the summer came to school. Unless the teacher was strong enough to whip the biggest boy, he usually resigned.

The teacher taught the little ones individually. There were no blackboards. Paper was scarce, and so the smaller children sometimes drew out the letters of the alphabet in a tray filled with moist sand. Slates were commonly used, because they could be cleaned with a bit of wet rag or even with a dry sleeve and used again and again. The more

Interior of a Log Schoolhouse

advanced pupils copied over and over in their writing books the sentence which the teacher first set down for them in a fair round hand.

There were few textbooks and a great variety among them. Each child brought whatever schoolbook he could find at home, for a book once purchased was passed on from the oldest to the youngest in a family. Classes stood in line to recite. If a pupil failed to answer a question correctly, he went to the foot of the class. It was considered a great honor to stand at the head at the end of a day's recitation.

These township or district schools, sometimes open only two or three months in a year because teachers were not available and because parents had insufficient money to support a longer term, were the only means of education in the country or in small towns. In Detroit there were teachers who took private pupils, and some of them taught advanced subjects.

Attempts were made by individuals and by groups of citizens to organize academies in which pupils could prepare to enter college. Charters were issued by the Territorial Council for twelve such institutions, but few of them were actually opened until after Michigan became a state.

One was Merrill's Select School, started in Ann Arbor by Thomas W. and Moses Merrill. In the initial number of the *Emigrant*, Ann Arbor's first newspaper, on November 18, 1829, appeared the following advertisement:

> Select school for young gentlemen and ladies in Ann Arbor Village. Reading, spelling, mental arithmetic, modern geography, and English grammar at $2.50 per quarter [three months]; including writing, practical arithmetic, ancient geography, history, philosophy, chemistry, logic, astronomy, the higher branches of mathematics, composition and declamation at $3.00; including the Latin & Greek languages, $4.50.
>
> The instructors pledge themselves to take a lively interest in their pupils' advancement in knowledge, in good habits and amiable deportment; and by a general superintendence regarding the intellectual, physical and moral welfare of those committed to their care, while at their boarding houses as well as at their class schoolroom, they hope to merit, as well as to receive the patronage of parents and guardians. Boarding may be obtained at $1.00 per week.

According to the advertisement, Thomas W. Merrill had the master of arts degree and had taught in New Hampshire; his brother had been a teacher in Albany, New York. In spite of the great variety of subjects offered, the low tuition fees, and the experience of the teachers, the school continued for only two years. Thomas W. Merrill moved to Kalamazoo, where he opened the Michigan and Huron Institute in 1836. This academy later became Kalamazoo College.

2

Although there was never a free public school in Michigan Territory, some persons were dreaming of a complete system of tax-supported schools from the first grade through a university. With this idea in mind, Judge Augustus B. Woodward drew up a plan which was adopted as a law by the governor and judges on August 26, 1817. The organization provided for was named by Judge Woodward the Catholepistemiad or University of Michigania.

This ambitious educational system was to consist of academies, schools, libraries, and museums, with the university at the top. Thirteen professorships were named. The Reverend John Monteith, Presbyterian minister, was appointed president, and the Reverend Gabriel Richard, Catholic priest, vice-president. To President Monteith were assigned seven of the thirteen professorships, and to Vice-President Richard the remaining six. The salary of the president was established by law at $25 a year and that of the vice-president at $18.75. For the financial support of the Catholepistemiad a 15 per cent increase of taxes was to be levied, and, following the custom of the time, four lotteries might be conducted to raise additional funds.

Neither the president nor the vice-president ever taught a class, but a building was erected in the fall of 1817 on the west side of Bates Street near Congress Street in Detroit. It was occupied for some years by a primary school and a classical academy conducted under the supervision of the university trustees.

Some persons have ridiculed this Catholepistemiad as the fantastic creation of an impractical dreamer. There is some truth in the criticism, for Michigan was not yet ready for so comprehensive a scheme of education; but Judge Woodward in his plan set forth four principles which were sound and which have become foundation stones of the public education system of Michigan and of other states as well.

These principles were, First, that it is the duty of the state to provide education for its people from the lowest grade through the university; second, that the system must be supported by taxation; third, that tuition fees for higher education should be low; and fourth, that the schools should be nonsectarian, that is, they should not be under the control of any religious denomination. Stated at a time when tuition fees had to be paid for even the most elementary education, and when every college and university in the country was maintained by a church, these ideas were considered radical. Today, however, the public schools, the state colleges, and the university practice Judge Woodward's principles.

The Legislative Council abolished the Catholepistemiad and established the University of Michigan by an act in 1821, but there was no real university until after Michigan became a state. As a means of support for the University, Congress in 1826 granted two townships, and the Ottawa, Chippewa, and Potawatomi Indians with whom Governor Cass made the Treaty of Fort Meigs in 1817 gave three sections.[1] These lands were the source of a valuable endowment. They were gradually sold, and the proceeds were used for the benefit of the University.

3

Regular church services for Protestants were not available during the early years in Michigan Territory. The population was small, and so many denominations were represented that none could support a minister. For a long time the only Protestant services were held by circuit riders—ministers who rode through the country on horseback, stopping to preach wherever they found an audience.

A Methodist congregation was organized in Detroit by the Reverend William Mitchell, a circuit rider, in 1810. During the War of 1812, there was no minister, but in 1815 the Reverend Joseph Hickox, another circuit rider, came to Detroit and revived the organization. Every third Sunday he preached in the Council House, going to the River Rouge, Monroe, and several points in Canada between times.

In 1818 the Methodists built a log church on the River Rouge, now in Dearborn, the first Protestant house of worship in the Territory.[2] Methodists in Detroit built a brick church on Gratiot Avenue in 1826, and a new one on Woodward in 1834.

Before the church on the River Rouge was built, another Protestant congregation was organized in Detroit. At the request of Governor Cass and some of the leading citizens, the Reverend John Monteith was sent by the American Board for Foreign Missions. The new minister, who had just been graduated from the Princeton Theological Seminary, preached his first sermon in the Council House on June 30, 1816.

The Reverend John Monteith was a Presbyterian, but the Protestant Society which was organized and which he served was interdenominational. The Society built a church on the east side of Woodward Avenue just north of Larned Street. Mr. Monteith left Detroit in July, 1821, and during the next three and a half years several ministers supplied the pulpit. By a majority vote in January, 1825, the Society became Presbyterian. The Reverend Noah M. Wells was the first pastor.

[1] The Regents of the University of Michigan, in recognition of this gift, established in 1932 five scholarships for Indian men and women.

[2] The Moravians, during the British regime, had a meetinghouse on the Clinton River.

Protestant Episcopalians organized a congregation in 1824 and built St. Paul's Church on Woodward just north of the Presbyterian Church. The Reverend Richard F. Cadle was the first minister.

A Baptist congregation, with the Reverend Henry Davis as pastor, began holding services in the University building in 1827. Three years later they built a frame church on the northwest corner of Fort and Griswold and replaced it in 1835 with a brick building.

Few Congregational churches were organized during the territorial period. Congregationalists found Presbyterian churches in many towns. Following the practice endorsed by the Plan of Union between the two denominations, they usually joined with the Presbyterians. Later, as Congregationalists became more numerous, they formed churches of their own. Among the early Congregational churches were one at Romeo founded by the Reverend Isaac W. Ruggles in 1828, one at Marshall established by the Reverend John D. Pierce in 1832, and one at Vermontville organized in 1836 by the Reverend Sylvester Cochrane.

The Lutheran Church in Michigan had its beginning in 1833 when the Reverend Frederick Schmid arrived at Ann Arbor from Germany in answer to a request for a minister. Because most of the Germans were farmers, the first church was built about a mile west of Ann Arbor on the Territorial Road. Pastor Schmid also served German congregations in Detroit and Monroe.

After the fire of 1805 in Detroit destroyed St. Anne's Roman Catholic Church, services were held in several places until the new St. Anne's on Larned Street was in a condition to be used. It was not completed until 1828.

Catholic churches outside Detroit were St. Anthony's in Monroe, St. Anne's at Mackinac, and a log church built in Northfield Township, Washtenaw County, in 1831 by Irish settlers. Their pastor was Father Patrick O'Kelly.

Congregation Beth El was not organized until 1850. It met at first above a cigar factory on Jefferson Avenue in Detroit.

Churches of the various denominations gradually were founded in the growing towns throughout the territory, but for many years a great many settlers had no permanent place of worship. For them the occasional circuit rider brought the only consolation of religion. So great was the longing of some for an opportunity to join in religious services that at the news of a meeting, perhaps twenty miles away, a settler would yoke his oxen and set out with his family on a journey that might require two or three days to go and return.

4

The predominance of the French-speaking people in Michigan was one reason for the late beginning of newspapers. Even though James M. Miller printed a part of his *Michigan Essay; Or the Impartial Observer,* August 31, 1809, in French, they showed no interest in it. Most of them were poor and many were unable to read. The English-speaking population was too small to support a paper, and so apparently only one issue of the *Essay* was published.

The first successful newspaper was the *Detroit Gazette,* which ran from 1817 until 1830. Two other newspapers, the *Michigan Herald* and the *Detroit Courier,* had a brief existence during the life of the *Gazette.* In 1831 the *Detroit Free Press* began publication as the organ of the Democratic party. It changed its allegiance in 1896, becoming a supporter of the Republicans.

The first paper issued outside Detroit was the *Michigan Sentinel,* published in Monroe in 1825. The *Emigrant* in Ann Arbor, 1829, was the second, followed by the *Oakland County Chronicle,* Pontiac, 1830; the *Michigan Statesman,* White Pigeon, 1833; the *Lenawee County Republican and Adrian Gazette,* 1834; and the *Kalamazoo Gazette,* 1837. Marshall, Constantine, and Niles also had newspapers during the territorial period.

These newspapers began publication in villages of only a few hundred inhabitants. Some were short-lived, but others continued for a number of years. All were four-page weeklies. The first page sometimes contained a column or two of advertising. The remaining columns were filled with articles or fiction. It might be called the magazine page.

Page 2 had editorials, state news, news of the territorial government, news from the East, and articles on politics. Newspapers were usually strongly partisan, the editor, whether Whig or Democrat, attacking the opposition furiously.

The third page frequently contained a column of local news, such as announcements of coming events. Stories of local happenings, however, rarely appeared, the editor apparently believing that everyone knew what had occurred in the community. On page 3 there might be also a column of news from Europe, but most of the space was occupied with advertisements, and page 4 usually was filled solidly with them. Because money was scarce, editors accepted farm produce in payment both for subscriptions and for advertising.

The year 1817 was notable for several cultural beginnings: the *Detroit Gazette* was first published, the Catholepistemiad was founded, and the Detroit City Library was incorporated. The library was open only to subscribers who bought shares of stock at five dollars each. The books were kept in the University Building.

Governor Lewis Cass and some of the leading citizens interested in the history of the territory organized in 1828 the Historical Society of Michigan. Among the members were Austin E. Wing, Dr. Zina Pitcher, Father Gabriel Richard, the Rev. Richard F. Cadle, and Henry R. Schoolcraft. Governor Cass was elected president.

The Society gathered for preservation manuscripts and objects of historical interest. Addresses delivered before the Society by Governor Cass, Henry R. Schoolcraft, Major Henry Whiting, and Major John Biddle were published in a book, *Historical and Scientific Sketches of Michigan*. This was a very creditable literary production for that early day.

Another organization of the period that deserves notice is the Detroit Young Men's Society, founded in 1833. Among the charter members were Jacob M. Howard, later a United States senator, and Dr. Douglass Houghton, a young physician. The society had its own library, and it held weekly meetings at which lectures and debates by the members were the principal features. In order to give the younger men opportunities to practice speaking, the Society retired to honorary memberships everyone who reached the age of thirty. Thereafter they might attend meetings and offer advice, but they were not permitted to debate or lecture. This organization was very popular, and many young lawyers, teachers, and politicians learned the art of speaking in the Society's rooms.

In spite of the foregoing examples of culture which have been mentioned, during the territorial period, Michiganians, considered all together, were uncouth according to eastern standards. That was to be expected because Michigan was a new country where everyone had to struggle for a living. There was little leisure for cultivating the fine arts of civilization and small means for promoting them; but there were educated men in the Territory, and men who had been leaders in various fields in their home communities. Even more important were young men and women with energy, enthusiasm, ambition, and vision. They would not be satisfied simply to make a living in Michigan; they wanted to make Michigan a good place in which to live.

5

Lewis Cass was governor of Michigan Territory from 1813 until 1831. After the War of 1812 Judges Woodward, Witherell, and Griffin returned and continued to serve until 1824, when Woodward and Griffin were not reappointed. Woodward was sent to Florida Territory as a judge. Solomon Sibley and John Hunt replaced them on the Michigan bench. William Woodbridge, a friend of Governor Cass, became secretary in 1814. During the frequent absences of the governor, Woodbridge acted in his place.

Governor Cass believed wholeheartedly in government by the people. Wanting them to have a voice in their government, he gave them in 1818 an opportunity to vote on the question of entering the second stage of territorial organization, in which they would elect a legislature and have a delegate in Congress. To the Governor's disappointment, a large majority voted against a change. The reason was that most of the inhabitants were French. They were satisfied with Cass's administration, and they had no desire to assume the responsibilities of even partial self-government.

In spite of the adverse vote, Congress in 1819 gave the people of Michigan the privilege of electing a delegate to sit in the House of Representatives. Like the delegates from other territories, he was permitted to speak in behalf of his constituents, but he had no vote.

William Woodbridge, who was secretary and collector of customs, was chosen delegate. He performed his duties satisfactorily, but when a clamor arose in Michigan because he retained his position as secretary, he resigned and returned to Detroit. Solomon Sibley replaced him in Washington. The delegate elected in 1823 was the Reverend Gabriel Richard. He served for one term, the only Catholic priest ever to sit in the House of Representatives.

Congress in 1823 passed an act by which the people were permitted to nominate eighteen men from whom the President would choose nine to sit as a legislative council. Two years later, the number was increased to thirteen, and in 1827 the voters were given the privilege of choosing the members directly. Michigan was now in the second stage of territorial government. Governor and judges attended to executive and judicial matters, and the council passed laws, which, however, were subject to the approval of Congress. Although an elected assembly might have been added, according to law, the people were satisfied with the council, and during the territorial period Michigan had a unicameral legislature.

Believing that local governments should be established and put into the hands of the people, in 1815 Governor Cass organized Wayne County with the boundaries of the area which had been purchased from the Indians by Governor Hull in 1807. Monroe County was organized in 1817, Macomb in 1818, Oakland in 1820, and St. Clair in 1821. Washtenaw and Lenawee counties were organized in 1826. These counties were in the southeastern part of the Territory and within the lines of the Hull purchase.

Townships were also established, sometimes while the population was sparse, only one to a county. As settlement increased, they were reduced in size to conform with the six-mile-square townships surveyed by the United States Government.

County and township governments were patterned on the systems prevalent in New England and New York. In New England, the town or township was the important unit, and the people met annually in town meeting to elect officers, vote taxes, and pass ordinances. In New York, the county was more important than the townships, and elected officers levied taxes and passed laws. Because most of the settlers had come from New York and New England, it is not surprising that a combination of the two systems developed.

In Michigan, the supervisor was the principal township officer. He and three other elected officers constituted the governing board of the township. The supervisors of all the townships, meeting together in the county seat, were the governing board of the county. In the townships settled by New Englanders, the town meeting was a regular feature of local government. Besides the supervisor, each township had a clerk, a treasurer, justices of the peace, constables, and other officers. The county had a clerk, a sheriff, a treasurer, a register of deeds, a prosecutor, and a coroner. Township and county government have changed little since the days of Governor Cass.

At first all the township and county officers were appointed by the governor. Cass disliked this arrangement, preferring that the people choose their own officers. At his request, in 1825 Congress passed an act giving the voters the privilege of electing all local officers except judges, clerks, and sheriffs. Even this act was not sufficient to satisfy the governor, who asked the people to vote for all township and county officers, promising to appoint as sheriffs, clerks, and judges those who received the greatest number of votes.

After more land had been purchased from the Indians, and settlers had moved into the south-central and southwestern parts of the Territory, additional counties were established and organized. The term "cabinet counties" is sometimes applied to Barry, Berrien, Branch, Calhoun, Eaton, Ingham, and Van Buren, all established in 1829 and named for members of President Andrew Jackson's Cabinet.[3] New counties organized were Cass and St. Joseph, 1829; Kalamazoo, 1830; Jackson, 1832; Allegan, Hillsdale, Lapeer, and Saginaw, 1835; Genesee, Kent, and Livingston, 1836. Before Michigan entered the Union in 1837, twenty-nine counties had been established. Seven, however, had not been organized, but were temporarily attached to a neighboring county. Four full tiers of counties north from the southern boundary had been established, and Saginaw County was the first in the fifth tier.

North of these counties there were few settlers in the Lower Peninsula. Across the Straits of Mackinac in the Upper Peninsula were Sault Sainte Marie and St. Ignace, and, in the Straits, Mackinac Island. According to the act establishing Michigan Territory, the western boundary was a line run northward from the southern bend of Lake Michigan through the middle of the lake, and then from the Straits of Mackinac to the international boundary line in Lake Superior. This line gave Michigan only a small portion of the Upper Peninsula.

In 1818, when Illinois was ready to become a state, Congress added to Michigan Territory all the remaining area of the original Northwest Territory in the Upper Peninsula and beyond Lakes Michigan and Superior to the Mississippi River. Governor Cass in 1818 established Michilimackinac County in the northern part of the Lower Peninsula and in the eastern part of the Upper Peninsula. West of it he established Brown County and Crawford County, in what is now Wisconsin, in the same year. Civil government at the time was provided for only those small areas which had been ceded by the Indians. Chippewa County in the Upper Peninsula was made from the northern part of Michilimackinac County in 1826. The county seat was Sault Sainte Marie. In 1829, Iowa County in southern Wisconsin was set apart from Crawford County.

Michigan Territory was a huge area, and in 1834 it received another large extension toward the west. By act of Congress all the land north

[3] William T. Barry was Postmaster General; John M. Berrien, Attorney General; John Branch, Secretary of the Navy; John C. Calhoun, Vice-President; John H. Eaton, Secretary of War; Samuel D. Ingham, Secretary of the Treasury; and Martin Van Buren, Secretary of State. Livingston County, organized in 1836, was named for Edward Livingston, Van Buren's successor as Secretary of State.

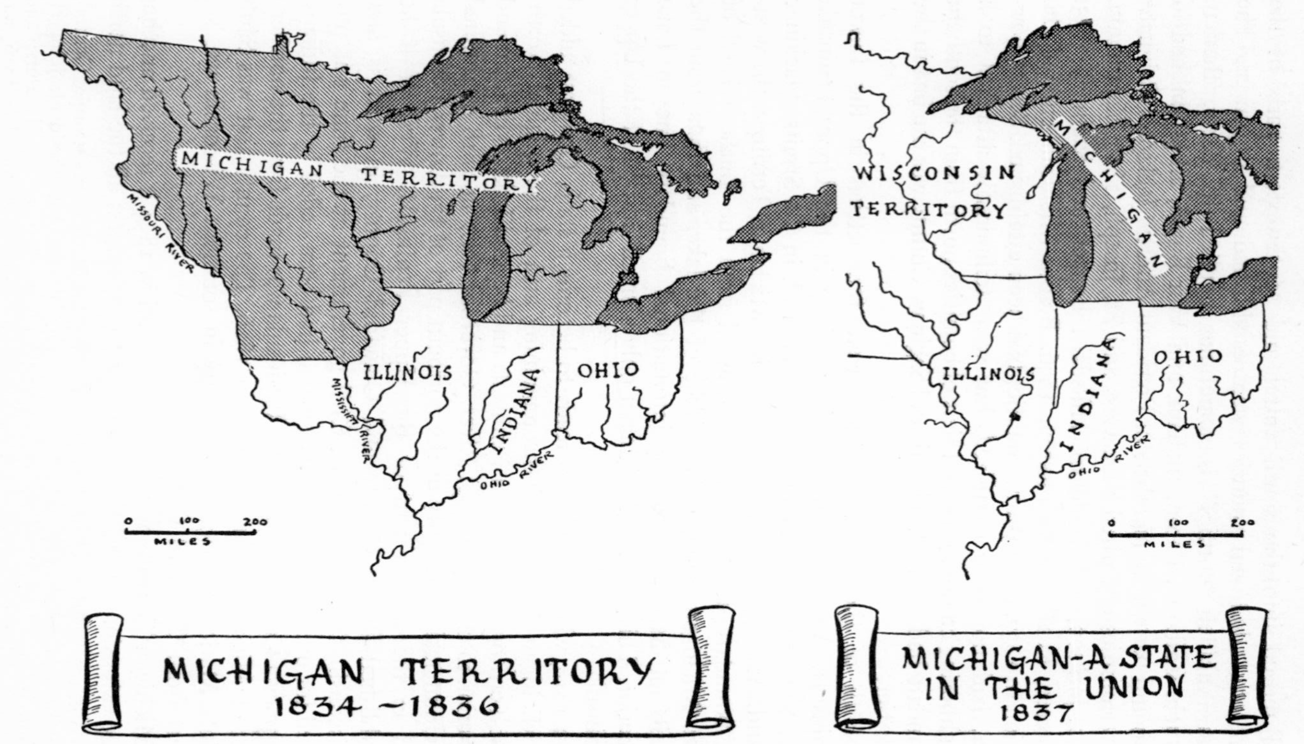
MICHIGAN TERRITORY
MISSOURI RIVER
MISSISSIPPI RIVER
ILLINOIS
INDIANA
OHIO
OHIO RIVER
0 100 200
MILES
MICHIGAN TERRITORY
1834 –1836
WISCONSIN
TERRITORY
MICHIGAN
ILLINOIS
INDIANA
OHIO
OHIO RIVER
0 100 200
MILES
MICHIGAN-A STATE
IN THE UNION
1837

of the state of Missouri and west of the Mississippi to the Missouri River, including the present states of Minnesota and Iowa and the eastern half of North Dakota and South Dakota, was attached to the Territory. Two counties were established in this area in 1834—Dubuque in the north and Des Moines in the south. In the same year the southern part of Brown County became Milwaukie County.

Governor Cass resigned his office in 1831 to accept the position of Secretary of War in President Jackson's Cabinet. During the eighteen years that the government of Michigan was in his hands, the Territory had progressed greatly. Instead of a wilderness with a few small settlements suffering from the horrors of war, it had become the scene of lively developments in farming, shipping, merchandising, and industry. The population had increased from 4,000 in 1810 to 31,000 in 1830. Governor Cass, through his understanding of the people and a sincere desire to advance their interests, was responsible for much of the progress. He had explored the Territory and published enthusiastic reports of its resources; he had purchased land from the Indians so that settlers could hew out farms for themselves in the forests; he had obtained from Congress appropriations for building roads; and he had got for the people as much self-government as was possible under the Ordinance of 1787. The Territory owed a debt of gratitude to Governor Cass.

13

The Boy Governor Does a Man's Job

The years from 1831 to 1837 were notable for many changes and exciting events in Michigan Territory. Leadership was in the hands of Stevens Thomson Mason, the Boy Governor. Under his guidance a constitution was adopted, Michigan became a state not recognized by Congress, and, finally, admittance to the Union was secured. During this period occurred the Black Hawk War, the Toledo War, two cholera epidemics, the operation of the first railroad, a great boom in real estate, and a tremendous growth in population.

General John T. Mason was appointed secretary of Michigan Territory in 1830. A member of the Mason family of Virginia, he had been living for some years in Kentucky. Stevens T. Mason, eighteen-year-old son of the new secretary, helped his father in the performance of his official duties, became well acquainted with the work, and made a favorable impression on Governor Cass.

In the summer of 1831 John T. Mason decided to go to Texas to look after some land claims there. He and Stevens T. went to

Washington and visited President Jackson. John T. Mason resigned his office and asked the President to appoint his son to the position. Pleased with the boy's evident ability, Jackson granted the request and named him secretary of Michigan Territory.

News of the appointment reached Detroit before Mason returned. Because he was an outsider and not yet of age, some of the leading citizens of Detroit called a meeting to protest against the appointment of "the stripling." After his arrival, a committee was sent to interview him and report. He received the members courteously and answered their questions, readily admitting that he was only nineteen years old.

After hearing the report of the committee, the leaders of the opposition drew up a memorial to the President, asking him to remove the boy from office. The Whig newspapers took up the issue and attacked the new secretary vigorously.

Mason acted wisely. First he wrote a long letter to President Jackson, explaining that the opposition to him was purely political and asking for the President's support. Then he published an address in which he promised to seek advice from older men and to serve the people faithfully. His frank appeal did much to disarm hostility, but the newspapers which were antagonistic to Jackson continued to attack him.

On July 24, 1831, Lewis Cass administered the oath of office to Stevens T. Mason, attended a farewell banquet arranged by citizens in his honor, and departed for Washington to serve as Secretary of War. Jackson appointed George B. Porter of Pennsylvania as governor. He did not reach Detroit until September 17, and he was frequently absent from the Territory thereafter. During these periods Mason was acting governor, and after Porter died in July, 1834, he continued to serve in that capacity, for Michigan never had another territorial governor. Because he was intelligent, industrious, and modest, he soon won the enthusiastic support of the people.

2

An Indian uprising in Northern Illinois and in Michigan Territory west of Lake Michigan occurred in the spring and summer of 1832. For a time it checked migration into the southwestern counties, and greatly exaggerated reports of widespread Indian hostility frightened settlers as far east as Detroit. The occasion of the disturbance was the crossing of the Mississippi River by Black Hawk and his "British band" into northern Illinois. This leader of the Sauk and Foxes was greatly feared. He was known to be resentful because he had been

Secretary Mason Taking the Oath of Office, 1831

forced to move beyond the Mississippi, leaving the villages and the cornfields of his people to the white settlers.

When he crossed over into Illinois near the mouth of the Rock River, Black Hawk was accompanied by about five hundred mounted warriors and an equal number of women and children. He declared that his purpose was to plant corn in his old fields, and the fact that he brought women and children with him makes it appear that he had no immediate intention of making war. Nevertheless, crossing the Mississippi eastward had been prohibited by treaty, and the settlers demanded protection.

The governor of Illinois called out the militia, and regulars were sent up the Mississippi River from St. Louis. Gathering a force of about four thousand men, General Henry Atkinson sent them up the Rock River in pursuit of Black Hawk. As he retreated, Black Hawk's band killed settlers who had not had time to escape. He called upon the other Indian tribes for assistance, but none rallied to his cause.

News of Black Hawk's depredations crossed Lake Michigan and spread through the settlements along the Chicago Road. Rumors ran riot from village to village and from farm to farm: Black Hawk himself was in Michigan; the Chippewa and Ottawa had joined him; the Potawatomi who inhabited the region were sharpening their hatchets to fall upon the settlers. Without waiting for orders, able-bodied men in some communities shouldered their guns and gathered to protect their families.

A request for assistance from the Indian agent at Chicago and increasing uneasiness among the people caused Acting Governor Mason to order Major General John R. Williams to call the militia near Detroit into service. About three hundred men, answering the call, assembled at Conrad Ten Eyck's tavern on the Chicago Road, now in Dearborn. Brigadier General Joseph W. Brown at Tecumseh mustered five companies from Clinton, Adrian, Tecumseh, Blissfield, and Palmyra and marched them to Niles. General Williams and his men started west on May 25.

Meanwhile a message from Chicago informed Mason that the dangers had been greatly exaggerated, and that Michigan troops would not be needed. The acting governor sent off a courier with orders for the militia to return. At Saline he overtook the army. General Williams ordered the men to return to Detroit, but, with his staff and a detachment of mounted men, rode on to Chicago. There was no need for going farther because sufficient settlers in Illinois had rallied to expel the invaders. General Brown released his men to return to their farms.

An overwhelming army of regulars and militia under General Atkinson drove the Sauk and Foxes across the Illinois line into the part of Michigan Territory that is now Wisconsin. Near the present city of Madison, Black Hawk made a brief stand. Forced to retire, he reached the Mississippi. There near the mouth of the Bad Axe River, while he was attempting to send women and children across to the western bank, the pursuing force overtook him. His offer to surrender was rejected.

An army transport, the *Warrior*, blocked escape by water. Caught between the guns of the steamer and the troops on shore, on August 2 the Indians were almost annihilated. Seeing that further resistance was useless, Black Hawk retired to the dells of the Wisconsin River. He was captured by two Winnebago and taken a prisoner to Prairie du Chien.

Black Hawk made peace with the government, and in 1833 he was taken on a tour of the East in order to impress him with the foolishness of defying the power of the United States. On his return journey he was brought to Detroit on July 4, 1833. There the whole town had gathered at the wharf to see him. Wearing a long blue coat, a white high hat, and spectacles, and carrying a cane, he conducted himself with dignity. The growth of the town since the War of 1812, when he had last seen it, amazed him. The next day Black Hawk paid a courtesy call on Acting Governor Mason.

Although Black Hawk's warriors never extended their attacks into the area of the present state, the war brought suffering and death into the territory. General Winfield Scott was ordered by President Jackson to lead United States troops from the East to take part in the Black Hawk War. Traveling from Fortress Monroe, Virginia, they embarked at Buffalo for Chicago.

On July 4, 1832, one of the transports tied up at Detroit. Suddenly, a number of the soldiers were stricken with cholera. Taken ashore for treatment, eleven died during the night. City authorities ordered the transport to leave the wharf, but the damage had already been done. The dread disease began to attack civilians, and on July 6 two died. Panic ensued. Many left the city to escape the mysterious sickness which struck without warning and killed its victims quickly.

So many became ill that the second floor of the Capitol was made into a hospital, and physicians in the city courageously attended the sick, although there was little they could do. Many died; some recovered. Father Richard also labored manfully, helping to care for the victims. A cart went through the city streets day and night, with attendants who cried as they went, "Bring out your dead."

Frightened Detroiters fled from what seemed to them a doomed city. To prevent introduction of the disease, other towns stationed armed guards on the roads to stop stagecoaches and individual travelers. At Ypsilanti, a coach from Detroit carrying passengers and the mail was halted by shooting one of the horses, and Secretary Mason, traveling west by the Chicago Road on official business, was arrested.

These precautions were not entirely successful. Near Fort Gratiot one of General Scott's transports stopped to put the sick ashore because there were too many to be cared for on the ship. Fearful of taking the disease, many of the soldiers who were not yet ill deserted and scattered throughout the countryside, spreading it among civilians. Of the outlying towns in which cholera appeared, Marshall suffered most. There, of the seventy inhabitants, eighteen were stricken, and eight died, among them the wife of the Reverend John D. Pierce.

The disease abated early in September. On the thirteenth of the month Father Gabriel Richard died, the last victim of the plague from which he had saved many sufferers by his unceasing toil. So ended the thirty-four years of service to Detroit and Michigan of this man who had been a mighty influence for good as priest, educator, and civic leader.

Another cholera epidemic appeared in Detroit in the summer of 1834. Though of shorter duration, it was more deadly than the former one. Seven per cent of the city's population died during the month of August.

The restlessness of the western Indians in general and the Black Hawk War in particular called attention to the need for a depot of arms, ammunition, and supplies for the western garrison posts closer to them than the existing ones. For that purpose, the United States Government selected a site on the Chicago Road near the River Rouge about ten miles west of Detroit.

Work was begun in 1833. Bricks were made of clay taken from a nearby pit and eleven buildings were erected around a square eight hundred feet on a side. The buildings were connected by a high brick wall which made a solid enclosure. Named the Detroit Arsenal, it was used by the government until 1873. The town of Dearborn grew up around it. For many years the commandant's residence on the corner of Michigan and Monroe was used as the city police station. In 1948 the building was given to the Dearborn Historical Commission to be maintained as a museum of local history.

3

In 1832, the year of the Black Hawk War and of the first cholera epidemic, the Legislative Council asked the inhabitants of the Territory to vote on the question of becoming a state. The number of ballots cast was small, but a majority favored statehood. The Legislative Council petitioned Congress to pass an enabling act giving the people the privilege of making a constitution for a state which would have for its southern boundary the line mentioned in the Ordinance of 1787 and in the act establishing Michigan Territory, that is, a line from the southernmost point of Lake Michigan due east to Lake Erie.

The claiming of the Ordinance line aroused the opposition of Ohio because, if it were granted, Toledo would be in Michigan. Ohio was building a canal to connect Lake Erie with the Ohio River, and Toledo was intended to be the northern terminus.

Strange as it may seem, the northern boundary of Ohio had never been established. When the constitution of the state was being written in 1802, the latitude of the southern extremity of Lake Michigan was unknown. Fearing that the Ordinance line might strike Lake Erie farther south than they wished, the delegates described the northern boundary as either the one provided by the Ordinance or, if that should strike Lake Erie below Maumee Bay, a line from the southern extremity of Lake Michigan to the northern cape of the bay. Congress admitted Ohio with this uncertain boundary, but in 1805 it established Michigan Territory with the Ordinance line as the southern boundary.

In order to settle the matter, Congress in 1812 directed that the Ordinance line be run. Action was deferred until after the war, when Edward Tiffin, surveyor general of the United States and formerly governor of Ohio, was ordered to have the work done. Following Tiffin's instructions, his deputy, William Harris, in 1817, marked the boundary desired by Ohio. The Harris line put Toledo in Ohio.

Governor Cass protested vigorously to the United States Government, and President James Monroe ordered a new survey in accord with the act which established Michigan Territory. In 1818 John A. Fulton ran the line, which fell below Toledo, putting it in Michigan. The land between the Harris and the Fulton lines, a tapering piece five to eight miles wide, was called the Toledo Strip. Michigan, of course, was satisfied, if Ohio was not; but Fulton's survey was inaccurate and Congress ordered a resurvey. The Talcott Line, named for the surveyor who ran it in 1834, was nearly identical with the Fulton Line.

Michigan seemed to have a clear title to the Toledo Strip. The official Talcott Line supported her contention, territorial officers had governed the disputed area, public land there had been sold from the Monroe land office, county courts of Michigan had sat there, and the inhabitants had voted in territorial elections. Political considerations, however, outweighed Michigan's rights. Michigan had only a nonvoting delegate in Congress; Ohio had senators and representatives. Indiana and Illinois, each of which had pushed its northern boundary above the Ordinance line, supported Ohio. President Jackson, at first, seemed to favor Michigan's cause; but an election year was approaching, and he could not afford to offend three states, with the possibility of losing their electoral votes. Until Michigan entered the Union, she would have no vote for President. Politically, her position was very weak.

To Stevens T. Mason it seemed that Michigan would never become a state if she had to depend on an enabling act by Congress. After Governor Porter died in July, 1834, Mason was acting governor again, and he began a campaign to make the territory a state. When the Legislative Council met in September, he asked that a census be taken as a first step. The returns showed that there were 85,856 people in the territory east of Lake Michigan.

Mason urged further action, calling attention to the clause in the Ordinance of 1787 which promised a territory having sixty thousand free inhabitants entrance into the Union after making a constitution and organizing a state government. Following the acting governor's instructions, the Council called a constitutional convention to meet in May, 1835. Mason declared that such measures were legal, and the people accepted him as their leader.

When word reached Michigan that Ohio authorities intended to extend their jurisdiction over the disputed strip on April 1, 1835, the Council passed an act providing penalties of fine or imprisonment against anyone, except territorial officers or officers of the United States, who might attempt to perform governmental duties there. In spite of this threat, Governor Robert Lucas of Ohio was determined to re-mark the Harris Line and to enforce Ohio Law in the Toledo Strip. To protect the surveyors he ordered militia to Perrysburg on the Maumee River.

Acting Governor Mason was equally determined to prevent what he considered invasion of Michigan's rights. Ordering General Joseph

W. Brown to Monroe to assemble the militia, he joined him there on April 1, 1835, to direct operations. The Toledo War was about to begin. The first move was to send General Brown as deputy sheriff with an armed posse into Toledo to arrest Ohio officials. Mason had decided not to use uniformed militia unless the sheriff's men were unable to enforce the law. After making some arrests and causing some damage to property, the posse returned to Monroe. One of the prisoners, Benjamin F. Stickney, refusing either to walk or ride, was tied on a horse and so delivered to the jail in Monroe.

Other raids were made on Toledo, and on April 26 another posse pounced upon Ohio's commissioners and surveyors rerunning the Harris Line in Lenawee County, fourteen miles south of Adrian. The commissioners escaped, but deputies from Tecumseh and Adrian captured nine of the party. All were released on bail except one who refused to furnish it. He was held in the county prison.

While these attempts to maintain the jurisdiction of Michigan Territory were taking place, two commissioners sent by President Jackson to negotiate with Lucas and Mason arrived on the scene. They reminded both governors that the President had warned them not to use force in trying to settle the dispute, and urged them to accept Jackson's recommendation that the matter be left to the decision of Congress in December. Although Lucas insisted on rerunning the Harris Line, he agreed to a suggestion by the commissioners that Michigan and Ohio govern the region jointly for the present. He had nothing to lose by waiting for action by Congress.

The commissioners tried to persuade Mason to have the charges against the Ohio officials dropped. He rejected the suggestion, and he refused to agree to joint government. He did agree to call a special session of the Council to lay the matter before it. Mason believed that the Council would support his stand, and he had no faith in Congress.

4

The constitutional convention met in the Capitol in Detroit on May 11, 1835, and it adjourned on June 24 after having completed its task. The constitution of 1835 was the best one Michigan has had. Like the Constitution of the United States, it provided a framework of government and left legislation to the legislature. Like the President, the governor was given the power to appoint judges and the principal officers of administration—secretary of state, auditor general, attorney general, and even county prosecutors—with the consent of the senate. The governor had great responsibilities, and he had sufficient power to meet them.

Although Michigan Territory had had a unicameral council, the constitution provided for a bicameral legislature. The house of representatives was to consist of from forty-eight to one hundred members; the senate was to have one third as many members as the house. Elections were to be held annually. Representatives were given terms of one year; senators, two years. The two houses elected the state treasurer. The people were given the privilege of electing the governor, lieutenant governor, members of the legislature, and local officials.

Article Ten dealt with education. One clause provided for a superintendent of public instruction to be named by the governor with the consent of both houses of the legislature. This provision is an indication of the importance which the delegates attached to the office. No other state constitution at the time contained such a clause. Elsewhere, the superintendent was a statutory officer whose position could be abolished by the legislature. The Michigan delegates made him a constitutional officer so that his position would be secure.

The same article also required the legislature to provide for a system of common schools to be open at least three months a year. The state was to give financial assistance. Actually, this clause did not guarantee free public schools. Rate bills were still issued, and the level of education varied greatly from district to district.

Article Ten also prescribed that the proceeds from the sale of land given by the United States for the support of schools should be put into a perpetual fund and the interest used to maintain schools. Income from lands granted for the University was required by the same article to be used only for the University.

The constitution contained a bill of rights meant to protect the liberties of the citizens, and qualifications for voting were liberal. Besides giving the franchise to all white male citizens above the age of twenty-one after a six months' residence, the constitution permitted all white male inhabitants to vote if they were twenty-one years old or over and were living in the Territory at the time the constitution was signed.

Amendments to the constitution might be made by a two thirds vote of each house of the legislature, ratified by a majority of the people voting on the proposal. A method was provided also for revising the constitution or making a new one.

A miscellaneous provision required the state government to encourage internal improvements, that is, transportation by roads, canals, and navigable waters. Although extravagant application of this clause almost bankrupted the state, the constitution, as a whole, was an excellent instrument of government.

Among the delegates who made the constitution were many able men. Some were already well known throughout the Territory; others reached high political positions later. Among those who had been in public life for a number of years were William Woodbridge and John Biddle, both Whigs of Detroit. Although the Democrats had a majority in the convention, Biddle was elected president. Another prominent Whig, but a newcomer in Michigan, was Townsend E. Gidley of Jackson County. Among the Democrats John Norvell of Detroit was leader of the liberals and Lucius Lyon, from Kalamazoo County, of the conservatives. Other delegates who had active parts in the convention were Edward Mundy of Washtenaw County, Ross Wilkins and John R. Williams of Detroit, Edward D. Ellis and Robert McCelland of Monroe, John S. Barry of St. Joseph County, John J. Adam of Lenawee, Hezekiah G. Wells of Kalamazoo, and Isaac Crary of Calhoun. Crary is especially notable for his report on education, which was written into the constitution and was the foundation upon which Michigan's school system was eventually established.

5

During June and July the Toledo War went on. Posses from Monroe County made several raids to arrest Ohio officials, and on one occasion Two Stickney,[1] resisting arrest, stabbed Joseph Wood, a deputy sheriff of Monroe County, and escaped. In July, Secretary of War Lewis Cass went to Detroit and tried to cool the belligerent ardor of his young friend, the acting governor. Mason, however, rejected his advice to have the cases against Ohio officials dismissed and was willing only to await the decision of the Legislative Council.

When the Council met in August, it supported the acting governor's stand and appropriated funds to carry on the contest. This action followed that of the Ohio Legislature, which had voted money to Governor Lucas. It had also organized Lucas County in the disputed area and named September 7 as the date for a session of court to be held in Toledo. The official record of such a session, the legislature believed, would prove that Toledo was within the jurisdiction of Ohio.

President Jackson, entirely out of patience with Mason, removed

[1] Benjamin F. Stickney was Two's father. He had named his sons One and Two in the order of their birth.

him from office on August 29, 1835. Before a successor arrived to take his place, a session of the court of common pleas of the second Ohio judicial circuit had been held in Toledo. General Joseph W. Brown, with about one thousand men, marched into Toledo on September 7, the day set for the meeting, but the Ohio judges had outwitted him. With an armed bodyguard they had quietly gone into town shortly after midnight, held a brief session of court, signed the record, and left. Their departure was hastened by the false report that General Brown was searching for them.

Later in the day, when the general arrived, he learned that he was too late. He retired with his soldiers to Monroe, where he dismissed them. The Toledo War was over, but the boundary remained undrawn.

The new secretary of Michigan Territory, John S. Horner of Virginia, handed Mason his credentials and entered upon his official duties on September 21, 1835. Relations between him and Mason were polite, but some residents of the Territory resented his supplanting of their fearless leader and expressed their feelings vigorously. Horner tried to carry out the President's instructions to have the suits against the Ohio officials dismissed, but the Monroe County prosecutor paid no attention to him. In March, 1836, Horner went to Wisconsin and was appointed secretary of that territory.

The constitution signed on June 24, 1835, provided that it should be laid before the people for ratification on October 5, and that an election of state officers and of a representative to Congress be held on the same day. The voters ratified the constitution and elected Mason governor, Edward Mundy lieutenant governor, and Isaac E. Crary United States representative. When the legislature met, the two houses chose Lucius Lyon and John Norvell as Michigan's first senators. Representatives and senators went to Washington and presented their credentials, but Congress refused to admit them. Although Mason called himself governor of the State of Michigan, the state could not enter the Union without the consent of Congress.

6

At the time, because both the North and the South wanted to keep an equal balance in the Senate, two states were always admitted together, one slave and the other free. Arkansas was asking for admission, and she was paired with Michigan.

When the question of Michigan's admission was raised, Ohio insisted that the boundary must be drawn according to her specification. Lyon, Norvell, and Crary could only sit as spectators and listen to the oral attacks on their state delivered by Ohio men. Lyon believed that Michigan should have compensation in the North, and he urged this solution informally upon senators and representatives.

A bill establishing the Harris Line as the southern boundary and a line along the Menominee and Montreal rivers as the western boundary was passed by the Senate in March, 1836, and sent to the House. The western portion of the Upper Peninsula was attached to Michigan as indemnity for the loss of the Toledo Strip.

An act to establish Wisconsin Territory with the Menominee–Montreal River line as its northeastern boundary was approved on April 20, 1836, but the debate on the Michigan bill continued. Ohio was determined that Michigan should specifically accept the Harris Line, and so the bill contained the provision that Michigan would be admitted only after a majority of delegates elected by the people to a convention for that sole purpose should give their consent. This bill was passed and signed by the President on June 15, 1836, when he signed also an act to admit Arkansas, which became Michigan's twin state.

When news that the law had been approved reached Michigan, bitter attacks were made on the terms it contained. The Upper Peninsula was characterized as "the sterile region on the shores of Lake Superior, destined by soil and climate to remain forever a wilderness." The editor of the *Free Press* called it "the region of perpetual snows—the ultima Thule of our national domain on the North," and Lucius Lyon suggested, "there we can raise our own Indians in all time to come and supply ourselves now and then with a little bear meat for a delicacy."

Complaints, of course, were of no avail, and the Legislature, obeying the demand of Congress, directed that the people elect delegates, who should meet in Ann Arbor on September 26. Governor Mason, who had so vigorously fought for the Toledo Strip, now advised the people to accept the terms required by Congress. Senator Lyon changed his mind and predicted that the Upper Peninsula in twenty years would be worth $40,000,000, and someone else expressed the opinion that "the whitefish of Lake Superior might be a fair offset for the lost bull-frog pastures of the Maumee." Whigs and conservative Democrats, however, bitterly opposed submission to Congress and urged the people to elect delegates who would vote "No" at the convention.

The Upper Peninsula, unwanted by Michigan, was greatly desired by the people west of Lake Michigan. Since 1829 they had petitioned Congress to establish the Territory of Huron, which would include the area south of Lake Superior. Many of the people in Michilimackinac and Chippewa counties preferred to be in the proposed Huron Territory. Petitions to Congress from Sault Sainte Marie complained that it was cut off from Detroit for six months of the year and that the government of Michigan had treated the northern region as a remote and neglected colony. Congress paid no attention to these pleas.

When the Convention of Assent, as it was called, met in Ann Arbor on September 26, it was soon discovered that a majority of the delegates were dissenters. After several days of angry debate, the delegates voted twenty-eight to twenty-one to reject the demand of Congress. They adjourned on September 30.

This decision expressed the resentment of Michigan people against Congress and Ohio, but it brought the state no nearer admission to the Union. Everyone realized that eventually assent would have to be given. Besides, there were practical reasons for entering the Union as quickly as possible. A surplus in the United States Treasury was to be divided among the states; territories would receive nothing. Then, too, Congress had promised to give Michigan 5 per cent of the net proceeds from the sale of public lands within her boundaries after she became a state.

These were strong inducements, and politicians who expected to be appointed to fill national offices in the state used their influence for assent. Governor Mason suggested another convention. The Democratic party organization urged the people in each county to elect favorably disposed delegates to a convention. This was done, the dissenters refusing to take part in what they called an illegal election. Monroe County, which was especially bitter over the loss of the Toledo Strip, elected no delegates.

On December 14, 1836, the second Convention of Assent met in Ann Arbor. After declaring that Congress had no constitutional right to require assent, the delegates decided, in the interest of Michigan and as proof of her desire for harmony among the states, to assent to the boundaries prescribed. They drafted a letter to the President reporting the decision of the people of Michigan.

Although the dissenters throughout the state jeered at the action of the delegates and, because of the bitter cold weather, nicknamed the meeting the Frostbitten Convention, the action was generally accepted as inevitable. President Jackson sent the report of the Convention to Congress with a recommendation that it be accepted. After several days of heated debate, a bill to admit Michigan was passed by both houses. It was signed by President Jackson on January 26, 1837. At last Michigan was a state within the Union, and a new star appeared in the flag.

PART IV

EXPLOITING NATURAL RESOURCES 1837–1860

— 14 —

Wildcats, Railroads, and Patriots

When Michigan became a state in 1837, the population was about 175,000. There were still many descendants of the French Canadians, but the majority of the inhabitants had come from New England and New York. Immigrants directly from Europe had not yet become numerous, but some Germans and Irish had already settled in the state. Twenty-two counties had been organized, all, except Mackinac and Chippewa, in the Lower Peninsula. Only the two southernmost tiers of counties were complete in 1837, but by 1840 two more were filled out, and Saginaw County was the first in the fifth tier.

Plenty of land was available for settlement, for, by treaties with the Indians, all except the western half of the Upper Peninsula had been acquired by the United States Government. The remainder was purchased in 1842. The land was surveyed and offered for sale at United States land offices within the state. Some settlers, without funds to purchase or unwilling to wait until attractive sites were placed on sale, occupied what they wanted as squatters.

Although most of the land belonged to the United States, the state also owned a considerable area. Section Sixteen of each township, by act of Congress was conveyed to the State for the support of schools, and seventy-two sections were given to aid in establishing a university. In addition, Congress gave Michigan five sections to help defray the cost of erecting public buildings and seventy-two sections where there were salt springs.[1] Congress also promised that 5 per cent of the net proceeds from the sale of public lands within its boundaries would be given to the state.

Besides all this, Michigan expected to receive an immediate gift of hard cash. In 1835 the national debt had been paid in full, and a surplus had begun to accumulate in the United States Treasury. Embarrassed by this unusual circumstance, Congress directed that all money over $5,000,000 in the Treasury on January 1, 1837, should be apportioned among the states according to their representation in the Electoral College[2] and distributed as an indefinite loan in quarterly installments. Michigan received $95,000 as the first installment, and two more were paid before the law was repealed in the fall of 1837 at the request of President Martin Van Buren.

An important natural advantage was Michigan's location in the heart of the Great Lakes region. The greater part of the outer boundary of the state was easily accessible by sailing vessels and steamships, and some of the rivers were navigable for a considerable distance inland. A steamer built at Grand Rapids in 1837 plied the Grand River between Lake Michigan and her home port, and other steamers were launched later.

By 1837 roads radiating from Detroit had been built to Chicago, to Toledo, to Flint, to Port Huron, and to Howell. There was also a highway from Monroe to Tecumseh, and the Territorial Road extended from Dearborn through Ann Arbor, Jackson, and Kalamazoo to St. Joseph on Lake Michigan.

The wealth of Michigan when it became a state was principally in agriculture. Lumbering had scarcely begun, and the fabulously rich deposits of copper and iron had not yet been discovered. There was, however, great prosperity. Money was plentiful, especially paper money, and during 1836 the sales of land by the United States at its offices in Detroit, Monroe, Kalamazoo, Flint, and Ionia had been

[1] Salt springs were valuable because they provided a local source of salt, making unnecessary the importation of this commodity. Michigan later became a foremost producer of salt, but the brine was obtained from deep wells instead of from springs.

[2] Michigan had three electoral votes—one for each of the two senators and one for the single representative.

greater than those in any other state. More than four million acres, one fourth of all the land sold in that year by all United States land offices, were sold in Michigan. Much was bought in large tracts to be held for future sale, for prices were rising.

2

Stevens T. Mason, the first governor of Michigan, was inaugurated on November 3, 1835. Young, enthusiastic, and affable, he was very popular. A patrician by inheritance, in politics he was a Democrat, and he was democratic in his concern for the general welfare. His message to the Legislature in January, 1837, contained recommendations for the enactment of laws on a number of important matters which he believed were necessary for the prosperity of Michigan. The newspapers supported the governor's program, and the Legislature enacted his recommendations into laws.

One important act created the office of state geologist and provided for a geological survey. The governor appointed Dr. Douglass Houghton, a brilliant young physician of Detroit, to this post. Dr. Houghton had come to Detroit in 1830 at the invitation of Governor Cass and others to deliver lectures on chemistry and geology. Although not yet twenty-one, he was a graduate of Rensselaer Polytechnic Institute and a member of its faculty. He also had been admitted to practice as a physician in New York.

His sponsors, who knew him only by reputation, were at first doubtful when they saw his youthful face and short stature. Their doubts soon vanished when they came to know him. A brilliant lecturer, a skilled physician, and a friendly person, Douglass Houghton quickly charmed everyone he met. He decided to stay in Detroit.

That he was hardy enough to endure rough living he soon proved by accompanying Henry R. Schoolcraft in 1831 on an expedition to Lake Superior and in 1832 to discover the source of the Mississippi River. Serving as physician and botanist, he had opportunities to examine the Upper Peninsula.

As state geologist, Houghton's first exploration resulted in the discovery of salt beds in the Saginaw River valley. His most important work, however, was accomplished in the Upper Peninsula, where, in 1840, he located some of the principal copper deposits, which he reported in February, 1841.

Dr. Houghton was appointed professor of chemistry, zoology, and mineralogy in the University of Michigan in 1839. Although his duties as geologist prevented him from teaching classes, he provided many specimens for the mineral collection of the University.

In 1842 Dr. Houghton was elected mayor of Detroit. In spite of his manifold duties he had taken an active interest in improving the school system, and while he was mayor he was also president of the board of education. He had supported Dr. Zina Pitcher in his fight for tax-supported schools, and it was during his year of office that the first free public schools in Detroit and in Michigan were set in operation.

At Dr. Houghton's suggestion the state geological survey and the United States land survey were carried on co-operatively, beginning in 1844. On September 19 of that year, William A. Burt, a deputy surveyor, looking for the cause of the remarkable deviation of the compass needle, discovered a rich deposit of iron ore on the site of the present city of Negaunee.

3

Governor Mason on March 20, 1837, signed an act of the Legislature providing for the organization of common schools. This act was based on the report of the first superintendent of public instruction. In July, 1836, Governor Mason had appointed the Reverend John D. Pierce to this office on the recommendation of Representative Isaac E. Crary. While living in Marshall the two men had studied a report on the Prussian school system, which they believed was the best, and Crary knew that Pierce had sound ideas.

Immediately after his appointment Pierce journeyed East and conferred with leaders in education about a school plan for Michigan. On his return he wrote a comprehensive report which laid down in detail a system which included primary schools, a university, and branches of the university as intermediate institutions. According to his plan, the schools and the university were to be free and supported by taxes. The law passed by the Legislature provided for schools in each district. No compulsion was attempted, but some financial assistance from the state was promised. Needless to say, free schools did not come at once, nor for many years; but Pierce's plan was an ideal which was finally reached and surpassed.

Through the efforts of Representative Crary in Washington, Congress gave the sixteenth section in each township to the state, instead of to each township, for the benefit of all the schools. These sections were placed in the hands of the superintendent of public instruction, and proceeds from their sale were put into the permanent primary school fund. Interest on the money in this fund was distributed to school districts.

The Legislature selected Ann Arbor as the seat of the state University, chiefly because a local land company offered forty acres free of charge. The law establishing the University followed closely the plan drawn by the Reverend John D. Pierce, a part of his report on a system of education for the state. The University was to have three departments—literature, science, and the arts, law, and medicine—and the governing body was a Board of Regents composed of twelve men appointed by the governor, who was ex-officio president of the Board, the lieutenant governor, the three judges of the supreme court, and the chancellor of the state. The seventy-two sections of land which previously had been granted by Congress were placed in the hands of a commissioner. Eventually they were sold for $547,000.

Four faculty residences and a combination dormitory, chapel, museum, library, and classroom building were erected, and the University opened in the fall of 1841 with two professors and six students. As the University was to be supported by the state, each student paid only an entrance fee of $10. Besides, he was charged $7.50 a year rent for his room. He made his own arrangements for board with a family in the town at a cost of $1.50 or $2 a week.

Student life in the University was very different then than now. The students lived in the building which later was called Mason Hall. Two shared a study, and each had his own bedroom opening into it. The boys chopped their own firewood and carried it up two or three flights of stairs. They swept the dirt from the floor out into the hall where it was gathered up by the janitor, Patrick Kelly, nicknamed "Professor of Dust and Ashes."

Every morning there was compulsory chapel, at 5:30 in spring and fall, and at 6:30 in the winter. Afterward the students attended a recitation before going to breakfast at a boardinghouse in the town. On Sunday they were required to attend one of the Ann Arbor churches. The number of students increased from the original six to eighty-nine in 1857.

The first two professors were the Reverend George P. Williams and the Reverend Joseph Whiting. Others were added as more students enrolled. Although the University was a state institution, for many years a large proportion of the faculty members were Protestant ministers.

The same law which provided for the University authorized the

Regents to establish branches to serve as preparatory schools for the University and to train teachers for the common schools of the state. Nine branches—in Pontiac, Monroe, Kalamazoo, Detroit, Niles, White Pigeon, Tecumseh, Romeo, and Ann Arbor—came under the control of the Regents, who gave them some financial support. Most of these schools had been organized earlier as local academies. Because the sale of University lands did not provide as much money as had been expected, support was gradually withdrawn from the branches, and no funds were granted after 1846. Some of the branches, nevertheless, continued as academies.

4

A banking law passed by the Legislature in the same session had disastrous consequences. Intended to make banking democratic, this act permitted groups of twelve or more men to establish a bank without the necessity of obtaining a special charter from the Legislature. There were at the time fifteen chartered banks in Michigan, probably enough to perform the financial services required by a frontier commonwealth. Money, however, had been in great demand during the real-estate boom of the past few years, and the establishing of banks which could issue notes that would pass as currency seemed an easy way to provide additional funds.

The act, with its later amendments, was considered a model. Strict provisions were included to protect depositors and receivers of notes from loss. Nevertheless, it was under this law that wildcat banks flourished in Michigan, and their notes became worthless pieces of paper.

Perhaps the law would have worked if times had been normal, but they were not. President Jackson's war on the Bank of the United States had resulted in relaxing restraints on state banks. His depositing of United States funds in some of these banks (in 1833) had increased their capacity to issue notes, and his specie circular (July 11, 1836), which ordered receivers to accept only gold or silver in payment for public land, helped caused a shortage of hard cash. Besides, demands by British creditors for payment of debts in gold threatened to reduce dangerously the supply of coin in the banks of New York City. To protect themselves, these banks suspended specie payment on May 10, 1837.

Banks throughout the country followed their example. Governor Mason called the Legislature in special session on June 12 to take

MINING–IRON (I) During the nineteenth century Michigan was one of the leaders in the mining of iron ore. From 1890 to 1900, Michigan produced more than any other state. In the early days of mining crude implements and techniques were employed, as seen in the use of a sledge hammer and hand drill, *above left. Above right:* Miners timbering a shaft to prevent cave-ins. *Right:* Scene from a shaft at the Cliff Mine, Ishpeming.

Charcoal was used to smelt ore in the early days. *Above:* Charcoal kilns, Menominee County. *Left:* Remains of a blast furnace, Garden Peninsula, Delta County.

MINING–IRON (II) In the Jackson Mine, the first in Michigan, the ore was quarried from the surface. *Center left:* The ore dock at Marquette, 1855 to 1868, was the first to have pockets and chutes. *Center right:* A lake freighter being loaded with iron ore at the Lake Superior and Ishpeming Railroad docks at Marquette. *Bottom:* Ore docks at Escanaba.

MINING—COPPER Copper has been for over a century an important Michigan product. *Above:* The Cliff Mine on Keweenaw Peninsula, one of the first copper mines in Michigan. *Center left:* The one-man drill. *Center right:* The picturesque Quincy Mine Shafthouse near Hancock. *Bottom left:* A mechanical scraper loading a tram car. Before efficient techniques were developed to separate the copper from the crushed rock, much copper was discarded along with the rock residue. At Lake Linden these stampings were dumped into the lake. *Bottom right:* A floating dredge pumps stampings from the lake to be reprocessed for copper.

FORTS IN MICHIGAN British and Americans fought over these Mackinac Island ramparts to control the Northwest Empire. *Right:* A plan of the fort. *Below:* Blockhouse at Fort Mackinac.

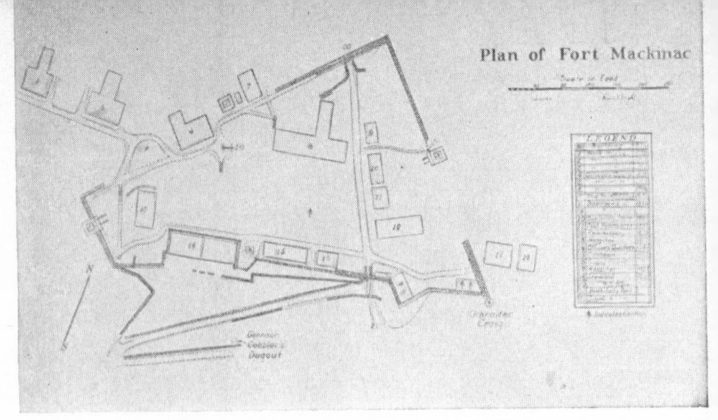

Fort Wayne was built in the 1840's to protect the Canadian-American frontier. *Left:* Original barracks at Fort Wayne. Fort Wilkins near Copper Harbor was built in 1844 to protect miners and to aid in the transfer and relocation of Indians. *Below:* A view of the officers' quarters in 1889 after the fort was abandoned.

LUMBERING (I) During the last half of the nineteenth century thousands of Michigan men spent part of the year in a lumber camp. Here are a few familiar scenes from that era. *Top left:* The mess shack was always a popular place in camp. *Top right:* The camp blacksmith was an important man in logging camps. *Center left:* The "Big Wheels," a Michigan invention, were a familiar sight in the pine woods. *Center right:* A logging train near Harbor Springs.

The log mark on the end of a log identified the owner. *Bottom left:* Some of the first marks used on the Muskegon River. *Bottom right:* Tools of lumbermen in the early days.

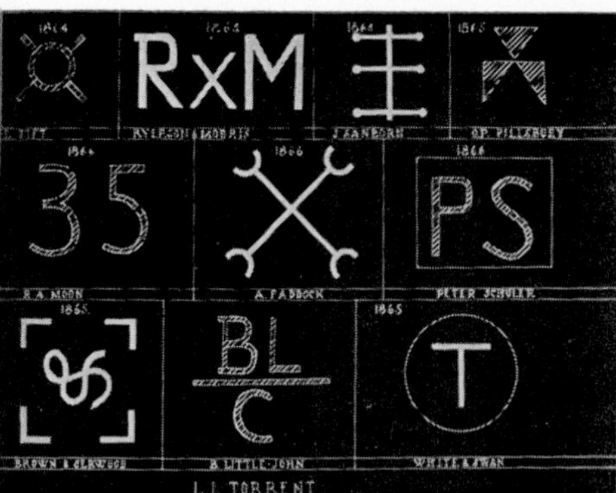

LUMBERING (II) The river drive was one of the most colorful and dangerous of logging operations. *Right:* A traction engine hauling logs to a river. *Below:* The beginning of a drive on the Muskegon River.

Log chutes were often used to get log into the river. *Above:* Log chute on Bi Manistee River. *Left:* Temporary dam were often built on small streams to ob tain water for floating logs. *Bottom lef* The last log drive on the Pine River. *Bot tom right:* Wanigans, floating cook shack accompanying a drive on the Muskego River.

LUMBERING (III) Schooners transported lumber from the mills to lake ports. *Left:* The lumber schooner, *S. O. Neff,* in tow entering Manistee Harbor. *Below left:* Louis Sands' mill at Manistee in 1898. *Below right:* Schooner *J. A. Holmes* loading tanbark on the Big Manistee River.

Lumbering still goes on in Michigan but new techniques are used. *Right:* Portable power saws save hours of labor. *Far right:* Trucks have replaced sleds and "Big Wheels" in transporting logs to mills. *Below:* This tractor hauled over two million feet of hardwood in two months.

SALT MINING Salt deposits were found under some lumber towns. Manufacturing salt from brine pumped from underground was economical because scraps from the mills could be used as fuel to evaporate the water. *Top left:* A salt derrick at the R. G. Peters Salt and Lumber Company at Eastlake on Manistee Lake. *Top right:* Barrels were made in the cooper shop for the salt. *Center right:* Packing salt in barrels. *Center left:* "Old Charlie" hauling a tram car of salt from the packing plant to the storage shed. *Below:* The steam barge *Normandie* clearing Manistee Harbor with a load of salt.

action in the emergency. A law was passed which relieved Michigan banks of the requirement that they pay out coin for notes. Here was an extraordinary opportunity to make money. New banks were quickly organized, apparently with the principal purpose of issuing notes which were not redeemable in cash. During the next eighteen months forty-nine were opened. Because of their vicious practices they were called wildcat banks.

Some of the banks were hidden away in the woods where the inspectors could scarcely find them. When discovered, their total resources might turn out to be a layer of silver dollars on the top of a keg filled with nails. Again, the same bags of coin were passed from

The Wildcat Bank of Shiawassee

bank to bank, just ahead of the inspector, and sworn to be the property of each bank. On one occasion the unexpected return of the inspector, after he had completed an examination, led to the discovery that the bank had in cash exactly $34.20 to support a note circulation of $20,000.

Closing the banks and selling mortgages on real estate which had been deposited with the state to protect note holders were of little avail, for the mortgages were on lots in paper cities or on other land at inflated prices, and the bottom had dropped out of the real-estate market. Finally the state supreme court in 1844 held unconstitutional the law under which the banks had been organized, thus relieving officers and stockholders of all legal liability. Wildcat bank notes were worthless. In 1845 there were only three banks in Michigan, all of them operating under special charters.

Michigan was not the only sufferer from an extravagant issue of bank notes. Inflation had been nationwide, and the panic of 1837, which came as the result of uncontrolled speculation, caused a depression which gripped business for nearly a decade.

5

In the spring of 1837 the prosperity of inflation seemed to be permanent. Everyone recognized the need for improved means of transportation to facilitate settlement and to carry produce to market; and everyone knew that because it was contrary to the principles of Jacksonian democracy for the national government to build roads, canals, or railroads, such internal improvements must be constructed by the states.

The people of Michigan were especially conscious of the benefits they had derived from the Erie Canal, which had been built by the state of New York, and they believed that their own state should undertake similar projects. As a result, the constitution of 1835 had made it the duty of the Legislature to appropriate funds for the improvement of roads, canals, and navigable waters.

In March, 1837, the Legislature passed a law providing for internal improvements to be built and operated by the state. The vote in the lower house was unanimous, and in the senate only one member opposed the bill. It was signed by Governor Mason, and the newspapers praised the legislators for their wise enactment. Indeed, Michigan was only following the lead of its sister commonwealths of the Old Northwest, which were already engaged in constructing internal improvements at public expense.

Excessive enthusiasm and political pressure caused the Legislature to adopt too many projects. Three railroads and two canals were planned to span the state from east to west. One railroad, the Southern, was to be built from Monroe to New Buffalo on Lake Michigan; another, the Central, from Detroit to the mouth of the St. Joseph River; and a third, the Northern, from Port Huron to Grand Rapids. Steamships on the Grand River would complete the connection of this line with Lake Michigan.

A canal was to be dug from Mount Clemens on the Clinton River to the mouth of the Kalamazoo, and another was to link the Saginaw River with the Maple, a tributary of the Grand. The Saginaw–Grand River Canal was to begin at the forks of the Bad River, fifteen miles above Saginaw, and terminate at the bend of the Maple, thirty-two miles from its confluence with the Grand River. Besides, a canal was to be constructed around the falls of the St. Mary's River between Lake Superior and Lake Huron.

A board of six commissioners of internal improvements was appointed to supervise the whole program. The Legislature authorized the board to purchase the rights of the Detroit and St. Joseph Railroad, which was already laying tracks. This became the Michigan Central, and under state ownership trains were run to Ypsilanti in January, 1838. Work was begun on the Southern at Monroe, but only preliminary grading was done on the northern line.

Construction of the Clinton-Kalamazoo Canal began in 1838. The story of the groundbreaking written by John H. Ingersoll, a reporter for the *Detroit Journal and Courier*, expresses the boundless optimism of the times. July 20, the date of the event, he asserted was "a day which will be recollected by the people of Michigan as the proudest that ever happened or can again transpire while her soil remains a component part of *terra firma*."

Ingersoll named the celebrities who had gathered at Mount Clemens for the momentous occasion: Governor Stevens T. Mason and other officials represented the state; Judge Ross Wilkins of the United States district court at Detroit and United States Marshal Conrad Ten Eyck represented the national government. Judge Christian Clemens, founder of the town which bears his name; John H. Stevens of Frederick; G. C. Leech of Utica; Ephraim Calkins of Shelby; and William Burbank of Rochester represented the towns which expected to prosper by proximity to the projected waterway.

The celebration was opened by the firing of a thirteen-gun salute at sunrise. Out-of-town guests who had arrived the night before and residents of Mount Clemens arose and made preparations for the great day. Settlers from the surrounding country drove into town, and even some Indians gathered to watch the curious proceedings and, perchance, beg a drink of liquor.

At 11 o'clock, the crowd assembled in the Court House Square and listened while a local lawyer delivered an oration in which he painted in glowing terms the benefits to be derived from the canal. As soon as he had finished, a parade was organized, headed by a band and the distinguished guests. All marched to the chosen site where the village of Frederick had recently sprung up near the old Moravian Mission settlement. Governor Mason made a few appropriate remarks, then took a spade and formally broke ground for the canal amid the cheers of the crowd and the firing of cannon.

6

To finance the program of internal improvements the Legislature authorized Governor Mason to negotiate a loan of $5,000,000. This was the amount that the governor had suggested in his message to the Legislature, a sum far too small to pay for the extensive program.

As soon as navigation opened in the spring of 1837, the governor went to New York to investigate the possibilities of selling bonds. By this time the financial picture looked dark, and he discovered that floating a loan would be difficult. In the fall he again went to New York, where he was told that the interest rate would have to be raised from 5½ per cent to 6 per cent.

Returning to Detroit, Mason induced the Legislature to pass the necessary amendment. After the revision he was able to place $1,500,000 worth of the bonds on a tentative basis. Oliver Newberry, the Detroit shipowner, took half a million dollars worth, and New York bankers expected to sell the remainder in Europe.

1837 was election year in Michigan. The Whigs nominated Charles C. Trowbridge, a young and successful businessman of Detroit, for governor, and the Democrats nominated Mason. The campaign was a bitter one. Although the Whigs had voted for the internal-improvements law in the Legislature in the spring, now that financial difficulties appeared they opposed the program and blamed the governor and his party for the ills that beset the state. When the votes were counted, it was found that Mason had won by the small plurality of 514. The Democrats retained control of both houses of the Legislature, but with reduced majorities.

In March, 1838, Governor Mason asked that he be relieved of the duty of selling the bonds and that a board be appointed to carry on negotiations. A bill was introduced for the purpose but failed to pass. Once again the governor set out for New York seeking a market for the bonds. There was need for action. European bankers had refused to take any of the issue, and Oliver Newberry reduced his subscription from $500,000 to $200,000. By this time contracts had been let, and the Legislature had already appropriated more than a million dollars.

In New York the governor, on June 1, 1838, made an agreement with the Morris Canal and Banking Company, which thereby became the agent of Michigan for the sale of the whole issue. For its services the company was to receive a commission of 2½ per cent. By this arrangement the state would receive less than the par value of the bonds. Governor Mason was severely criticized for this provision, contrary to the law which specified that the bonds must be sold at par. He agreed to it only because the money was needed at once and because the officers of the company assured him that the bonds would sell at a premium, thus returning the equivalent of the par value. Considering the stringency of the money market at the time, only the governor's inexperience, his supreme optimism, his knowledge of the urgency of the occasion, or a combination of all three could have made him believe such assurances.

The main thing was that he actually obtained $110,397 in bank notes, which he locked in a small trunk. Then with Theodore Romeyn, a lawyer of Detroit, by ship, railroad, stagecoach, and canal boat, he set out for home. During the whole trip the trunk was always in his possession unless it was carefully stowed away in a baggage car or in the cabin of the captain of the ship. There was only one exception. Romeyn was left in charge of the trunk in his hotel room one evening while Governor Mason was out.

After his arrival in Detroit the governor was informed that $4,630 were missing from the trunk. The Morris Company was notified. On the same day that the governor's letter was received, a package was delivered to the office of the company containing all except $50 of the missing money. Governor Mason paid that sum from his own pocket so that the state sustained no loss, but his opponents made great political capital of the mysterious disappearance and reappearance of the money. Some suspicion was directed toward Romeyn, but the governor refused to accuse anyone. The mystery was never solved.

Up to this time the state had been issuing bonds only as the money was required. In November, 1838, the Morris Company, apparently desirous of collecting the $125,000 commission, informed the governor that the only way by which the state could obtain more cash was to make a quick sale. It offered to take one fourth of the bonds, the Bank of the United States in Pennsylvania taking the remaining three fourths. Payments of $250,000 quarterly were promised. Although Mason was disappointed, he agreed to the sale as a necessity, and all the bonds of the State were delivered to the company. The result of this action will appear later.

7

In addition to the manifold duties of the governor in administering the domestic affairs of Michigan, during the latter part of 1837 and the whole of 1838 he was burdened with a grave international problem

In December, 1837, revolts against the authorities began in both Upper and Lower Canada. Known as the Rebellion of 1837 or the Patriot War, it was an attempt by the French in Lower Canada to overturn the British government and gain independence, and by the British in Upper Canada to remove from power a selfish ruling group.

In Lower Canada, the rebellion was soon put down by force; but in Upper Canada, suppression was not so prompt. There native-born British subjects and Americans who had moved to Canada were determined to put an end to abuses and have a share in the government.

In Upper Canada a comparatively small group controlled government offices, real estate, and nearly all business. They were descendants of Loyalists who had fled from the United States during the Revolution, and who had been granted land and other favors by the British government. This oligarchy, which was called the Family Compact, muzzled the press, ignored petitions for redress of grievances, and discouraged education for the poorer people.

A leader of the opposition was William Lyon Mackenzie, editor of the *Colonial Advocate* in Toronto. From 1824 onward he carried on in his newspaper a vigorous attack on the Family Compact, demanding representative and responsible government. Elected to the Assembly five times, he was five times expelled by the supporters of special privilege.

Convinced that only by an appeal to arms could the grievances of the people of Upper Canada be redressed, Mackenzie directed an attack on Toronto in December, 1837. His troops were defeated, and he was forced to flee to the United States. The people of Buffalo, remembering the War of 1812, received him with enthusiasm and offered support against a repressive aristocratic government.

The rebellions in Canada were not isolated outbreaks but a part of a general pattern of revolt against domination from without and special privilege within. The 1830's were a time of revolution in Europe, and in both America and England the little people were demanding a greater voice in government. There had been the July Revolution in France, the Belgian war for independence, the Polish revolt against the Russian overlord, and uprisings in the Italian provinces against the Austrian Empire. By 1832, the Greeks had won their independence from Turkey.

The people of the United States were deeply sympathetic with these movements in Europe, and during the administrations of Andrew Jackson they made their strength felt in politics. In 1836, Texas won its independence of Mexico and President Jackson recognized it as a nation in 1837. To many Americans the revolt in Canada appeared to be the beginning of the end of British dominion in North America.

Mackenzie obtained both financial support and volunteers in New York. Although he was arrested and imprisoned for violating the neutrality law of the United States, his followers continued to harass the Canadian authorities by raids across the border. Guerrilla bands, composed of refugees from Ontario and American sympathizers, were especially active along the Michigan frontier.

Shortly after the rebellion broke out, the United States Department of State requested Governor Mason to arrest all persons concerned in hostile demonstrations against the British government. As a warning the governor issued a proclamation reminding American citizens of their obligation to obey the neutrality law.

Although they were only a small minority of the population, the supporters of the rebel cause in Michigan were too numerous for the governor to arrest. On January 1, 1838, they held a mass meeting in Detroit and collected funds to assist the rebels, or Patriots, as they called themselves. Five days later a gang of them broke into the Detroit jail and carried away 450 stands of arms which had been deposited there for safekeeping. They then seized the schooner *Ann* at a Detroit wharf; put aboard muskets, cannon, and 130 men; and sailed for Gibraltar to prepare for an invasion of Canada.

It was the duty of the United States Government, of course, to seize the *Ann* and prevent an attack on a friendly nation. General Hugh Brady, commander of the military district of the Lakes, had his headquarters in Detroit, but he had no troops. On that account the United States District Attorney called upon Governor Mason for aid in taking the *Ann* into custody.

The governor called out the militia and, because their muskets had been stolen, marched them to Dearbornville, where they were equipped with arms from the United States arsenal. After marching back to Detroit, on January 8, they embarked in two ships and sailed for Gibraltar. When they arrived, the *Ann* had already left for Canada.

The British and the Canadian governments complained bitterly against the United States because it did not use military force to disperse the rebels. The real reason was that the United States had too few troops to patrol the border from Maine to Michigan. At that time the whole strength of the regular army was only five thousand men stationed at scattered posts, and nearly three fourths were in Florida fighting the Creeks and Seminoles. Even so, on January 27,

1838, three companies of regulars reached Detroit. In spite of their presence, the Patriots attempted another invasion of Canada.

On February 24 they crossed the Detroit River on the ice to Fighting Island in Canadian waters. When General Brady learned of this movement, he led his troops down the river and stationed them opposite the island with orders to arrest any armed men on their way to or from the Patriot position. Then, when the British commander threatened to pursue the rebels into American territory, General Brady set up markers to designate the boundary line and prepared to repulse any invasion by British troops. Next day, when the British opened fire with artillery on the Patriots, they replied for a time; but when the British began to advance, they broke and fled to the Michigan shore, where General Brady's men disarmed them and arrested the leaders.

Trouble on the border flared up again in December, 1838. On the second day of the month, General Brady dispersed a force of Patriots east of Detroit and confiscated their arms. Undaunted by this reverse, a company of them seized the steamer *Champlain* at a Detroit wharf at two o'clock in the morning of December 4, sailed for the Canadian shore, and landed above Windsor. Surprising the troops in the Windsor barracks, they captured most of them and set fire to the building. They then started for Sandwich. Meeting Dr. John J. Hume, an army surgeon, on the road, they killed him. When Colonel John Prince, who was advancing with the militia to meet the invaders, learned of this wanton murder, he immediately ordered a firing squad to execute four prisoners his men had captured.

Troops from Fort Malden hastened to the scene of action, and soon all the Patriots were killed, captured, or fleeing for their lives. This Battle of Windsor was the last engagement of the rebellion.

Governor Mason was blamed by some for not having taken stringent enough measures against the Patriots, and by others for interfering with a movement to free Canada from a despotic oligarchy. There is no doubt that he sympathized with the rebels, but his official attitude was correct and, considering the limited means at hand, he probably did as much as was possible to prevent hostilities against Canada. Dr. Edward A. Theller, a leader of the Patriots, later explained that Governor Mason's "democracy prompted him to pray for the success of the cause while the dictates of duty impelled him to counteract the effort. . . ." However that may be, it is certain that the frequent alarms increased the burdens of his office.

In conclusion, although the Patriots failed to overthrow the Family

Compact, their resistance called attention to the abuses which existed. The British government sent Lord Durham to investigate the situation, and as a result of his report the Act of Union was passed in 1840, and representative and responsible government soon followed.

During the rebellion the British had armed several vessels on the Great Lakes, a violation of the Rush-Bagot Agreement of 1817, which limited such ships to one of one hundred tons or less mounting an eighteen-pound cannon on Lake Ontario, and two on the Upper Lakes.

The United States Government in turn had an iron steamship of five hundred tons burden constructed at Pittsburgh. The parts were carried to Erie, Pennsylvania, where they were assembled. Launched during the summer of 1844, she was the first iron warship on the Upper Lakes. This ship, which was named the *Michigan,* carried two eight-inch guns and four thirty-two-pounders.

In 1905, when a new cruiser, the *Michigan,* was commissioned, the old ship was named the *Wolverine.* She was used by the Naval Reserve as a training ship until 1923, when she was tied up at Erie. During 1948 and early 1949 a campaign to raise funds to restore her was carried on. Because sufficient money could not be obtained, the *Wolverine* was towed to a scrap yard for dismantling in June, 1949.

Another result of the Rebellion was the authorization of Fort Wayne in 1841. Built on the Detroit River at the foot of Livernois Avenue in Detroit, it was completed in 1851, a square-bastioned fortress with barracks constructed of stone. Fort Wayne never fired a hostile shot.

In May, 1949, the United States Government transferred the title of Fort Wayne to the city of Detroit on condition that it be maintained as a historical monument. The stone barracks have been turned into a museum, and the fortifications are open to visitors.

— 15 —

End of Internal Improvements: Logging Begins

By the fall of 1839, the nation was in the painful grip of the panic. In Michigan wildcat banknotes had depreciated, prices of farm produce had fallen, land which had formerly been selling at inflated figures now had no purchasers, and mortgages were being foreclosed. Construction of the railroads and canals, which had been begun with high hopes for the future, lagged for lack of funds.

In the widespread dissatisfaction and even misery, the Whigs saw their opportunity to gain control of the state government. Meeting in Marshall, the party convention blamed all the current suffering on Governor Mason and the Democrats, and nominated William Woodbridge of Detroit for governor.

Woodbridge was a conservative Whig who had come to Michigan after the War of 1812 as secretary of the Territory. Later he had served as territorial delegate to Congress and as a judge of the territorial supreme court. He was a stern, retiring, scholarly man, anything but the typical politician. Nevertheless, he was ambitious for office, and the people trusted him for his honesty and strength of character.

Governor Mason had no desire to run again, and his party by this time, controlled by the conservative element, looked upon him as a liability. For governor they nominated Elon Farnsworth, chancellor of the state, an able and highly respected lawyer. The campaign, as usual, was carried on with uncomplimentary name-calling by the party newspapers. Governor Mason, who formerly had been almost idolized, was now called a worthy successor to Benedict Arnold, and Woodbridge was held up to popular scorn as a tyrant judge, a disfranchiser of the poor, and an office seeker in his dotage.

There was little doubt as to the outcome of the election. The radical Democrats, dissatisfied with the conservative candidate of their party, supported the Whig ticket, and people who blamed the Democrats for the panic voted hopefully for the opposition, which promised sweeping reforms. Woodbridge won the governorship, and the Whigs elected a majority to both houses of the Legislature.

Unhappy because of his fall from popular favor, in the autumn of 1841 Stevens T. Mason moved to New York. In 1838 he had married Miss Julia Phelps of that city, and he began the practice of law there. He died on January 4, 1843, at the age of thirty-one. In 1905 his remains were buried in Detroit on the site of the old Capitol. Three years later a bronze statue was placed upon his tomb.

2

Lack of money had forced a reduction in the advance of internal improvements, but some progress had been made. By the end of 1839, 110 miles had been cleared for the line of the Northern Railroad, the Southern had reached Adrian, and the Central ran its first train to Ann Arbor on October 17.

A great celebration was organized in honor of the event. According to the Ann Arbor *Western Emigrant* (October 23, 1839), "People came from all quarters, to witness the arrival of the cars for the first time at our new and beautiful depot. . . ." At noon the train from Detroit arrived bringing the Brady Guards and other visitors. A parade was formed which proceeded to the Courthouse Square, where tables were set for a banquet. After the meal toasts were drunk, among them one to Ann Arbor in the following words: "Appropriately selected as the literary emporium of this beautiful peninsula, may the streams of learning and science gush from the surrounding hills, as from the seven hills of the Imperial City, refreshing and purifying the whole land."

Both the Clinton and Kalamazoo and the Saginaw canals were under construction, and the Grand and Kalamazoo rivers had been made navigable, the first as far as the rapids, and the second to Allegan.

The only project which was a complete failure was the canal around the rapids of the St. Mary's River. A contract for construction had been made in September, 1838. In May, 1839, the contractor appeared at the Sault with a gang of workmen and began to dig. He was warned by the commandant of Fort Brady not to interfere with the millrace of a sawmill used by the post. Disregarding the warning, the contractor continued his operations in such a way as to endanger the flow of water to the mill. When he refused to desist, an officer appeared with a detachment of regulars and forcibly removed the workmen from the scene.

In August, Michigan and the War Department reached an agreement on the route of the ship canal, but the contractor refused to resume work, and the project was abandoned. It is believed that the contractor, not liking the job and fearing that the state would not be able to pay for the work, intentionally caused the interference of the military officers.

According to the agreement with Governor Mason, the Morris Canal and Banking Company continued to pay the quarterly installments of $250,000 until January 1, 1840. It defaulted on April 1, and sometime later both this company and the Bank of the United States of Pennsylvania, which had joined with it as a purchaser of the bonds, failed. When the state demanded that the bonds on which the holders had advanced no money be surrendered, it was discovered that the two banks had deposited the bonds with bankers in England as security for loans of their own.

These bonds had a face value of $2,200,000 and, of course, were a debt against the state, although it had received no return from them. It was finally decided that principal and interest would be paid only on bonds for which the state had been paid. Some writers have called this a policy of repudiation. As a matter of fact it did for a time injure Michigan's reputation as a borrower, but Judge Thomas M. Cooley expressed the opinion that it was an equitable arrangement.

Michigan had company in her misery. The other states of the Old Northwest also had plunged recklessly into the construction of unnecessary internal improvements. Ohio, Indiana, and Illinois planned and began construction of roads, canals, and railroads, many of them located because of political pressure and leading nowhere. Most of the work was paid for by borrowed funds. Like Michigan, Indiana lost money by dealing with the Morris Canal and Banking Company. By 1840, the credit of these states had been ruined because they were unable to pay their debts.

In spite of their promises of reform, the Whigs were able to accomplish little in the way of improving conditions within the state. The United States Government gave Michigan five hundred thousand acres of land in 1841 to be sold for the benefit of internal improvements, but the demand for land was so slight that not more than fifty cents an acre could be realized on sales.

3

The Presidential campaign of 1840 was the most exciting one up to that time. Martin Van Buren was renominated by the Democrats, and the Whigs chose as their candidate William Henry Harrison. Henry Clay was the logical candidate, but he had made many political enemies during his long years of service in Congress. Harrison, who was sixty-eight years old, had been long in retirement, living in his fine big house on the bank of the Ohio River. He had taken no part in discussions of public questions, and he remained silent during the campaign.

After he was nominated, a Democratic editor expressed the opinion that if Harrison were given a pension and a barrel of hard cider, he would be content to retire to a log cabin for the rest of his days. Shrewdly seizing this idea, the Whig leaders hailed Harrison as a man of the people, a sturdy frontiersman who would bring common sense into the national government.

The Whigs praised Harrison also as a military hero, magnifying for their purpose the battles of Tippecanoe and the Thames. As a running mate they chose John Tyler of Virginia, a former states' rights Democrat, to attract the southern vote. "Tippecanoe and Tyler too" became the party's slogan.

In every town the Whigs set up a log cabin with a coonskin nailed to the door and a barrel of hard cider invitingly open. The cabin in Detroit was on the corner of Randolph and Jefferson. Great parades and meetings were organized throughout the country. On May 29 some Michigan Whigs attended a party rally on the site of the Battle of Tippecanoe, and many more were at the great Fort Meigs gathering on July 11.

Five steamships sailed from Detroit crowded with enthusiastic partisans, the Erie and Kalamazoo Railroad carried many to Toledo, and others from the southern counties of Michigan made their way to Fort Meigs in wagons. There they whooped it up for Old Tip and Ty, and they patiently listened while Harrison spoke for more than two hours. Another big rally was held in Detroit on September 30.

"Tippecanoe and Tyler Too" Campaign—Log Cabin in Detroit, 1840

The excitement of the campaign helped people forget the hardships of the financial depression, but Whig leaders continued to remind them that the Democrats were responsible for it. Hard times alone were enough to defeat Van Buren, but in spite of the vigorous campaign in Harrison's behalf his popular majority was only 150,000. In Michigan he received but 1,800 more votes than his opponent.

The triumph of the Whigs was short-lived. Harassed by impatient office seekers, Harrison became ill and died a month after the inauguration. John Tyler, "President by accident," reverted to Democratic principles, and the Whigs read him out of the party.

4

The Michigan Legislature elected Governor Woodbridge to the United States Senate in February, 1841, and his term of office was completed by Lieutenant Governor James Wright Gordon. The Whigs were defeated in the fall election of 1841. Dissatisfied with the administration, the people returned to their Democratic allegiance and elected as governor John S. Barry of Constantine, St. Joseph County. Barry was a successful merchant, economical and conservative in his personal affairs, and equally so in managing the business of the state. So well did he discharge the duties of his office that he was re-elected in 1843.

During Barry's administrations, for a time, construction was continued on the Central and the Southern railroads and on the Clinton-Kalamazoo Canal. Canal building was stopped when the twelve miles from Mount Clemens to Rochester had been excavated. For a few years boats ran as far west as Utica, and the canal furnished water power for a gristmill.

Today the course of the canal may easily be followed. Water in the six-mile section from Rochester to Utica still serves as power for a mill. The section of equal length from Utica to Mount Clemens, however, has gradually filled in until it is now only a drainage ditch.

In 1843 the Legislature set the western limit of the Southern Railroad at Hillsdale and of the Central at Kalamazoo. Hillsdale was reached in that year, and Kalamazoo in February, 1846. By that time the total internal-improvements debt was $4,121,720.79.

The experiment in railroad building by the state had not been successful. Perhaps, if conditions had been normal, the results would have been different; but political pressures of people in various parts of the state for the construction of lines in their region, whether economically practical or not, would undoubtedly at any time have led to overbuilding.

By 1846 it was the general opinion that Michigan should withdraw from the railroad business, and so the Legislature in that year sold the two partially completed lines. The Southern was bought for $500,000 by a private corporation. Another private company purchased the Central for $2,000,000.

Eastern financiers raised money to buy the Michigan Central, and they engaged James F. Joy, a young attorney of Detroit to represent them. A native of New Hampshire, Joy was a graduate of Dartmouth

College and of Harvard Law School. He had come to Detroit in 1836 and was associated with Senator Augustus S. Porter as a lawyer.

At his request the Legislature in 1846 granted a charter to the new company. By its terms the Central was to be extended to New Buffalo instead of to St. Joseph, as originally planned. The company reached New Buffalo on Lake Michigan within two years, constructed a harbor, and made connections by ships with Chicago. John M. Forbes was president of the Michigan Central and John W. Brooks, a young civil engineer, was general superintendent.

James F. Joy's connection with the Michigan Central led him farther and farther into the railroad business. In later years he promoted other lines in Michigan, and he became one of the leading figures in extending railroads westward.

5

Except for numerous prairies and oak openings in the southern counties, Michigan was heavily wooded. The timber was at first cut for stockades, for cabins, and for firewood; later, to clear the land for cultivation. The surplus was burned as rubbish. To those who wanted to begin farming, the dense forest was not attractive. Settlers hated the big trees as obstacles that interfered with their immediate need for land on which to grow crops.

Although houses were usually built of logs, at Detroit some were of frame covered with boards. Planks were needed too for various purposes. At first they were obtained by whipsawing. A log was laid over a pit above which a platform had been built. Boards or planks were taken off by two sawyers, one in the pit and the other on the platform pulling the saw up and down.

The first type of saw operated by water power moved up and down like the whipsaw. It was held firmly in place by a heavy wooden frame called a gate or a sash. When several saws were set side by side in the sash so that a number of planks could be made simultaneously, it was called a gang of saws. The sash was very heavy and consumed much of the power produced by water wheel or steam engine.

An improved form of the up-and-down saw was the muley, which operated without the sash. It could be used also in gangs and it doubled the output of mills in which it was installed. Next came the circular saw, which was more efficient than the muley because it produced lumber much more rapidly. Later the band saw was used because it made a narrower cut and wasted less of the log in sawdust.

Sawmills operated by water power were in use at Detroit quite early. A prisoner there during the French and Indian War, in 1757, reported that two were working. A stand of pine on the Pine River, which flows into the St. Clair River, was the source of building material for the Detroit region. Logs could easily be floated down to the mills.

Settlers came into Michigan in large numbers during the late 1820's, and promoters looked for likely spots where they could lay out town sites. They always chose places where a stream could be dammed to operate a gristmill and a sawmill. Many small mills were built to supply the local demand for boards and planks as settlements fanned out from Detroit; but it was not until the 1840's and 1850's that commercial logging and lumbering began. Then steam-power mills turned out lumber in great quantities for wholesale distribution to distant markets.

The timberland of the Lower Peninsula can be divided roughly into two regions. Below an irregular line drawn from St. Clair to Muskegon occurred mostly hardwoods: oak, beech, maple, elm, hickory, walnut, ash, and others. North of this line were the pines, with some intermingling of hardwoods. Michigan white pine, the finest of which was called cork pine, was the best in the world. These great trees grew to a height of one hundred and fifty feet and many were three or four feet in diameter.

A glance at the map of Michigan will help explain the natural advantages enjoyed by lumbermen in the state. Many rivers flow from a central divide either into Lake Huron or Lake Michigan. Of the former there are the Pine; the Black; and the Saginaw, which with its tributaries, drains more than three thousand square miles; the Au Sable; the Thunder Bay; and the Cheboygan.

On the western side of the state in the former pine region are the Muskegon, the White, the Pentwater, the Pere Marquette, the Lincoln, the Great Sable, the Manistee, the Betsie, and the Boardman. Logs cut along these streams or their tributaries were piled on the banks during the winter. When the spring thaw came the logs were rolled into the swollen creeks and rivers to float down to towns near the mouth, where the mills converted them into lumber which was loaded on vessels to be carried to various ports around the Lakes. There were stands of pine also among the hardwoods south of Muskegon, and millions of feet were floated down the Grand and the Kalamazoo rivers to mills at Grand Rapids, Grand Haven, Allegan, and Saugatuck, but the great pine forests were farther north.

6

When lumbering began, the number of fur-bearing animals had been so greatly reduced that fur trading had seriously declined. Under the circumstances it was natural that men who had been active in gathering and selling furs should enter the new industry. They knew the woods, they liked outdoor life, and they were able to endure the hardships necessary in getting out the logs. Clerks and agents became lumbermen, and *voyageurs* exchanged canoe paddles for axes.

On the east coast logging and lumbering moved from St. Clair to Port Huron, to Flint, and to Saginaw, which had a steam sawmill in 1834. It was built by Harvey Williams for his nephews Ephraim S. and Gardner D. Williams, agents for the American Fur Company. Seeing the decline of the fur business, these men remained to become the founders of the industry which was to make Saginaw famous. This mill was small and produced lumber for local use only. The Williamses continued in the business, although Ephraim moved to Flint in 1840.

Other pioneer lumbermen of the region were Albert Miller, who built a mill at Portsmouth near the mouth of the Saginaw River in 1836; George Hazleton, who had mills on the Flint River in 1840; and Charles Merrill. Bay City, at first called Lower Saginaw, had a mill in 1847. By 1860, there were seventy-two mills on the Saginaw River and its tributaries, and Saginaw was the first great center of the Michigan lumber industry. The combined production of the Saginaw Valley in 1860 was more than 131 million board feet. Schooners and steamships tied up at the wharves of Saginaw and Bay City and sailed away loaded with lumber for Detroit, Toledo, Cleveland, and Buffalo.

On the west coast the industry also moved northward and inland, every river eventually carrying its quota of logs to Lake Michigan. The beginnings, as on the other side of the state, were small. Typical of the successful lumberman was the career of Charles Mears. In 1836 he and two brothers came out from Massachusetts and opened a store in Paw Paw.

Becoming restless, Charles and one brother the next year floated down the Paw Paw River to the St. Joseph, out to Lake Michigan, and paddled up the coast to White Lake, where Whitehall is now situated. On the bank of Silver Creek, a tributary of the White River, they built a cabin. The brother remained there while Charles went east for mill machinery. In the fall he returned and built a mill on the southeast shore of White Lake. Knowing that he must have a market for his lumber, in 1838 Mears had a sloop, the *Ranger*, built at St. Joseph, and the same year he sent a cargo to Chicago.

Charles Mears steadily expanded his activities. In 1844 he built another mill on Duck Lake just south of White Lake, and in 1849 a third on Black Creek just above Pere Marquette, now Ludington. Later, in 1863, when he was a state senator, he had the name changed to Lincoln River. In 1850 Mears opened his own lumberyard in Chicago. He continued to buy land, and in 1854 he established a mill on the Great Sable.

In order to assure adequate transportation for his increasing production, in 1856 he had a steamer built at Cleveland. It carried passengers, mail, and lumber to Chicago and brought back supplies. In 1857 Mears owned a mill also at Pere Marquette. Mears was a stanch Republican and an admirer of Abraham Lincoln. When the Republican Convention which nominated Lincoln met in the Wigwam in Chicago in May, 1860, part of the decorations consisted of evergreen boughs carried by one of Mears's ships from Michigan forests.

The first sawmill on the Muskegon River began to operate in 1838, and three mills were running on Muskegon Lake in 1840. George and John Ruddiman, Theodore Newell, Martin Ryerson, and Henry Knickerbocker were early operators, and Delos A. Blodgett was rising to prominence during the latter part of this period. Charles H. Hackley began working as a laborer in 1856. Three years later he and his brothers and their father were in the sawmill business for themselves. By 1860, Muskegon was producing 75 million board feet of lumber, the largest output on the west coast of Michigan.

Pentwater had a mill in 1850 built by William M. Ferry, and another in 1853 owned by Edwin R. Cobb and Andrew Rector. Charles Mears began sawing there in 1856.

On the Manistee River the first mill was built by John Stronach and his sons in 1841. Four years later Joseph Stronach erected a steam mill on Manistee Lake, and Roswell Canfield put one in operation in 1848. Other mills were soon built around the lake to saw the logs which were floated down the river.

Logging in the Grand Traverse region began in 1847 when William Boardman purchased land where Traverse City now stands, and his son Horace began logging. In 1851 Hannah, Lay and Company, a Chicago firm, bought out the Boardmans and commenced extensive operations.

Lumbering in the Upper Peninsula was in its infancy. A few mills provided lumber for local building needs, largely in the copper and iron mining regions. At Escanaba Daniel Wells, Jr., and Jefferson Sinclair built a mill in 1846. Nelson Ludington and his brother Harrison joined the partners in 1848 and bought them out in 1857. This was the beginning of N. Ludington and Company. Mills on the Menominee River, which later became one of the greatest carriers of logs, were built in the 1840's, at first on the Wisconsin side. In 1856 Abner Kirby built a mill at Menominee. Three years later Samuel M. Stephenson joined him as a partner. Augustus A. and William O. Carpenter invested in the business, which in 1861 became Kirby, Carpenter and Company.

The statistics of lumbering in Michigan for the period 1840-1860 are not very impressive when compared with those of the later period, but they do show how rapidly the industry was growing. For example, in 1840, there were five hundred mills operating, and in 1860, nearly one thousand. The value of forest products in Michigan in 1840 was $1,000,000; in 1860 it was $6,000,000. Nearly 800 million board feet of lumber were sawed. The industry was important, but not until after the Civil War did it reach its peak.

— 16 —

Copper Boulder and Iron Ore Mountain

The presence of copper in the Upper Peninsula had been known from the earliest days of exploration. Because it was found in the pure state, the Indians were able to hammer pieces into ornaments, tools, and weapons. These attracted the attention of Champlain and later French leaders, but, although explorers searched for the source of the metal, no mining was done during the French regime.

After the British occupied Fort Michilimackinac at present Mackinaw City, in 1761, fur traders in the North Country began prospecting for copper. Alexander Henry, who survived the massacre at the fort in 1763, heard of a great mass of copper on the bank of a river flowing into Lake Superior. Paddling along the south shore of the lake, he entered the Ontonagon River and saw the conglomerate boulder, which consisted of pure copper imbedded in rock. Believing that it had rolled out of the river bank, Henry organized a company which began mining operations on the Ontonagon in 1771. After one season of unrewarding labor, the project was abandoned.

In 1820, some members of Governor Lewis Cass's party, exploring the shores of Michigan, visited the Ontonagon boulder, and Henry R. Schoolcraft, geologist with the expedition, described it in his account of the journey published in 1821. This report helped keep alive interest in the mineral resources of the Upper Peninsula.

Schoolcraft was in the Upper Peninsula again in 1831 and 1832. Dr. Douglass Houghton accompanied him on both occasions, and in 1831 he went up the Ontonagon River to see the boulder. He hacked off bits of the native copper and carried them away as specimens. On this expedition, he had also examined the rocks on Keweenaw Peninsula and found traces of copper.

These previous experiences made Houghton eager to explore the Upper Peninsula after he became state geologist in 1837. Although his report to the Legislature in 1841 contained a warning that quick riches would not be found on the shores of Lake Superior, news that he had found extensive copper deposits in the northern part of Michigan quickly reached the East.[1]

As a result of Houghton's report of 1841, men began entering the north country seeking copper. Legally they had no right to dig, for the land west of the Chocolay, or Chocolate River, and the Escanaba still belonged to the Indians. The government, however, by the Treaty of La Pointe in October, 1842, acquired from the Indians all the remaining land within the boundaries of Michigan.

One of the first to reach the Upper Peninsula in the summer of 1841 was Julius Eldred, a businessman of Detroit. For him the attraction was the Ontonagon boulder. Believing that people would pay to see this natural curiosity, he was determined to remove it to Detroit and put it on exhibition. He made his way to the Ontonagon River, examined the boulder, and made plans to carry it away. To a Chippewa chief who asserted some sort of claim to it, he paid $150.

The next summer he was back again with tackle to move the boulder, but the 6,000-pound combination of copper and rock resisted his efforts. Defeated but undismayed, he returned to Detroit and prepared a sturdy car and two twenty-five foot sections of track for a second attempt.

When Eldred arrived, he found to his surprise that a Colonel Hammond had taken a permit to mine on the land where the boulder lay and had sent James K. Paul and a party of miners to hold it. Jim Paul was a pretty tough character, and so Eldred bought the boulder

[1] Dr. Houghton was drowned on October 14, 1845, when the boat in which he was approaching Eagle River capsized in a storm. He was only thirty-six years old.

again, paying $1,365. He also obtained a permit from General Walter Cunningham, the government agent.

Then the work of removal began. With block and tackle the boulder was dragged up the cliff. Placed on the car which Eldred had brought, it was inched along the tracks by the use of cables attached to trees. After advancing fifty feet, the car was halted while the rear section of track was carried ahead and relaid. Hills and hollows made progress slow over the trail. At last, after more than four miles, they reached

The Ontonagon Boulder

the open river and swung the boulder onto a raft and floated it down to Lake Superior.

The government agent, meanwhile, had received an order from the Secretary of War to seize the boulder. In spite of Eldred's protests, he did so; then, feeling sorry for the man who had spent so much time and money on his project, he permitted him to ship it to Detroit. There Eldred placed it in a room on Jefferson Avenue and charged an admission fee of twenty-five cents to see it.

Seized again by order of the Secretary of War, the boulder was taken to Washington. Eldred accompanied it to the capital and filed a claim for his expenses. Finally the War Department paid him $5,664.98. The boulder was exhibited in the Smithsonian Institution for many years. Now it may be seen in the Natural History Building of the National Museum. The newspaper publicity attending the removal of the boulder created widespread interest in the copper region.

2

In order to make provision for the orderly registration of mining claims, the government stationed a mineral agent at Copper Harbor on the Keweenaw Peninsula in 1843. At first prospectors were permitted to lease for three years tracts of nine square miles. The leases were renewable. A royalty of six pounds of copper out of every hundred had to be paid to the government. On March 1, 1847, Congress passed a law permitting the outright sale of mineral lands in quarter sections.

It was believed in Washington that the miners should be protected from the Indians who still inhabited the Upper Peninsula; and so Fort Wilkins, named for the Secretary of War, was built near Copper Harbor between Lake Fanny Hooe and Lake Superior. General Hugh Brady, commanding the Fourth Military Department, went from Detroit with Captain R. E. Cleary and companies A and B of the Fifth Infantry Regiment to supervise the construction of barracks and a stockade in 1844.

As it turned out, the fort was not needed, for the Indians were friendly and not nearly so dangerous as the miners when they were on a drunken spree. When the Mexican War began in 1846, the garrison was ordered away and the fort was unoccupied, except by caretakers, until 1867. Final evacuation of the fort was ordered in 1870. The counties of Keweenaw and Houghton later purchased the tract of land from the government and deeded it to the state. Today, the stockade and the buildings have been restored, and Fort Wilkins is a very attractive state park.

Although prospectors were in the Upper Peninsula in 1841 and 1842, the boom years were 1843 to 1846. Expecting to find masses of virgin copper to be had for the taking, men swarmed into the copper country. It was the first great mining rush in the United States. During the summer of 1843, the government mineral agent at Copper Harbor issued more than one hundred permits. Prospectors soon learned that copper hunting was hard work. Swamps sometimes blocked their way, and cedar thickets were so dense that a path had to be hacked out with axes. Supplies were expensive, mosquitoes were ferocious, and the severe winter weather discouraged all but the most hardy from remaining throughout the year.

Many copper-mining companies were organized, some to operate and others simply to sell stock to speculators. Capital was invested by men in eastern cities, particularly Boston.

In 1844 the Lake Superior Copper Company was formed by a group of Boston financiers who sent Dr. Charles T. Jackson to manage their operations. His overly optimistic reports encouraged others to invest money in copper mines. The first company and its successors continued to operate at a loss until 1849, when it went into bankruptcy. Although $2,500,000 had been spent, only $20,000 were paid in dividends.

Another company, the Pittsburgh and Boston, founded in 1844, was more successful, although it too nearly failed before rich deposits were discovered. A great deal of money had to be spent before any return could be expected. Transportation costs for food and equipment were high, labor was scarce, and managers conducted operations largely by the method of trial and error.

The Pittsburgh and Boston Company was fortunate. Near the village of Eagle River its workmen, following a vein, opened the Cliff Mine and found a mass of native copper. Other masses, weighing from one hundred to one hundred and fifty tons, were discovered along with many nuggets of silver, and the company paid a dividend in 1848, the first in the district. The Cliff Mine was the richest of the early ventures until about 1860, when profits began to dwindle. Before it was discontinued in 1870, it had paid its stockholders $2,627,660, a little over 2,000 per cent on the capital investment.

The practice in mining copper was first to sink a shaft beside a vein of the metal. From the shaft, tunnels were then driven horizontally at various levels. To break through the rocks, holes were bored with hand drills and sledge hammers, then black powder was tamped into the holes and exploded by fuses. The debris from the explosion, rock and copper, was hauled to the shaft in wheelbarrows.

Rock and copper were raised to the surface by a windlass consisting of a large drum mounted vertically on an axle. A long beam was attached to the bottom of the drum, and a horse hitched to the end of the beam walked in a circle, winding around the drum a chain which hauled a bucket up the shaft. Steam hoisting engines were introduced during the 1850's. Nearby, a stamp mill crushed the rock and released the copper.

The Cliff and other early mines near the tip of the Keweenaw Peninsula depended on mass copper for their dividends. A similar region was in the vicinity of the Ontonagon River. There mining was begun in 1843 by men recruited largely from the lead mines of Illinois and Wisconsin. The most spectacular success was achieved by the Minesota Mine, which was opened in 1847. There was found the largest single mass of native copper ever discovered. It weighed nearly five hundred tons.

In spite of the eagerness to amass wealth in the copper region, the prospectors and miners took time for important celebrations. William W. Spalding, a prospector in the Ontonagon region, entered in his diary an account of how he and others observed the Fourth of July in 1846 at the mouth of the Iron River. Spalding read the Declaration of Independence, and another member of the party delivered a patriotic oration. A table had been set under a bower of evergreen branches, and thirty-three men sat down to a good dinner. In that faraway part of Michigan, the nation's birthday was fittingly remembered.

The town of Ontonagon had its beginning with the arrival of James K. Paul, Nicholas Miniclier, and several others from the lead mines in 1843. Jim Paul squatted on a claim at the mouth of the river; he later purchased it and platted the town.

The United States Government established a mineral agency on the ground in 1844, and when miners began to arrive, Paul turned his cabin into a hotel. The host was hardy enough to manage his guests, who were a rough lot.

About a mile above the mouth of the river, Daniel S. Cash opened a store in which his nephew, William W. Spalding, became a partner. Spalding also engaged in mining and hauling ore on boats from the Minesota Mine to the lake. Cash began farming on a small scale and increased his plantings when his experiment proved to be successful. He was the first farmer in that part of the state.

The third Michigan region in which copper was produced was in the neighborhood of Portage Lake. Here the copper was found in small fragments in the lava flow and in conglomerate formation rather than in great masses. The early prospectors were not favorably impressed by the traces of the metal they uncovered there, but the Quincy and the Pewabic mining companies explored the region in the late forties and early fifties. In 1856 the rich Pewabic Mine was opened, and within the next few years the Quincy Mine and the Franklin Mine began producing.

The neighboring towns of Houghton and Hancock were begun during the 1850's. Ransom Sheldon was the founder of Houghton. With C. C. Douglass he bought land around Portage Lake, and in 1852 he opened a store on the south side. That was the beginning of Houghton. The next year Sheldon built a sawmill.

Captain Douglass owned land just across from Houghton. A store was built in 1858, and in 1859 Douglass platted the town of Hancock. Both towns grew as the mines on the shores of Portage Lake were developed.

Before the Civil War the Cliff, the Minesota, the Pewabic, the Quincy, and the Franklin mines were the most successful financially. Many other companies went bankrupt, and investors had nothing to show for their money but beautifully engraved certificates of stock. By 1849 it was evident to individual prospectors that the tales of easy wealth which had drawn them to the Upper Peninsula were wholly fanciful. Without vast resources of capital, mining could not be carried on profitably, and even many well-financed operations failed. Men who were willing to work for the mining companies remained, but the restless ones, hearing of the discovery of gold in California, left Michigan to try their luck in another Eldorado. Many a forty-niner had served his apprenticeship in the copper country of Michigan.

During the first ten years of operation, 1845 to 1855, the copper mines produced 13,419,000 pounds of metal. Output increased until in 1860 alone it was 11,792,000 pounds, and the value of the product was $2,690,000. Thirty-three companies were employing 3,681 men, and the capital invested was estimated at $4,053,000. Copper mining was becoming big business in Michigan.

3

In contrast with the long-time knowledge that copper existed in the Upper Peninsula, the presence of iron ore in large quantities was entirely unknown until 1844. The principal reason was that the iron, unlike the copper, did not occur in the pure state but in the form of ore, which to the Indians and the early explorers alike, was simply an unusually heavy kind of rock.

The discoverer of iron in Michigan was William A. Burt. A deputy surveyor under Douglass Houghton, he was running township lines in the Upper Peninsula. In the fall of 1844 Burt and his party made camp at the eastern end of Teal Lake. One of his assistants was Jacob Houghton, a brother of Douglass. On September 19, while surveying the line south between ranges 26 and 27 west, Burt was surprised by the peculiar movements of the needle of the magnetic compass. Frequently changing direction, it was as likely to point to the south as to the north.

When the needle of the magnetic compass finally pointed southwest, Burt asked his assistants to hunt for the cause of this phenomenon. After a few minutes each returned with pieces of iron ore gathered from numerous outcroppings. The site was south of Teal Lake, where Negaunee now stands.

Under the circumstances, the party was fortunate in having a solar compass which had been invented by Burt. Using the sun for indicating direction, it was reliable when the magnetic compass became erratic. In that region rich with iron ore the surveyors had to depend entirely on Burt's solar compass.

Before the news of Burt's discovery had come out of the North, a company organized to mine copper became interested in the iron which he had found. In Jackson, Michigan, Philo M. Everett, a storekeeper, and some of his friends formed the Jackson Mining Company in July, 1845. Carrying permits to locate mining claims, Everett and three companions proceeded to Sault Sainte Marie. There they heard of a mountain of some sort of ore near Teal Lake.

Everett bought a boat, engaged Louis Nolan, a local pilot, and sailed to the mouth of the Carp River, where Marquette now stands. Failing to find the mineral, Nolan suggested that they go on to L'Anse on Keweenaw Bay and ask Marji-Gesick, a Chippewa chief, to guide them to it. They found Marji-Gesick, and he readily agreed to show them the heavy stones which they were looking for.

They returned to the mouth of the Carp River and, after traveling twelve or thirteen miles through dense forests and over great bare rocks, came to Teal Lake. Leading them away from the lake toward the south, the Chippewa brought them to the foot of a hill. There lay a tall pine tree that had been thrown down by a storm. Among the roots many pieces of rich ore were visible. Negaunee later was built on the site, and in memory of this event an uprooted stump appears on the city's seal.

A little farther on was a ridge of bare rock, Everett called it "a mountain of solid ore, 150 feet high." Believing that he had found a valuable mining site, he took some specimens of ore and sailed to Copper Harbor where he entered his location in the office of the government mineral agent. The next year two other members of the Jackson Company, Abram V. Berry, president, and Frederick W. Kirtland, secretary, went to Teal Lake and built a cabin where they left a man to hold their claim.

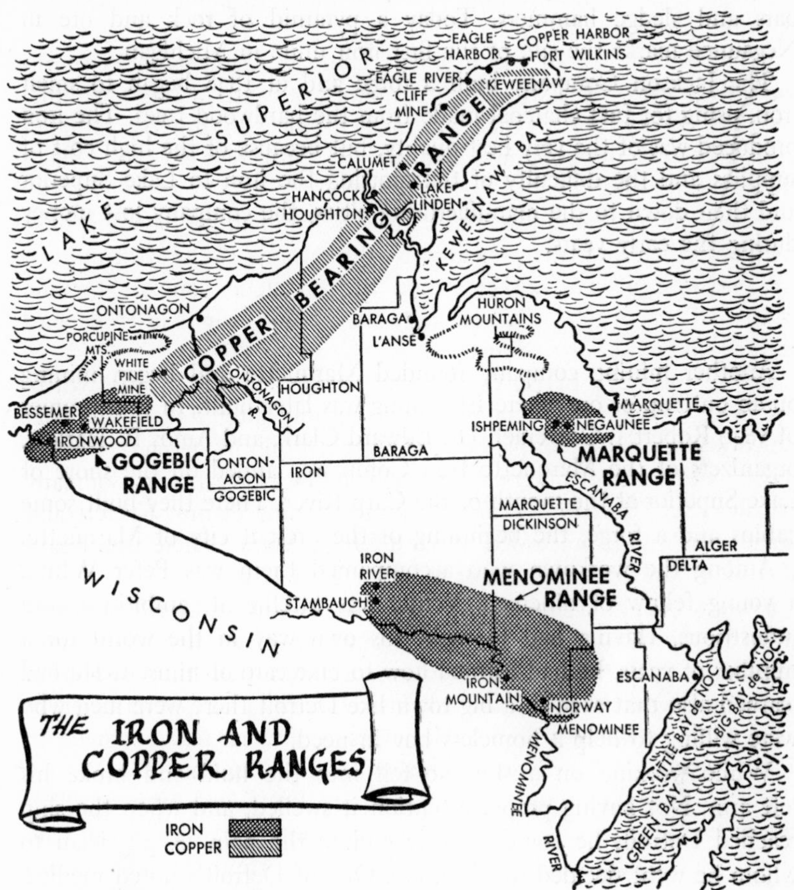

The officers gave Marji-Gesick a small share in the company in return for having guided Everett to the iron ore. Unfortunately for the chief, he forgot about the piece of paper with writing on it which he received at the time. After his death, his daughter Charlotte found it and tried to collect the money that was due. The original owners had sold their stock, and the new company refused to honor her claim. Philo M. Everett, no longer a stockholder in the Jackson Mining Company, did all he could to help her, and finally the Michigan Supreme Court decided that she was entitled to the share in the company which had been given to her father.

In 1847 the Jackson Mining Company began getting out ore. Because it was above ground, all they had to do was break it up with bars and sledge hammers. Today a pyramid of rock and ore in Negaunee marks the site of the first iron mine in Michigan.

The Jackson Company built a forge and in 1848 began to smelt iron, using for fuel charcoal made from the hardwood trees. The iron produced was of the very best quality, but because of the high cost of supplies and the difficulty of transporting the iron to Lake Superior and then down to the manufacturing cities, the company lost money during the early years.

4

Another mining company founded Marquette and began mining on an outcrop of ore where Ishpeming was later built. In the summer of 1849 Robert J. Graveraet, Dr. Edward Clark, and Amos R. Harlow, organizers of the Marquette Iron Company, landed on the shore of Lake Superior at the mouth of the Carp River. There they built some cabins and a forge, the beginning of the present city of Marquette.

Among the workmen who accompanied them was Peter White, a young fellow of nineteen. White was intelligent, ambitious, and industrious. Having had to make his own way in the world for a number of years, he had learned how to take care of himself. He had learned also that even in a big town like Detroit there were men who were willing to help a homeless boy in need.

While working on a ship he fell into the hold and broke his left arm. Not having proper attention it swelled, and when the ship reached Detroit, he could scarcely endure the pain. A physician to whom he went decided to amputate. One of Detroit's noted medical men, Dr. Zina Pitcher, happened to arrive just as the operation was about to be performed. Determined to save the arm, he took White in charge, reduced the swelling, and set the bone properly. He also found a position for him in a Detroit store. Peter White never forgot Dr. Pitcher's friendly service.

White had worked in stores in Mackinac and Detroit, he had sailed aboard lake vessels, and he had been a clerk on a lighthouse construction job. In 1849 he was at Mackinac when Robert J. Graveraet stopped there to engage men to go to the iron region. White had long been interested in the Upper Peninsula, and so he went gladly.

At first he helped break out ore from the hill two miles beyond the Jackson mine; then he took a hand in whatever work was going forward on the shore at Marquette. When the Marquette Iron Company opened a store in 1850, Peter White was put in charge. He was also mail clerk. During the winter he and two Indians carried the mail overland between Marquette and L'Anse, traveling on snowshoes through the bitter cold.

In 1853 Peter White started a bank, in 1857 he was appointed register of the land office and collector of the port, and in the same year he entered the State Legislature. To get to Lansing, he had to make the first part of his journey from Marquette to Escanaba on snowshoes. Before 1860 Peter White was a very influential person, and his influence continued to grow with the years.

5

A third company which was destined to absorb the first two, was organized in 1847. Fifteen men, including Samuel L. Mather, a young lawyer, and Dr. Morgan L. Hewitt, a physician, were incorporators of the Cleveland Iron Company, now the Cleveland-Cliffs Iron Company. Claiming the same outcropping as the Marquette Iron Company, at what is now Ishpeming, the Cleveland group appealed to the United States Government. Proof of earlier occupancy by a tenant was produced, and in 1853 the Cleveland Company took over the property from the Marquette Company. Like the others, the Cleveland Company smelted iron in forges and found it unprofitable.

To solve one of the problems, they built a plank road over the steep and rocky grades from Ishpeming to Marquette in 1855. Hauling out ore was somewhat easier, but not much. Finally, in 1857, a steam railroad constructed by Heman B. and Samuel Ely made possible the safe and rapid carrying of great quantities of ore to the loading docks at Marquette. Mining increased at both Negaunee and Ishpeming. At the latter place the Lake Superior Iron Company, organized by the Ely brothers and John Burt and his brothers, also was producing ore.

At first ore was unloaded on the docks at Marquette and hauled aboard ships in wheelbarrows, a slow and expensive process. To make the loading easier and quicker, the Cleveland Iron Company in 1859 built a new dock reaching out four hundred feet into the harbor. On the dock was built a high trestle with tracks for cars from the mines. Under the tracks huge bins caught and held ore dumped from the cars. Ships tied up beside the dock, hatch covers were removed, and ore from the bins poured down through the hatches into the holds of the ships. The new dock, and others like it, speeded the return of ore-laden ships to the furnaces on the lower Lakes.

17

Charles T. Harvey Builds the Locks

THE PEOPLE of Michigan for years had been interested in having a canal built around the rapids of the St. Mary's River so that ships might pass easily from Lake Huron to Lake Superior. Because the contractor had refused to carry out his agreement with the state in 1839, the first attempt had failed. Transportation for the increasing number of passengers and for the copper and iron which were being mined was wholly inadequate.

At first there were only two sailing vessels on Lake Superior, the *Algonquin* and the *Astor*. The latter was lost in a storm in September, 1844. The next year six schooners and the steam propeller[1] *Independence* were dragged over the portage around the Sault, and in 1846 the *Julia Palmer*, a side-wheeler, also was transferred from Lake Huron to Lake Superior in the same manner.

During the following nine years five additional ships crossed the portage. Cargoes, however, had to be unloaded, hauled overland, and

[1] This term was used to distinguish steamships driven by a screw propeller from those driven by paddlewheels.

then loaded again. A tramway built around the rapids in 1851 made the transfer easier, but ships were still compelled to load and unload.

Hoping to obtain assistance in building a canal, the state petitioned the national government. At first there was opposition in Congress to the idea. Ignorance of the need for a canal and of the geography of the region appeared in the debates. When Senator Henry Clay objected to such a project on the ground that "it is a work quite beyond the remotest settlement of the United States, if not in the moon," Senator John Norvell of Michigan informed the Senator from Kentucky that steamboats for years had been sailing to the foot of the rapids. Finally, in 1852 Congress passed an act granting 750,000 acres of public land to the state to defray the cost of construction.

Charles T. Harvey, a young man who was spending the summer at the Sault for his health, immediately became interested when he heard of the act of Congress. He had visited the mines at Negaunee and Ontonagon and had been impressed with the importance of building a canal.

Harvey was western representative of the Fairbanks Scale Company of St. Johnsbury, Vermont. Appealing to Erastus Fairbanks and Joseph P. Fairbanks, his employers, he enlisted their interest in the project. They induced other eastern capitalists to join with them, and they engaged James F. Joy of Detroit to put a suitable bill through the Michigan Legislature. The bill was passed on February 5, 1853. Two months later the bid of the associates was accepted, and they organized the St. Mary's Falls Ship Canal Company to carry out the terms of their contract with the state. The canal was to be completed in two years.

The company appointed Charles T. Harvey general agent in charge of operations. After engaging men and buying horses, tools, and supplies, he reached the Sault on June 1, 1853, and work commenced the next day. The task before him would have frightened anyone less energetic than Harvey. Miles away from sources of supply, he had to try to anticipate every need. Because shipping ceased early in the fall, it was necessary to build warehouses to hold whatever was required during the winter. Harvey built shanties, messhalls, and a hospital for the men. At one time sixteen hundred laborers were working on the canal.

Short winter days and temperatures sometimes thirty or forty degrees below zero were serious handicaps. Because much of the cut was made through solid rock, progress was slow. Equipment broke down and had to be repaired on the spot. Although the company engaged several engineers to direct the work, they were absent a great deal, and the responsibility fell upon Harvey. Every day he could be seen driving his mouse-colored pony along the line of the works, overseeing the whole job.

Under Harvey's tireless supervision, the canal was completed on time. Two locks, each 350 feet long, 70 feet wide, and 13 feet deep, raised and lowered ships from one lake to the other. The first vessels passed through in June, 1855.

The cost of supplies at the mines and the expense of shipping copper and iron ore to the manufacturing cities were drastically reduced. The result was a great increase in mine production. The shipment of iron ore in 1855 was only 1,449 tons. In 1860 it had increased to 114,401. The quantity of copper shipped increased from 5,820,000 pounds in 1855 to 11,792,000 in 1860.

The Sault Canal was operated by the state, and tolls were charged for passing through. During the first year $4,374 were collected, and in 1860, $24,660.

Harvey and other agents of the Ship Canal Company shrewdly selected some of the best timber and mineral land in the two peninsulas as compensation for building the waterway. In doing so they were simply carrying out the terms of the contract with the state, which permitted the company to select any land which had not been granted.

After having served his apprenticeship at the Sault, Harvey continued to undertake engineering projects. One of his achievements was building the first elevated railroad in New York. He lived to participate in the semicentennial waterway celebration at Sault Sainte Marie in 1905.

2

Before railroads had developed from short stub lines, connecting only two or three towns, into long-distance integrated systems, steamships were the great carriers of merchandise and of immigrants to the West. Three of the leading Michigan shipowners of this period were Oliver Newberry of Detroit and the two Wards, Captain Sam and his nephew, Eber Brock Ward. These men operated both sailing vessels and steamships, the latter equipped with luxuriously furnished cabins and salons for passengers. Both Newberry and Sam Ward had settled in Michigan in 1820. The former became a merchant in Detroit, the latter a shipbuilder at Marine City on the St. Clair River.

Newberry was a shrewd businessman, a bachelor, and somewhat

eccentric. He let his hair grow long, and his tall hat was always stuffed with bills, drafts, and banknotes. He was a man of few words, but he made his meaning clear. As his trade increased, he established his own shipyard at Detroit and built sailing vessels to carry his own and others' merchandise. His ships carried supplies to army posts, and they found profitable cargoes at various ports on the Lakes.

In 1830 Newberry had an agent at Chicago, and within a few years he had a dock and warehouses there. He built his first steamship in 1833 and named her the *Michigan*. Thereafter he built a number of steamers, all noted for their fine accommodations for passengers. He continued to be an influential shipowner until the 1850's, when the railroads took away much of the freight and passenger business.

Captain Chesley Blake was the commodore of Oliver Newberry's fleet. A giant of a man, six feet three inches tall, with broad shoulders and a deep chest, when he appeared on the pilothouse roaring out his orders as his ship came up to the wharf, he was the perfect picture of a sea captain.

Blake boasted that during forty years he had never scratched the paint on a ship nor once touched bottom. Even Newberry, who had a short temper himself, was usually careful how he issued orders to Blake. Once, after Newberry had criticized his handling of a ship, Captain Blake retaliated by sailing away while his employer was ashore on Mackinac Island. Although he frequently threatened to leave Newberry's employ, he never did.

Captain Sam Ward came to Michigan from Vermont. Settling at the mouth of the Belle River, now Marine City, he built a small schooner, the *St. Clair*, and sailed about the lakes, trading as he went. He even made one trip through the Erie Canal and down to New York. Joined by his young nephew Eber Brock Ward, he began to build steamships. One of them, the *Sam Ward*, was dragged across the Sault portage in 1853 and launched in Lake Superior. Together the Wards built fourteen steamships up to 1854, and Eber B. built twelve steamers and three propellers. They were the largest shipowners on the lakes.

Eber B. Ward was aggressive, impatient, and ambitious. He had cold blue eyes, a ruddy complexion, and an iron jaw. Always alert to new possibilities for business, he had ships ready to carry passengers across Lake Michigan when the Michigan Central Railroad reached New Buffalo. He also recognized in advance the great future for traffic on Lake Superior after the Sault Canal should be opened, and he was prepared to take a large share in it.

Realizing that the railroads which made through connections between New York and Chicago in 1852 would take passengers and freight from his steamships, he looked for new enterprises. He invested largely in timberland and sawmills, and in 1853 he organized the Eureka Iron and Steel Company. At Wyandotte the company built a blast furnace and rolling mills to make use of the iron from the Lake Superior mines.

Eber B. Ward had a sister who was a remarkable woman. Known to everyone as Aunt Emily, she brought up her brother and two sisters after their mother died. Later, she reared the children of her two sisters. Always ready to assist persons in need, she could depend upon her brother or her Uncle Sam to give as much money as she wanted for charitable purposes. At her request, Eber B. Ward built a school at Marine City, engaged a teacher, and opened it free of charge to girls selected by Aunt Emily, who served as housemother.

3

The completion of the Michigan Southern and the Michigan Central railroads, both of which reached Chicago in the summer of 1852, was a threat to the passenger business of steamships. Two years later when the Great Western, running from Buffalo to Windsor, Ontario, opposite Detroit, completed through rail connections with the East, the doom of the luxury liners was sealed. In 1855 a line passing south of Lake Erie from Buffalo to Toledo gave travelers another route to Chicago by way of the Erie and Kalamazoo and the Michigan Southern.

Other railroads were built in Michigan before 1860. One of them was the Detroit and Milwaukee, which reached Grand Haven in 1858. The third railroad to cross the state, it developed from the Pontiac and Detroit Railroad, which was chartered in 1830, but which did not reach Pontiac until 1843.

Another railroad was constructed from Detroit to Toledo in 1856 and leased to the Michigan Southern. The last in this period was the branch of the Grand Trunk from Detroit to Port Huron, which was opened in 1859. By crossing the river to Sarnia, passengers could travel through Canada to New England. The Grand Trunk was the third line making through connections between the East and Chicago.

Railroads were given assistance indirectly by the United States. In 1856 Michigan received from the national government nearly three million acres of public land to be granted in aid of railroad building in both peninsulas. By 1860, there were in the State eight hundred miles of railroad.

Railroads brought prosperity to towns and to agricultural regions as well. Nevertheless, they also aroused some hostility, which in Michigan resulted in the famous Railroad Conspiracy Case tried in Detroit in 1851.

Farmers along the line of the Michigan Central Railroad, especially between Grass Lake and Jackson, were bitterly antagonistic to the

Attack on a Michigan Central Train, Grass Lake

management. Because neither the railroad right of way nor the fields were fenced, cattle, horses, hogs, and sheep wandered onto the tracks and were killed. The railroad company refused to pay more than half the value of the animals, and farmers who were not satisfied had to sue in the courts.

Hostility toward the railroad company became so strong that those who considered themselves unfairly treated began to place obstructions on the tracks, tear up the rails, and shoot at the train crews. Traveling on the Michigan Central became so dangerous that passenger traffic declined. Among those who carried on these attacks were some of the leading citizens of the region, and Abel F. Fitch, who was believed to be the head of the conspiracy, was a well-to-do farmer of Michigan Center.

Early in the morning on November 19, 1850, the freight depot of the Michigan Central in Detroit burned. Convinced that Fitch and his neighbors were responsible, the company sent out detectives, who brought charges against forty-four men. They were arrested, jailed in Detroit, and put on trial in May, 1851. Eminent lawyers engaged by the Michigan Central assisted the state in the prosecution, and the defendants retained William H. Seward of New York as their chief counsel.

Continuing through the summer months, this celebrated trial ended in September with the conviction of twelve men, who were sentenced to prison terms of from five to ten years. Fitch, who was accused of plotting the destruction of the depot, died during the trial. There is no doubt that he was active in the attacks on the trains, but many believed that the testimony linking him with the fire was perjured.

Although the trial put an end to attacks on the trains, hatred of the Michigan Central continued unabated for many years. Other buildings were burned, but, though officials believed that friends of Fitch were responsible, none of them was ever arrested.

Before the Civil War, manufacturing was not of primary importance in the economy of Michigan. The 1860 census reported the capital invested in manufacturing, including flour and sawmills, as only $35,303,590, and the number of employes as 22,827. The value of manufactured goods produced was $33,068,071.

Detroit, of course, was the principal industrial center. It had steam sawmills, foundries, and machine shops, and manufactured steam engines, agricultural implements, steam boilers, stoves, furniture, and chemicals.

In Port Huron there were shipyards, lumber mills, and foundries. Saginaw had five sawmills and Bay City fifteen. In Flint there were lumber mills, one foundry, one machine shop, and a company making sashes, blinds, and doors. The principal industry of Grand Rapids was the production of stucco and plaster from gypsum dug in the pits not far from town. There were also small machine shops, a wagon works, a pottery, and a woolen factory. Kalamazoo manufactured carriages, mill equipment, steam engines, stoves, pianos, and melodeons. Before 1860 most of the products were sold within the state. Factories were small. The owner was usually the manager, and he worked along with his employes.

4

During this period the wealth of the state was largely in the farms and their products. Most of the work was still done by hand even though some machinery had been invented. Agricultural magazines advertised mowing machines for cutting hay, reapers for harvesting grain, and threshing machines powered by a horse walking on a treadmill.

Inventors were busy trying to produce machinery for large-scale farming. Many were building reapers. Cyrus H. McCormick patented one in 1834, and Hiram Moore another two years later. Moore lived in Climax, Kalamazoo County. A young lawyer, John Hascall, was associated with him in his work, and Lucius Lyon invested money in it.

The machine was given a trial in Lyon's wheat fields on Prairie Ronde near Schoolcraft during the summer of 1839. A huge unwieldy contraption, it required sixteen or eighteen horses to move it. It was really a combine; that is, as it rolled across the field, it cut off the heads of the wheat, threshed out the grain, and collected it in bags. With this machine a farmer could harvest twenty to thirty acres a day. Unfortunately, it broke down too frequently to make its operation highly profitable.

Moore continued to tinker with the machine as long as Lyon was able to provide money for experiments. Patent suits between Moore and McCormick were expensive, and finally Lyon was unable to contribute further cash. Moore gave up, but by 1850 McCormick was producing harvesters on a large scale in his Chicago factory.

In spite of the inventions which have been mentioned, few farmers used them during this period. They were expensive, and farmers had little cash to spend. The age-old practice of agricultural production by simple implements in the hands of men and boys continued for many years.

There were journals for the farmer who wanted to learn new and better methods of doing his work. The first published in Michigan was the *Western Farmer*, which appeared in Detroit on January 20, 1841. After several changes of ownership it became the *Michigan Farmer*. This journal, sometimes issued monthly and sometimes semimonthly, contained a great variety of information for the farmer and his wife. New practices which had proved successful in Europe or in America were described in detail.

How to make use of waste products, for example the pressing of lamp oil from pumpkin seeds, was a feature of the magazine. Although the editor did not express an opinion about the matter, he did publish a letter from a man in Lapeer County who told of making silk from the cocoons of silkworms and urged other Michiganians to engage in the profitable business of silk culture. There was always a women's section in the *Farmer* with recipes, hints about clothing, and even instructions on table manners.

How many farmers' wives read this or any other journal cannot be known. Some undoubtedly did, and one wrote a long complaint in verse, beginning:

> It's work, work, work, the livelong day,
> No rest from toil, no time for play,
> Altho' we're up before the sun,
> 'Tis nine at night e're work is done.

The editor of the *Michigan Farmer* printed it above her pseudonym, "Ann of the Farm."

Some men also recognized the hardships of a farmer's wife and the narrowness of her sphere. The writer of an article which appeared in the *Michigan Farmer* in 1852 asserted:

> The life of the farmer's wife is one of confinement and unremitting toil. From early dawn until late at night it is nothing but mend and botch,[2] cook and bake, wash and sweep, churn and make cheese, wait upon her husband and his band of laborers, bear children and nurse them. No time for relaxation or enjoyment, or the improvement of her mental or social faculties is found. As the means of the farmer and his family increases, the *husband* becomes more noticed, and his circle of acquaintances and friends enlarges; he daily meets his associates and mingles with the world, but his wife toils on in the old dull routine, with nothing to break in upon the monotony of her existence, except perhaps the advent of another child, or the death of one to whom her heart is bound in the strongest ties.

This is probably a pretty accurate picture of the dreary life of women on the farms of Michigan. In spite of hardships, many of them had hope for the future; and they inspired their children with the will to improve their condition.

[2] Patch.

— 18 —

Politics, Immigration, and Education

GOVERNOR JOHN S. BARRY'S two terms in office ended in 1845. Another Democrat, Alpheus Felch of Ann Arbor, was elected to succeed him. A native of Maine and a graduate of Bowdoin College, Felch had come to Michigan in 1833 and settled in Monroe. Ten years later he removed to Ann Arbor. Before he was elected governor, he had already served the state as a member of the Legislature, as bank commissioner, as auditor general, and as a justice in the supreme court.

During his first year in office the Mexican War began, and the War Department sent him a requisition for ten companies of volunteers to be ready when the President should ask for them. Thirteen companies were easily raised, but none of them was called except the Brady Guards of Detroit, who were sent to relieve the regulars at Mackinac and Fort Brady.

Finally, in October, 1847, the President called for a regiment of volunteers, which reached Mexico after hostilities had ceased. Company K of the Third Dragoons, in which Lewis Cass, Jr., was a major, and three companies of the Fifteenth United States Infantry, all from Michigan, took part in the battles around Mexico City.

In 1847 the Legislature elected Governor Felch United States senator, and the lieutenant governor, William L. Greenly, served in his place. After completing his term in the Senate, Felch was sent to California as a commissioner to examine land claims, and from 1879 to 1883 he was Tappan Professor of Law in the University of Michigan. He died in Ann Arbor in 1896 at the age of ninety-two.

In 1847 the Legislature took up the problem of permanently locating the state capital as provided by the constitution. The people of Detroit wanted to retain it, but most of the legislators believed

Building the First State Capitol, 1847

that it should be moved to a more central place. Many towns lobbied vigorously to have the capital established within their limits. Local pride made agreement on any one of them impossible.

After long debate and a great deal of parliamentary maneuvering, the Legislature voted to place the capital "in the township of Lansing in the County of Ingham." There was not even a log cabin on the site. A capitol building was quickly erected, and the Legislature in 1848 met in the new town. It was at first called Michigan, but after a few months the name was changed to Lansing.

In the election of 1847, Epaphroditus Ransom, a Democrat of Kalamazoo, was chosen governor. He had been an associate justice of the state supreme court from 1836–1842 and chief justice since 1843.

Governor Ransom was a great believer in the benefits to be derived from plank roads. During his administration he signed charters providing for the incorporation of about fifty plank road companies.

These roads were made of oak planks three inches thick laid crosswise on heavy stringers, or directly on the ground. Warping of the planks made the roadbed uneven, and rotting of the wood made it dangerous to horses. The Detroit and Pontiac, the Detroit and Saline, and the Detroit and Howell were the most important plank roads. The chartered companies set up toll gates where fees were collected for the use of the road—two cents a mile for two-horse vehicles and one cent for those drawn by one horse. Toll roads were operated by private corporations for many years, but gravel for surfacing was later substituted for the unsatisfactory planks.

Lewis Cass was the Democratic candidate for President in 1848. He had resigned as territorial governor of Michigan in 1831 to become Secretary of War in President Jackson's Cabinet, where he remained until 1836, when he was named minister to France. He gave up that position in 1842 and returned to Michigan. In 1845 the Legislature elected him United States senator. He resigned in 1848 to run for the Presidency.

General Zachary Taylor of Louisiana was nominated by the Whigs. Both parties were threatened with destruction by the problem of slavery in the new region acquired by the Mexican War. Some demanded that slavery be excluded; others that it be protected by the national government; and Cass, in his famous Nicholson letter of December 24, 1847, favored permitting the people of each territory to decide for themselves whether they would have slavery or not.

This doctrine was given the name of "popular sovereignty" or "squatter sovereignty," and Cass was held up to scorn by antislavery men as a compromiser whose only purpose was to gain southern votes. Such an interpretation was unfair. It is true that Cass wanted to be President, but he had always believed in permitting the people to make decisions on important local matters for themselves, a belief which he had consistently practiced while governor of Michigan Territory.

In New York a faction of the Democratic party under the leadership of Martin Van Buren, called by their opponents "Barnburners," refused to accept Cass as the nominee. They joined with the antislavery Free-Soil party, which nominated Van Buren for President. Michigan gave its electoral vote to Cass, but enough votes were cast for Van Buren in New York to throw that state and the election to Taylor.

Cass was sent to the Senate again in 1849 and 1851. Named Secretary of State by President Buchanan, he held that post until December 14, 1860, when he resigned because he could not agree with the President's policy of permitting the southern states to secede without attempting to preserve the Union.

2

The State Legislature in 1849 decided to place on the fall ballot the question of revising the constitution. A large majority voted for a revision. At the same time John S. Barry was again elected governor, the only man in the nineteenth century to hold the office three times.

The Constitutional Convention met in Lansing on June 3, 1850, and the voters in November, by a huge majority, approved the constitution which it drew up. An amendment submitted separately at the same time, which would have given Negroes the suffrage, was rejected by a vote of 32,000 to 12,000.

The new constitution differed from that of 1835 in many respects. One can see at a glance that it is twice as long. The greater length was the result of incorporating in the document many restrictions on the powers of the legislature and the governor. For example, stock in any corporation engaged in building internal improvements must not be purchased; no special laws might be passed chartering corporations; banking laws would take effect only after a majority of the people had voted their approval; laws for suspending specie payment were prohibited; and borrowing in the name of the state was to be limited to a total of $50,000.

Salaries of state officers were set at a very low figure, $1,000 a year, for instance, for the governor, and might not be increased except by amending the constitution. This, of course, was a foolish provision which caused a great deal of trouble; but it reflected the lack of confidence which the people had in their representatives. Some of the other restrictions, however, were wise, based as they were on unhappy experiences during the previous fifteen years.

The legislature was to be elected biennially in even-numbered years instead of annually, and biennial sessions were provided for.

The powers of the governor were reduced. All state officers, including judges and the Regents of the University, were to be elected; and the governor was made ineligible to receive any appointment to office from the legislature during the term for which he had been elected. This was to prevent him from resigning to become, for example, a United States senator.

The constitution of 1850 contained no separate bill of rights, but the liberties of individuals were protected by provisions scattered through the document. Demands for the recognition of women's rights resulted in a clause which gave to married women complete control of any property they had acquired before their marriage.

In order to satisfy the demand by prohibitionists that the sale of liquor be forbidden, the Convention adopted the following section: "The Legislature shall not pass any act authorizing the grant of license for the sale of ardent spirits or intoxicating liquors." Instead of prohibiting the trade, this clause resulted in the unregulated sale of liquor.

In addition to white male citizens over twenty-one years of age, aliens who had declared their intention to become citizens of the United States and civilized male Indians were given the suffrage.

Free schools were to be maintained for at least three months each year, beginning five years after the adoption of the constitution. In spite of this provision, it was only in Detroit that there were really free schools, for rate bills were still collected elsewhere. A novel feature was the requirement, the first in any state constitution, that the legislature establish an agricultural college. This constitution was the fundamental law of Michigan until January 1, 1909.

Michigan had come a long way from the Panic of 1837, the financial troubles of the succeeding years, and the abandonment of the internal-improvement program. When the new constitution was adopted, the state was out of debt. The treasurer's report in December, 1850, showed a cash balance of $36,057.85. Two years later the surplus had increased to $116,555.21. It was used to help redeem the internal-improvement bonds.

The first governor elected under the constitution of 1850 was Robert McClelland of Monroe, a Democrat. He was a native of Pennsylvania and a graduate of Dickinson College who had come to Michigan in 1833. A member of both constitutional conventions, he had been also three times a representative in the legislature, and a member of Congress for six years.

The constitution had provided that the governor elected in 1851 should serve for only one year in order to move the state election to the even years. In the election of 1852 Governor McClelland ran again and defeated Zachariah Chandler, a merchant of Detroit who had recently entered politics. In March, 1853, President Franklin Pierce appointed McClelland Secretary of the Interior, and he resigned to join the President's Cabinet. Lieutenant Governor Andrew Parsons completed the term of office.

3

Up to this time the Democrats in Michigan had won every election except in 1839, but the antislavery agitation in the North was bringing about the dissolution of both the Whig and the Democratic parties, and a new national party, born in Michigan, was about to make its appearance.

In Michigan and some other northern states the Liberty party had nominated James G. Birney for President in 1840. In 1841 he became a resident of Bay City, Michigan, and ran for governor in 1843, polling 2,776 votes. Michigan gave him 3,632 votes in the presidential election of 1844.

The strong abolitionist stand of the Liberty party alienated the more conservative antislavery people, and it was replaced in the election of 1848 by the Free-Soil party, which opposed the extension of slavery into the territories. Van Buren received 10,389 votes in Michigan as the Free-Soil candidate.

The growing strength of the opposition in Michigan to the extension of slavery was shown in 1849 when the same Legislature which elected Cass senator passed resolutions directing him and Senator Felch to support the Wilmot Proviso.[1] Cass's threat to resign rather than to vote for that measure caused an about-face in the Legislature, which gave him and his colleague freedom of action to maintain and promote the best interests and the tranquility of the nation.

The Compromise of 1850 was the cause of further discord. Michigan, like other northern states, passed personal-liberty laws to protect Negroes against the stringent Fugitive Slave Act which was a part of the Compromise. State officers were forbidden to assist United States officers in apprehending alleged escaped slaves, county jails were ordered not to receive them as prisoners, prosecuting attorneys were

[1] The Wilmot Proviso was an amendment offered by Representative David Wilmot of Pennsylvania in 1846 to a bill appropriating money to buy territory from Mexico. The amendment would have prohibited slavery in the region acquired from Mexico. Cass believed that the inhabitants of a territory had the right to decide whether they wanted slavery or not. The amendment was frequently debated, but it was not passed.

required to defend them when they were taken to court, and they could not be given up unless two witnesses swore to their identity.

The attack on slavery became a moral crusade in which the Protestant churches took a leading part. Congregationalists, Methodists, Baptists, and Presbyterians denounced slavery as a crime and a sin. The last three denominations, because they had many churches both in the North and the South, split into regional organizations on the question—the Presbyterians in 1837, the Methodists in 1844, and the Baptists in 1845. In Michigan, Ohio, New York, and Pennsylvania, the more radical Methodists, impatient at the delay in breaking with slaveholders, seceded from the denomination several years before the national breach and formed the Wesleyan Methodist Church (in Michigan in 1841).

During the 1840's and 1850's many persons in Michigan were active agents of the Underground Railway. Reaching from the Ohio River to Canada, this organization assisted escaped slaves to avoid capture by their masters. In every town of the southern tiers of counties, men and women hid Negroes in their houses or barns, fed and clothed them, and passed them along secretly to the next station. The Quakers were particularly active in the Underground.

Although both Democrats and Whigs had left their parties to vote with the Free-Soilers, the Whigs suffered the greater loss. Both of the old parties tried to keep their members in line, but in 1854 the passage of the Kansas-Nebraska Act, nullifying the Missouri Compromise and opening the new territories to slavery, united the anti-slavery elements of both parties.

A convention assembled in Jackson on July 6, 1854, composed of anti-Nebraska Whigs, anti-Nebraska Democrats, and Free-Soilers. The leaders were Kinsley S. Bingham, Hovey C. Clarke, Isaac P. Christiancy, and other Democrats; and Zachariah Chandler, David S. Walbridge, Jacob M. Howard, and other Whigs. Because the assemblage was too large for any hall, meetings were held outdoors under the oaks. The convention passed resolutions to fight the extension of slavery and to adopt the name Republican for the new party. They nominated a slate of candidates for all state officers, headed by Kinsley S. Bingham of Livingston County, for governor. This was the first state-wide convention of the Republican party.

In the fall election the Democrats nominated John S. Barry, who already had served three terms. He was defeated by Bingham, and the Republican ticket was elected, including a majority of the state senators and representatives, and three of the four United States representatives. From 1854 onward Michigan was almost solidly Republican, electing only two Democratic governors, Winans in 1890 and Ferris in 1912 and 1914, until 1932. In presidential elections Michigan never gave all her electoral votes to a Democrat from 1856 until 1932.

Governor Bingham had come to Michigan from New York and taken up land in Livingston County in 1833. He had served in the state legislature from 1837 to 1842 and in the United States House of Representatives from 1846 to 1850 as a Democrat. Strongly opposed to slavery, he had voted for the Wilmot Proviso. It was during Bingham's term of office that the Republican legislature passed the personal-liberty law. Governor Bingham was re-elected in 1856, and John C. Frémont, the Republican nominee for President, received a majority of the popular vote in Michigan.

A feature of the national campaign of 1856 was the Republican rally for Frémont in Kalamazoo at which Abraham Lincoln of Illinois was one of the speakers. Although he had been a member of Congress, at the time he was not well known outside his own state. On this occasion his attack on slavery was so moderate that many in the audience were displeased, and Zachariah Chandler was completely disgusted with Lincoln.

When Lewis Cass resigned from the Senate to enter President Buchanan's Cabinet in 1857, the Legislature chose the Republican Zachariah Chandler as his successor; and in 1858, Moses Wisner of Pontiac, a Republican, was elected governor. In 1859 ex-Governor Bingham was sent to the Senate as Chandler's colleague.

In the election of 1860 in Michigan, Lincoln received 87,457 votes; Douglas, 66,163; Breckenridge, 805; and Bell, 373. Austin Blair, a lawyer of Jackson, was elected governor.

4

The population in 1840 was 212,267; in 1850, 341,591; and in 1860, 749,113. Most of the people were descendants of the original Canadians, immigrants from Canada, and newcomers from New England, New York, and other eastern states, with some from Ohio, Indiana, and farther south.

Immigration from Europe on a large scale began in the 1830's and continued in great numbers thereafter. The largest group was from the British Isles. The English and the Scots mixed rather easily with the native elements because they spoke the same language. The Irish, of course, had the same language, but being poor, as a rule, they settled in cities where at first they worked as laborers, or they found jobs digging canals and building railroads. They were clannish, tending to live together. The potato famine of 1845 sent thousands of Irish men and women to the United States. Many came to Michigan. A number were engaged in fishing on the west coat around Charlevoix before 1860.

One group from England should be especially mentioned—the Cornishmen who were brought to the Upper Peninsula to be captains and workers in the copper mines. Known as Cousin Jacks, they played an important part in the development of the mineral regions.

The Germans were the next largest group of European birth. A few had settled in Michigan during the British regime, and others had joined them. By 1833 there were sufficient Germans in Ann Arbor and on the surrounding farms to support a pastor. In answer to a request to the homeland, the Reverend Frederick Schmid was sent to them in that year. He established and served Lutheran churches in Washtenaw, Wayne, and Monroe counties.

Most of the Germans were farmers with sufficient money to purchase land of their own. Others worked as hired hands until they had saved enough money to buy forty or eighty acres. There were also among the German immigrants skilled artisans who settled in the cities.

The Reverend Mr. Schmid had a hand in the settling of the Saginaw Valley. Asked for advice by a Lutheran minister in Germany who wanted to come to Michigan to carry on missionary work among the Indians, he suggested the Saginaw country, which he had visited at various times. As a result, the Reverend August Craemer in 1845 led a party of fifteen from Franconia in Bavaria to a spot on the Cass River where he founded Frankenmuth.

Other congregations came out under the leadership of their ministers and founded Frankentrost in 1847, Frankenlust in 1848, and Frankenhulf in 1851. These people, like those in Washtenaw and Monroe counties, were sturdy and prosperous farmers. So desirable did they seem to be as residents of Michigan that the Legislature appropriated public lands to raise funds to build roads into the Saginaw country.

Another agricultural settlement of Germans was founded in Clinton County about twenty-five miles northwest of Lansing. Under the leadership of the Reverend Anton Kopp, a small group of Catholics from Westphalia established a settlement with that name in 1836. Their struggle to make a home in the wilderness was more difficult than that of their fellow countrymen who have been mentioned, for the Westphalians were very poor, and the land that they acquired was practically cut off from the settled parts of the state. As in the other regions, new immigrants from Germany were attracted to Westphalia.

Another wave of German immigrants came to the United States and Michigan as the result of the unsuccessful revolution of 1848. Many of the leaders were intellectuals who settled in cities. Detroit received a number, of whom Dr. Herman Kiefer was the most notable. He was a physician, a civic leader, and a Regent of the University of Michigan.

These Germans brought their culture with them. In Detroit they organized the Harmonie Society in 1849, devoted to choral music; the Socialer Turnverein in 1853, for physical development and political discussion; and the Theater-Verein also in 1853, for the production of German comedies and dramas. They also established several newspapers. Although the Germans soon became Americanized, they continued to contribute a great deal to the development of social life, especially in music, art, and the drama.

In 1846 the first Dutch colony came to Michigan. Under the leadership of the Reverend Albertus C. Van Raalte, his wife, their five children, and fifty-three followers left the Netherlands in October, 1846, for America. Most of them were poor people suffering from adverse agricultural conditions. As dissenters from the state church, they were also fleeing from religious persecution.

Van Raalte intended to settle in Wisconsin, but he and his flock stopped in Detroit for the winter. There, some leading citizens, becoming interested in this sturdy band of immigrants, induced him to remain in Michigan. Some of the men worked at Marine City helping to build one of Eber B. Ward's steamships.

In the spring Van Raalte established his settlement at the mouth of the Black River, the beginning of the city of Holland. There was much similarity between this colony and that of the Pilgrims who had settled Plymouth more than two hundred years earlier. The newcomers suffered hardships and want because of the unfamiliar surroundings. Again, at first all property was held in common, and all sorts of problems were decided in church meetings. Like the Pilgrims, they found that the communal system was not satisfactory and changed to individual ownership. These Hollanders were eager to provide an education for their children. In 1851 they founded an academy which became Hope College.

Other ministers, bringing their congregations with them, founded Zeeland, Vriesland, and Overisel. In addition, Grand Rapids, Grand Haven, Muskegon, and Kalamazoo became notable as centers of Dutch population. These people, while retaining many of their Old World customs, soon became loyal Americans, and contributed another element to our national culture.

In 1848 the Legislature appropriated four thousand acres of internal-improvement land, of which the proceeds were to be used for building a pier at the mouth of the Black River, and three thousand more to build roads into the Dutch settlements.

5

In spite of the fact that many foreigners came to Michigan after 1840, there was much vacant land to be sold, and it was believed that other states were attracting many who would have settled in Michigan if they had known of the opportunities awaiting them. To remedy this condition, the Legislature in 1845 provided for an agent to prepare a pamphlet in English and German, and go to New York. There, with the aid of an interpreter, he would try to direct desirable immigrants to Michigan. John Almy of Grand Rapids was appointed to the position. He published a pamphlet, distributed five thousand copies in Europe through United States consuls and emigration societies, and placed several thousand more in the hands of immigrants in New York. Because funds for only one year had been appropriated, the office was discontinued.

In 1849 the Legislature again provided for an immigration agent in New York. Edward H. Thompson of Flint, who was appointed, prepared a booklet of forty-seven pages in German and English entitled *The Emigrant's Guide to the State of Michigan* or *Des Auswanderers Wegweiser nach dem Staate Michigan*. One edition of seven thousand copies was published at state expense, and a second of the same number was paid for by Saginaw County. As a result land sales in the Saginaw Valley greatly increased. Thompson's appointment was for only one year, but a commissioner of immigration was provided for again in 1859 and 1860. The outbreak of the Civil War caused the abandonment of the office for ten years.

6

There was another group settlement in Michigan in 1847. The people were not foreigners; they were Mormons, and their peculiar customs aroused antagonisms which led to their destruction. The leader of the colony was James J. Strang, a follower of Joseph Smith, who had founded the Church of Jesus Christ of Latter-day Saints, generally known as the Mormon Church. When Smith was assassinated in 1844, Strang attempted to become his successor; but Brigham Young got control of the organization and led the majority of the Mormons to Utah.

Strang first founded the settlement of Voree in Wisconsin for those who accepted him as their leader; then, in 1847, he established his headquarters on Beaver Island in Lake Michigan, whither he had been directed, he asserted, by a revelation from God. There he developed a communal economy centered about the religious organization.

A revelation from God in 1849 commanded Strang to institute the practice of polygamy. In obedience to the command, Strang, who already had a wife, married another. He continued adding wives to his household until he had five.

The Lord also revealed to Strang that he should rule on earth as God's viceroy; and so on July 8, 1850, with great ceremony, Strang, wearing a red robe, was crowned king in his capital of St. James. It is interesting to notice that the "king" accepted election to the offices of justice of the peace and township supervisor under Michigan law, and served two terms in the Michigan legislature from 1852 until 1856. At Lansing he was regarded as a very capable legislator.

Trouble with the Irish fishermen on the mainland opposite Beaver Island led to charges by his enemies that he was guilty of counterfeiting, trespass on United States lands, treason, and robbery of the mails. The USS *Michigan* appeared at the wharf of St. James in May, 1851. Strang and thirty-one of his followers were arrested, taken to Detroit, and tried in the federal court. Serving as attorney for himself and the others, he won acquittal for all of them. Even the Detroit newspapers, which were hostile to the Mormons, commented favorably on his ability as a lawyer.

Strang's autocratic rule aroused the hatred of some of his followers. One, who believed that he had been injured by the "king," plotted his death, and used an officer of the United States Navy to accomplish his purpose. By previous arrangement, the USS *Michigan* called at St. James on June 16, 1856, and the captain summoned Strang to come aboard. Two assassins, who were lying in wait, shot him as he stepped upon the wharf. Then they fled aboard the ship, which carried them to Mackinac Island where they were permitted to go free.

Strang, who had been mortally wounded, was removed to Voree, where he died on July 9, 1856. Mobs from the mainland raided the island, attacked the Mormons, herded them on ships, and sent them away. Then they took or destroyed their property. Today on Beaver Island, St. James, Lake Geneserath, and the King's Highway are names which remain to recall the rule in Michigan of King James I.

7

In spite of laws and land grants, the common schools in Michigan made little progress before 1860. Detroit alone, beginning in 1842, had free schools. Its board of education opened the first high school in 1844 in the old University Building on Bates Street, but it continued for only a short time. In 1848 the old Capitol on Griswold Street was acquired by the city and used to house a union school, that is, a graded school. In 1858 high-school classes were added. The enrollment at first was only twenty-three—all boys, for girls were not admitted until 1860. In view of the strong abolition sentiment in Michigan during the ten or fifteen years before the Civil War, it is an interesting fact that in 1839 a separate school was provided for Negroes, and they were not permitted to attend school with white children until 1869.

Secondary education, as a rule, could be had only in private academies and, for a time, in the nine branches of the University. When state support was withdrawn from the branches in 1846, some closed, but others were kept as private schools. The one in Kalamazoo, which had opened in 1836 as the Michigan and Huron Institute, continued as the Kalamazoo Literary Institute. The principal, the Reverend James A. B. Stone, was a very capable educator; and his wife, Lucinda Hinsdale Stone, an unusually gifted woman, conducted a female seminary in conjunction with the Institute. In 1855 it obtained a charter from the Legislature incorporating it as Kalamazoo College. Most of the founders were Baptists.

A Baptist college was the first in Michigan to grant academic degrees to women. Michigan Central College, which was established at Spring Arbor, near Jackson, in 1844, in 1851 awarded degrees to several women graduates. It removed from Spring Arbor and opened in 1855 at Hillsdale as Hillsdale College.

Other denominations also sponsored colleges. Wesleyan Seminary, opened at Albion in 1843 by the Methodists, became Albion College. Olivet was founded in 1844 by Congregationalists from Oberlin College in Ohio. Like its parent institution it was strongly abolitionist, and it was considered very radical.

When the educational system of the state had been planned, the expectation was that sufficient teachers for the common schools would be prepared in the branches of the University. The abandonment of the branches by the Regents in 1846 for lack of funds soon led to a demand for a state-supported school to train teachers. As a result, the Legislature in 1849 provided for the Michigan State Normal School under the management of the State Board of Education.

Ypsilanti was chosen as the site of the school, and the people of the town provided a three-story brick building finished with stucco. Dedication ceremonies were held on October 5, 1852. The Reverend John D. Pierce delivered the address, and Isaac E. Crary, president of the Board of Education and partner with Pierce in founding the school system of the state, pronounced words of dedication.

Adonijah S. Welch was principal of the Normal School. The first activity was the holding of a teachers' institute, which was attended by 250 teachers of the state. At the close of the institute the Michigan State Teachers' Association was organized. Classes in the Normal School were first held on March 29, 1853.

The Legislature in 1855, urged to action by the Michigan Agricultural Society, passed an act for establishing Michigan Agricultural College. A site was selected in the country nearly four miles from Lansing. In a heavily wooded area a clearing was made and three brick buildings were erected. One contained an auditorium, laboratories, and classrooms; the second was the dormitory; and the third was the barn. They were completed early in 1857, and the college was opened with dedication ceremonies on May 13. It was the first state college of agriculture in the United States.

By the act of the Legislature, the college was under the Board of Education, which governed the State Normal School. At the dedication, Hiram L. Miller, president of the Board, spoke briefly. He was followed by President Joseph R. Williams of Constantine, who delivered an address on the need for a college of agriculture. The final speaker was Governor Kinsley S. Bingham, himself a successful farmer. The governor in his speech emphasized the great opportunities for educated young farmers.

The entering class consisted of sixty-one men. Tuition was free to residents of the state, but students had to pay for board and books. They were able to earn a large share of expenses because each was required to work on the farm three or four hours a day, besides attending classes. The rate of pay was ten cents an hour. At first most of the work consisted in felling trees and pulling stumps to prepare the land for crops.

President Williams and five others were the faculty. The president was originally a Massachusetts man and a graduate of Harvard. The courses included English, chemistry, botany, animal and vegetable physiology, entomology, geology, and veterinary arts.

The college made little progress during the early years. Because much of the land was swamp, mosquitoes flourished and students became ill with ague. Ditching eventually eliminated the disease. Inadequate funds were also a handicap. Dominated by farmers, many of whom believed that providing book learning was a waste of tax money, the Legislature at first appropriated too little toward the support of the institution. The growth of the college really began during the period after the Civil War.

The University of Michigan grew slowly. Although the South Wing, exactly like the North Wing, or Mason Hall, had been built in 1849, the enrollment in the Literary College in 1851–1852 was only 57. There were during the same year, however, 127 students in the Medical School, which had opened in its own building in 1850.

Dr. Zina Pitcher, one of the Regents, was largely responsible for the founding of the Medical School. In keeping with the practices of other similar institutions of the time, the requirements for entrance were easy to meet. Degrees were conferred upon students who attended two six-month courses of lectures, presented a thesis on a medical subject, and passed the final examinations. They must also have served an apprenticeship with a physician for three years.

One of the reasons for the unsatisfactory condition of the University was lack of a permanent head. Each year the faculty of each college elected one of the members to take charge. Under these circumstances there could be no continuing policy, and the institution simply drifted along.

The new state constitution required the Regents to choose a president, and in 1852 they appointed the Reverend Henry Philip Tappan of New York. Dr. Tappan had taught in the University of New York City, and he had published books on philosophy. Having studied the educational systems of Europe, he believed that the Prussian system was the best. He knew that the Reverend John D. Pierce had used that system as a model in organizing the schools of Michigan, and he was eager for the opportunity to put the theory into practice.

The Literary College had only the classical course taught by the recitation method as in high schools and academies. In this, Michigan was following the current American custom, for the universities in the East used the same practice. President Tappan was determined to develop a real university. To the classical course he added a scientific course leading to the degree of bachelor of science, and a "partial course" for those who wanted to select their own subjects without seeking a degree. He also planned to organize advanced work for graduates.

Believing that an astronomical observatory was necessary for the University, President Tappan raised the money for it largely by appeals to wealthy persons in Detroit. Then, resolved to have the best equipment possible, he went to Berlin, where he purchased a telescope. He also engaged Professor Franz Brünnow to teach astronomy. The observatory was ready for use in 1854.

To further the President's purpose of increasing scientific instruction, the Regents in 1853 appointed Alexander Winchell professor of physics and civil engineering. Three years later the chemical laboratory was erected.

When President Tappan took office, there were, in addition to the four faculty houses, three buildings on the campus: North Wing (Mason Hall), South Wing (1849), and the Medical Building (1850). Because the President wanted rooms for a library and for fine arts and natural history collections, in 1856 he abolished the dormitory system and sent the students to live in town.

The Law School opened in 1859. The first faculty consisted of Justice James V. Campbell of the state supreme court, Thomas M. Cooley, soon to be elected to that court, and Charles I. Walker, a Detroit attorney. To enter, a student had to be at least eighteen years old, and he had to present a certificate of good moral character. To qualify for a degree, he had to attend two terms of lectures of six months each.

By 1860, the University had made notable progress under the guidance of President Tappan, and he was making the alumni and the people of the state proud of the institution.

8

Throughout the country, the period from 1830 to 1860 was marked by much agitation for the reform of various existing conditions. The reform movement in the North that attracted the most attention and aroused the greatest bitterness was the antislavery crusade which has already been discussed.

There were numerous organizations working for temperance in the use of liquor or for prohibition of its manufacture and sale. Maine became legally dry in 1846, and Ohio in 1850. The denial to the Michigan Legislature of the power to license liquor establishments written into the constitution of 1850 was the result of pressure by groups throughout the state. When it was found that this provision permitted liquor dealers to operate without control, a prohibition law was demanded.

The Legislature in 1853 passed an act forbidding the manufacture or sale of liquor in the state and laid it before the people in the fall election. A majority voted favorably, but the supreme court held the law unconstitutional because it had been adopted by referendum. A law passed in 1855 was not enforced, and it was repealed in 1875.

Another field for reform was women's rights. Demands were made for equal educational opportunities for women, for equal suffrage, and for the right to control their own property. Admission to the University was denied until 1870, but the constitution of 1850 gave married women the right to use or to dispose of their own property without the consent of their husbands.

During this period labor was organizing to some extent and demanding higher wages, shorter hours, better working conditions, free schools, and the repeal of laws that sent men to prison because they could not pay their debts. The first strike in Michigan occurred in 1837 when carpenters paraded the streets of Detroit with banners bearing the jingle "Ten hours a day, And two dollars for pay." In spite of such protests, long hours and small wages continued to be the rule; but in 1839 the Legislature abolished imprisonment for debt, except in case of fraud.

Besides the carpenters' union, which has been mentioned, printers, stonecutters, and iron molders were organized before 1860. The Panic of 1857, however, practically wiped out the unions, and they had to begin all over again.

9

The period 1837 to 1860 was an important one in the development of Michigan. Population increased enormously. For the first time settlers included thousands of people directly from Europe, especially from the British Isles, Germany, and Holland.

There was a marked improvement in transportation. Plank roads, although they had some undesirable features, were preferable to ruts and mudholes. Better still, there were three railroads which crossed the state. Besides, after 1852 it was possible to go quickly by rail either to New York or Chicago. Perhaps the most remarkable feature of all was the Sault Canal, which made easily available the mineral wealth of the Upper Peninsula.

People were able to live more comfortably. As sawmills increased, frame houses covered with siding replaced the log cabins, and some houses were built of brick or stone. During the 1840's houses like Greek temples with tall white columns in front were erected by the wealthy, and many of them can still be seen in the southern part of the state. Floors were carpeted, and fine furniture took the place of homemade tables, chairs, and stools. Stoves both for heating and cooking were widely used, making the houses more comfortable for the family and more convenient for those who prepared the meals. The larger towns made improvements for the health and safety of the residents. Waterworks were built, some street paving was done, and volunteer fire companies were organized. The streets of Detroit, Grand Rapids, and Kalamazoo were lighted by gas lamps.

It was during this period that both copper and iron mines were opened and began to produce profitably. Lumbering also had its commercial beginning, and manufacturing first became of some importance. All of these activities, however, increased enormously during later years.

In the field of government and politics, a new constitution was adopted in 1850 which had what were said to be more democratic features than the first one. All state officers were elected by the people, and the powers of the governor and of the legislature were limited. Some of these limitations had unfortunate results. For example, the state was not permitted to build roads.

In 1854 the Republican party was organized in Jackson, and it broke the almost exclusive hold of the Democrats on the state. The political career of Lewis Cass, a Democrat, soon came to an end, and Zachariah Chandler, a Republican, became the political leader in Michigan.

Reforms were earnestly campaigned for, but during this period neither women nor workingmen, white or black, received much consideration.

Great advances were made in education. Even though only Detroit had free schools, the time was approaching when they would be available throughout the state. In the field of higher education there was much progress. Denominational colleges were founded, the State Normal School and the Michigan Agricultural College were opened, and President Henry Philip Tappan was making over the University. Michigan was progressing remarkably both in substance and in opportunities for education.

PART V

BEGINNINGS OF INDUSTRIAL DEVELOPMENT 1860–1890

— 19 —

The Civil War and Increased Production

WHEN SOUTH CAROLINA and the other states of the deep South seceded (1860–1861), in the East there was strong sentiment for letting them leave the Union peaceably. Businessmen particularly hoped that there would be no war, and workingmen were for peace. At a national convention in Philadelphia in February, 1861, resolutions were passed opposing measures that would precipitate hostilities, and Horace Greeley, the influential editor of the *New York Tribune,* favored peaceful separation.

In Michigan the official reaction to secession was quick and sharply critical. In his exaugural address, Governor Moses Wisner on January 1, 1861, declared: "This is no time for timid and vacillating counsels when the cry of treason and rebellion is ringing in our ears. . . ." He asserted it to be the fixed determination of Michigan that "The Federal Constitution, the rights of the States, and the Union of the States *must and* SHALL BE PRESERVED."

The next day Governor Austin Blair in his inaugural said: "The Union must be preserved and the laws must be enforced in all parts of it at whatever cost. . . . Secession is revolution, and revolution in the overt act is treason and must be treated as such. . . . I recommend to you [the Legislature] at an early day to make manifest . . . that Michigan is loyal to the Union, the Constitution and the laws, and will defend them to the uttermost; and to proffer to the President of the United States *the whole military power of the State* for that purpose." The Legislature exceeded the recommendations of the governor by passing a resolution pledging not only the military power but also the material resources of the state to support the United States Government.

In February, after seven states had seceded, Senator Zachariah Chandler wrote to Governor Blair: "Some of the manufacturing states think a fight would be awful. Without a little bloodletting, this Union will not, in my estimation, be worth a rush."

Lewis Cass left Buchanan's Cabinet in protest against the President's do-nothing policy, and he supported the Union as a War Democrat. In spite of his advanced age, he spoke at patriotic rallies, and he lived to see the Union re-established. He died on June 17, 1866, at the age of eighty-four.

The firing on Fort Sumter, April 12, 1861, and its surrender by Major Robert Anderson aroused the North to action. President Lincoln's call for volunteers was answered promptly in Michigan.

The reasons for Michigan's enthusiasm for war were that comparatively few Southerners lived in the state; little direct trade had been carried on with the South; churches had been actively engaged in arousing hatred of slavery; raids of slaveowners into Michigan had made people hostile to all their kind; the Republicans had been campaigning against the extension of slavery since 1854.

A special session of the Legislature in May, 1861, authorized the governor to raise ten regiments of volunteers and to borrow $100,000. The first regiment was assembled at Fort Wayne and arrived in Washington on May 16. Three more regiments left before the end of June, and by December, 1861, thirteen regiments of infantry, three of cavalry, and five batteries of artillery had been sent to the front.

In the summer of 1862 recruits were difficult to find because people were discouraged by the prolonged and unsuccessful course of the war and because men in factories were receiving high wages. Army pay offered no incentive. In the beginning, privates received $13 a month, and later the amount was increased to only $16. So strong did opposition to the war become that in Detroit a mob broke up a

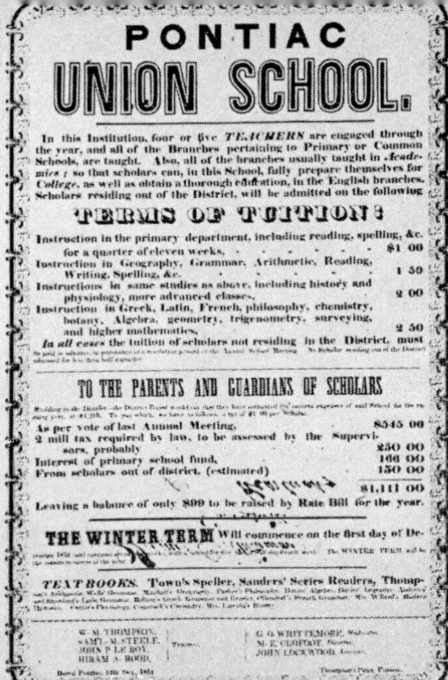
PONTIAC

UNION SCHOOL.

In this Institution, four or five *TEACHERS* are engaged through the year, and all of the Branches pertaining to Primary or Common Schools, are taught. Also, all of the branches usually taught in *Academies*; so that scholars can, in this School, fully prepare themselves for *College*, as well as obtain a thorough education, in the English branches. Scholars residing out of the District, will be admitted on the following

TERMS OF TUITION:

Instruction in the primary department, including reading, spelling, &c. for a quarter of eleven weeks,	$1 00
Instruction in Geography, Grammar, Arithmetic, Reading, Writing, Spelling, &c.	1 50
Instructions in same studies as above, including history and physiology, more advanced classes,	2 00
Instruction in Greek, Latin, French, philosophy, chemistry, botany, Algebra, geometry, trigonometry, surveying, and higher mathematics,	2 50

In all cases the tuition of scholars not residing in the District, must

TO THE PARENTS AND GUARDIANS OF SCHOLARS

As per vote of last Annual Meeting,	$545 00
2 mill tax required by law, to be assessed by the Supervisors, probably	250 00
Interest of primary school fund,	166 00
From scholars out of district, (estimated)	150 00
	$1,111 00

Leaving a balance of only $99 to be raised by Rate Bill for the year.

THE WINTER TERM Will commence on the first day of De-

TEXTBOOKS. Town's Speller, Sanders' Series Readers, Thomp-

W. M. THOMPSON,
SAM'L M. STEELE,
JOHN P. LE ROY,
HIRAM A. ROOD,

G. O. WHITTEMORE,
M. E. CROFOOT,
JOHN LOCKWOOD,

EDUCATION Union schools were common in the nineteenth century in Michigan. *Top left:* Broadside advertising the Pontiac Union School. *Top right:* Union school at Niles. *Center:* Interior of a country school near Grand Rapids in 1908. *Below right:* Exterior of a typical country schoolhouse. *Bottom left:* Title page of a catalogue of a select school for young ladies, Ann Arbor.

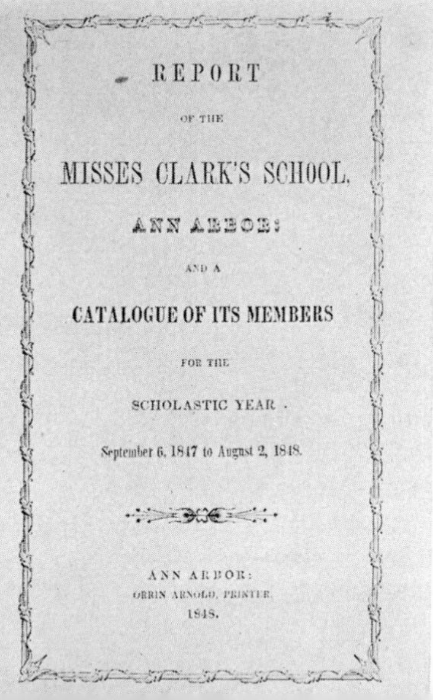
REPORT

OF THE

MISSES CLARK'S SCHOOL,

ANN ARBOR;

AND A

CATALOGUE OF ITS MEMBERS

FOR THE

SCHOLASTIC YEAR

September 6, 1847 to August 2, 1848.

ANN ARBOR:

ORRIN ARNOLD, PRINTER.

1848.

LAKE TRANSPORTATION (I) With over 2,000 miles of coastline, Michigan enjoys the advantage of cheap water transportation. *Right:* A canoe, used by Indians on the lakes and rivers of Michigan, transporting traders from Mackinac to Lake Superior. *Below:* Thousands of settlers arrived in Michigan on steam vessels like the *R. N. Rice* in the nineteenth century. *Center left:* Launched in 1844, the *Michigan* was the first iron warship on the Upper Lakes.

Iron whalebacks appeared on the Great Lakes in 1888. *Above:* A steam whaleback enters the Poe Lock at Sault Sainte Marie. *Left:* Lumber and tanbark were carried by schooners like the *Day Spring,* which is shown sailing up the Manistee River in 1890.

AKE TRANSPORTATION (II) To eet the demand for Lake Superior n ore, larger ships were built. *Above:* huge bulk freighter used on the Lakes day. *Right:* The Coast Guard ice-eaker, *USS Mackinac,* is shown head-g up the Detroit River to clear the annel for spring navigation. *Below ft:* Lighthouses, like the one at Sable oint on Lake Michigan, dot the shore-ie of Michigan. *Below right:* State-vned ferries like the *Vacationland* uttle passengers back and forth across e Straits of Mackinac.

WAR MEETINGS!

The crisis is upon us! The Government wants men NOW! We must immediately enlist, or be drafted. What patriot can wait for a draft when his country calls? Come, men of Old Livingston, come and join the Grand Army of the Union. There is now a chance to enlist and receive your bounty, but that chance will soon be gone. There will be a War Meeting at

ON

Turn out to the meeting, and add your names to the muster-roll of the UNION. A recruiting officer will be in attendance.

LUCIUS H. IVES,
RECRUITING OFFICER FOR THE 23D REGIMENT.

RECRUITS WANTED
FOR THE
1st REGIMENT OF U. S. SHARP-SHOOTERS

The undersigned will be at

On **186**

for the purpose of enlisting men for the First Regiment of United States Sharp-Shooters, now at Washington. None but good able-bodied men will be received.

The Regiment is to be armed with Sharpe's improved Target Rifles, which are to be furnished the Regiment by the 20th inst.

Headquarters at the City of Lansing, two doors below Bailey's Bank, on Michigan Avenue.

Recruits will be received for about THIRTY DAYS only.

J. H. BAKER,
1st Lieut. Co. C., 1st Regt. U. S. S. S.

Lansing, February 10th, 1863.

CIVIL WAR By the summer of 1862 recruits were difficult to find because people were discouraged by the prolonged and unsuccessful course of the war. To stimulate interest in army life and increase enlistments, patriotic meetings were held and bounties offered for recruits, as indicated in broadsides on this page. *Right:* War dispatch from the Detroit *Free Press*, June 25, 1863.

RALLY ROUND

THE FLAG, BOYS!

100 MEN WANTED!!
For the 23d Mich. Infantry.

Enlist before April 1st, secure the Government Bounty of $300 00,

AND "KEEP OUT OF THE DRAFT!"

Government Bounty, $300; State Bounty, $100; Town Bounty, $100.
Apply to WM. SICKELS, St. Johns, or

O. L. SPAULDING,
Lieut. Col., 23d Mich. Infantry, Corunna.
March , 1864.

("REPUBLICAN" PRINT, ST. JOHNS.)

THE LATEST
BY TELEGRAPH.

OUR SPECIAL DISPATCHES.

Heavy Skirmishing on the Potomac.

THE SIXTEENTH MICHIGAN LOSE TWENTY MEN.

Captain Mott Mortally Wounded.

Lieut. Cook and Sergt. Hilton Severely Wounded.

EWELL'S WHOLE CORPS SAID TO BE IN PENNSYLVANIA.

Reported that the Rebels are Marching on Harrisburg.

THEY ARE IN FORCE AT MERCERSBURG.

The Position of the Rebel Army on the Potomac.

Reported that Grant was to Commence Throwing hot Shot on the 20th.

REBEL ACCOUNTS REPORT HEAVY SKIRMISHING AT VICKSBURG.

HEAVY REINFORCEMENTS HAVE REACHED GRANT.

Feared the Rebels are Preparing to Blow up the Works on Our Entering.

ASSAULT MADE UPON PORT HUDSON,

Position Gained Within 100 Yards of the En-

RAILROADS AND INTERURBANS *Top:* A train of the Detroit, Lansing and Lake Michigan Railroad in 1874. *Center left:* Shay's logging train near Harbor Springs in the late nineteenth century. *Center right:* The first horsecar in Grand Rapids late in the nineteenth century. *Bottom left:* Interurban electric cars in 1914. *Bottom right:* Ann Arbor electric streetcar.

MASS
MEETING!

AT MASON, SEPT. 9th, 1854.

To the People of Ingham County, without distinction of Party:

In view of the recent action of Congress in regard to the organization of Nebraska and Kansas Territories, and the evident designs of the Slave power to attempt still further aggressions upon Freedom, we invite all our Fellow Citizens, without reference to former political associations, who think that the time has arrived for a Union at the North, to protect Liberty from being overthrown and down-trodden, to assemble in

Mass Convention,

On Saturday, the 9th day of September next, at 10 o'clock A. M., at the Court House, in the Village of Mason, for the purpose of putting in nomination suitable persons to fill the County offices, Representative

GO EARLY AND GET A SEAT!

1776. 1866.

GOV. H. H. CRAPO,

AT BIDWELL'S HALL

Thursday Evening, October 4th,

Will address the CITIZENS GENERALLY, upon the Political Issues of the day, at 7 o'clock.

COME ONE! Come All!! COME EVERYBODY and hear him!!!

POLITICS AND GOVERNMENT Before radio and television political candidates relied more on political rallies and meetings than they do today. Broadsides above announce such meetings. *Right:* Shiawassee County Courthouse, built in 1903. *Bottom:* State Capitol Building at Lansing, built in 1872.

CITY AND TOWN LIFE Life in the cities and towns of Michigan has changed considerably in the last century. Pictures on this page reflect the conditions of the earlier era. *Above:* An early mining town, Ironwood, in 1885. *Right:* Battle Creek in the 1850's. *Below:* Singapore, near the present Saugatuck on Lake Michigan, has for years been completely covered with 15 to 20 feet of sand. *Bottom left:* Police patrol in Grand Rapids. *Bottom right:* Harbor Springs' water supply system.

SOO CANAL The construction of locks at the St. Marys Rapids at Sault Sainte Marie was of tremendous significance to the industrial life of Michigan. It was of especial importance to the mining of iron and copper in the Upper Peninsula. *Above:* The old state locks built in 1855.

Center: Ships passing through the modern locks. *Lower right:* The rapids of the St. Marys River.

patriotic rally on July 15, 1862. Only by giving bounties to volunteers could new regiments be enlisted.

In 1862, the United States Government offered a bounty of $100 to each volunteer. Two years later this sum was raised to $300 for recruits and $400 for veterans. States, counties, and cities offered bounties also, so that sometimes a volunteer could collect $1,000 in advance. This practice led to bounty jumping. Dishonest men would collect the bounties in one neighborhood and, instead of enlisting, disappear and go through the same performance somewhere else.

On March 3, 1863, Congress passed a draft act which applied to districts which failed to furnish their quota of volunteers. Single men twenty to forty-five years old and married men twenty to thirty-five were subject to call. A drafted man might avoid service by hiring a substitute or by paying $300. This law, because it was unfair to men who could not afford to pay a substitute, resulted in riots in New York and other cities, including Detroit.

In the same year the Michigan Legislature authorized a state bounty of $50. By 1865, when quotas could be filled only with great difficulty, the Legislature voted a bounty of $150 and authorized the townships to offer $100.

War weariness caused much opposition to President Lincoln. Henry H. Crapo of Flint, a Republican candidate for governor, was elected in 1864, and Lincoln carried Michigan; but ten counties—Bay, Delta, Livingston, Macomb, Monroe, Oakland, Ottawa, Saginaw, Washtenaw, and Wayne—gave majorities to General George B. McClellan, the Democratic nominee. Even the soldiers in the Ninth Michigan Cavalry cast a majority of fourteen votes for him.

The people at home during the war co-operated to make life more pleasant for the soldiers in the field. The Michigan Branch of the United States Sanitary Commission, the Ladies' Soldiers' Aid Society, and the Michigan Soldiers' Relief Society assisted needy families of soldiers; sent packages of food, bandages, and medical supplies to the hospitals and to the men in Michigan regiments. The Michigan branch of the United States Christian Commission supported agents who visited the men, caring for their physical and spiritual needs.

During the war Michigan contributed thirty regiments of infantry, eleven of cavalry, one of artillery, one of engineers, and one of sharpshooters, a total of more than 90,000 men. Michigan regiments fought in all the principal battles, and monuments in their memory stand on every battlefield.

The most picturesque officer from Michigan was George A. Custer, a brigadier general at the age of twenty-three. At Gettysburg, mounted as usual on the fastest horse he could find, he led the Michigan Cavalry Brigade in a wild charge, his long golden locks, streaming out from under his broad-brimmed hat, serving as a guidon for his men. Remaining in the army after the Civil War, Custer was killed by the Sioux under Sitting Bull in the Battle of the Little Big Horn River in Montana in 1876.

A famous exploit by Michigan troops was the capture of President Jefferson Davis of the Confederacy by Lieutenant Colonel Benjamin D. Pritchard and the Fourth Michigan Cavalry near Irwinsville, Georgia, on May 10, 1865. Learning that the fleeing president was encamped in the woods with his family and a military escort, Colonel Pritchard surrounded them under cover of darkness. As daylight broke, the colonel with a small detachment dashed into the camp and captured the whole party without firing a shot. Davis hastily put on his wife's cloak and covered his head with her shawl; but his disguise was easily penetrated, and he admitted his identity. Colonel Pritchard delivered the captured president a prisoner to Fortress Monroe.

2

The Civil War brought desolation to the South, but in the North it encouraged manufacturing and produced a hectic prosperity. Michigan profited immensely by the unusual war-created demand for products of field, forest, factory, and mine. The Civil War so greatly increased the demand for copper that the price rose from twelve cents a pound to fifty-five, and there was prosperity in the copper country.

Prosperity, however, was not permanent for some parts of the area. Of the three regions in which copper was found, the one nearest the extremity of the Keweenaw Peninsula was worked out first. The great Cliff Mine closed in 1887, and only a few others continued to operate. Copper Harbor was deserted, and Eagle Harbor declined in population. The second region, in the vicinity of the Ontonagon River, was played out by 1890 when its rich fissure veins had been emptied. The third, the Portage Lake region, really began to be productive during the period 1860–1890, and continued to be the richest source of copper for many years. Here it was the Calumet and Hecla Company's mines which became world-famous.

The Calumet Mining Company was organized in 1861 by Edwin J. Hulbert, discoverer of the rich conglomerate. Production began in 1864, and Hulbert opened the Hecla Mine in 1866. He had been a successful prospector, but he was an incompetent manager. In order to save the property from bankruptcy, the company removed him in 1867 and put in his place Alexander Agassiz, the zoologist, son of the naturalist Louis Agassiz. The Calumet and Hecla mines were combined in 1871 under his direction, and others were added to form the Calumet and Hecla Corporation. So rich were the conglomerate deposits and so capably did Agassiz manage the mines that they were fabulously productive. The office of the company was in Boston, and the profits went to the stockholders there. During this period the Pewabic, Quincy, Osceola, Franklin, and Allouez mines were being profitably operated. Boston money was invested in most of them.

Improved methods of mining made quantity production cheaper. During the 1870's more powerful explosives were used for blasting, and in the 1880's air drills replaced the laborious use of the hand-power drill. Larger and more efficient steam engines provided power for hoisting and for crushing copper-bearing rock. In order to locate new lodes, companies began using diamond drills which brought up cores showing the composition of the rocks through which they passed.

In 1880 the output of all the Upper Peninsula mines was 49,601,000 pounds of refined copper, and the net earnings were greater than those of precious-metals mines in California, Colorado, or any other state. Up to 1887, Michigan was the greatest copper producer in the nation. After that year Montana, Arizona, and other western states took the lead.

From the beginning nuggets of silver were frequently found with the copper. Considering them to be a sort of bonus, the miners usually pocketed them. Even so, the companies got some of the precious metal, for it was reported in 1887 that $3,500,000 worth of silver had been produced by the mines in the Upper Peninsula.

Some gold also was discovered, and the Ropes Mine near Ishpeming between 1883 and 1897 produced about $650,000 worth. Mining finally ceased because the cost of production was greater than the value of the gold. In 1888 the Michigan Gold Mining Company in the same region also produced some gold, but it too ceased operations because of the high costs. Michigan never became a large-scale producer of the precious metals.

During this period transportation was facilitated by the opening of the Portage Lake and Lake Superior Ship Canal through the Keweenaw Peninsula. As in the construction of the Sault Canal, the state let out contracts and Congress provided funds by a grant of land. The southeastern connection was completed in 1860, and the northwestern in 1873. This new waterway brought freighters to Houghton and to Hancock, and it provided a shorter and a safer route for ships bound for Ontonagon, Ashland, Duluth, and Superior. In 1881 Michigan transferred ownership of the waterway to the national government.

3

The Jackson, the Cleveland Cliffs, and the Lake Superior mines at Negaunee and Ishpeming in the Marquette Iron Range continued to produce iron ore. The type of mining changed, however. Instead of simply quarrying, as had been the practice at first, after 1870 it became necessary to sink shafts and run drifts through solid rock to get at the ore. As in the copper mines, power drills and hoisting machinery were necessary equipment. New mines were opened and new towns sprang up around them—Republic, Champion, Michigamme, and others. Production, which had been only 114,000 tons in 1860, increased to 1,945,000 by 1880. A second railroad, built from Negaunee to Escanaba (1864), gave the mines an outlet on Lake Michigan in addition to the one on Lake Superior at Marquette. This line became a part of the Chicago and Northwestern Railroad.

A new source of iron ore was tapped in 1877 when mines were opened on the Menominee Range. Iron Mountain, Iron River, and Crystal Falls became the principal mining centers. In 1880 fifteen mines produced 560,950 tons of ore, which were carried by rail to the loading docks at Escanaba.

The third iron district was opened in this period on the Gogebic Range in the extreme western part of the Upper Peninsula. J. L. Norrie and others found rich ore deposits in 1881, but development was slow at first because of the isolation of the region and the lack of transportation. The Milwaukee, Lake Shore and Western, which reached Ironwood in 1884, made possible the shipment of supplies and ore. The Colby Mine began producing in 1884, and the Norrie Mine was opened the next year. Ironwood, Bessemer, and Wakefield were the centers of production on the Gogebic Range. The ore was carried by rail to Ashland, Wisconsin, where it was transferred to ships.

The output of iron increased because of the demands of the Civil War, and the opening of mines in the two additional regions made Michigan the leading ore-producing state. By 1890 the mines of the three regions were shipping more than eight million tons annually to the smelters around the Lakes.

4

The greatly increased production of the Upper Peninsula mines induced the building of larger ships and new types for carrying ore. At first the ore was packed in barrels or simply dumped on the decks of sailing vessels or steamships, but in 1869 the *R. J. Hackett* was designed and built expressly as an ore carrier. She was a wooden steamship with all her machinery placed in the stern and her bridge forward, leaving the space between for hatches through which ore could quickly and easily be loaded from the high bins on the docks at Marquette and Escanaba. Other shipbuilders followed suit in constructing similar vessels.

The first commercial iron ship on the Lakes was launched in 1862. Because such ships could be made larger than wooden ones, they gradually displaced them. The *Onoko*, built in 1882, was the first of the iron bulk freighters. She was 287 feet long.

The iron whaleback ship first appeared in 1888. Riding low in the water with a rounded topside, it resembled a submarine. The designer and builder, Captain Alexander McDougall, believed that his ship could not be destroyed by wind and water. Although he had a great deal of difficulty in convincing others of the practicality of this new type of ship, whalebacks became quite common on the Lakes; but they were finally supplanted by the huge bulk freighters, which are economical to operate. Two or three of the whalebacks, however, were still sailing in the 1940's.

The great demand for Lake Superior iron ore and the increasing length of ships made necessary new and larger locks at Sault Sainte Marie. In 1877, because the work was of national importance, the United States Government began building the Weitzel Lock, which was opened in 1881. In the same year, Michigan transferred the Soo Canal to the United States. The lock was 515 feet long and 80 feet wide. Ships were raised and lowered in one stage instead of in two, as was formerly the case, and no toll was charged. In 1887 the Poe Lock was begun, and it was placed in service in 1896. It is 800 feet long and 100 feet wide. The old state locks were destroyed to make room for the larger Poe Lock.

5

Railroad building was greatly increased by national land grants. In 1856 and 1857 Congress gave Michigan 3,775,000 acres of land to distribute to railroads. In the Upper Peninsula the railroad from Marquette to Ishpeming was extended to L'Anse in 1872 and to Houghton in 1883. It was known as the Marquette, Houghton and Ontonagon.

Another line, the Peninsular, was built from Negaunee to Escanaba in 1864. It became a part of the Chicago and Northwestern and gave the Upper Peninsula a direct route to Chicago in 1872. Branches of this road ran to the iron mines in the Menominee Range. Railroad traffic to and from the Upper Peninsula was with Milwaukee and Chicago.

In order to provide a rail connection between the two peninsulas, Michigan capitalists built the Detroit, Mackinac and Marquette Railroad, which reached St. Ignace from Marquette in 1881. Ferries across the Straits carried cars to the Jackson, Lansing and Saginaw Railroad terminal at Mackinaw City. It was hoped that these lines would divert Upper Peninsula traffic from Milwaukee and Chicago to Detroit and other Michigan cities and help bind the two peninsulas in a closer union.

In the Lower Peninsula a number of new railroads were built to reach the rapidly developing lumbering centers. Among them were the Flint and Pere Marquette from Saginaw to Ludington, at the mouth of the Pere Marquette River; the Grand Rapids and Indiana from Fort Wayne to Petoskey; the Chicago and Western Michigan from New Buffalo to Pentwater; and the Toledo, Ann Arbor and North Michigan to Frankfort. Ferries across Lake Michigan were operated by the T.A.A. and N.M. from Frankfort to Kewaunee, Wisconsin, beginning in 1892.

The T.A.A. and N.M. was the first to carry loaded freight cars across as large a body of water as Lake Michigan. The loss of time and the expense of unloading cars at Frankfort, loading a ship, unloading the ship at Kewaunee, and loading cars there caused James Ashley, president of the railroad, to have two wooden car ferries built in 1892. Each ferry could carry twenty-four freight cars. At first shippers were reluctant to trust their goods to the ferries, but Ashley soon convinced them that they were safe. Accidents, however, did happen. In November, 1895, while ferry *Number 1* was crossing from Kewaunee to Frankfort in a storm, the cars broke their fastenings and seven went over the stern into the lake. The T.A.A. and N.M. later ran ferries from Frankfort to Manitowoc, Wisconsin, and Menominee and Manistique, Michigan. Beginning in 1897 car ferries were operated by the Pere Marquette Railroad from Ludington to Kewaunee, Manitowoc, and Milwaukee, Wisconsin.

At Detroit, beginning in 1866, a railroad ferry carried freight and passenger cars across the river to connect the Canadian Great Western with the Michigan Central. Because this method was slow, there was much talk of building a bridge or a tunnel to speed the crossing. Shipowners opposed a bridge, and so James F. Joy obtained permission in 1871 to dig a tunnel. The excavating was begun at the foot of St. Antoine Street in Detroit, and the tube had been completed for 135 feet when the workmen struck a pocket of hydrogen sulphide gas and refused to continue. In 1891 the Grand Trunk constructed a tunnel between Port Huron and Sarnia, Ontario, and the Michigan Central finally completed a tunnel under the Detroit River in 1909.

6

During the period 1860 to 1890, lumbering in Michigan increased enormously. Moving ever northward and farther inland, loggers made use of every stream in the Lower Peninsula, and production in the Upper Peninsula added millions of board feet to the output of the state. Because many stands of pine were not accessible by water, beginning in 1877 operators built narrow-gauge railroads into the woods, and the land was systematically stripped of its pine forests.

Boom companies impounded the logs near the mouths of rivers, sorted them, and rafted them to the owners' mills, where whirring saws sliced the logs into lumber. Nearly every year was marked by an increase until 1888, when 4,292,000,000 board feet of lumber were sawed, the peak of production in the state. In addition, millions of shingles, staves, pickets, railroad ties, and squared timbers were manufactured. After 1888 there was a steady decline, but in 1900 Michigan was still ahead of every other state in the output of lumber.

There were several reasons for the phenomenal increase in the production of Michigan white pine. First of all, it was the best in the world, and it was consequently in great demand. Second, the country was growing rapidly, towns and cities were springing up, especially in the Midwest, and Michigan lumber was required for building houses. Chicago, the important distributing center in that region, was easily reached by cheap water transportation. Incidentally, materials from the mills of Michigan were used to rebuild Chicago after the disastrous fire of 1871.

The output of mills was greatly increased by the use of improved machinery, especially by the introduction of circular saws and band saws. A constant supply of logs was assured after narrow-gauge railroads were run into the woods by the lumber companies to reach distant stands of timber. Then it was not necessary to await the spring freshets to carry logs to the saws. The building of new railroads farther north into the state made possible the shipment of lumber to outside markets all year round instead of only during the season of navigation when the Lakes were open.

Another reason for increased production was the coming of eastern operators and the investment of eastern capital. The decline of lumbering in Maine turned the attention of many producers to Michigan. During the 1850's Royal C. Remick, Charles Merrill, Thomas Merrill, Simon J. Murphy, Sewell Avery, and others from Maine began buying timber lands in the Saginaw Valley. Their experience and their financial resources helped increase production.

The huge profits which could be made in Michigan induced many men to engage in logging and in the manufacture of lumber. Of course, there were failures. Mills frequently burned, a winter's cut of logs was sometimes left stranded in a stream for lack of water, or smaller operators were unable to pay their bills and went bankrupt. The larger producers reaped fabulous fortunes from the forests. Even the Panic of 1873, though severe, was only a temporary reverse.

One reason for the profits in Michigan lumber was the cheap and convenient water transportation. Most of the logs could be floated to the sawmills, and the lumber could be carried by steamer or schooner to the principal ports of the Great Lakes. Individual ships took on large cargoes, and strings of as many as six schooners towed by a tug hauled great quantities of lumber at little expense.

Another reason for the great profits in lumbering was that land was cheap and easily obtainable. The United States Government gave Michigan more than thirteen million acres of land, about 40 per cent of the land area of the state, for education, internal improvements, government buildings, and railroads. Sometimes, as in the case of the Sault Canal, the state granted land to a company in return for completing a specific project. Other land was sold at low prices, and more than five million acres were given to railroads as subsidies. Usually the odd- or even-numbered sections on each side of the right of way to a depth of six miles were assigned to the railroads. In order to raise money to defray the cost of construction, some of these lands were sold for what they would bring. Besides, warrants for land, given as a bounty to men who had served in the armed forces during a war, could be bought cheap.

The Homestead Act of 1862 was another means of transferring public lands to private owners. By its provisions, any American could claim from the United States 160 acres of land free in return for five years' occupancy and a fee of $10 for registration, or for $1.25 an acre and fourteen months' residence on it. Lumber companies were glad to pay the $1.25 purchase price and let the homesteaders keep the land. The state sold its own school grants and other land as rapidly as possible, sometimes for as little as thirty cents an acre. Only one fourth of the purchase price was required as down payment, and no taxes were due until after the whole had been paid. Lumbermen bought this land for the timber, stripped it, and abandoned it as worthless. An even less expensive practice was called "logging a round forty." A company would lease a forty-acre tract, and then, ignoring survey lines, would slash in all directions as fast and as far as possible.

7

On the Lake Huron side of Michigan, logging continued in the regions that had earlier been opened and advanced inland and northward. Port Huron had been one of the earliest lumber centers. Annual production rose to a high point of 56,000,000 board feet in 1873, then fell off rapidly. It has been estimated that the total output was 302,710,000 feet.

Production in the Saginaw Valley increased enormously. Experienced operators from Maine extended their holdings of timber lands and their cutting of pine. Rail transportation carried millions of feet of logs from regions beyond the streams. During the 1870's, the Flint and Pere Marquette, the Saginaw and St. Louis, and the Jackson, Lansing and Saginaw helped load the millponds with logs. Towns situated on both a railroad and a stream became important lumber centers. Midland, for example, on the Pere Marquette Railroad and the Tittabawassee River, in 1873 had twenty-seven mills.

In the Saginaw region, besides the men who have been mentioned, important operators were Jesse Hoyt, Aaron T. Bliss, Wellington R. Burt, David Whitney, James H. Hill and his sons Arthur and William H., James Shearer, C. F. Marston, Augustus H. Mershon and his son William B., and Henry Howland Crapo.

When mill operators saw that the pine was beginning to fail in the Saginaw Valley, many purchased land on Georgian Bay or on the Canadian shore of Lake Huron. The logs were floated in great rafts to the mills of Bay City and Saginaw. In this region the high point of production was reached in 1882, when more than a billion board feet of lumber were sawed. Because of the demand for ships and the abundance of timber, Saginaw and Bay City became shipbuilding centers. After a time steel ships as well as wooden ones were constructed.

Northward, mills were built during this period at Tawas City, Oscoda, Harrisville, Ossineke, Alpena, and Cheboygan. The Au Sable River carried great quantities of logs to Oscoda. There Henry Martin Loud and his sons were the largest operators.

Alpena, at the mouth of the Thunder Bay River, became a great mill town. One of the earliest lumbermen was George N. Fletcher, and together with his sons he remained one of the biggest producers. Others at Alpena included F. W. Gilchrist and Albert Pack. The largest annual production of lumber was sawed in 1888—215,000,000 board feet.

Cheboygan reached its peak of production later than the towns farther south. In 1873, 41,000,000 feet were cut, and the high mark of 127,540,000 feet came in 1890. Today a mountain of sawdust a thousand feet long stands as a silent reminder of the screaming saws of Cheboygan's mills.

8

On the west coast of Michigan the movement northward and inland progressed as it did on the east coast. The Grand River and the Kalamazoo had early begun to carry logs. They were the first to decline, for the heavy pine stands were farther north. Before 1890, Kalamazoo and Allegan had begun to manufacture paper from wood pulp.

Grand Rapids reached its high production in 1873 with 56,000,000 feet. Afterward, hardwood was cut, and Grand Rapids became the furniture center of Michigan.

Lumber from Grand Rapids was rafted down to Grand Haven for shipment, and logs were floated down the Grand River to the mills of Grand Haven. There Gilbert and Sons and William M. Ferry and Sons were the largest producers. In 1882, Grand Haven sawed 192,000,000 feet of lumber, its largest output. By 1890, production had declined to 32,000,000.

At Muskegon the number of mills increased and poured out every year larger and larger quantities. In 1873 they sawed 329,689,000 board feet, and in 1887, the peak year, 665,449,000. This was the largest production of any city in Michigan. Prominent mill operators were C. H. Hackley and Company, McGraft and Montgomery, Tillotson and Blodgett, Ryerson, Hills and Company, and Mann and Moon.

Whitehall and Montague on White Lake and Pentwater continued to produce lumber. Charles Mears, James Ludington, and Louis Sands had mills at Pentwater. The town of Ludington at the mouth of the Pere Marquette River was at first called Pere Marquette. Later it took the name of one of its prominent lumbermen, James Ludington. Horace Butters, Delos Filer, and Justus Stearns had mills in Ludington, and Charles Mears had one nearby on Lincoln Lake.

Next to Muskegon, Manistee was the greatest lumber producer on the west coast. The Manistee River with its tributaries flowing through eight counties in the best pine area carried millions of logs to the mills on Manistee Lake. The top production figure was 300,000,000 board feet in 1892. During this period the largest lumber companies were Buckley and Douglas, Canfield and Wheeler, Delos Filer and Sons, Charles F. Ruggles, and Louis Sands.

Sands was a Swedish immigrant who had come to the United States in 1853 and had worked his way out to Michigan. Employed at first as a laborer, he gained experience and saved sufficient money to take small logging contracts. He rapidly expanded his operations and in 1878 acquired a mile of frontage on Manistee Lake and the Manistee River. Sands built ships to carry his lumber to market and ran a narrow-gauge railroad into the woods to bring out the logs. Salt beds were discovered under Manistee in 1879, and Sands was among the mill owners who began manufacturing salt, using scrap wood to fire the evaporating kettles. His other interests were a bank, a gasworks, and an electric plant in Manistee. This immigrant made good use of the opportunities he found in his adopted country.

In Traverse City, and in fact in the whole Grand Traverse region, lumbering was dominated by Hannah, Lay and Company, which had built a mill in 1851. The firm had a lumberyard in Chicago which was managed by A. Tracy Lay, while Perry Hannah supervised the logging camps and mills in Michigan. Hannah, Lay and Company built a store which grew into a large mercantile establishment. They also operated a bank and a flour mill in Traverse City. In 1887 the company sold its timber lands and mills to John Torrent of Muskegon, retaining its store.

9

In the Upper Peninsula, Menominee was the principal lumber center. Kirby, Carpenter and Company, Ludington, Wells and Van Schaick, the Menominee Bay Shore Lumber Company, and the Girard Lumber Company were the largest producers.

Another large center of lumber production was Escanaba, where the

N. Ludington Company was the dominant firm. On Ford River, not far from Escanaba, the Ford River Lumber Company had a large mill. Manistique had mills owned by the Chicago Lumber Company and the Western Lumber Company. Near the town the Delta Company and the North Shore Company added their production to the total, which put Manistique among the important lumber towns. Other Upper Peninsula towns which produced lumber for export were Baraga, Chassell, Dollarville, Grand Marais, Seney, Munising, Pequaming, Sault Sainte Marie, St. Ignace, and Ontonagon.

In the Michigan woods there were opportunities to make great fortunes. The names of some of the successful lumbermen have already been mentioned. Many of them began as laborers. Thousands of others worked for short periods or for many years, leaving no record of their labors except in the payroll books of a logging company. They were the men who got out the logs and sawed the lumber. At first they were largely Americans and French Canadians. Then came Germans, Swedes, Norwegians, Danes, Finns, and Poles. To most of them, life in the woods was a new experience, but they learned rapidly and gloried in the hardships that only rugged men could endure.

In the fall of the year, the lumberjacks, or shanty boys as they were called at first, by ship, train, or wagon traveled to the town nearest the camp in which they were going to work. Shouldering their turkeys (denim bags containing their clothes and other possessions), they set out on foot along the rutted road for the camp that would be their home during the winter.

The lumber camp was established in an area of pine near a river or a tributary. It consisted of a bunkhouse, a messhall and kitchen in one building, a separate office, and stables. Logging was carried on during the winter because then the logs could be hauled on sleds over the snow to the river bank.

To make hauling easier, a sprinkler sled was driven over the logging road to make a smooth ice surface. The sleds, piled high with great logs, were drawn by oxen or horses. On down grades, sand was thrown on the ice to prevent the sleds from going too fast and running over the horses.

When there was no snow, logs were hauled by Michigan logging wheels. Developed and manufactured by Sylas C. Overpack in Manistee, these big wheels were ten feet in diameter, with steel tires six inches wide. The tongue was sixteen feet long. Sturdily constructed for hard usage, the big wheels with tongue and axle weighed a ton. For many years they were in great demand in Michigan and other lumber-producing states.

For hauling, the wheels were run astride a pile of four or five logs on a skid. The tongue was raised to a vertical position, and a heavy chain was slipped under the logs and fastened to hooks on the top of the axle. When the tongue was pulled down parallel to the ground, the logs were raised from the skid. A second chain around the forward end of the logs was attached to the tongue to hold it down. The driver sat on a board which extended back from the axle. One team of horses or oxen could draw a load of logs slung under the axle of the big wheels.

The lumberjacks were up at daybreak, ate a hearty breakfast, and were out in the woods as soon as it was light. The great pines were felled, branches were trimmed off, and the huge trunks were sawed into lengths that could be handled. At noon the cook brought a hot lunch to the men.

When the men returned to the camp at dusk, they removed their heavy clothes and hung them up to dry. They then had a hot supper. Afterward, for an hour or so they amused themselves before it was time to go to bed. There was always a fiddler in camp, and the jacks performed jigs or buck-and-wing dances to amuse their fellows. Stag dances were another diversion, with husky, bearded shanty boys as "women" partners.

Whenever the men sat around the stove in the bunkhouse, someone was sure to tell a story. Others followed, and each would try to outdo his mates in the exaggeration of a tall tale. Unbelievable exploits of real or mythical characters, told with tongue in cheek, were loudly applauded or jeered by the audience, who were always eager for more. Paul Bunyan and his Blue Ox Babe figured in these story-telling sessions, at least during the later years. Wherever or whenever the legends about this gigantic woodsman originated, they are now the best known of lumberjack lore.

In the spring when the streams were swollen by melting snow and heavy rains, the logs which had been piled along the banks were rolled into the water. Bobbing, spinning, plunging, and crashing together, they sped down the stream. Men called "river hogs" followed them on the banks, setting adrift any that floated ashore and breaking up jams at curves and shallow spots. This was dangerous work to which only experienced men were assigned. Finally, the logs reached the mills near the river's mouth, where they were dragged out of the water and sawed into lumber.

When numerous companies piled their logs on the banks of a

stream, identification became necessary. Each company adopted a distinctive design which was put on the ends of their logs by the stroke of a heavy hammer. Boom companies were organized, one on every large stream, to handle the floating logs. They took charge of the spring drive from the rollways to the mills.

Lumberjacks Dancing a Jig

Near the mouth of the river, a large boom formed of logs chained together captured the floating logs as they came down. Skilled rivermen with steel calks in the soles of their boots sorted the logs according to the marks. When enough logs with the same mark had been collected, they were made into a raft and floated to the owner's mill. The Tittabawassee Boom Company was the leading one in the state.

In 1882, the year of its greatest activity, it sorted and delivered 600,000,000 feet of logs.

The lumberjacks reached the milltown soon after the logs arrived. Their pockets bulging with their winter's pay, many could not resist the temptations of the saloons and gambling dens. Drunken fights broke out, and sometimes a crowd of intoxicated jacks cleared the streets temporarily and took over the town. On these occasions constables usually kept out of sight.

The rowdy element among the jacks made so much commotion that they gave a bad name to the whole lot. Many of the men in the logging camps were sober individuals who were ambitious to learn the business and to begin operations themselves after they had experience and had saved enough money. Others were farmers who spent the winter in the camps to accumulate some cash with which to buy additional land. They shunned the saloons and carried their wages home with them.

10

For many years it seemed that the supply of Michigan pine was inexhaustible. More and more companies entered the woods, and production of lumber increased. Then one operator after another found that the supply was dwindling. For a time huge rafts of logs from Canada provided stock for the mills of Bay City and Saginaw. Then lumbermen began to move—to the western shore of Michigan, to the Upper Peninsula, to Wisconsin, and even to the Pacific Coast. In 1890, there was still a great deal of pine in Michigan, but production was decreasing every year.

As a rule, after the pines were cleared from an area, nothing was left but slashings from the great trees, and smashed remains of trees too small to cut. The ground was littered with tops and branches which dried and became prime fuel for a forest fire. The loggers had no thought for the future. "Cut and get out" was their motto. There was sharp competition, and to make money they believed that they had to clear the land as quickly as possible.

Because of the careless methods of production, fires broke out from time to time in numerous places. The first great forest fires occurred in 1871. Drought and extremely hot weather during summer and fall prepared the woods for burning. On October 8, men from Holland fought small fires in the woods near town. During the night a high wind rose and flames raced into the outlying streets. Roused from sleep, the inhabitants fought the fire and tried to carry away their possessions.[1] So rapid was the spread of the flames that many took to Black Lake in boats to save their lives. Most of the town was wiped out, and horses, cattle, and pigs were killed. Only one person was killed, but three hundred families were left homeless.

Farther up the shore of Lake Michigan, Manistee also was a fire victim, half the town being destroyed by a conflagration. From these fires on the western shore, flames driven by strong winds swept across the state, laying waste forests, fields, and farms in Lake, Osceola, Isabella, Midland, Saginaw, Tuscola, Sanilac, and Huron counties. Eighteen thousand persons saw their homes destroyed. Relief committees appointed by Governor Henry P. Baldwin aided the destitute, and assistance was provided by people throughout Michigan and from every part of the country.

Forest fires continued to destroy valuable timber, and in September, 1881, another great conflagration swept across a wide area. Again, as ten years previously, a severe drought had dried up streams and swamps, and had turned slashings into easily combustible tinder. Small fires were burning in numerous spots in Lapeer, Tuscola, and Huron counties. A gale from the southwest on September 5 spread these fires and sent them racing through the woods. Nothing could stop the devastating wall of flame. Men, women, and children fled for their lives, many taking refuge in Lake Huron.

For three days the fires continued destroying farm buildings and towns in their path. Tall trees burned like great candles, and flames fed by rising gases billowed and roared high in the air. Smoke and flying ashes obscured the sun and, except where the crackling flames cast a lurid light, it was dark at noonday.

This time 125 lives were lost; thousands of people were homeless and without food. Again the people of the state and of the nation sent aid. The American Red Cross, then newly organized, gathered blankets, clothing, and other necessaries for the suffering refugees. Clara Barton directed the relief activities from her headquarters in Dansville, New York. This was the first great disaster in which the Red Cross lent a helping hand, and its prompt service attracted favorable attention to Miss Barton and her little band of earnest assistants.

[1] The great Chicago fire also began on October 8.

20

New Directions

After the Civil War Michigan attracted many persons who were seeking a pleasant place to spend the summer. Steamship and railroad companies published illustrated booklets extolling the natural beauty, the numerous lakes, and the excellent fishing, especially in the northern parts of the state. Petoskey, Charlevoix, Sault Sainte Marie, and Mackinac Island were among the places recommended.

Mackinac Island had been visited by tourists even before the fur trade closed. During the 1850's some cottages were built, and summer residents found the climate delightful. After the Civil War the island became even more popular as a resort. Hotels were erected and roads leading to various points of interest were laid down. In 1894 the garrison was removed and the fort was given to the state. The next year nearly the whole island was made a state park.

Charges in the resorts were moderate. The highest advertised rate for board and room in a hotel on Mackinac Island or at Petoskey was three dollars a day or eighteen dollars a week. At Petoskey board and room could be had for as little as six dollars a week.

The railroad brochures emphasized the opportunities for hunting and fishing in Michigan. Fish and game were abundant, and there were practically no limits to the number of wild turkey, grouse, duck, quail, pigeon, deer, and fish which the sportsman might take. Although as early as 1859 the Legislature had passed a law intended to conserve fish and game by establishing closed seasons, no effective means of enforcement were provided.

The Fish Commission, appointed in 1873, was occupied principally in trying to increase the number of lake trout and whitefish in the Great Lakes for the benefit of commercial fishermen. Hatcheries were built and fingerlings were planted in the Lakes. The commercial fishermen gladly accepted this service by the state, but they refused to obey laws limiting the size of mesh in nets. They were interested only in the largest possible catch, regardless of the future of the industry.

Even the appointment of a state fish and game warden in 1887 had little effect on the enforcement of the laws against either professional or amateur hunters and fishermen. Some species became scarce, and two, the wild turkey and the passenger pigeon, were exterminated.

The passenger pigeon was a beautiful bird. It had a long graceful neck, narrow wings, and long tail feathers. Its head and neck were royal purple shading into light blue, with a velvety sheen on the back and wings. The throat and breast were a reddish-brown fading into pink. Bluish-black tail feathers were tipped with white.

At one time passenger pigeons appeared each spring throughout the Middle West and the East. Flying in compact masses, they streamed through the sky like great dark clouds. So numerous were the birds that a flock sometimes required several hours to pass over an observer. The forests of Michigan were one of their favorite haunts, and it was in Michigan that the last great nesting was made.

Early in the spring the huge flocks appeared. Finding a wooded area that offered food and protection, they alighted in the trees by the million. Fifty or more nests were sometimes built in a single tree, and branches snapped off with the weight of roosting birds. Beechnuts and acorns were their principal food. Every morning the birds flew out in swarms to a feeding place, coming back in the evening to their nests.

At first only Indians and nearby settlers hunted the birds for food, and the number taken was inconsequential. Then market hunters began to follow the flocks. News of their nesting was reported widely, and men came to Michigan from as far away as Maine and Texas to slaughter the passenger pigeons. Guns were of little use, for the birds flew high. Long poles were used to knock squabs from their nests, trees were cut down, and grain was scattered in open places where nets had been set to fall upon and trap the feeding pigeons.

The dark woods teemed with terror-stricken pigeons nearly deafening the hunters with the beating of their wings and with their shrill cries. Squabs and full-grown birds were knocked to the ground, their heads were wrung off, and the bleeding bodies were tossed into bags. Some of the pigeons, especially those caught in nets, were carried away to be sold as targets for sportsmen in trapshooting.

The dead birds were taken to a railroad station or a port, packed in barrels, and shipped to Chicago, Detroit, and other cities where they were served as delicacies in hotels and restaurants.

The last great nesting in Michigan occurred in 1878. So large was the flock that it occupied an area forty miles long and from three to ten miles wide. Hundreds of hunters entered the woods, and it was estimated that three million dead birds and eighty thousand live ones were shipped from the region. How many were left dead in the woods will never be known.

During the 1880's smaller flocks of pigeons appeared, and in 1888 a moderately large one passed over Cadillac. Even in the early 1890's, small flights were reported, but the pigeons soon became extinct. The clearing of the forest and the settling of the land contributed to the decline and disappearance of the species; but the wanton slaughter, with no regard for even the insufficient laws passed for their protection, was certainly an important factor in the extermination of the beautiful birds which had chosen Michigan as their favorite nesting place.

2

The population of the state continued to increase rapidly. In 1860 it was 749,113; in 1870, 1,184,059; in 1880, 1,636,331; and in 1890, 2,093,889. The growth in the number of foreign-born residents was a notable feature. Canadians, the largest element, had increased from 36,000 in 1860 to 181,000 in 1890. The Germans were second. Numbering 38,000 in 1860, there were 135,000 of them in 1890. Englishmen increased from 25,000 to 55,000, Scots from 5,000 to 12,000, and Irish from 30,000 to 39,000. The last reached the peak of 43,000 in 1880, and the number had declined by the date of the next census. This was the only foreign-born group which did not continue to increase. The Dutch element had grown from 6,000 to 29,000.

During the period 1860 to 1890 the Scandinavians first became numerous, and the peoples of southern and eastern Europe began to appear in the census returns. In 1860 only 440 Norwegians, 266 Swedes, and 192 Danes were reported; thirty years later these nationalities had increased respectively to 7,000, 27,000, and 6,000. No Finns were shown in the census report, but they were probably included among the Russians, as they were subjects of the Czar. There were some in the Upper Peninsula, for in 1864 a mine agent who had been sent to northern Europe to engage workmen brought a group of Norwegians, Swedes, and Finns to Hancock, and in 1871 a Chicago newspaper reported that the Finns had begun their migration to America. There were sufficient Finns in the North Country to warrant the establishment of a newspaper in their language in Hancock in 1876, and in 1889 the Michigan commissioner of labor and industrial statistics reported 386 Finns employed in the copper mines.

The number of foreign-born from southern and eastern Europe was still comparatively small at the end of this period. The sixty-eight Russians reported in 1860 had by 1890 increased to 11,889, the Poles from 112 to 15,669, and the Italians from 78 to 3,088. Hungarians first appeared in the Census of 1870, when 144 were counted; in 1890, there were only 637. Bohemians, too, were first reported in 1870. There were 1,179 in Michigan then, and 2,311 in 1890. Michigan in 1890 was still drawing its immigrants almost entirely from northern and western Europe, peoples who were easily assimilated into the resident population.

After the Civil War the state government resumed its campaign to bring foreigners, especially Germans, to Michigan. In April, 1869, the Legislature authorized Governor Henry P. Baldwin (1869–1873) to appoint an agent to reside in Germany and another to act for the state in New York City. The governor appointed Max H. Allardt, who had been born in Germany but had lived in the United States since he was a child.

Allardt was in Germany from 1870 to 1875, where he published a periodical entitled *Der Michigan Wegweiser* (*The Michigan Guidebook*) and a pamphlet, *Michigan, Its Advantages and Resources with a Complete Map of the State* (*Michigan, Seine Vorzuge Und Hulfsquellen, und Vollstandiger Karte des Staates*).

Although the Franco-Prussian War reduced emigation for a time, the number of immigrants increased appreciably. Nevertheless, Governor John J. Bagley (1873–1877), believing that the results were not worth the expense, recalled Allardt late in 1874.

In 1881, following the recommendation of Governor David H. Jerome, the Legislature again provided for a commissioner of immigration. He published a pamphlet entitled *Michigan and Its Resources* which was widely circulated. It was first translated into German and

Dutch, and in 1884 editions in French and Swedish were issued. This pamphlet was credited with bringing many immigrants to the state. Governor Josiah Begole, although he had at first praised the commissioner for his achievements, in 1885 decided that the office should be abolished. The cost, about $11,500 a year, he believed was too great, and the large number of immigrants coming to Michigan were taking jobs from native workmen. The law was repealed in 1885 because the commissioner had done his job too well.

The wages and prices listed in *Michigan and Its Resources*, published in 1881, are interesting reading today. Carpenters were paid from $2 to $3 a day, bricklayers $2.50 to $3, woodcutters $22 to $26 a month with board, farm hands $16 to $25 a month with board, and female domestics $1.50 to $3.50 a week with board.

Prices were low, although they varied considerably, being higher usually in the Upper Peninsula than in Detroit. Roast beef was quoted at from ten to sixteen cents a pound, corned beef five to ten cents, fresh pork ten to fifteen cents, ham ten to eighteen cents, chickens eight to eighteen cents, butter twenty to thirty-five cents, coffee fourteen to thirty, sugar ten to twelve and a half, potatoes forty cents to a dollar a bushel, milk four to eight cents a quart, eggs twelve to thirty cents a dozen, and board could be had for from $3 to $5 a week.

Although Michigan was eager to attract sturdy, industrious immigrants, one issue of the book (1893) carried the following warning: "Emigrants who float in with the tide will not find Michigan their El Dorado. . . . The Lord hates a lazy man, and the law takes care of the dishonest. Michigan is a hive of industry, with no use for drones."

3

Labor unions had been disrupted by the Panic of 1857, but new ones sprang up during the Civil War and afterward. The powerful Brotherhood of Locomotive Engineers had its beginning in Marshall, Michigan, where William D. Robinson in 1863 held meetings of Michigan Central Railroad engineers at his home to consider how they could increase their pay and improve working conditions. A convention of delegates in Detroit on May 15, 1863, organized the Brotherhood of the Footboard, a name that was changed to Brotherhood of Locomotive Engineers the following year. Robinson was the first Grand Chief Engineer.

Other unions founded during the 1860's were the Iron Molders,

Machinists and Blacksmiths, Cigarmakers, Carpenters, and Plasterers. On July 4, 1865, union workingmen held their first parade in Detroit. The growth of unions in Michigan at this time resulted largely from the capable leadership of Richard Trevellick. To strengthen the movement, he combined the separate unions of Detroit into an assembly. So dangerous did this alliance of workingmen appear to employers that they formed a general association to protect their interests. The Panic of 1873, by causing widespread unemployment, for a time weakened the labor movement in Michigan and throughout the nation.

One of the most influential labor organizations in American history rose to power, declined, and disappeared during this period. Founded in 1869 by Uriah Stephens, the Knights of Labor soon had a large membership. Organized like a lodge, with password, grip, and secret ritual, it was open to all workers without regard to occupation. The only persons barred from joining were liquor dealers, professional gamblers, lawyers, and bankers, a strange assortment. Beginning in 1878, when Terence V. Powderly became Grand Master, the Knights had a phenomenal growth.

A branch was established in Detroit in 1878. Charles Joseph Antoine Labadie, called "the gentle anarchist," was the leader. Jo Labadie somewhat resembled Buffalo Bill in appearance. He had a white mustache and a white goatee, and he wore a large felt hat and a Windsor tie. Jo was part Indian, part French—a real Michiganian. He was a journalist and a poet, and he set his writings in type and printed them on his own press. An incurable idealist, he hated governments but loved people.

Labadie was a poet, but he had practical ability, and he organized assemblies in Detroit and in a number of outlying towns. Saginaw and Bay City became strongholds of the Knights. The newspapers in 1886 credited the organization with 25,000 members, but there were probably no more than 10,000.

Believing that the most good could be accomplished for workingmen by promoting favorable legislation, the Knights entered politics and in 1886 elected thirty-eight members to the State Legislature. By combining with others who were in sympathy with their principles, they were able to enact a law providing for compulsory school attendance, a child-labor law, and laws requiring safety devices in factories and inspection of mines. A law of 1883 established the Bureau of Labor, headed by a commissioner. Although he could do no more than gather and publish facts about industries in the state, his findings provided useful material for leaders who were demanding reform.

The child-labor law of 1885 forbade the employment of children under the age of ten in a factory, warehouse, or workshop, and the employment of any person under eighteen for more than ten hours a day or sixty hours a week. Children under fourteen were not to be employed unless they had attended school during at least four of the preceding twelve months.

According to the commissioner of labor's report on the furniture industry in 1890, children began to work at the age of thirteen. Their earnings were estimated at from $100 to $175 a year. Women earned no more than $300, and men about $500. House rent at that time varied from an average of $7.56 a month in Detroit, to $6.58 in Grand Rapids, to $5.67 in smaller towns.

Although the national organization of the Knights of Labor was opposed to strikes, many strikes were led by Knights. The most spectacular one during this period in Michigan was the lumber-mill strike in the Saginaw Valley in 1885. Believing that the ten-hour law passed in the spring was to take effect on July 1, instead of in September as was the fact, the employes walked out when their demand for a ten-hour day at the same wage was rejected. The leaders, chanting the slogan "Ten Hours or No Sawdust," soon shut down every lumber mill and saltworks in the Valley.

Governor Russell A. Alger sent militia to the strike-bound region to maintain order, and the operators hired 150 Pinkerton agents whom they had sworn in as deputy sheriffs. This was the first occasion in the state that militia and Pinkerton men were used against strikers. Under the circumstances there were numerous acts of violence. Finally, after three months, the operators obeyed the new law, and the workmen got their ten-hour day.

The Knights of Labor began to break up in 1888. There were too many diverse elements which were difficult to control, and unskilled workers had little money to pay their dues. Besides, the Knights lost a railroad strike in 1886, and they were blamed, unjustly, for the deaths in the Haymarket Riot in Chicago on May 4 of the same year.

Skilled craftsmen had, from the beginning, disliked the indiscriminate membership of the Knights. Because they were the aristocrats of labor, the skilled men wanted to protect their own trades against inroads by unskilled workers. To accomplish their purpose, craft unions joined together in 1881 in the American Federation of Labor.

Jo Labadie soon became a leader in the new movement, and in 1889, when the Michigan Federation of Labor was organized, he was elected the first president. By 1890, labor, at least in certain crafts, was strong enough to exert pressures for the betterment of working conditions.

4

In the industrial development of this period, lumber and lumber products were most important. Furniture, wagons, and carriages manufactured in Michigan became widely known. Shipbuilding flourished, especially in Bay City, Grand Haven, and Detroit.

Salt was produced in connection with the lumber mills. Douglass Houghton had found salt springs in the Saginaw region, but little was done to develop this resource until the State Legislature by a law of 1859 promised a ten-cent-a-bushel bounty when a company had produced 5,000 bushels. Operations were begun at once. The East Saginaw Salt Company turned out 53,000 bushels in 1860, and three times as much the next year. Other companies were organized, and when the increasing output threatened to empty the state treasury, the Legislature repealed the bounty law in 1861.

During this period the production of salt was closely linked with lumbering, for slab wood and other scrap from the mills were used as fuel to evaporate the water from the brine. By 1880 Michigan was making half of the salt in the nation, and the output in 1890 was more than 3,800,000 barrels. Besides Saginaw, St. Clair, Midland, Manistee, and Port Huron also had become salt-producing centers.

After the Civil War manufacturing increased in Detroit and other cities. Detroit continued to produce locomotives, steam engines, and stoves. The building of freight cars was begun about 1860. A few years later John S. Newberry and James McMillan became leaders in this industry. George M. Pullman first built his palace cars and sleeping cars in Detroit, and his plant was operated there until about 1890, when he moved to Chicago.

During this period Detroit became an important center for the production of drugs, varnish, paint, shoes, and seeds. Frederick Stearns began the manufacture of pharmaceuticals early in the 1860's, and the firm which became Parke, Davis and Company was organized in 1867 by Hervey C. Parke, George S. Davis, and Dr. Samuel P. Duffield. The Berry brothers, Joseph H. and Thomas, were pioneers in the production of varnish; and Dexter M. Ferry developed the growing and selling of farm and garden seeds into a large industry. There were several shoe factories in Detroit. The firm of Pingree and Smith, organized in 1866 by Hazen S. Pingree and Charles H. Smith, was one of the largest.

Grand Rapids had a variety of industries, including factories making freight cars, elevators, pumps, paint, varnish, tools, and surgical instruments. Furniture made in Grand Rapids was sold in all parts of the world. Flint became known as a center for the manufacture of wagons and carriages. In Kalamazoo, Dr. William E. Upjohn began manufacturing pharmaceuticals, and the production of paper was becoming important. Detroit, Grand Rapids, and Kalamazoo had horse-drawn streetcars. By 1890 all these cities, and some of the smaller ones also, had telephones and electricity.

Electric street lights replaced gas lamps, first in the business districts and later in the residential sections of cities. The earliest electric lighting was by arc lamps. In Detroit tall steel towers, some of them 150 feet high, were erected on lower Woodward Avenue and on Jefferson Avenue in 1881. The arc lamps were fastened to the tops of them. Because of their altitude, one observer asserted that they threw more light on the sky above than on the earth beneath. Some of the downtown stores installed arc lamps during the 1880's.

The Edison Illuminating Company of Detroit was organized in 1886. It installed incandescent electric bulbs, the invention of Thomas A. Edison, a former resident of Michigan.

Born in Ohio in 1847, Tom Edison had moved with his parents to Port Huron when he was seven years old. He was an inquisitive youngster, interested in many things; but he was bored by his lessons in school. There was nothing in them about what he was eager to know. Provoked by his inattention, his teacher finally sent him home with the comment that he was too dull to learn anything.

Tom's feelings were hurt. His mother, who had been a teacher, comforted him, and undertook his education herself. His father encouraged him to read widely, and when he was only nine years old he was studying books on history and natural science. In the basement of their big old house on the military reservation of Fort Gratiot, Tom set up a chemical laboratory. All his pocket money went for books and chemicals.

When Tom was twelve years old, the Grand Trunk Railroad ran its first train from Detroit to Port Huron. A restless boy, always eager to try something new and to keep himself occupied, Tom saw in the railroad a great opportunity. Although Samuel Edison, his father, had a prosperous business in feed and grain, and there was no need for the boy to work, he wanted to earn more money to buy laboratory equipment. He got permission from the conductor to sell candy, peanuts, and popcorn on the train, then asked for his parents' consent. They tried to discourage him, but, seeing how determined he was, they let him have his way.

Tom rode to Detroit in the morning, selling his wares to the passengers. While waiting for the train to return in the evening, he spent his time in the city library. Rashly he decided to read every book in the building, but he gave up that plan after reading through several shelves. To add to his business, he bought newspapers in Detroit and sold them on the train, at the stations along the way, and in Port

Tom Edison's Laboratory at Port Huron

Huron. When other trains were added on the line, he hired boys to work on them.

Tom continued his experiments. He and a chum constructed crude telegraph instruments modeled after the ones he saw in the railroad stations, strung a wire between their houses, and carried on halting conversations. One day at Mount Clemens, while waiting for the train to start, he saved the son of the telegraph operator from being run over by a string of freight cars. In gratitude, the operator offered to teach Tom telegraphy. Always eager to learn things that interested him, the boy gladly accepted.

To help occupy his spare time on the long train ride every day, Tom set up a laboratory and a printing press in the baggage car. On the press he printed the *Grand Trunk Weekly Herald*. One day when the car hit a rough spot in the tracks, the chemicals were upset. A stick of phosphorus burst into flames and set the car on fire. The conductor was furious. At the next stop, Smith's Creek, he threw press and laboratory out the door and ordered Edison to follow them.

When he was seventeen, Edison left home to earn his living as a telegrapher. He was a skilful operator, but he was more interested in improving the equipment than in sending and receiving. As a result, he lost one position after another and wandered from city to city.

While working as a telegrapher, he invented an electric vote recorder for legislative chambers, a printing telegraph, and a method of sending two messages over a wire at the same time. In 1869 he sold his patents for $40,000. To the young inventor, this was a fortune.

Edison set up his own shop in Newark, New Jersey, in 1870, and hired skilled workmen to fashion his ideas into new machines. Six years later he moved to Menlo Park, New Jersey, where he had built a laboratory. There, in 1879, after thousands of failures, he finally was successful in perfecting the incandescent electric light bulb. It was hailed as one of the greatest inventions ever made. Companies were organized in large cities to provide lighting with the new bulbs.

In Detroit Henry Ford was chief engineer for the Edison Illuminating Company during the 1890's. After he had built his first automobile in 1896, he was introduced to Edison at a company convention. The Wizard of Menlo Park, as he was called, listened intently to Ford's description of his car. He asked a few questions about the engine. Then he told the young man that he had a good idea which he should develop. Ford was greatly encouraged, and the two men became close friends.

In 1929 the Golden Jubilee of Electric Light was celebrated. Dearborn was the official headquarters. There, in preparation for the event, Henry Ford had had reconstructed Edison's Menlo Park laboratory, equipped just as it had been in 1879. Thomas A. Edison went to Dearborn and, as a part of the celebration, he repeated the final successful experiment of making the first incandescent bulb. President Herbert Hoover was one of the distinguished guests at the celebration. Today visitors to Ford's Greenfield Village in Dearborn may see the laboratory and the other buildings in which Edison worked to produce the electric lamp and many other important inventions.

5

Between 1860 and 1890 farmers moved into the northern counties of the Lower Peninsula and into the Upper Peninsula, and it was during this period that farming became a great industry. Previously, crops were grown to supply the farmer's family, and surpluses, if any, were sold in the immediate neighborhood. The clearing and cultivation of more land had made larger surpluses possible, and the numerous railroads in the state provided transportation to carry them to distant markets. Farmers who could send the produce to a lake port had an advantage of cheaper shipping costs.

The largest Michigan farm crop, and the most valuable, was wheat. Shipments out of the state returned more money to the farmers than the total of all other surplus crops combined. Corn, oats, barley, buckwheat, and hay were raised in large quantities, and along with wheat the value of these products per acre was greater in Michigan than in any other state. All the grains except corn were grown in the Upper Peninsula as well as in the Lower.

Potatoes, beets, turnips, carrots, and other garden vegetables returned good yields both below and above the Straits of Mackinac. It was observed, however, that in the Upper Peninsula farmers and gardeners from the northern countries of Europe, Scandinavians and Finns, were most successful. Near the cities, truck and market gardening were extensively practiced.

Because of the glaciers, Michigan has a great variety of soils. Gradually farmers learned that special crops would thrive on what had been considered waste land. For example, swamps, when drained, provided a deep rich soil for celery, cranberries, and peppermint. Before 1890, Michigan was producing more peppermint oil than all the other states together. Celery also became a cash crop with Kalamazoo as the principal center. In the fertile muck fields around the city, three crops a year could be raised. Although celery was not shipped in any quantity before 1878, by 1890 it had become a great article of export. At the height of the season daily shipments of thirty or forty tons were made from Kalamazoo. An excellent quality of celery was grown also near Newberry, in the Upper Peninsula.

During this period the fruit belt had its beginning as a commercial producer of apples, peaches, pears, plums, and cherries. On the western side of the state, between the Grand Traverse region on the north and the St. Joseph River on the south, a strip of land about forty miles wide was especially productive. Its advantage was the proximity of Lake Michigan which tempered the west winds blowing over it.

Even before the Civil War, pioneer farmers who planted small orchards discovered the suitability of soil and climate for raising fruit. After 1860 commercial production developed rapidly. As in the case of lumber, Chicago was the nearest and largest market, but railroads also carried fruit to Detroit and into Indiana and Ohio. Fruit was grown in other parts of the state, but not on so large a scale as in the fruit belt. Grapes, strawberries, raspberries, and blackberries also were produced commercially.

Cattle were raised for beef, as horses were replacing oxen for draught purposes, and dairy farming was still in the future. Nearly every farmer had a flock of sheep which provided both meat and wool. Throughout the southern part of Michigan there were numerous woolen mills which spun the wool and made the yarn into cloth.

Although the early 1870's were a period of hard times for the farmers, conditions improved and they had more money to spend. New and better tools and machinery were used on more and more farms. For the farmer's wife there were washing machines and sewing machines. For use in the fields there were the self-binding reaper, the Oliver chilled-steel plow, the corn planter, and the wheat drill. On numerous farms windmills were erected to pump water for the animals and for use in the house. In spite of these new contrivances, farmers and their families were still largely isolated, and it was only the most successful who were able to afford all of the labor-saving devices.

In 1872 an organization came to Michigan which promised both social and economic benefits to the farmer. The Patrons of Husbandry, founded in 1869 by Oliver H. Kelley, spread rapidly throughout the states. Among the purposes of the founder were to make the daily lives of men and women on the farms better and happier, to encourage education, to improve economic conditions, to make farm life more attractive, and to induce children to remain on the farms. The local lodge was a Grange and members were usually called Grangers.

Women as well as men were admitted to the Granges, and the social features of the organization helped relieve the monotony of farm life. To improve the economic condition of the farmer, the Patrons urged certain reforms, especially regulation of railroad rates, which were excessive. Members were urged to elect candidates who promised the desired reforms, but the Patrons neither formed a third party nor supported either of the leading parties as such. In the West, because the farmers were suffering from adverse economic conditions, the

Patrons became quite radical in their demands for reform. In Michigan, however, where the farmers were relatively prosperous, the organization was conservative.

As a means of saving farmers money, the Patrons advised establishing co-operative stores. A number of them were opened, selling everything from groceries to farm machinery. Those that were well managed prospered for a time, but they failed one by one, and before 1890 the experiment had been abandoned. Marketing of farm crops on a co-operative basis flourished for a short time also. In both cases failure resulted from a declining membership in the Granges, difficulties of borrowing money on favorable terms, and poor management. Nevertheless, the Patrons continued as an organization, their influence was frequently felt by the Legislature, and in later years co-operatives which they fostered were successful.

Another farm group called the Patrons of Industry was established in Michigan in 1887. Appealing to farmers who were dissatisfied with the conservative stand of the Grangers, the Patrons of Industry were active in politics. In 1892 they joined with the radical Populist party in demanding fundamental reforms, but the Patrons of Industry soon declined, and by 1896 the organization had ceased to exist.

— 21 —

End of an Era

FREE SCHOOLS in Michigan were at last made a reality by an act of the Legislature approved on April 3, 1869. Instead of having to depend upon tuition payments, schools were supported by local taxes and by state aid. Attendance increased, but there were still many children not in school. Compulsory attendance laws of 1883 and 1885, which required a minimum of four months' schooling, were not enforced.

Union schools became common after 1860. They were graded schools with frequently an added year or two of advanced work. By 1870 about a dozen high schools existed. Many taxpayers believed that they should not be required to support education beyond the elementary grades. To prove this theory, some Kalamazoo property owners took the matter to court. In 1874, the supreme court of the state, Justice Thomas M. Cooley writing the opinion, held that high schools were legitimate establishments under the school law. After this decision in the Kalamazoo case, high schools increased rapidly.

At the University of Michigan, President Henry P. Tappan was successful in raising the standards. Students and alumni understood what he was doing, and they approved. So did many others, but he antagonized some members of the faculty by his sharp criticism, he aroused the hostility of some newspaper editors by his frequent references to the perfection of the Prussian system of education, and he clashed with the Regents on the government of the University. The Board elected in 1858 was determined to rule. Although only three of the members had any college education, they interfered with the management of even minute matters. Dr. Tappan's imperious nature made agreement impossible. On the afternoon of Commencement Day, June 25, 1863, at the annual meeting, the Board demanded his resignation. Dr. Tappan resigned and spent the remainder of his life in Europe.

The Regents elected as his successor Dr. Erastus O. Haven, a Methodist minister who had been a member of the faculty from 1852 to 1856. President Haven was an active, energetic, and kindly person who was able to heal the wounds caused by the brutal dismissal of President Tappan. It was during his administration in 1867 that the Legislature voted a tax of one twentieth of a mill on each dollar of taxable property to be levied for the support of the University. This was the beginning of dependable state aid. The enrollment in 1867 was 1,255, the largest in any American university.

In 1869 President Haven resigned to become president of Northwestern University, and Professor Henry S. Frieze was acting president until 1871. It was during his administration that women were first admitted to the University. Although petitions on the subject had been received since 1850, it was not until January 5, 1870, that the Regents adopted a resolution recognizing the right of every Michigan resident possessing the requisite qualifications to attend the University. Miss Madelon L. Stockwell of Kalamazoo was admitted in February, 1870, and in the fall eleven others entered the Literary College, three Pharmacy, two Law, and eighteen Medicine.

Professor Frieze was anxious to be relieved of his administrative duties. In 1871 the Regents appointed Dr. James B. Angell president. A graduate of Brown University, he had studied in Europe, had taught at Brown, and had been editor of the *Providence Journal*. Since 1856 he had been president of the University of Vermont.

In 1880 President Rutherford B. Hayes sent Dr. Angell to China as minister plenipotentiary to negotiate a treaty. He performed this service successfully and returned to Ann Arbor in 1882.

President Angell correlated the various departments and set up the elective system, which permitted specialization during the third and fourth years. He also organized the Graduate School in the Literary College. In 1879 he established a chair in the science and art of teaching, the first in any American university. Dr. Angell continued to serve as president until 1909.

Because he was nationally known, President Angell brought great prestige to the University. He soon won the support of alumni and legislature and obtained funds for a much-needed building program.

The Law Building, later named Haven Hall, was erected in 1863. University Hall, connecting Mason Hall and South Hall, was completed in 1875, the museum in 1879, the engineering shops in 1882, the library in 1883, and the physics laboratory in 1887.

2

During the first few years, Michigan Agricultural College had a precarious existence. The difficulties attending the operation of a school outside a town on uncultivated land had been underestimated, and there were strong differences of opinion as to curriculum and management.

In 1861 control by the Board of Education was terminated and the Legislature provided for a Board of Agriculture of six members to govern the college. This fundamental change marked the beginning of stability and advance for the institution.

Under the Morrill Act, passed by Congress in 1862, the state received a grant of 240,000 acres of public land which served as an endowment for the college. In compliance with the requirements of the act, military drill for students was begun in 1863.

Theophilus C. Abbot, a member of the faculty, became president in 1862 and continued in office until 1884. During his administration the college progressed. Besides training young men for agriculture, the college held winter farmers' institutes which brought men actively engaged in farming to the campus for instruction in special subjects. Women were admitted as students in 1870.

New buildings were erected to house a greater number of students and to provide additional laboratories and classrooms. Williams Hall, a chemical laboratory, a botanical laboratory, a greenhouse, a library, and an astronomical observatory were built during this period.

Edwin Willits was appointed president in 1885. A graduate of the University of Michigan, he had been teacher, newspaper editor, representative in Congress, and member of the State Board of Education. When he was appointed, he was principal of the State Normal School at Ypsilanti.

Willits was a man of great energy and enthusiasm. Eager to make the college more helpful to farmers of the state, he used his influence in Washington to help the Hatch bill through Congress. This act provided funds for the support of agricultural experiment stations. In 1889 Willits resigned to become assistant secretary of agriculture under President Benjamin Harrison. His successor was Professor Oscar Clute.

A new state institution of higher learning, the Michigan Mining School, was established in 1886 at Houghton, in recognition of the need for trained mining engineers. By the act of the Legislature which provided for the school, it was placed under the direction of a Board of Control. Tuition was free to Michigan students.

When it opened on September 15, 1886, Albert Williams, Jr., was principal. Because no building was provided, classes were first taught in the town hall. Dr. Marshman E. Wadsworth was appointed director in 1887. When the original quarters became too small, four rooms in the Odd Fellows Building and a large skating rink were rented. Jay A. Hubbell, who had been active in establishing the school, gave a tract of land, and a building was erected in 1889. From the beginning, the policy of the school emphasized practical work in laboratories, shops, and mines.

3

Madelon L. Stockwell, the first University of Michigan coed, had been prepared and encouraged by a remarkable woman, Lucinda Hinsdale Stone. She was the wife of Dr. James A. B. Stone, president of Kalamazoo College. As a girl in New England, Lucinda Hinsdale had been eager for more than a grade-school education. She managed to gain admittance to an academy for boys and prepared for college, only to be denied admission. At Kalamazoo she founded and directed the women's department of the college.

Mrs. Stone was also a leader in the formation of women's clubs. The first Ladies' Library Association in Michigan, founded in Kalamazoo in 1852, grew out of Saturday evening discussions of new books at the Stones' home. In 1879 the ladies erected a building to house their books and to serve as a cultural center. A number of other library associations and literary clubs were organized in Michigan during this period through the influence of Mrs. Stone: at Battle Creek in 1864, at Ann Arbor in 1866, and Ypsilanti in 1868, at Grand Rapids in 1869, and at Schoolcraft in 1879.

The women raised money by sponsoring lectures and plays, and by wheedling contributions from their husbands. The libraries they established usually were later taken over by the towns.

Women's clubs, with a cultural purpose, were organized during the seventies, following the establishing of the first club in Kalamazoo in 1873. Members read papers, and speakers from outside the group were engaged. Mrs. Stone considered these clubs as a means for continuing the education of women. She made her influence felt throughout the state by her newspaper articles, especially her "Club Talks" in the *Detroit Post and Tribune*.

Another woman, who had a much wider influence than Mrs. Stone, got her early education and her inspiration in Michigan. Dr. Anna Howard Shaw was born in England in 1847 and came with her family to Massachusetts in 1852. Seven years later the Shaws settled on a farm in the Michigan woods about nine miles from Big Rapids. Anna had little opportunity to obtain a formal education, but she read a great deal, and she practiced making speeches from stumps in the woods.

When Anna was fifteen, she began to teach school at two dollars a week, boarding around with the pupils' families. Later she went to live with an older sister in Big Rapids. One Sunday in church she listened to a woman preacher. She at once decided to become a preacher herself and talked with the woman about preparing for the profession. Her advice was to go to school.

Anna attended the Big Rapids High School, and her parents offered to send her to the University of Michigan if she would give up the silly idea of preaching. But, determined to be a preacher, she obtained a license from the Methodist Episcopal Church and delivered her first sermon at Ashton, Michigan, when she was twenty-three years old. Two years later she entered Albion College, from which she was graduated. In 1876, although she was penniless, she enrolled in Boston Theological Seminary and made her own way until she had completed the course. After the Methodist Episcopal Church had refused ordination because she was a woman, she was ordained by the Methodist Protestants.

Not satisfied that she was doing as much good as possible, she entered Boston Medical School and was graduated in 1885. At first she engaged in social work; then she began lecturing for the cause of temperance and woman suffrage. Susan B. Anthony induced her to give all her time to the suffrage movement, and she became one of the national leaders.

A third woman who accomplished great things in Michigan and elsewhere was the Reverend Caroline Bartlett Crane. Her work in

Michigan began at the end of the period 1860–1890, and continued for many years. Born in Wisconsin in 1858, Caroline Bartlett attended college, became a newspaper reporter, and finally a minister in the Unitarian Church. Her first charge was in Sioux Falls, South Dakota, and in 1889 she accepted a call to the First Unitarian Church of Kalamazoo. Mrs. Lucinda Hinsdale Stone was an active member.

Caroline Bartlett believed in "pure and practical religion" and it was her aim "to help establish truth, righteousness and love in the world." In 1894 her congregation erected a new building planned to provide for various services to the community. One purpose was to initiate programs which might later be carried on at public expense. It was called The People's Church.

Under Miss Bartlett's direction, trained teachers conducted a public kindergarten and classes in domestic science and manual training. When parents discovered the usefulness of such activities, they urged their adoption by the School Board. In 1899 these programs were added to the curriculum of the Kalamazoo schools. Other organizations conducted in the church were a club for Negroes and gymnasium classes for women.

In 1896 Miss Bartlett married Dr. A. W. Crane, a physician and a member of the church. She, her husband, and others founded the Unity Club to study local civic problems. Enlisting the assistance of college professors, physicians, and other interested persons, they investigated the city water supply, sewage disposal, the efficiency of police and fire departments, conditions in factories and in the schools, and facilities for recreation. Members of the club prepared and read reports, and the findings were used to help improve conditions in Kalamazoo. Other communities, becoming acquainted with the program, borrowed the information for their own use.

In 1898 Mrs. Crane resigned her pastorate because of failing health. She did not, however, lose interest in local affairs. Three years later she organized the Women's Civic Improvement League, which studied the problems of sanitation and public relief. Their investigation of conditions in slaughterhouses resulted in the passage of a state meat inspection law. Mrs. Crane's fame spread to other cities, and she was called upon to make sanitary surveys in a number of them.

Among the cultural activities of the period were local lyceums, addresses by eminent literary men, and theatrical productions. In 1876 at Bay View a summer Chautauqua was established with courses of lectures and musical programs.

An interesting development was the building of opera houses.

Beginning in the seventies, nearly every town sooner or later had a building or a hall in which plays or other entertainments were held. The name opera house was not exactly descriptive, for operas were seldom heard even in the cities. It was adopted because it sounded cultural, and because the term theater was distasteful to many persons.

In the smaller towns the opera house usually occupied the second floor of a store building. It had a stage and at least the minimum

The Howell Opera House, Interior, 1885

essential equipment for presenting plays. Increasing wealth relaxed some of the prejudice against theatrical presentations, and improved means of transportation made possible the booking of touring stock companies by even small-town opera house owners. *Uncle Tom's Cabin* was the most popular play, drawing a full house every time it was enacted. Besides offering professional productions, lectures, and concerts, the opera house also was open to high-school commencement exercises and to local-talent entertainment.

Detroit, of course, was large enough to attract the famous actors and actresses of the day: Helena Modjeska, Mary Anderson, E. H.

Sothern, Joseph Jefferson, and Edwin Booth. A native son, Bronson Howard, became a playwright of international reputation. Howard's first play, *Fantine,* had its premiere in Detroit in 1864. *Saratoga* ran for more than one hundred performances in New York; then, under the title *Brighton,* it was played 240 times in London. A German translation was popular in Berlin. Other plays written by Howard were successfully produced in the United States and Great Britain.

4

In politics the period 1860 to 1890 was marked by the rule of the Republican party ably supported by members of the Grand Army of the Republic, Union veterans of the Civil War. Waving the bloody shirt served instead of issues. Democrats were branded as rebels and traitors.

During this period the Republicans lost the governorship only twice. In 1882, a fusion of Democrats and Greenbackers elected Josiah W. Begole, a former Republican, in the contest with Governor David H. Jerome. Begole was a well-to-do farmer who lived near Flint. He had been a state senator in 1871 and 1872, and in the latter year he had been a delegate to the National Republican Convention. He later served as a member of the Forty-third Congress. All the other officers elected that year were Republicans.

The second defeat of the Republicans was more serious. In 1890 the Democrats elected as governor Edwin B. Winans, a prosperous farmer of Livingston County, and all the other state officers. They also named seven of the eleven representatives to Congress.

Although Michigan gave its electoral vote in 1884 to James G. Blaine, Grover Cleveland was elected President. He appointed Don M. Dickinson of Detroit Postmaster General, and the Democrats of Michigan had a brief taste of the sweets of national patronage.

During this period, up to 1879, Senator Zachariah Chandler was the political boss of Michigan, and his influence extended much farther. He was one of the Radical Republicans who opposed Lincoln's lenient policy toward the South. Along with the others, he attacked President Andrew Johnson when he attempted to implement Lincoln's policy, and he was one of the leaders in procuring the impeachment and trial of the President in 1868.

Chandler was aggressive, intolerant, and narrowly partisan. He was a good hater who punished his opponents by the use of patronage. His enemies called him coarse, ignorant, and unscrupulous; his supporters trusted him because he fiercely defended the Union.

Entering the Senate in 1857, Chandler served three terms. Much to his chagrin he was defeated in 1875 by a combination of Democrats and younger Republicans who resented his aggressiveness and his handling of the patronage. They elected in his place Supreme Court Judge Isaac P. Christiancy, who had been a Democrat and a Free-Soiler before 1854, a much more moderate person than Chandler. President Ulysses S. Grant appointed Chandler Secretary of the Interior in 1875, and he held that position until 1877.

In 1876 Chandler was chairman of the Republican National Committee. Determined that Hayes should be President, on the day after the election, when the result was still uncertain, he sent out a telegram from party headquarters to the newspapers: "Rutherford B. Hayes has received 185 electoral votes, and is elected." As a matter of fact Hayes had only 165 uncontested votes and Samuel J. Tilden, 184. Twenty votes were in dispute, seventeen of them in South Carolina, Florida, and Louisiana, in which United States troops were still maintained. Tilden needed only one vote to win; Hayes needed all twenty. Chandler used his influence to win the southern votes for Hayes.

An electoral commission consisting of five Supreme Court justices, five senators, and five representatives, eight of whom were Republicans and seven Democrats, gave the twenty disputed votes and the election to Hayes. When Hayes withdrew the federal troops from the three states, thus permitting them to return Democratic majorities, Chandler denounced him as a traitor to his party. The new president named Carl Schurz, civil service reformer, as Chandler's successor in the Interior Department. In 1879 Chandler was again elected Senator. He died in December of that year.

During this period two new political parties appealed to dissatisfied voters for support: the Greenback party and the Prohibition party. The Greenback party was organized in 1876. It demanded that "greenbacks," or United States Treasury notes, issued during the Civil War as an emergency currency in the amount of $450,000,000, should remain in circulation and that more should be issued to relieve the shortage of money. Congress, however, in 1875, under the influence of the "sound money" interests, passed a law providing for the resumption of specie payments on January 1, 1879, that is, the exchange of gold for greenbacks. A law of 1878 provided that the $346,681,016 of outstanding greenbacks should remain in circulation. When Congress began to accumulate a gold fund to meet the eventual demand for exchange, greenbacks passed at par value.

This policy of Congress in freezing the amount of money when industry was growing and additional cash was required was greatly to the advantage of bankers and creditors in general. Debtors who had borrowed cheap greenbacks had to repay their debts in dearer money. For example, because the scarcity of cash reduced prices, farmers had to sell more bushels of wheat than before to pay their mortgages or other debts.

In Michigan Democrats and Greenbackers fused in 1882 to elect Josiah Begole governor, and in 1884 the two parties won seven of the eleven seats in Congress.

The Prohibition party was pretty strong, polling, in 1890, 25,000 votes, its greatest total. The Republicans, eager to win their support, in 1886 promised a vote on state-wide prohibition. A constitutional amendment placed on the ballot the next year was defeated by the vote in Wayne County and in the Upper Peninsula. There is no doubt that the vote was managed by the machine in Detroit, and in Gogebic County more votes were cast against the amendment than there were voters in the county. Although this attempt to outlaw liquor failed, a local-option act was passed in 1889, permitting counties to vote themselves dry.

5

In the field of national government there were a number of important and exciting issues. During more than half of the period 1860–1890, the questions of the status of the newly liberated Negroes and the treatment of the southern states occupied men's minds. The mild policies of Lincoln and Johnson toward the South were reversed by the Radical Republicans under the leadership of Senator Zachariah Chandler and others. United States troops were quartered in the states which had seceded, and by the Thirteenth, Fourteenth, and Fifteenth Amendments to the Constitution, Negroes were given their freedom, protection of their civil rights, and the privilege of the ballot. The last United States garrison was withdrawn from the South in 1877.

During Grant's administration, corruption in government flourished. The President, who was honest himself, was naïve in political matters and easily managed by corrupt advisers. Senator Chandler was an exception. Although he was a devoted supporter of the administration, he was honest. Corruption and ineptitude in Washington caused numerous Republicans to break with the party and nominate Horace Greeley, the New York newspaper editor, for President in 1872. Austin Blair, who had been governor of Michigan during the Civil War, led the Liberal Republican-Democratic coalition ticket in the state in 1872. Grant's reputation as the general who had saved the Union won him the Presidency again.

Continued corruption led to a demand for civil service reform, the selecting of appointive government officers because of merit instead of on the recommendation of a political leader. Senator Chandler, who was expert in using the patronage to strengthen the party and to maintain his own position, bitterly fought the proposed reform. The assassination of President Garfield by a disappointed office seeker caused a strong popular revulsion against the spoils system. Congress in 1882 passed the Pendleton Act, which created the Civil Service Commission and marked the beginning of the merit system in the national government.

Other important issues were the maintenance of the gold standard, the tariff, and the regulation of the railroads. The Republicans upheld the gold standard and the protective tariff. Long-continued protests against the unfair practices of the railroads finally induced Congress in 1887 to pass the regulatory Interstate Commerce Act. Judge Thomas M. Cooley of Michigan was appointed chairman of the Interstate Commerce Commission when it was established under the provisions of the act. All of the national issues which have been mentioned influenced state politics to some extent.

In the state, prominent issues during the period were a new constitution, municipal aid to railroads, woman suffrage, Negro suffrage, prohibition, hours of labor, regulation of railroads, and ballot reform.

The constitution of 1850 provided that in 1866 the question of revising the constitution should be placed on the ballot. A majority voted in the affirmative and a convention assembled in 1867. The revised constitution which was written was rejected at the polls in 1868. Opposition to three sections is believed to have caused the people to vote against the revision: higher salaries for state officers, permission for municipal aid to railroads, and authorization of Negro suffrage. A section prohibiting licensing of liquor establishments, which was voted on separately, was defeated. In 1873, by vote of the Legislature, a commission was assembled to revise the constitution. This revision was rejected by the voters in 1874, and the constitution of 1850 remained in force.

The Republicans favored permitting cities and townships to issue bonds and give the proceeds to railroad companies which promised to build lines to serve them. Although there was no assurance that the railroads would ever be built, payment of interest and principal on the bonds would be made from taxes. Bills passed by the Legislature authorizing the issuing of bonds were vetoed by Governor Henry H. Crapo, himself a Republican, because he believed they were not in the public interest. The bills were passed over his veto; but in the decision on the Salem case in 1870, the Michigan Supreme Court held that the people could not be taxed for the support of railroads nor of any other private business.

The adoption of Negro suffrage in Michigan, in spite of the fact that Senator Chandler and other Radical Republicans had forced it on the South, was delayed until 1870, when both the Fifteenth Amendment to the Constitution and an amendment to the state constitution were ratified.

Associations favoring woman suffrage were active, but they accomplished nothing during the period. Nevertheless, two women did vote in Michigan in 1871—Miss Mary Wilson in Battle Creek and Mrs. Nannette B. Gardner in Detroit. A wealthy widow and a taxpayer, Mrs. Gardner convinced an alderman that he should register her because she had no husband to protect her interests.

On election day, April 3, 1871, Mrs. Gardner, accompanied by her small son and two women friends, drove to the polling place in her carriage. In one hand she held a vase of flowers, and in the other a ballot "which she had decorated with various appropriate devices." When it was discovered that she had registered, she was permitted to vote without further question. Mrs. Gardner, delighted with the courtesy of the election inspectors, gave them the vase of flowers. Mrs. Gardner was permitted to vote as long as she lived in Detroit. She alone had that privilege because no other woman was able to get herself registered.

6

Regulation of railroad rates to prevent exorbitant charges for freight and passenger traffic and discrimination between places and among shippers was attempted by many states. Some legislatures passed severe laws establishing rates which the railroad companies claimed were ruinous.

In Michigan railroad regulation was mild in comparison. A law of 1873 provided for a commissioner of railroads whose duties consisted of inspecting tracks and bridges, requiring reports from all the companies, publishing statistics, reporting failures to obey state laws, and making recommendations to the Legislature for new legislation.

The commissioner's reports indicate that there were few complaints about discrimination in rates between various towns, and he expressed the opinion that charges were lower in Michigan than in any other state, with the possible exception of Ohio. He asserted that Michigan shippers were discriminated against by the great trunk lines, being compelled to pay higher rates on goods sent East than other shippers farther West. There was nothing that the Legislature could do to protect its people from such practices, for regulation of commerce between the states was a subject reserved to the national government. The necessity for action in this field led to the establishing by Congress of the Interstate Commerce Commission in 1887.

One of the important reforms of this period was the adoption of the Australian ballot for voting in elections. Previous to the passage of laws in 1889 and 1891, each party had provided ballots on which were printed the names of its candidates. With this system, it was easy for political bosses or employers to see how each man voted, and to punish him if he used the wrong ballot.

For some years there had been a demand for a secret ballot, but men who profited by controlling elections vigorously opposed any change. They declared that it was cowardly to sneak behind a curtain to vote. Every red-blooded American, they asserted, should be proud to let everyone know for whom he cast his ballot. In spite of bitter opposition by an influential minority, laws of 1889 and 1891 provided for a ballot printed by the state or local government which contained the names of all candidates. The voter marked his ballot in a booth, folded it, and saw the clerk deposit it in the ballot box. This law made it more difficult for bosses to control the vote.

7

The period 1860 to 1890 is notable for important developments in Michigan. Although the Civil War had an unsettling effect on business for a time, it eventually stimulated all sorts of production. A great increase in the demand for iron, copper, lumber, foodstuffs, and manufactured goods induced an enormous output of materials from mines, forests, farms, and factories. The Panic of 1873, brought on by overexpansion, caused a temporary setback to economic development, but recovery was rapid and prosperity returned.

Mining continued to be an important industry in Michigan. Besides the mines in the Marquette Range, new ones were opened in the Menominee and the Gogebic ranges, and Michigan led the nation in production of iron ore. Although some copper mines were worked out, those in the Portage Lake region, especially the Calumet and Hecla groups, increased the output so that until 1887 Michigan was first among the states as a copper producer.

Logging and lumbering were extended north along the shores of Lakes Huron and Michigan and into the Upper Peninsula. In 1888 production reached the peak of more than four billion board feet of lumber. Great fortunes were accumulated by successful lumbermen. Careless and wasteful logging left combustible debris in the woods, and great forest fires, especially in 1871 and 1881, devastated wide areas in the state.

Demand for more foodstuffs, the extension of railroad lines, and the clearing of land by the lumbermen caused an expansion of farming. Except in the newly occupied regions, farmers produced surpluses for sale, and farming became an industry rather than simply a means of providing subsistence. Diversified agriculture was the rule, but certain regions specialized in products suited to the soil and climate. The counties along the shore of Lake Michigan from Grand Traverse Bay southward became noted for fine fruits, and Kalamazoo was the center of the celery-growing industry.

Greater wealth permitted many farmers to purchase some of the machinery which made their work lighter and increased production. The Patrons of Husbandry gave farmers an opportunity to co-operate to improve their condition, but the Grangers in Michigan were not so radical in demanding reforms as were those farther West. The Grange meetings, which were attended by women as well as men, provided some social opportunities for farm wives. Poor roads kept country people isolated, and many young men and women went to the cities seeking a more interesting environment.

Industries of all kinds expanded rapidly after 1860. Michigan became noted for the manufacture of furniture, wagons, carriages, railroad cars, agricultural implements, shoes, stoves, and drugs. There were jobs in towns for immigrants and for people from the country. Dissatisfaction with wages and working conditions led to the founding of unions. During this period the Knights of Labor, which accepted all sorts of workingmen, had its rise and decline.

The Knights were succeeded by the American Federation of Labor, a combination of craft unions which admitted only skilled men to membership. Strikes were numerous, but usually of short duration and rarely successful. Industrialists banded together to resist the demands of their employes. By supporting candidates favorable to their cause, unions won some victories in the State Legislature. Laws were passed limiting child labor, reducing the hours of labor to ten a day, and requiring inspection of mines.

Railroads were extended throughout the state in both the Upper and the Lower peninsulas to carry the increased production of forests, fields, mines, and factories. The two peninsulas were connected by railroads and car ferries across the Straits of Mackinac. The state gave the Sault Canal to the national government. A new single lock was built, construction of another was begun, and the collection of tolls was abandoned.

The public schools of Michigan during this period were made free to all pupils. Union schools and high schools provided better and more advanced education for the children of the state than had been available earlier. Many children, however, were not in school because the compulsory-attendance law was not enforced.

In 1886 the state opened a new institution of higher learning, the Michigan Mining School at Houghton in the Upper Peninsula.

The increase in wealth and advances in technology made living more comfortable and convenient, at least in the cities. Streets were paved, electric lights were installed, and the three largest cities had streetcars. Central heating began to replace fireplaces and stoves, and bathrooms were equipped in some houses. Telephones could be had, but they were used largely for commercial rather than social communication.

With increasing wealth came the desire to build larger and more ornate houses. Not satisfied with the simple dignity of the colonial style, rich men vied with each other to build mansions which they believed were in keeping with their position in society. Huge houses with towers, cupolas, Gothic windows, scrollwork in wood or cast iron, sprang up in every town. Other residents imitated their wealthier fellow townsmen by building similar dwellings of smaller size. Many of the large houses are still standing, mute testimony to the fact that increased wealth did not necessarily make for good taste.

During this period the Republican party, which had begun as a radical organization demanding reform, became entrenched in power and conservative in its policies. The Democrats were the opposition party, but they were unable to convince the voters that they should be given the reins of government. The Greenback party, which favored a more liberal money program, joined with the Democrats to elect Josiah

Begole governor in 1882, and the Democrats put Edwin B. Winans in office in 1890. With these exceptions, the Republicans dominated the political scene between 1860 and 1890.

During these years developments in mining, lumbering, farming, and industry were preparing the way for even greater production in the future, except in lumber. The trend from a predominantly extractive economy to one of manufacturing had begun.

PART VI

CHALLENGE TO DEMOCRACY 1890–1920

— 22 —

Hazen Pingree, Idol of the People

THE REPUBLICANS won the election of 1888, and Benjamin Harrison succeeded Grover Cleveland as President. Cleveland was re-elected in 1892. Shortly after he was inaugurated in March, the Panic of 1893 broke. One cause was the extravagance of Congress, which almost emptied the Treasury. Another was the issuing of great numbers of Treasury notes, based on silver but redeemable in gold. These notes drained so much gold from government vaults that many persons believed the gold standard could not be maintained. Fear of unfavorable conditions caused people to hoard their money.

There were other reasons for the Panic of 1893. During the preceding five or six years the farmers of the South and the West had seen their purchasing power steadily decline, and all sorts of business dependent on their trade had suffered. Besides, there had been overexpansion of industry through the growth of the great trusts and the overbuilding of railroads. The investment resources of the country had been strained by these developments, and gold had been withdrawn by European investors because of a financial crisis abroad.

President Cleveland finally induced Congress to repeal the Sherman Silver Purchase Act, which had continued to drain gold from the Treasury, but he accomplished his purpose only at the expense of alienating southern and western Democrats. In the South and in the West, the farmers, convinced that they would have to gain control of the government to improve their condition, organized into alliances and elected governors, legislators, and a few members of Congress.

In 1892, determined to break with the old-line parties, the leaders called a convention in Omaha in July, organized the People's party, and planned a national campaign. Their platform demanded free and unlimited coinage of silver at the old ratio of sixteen to one; a flexible currency system controlled by the government instead of by the bankers; a graduated income tax; postal-savings banks; public ownership and operation of railroads, telegraph, and telephones; immigration restrictions; an eight-hour day; direct election of senators; the Australian ballot; and the initiative and referendum. This was considered a very radical program.

The 1892 presidential candidate of the Populists, as the party came to be called, was James B. Weaver of Iowa, who polled more than a million popular votes and received twenty-two in the Electoral College. These were from western states, for the Southerners remained loyal to the Democratic party in spite of Cleveland's hard-money principles.[1]

In 1896 the Democrats adopted the program of the Populists and nominated Williams Jennings Bryan. The Populists nominated him also. Almost terrified by this combination, the Republicans charged their opponents with anarchism and sedition. They raised and spent a huge campaign fund estimated at $16,000,000 and elected their candidate William McKinley. The Republicans retained control of the government until 1913, when Woodrow Wilson became President. Meanwhile, Theodore Roosevelt (1901–1909) talked a great deal about reform, but he accomplished little because conservative Republicans controlled Congress. He did arouse in the people a greater interest in government and demands for change. Some advances were made, but most of them occurred during the administration of William Howard Taft (1909–1913).

In 1898, the United States, by defeating Spain in a short war, proved that she had become a world power. For better or for worse she acquired colonies and assumed the white man's burden.

[1] Cleveland believed in maintaining the gold standard instead of increasing the quantity of currency by the addition of "soft money"—paper money and cheap silver.

Throughout these years there was a great increase in the population of cities, resulting from unrestricted immigration from Europe and a movement from the rural districts.

The rapid growth of industry and of industrial combinations too strong for state governments to control led to attempts by Congress, in the Interstate Commerce Act of 1887 and the Sherman Antitrust Act of 1890, to regulate them or reduce their size. Because the railroads and other industries controlled the Senate, and because the Supreme Court was exceedingly conservative, the national government was almost as helpless as were the states.

To match the huge aggregations of capital found in the steel, mining, and railroad companies, labor organized on a large scale and fought for improved conditions. At that time, because the courts were usually hostile to unions, the leaders believed that the only way to win better conditions for workingmen was by violence.

During the period 1890 to 1920 Michigan followed the political pattern established in 1854, electing Republican state administrations with few exceptions and contributing her electoral vote to Republican presidential candidates. On one occasion, in 1892, five electors voted for Cleveland and nine for Harrison. This result was made possible by a law of the Democratic Legislature in 1891 which provided that presidential electors should be chosen by congressional districts. The Republicans regained control of the state government in 1892 and repealed the law, returning to the practice of choosing a solid block of electors of the party which cast a majority or a plurality of votes in the state at large.

There were also one other exception to the rule in a presidential election and two in elections of state officers. The electoral vote was cast in 1912 for Theodore Roosevelt, who was running as a Progressive against Taft and Wilson; and in the same year, and again in 1914, the people elected Woodbridge N. Ferris, a Democrat, governor. The Legislature, however, was Republican.

2

Of the Republican governors, one in particular distinguished himself, although he was thoroughly disliked by the leaders of his party. That man was Hazen S. Pingree.

Pingree began his political career in 1890 as mayor of Detroit. Up to that time he had been a successful businessman, the senior partner of the shoe-manufacturing company, Pingree and Smith, and had taken no part in politics. His home, a great stone mansion on Woodward Avenue, stood on the site of the present Horace H. Rackham Educational Memorial Building.

Hazen Pingree was born in Maine in 1840. When the Civil War began, he was working in a shoe factory in Massachusetts. Enlisting immediately in an artillery regiment, he fought in several battles until he was captured by the Confederates and imprisoned in the Andersonville, Georgia, stockade. Pingree made the acquaintance of prisoners from Detroit who spoke so enthusiastically about the opportunities there that after the war he moved to that city. For more than a year he worked at his trade. Then he entered into a partnership with Charles H. Smith in 1866 and began on a small scale to manufacture shoes. The firm of Pingree and Smith prospered until by 1890 it was doing a business of more than $1,000,000 a year.

Although Michigan could be counted on to go Republican in national elections, and usually in state elections also, Detroit was in the hands of the Democrats. A group of influential businessmen, who hoped to change the complexion of the city government, in 1889 cast about for a Republican who might attract sufficient votes to win the election. Their choice fell upon Hazen Pingree, who, after some hesitation, agreed to run for mayor. He was elected in 1889 and re-elected three times afterward, but not with the support of the men who had induced him to run in the first election.

Hazen Pingree was a businessman. He was experienced in buying and selling, and he was accustomed to giving and receiving his money's worth. He immediately began an intensive examination of the affairs of the city, and found that it was being badly cheated. For example, he discovered that the few paved streets were full of holes because the paving had been poorly done; two electric companies were squabbling over the privilege of lighting the streets and bribing aldermen for the lucrative business of overcharging the city; good building lots held by wealthy citizens waiting for a rise in price were assessed at acreage rates, factories and downtown business buildings were lightly assessed, while the lots of homeowners were valued much more highly in proportion for tax purposes; the gas company was charging almost twice as much in Detroit as was charged in other cities; the street railway company, in spite of the fact that it was using ancient horse-drawn cars instead of the electric cars which most cities had at that time, was charging a five-cent fare and paying the city nothing for its franchise which was worth five or six million dollars.

As soon as he had gathered the facts, the mayor began his campaign to remedy the abuses. Of course the intrenched interests which had obtained special privileges from the corrupt city council defied him. His Honor was not surprised by this reaction, but he was a little bewildered when many of the best people turned against him. He soon discovered the reason. These men were stockholders in the corporations which were robbing the people, and they were the owners of choice parcels of land on which they were paying only nominal taxes. They were angry, and their feelings were hurt. Pingree, they had thought, was one of them. Now he was trying to cheat them of their privileges. He was a traitor to his class.

They snubbed him socially, removed him from the board of the Preston National Bank and influenced banks in Detroit to refuse his business so that he had to do his banking in New York, and opposed his renomination and re-election. But it was impossible to defeat him, for the people recognized him as their friend, and they supported him enthusiastically. One of Pingree's greatest services as mayor was to awaken the citizens to their duty as voters. Obeying his injunction to take part in the caucuses and to go to the polls, the people of Detroit learned that the popular will can be enforced if it is exerted continuously. Three times Pingree was re-elected mayor. The third time he received 67 per cent of the popular vote.

Besides the powerful business and industrial interests and the Republican party organization controlled by Senator James McMillan, the newspapers also were against Pingree. When they refused to publish his proclamations and printed distorted stories about his policies, he had broadsides printed and set up on billboards on the Michigan Avenue side of the City Hall. The passers-by sometimes lined up for blocks to wait for a chance to read them.

The mayor first brought the gas company to heel. Discovering that it had been violating the terms of its charter, he threatened suit to cancel it. When the company officials learned that he could not be influenced by a proffered bribe of $50,000, they gave up and reduced the rate from $1.50 per thousand cubic feet to eighty cents, as he had demanded, thus saving the people of the city thousands of dollars.

When he was unable to induce the electric companies to lower their charges, he established in 1895 a municipal lighting plant of which the present greatly enlarged system is the direct descendant. The young engineer whom he chose to build and manage the plant was Alex Dow, who later became head of the Detroit Edison Company. Lighting by the municipal plant cost $36 a year per lamp. In 1889 the charge had been $140.

During the whole period of his incumbency as mayor, Pingree fought the street railways. He found that they paid only 1½ per cent of their gross earnings in taxes to the city. In 1890, this amounted to $12,000. He believed that they should pay taxes on a fair assessment of their real and personal property, and that they should reduce the fare to three cents. When the companies refused, and he found he was powerless because they had a thirty-year franchise which would not expire until 1909, he induced a syndicate to build a three-cent line in 1895. His triumph was short-lived, however, for within less than two years the line was bought by the company which Pingree had been fighting.

Hazen Pingree was a man of broad and deep sympathy. The plight of thousands of men out of work, and their families, following the Panic of 1893, moved him mightily. He not only felt sorry for them but he took intelligent measures to relieve their want. Believing that these people would be glad for an opportunity to grow their own food, he advertised for the loan of vacant lots. Owners offered more than could be used for gardens, but pleas for money to buy seeds and tools resulted in meager donations.

When a special collection taken in the churches of the city amounted to only $13.80, the mayor sold his favorite saddle horse at auction for $380 and put the money into the fund. Pingree's potato patches, as they were called, served a useful purpose in Detroit, and his plan was adopted by a number of other cities. Even this project, however, did not change the attitude of his enemies. Downtown department stores refused to display in their windows vegetables from the gardens. Owners explained to the mayor's representative that to do so might make them appear to be supporters of Pingree, and offend some of their best customers.

3

Hazen Pingree found that control of the Legislature in Lansing by conservative Republicans interfered with his reform plans in Detroit. For example, he wanted direct primary elections; he wanted to compel the railroads to pay taxes on their property in Detroit; and he wanted home rule for cities so that Detroit and other municipalities could purchase street railways or other utilities and operate them for the people's benefit. He decided that to carry out his program he must be elected governor.

In 1896 Pingree obtained the Republican nomination for that office. The question naturally arises, Why did Senator James McMillan, party chief, and other influential leaders permit the nomination of this man whom they so thoroughly feared and abhorred? The answer is that they needed his vote-getting power to pull the Republican ticket through and to prevent the state from going to Bryan. The party leaders were confident that a majority of the state senators, who came to be known as the "Immortal Nineteen," would block any of Pingree's dangerous proposals. And so it almost turned out.

When Pingree took office as governor in January, 1897, his term as mayor of Detroit still had a year to run. Believing that he could accomplish his purposes more easily by occupying both offices, for more than two months he was mayor and governor. Then on March 20, 1897, the state supreme court ruled that he must give up one or the other. He thereupon resigned as mayor.

The new governor's principal attack was upon the favored position of the railroads in regard to taxation. Unlike other industries, they paid no tax on their real estate, buildings, and equipment, but only about 2 per cent of their annual earnings. This condition was a result of the desire of the legislatures in the early days to encourage railroads while they were in their infancy. Even though the railroads had been granted 5,000,000 acres of land to help pay the cost of construction and had long ago reached a prosperous maturity, they were still almost tax exempt, thanks to the pressure of their powerful lobby on the legislators.

Pingree's idea that the railroads should pay higher taxes was nothing new in the state. Beginning in 1877 governors Bagley, Croswell, Luce, Winans, and Rich had asked for action by the legislature but had accomplished nothing. The new governor was determined to make a fight to the finish. He had no desire to injure the railroads, but he insisted that they pay their proportionate share of the cost of state government. The additional revenue would be deposited in the primary-school interest fund, providing more adequate support for public schools.

When in the regular session of the Thirty-ninth Legislature the House passed his railroad-tax legislation and the Nineteen Immortals in the Senate defeated it, he called a special session in which the performance was repeated. Pingree was re-elected in 1898 and had the measure reintroduced. This time it passed, but the state supreme court declared it unconstitutional.

The governor now demanded a joint resolution of the Legislature to place on the ballot an amendment which would make his tax plan legal. The Senate blocked the resolution in the regular session and in a special session. The legislature, in a second special session called shortly before the election of 1900, passed the resolution. It was placed on the ballot and received a popular majority of 380,000 votes. Pingree called a third special session to pass a law which would implement the amendment. The Senate refused. The governor would have called a fourth special session if there had been time. As it was the end of his second term, he retired from office without the law for which he had worked so assiduously; but in 1901 such a law was passed and to him belongs the credit.

Pingree failed to obtain a general law for direct primary elections, but in 1899 a local law permitted Detroit and Grand Rapids to use this method of making nominations. Finally, in 1905 a general law was passed, but it was intentionally made impractical. A real primary system was provided in 1909.

Pingree failed also to obtain home rule for cities; but the new state constitution which was adopted in 1908 provided for home rule, and it specifically authorized cities to acquire and operate public utilities. Although these reforms were delayed, they were the fruit of Hazen Pingree's persistent endeavors.

4

Pingree has been largely overlooked by historians of the reform movement in cities and states. There are two reasons, perhaps. One is that that he was not a political theorist or a philosopher. He subscribed to no "ism." It was realities that aroused him to action. When he found that the people were being robbed and cheated by powerful corporations and leading citizens, he set himself to remedy what he considered to be an evil situation.

A second reason why he has been ignored is that he does not fit readily into the reform picture. Instead of being in office simultaneously with Golden Rule (Samuel M.) Jones and Brand Whitlock of Toledo, Mark Fagan of Jersey City, Fremont Older of San Francisco, Robert M. La Follette of Wisconsin, Theodore Roosevelt of New York, and Tom Johnson of Cleveland, he antedated all of them.

Tom Johnson was manager of the street railway lines in Detroit while Pingree was mayor, and, although they were on opposite sides, Johnson learned to admire him. Later, as mayor of Cleveland, he won cheap transportation for the people of that city. Golden Rule Jones, too, after Pingree's death wrote that he had been inspired by the Detroiter's fight for reform. As for Theodore Roosevelt, when Pingree was governor, the younger man was a strictly regular Republican with abounding scorn for those who failed to follow the party line. Some years were to pass before he saw the light and was converted to the necessity for reform.

During the campaign of 1896, for example, Roosevelt wrote: "The conduct of Pingree in Michigan, however, is most unfortunate. He has hardly supported McKinley at all, and his men are trying to trade so as to carry him [Pingree] through at all costs; while on the other hand I did not meet a decent Republican in the State who intended to vote for him. The scoundrel actually asked the Bryan people to let him introduce Bryan at his great meeting in Detroit."

In the eyes of some wealthy men of Detroit, Hazen Pingree was a traitor to his class; as Theodore Roosevelt saw him, he was a traitor to his party—altogether a pretty low sort of creature. But the people who elected and re-elected him had a different opinion. As had been said of Grover Cleveland, they might also have said of Pingree: "We love him for the enemies he has made."

5

The War with Spain occurred during Pingree's first term as governor. Among the causes of the war were sympathy for the Cubans, aroused in part by propagandists from Cuba and to a greater extent by the yellow press, of which Hearst's *New York Journal* and Pulitzer's *New York World* were the leaders; a feeling of national strength and a desire to show the world how strong the nation was; the eagerness of some politicians like Henry Cabot Lodge and Theodore Roosevelt to make the United States into a world power; resentment against Spain for actual atrocities, for the more numerous ones manufactured by the newspapers, and for the sinking of the *Maine*[2] in Havana Harbor on February 15, 1898.

Although the Spanish government accepted all the demands for reform in Cuba which President William McKinley made, he asked Congress to declare war because he was afraid that his party would repudiate him if he maintained peace. He signed the war resolution on April 20, 1898.

Russell A. Alger of Michigan was Secretary of War. During the Civil War he had enlisted in the Second Michigan Cavalry and had risen to the rank of general. After his return home, Alger engaged in

[2] It was believed that the *Maine* was sunk by the Spaniards, but no proof was ever discovered.

the lumber business and accumulated a large fortune. He was elected governor in 1884.

The War Department was unbelievably inefficient. Offices were filled with spoilsmen, and Alger had no vigorous young assistant like Theodore Roosevelt, who had put the Navy in top condition. The Secretary was a capable administrator, but he was unable to overcome the inertia which had developed over a long period of inactivity. The tasks of equipping the troops, furnishing them with supplies, and transporting them to camps and to Cuba were badly managed. After the war, so great was the volume of criticism poured upon the Secretary that he had to resign to save the President from embarrassment.

The President's call for five regiments of volunteers from Michigan was answered by the organization of the 31st, 32nd, 33rd, 34th, and 35th infantry regiments. The 33rd and 34th took part in the Cuban campaign. The 31st after the war served in Cuba on police duty, and the remaining two regiments saw service in southern camps.

General William R. Shafter, a native of Kalamazoo County, was in command of the expeditionary force in Cuba. He managed the brief campaign as well as could be expected of a man sixty-three years old who was so ill that he seldom was able to get his three hundred pounds of flesh and bone aboard a horse. In addition to illness, tropical heat, spoiled rations, and yellow fever, he had to contend with irresponsible newspaper correspondents and Colonel Theodore Roosevelt. The latter was an unfailing source of information for the newsmen. They disliked Shafter, who told them only as much as he believed they should know and was irritated by their insistence for more. Dispatches to the newspapers reflected their displeasure with him, but Colonel Roosevelt received more friendly treatment.

Although Governor Pingree was opposed to war with Spain, when it came, he loyally supported the President. He established a camp at Island Lake, near Brighton, and lived there with the Michigan troops during the summer of 1898. He visited the regiments at Chickamauga, Georgia, and when he discovered that the men were living on salt pork and hardtack, he demanded that the War Department provide better rations. When he learned that the sick at Montauk Point, Long Island, were not being properly cared for, he dispatched nurses to the camp. After the war, the governor sent special trains to carry the sick and wounded back to Michigan.

Michigan had a Naval Brigade, organized in 1895, which was composed of young men from Detroit, Ann Arbor, Saginaw, and other Michigan cities. In the summer they had gone on cruises on the training ship USS *Yantic*. When the Navy Department called for volunteers, the Naval Brigade enlisted. Professor Mortimer E. Cooley, later dean of the College of Engineering of the University of Michigan, a graduate of the Naval Academy, was chief engineer. There were forty-six University of Michigan men in the group. Sent to Norfolk, Virginia, they were assigned to the USS *Yosemite*, a converted merchantman rated as an auxiliary cruiser.

The captain was Lieutenant Commander W. H. Emory, a regular Navy officer. Among the crew were Woolsey M. Campau, Truman H. Newberry, Edwin Denby, Henry B. Joy, and other young men of the

The U.S.S. Yosemite Sinking the Antonio Lopez in 1898

leading families of Detroit. Newberry and Denby later served as Secretary of the Navy.

According to the recollection of Dean Cooley, reported in his autobiography *Scientific Blacksmith*, every member of the crew cheerfully performed the most menial tasks and considered the whole period of service at sea in the nature of an excursion. Another writer, however, heard a different story. He wrote: "Unfortunately the vessel was in command of a naval officer who considered it his main duty to train well-born landsmen to become common sailors. There was no sympathy between the captain and his crew. . . ." Perhaps the commanding officer wanted to impress upon his excursion-minded charges the grain of truth in General Sherman's epigram about war.

The *Yosemite* was first engaged in convoy duty between Norfolk, Virginia, and Tampa, Florida; then she sailed for Cuba. From there she was dispatched to Puerto Rico with orders to blockade San Juan Harbor. On June 28 the *Yosemite* attacked and set afire the *Antonio Lopez*, an armed blockade runner supported by a torpedo boat and the guns of the harbor forts. Fortunately, not a shell struck the *Yosemite*, which was entirely unprotected by armor. The crew was awarded double prize money[3] and the Sampson Medal[4] for this action.

In Michigan the Military Board scandal made trouble for Governor Pingree. Members of the Board entered into a conspiracy with the Henderson-Ames Company of Kalamazoo to defraud the state. After the war, unused uniforms were sold at a salvage price to a dummy company which turned them over to Henderson-Ames. Labels were changed and the uniforms were sold to the Michigan quartermaster at full price.

When the fraud was discovered, the Henderson-Ames men confessed their part in the transaction and made restitution. Two members of the Military Board were sent to prison and another was fined. Although Governor Pingree knew nothing of the conspiracy, his opponents made great political capital of the scandal. Angered because the Henderson-Ames men were not prosecuted, he pardoned the two members of the Board who had been imprisoned, on condition that they repay the state the money which they had received. In taking this action the governor believed that he was simply serving the cause of justice.

After leaving office on January 1, 1901, Governor Pingree sailed for England, then made a tour of South Africa. On his return to London he was taken ill and died there. His body was brought back to Detroit, and a great public funeral was held. Eulogies were pronounced by friends and foes, alike, and the State Legislature passed a resolution testifying to his sterling character. Later a great bronze statue, paid for by public contributions, was erected in Grand Circus Park. Part of the inscription describes him as "The Idol of the People."

[3] Prize money is a portion of the proceeds from the sale of a captured ship, which is divided among the officers and men who made the capture.

[4] Named for Admiral William T. Sampson, who was commander of the North Atlantic Squadron which destroyed the Spanish fleet off the southern coast of Cuba on July 3, 1898.

— 23 —

The Progressive Movement

DURING THE early years of the twentieth century a movement for reform in government and in business practices swept across the country. Among the leaders in state and city government were Governor Hiram Johnson of California, Governor Robert M. La Follette of Wisconsin, Governor Joseph W. Folk of Missouri, Mayor Brand Whitlock of Toledo, and Mayor Tom Johnson of Cleveland. In the national field William Jennings Bryan, Robert M. La Follette, Theodore Roosevelt, and Woodrow Wilson were leaders.

Not one of these men had any complaint against the democratic form of our government. All of them had an abiding faith in the worth of democracy. Their complaint was that it didn't work; that while the citizens had the right to choose their representatives, too often the nominations were dictated by political bosses in the pay of powerful financial and industrial corporations. As a result governing agencies frequently were operated for selfish interests instead of for the general welfare. The reformers wanted not only government by the people but also government for the people.

In order to accomplish this purpose they labored to give the people a more direct voice in the government by means of the initiative and referendum, direct primaries for nominating state and local officers, recall of elected officers, and popular election of United States senators.

The reformers in state and nation also attempted to serve the general welfare by reducing the power of trusts and other combinations, which, in many cases, controlled the government. Theodore Roosevelt and William H. Taft tried trust busting without satisfactory results. Laws for regulating railroads, banks, and industries were somewhat more successful. For example, the Interstate Commerce Act, 1887, the Elkins Act, 1903, the Hepburn Rate Act, 1906, applied to railroads; the Federal Reserve Act, 1913, regulated banks and the supply of money; and the Clayton Antitrust Act, 1914, prohibited unfair practices in commerce. The Underwood Tariff, 1913, was intended to reduce prices to the consumer; and the Sixteenth Amendment, 1913, which empowered Congress to levy an income tax, was for the purpose of laying a fair share of the cost of government upon the shoulders of those best able to pay.

The most important national acts were passed in 1913 and 1914 during the first term of Woodrow Wilson. He deserves much credit; but he profited from the agitation of the Populists, Bryan, La Follette, and Theodore Roosevelt.

2

Governor Pingree's successor in Michigan was Aaron T. Bliss, a wealthy Saginaw lumberman and conservative Republican. His principal opponents in the campaign preceding the Republican Convention at Grand Rapids were Dexter M. Ferry of Detroit, head of a seed company, and Justus S. Stearns of Ludington, a lumberman. The three were reputed to be multimillionaires. Chase S. Osborn, a newspaper publisher of Sault Sainte Marie, who was also seeking the nomination, charged that they spent $750,000 in order to win the top position on the party ticket. According to Osborn, delegates were offered as much as $3,000 for a vote in the convention.

Although Bliss was renominated and re-elected in 1902, the extravagant use of money to buy the nomination had aroused the people to demand primary elections. Both parties that year, recognizing that the time for reform had come, endorsed the primary system in their platforms, and in 1903 the Legislature passed three local acts permitting the holding of primaries in Kent, Muskegon, and Wayne counties. A general law which proved to be unworkable was enacted in 1905, and it was not until 1909 that a satisfactory statute was passed.

The next governor, Fred M. Warner, served three consecutive terms from 1905 to 1911. He was a very successful farmer and businessman who had gained some political experience as a state senator, and as secretary of state from 1901 to 1905. A conservative himself, he was supported by the conservative Republican organization.

The demands for reform which had brought about the correction of some social, economic, and political abuses in a number of states became insistent in Michigan. There was strong pressure by various groups for the initiative and referendum in state government, home rule for cities, votes for women, and prohibition of the manufacture and sale of liquor. Dissatisfied with the constitution of 1850, a majority of the voters in 1906 asked for a convention to make a new one. Meeting on October 22, 1907, the convention completed its work on February 21, 1908.

Occupations of the members of the convention indicated how the social, economic, and political life of the state had changed during the past fifty-seven years. Of the total membership, the majority were lawyers. Business and organized labor were represented, and there were only seven farmers. Although the Democrats had dominated the convention of 1850, in 1907 all except eight of the members were Republicans.

Leaders in the convention decided to revise the old constitution instead of trying to write an entirely new instrument of government, and so the constitution of 1908 contains many of the unsatisfactory features of its predecessor. Some improvements were made, and provisions in keeping with the current demands for reform were inserted.

The form of the constitution was better than that of the preceding one. The material was arranged logically, with sections on the same subject grouped together. The influence of progressive thinking was responsible for a number of innovations. Although woman suffrage was not granted, women who were taxpayers were permitted to vote on bond issues or the expenditure of public funds. Finally, in 1920, after the Nineteenth Amendment to the United States Constitution had been ratified, an amendment to the Michigan constitution gave women the privilege of voting without restriction.

Special provisions were made for the welfare of women and children. To protect them from exploitation by employers, the Legislature was empowered to pass laws limiting their hours of labor in factories and regulating the conditions under which they worked. Delinquent and dependent juveniles were placed under the jurisdiction of probate judges so that they would not be dealt with in the criminal courts.

Among the progressive measures which had been adopted by several states were the initiative and the referendum. The initiative gave to the voters the privilege of placing a bill on the ballot and making it a law by a majority vote at the polls. The referendum permitted the voters to repeal an unpopular law which had been passed by the legislature. Although the conservative element in the convention was strong enough to prevent either of these devices from being included in the new constitution, the legislature was given the right to refer to the people laws which it had passed. Progressives continued to demand the adoption of these plans which placed legislation in the hands of the people. As a result, in 1913 the initiative and the referendum for legislative matters and the initiative for constitutional amendments were made a part of the constitution.

Some of the progressive ideas which Hazen S. Pingree had advocated as mayor and as governor were written into the new constitution. Cities and villages were given home rule; that is, under a general law of the legislature, the voters of villages and cities were given the privilege of drawing up their own charters. Municipal ownership and operation of public utilities, such as street railways and electric power plants, also were permitted.

The constitution of 1850 prohibited the state from engaging in any works of internal improvement. By interpretation, this restriction was held to mean that the state could not build roads. An amendment in 1905 had given that power to the state. In the new constitution the Legislature was given permission to provide for the construction of roads and for the protection and reforestation of lands owned by the state.

The progressive features of the constitution which have been mentioned were in keeping with the forward-looking spirit of the times, but statutory matters from the older document were retained. Reflecting a distrust of the Legislature, the constitution makers specified the manner in which fuel, stationery, and printing should be purchased, and salaries of state officers and legislators were fixed so that they could be changed only by amendments. Compensation for the governor was increased from $1,000 to $5,000, and that of most of the others was raised to $2,500. Although those salaries may have been adequate at the time, changing conditions made them pitifully small. Nevertheless, it was not until 1948 that an amendment permitted the legislators to determine their own compensation and that of state officers. As a result, the governor's salary was raised to $22,500, a sum more nearly consistent with the heavy duties of the chief executive of a great state.

ENTERTAINMENT Recreation has always been an important aspect of the social life of Michigan, as evidenced by the pictures on this page. *Above:* Several members of the Grand Rapids Bicycle Club about to start on a tour in the 1880's. *Center left:* The famous Kerredge Opera House at Hancock. *Center right:* A baseball game between Detroit and Chicago on June 19, 1886, at Recreation Park in Detroit.

Bottom left: Great Lakes cruise ship at dock at Harbor Springs. *Bottom right:* Motorcar sight-seeing trip in the early 1900's.

HIGHWAY DEVELOPMENT Mud roads like those shown above were common in Michigan at the turn of the century and later. Now expressways and superhighways handle thousands of vehicles daily. *Right:* A view of the Detroit Industrial Expressway near Ypsilanti.

Below: The main road in Dexter in 1890 was unfit for travel during many months of the year. The good-roads movement brought many needed improvements. *Bottom:* The same scene fifty years later.

WINTER ARRANGEMENT

FOR 1866-7.

WHILE THE SLEIGHING IS GOOD

—A—

LINE OF STAGES

WILL RUN FROM

Traverse City to Muskegon,

—IN—

3 DAYS.

Leaving TRAVERSE CITY every Monday, Wednesday and Friday, at 7 o'clock A. M.
Returning Leave MUSKEGON every Tuesday, Thursday and Saturday, at 7 o'clock A. M., stopping both ways, for the night, at Manistee and Pentwater,
And, to take on and leave off passengers or freight, at White Lake, Pere Marquette, Lincoln, Freesoil, Norwalk, Pleasanton, Benzonia, Homestead, Sherman's or any other point on the route.

:o:

☞ Express goods carried with safety and responsibility.

:o:

Accommodations as GOOD, Fares as LOW, and QUICKER TIME than by any other line.

STEWARD & DAILY,
ROOT & COLLINS,
PITTENGER & CO.

TRAVEL Plank roads were popular in Michigan in the nineteenth century. *Above right:* A view on the Detroit and Erin plank road, in Erin Township. In the early days one had to pay a toll to use certain roads. *Center right:* Tollhouse on Jefferson Avenue at Baldwin in Detroit.

Good Intent Line

OF COACHES.

Tri - Weekly

LineBetween

KALAMAZOO, BATTLE CREEK & GRAND RAPIDS,

Stagecoaches ran between many Michigan cities in the nineteenth century. *Left:* A broadside of the Good Intent Line. *Below:* One of its stages in Plainwell in 1865.

BRIDGES AND FERRIES Ferries were used extensively on Michigan rivers before bridges were built. *Top left:* The Bridge Street Ferry on the Grand River in Grand Rapids. Later crude bridges were built like the one pictured, *top right,* which spanned the Montreal River between Ironwood, Michigan, and Hurley, Wisconsin, in 1885. The covered bridge, common a century ago, is today a relic. *Above right:* One of the few remaining in Michigan today near Lowell on the Flat River.

Above left: The Ambassador Bridge joining Detroit and Windsor, Ontario. *Below:* The Blue Water Bridge spanning the St. Clair River and connecting the U.S. and Canada at Port Huron, Michigan, and Sarnia, Ontario.

CONSERVATION To protect the natural resources of Michigan a conservation program was initiated late in the nineteenth century. *Right:* Virgin timber in the Porcupine Mountains. *Below left:* Devastation by forest fires between Grayling and Kalkaska. *Below right:* Modern forest planting methods typical of operations by the Forestry Division of the Conservation Department.

Left: Pine plantation at the Au Sable Sta Forest under control of the Forestry Div sion of the Conservation Department.

Wildlife has always been abundant i Michigan. *Below left:* Beavers were sough after by early traders and Indians for pelt *Below center:* Bull moose in Lake Ritchi on Isle Royale. *Below right:* Deer feeding

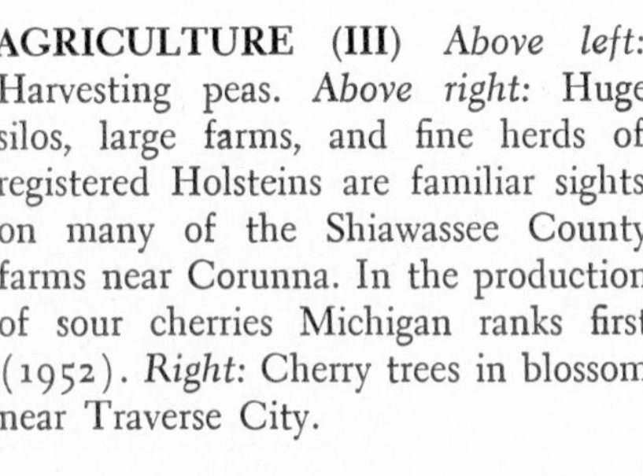

AGRICULTURE (III) *Above left:* Harvesting peas. *Above right:* Huge silos, large farms, and fine herds of registered Holsteins are familiar sights on many of the Shiawassee County farms near Corunna. In the production of sour cherries Michigan ranks first (1952). *Right:* Cherry trees in blossom near Traverse City.

Bottom left: Duck farm at Alma. *Bottom right:* Grain elevator at Saginaw.

AGRICULTURE (II) Michigan ranks eleventh (1952) in hay production. *Left:* Men loading hay. *Center right:* Baling hay. In the production of tomatoes for market Michigan ranks third compared with other late-producing states. *Center left:* Men picking tomatoes at the Mt. Pleasant State Hospital in 1944.

Corn harvesting in Michigan is rapidly changing. Today most corn is husked by either a corn picker from the stalk or it is hauled from the shock to the barn and run through a shredder. Very little is now husked by hand as shown in the photo, *bottom right*. Michigan ranks fifth in the production of sugar beets. *Bottom left:* Cultivating sugar beets in Tuscola County.

GRICULTURE (I) Farming has always een an important industry in Michigan. Beause of the diversity of crops grown in the ate, Michigan's high rank in the production f agricultural products has often been underestimated.

Crude farming implements were used in the ineteenth century to harvest wheat. *Right:* armer using a cradle.

Above: Hiram Moore (in top hat) and his famous combined harvester in the 1840's. Familiar farm scenes: *Left:* Gathering sap for making maple sugar and syrup. *Below:* Early threshing machine. *Bottom:* Spring plowing.

3

Although Governor Warner was a conservative, he was carried along by the reform movement, and he became a leader in the demand for change. During the six years that he was in office, the Legislature passed laws levying heavier taxes on railroads and reducing their passenger and freight rates, increasing the taxes of telephone and telegraph companies, regulating insurance companies, conserving natural resources, providing for food inspection, requiring safety measures in factories, limiting the hours of labor of employes under eighteen to ten hours a day or fifty-four a week, prohibiting the employment in manufacturing or mercantile establishments of children under fourteen, giving the people the right to nominate candidates for certain offices in primary elections, and establishing a state highway department.

In his exaugural message, written when he was about to relinquish his office to his successor, Governor Warner pointed with pride to the progressive measures which had been enacted during his three terms as governor, asserting that in no similar period in the history of the state had so much beneficial legislation been provided for the general welfare. As a matter of fact, he was right.

Nevertheless, many persons believed that Governor Warner was responsible for laxity of management and a good deal of the corruption that had developed during his administrations. Besides, the state was a half-million dollars in debt. For these and other reasons the Republican party was badly split; and when Warner ran for his third term in 1908, he won by only a small plurality. There was strong opposition to him in the primary campaign of 1910.

4

The successful contender for the Republican nomination in 1910 was Chase S. Osborn. Beginning his campaign in 1909, he took as his slogan: Anti-Warnerism, Harmony, and a New Deal for Michigan. In his platform he promised to correct the abuses which had developed under Governor Warner, to bring harmony to the Republican party, and to give Michigan the sort of government which she deserved. Colonel Frank Knox, a newspaper publisher of Sault Sainte Marie, was his campaign manager.

Osborn's Democratic opponent in the election was Lawton T. Hemans of Mason, formerly a state legislator, and a member of the

Constitutional Convention of 1907–1908. Osborn defeated him by a plurality of only 43,033 votes. In general Osborn received fewer votes than other candidates of his party because the Republican organization, ignoring his plea for harmony, was against him. Besides, because Governor Warner had appointed him to the Board of Regents of the University, some people feared that he was really a Warner man.

Chase S. Osborn was an aggressive, able, and colorful person. Before 1910 he had had a varied career. As an explorer, authority on wild life, author, public speaker, and newspaperman, he was known throughout Michigan and far beyond the borders of the state.

After working as reporter and editor in Indiana, Illinois, and Wisconsin, he became publisher of a weekly newspaper in Florence, Wisconsin, at the age of twenty-four. Three years later he bought the *Sault Sainte Marie News*, which he published until 1900, when he sold it to Colonel Frank Knox. In 1902 he bought the *Saginaw Courier-Herald*, but he remained a resident of Sault Sainte Marie and an enthusiastic booster for the Upper Peninsula.

Osborn's unsuccessful attempt to win the Republican nomination in the millionaires' campaign of 1900 has already been mentioned. After that experience, which taught him that money was needed for success in politics, he decided that in order to be independent, he would have to make a fortune before running again. And so, during the next ten years he applied himself to that task. Most of his wealth was acquired by discovering iron deposits and selling them to mining corporations. When he ran for governor in 1910, he was reputed to be a millionaire. At any rate, he had sufficient money so that he could be independent of those who would have been willing to advance campaign funds in return for special privileges.

Before he became governor, Osborn had held three state offices by appointment. Governor John T. Rich had named him fish and game warden in 1894, and he served until 1899, energetically enforcing the law and promoting additional legislation for the protection of the wild-animal life of the state.

From 1899 to 1903 he was state railroad commissioner. Appointed by Governor Hazen Pingree, he became an admirer of that unorthodox Republican and learned some valuable political lessons. Through his vigorous efforts, the Legislature was induced to lower passenger fares, and he inaugurated a program of grade separations for the public safety.

His third position was Regent of the University of Michigan. Governor Warner appointed him in 1908 to fill the unexpired term of Peter

White, who died in that year. As a Regent, he took an active and friendly interest in the affairs of the University, which in later years received numerous benefactions from him.

Chase Osborn had made many promises in his platform. One of them was that he would not seek a second term. He wanted to devote all his time to the interests of the state instead of spending the second year in office, as was usually the case, working for re-election. Not having to consider the effects of his actions on pressure groups that might try to defeat him, the governor set out fearlessly to carry his program into effect.

Bitterly hostile to the "booze interests," as he called them, he had legislation passed which prohibited distillers, brewers, or wholesalers from owning saloons. This action was intended to reduce their powerful influence in local politics. Believing that women should have the vote, he induced the Legislature to pass a resolution to lay the matter before the people. It was voted down.

The governor, favoring what he called a reasonable conservation program, managed to have acts passed which provided state aid for county agricultural schools and for the teaching of agriculture in the public schools. In the field of labor, Osborn got adequate authority for the labor commissioner so that he could enforce the provisions of the labor laws, and he was responsible for the passing of Michigan's first workmen's compensation act.

One of Osborn's campaign promises was to economize and to give the state an efficient administration. By abolishing unnecessary offices, by cutting surplus employes from the payroll, and by careful management of the state's business, he not only wiped out the half million-dollar debt but he left a surplus of nearly half a million dollars in the treasury when he retired from office at the end of 1912.

5

Osborn had been an admirer of Theodore Roosevelt since the turn of the century. It was not surprising, then, that he was one of the seven governors who urged Roosevelt to run for President in 1912. Convinced that the people of Michigan favored Roosevelt and knowing that the Republican party machinery of the state was in the hands of Taft men, the governor called a special session of the Legislature in the spring of 1912 and had a presidential preferential primary bill introduced. He urged that it be given immediate effect by a two-thirds vote so that the people would have an opportunity to name their choice for President at the polls before the National Republican Convention met in Chicago on June 18. If that had been done, the delegates from Michigan would have been bound to vote for the candidate who received the majority in the primary.

The Legislature passed the bill, but the "Immortal Thirteen" in the Senate, political opponents of Osborn and favorable to Taft, made it impossible to obtain a two-thirds majority. As far as the 1912 nomination was concerned, the act was useless; because, like other ordinary legislation, it did not take effect until ninety days after the Legislature adjourned.

April 11, 1912, was the day set for the meeting of the State Republican Convention at Bay City. The principal business there would be the choosing of six delegates at large to go to the National Republican Convention in Chicago. Because it was believed that the twelve delegates chosen in the congressional districts would be evenly divided for Taft and for Roosevelt, each faction of the party was determined to gain control of the State Convention and name the six delegates at large so as to have a majority at Chicago.

Frank Knox, a Roosevelt man, was chairman of the Republican State Central Committee; Paul King, a Taft man, was secretary; and a majority of the committeemen were for Taft. A split in the party in Wayne County and in Calhoun County had produced two contesting delegations to the convention at Bay City. Since these delegations were large enough to determine the result in the convention and since the State Central Committee had the right to decide which group should be seated, the first struggle for power took place in the committee.

The night before the convention, Secretary King called a secret meeting to which Chairman Knox was not invited. Seventeen of the twenty-four members attended. Robert H. Shields of Houghton acted as chairman, and by a vote of fourteen to three the committee deposed Truman H. Newberry as temporary chairman of the convention. He was a Roosevelt man, having served as Secretary of the Navy in Roosevelt's Cabinet, and it was feared that he would manage affairs so that the Roosevelt delegates from Wayne and Calhoun counties would be seated. Grant Fellows of Hudson was named to replace him, and the committee decided to seat the Taft delegation. When Frank Knox learned of the meeting, he declared that it was illegal.

Governor Chase S. Osborn was unable to attend the convention because he had broken his foot in an accident. Knowing that there was likely to be trouble, he ordered out the Bay City company of the National Guard, directing its captain to co-operate with the mayor.

The convention was to meet at 10.30 A.M. in the armory. When the delegates arrived, police and national guardsmen prevented them from entering the building. Robert H. Shields, Paul King, and other Taft committeemen, however, were admitted by a side door. A little later Frank Knox and former Senator Albert J. Beveridge of Indiana, who had been invited to address the convention, were permitted to enter. Knox vigorously protested the committee's action. Shields, who was acting as chairman, ignored him and ordered the guards to admit only

The Bay City Convention in Turmoil

the delegates who had cards signed by Paul King. Taft supporters swarmed into the armory through the front doors, and some Roosevelt men managed to get in through basement windows and transoms. Noisy disorder prevailed throughout the hall.

Both Shields and Newberry appeared on the platform, and each tried to gain the attention of the delegates and open the convention. During the commotion, W. D. Gordon of Midland, a Roosevelt supporter, sprang to the stage and attempted to address the meeting. John F. Cremer of Marquette, a Taft man, grappled with him and threw him from the stage.

Then there was bedlam. Fights between Roosevelt and Taft partisans broke out all over the floor. Police and militiamen finally separated the combatants, but it was impossible to bring the convention to order.

During the fighting, additional Roosevelt men entered the hall. Convening in one corner, the delegates who favored Roosevelt organized as a convention, elected six delegates at large, and adopted a resolution instructing them to vote for Roosevelt. Many of them then left the hall. Knox also left with Beveridge, who had had no opportunity to deliver his address.

Grant Fellows finally called the remaining delegates to order, six delegates at large were elected and instructed for Taft, and Alex J. Groesbeck was named state chairman in place of Frank Knox.

When the National Republican Convention met in Chicago, it was dominated by Taft men, and the credentials committee refused to seat contesting Roosevelt delegates. Many of those from Michigan attended the Progressive Convention, which nominated Roosevelt.

When Roosevelt bolted the Republican party and ran as a Progressive, Osborn did not follow him. As much as he admired the former President, he could not bring himself to leave the party. He was dissatisfied with the conservative leadership, but he believed that necessary reforms could best be achieved by the party if it were led by men with progressive ideas. Osborn did take the stump for Roosevelt late in the campaign, but not in Michigan. He spoke in Illinois, Missouri, Indiana, and Oklahoma.

The Progressives met at Jackson and nominated a full state ticket. In the election of 1912, Theodore Roosevelt received a plurality of the popular vote in Michigan, and the electoral vote of the state was cast for him. This was the first time since 1852 that Michigan, in a presidential election, had strayed from the Republican fold.

6

The Republicans won all the state offices except that of governor. For that office the Republican candidate received more than 169,000 votes and the Progressive more than 152,000, a total of 322,000. The split made possible the election of a Democrat, Woodbridge N. Ferris, with 194,000 votes. Governor Ferris was a teacher. He had organized and conducted business schools in New York State and in Illinois, in which both he and Mrs. Ferris taught. They moved to Big Rapids, Michigan, in 1884 and opened the Ferris Industrial School. Fifteen years later the name was changed to Ferris Institute.

This was an unusual school. There was no entrance requirement except a willingness to study. The curriculum included high-school subjects, commercial courses, teacher training, and pharmacy. Ferris and his wife took a personal interest in the students, and when he ran for office, thousands of them and their friends voted for him.[1]

Governor Ferris described himself as "constitutionally a radical, a 'natural born' fighter, prone to favor extreme measures, in order to secure reforms." He gave credit to his wife for teaching him "patience and wisdom."

As governor he advocated progressive measures: popular election of United States senators, a corrupt-practices act, ballot reform, good roads, increased power for the state over public utilities, appointment of all state officers except governor, and the initiative, referendum, and recall. The last three measures, as has previously been noted, were adopted by the people in 1913.

Ferris was the Democratic candidate in 1914, and the Republicans nominated Chase S. Osborn. The Progressives also had a candidate, Henry R. Pattengill. He received more than 36,000 votes, and Osborn more than 176,000, a total of 213,000. Ferris, who received 212,000, had a plurality and became governor for a second term.

The question may be asked, Why did a Democrat win a second time in a strongly Republican state like Michigan? There are several reasons. In the first place, the Progressive candidate took some of the votes which Osborn might have expected to receive. Second, Osborn had left the country in 1913 on one of his world tours and he was away during most of the campaign. Third, conservative Republicans would not support Osborn because they knew that they could not control him. As he once explained in a letter: "Everyone agreed to the fact that he [Osborn] would not stand hitched."

Governor Ferris was a stanch advocate of prohibition. He was dry personally, as well as politically, in sharp contrast to many other office holders. During his second term, in 1916, the people adopted a prohibition amendment to the state constitution. By that time forty-five of the eighty-three counties had voted themselves dry under the local-option law of 1889. The Legislature passed a prohibition act in 1917, and it went into effect in 1918.

The war certainly helped speed the process of adopting prohibition in Michigan, in other states, and in the nation as well; but it was the culmination of a long campaign and the result largely of the lawless acts of the saloonkeepers, brewers, and distillers. During the years

[1] Ferris Institute in 1949 became a state-supported school.

immediately preceding prohibition, newspapers were filled with stories about the control of local government by the liquor interests and their immunity to the ordinary processes of the law.

7

In 1916 Albert E. Sleeper, a Republican, was elected governor with a clear majority of nearly 100,000 over his Democratic opponent, Edwin F. Sweet. Pattengill, who again ran as a Progressive, received only ninety-five votes. Governor Sleeper was a banker in Bad Axe and a regular Republican. He had represented the twentieth senatorial district in the legislatures of 1901–1902 and 1903–1904, and he had been state treasurer from 1909 until 1913. The United States entered the World War in 1917, and Governor Sleeper was occupied largely with matters related to military and industrial participation by the state.

An unusual campaign for a seat in the United States Senate was carried on in 1918. Truman H. Newberry, Henry Ford, and Chase S. Osborn ran in the Republican primary. Ford ran in the Democratic primary also. Newberry was nominated by the Republicans, Ford by the Democrats. Newberry won the election. He was prosecuted for spending more money in the primary campaign than was permitted by the National Corrupt Practices Act, which fixed the figure at $10,000. There was no doubt that he and his supporters had spent the money, about $195,000; but when the case finally reached the Supreme Court, it held by a five-to-four decision that Congress had no power to regulate nominations. The Corrupt Practices Act, it decided, applied only to elections, not to the primary.

Newberry was admitted to the Senate, but the Republicans, disturbed by Democratic charges that he had bought his seat, passed a resolution condemning the use of large sums of money in elections. The Democrats continued to snipe at Newberry until in 1922 he resigned from the Senate. Governor Alex J. Groesbeck[2] appointed James Couzens, former associate of Henry Ford, former police commissioner, and mayor of Detroit, 1919–1922, as his successor. In 1924 he was elected to fill the unexpired term and for the full term. As a senator, Couzens was a progressive Republican.

[2] Alex J. Groesbeck was governor from 1921 to 1927.

— 24 —

Economic Developments

DURING THE 1890's new iron mines were opened, and the three ranges —the Marquette, the Menominee, and the Gogebic—poured out increasing quantities of rich ore. The Panic of 1893 caused a temporary stoppage. Nearly all the mines in the Upper Peninsula closed in the summer of 1893. In the spring of 1894, the mines at Ironwood opened, paying reduced wages. According to the operators, the miners had requested the reopening, offering to work at rates based on the price of ore. Nevertheless, the men struck in June for higher wages, and all the mines closed.

On July 1, the Norrie Mine began to load cars from its stockpile under the protection of the sheriff of Gogebic County. Two days later about one thousand men marched to the mine to try to induce the steam shovel operators to quit. A fight soon began, shots were fired, and a few men were slightly wounded.

The sheriff appealed to Governor John T. Rich for troops. He sent five companies of the Fifth Regiment, Michigan National Guard, which arrived on July 4. The state labor commissioner reached the strike scene on July 8 and tried to get the men back to work after he was satisfied that the corporations were paying as much as the price of ore warranted. The men refused.

The work of loading the cars was resumed on July 16 under protection of the troops. Strikers who interfered were arrested. When the leader of the strike was jailed, the men began to return to work, and the national guardsmen left on July 30.

The mines recovered gradually from the effects of the panic, and Michigan retained the leadership in production until 1900, when the output rose to nearly ten million tons. In that year, however, the open-pit mines of the Mesabi Range made Minnesota the foremost iron-producing state. Although the mines of Michigan disgorged still larger quantities of ore, reaching the peak of eighteen million tons in 1916, the state never again reached the top position.

2

Copper production followed a course similar to that of iron. Tonnage increased, but the percentage of the United States output of the metal decreased. After 1887, Michigan lost its first place to Montana. In 1906 Arizona took the lead. Nevertheless, production in Michigan was constantly rising. In 1887 it had been only 75,793,000 pounds, in 1900 it was 155,617,000, and in 1916 the high point of 266,839,000 pounds was reached.

At the turn of the century there was prosperity in the copper country. One manifestation of it was the building of ornate opera houses. Previously there had been small theaters in Houghton, Hancock, Lake Linden, and Calumet. Local pride, however, demanded theaters in which first-class performances could be presented, and ample funds were available to build them. Two were especially notable.

In Calumet, the Red Jacket Opera House was completed in 1900. Constructed of stone, it was an imposing building. The interior was decorated in the style of Louis XIV. The floors were carpeted, and incandescent electric bulbs were used for light. The first production was *The Highwayman*, by De Koven and Smith, played by the Broadway Opera Company. Seats for the opening performance sold for $25.

The other playhouse was the Kerredge Theater in Hancock, built by William Kerredge and his son, Ray. It was a brick building with Renaissance decorations, lighted by electricity. When it opened in 1902, box seats cost $40 and seats in the orchestra were $10. Both theaters booked New York productions. Besides the popular shows, such as *Way Down East*, Shakespeare and the opera *Faust* were played to full houses. Among the noted performers who appeared in Hancock and Calumet were Fritz Kreisler, Maude Adams, Sarah Bernhardt, Frances Alda, and Alma Gluck. The towns in the copper country supported entertainment of a higher quality than did places of the same size in the Lower Peninsula.

A notable decline occurred in 1913 and 1914, when some of the mines were closed and others were working with reduced forces. This condition was caused by the strike which began in July, 1913.

Many of the employes belonged to the Western Federation of Miners. Formerly an affiliate of the Industrial Workers of the World, since 1911 it had been in the American Federation of Labor. The union, however, was not recognized by the mine owners.

The miners struck when the operators refused to grant their demands: an eight-hour day, abandonment of the one-man drill and a return to the two-man drill, a minimum wage of $3.50 a day, and recognition of the union. Charles W. Moyer, president of the Western Federation, led the strike in person.

A "Citizens Alliance" was formed to preserve order, and violence flared between this group and the strikers. The sheriff of Houghton County appealed to the governor for troops. Assured by individuals whose judgment he trusted, that order could not be maintained without them, Governor Woodbridge N. Ferris sent the entire Michigan National Guard to the copper country.

Violence, however, continued, and the bitter feeling between the operators and the miners was increased by a tragedy on Christmas Eve. While families of the strikers were attending a party in a large hall in Calumet, someone shouted "Fire." In the panic that followed, seventy-three women and children were trampled to death. Word was soon spread about that an agent of the operators had raised the false alarm. No evidence whatever was produced to support the charge, but the tragedy increased the tension between miners and operators.

Efforts were made by the governor and by the United States Secretary of Labor to mediate the strike, and a congressional committee visited the affected area and published a report. Refusal of the operators to deal with the union prevented any negotiations. Finally Moyer was savagely beaten by men of the Citizens Alliance, shot in the back, and put on a train bound for Chicago, with a warning to stay away from the Upper Peninsula.

In the spring of 1914, the men began going back to work. The mines were put on an eight-hour basis, a minimum wage of $3 was guaranteed, and a modification of the one-man drill was provided. The operators, however, refused to recognize the union, and it soon disappeared from the copper country.

As mining continued, shafts were sunk deeper and deeper. Calumet and Hecla's Red Jacket shaft reached a depth of 4,920 feet in 1902, and the Quincy shaft was 5,280 feet below the surface. These were the deepest mines in the world.

Because costs of production increased as the shafts were driven farther down into the earth, the directors of Calumet and Hecla decided to acquire control of additional companies so that economies could be realized by centralized management. In 1905 they began purchasing stock of the Osceola, Isle Royale, Tamarack, Ahmeek, and other mines. Some companies were bought outright, and in 1918 Calumet and Hecla was producing 60 per cent of Michigan copper. The other large companies, the Copper Range Consolidated and the Quincy, together produced 32 per cent. Nearly all the output of Michigan copper came from the mines of these three companies.

3

Michigan continued to be a leader in the production of salt. Midland, Saginaw, Bay City, Wyandotte, St. Clair, Port Huron, Manistee, and Ludington were the principal centers. To get salt, pools of natural brines are tapped, or steam is forced down into beds of rock salt to make an artificial brine. The salt is separated from the brine by evaporation. It has been estimated that the salt reserve underground in Michigan is sufficient to supply the entire world.

Many valuable products besides table salt are made from the brines pumped out of the ground. For example, the Solvay Process Company of River Rouge, the Michigan Alkali Company, and the J. B. Ford Company of Wyandotte make soda ash, caustic soda, baking soda, calcium chloride, magnesium, bromine, and other chemicals. All these companies were founded during the 1890's.

Midland is a town famous for chemicals extracted from brine. Formerly a center of the lumber industry, it is now the home of the Dow Chemical Company, which was organized in 1890. The great development of this firm is based on the genius of Dr. Herbert H. Dow, the founder, who perfected an electrolytic process for separating bromine, chlorine, and other elements. The company also makes metallic magnesium from brine, and it manufactures most of the aspirin used in this country, shipping it in bulk to processors who press it into tablets and package them for sale. The Dow Company today produces hundreds of chemicals.

Another Michigan mineral is coal. According to geologists, there are 125,000,000 tons of soft coal underground. Most of it will remain there, for the thin veins are overlaid with so great a deposit of glacial sand and gravel that the coal cannot be mined economically.

For more than a hundred years some coal has been produced. The first was mined near Jackson in 1835. Other operations were carried on at Grand Ledge and elsewhere in Eaton County before the Civil War.

Coal mines were opened in the 1890's at Saginaw, Bay City, and St. Charles. Between 1900 and 1911 more than thirty were active. Peak output was reached in 1907, when 2,035,858 tons were taken out of the ground. Afterward the production decreased gradually. In April, 1952, the Swan Creek Mine in Saginaw County, the only active mine in the state, was closed, and Michigan's coal-mining industry expired.

4

After 1888, there was a gradual decline in output of lumber in Michigan. The value of forest products fell from a high of $85,000,000 annually to $55,000,000 in 1900; the number of workers employed, from 54,000 to 25,000.

In the Upper Peninsula production was high for some years. Menominee held the leading position, and the Kirby, Carpenter Company was the biggest producer of lumber. Manistique was next, followed by Grand Marais and Baraga. Other active centers were Ontonagon, Pequaming, Seney, Escanaba, Nahma, and Hermansville.

C. J. L. Meyer, a lumberman from Wisconsin, founded Hermansville in 1878 and began sawing pine. In 1883 he organized the Wisconsin Land and Lumber Company, which acquired large tracts of timber in the Upper Peninsula. When the pine began to fail, Meyer developed machinery to process hard maple into fine flooring. From 1887 onward, the mills at Hermansville sawed chiefly hardwood, but pine, cedar, and hemlock on the Company's lands were also made into lumber. Dr. George W. Earle, Meyer's son-in-law, succeeded him as president of the company.

There were still a few large stands of pine in the Lower Peninsula. One of the most remarkable centers after 1900 was Deward in the northwest corner of Crawford County on the Manistee River. David Ward, cousin of Eber B. Ward and a famous lumberman, owned a tract of timberland of about 90,000 acres in that region which he estimated would require twenty to thirty years of heavy lumbering to exhaust. In 1900 he died, and in his will he stipulated that his estate be settled within twelve years. The three executors, a son, a grandson, and a son-in-law, decided to clear the land in that time.

They chose the site of the lumber town in the heart of the forest and named it for David Ward—Deward. They had a great mill built designed to do the job in the most economical and speedy manner. It started sawing in September, 1901. For a year it ran day and night without repairs, turning out 200,000 feet of lumber every twenty-four hours. The greatest year's production was 52,000,000 feet. Logs were brought in by rail, and the lumber was shipped by rail to East Jordan, where it was loaded on barges and carried to Chicago and other lake ports.

Deward was an attractive lumbering town. Cottages were built for the workmen and their families. There were a company store, a schoolhouse, a Swedish church, and a community hall, but no saloons. It was a quiet, industrious community of eight hundred inhabitants. The local baseball team was called the Bush Rangers. There was a roundhouse for repairing the engines and the cars, and a part of the town was occupied by railroad men.

The executors of David Ward's will accomplished their purpose. So efficiently did their logging and sawing operations progress that the land was cleared in twelve years. On March 16, 1912, the mill was shut down for lack of logs to saw; it was dismantled and hauled away. Some of the villagers remained, but now the place is deserted, a ghost town. Until very recent years, Deward was shown on the maps of Michigan, but the population was given as zero.

The cutover lands of the pine regions either reverted to the state for nonpayment of taxes or remained in the hands of lumbering or railroad companies. Both of the latter carried on extensive advertising campaigns to sell to prospective farmers. They were assisted by local chambers of commerce and other booster organizations.

Lumbering had almost ceased in Oceana County by 1882, and Pentwater was looking for industries to replace the lumbermills which no longer received sufficient logs to keep them busy. Mason County in 1891 issued a pamphlet entitled *The Advantages of the City of Ludington.* It extolled the fertility of land in the county which could be purchased for from $5 to $20 an acre.

In 1899, lumber companies in Manistee were promoting the sale of their land through agents, and the Manistee and Northeastern Railroad and the Flint and Pere Marquette Railroad were publishing statements in praise of their cutover lands.

Another promotional campaign of a more comprehensive scope was begun in 1909 by the Western Michigan Development Bureau of Traverse City. Taking all of the western part of the state from

Muskegon to Mackinaw City as its field, it sought by bulletins and by illustrated lectures to lure farmers to this region. Efforts to attract settlers were carried beyond the boundaries of Michigan into neighboring states.

As a result of these and other advertising programs, many men bought cutover lands. A number of them were foreigners from eastern Europe who had been in the United States long enough to earn sufficient money in factories or mines to purchase a farm. Some remained, but many were starved out after a few years. The light sandy soil with its thin layer of leaf mold would produce one or two crops. Then the fertility was gone. Most of the former pine lands are good only for reforestation or grazing.

5

In 1913 the Legislature passed an act providing for a commissioner of immigration and a deputy. Their duties were to collect and compile information relative to the advantages and opportunities afforded by the state to farmers, merchants, manufacturers, and home and pleasure seekers, and to distribute the information. The chief object of the commissioner was to encourage settlement upon Michigan's good agricultural lands by arousing residents of the state to appreciate the opportunities available, and to attract people from other states, Canada, and central and northern Europe.

The commissioner of immigration in 1914 published a book entitled *Michigan, the Land of Plenty*, dealing with agriculture, mining, and manufacturing. In it the statement was frankly made that sandy, cutover land was not suitable for agriculture. "It is a great misfortune for Michigan, that some of her pure sand lands have been sold by unscrupulous speculators to city citizens, who have been parted from their savings of years and left without experience or a soil with which to recoup their lost savings."

The State Legislature in 1899 took notice of the problem of cutover lands and of diminishing forests by creating the Michigan Forestry Commission of three persons, including the commissioner of the State Land Office. The Commission was directed to "institute inquiry into the extent, kind, value, and condition of the timber lands of the State; the amount of acres and value of timber that is cut and removed each year and the purpose for which it is used; the extent to which the timber lands are being destroyed by fires, used by wasteful cutting or consumption, lumbering, or for the purpose of clearing the land for tillage. It shall also inquire as to the effect of the diminution of timber and wooded surface of this State in lessening the rainfall and producing droughts, and the effects upon the ponds, rivers, lakes and the water-power and harbors of the State, and affecting the climate and disturbing and deteriorating natural conditions." The Commission was required also to make a study of second-growth timber, overflowed and stump lands, and to lay before the Legislature a forestry policy for the state. To defray the expenses of the Commission in the performance of these important duties, the Legislature appropriated the insignificant sum of $2,000 a year.

The Legislature established a permanent forest preserve in 1901, consisting of tax-delinquent and swamp lands in Crawford and Roscommon counties; and in 1903 the commissioner of the State Land Office was given charge of "all matters relating to the preservation of the forests of this state and to the prevention and suppression of forest fires." The direction of this work was made an immediate responsibility of the chief fire warden, appointed by the land commissioner, who had deputy fire wardens in various parts of the state. Largely because of a lack of funds, the law was of little use.

Another act of 1903 provided for a forestry warden, with deputies who were to supervise and reforest the state preserve. Filibert Roth, who was the professor of forestry at the University of Michigan, was the first warden. He began the work of reforestation in 1904.

In 1909 the Public Domain Commission was established, composed of a number of ex-officio members, including the commissioner of the State Land Office. The new Commission appointed the state game, fish, and forestry warden and the state forester. A nursery for growing seedlings was opened at Higgins Lake, cutover lands were planted with trees, and measures were taken to prevent and fight forest fires; but the results were small. By 1920, only 9,000 of the 10 to 12 million acres of cutover land had been replanted, and forest fires continued to destroy great areas of timber. Lack of co-ordination, lack of specialization, and lack of funds were responsible for the poor results.

The United States Government assisted in the important work of protecting growing timber. In 1909 it established the first national forests in Michigan in Iosco County along the Au Sable River and in the Upper Peninsula west of Sault Sainte Marie. Consisting of about 100,000 acres, these forests were guarded by rangers. Financial assistance to states for protecting their forests was provided in an act passed by Congress in 1911.

6

Closely related to the subject of reforestation and protection of the standing timber were the problems of preserving the wild life of the state. Beginning in 1859, the Legislature passed laws to protect deer, wild turkey, grouse, duck, and quail by establishing limited hunting seasons. Indians, who were dependent upon hunting for their food, were expressly excluded from the provisions of the law. Later laws protected fur-bearing animals by limiting the period during which they might be taken, and bag limits were set for all sorts of game. Songbirds were given complete protection. These laws were passed at the insistence of sportsmen's organizations and the Michigan Audubon Society, but for many years no adequate means of enforcement were provided.

In 1887 a fish and game warden was given the responsibility of enforcing the laws, but governors usually appointed men who would use their deputies in the counties to build a state-wide political machine. Local opposition to enforcement of the laws discouraged the politically minded wardens from doing their duty. A notable exception was Chase S. Osborn, fish and game warden from 1895–1899. Interested himself in the preservation of wild life, he traveled about the state seeking violators of the laws and taking them into court. Nevertheless, illegal hunting continued. The wild turkey was extinct in Michigan by 1890, and the passenger pigeon by 1900.

Attention to the protection of fish began in 1859. At the demand of sportsmen, the Legislature forbade the use of nets in the streams and lakes of southern Michigan. Seasons for fishing were limited by later laws, and a minimum size was set for fish that might be taken. Special efforts were made to protect trout and grayling. The latter was a native game fish, very numerous in northern streams.

To protect the commercial fisheries of the Great Lakes contiguous to Michigan, the Legislature in 1865 passed a law regulating the size of the mesh of fishermen's nets. As no means of enforcement were provided, the fishermen ignored the law and demanded that the state establish hatcheries to increase the number of whitefish and lake trout. In 1873 the Fish Commission was appointed. It established hatcheries for both commercial fish and pan and game fish. Without agents to enforce the laws, there was a continuing decrease in the catch of whitefish and lake trout and of game fish. By 1900 the grayling had disappeared from the streams of Michigan, except in the upper reaches of the Manistee River. The Commission, however, was successful in increasing the number of brook trout by stocking the streams with fingerlings from the hatcheries.

Because politics interfered with enforcement, little was accomplished in the protection of fish and game until after the establishment of the Conservation Commission in 1921. This new body assumed the duties of the various enforcement and replacement agencies, taking charge of fish, game, forests, and other state lands. A director appointed by the Commission was responsible for all such activities. After 1929, especially, the Conservation Department carried on a successful and intelligent program of rehabilitation of the cutover lands and the protection of wildlife in the state.

A Michigan Summer Resort, 1900

The popularity of Michigan summer resorts on Lake Huron, Lake Michigan, Lake Superior, and on inland lakes continued to grow. Railroads, steamships, and interurbans carried increasing numbers of vacationers to hotels, cottages, and camps. Before 1920, a few owners of automobiles drove to resorts that were not too far from their homes.

7

Agriculture in Michigan advanced both in the number of acres under cultivation and in the value of farm products. Some important changes occurred. Increased use of machinery released more and more men from farm work to seek employment in the growing industries of the cities. Growth of urban population was responsible for specialization in truck and garden farming, and a great expansion of dairying. Because more feed for horses and cattle was required, corn and oats became the principal crops, replacing wheat in the leading position. Besides, cheap production on the great wheat ranches of the West made the growing of wheat in Michigan less profitable.

Beginning during the 1890's, corn, wheat, oats, and other grains were made into new kinds of breakfast foods. The center of production was Battle Creek. Since 1876, Dr. John Harvey Kellogg had been in charge of the sanitarium where he emphasized the value of a vegetable diet. A former patient of Dr. Kellogg, C. W. Post, began the manufacture of health foods in 1895, and he organized the Postum Cereal Company the next year. W. K. Kellogg, a brother of Dr. John Harvey Kellogg, soon afterward established the Kellogg Toasted Corn Flake Company. Both firms produced attractively packaged, ready-to-eat breakfast cereals which became famous throughout the nation.

A new farm product was sugar beets. After experiments begun in 1890 by the Michigan Agricultural College had shown that beet culture was successful, farmers in the southern counties began to plant beets extensively. The Saginaw River Valley was best suited for this crop, and it became the principal center of production. The first beet sugar refinery was put in operation in Bay City in 1898. In 1920 more than a million tons of beets were processed by sixteen refineries. The output of sugar for that year was 165,899 tons.

8

Farmers and others who had occasion to use wagons or carriages for transportation had much to complain about, for in general the roads in Michigan in 1900 were in bad condition. There were still some plank roads which had been chartered under state law and which charged toll. Planks had been replaced by gravel, and some of these roads were in fair condition, but they usually were only from five to ten miles in length. Because the income from most of them was inadequate, they were permitted to lapse into disrepair. All the private road companies disappeared shortly after 1900.

Except for these toll roads, all roads in Michigan until 1893 were under township control. Little money was available, and residents worked out their road tax by appearing on the job with their neighbors, bringing with them picks, shovels, wheelbarrows, and teams. Necessarily, the road building was pretty primitive. In order to provide sufficient funds and skilled supervision, larger districts than townships were needed.

In 1893 the Legislature empowered counties to elect or appoint a road commission and adopt country-wide road administration. Counties were slow to take advantage of this law, but by 1914, fifty-nine had county road systems. Minor roads, however, were still maintained by working out the tax.

In Michigan and elsewhere in the United States there was a bicycle craze during the 1880's and 1890's. Clubs were formed, and besides riding in towns and cities, men and women made long trips. Prizes were awarded to those sturdy cyclists who rode one hundred miles in one day—small golden bars—and silver bars for fifty miles. So great was the desire for distinction that some riders earned a number of bars, which they wore on their shoulders as evidence of their prowess.

For long-distance riding, fairly good roads were necessary, and the cyclists throughout the country campaigned for improvements. The leader of the movement in Michigan was Horatio S. Earle, chief of the League of American Wheelmen in Michigan in 1899, and national president in 1901. He was also a member of the state senate, where he sponsored a resolution which provided for a committee to investigate and report to the next Legislature on means of improving the highways. Governor Bliss appointed the committee with Earle as chairman. The committee at once named Frank F. Rogers, of Port Huron, state highway engineer without salary, because no money had been appropriated.

The constitution of 1850, it will be recalled, prohibited the state from engaging in any work of internal improvement. This was interpreted to mean that the state could not build roads. Horatio S. Earle campaigned so effectively to have this bar removed that in April, 1905, the people voted to amend the constitution to permit "the improvement of public wagon roads."

The Legislature at once passed a law establishing a State Highway Department and providing for payment of state funds to counties which met construction standards. Governor Fred W. Warner in 1905 appointed Earle highway commissioner, and he named Rogers his deputy.

In 1905 the state began to apply the proceeds from automobile license fees to the building of roads, but the construction was still carried on by the counties with aid from the state. In 1917, in order to meet the requirements of the Federal Aid Act of 1916, the State Highway Department was given full control of the construction and maintenance of state trunk-line roads. In 1919 the people voted for an amendment to permit the state to borrow $50,000,000 for a comprehensive highway building program. The good roads of Michigan had their origin in this program.

Macadam and gravel roads were dusty and could not withstand the heavy traffic of an increasing number of automobiles and trucks. Experiments with various materials were carried on, and in 1909 the first mile of concrete road in the world was laid on Woodward Avenue in Detroit from Six Mile Road to Seven Mile Road. Engineers from other states and countries who came to examine this pavement found that it was superior to macadam or gravel. The building of concrete highways spread from Wayne County throughout the world.

— 25 —

Putting the World on Wheels

MANUFACTURING INCREASED enormously during the period 1890 to 1920. As one would expect, some of the important industries in Michigan were based on the use of wood. In 1909 the state was first in the production of refrigerators and second in the production of furniture. It ranked first also in the manufacture of showcases, and second in the output of billiard tables. It was first in the manufacture of salt and essential oils of mint; second in food preparations, drugs and patent medicines, cash registers, and calculating machines; and third in beet sugar, brass and bronze products, fur goods, flags and banners, steel springs, stoves, and furnaces.

At the top, as far as the state and the nation were concerned, was a comparatively new industry, the manufacturing of automobiles. Although the first automobile made in Detroit had appeared on the street as recently as 1896, by 1904 Michigan had taken the lead in production over other states. In 1909 the state was still ahead, and it had increased its percentage of the national output. At home, too, it had attained top position, for the value of automobiles and parts manufactured in Michigan in that year was $96,651,451, far above that of any other industry in the state.

The automobile had its origin in Europe. Gottlieb Daimler, a German, invented the internal combustion engine and applied it to transportation in 1886. Carl Benz, another German, also was an early maker of automobiles, and French manufacturers soon entered the field.

In the United States, the first practical car propelled by an internal combustion engine was built in 1893 by Charles E. and J. Frank Duryea of Springfield, Massachusetts. The next year the Apperson brothers in Kokomo, Indiana, made a car designed by Elwood Haynes. On March 6, 1896, the first successful car built in Detroit appeared on the streets of the city. It was driven by Charles B. King, who had built it in a machine shop. Henry Ford's car made its debut three months later, on June 4. King was more interested in art and music than in automobiles, and he soon retired from the field; but Ford continued to experiment, and he finally became the greatest single producer of motor cars.

2

The first automobile company organized in Michigan was the Olds Motor Vehicle Works, in which Ransom E. Olds and Frank Clark of Lansing were partners. Olds's father made gasoline engines and Clark's father made carriages. The sons combined the two and produced their first car in 1898. Clark sold out to Olds, who obtained sufficient capital to establish a factory in Detroit in 1899. Like most other cars of the period, it had only one cylinder; but it ran, and the Oldsmobile was a very popular car. Four hundred were built in 1901, and 2,500 in 1902. It was the first car produced in quantity. After a fire destroyed the factory in 1902, Olds moved to Lansing.

The first automobile show was held in Madison Square Garden, New York, in 1900. All the cars were shipped by rail. The next year, Olds asked Roy D. Chapin, a young employe, to drive an Oldsmobile to New York for the show. He finally made it, in a week. After driving through Canada, he crossed over to Buffalo. In New York State the roads were so bad that he used the tow path of the Erie Canal as long as he could. He had to make many repairs on the way, and he smashed a wheel when the car skidded on a wet asphalt pavement in New York City. Although Alexander Winton had driven one of his cars from Cleveland to New York in 1899, Chapin's drive was the longest up to that time. Chapin later became one of the founders of the Hudson Motor Company and, still later, its president.

3

Ford made two false starts before he was successful in producing automobiles commercially. In 1899 the Detroit Automobile Company was organized with Ford as chief engineer and one of the owners. In 1901 because of differences of opinion as to policy, Ford withdrew and the company was reorganized as the Cadillac Motor Company with Henry M. Leland as production manager. Leland was an experienced manufacturer of engines. At Cadillac he first developed interchangeable parts through precision methods.

Ford seemed to be interested principally in producing fast and powerful racing cars. They got publicity, but they were useless for sale. He raced the famous 999 himself. Then he hired Barney Oldfield, who broke the record in 1902. After withdrawing from the Detroit Automobile Company, Ford organized the Henry Ford Automobile Company, which failed in 1902.

In 1903 the Ford Motor Company was incorporated with a capitalization of $100,000. Only $28,000 was paid in cash. The principal financial backer was Alexander Y. Malcolmson, a coal dealer, who had faith in Ford's ability to produce cars. James Couzens, an employe of Malcolmson, managed to scrape together $2,000, which he invested in the corporation, and Malcolmson put him in charge of the business affairs of the new company to protect his interests.

Others induced by the coal dealer to invest were John S. Gray, banker, and John W. Anderson and Horace H. Rackham, lawyers. Ford had 25 per cent of the common stock and the Dodge brothers, John F. and Horace E., were assigned shares in return for manufacturing engines and other parts for the Ford car. At that time no expensive factory buildings were required, for everything was made by Dodge and other suppliers and simply assembled in the small shop on Mack Avenue at Bellevue in Detroit.

During the first year of operation, 1,708 cars were produced, and the profits were $280,000. Although returns on the investment continued to be very large, Malcolmson became dissatisfied and sold out his interest to Ford in 1906, giving the latter 51 per cent of the stock.

Ford was convinced that most people wanted cars primarily as a means of transportation, and that if he could make them cheaply enough he would find a ready market. In 1908, therefore, he began the production of the Model T, in his new factory in Highland Park. It was a sturdy, inexpensive machine. Although the average price of an automobile in that year was $1,926, the Model T sold for $950. Assembled in a plant designed for mass production, 10,600 cars were turned out the first year. By 1913 the annual output was nearly 200,000 and the price had been reduced to $550. In 1915 the cheapest model sold for $360.

In January, 1914, it was announced that five dollars would be the minimum pay for an eight-hour shift at Ford's. As a result men flocked to the Highland Park plant from all over the country. Fire hoses had to be used to disperse a mob of ten thousand that stormed the employment office. Other manufacturers in the Detroit area condemned Henry Ford as a disturber of industrial stability. Some newspapers, among them *The New York Times*, found fault with the plan. Their comments gave Ford a great deal of free publicity. It was soon disclosed that the new rate of pay applied only after a man had worked for six months. This provision helped to reduce the labor turnover and to increase production.

Desiring to have a free hand in managing the business, in 1919 Ford bought out all the stockholders for more than $100,000,000. The Dodge brothers received $25,000,000; Horace H. Rackham, in return for his $5,000 investment, $12,500,000; and James Couzens, who had remained with Ford and who had had a great share in making the business a success, $29,308,857.80. Each of these men also had been receiving large annual dividends.

4

Another pioneer in the automobile industry was David D. Buick, an able inventor and mechanic but a poor businessman. The Buick Company began manufacturing in Detroit in 1902, but production languished for lack of money. The next year James H. Whiting of the Flint Wagon Works bought the business and moved it to Flint. He sold out to the Durant-Dort Carriage Company of Flint in 1904. William C. Durant, head of the company, was a successful carriage manufacturer. Now he began a spectacular career of promotion, during which he made and lost millions himself and became the founder of the General Motors Corporation.

Durant was a small, inconspicuous, quiet person with a fertile imagination, ability to convince people, a tenacious purpose, and the stamina, so legend has it, to work at top speed twenty-four hours a day.

Unlike the roaring, heavy-fisted, hard-drinking Dodge brothers, he neither smoked nor drank. Although he spoke softly, he made himself heard.

With the idea of stabilizing the automobile industry by a strong combination, in 1908 Durant established the General Motors Company with Buick as the basis. Capitalization was $12,500,000. Soon he acquired the Olds Motor Works. Durant even tried to buy the Ford Motor Company to add to General Motors in 1908. Ford, who was in poor health at the time, was willing to talk with him. Durant offered $8,000,000. Ford agreed to sell, for cash. Durant failed to raise the money, and Ford stayed in business.

In 1910 Cadillac and Oakland were added to General Motors. Parts and accessory manufacturers were also brought into the combination, which was simply a holding company. Rapid expansion made additional capital necessary. When Durant applied to New York bankers in 1910, they advanced $15,000,000 on condition that they have control of the company for five years. He had to agree because he needed the money; and, of course, he was no longer boss of General Motors. It looked as if Durant's meteoric career were at an end.

In 1911 the Chevrolet Motor Car Company was incorporated. Durant soon bought it and moved it from Detroit to Flint. He induced many holders of General Motors stock to exchange it for Chevrolet stock. He also quietly purchased General Motors shares on the open market. As a result of these maneuvers, Chevrolet was the owner of a majority of General Motors common stock in 1916 when control by the bankers was released; and Durant, president of Chevrolet, again became president of the new General Motors Corporation. He had used Chevrolet for his purpose this time as he had used Buick in the beginning.

Durant was forced out of General Motors by the financial crisis in the brief depression of 1921. Again he began gathering automobile companies into a combination. This time he was not so successful as before. The great depression of 1929 ruined his ambitious plans, and he retired at the age of seventy-four.

5

The last of the Big Three, the Chrysler Corporation, was a later development which grew out of a combination of two early Detroit companies, the Maxwell and the Chalmers. When they were faced with financial collapse, Walter P. Chrysler, a former General Motors man, was engaged in 1922 to reorganize the affairs of these two companies. They were united in the Maxwell Motor Corporation, which continued until 1925, when Chrysler Corporation was organized. Both the Maxwell and the Chalmers were discontinued, and the Chrysler cars appeared. Plymouth was developed by Chrysler as a contender in the low-price field, and De Soto as a middle-price car. K. T. Keller, a production man, and Fred M. Zeder, an engineer, were capable assistants to Chrysler. After his death in 1940, Keller became president of the corporation.

6

Other Michigan companies which survive, at least in the names of their cars, are the Dodge, the Hudson, and the Packard. Dodge Brothers, Incorporated, was organized in 1914 by John F. and Horace E. Dodge. Their cars were the first to have all-steel bodies. The company was acquired by Chrysler in 1928.

J. L. Hudson, a Detroit merchant; Roscoe B. Jackson; Roy D. Chapin of Chalmers; and Howard E. Coffin, also of Chalmers, were the founders of the Hudson Motor Company in 1909. Believing that people would prefer closed cars to open ones, if they were not too expensive, in 1921 Hudson built the Essex, a moderate-priced car with a closed body. Its immediate popularity began the change to closed-body cars. Roy D. Chapin was president of Hudson Motors from 1910 until his death in 1936.

The Packard car was originally made in Warren, Ohio, by two brothers, J. W. and W. D. Packard, who had a manufacturing establishment there. They had been interested in automobiles as early as 1893. In 1898, they bought a Winton, dismantled it, and decided they could make a better car. The first one was ready in 1899.

In 1901, Henry B. Joy and his brother-in-law, Truman H. Newberry, saw a Packard in New York and were impressed by the ease with which it started. This was an important consideration in the days before Charles F. Kettering's electric starter became a regular part of the equipment. Starting an engine with a crank required a certain knack, and a good deal of agility; for if the spark was not properly set, the engine would backfire and spin the crank in reverse. Unless the cranker let go and got out of the way, he would have a broken wrist.

Henry B. Joy bought a Packard and was so pleased with it that he wanted an interest in the company. He believed that production should be increased. The Packards were willing, but they didn't have the necessary capital. Joy induced a number of Detroiters to join him in putting money into the concern. They included Frederick M. and Russell A. Alger, Jr., Truman H. and John S. Newberry, Richard F. Joy, Philip S. McMillan, and Dexter M. Ferry, Jr. Because they had the controlling interest, they moved the company to Detroit in 1903.

The companies which have been mentioned are those which prospered. Many others, more than one hundred of them in Michigan, failed after a brief existence. The cars which they produced have long

An Early Automobile—1902 Model

since vanished from the roads, and even the names of many have been forgotten.[1]

Some which were built for a few years in Detroit were the Saxon, 1914 to 1922; the Flanders, 1911 to 1912; the Abbott, 1909; and the Brush, 1907 to 1909. Other cities of Michigan also manufactured cars which have been forgotten. In Kalamazoo, the Roamer was built from 1916 to 1926; in Saginaw, the Marquette in 1912; in Jackson, the Earl from 1922 to 1924; in Adrian, the Lion in 1914; and in Marysville, the Wills-St. Claire from 1921 to 1926. Today some models of these cars may be found in the garages of collectors of early automobiles.

[1] It has been estimated that 2,500 different-named cars were manufactured in the United States at one time or another.

7

Before 1920, long trips were only for those who were willing to suffer some inconveniences, and who had great physical endurance. Outside the cities, gasoline stations and repair shops were not numerous, and the roads were either of dirt or macadam. In dry weather the wheels raised clouds of dust, and in the spring or after heavy rains cars were likely to sink axle deep in the mud. Early cars had neither windshields nor tops. Driver and passengers alike wore long linen dusters and goggles. A man frequently wore a leather cap, and a woman tied a scarf over her hat to keep it from blowing away. Even after windshields and tops were provided, the flapping side curtains let in dust and rain. There were so few route markers that the automobilist was likely to lose his way. It was only after good roads were built in the 1920's and afterward that long-distance driving became a pleasure.

Laws in Michigan and in other states threatened to make automobile riding a burden rather than a pleasure. Before 1900, steam-driven traction engines clanking noisily along from farm to farm, where they furnished power for threshing wheat, were the only mechanical vehicles which used the roads. Horses were usually afraid of them.

In Michigan a law required that an attendant walk some distance ahead of any carriage or traction engine propelled by steam to warn drivers or riders of its approach. The engine had to be stopped until the attendant had led the horse past. At night, according to the law, the attendant had to carry a red lantern.

When it is recalled that some of the early automobiles were propelled by steam engines, it can easily be imagined what effect this law might have had on the development of the new means of transportation. As a matter of fact, an amendment in 1903 exempted automobiles from the provisions of the law.

The first comprehensive act regulating the use of automobiles in Michigan was passed by the Legislature in 1905. Each owner was required to register his car with the secretary of state. The secretary issued a small metal disk stamped with a number which the owner had to attach to the car. Besides, he had to have that number painted on the back of his car in figures three inches high.[2] Before operating a car, one was required to obtain a driver's license from the secretary of state.

The law of 1905 set the maximum speed at twenty-five miles an

[2] It was not until 1910 that the secretary of state furnished two "number plates."

hour on the highways and eight miles an hour in the business districts of towns. It provided that when a horse-drawn vehicle approached on the road, the driver of a car had to reduce his speed to ten miles an hour. If the horse appeared to be greatly frightened, the automobilist was required to pull off the road and stop the engine until the horse had passed. Although this section remained in the statute book for many years, horses gradually became accustomed to automobiles, and the law was not enforced.

The automobile amazingly influenced the American way of life. Even before World War I, when there were only five million cars in use, the effects were widespread. The automobile created a great variety of jobs in factories of many kinds and in repair shops. It induced an increased production of iron, steel, copper, rubber, leather, oil, and gasoline. As cars became less expensive more and more people purchased them, and they gave to a part of the population a greater mobility. City residents could drive into the country, and farmers could more easily go to town. Surburban residential districts began to develop because people could drive a considerable distance to work.

Trucks and buses propelled by gasoline engines also caused social and economic changes. Farmers used trucks to carry their produce to more distant markets than before, and perishable foods were available to consumers in better condition. Because they were cheaper to operate than steam or electric railways, trucks and buses took passengers and freight from those transportation lines. Besides, trucks provided door-to-door delivery, and buses could easily change their routes to serve new communities.

Although steam railroads did not feel the competition greatly before 1920, interurban electric railways were nearly ruined. The steam lines retained their long-distance passenger and freight traffic and the heavy local freight. The interurbans, however, depending on short hauls, could not compete successfully with the new vehicles propelled by gasoline engines.

Electric interurban lines developed rapidly in Michigan during the 1890's. Requiring a lighter roadbed and less expensive equipment than the steam railroads, they cost less to operate. Low fares, frequent service, and high-speed cars attracted passengers. The first interurban in Michigan began running between Ann Arbor and Ypsilanti in 1890. Although a steam engine was used at first, in 1896 cars propelled by electric motors replaced them.

In Michigan the principal lines fanned out from Detroit. After the system had fully developed, it was possible to travel from Detroit to

Monroe and Toledo, to Mount Clemens and Port Huron, to Flint and Saginaw, to Ypsilanti, Ann Arbor, Jackson, Battle Creek, and Kalamazoo.

There were lines also from Grand Rapids to Holland and Saugatuck, and to Grand Haven and Muskegon. From St. Joseph one could go by interurban to South Bend, Indiana, and from Adrian to Toledo, Ohio. In the Upper Peninsula there was a line from Negaunee to Ishpeming, and another from Houghton to Lake Linden and Hubbell. Interurbans carried freight as well as passengers.

The tracks were usually laid beside the highways, and there were numerous grade crossings. Because the interurbans ran at high speed, many accidents occurred at the crossings. By 1912 the electric cars had reached the peak of their popularity. As automobiles, trucks, and buses became more numerous, interurbans began to lose traffic. During the 1920's they disappeared.

Today the only trace of this formerly important means of transportation is the graded roadbed overgrown with grass which may still be seen beside some highways in the southern part of the state. Where roads have been widened, even that evidence has been destroyed. Interurban electric lines in Michigan and elsewhere were victims of progress.

— 26 —

Michigan in World War I

UNITED STATES census reports contain evidence of the rapid growth of population in Michigan. In 1890 it was 2,093,889; in 1900, 2,420,982; in 1910, 2,810,173; and in 1920, 3,668,412. During the thirty-year period the increase was more than a million and a half. Of this number, more than 850,000 were added between 1910 and 1920.

The growth of population can be accounted for by the natural increase by birth, by the coming of Americans from other states, and by immigrants from Canada and Europe. Although Canadians, people from the British Isles, Germans, Dutch, and Scandinavians continued to settle in Michigan in large numbers, after 1900 there was a great increase of people from southern and eastern Europe—Poles, Greeks, Italians, and Hungarians.

The principal reason for the rapid growth in population was the development of industry in Michigan. Factories increased in number and in size, and there was a great demand for workmen. That is why most of the newcomers found jobs and homes in the cities. Statistics of city populations show the effects of the multiplication of manufacturing plants. Detroit, with nearly a million inhabitants in 1920, was almost five times as large as it had been in 1890. During the same thirty years, the population of Flint increased ninefold, that of Pontiac fivefold, and of Kalamazoo and Grand Rapids twofold. It is significant that the greatest growth appeared in the cities which made automobiles. Saginaw and Monroe grew slowly, while Manistee and Menominee declined in population.

In the Upper Peninsula, the counties in which iron and copper were produced increased in population. The northern counties of the Lower Peninsula, in general, showed a small increase as a result of settlement on cutover lands. The southern counties, on the other hand, except those which contained industrial cities, declined. Greater use of agricultural machinery released many persons from work on the farms, and the cities offered a more attractive life as well as jobs in factories.

The trend of population from country to cities was notable. In 1890, only 35 per cent of the people of the state lived in towns or cities of 2,500 inhabitants or more, and 65 per cent lived in villages or on farms. By contrast, in 1920, the ratio was almost reversed. Sixty-one per cent were living in towns or cities, and 39 per cent in villages and on farms. This shift to large cities of people accustomed to life in the country or in villages resulted in many serious problems of health, safety, education, labor relations, and transportation. Because the cities alone were unwilling or unable to solve them, the state assumed greater and greater control, and even the United States Government began to expand its regulations and services.

2

During this period Detroit adopted a new city charter and acquired the street railway system. Need for change in the city government was obvious to those who believed that the people should rule; but many respectable men refused to take part in politics because they felt it would be degrading.

Elections were controlled in many precincts by corrupt boards on which the liquor interests were always well represented. In the Fourth Precinct of the Ninth Ward, called Batty McGraw's precinct, the board consisted in 1914 of a saloonkeeper with his two bartenders, another saloonkeeper with his bartender, and a machinist. This board practiced all sorts of election frauds, including re-marking ballots and casting votes for absentees.

The most notorious of the controlled precincts was the First of the First Ward. This precinct, on the east side of Woodward Avenue at the river, was presided over by Billy Boushaw. Billy ran a combined saloon and flophouse for floaters who cheerfully voted as he asked them to. In the election of 1914, every vote in this precinct was controlled.

There were some respectable citizens of Detroit, however, who were willing to take an active part in politics in order to rescue the city from control of saloonkeepers, the Detroit United Railway, and other special interests. The most notable was Henry M. Leland, automobile engineer, founder and first president of the Detroit Citizens League, organized in 1912. A lawyer, Pliny W. Marsh, was secretary and the active director. Other leading citizens who helped finance the League and who worked for decent government were Ralph Stone, Tracy W. McGregor, John C. Lodge, Harold H. Emmons, and Divie B. Duffield. They established the *Civic Searchlight*, a publication which contained nonpartisan information about candidates for office, and recommended those whom they believed best qualified. An election law passed by the State Legislature in 1915 abolished the corrupt election boards and paved the way for better government.

In 1918 the people of Detroit adopted a new charter which provided for nonpartisan elections in odd years. The only elected officers are the mayor, clerk, treasurer, and a nine-man council elected at large. The council meets every day, and committees are always in touch with every aspect of city government.

The mayor appoints all heads of departments and may remove them at will. Thus, full authority and responsibility for efficient government are in his hands. The people are protected by the right to recall the mayor or any other of the elected officers. James Couzens was the first mayor chosen under the new charter.

The fight which Mayor Pingree had inaugurated against the street railway company continued. The Detroit United Railway wanted a new long-term franchise, but the city refused to grant it. When all the franchises had expired, the company continued on a day-to-day agreement. That meant that at any time it could be prohibited from using the streets; but if that were done, the people would have no transportation.

The D.U.R. refused to build lines to serve the new surburban developments unless a franchise was granted. In election after election the settlement of the street railway dispute was an issue. The D.U.R. always attempted to elect friendly aldermen.

Finally, after Couzens became mayor, a solution was reached. He led the fight vigorously and attracted supporters as Pingree had done. In the spring of 1920, the voters authorized the building of competing municipally owned lines, and in 1922 they voted to purchase the D.U.R. equipment for $19,850,000, a great reduction from the $31,-

500,000, which the company had previously asked. The city extended car and bus lines into sparsely populated sections to provide transportation, even though they might operate for a time at a loss.

Other cities, at about the same time, adopted more efficient forms of government. For example, in 1916 the people of Grand Rapids approved a new charter which provided for an elected commission of seven men instead of the twenty-four aldermen under the previous charter. They elected one of the members mayor, and chose a manager who had complete charge of municipal administration. In 1918 Kalamazoo also adopted the commission-manager form of government. Incidentally, Michigan has more cities under managers than any other state.

3

Education in Michigan improved considerably, especially in the cities. School buildings were erected with facilities for a variety of studies including music, art, manual training, and domestic science. Nearly every one had a gymnasium, and some had swimming pools.

In the country, smaller financial resources and conservatism retarded advance. One-room schools built during the 1870's or the 1880's continued in use, and some are still in service at the present time. A law of 1895 required all children from seven to sixteen years of age to attend school a minimum of four months each year, and a truant officer in each district was appointed to enforce the law. A new law in 1905 made attendance compulsory for the full term fixed by the district in which the children lived. Under these laws, most of the boys and girls of the state received at least the rudiments of an education.

Lengthened terms and more adequate buildings were important, but even more so was the raising of the standards for teachers. To increase the means of teacher training, three new normal schools, in addition to the original one at Ypsilanti, were founded. Central State Normal School, which opened in Mt. Pleasant as a private institution in 1892, was taken over by the state in 1895. Four years later Northern State Normal was established at Marquette in the Upper Peninsula, and in 1904 Western State Normal was opened in Kalamazoo.

4

Outbreak of World War I in August, 1914, took Americans by surprise. Ignorant of European affairs and engrossed in their own pursuits, most Americans believed that the war was none of their business. From the beginning there was sympathy for the Allies, especially Great Britain, France, and Belgium. Nurtured by shrewd propaganda against Germany and strengthened by our economic interest as the Allies borrowed money and purchased vast quantities of foodstuffs and munitions in the United States, the feeling of attachment became even stronger.

Great Britain's naval blockade, which caused her to seize ships and cargoes bound for Germany or for neighboring neutral countries, caused irritations and resulted in notes of protest from President Woodrow Wilson. On the other hand, Germany's submarine campaign, in retaliation for the blockade, sank merchant ships without warning and killed Americans. The sinking of the British liner *Lusitania* on May 7, 1915, cost the lives of 1,198 persons, including 128 American citizens. Theodore Roosevelt and others demanded immediate war with Germany, but President Wilson asked only for reparations and for a promise that ships would not be sunk until the safety of passengers had been provided for. The promise was given, and for a time there was peace.

Even though preparations for eventual hostilities were hurried forward, the slogan of the Democratic party in the campaign of 1916 was "He kept us out of war," and Wilson was re-elected. Announcement in January, 1917, by the German government of unrestricted submarine warfare caused the President to break off diplomatic relations. During March five American ships were sunk, and on April 2 the President asked Congress for a declaration of war against Germany. Congress complied with a joint resolution on April 6, 1917.

Americans entered the war with great enthusiasm. Deeply stirred by the idealistic pronouncements of President Wilson, they were willing to sacrifice comfort, money, and even their lives in what they believed was a holy crusade, a war against the forces of evil. Nearly everyone was sure that the world would be a better place to live in after the victory had been won.

In Michigan Albert E. Sleeper, a Republican, was elected governor in 1916. Late in March, 1917, when war seemed imminent, the governor called a conference of state officers to consider what action should be taken in the event of hostilities. The War Preparedness Board was set up, and the Legislature voted a war loan of $5,000,000 at the request of the governor. This money was used to organize the Michigan State Troops to replace the National Guard units which were on the Mexican border and were expected to be sent overseas, to aid the families of men in the service, to provide assistance to returning veterans, and to help farmers produce larger crops of necessary foodstuffs.

Because it was believed that additional protection from lawless elements or foreign saboteurs might be necessary during the war, the Michigan State Police force was organized. The duties of these men were to co-operate with state and local officers in detecting crimes, arresting criminals, and preserving law and order. The State Police force became a permanent law enforcing agency, and it is one of the best in the nation.

The 11th National Guard Division composed of Michigan and Wisconsin men had been ordered to the Mexican border in June 1916 with other national guard and regular army units to participate in the hunt for Pancho Villa, who had conducted murderous raids across the boundary into the United States. After war on Germany had been declared, the Michigan-Wisconsin organization became the 32nd Division. The 1st Michigan Ambulance Company was detached from it and became the 168th Ambulance Company of the 42nd Division, nicknamed the "Rainbow" because it consisted of units from all the national guard divisions.

The 32nd Division was sent to Camp MacArthur at Waco, Texas, in September, 1917, to train for service overseas. Some of the units embarked in January, 1918, and by the middle of March all had reassembled in France. The division took over a quiet sector near Belfort in May. In July the 32nd was transported to the fighting front and went into action on the Ourcq River, taking part in the great Aisne-Marne offensive against the German army. General William G. Haan was in command.

The 32nd, nicknamed the "Red Arrow Division," participated also in the Oisne-Aisne and the Meuse-Argonne offensives. One of the best combat divisions, its casualties totaled 2,898 killed and 10,986 wounded. Officers and men were awarded 134 Distinguished Service Crosses. After the Armistice on November 11, 1918, the 32nd served in the Army of Occupation at Koblenz on the Rhine until April, 1919.

5

Although thousands of young men enlisted voluntarily in the regular army and in national guard units, it was evident that several million would be needed. Convinced that an honest draft system was the best way to provide recruits, Congress in May, 1917, passed the Selective Service Act. All men between the ages of twenty-one and thirty were required to register. Local draft boards made up of civilians classified the registrants, and a drawing of numbers in Washington determined the order in which those available for service should be called. Quotas were set for each state. Able-bodied unmarried men without dependents were drafted and sent to camps for training.

Camp Custer near Battle Creek was built in 1917, and drafted men from Michigan and Wisconsin began to arrive there in September. They were organized into the 85th Division, trained, and shipped to England in July, 1918. Several units, the 339th Infantry, the first battalion of the 310th Engineers, the 337th Field Hospital, and the 337th Ambulance Company, were detached and sent to Archangel, Russia. There, with other Allied troops, British, French, and Canadian, they fought against the forces of Soviet Russia. Because of the rigorous weather, the 339th and the supporting units were nicknamed the "Polar Bears." They returned to Michigan in July, 1919. The remainder of the 85th Division crossed to France and its men were used as replacements in other American units.

In 1918 the age of men subject to the draft was lowered to eighteen and raised to forty-five. Young men were permitted to continue their education in college at government expense. They were enrolled in the Students' Army Training Corps, issued uniforms, and given military training in addition to their academic studies. This arrangement was advantageous to students and colleges alike. Without it many of the smaller colleges would have had to close for the duration of the war. There were 1,200 in the SATC at Michigan Agricultural College and nearly 4,000 at the University of Michigan.

Michigan contributed mightily with her fields and factories toward winning the war. Farmers increased their production of foodstuffs, and the factories poured out a prodigious stream of mechanical equipment needed by a modern army. Among the most important products were airplanes, Liberty engines, tanks, trucks, and shells. Even Henry Ford, who had sponsored the Peace Ship in 1915 and had himself accompanied the strange assortment of zealots who sailed on the *Oscar II*, determined to get the boys out of the trenches by Christmas, subordinated his hatred for war to his patriotic duty and turned out Eagle boats on the River Rouge.

On the home front there was continued enthusiasm which sometimes got out of hand. Slackers and pro-Germans were threatened with violence, and a few were roughly handled. The homes of persons who refused to buy Liberty Bonds were daubed with yellow paint, and the teaching of German in schools was abandoned. More constructive endeavors were the participation in all sorts of drives to raise money for the government and for soldier welfare agencies. Thousands of men, women, and children worked as volunteers in the five campaigns to sell Liberty Bonds and Victory Bonds. Michigan exceeded its quota every time, by 140 per cent in the second Liberty Loan drive.

Many volunteered their services to assist in raising funds for the Red Cross, the YMCA, the YWCA, the Knights of Columbus, the Salvation Army, the Jewish Welfare Board, the Camp Community

War Workwomen in a Detroit Factory

Service, and the American Library Association. All these organizations were engaged in providing services for the soldiers in camp and near the front. Thousands of dollars were generously contributed to aid those agencies in carrying on their work.

The Armistice signed by the Allies and Germany silenced the guns in Europe on November 11, 1918. Spontaneous celebrations at news of the victory occurred in every town and city in the United States. The war was over. The Kaiser had been dethroned, and the world had been made safe for democracy. There were insistent demands that the soldiers overseas be brought home immediately. The fine spirit of sacrifice and co-operation with other peoples which had characterized the nation during the war broke down.

A majority of Americans apparently were determined to withdraw from participation in world affairs. In spite of the pleas of President Wilson and other leaders, the Senate refused to ratify the Treaty of Versailles, which contained the Covenant of the League of Nations. "Return to Normalcy" was the slogan of the Republican party in the election of 1920 which placed Warren G. Harding in the White House. In Michigan, Alexander J. Groesbeck, a Republican, was elected governor.

6

The period 1890 to 1920 was marked by many social, political, and economic changes. In Michigan, up to 1890, economic activities consisted principally of the primary extractive processes: fishing, farming, lumbering, and mining. From 1890 to 1920 these activities continued and, except for lumbering, increased in quantity and in value of the output; but manufacturing developed rapidly and outstripped all the others in the value of its production. In this field the automobile industry had a phenomenal growth. It became the leading industry and the number of automobiles produced in Michigan was greater than that in any other state.

The increase in manufacturing caused a shifting of population from the rural districts to the cities. Detroit, Grand Rapids, Flint, and Pontiac grew rapidly. There was a slight decrease in the population of the southern tiers of counties, except for those which contained large cities, because the use of more machinery on the farms released men for work in factories. In the northern counties of the Lower Peninsula the population increased as the result of the occupation of cutover land by people who tried to develop farms. In the Upper Peninsula the population increased because of the demand for both iron and copper.

During this period immigration to the United States was unrestricted in spite of protests by workingmen. Foreigners continued to come to Michigan, but new nationalities predominated. While the number of Scandinavian immigrants was sufficient only to maintain the level previously reached, there was a marked increase in the number of Poles, Hungarians, Greeks, and Italians. Fewer Scots, Irish, and English came to Michigan.

Pingree's fight as mayor of Detroit and governor of Michigan to abolish abuses, to equalize the burdens of taxation, and to give the people a more direct voice in their government accomplished little during his administrations, but he aroused the people to demand reforms which came later.

Michigan had three progressive governors after 1900 whose careers paralleled those of the progressive presidents, Theodore Roosevelt, William H. Taft, and Woodrow Wilson: Warner, Osborn, and Ferris. A new constitution, approved by the people in 1908, contained a number of progressive features, and by amendments the initiative, referendum, recall, woman suffrage, and prohibition of the manufacture and sale of liquor were added to it.

During this period a beginning was made in the conservation of natural resources, a state highway department was established, railroads were more strictly regulated, insurance companies came under state supervision, women and children were given additional protection, and a workmen's compensation law was enacted.

The year 1917 marked the end of reform in both state and nation. World War I began in 1914, and, although the United States was officially neutral for nearly three years, the attention of the national government was directed largely to foreign affairs. In Michigan and in other states the demand from abroad for unprecedented quantities of food and manufactured products brought full employment and great prosperity. To a large extent people were satisfied with conditions as they were.

Then in 1917 we declared war on Germany. Nearly everyone was certain that we would lick the Kaiser, make the world safe for democracy, and live happily ever afterward. Victory was won in 1918 after a prodigious national effort in which Michigan loyally played her part. Immediately, throughout the country enthusiasm for co-operation in world affairs evaporated, the Senate rejected President Wilson's League of Nations Covenant, and the Republicans won the election of 1920 with the slogan, "Return to Normalcy." In Michigan Governor Albert E. Sleeper completed his second term in office, and Alexander J. Groesbeck became his successor.

PART VII

ECONOMIC ACHIEVEMENT AND SOCIAL PROGRESS 1920–1950

— 27 —

The Prosperous 1920's

The spirit of sacrifice and the high idealism which had carried the American people through World War I evaporated after victory was won, and a return to normalcy seemed to mean a suspicion of both ideas and ideals and a grim determination to make money. President Wilson's vision of world-wide co-operation was replaced by the illusion that prosperity is attained by national selfishness.

Graft and corruption on a scale previously unknown developed in the Harding administration, and a majority of the people paid little heed when they learned the facts. Moral values had become debased during the war, and nearly everyone, it seemed, wanted to get rich regardless of the means involved. Lawlessness became widespread. Enforcement of the prohibition laws, which at first was fairly successful, broke down, and bootleggers became prosperous and powerful.

The Detroit area, because of its proximity to Canada, was an important center of the bootlegging industry. On the Canadian side of the river, speedboats took on cargoes of liquor, filed with the customs officers clearance papers showing the West Indies or Mexico as their destination, and waited for a signal from the American side. On the river the United States Customs Patrol, nicknamed the "Prohibition

Navy," watched for bootleggers' boats. Catching them was difficult, for the river was nearly seventy miles long and only half a mile wide. Under cover of darkness fast boats could cross unseen in a few minutes. Those that were intercepted were confiscated, and the crews were held for trial in the United States District Court in Detroit.

Along the waterfront, especially in the downriver communities of River Rouge, Ecorse, and Wyandotte, the big dealers in contraband liquor had elaborate systems for receiving the cargoes. Their agents ranged along the shore watching for city police and United States officers. When the coast was clear, they signaled the skippers of the boats to cross. Speedy trucks carried the cases to well-guarded garages.

Some operators had boathouses built so that the smugglers could slip inside and close heavy doors behind them. Above was the office and a garage opening on Jefferson Avenue or the River Road. Trucks were loaded, armed guards put aboard, and when spies gave the word the trucks roared out, usually headed toward Chicago; for much of the liquor that crossed the river was purchased by out-of-town buyers.

On the road the drivers tried to avoid sheriffs, state police, and United States agents. Bribes sometimes cleared the road for the trucks. Hijackers were a more dangerous hazard. Tough underworld characters, perhaps bootleggers themselves, they preyed upon the illegal cargoes, knowing that those they robbed would not report them to the police. Sometimes they captured a load of liquor without a struggle, but frequently they had to shoot it out with the guards.

Bootleggers settled scores with hijackers in their own fashion. Hired killers were put on their trail, and many died by a shotgun blast. Because both bootleggers and hijackers sometimes worked in gangs, the killing of one man often led to a feud, and a dozen might die before the affair was settled.

The Giannola and the Vitale gangs were two of the most notorious. Sam and Tony Giannola and John Vitale, Sicilians, sold beer and fruit in Wyandotte before the prohibition era. By using strong-arm methods, they drove competitors out of business and became the bosses of the Sicilian community.

With this lawless background, they took naturally to bootlegging and hijacking. Wanting to be a boss in his own right, John Vitale left the Giannolas and took some of the gang with him. There was bad feeling between the gangs, and soon the Giannolas hijacked a big load of Vitale's whisky. Vitale swore vengeance. Tony Giannola was shot by his own bodyguard while attending a wake. Sam laid a trap for Vitale. A blast of shotgun slugs missed him but killed his brother-in-law. One of Vitale's henchmen was murdered and Vitale's son was wounded. Then Sam Giannola was shot to death. The feud continued until Vitale and his son were killed.

There were other murderous gangs, too. The Purple Gang, the River Gang, and the West Side Gang were some of them. Warring on each other and shooting it out with police, they were deadly menaces in the community. Some of the hoodlums who escaped the bullets of their enemies were arrested and sentenced to long terms in prison. Hundreds of cars and trucks and a few airplanes used for transporting liquor were confiscated.

Besides the liquor that was brought across the river, greater quantities were produced in the cities and in the rural districts. Garages, abandoned factories, and barns were used as breweries and distilleries. The stuff they produced was usually filthy, and some of it was poisonous, but there were always purchasers. In certain circles it was considered smart to have a large supply of liquor, and some men boasted of the exploits of their bootleggers. Many persons who could not afford to pay bootleggers' prices made wine and beer at home.

Prohibition gave a special opportunity for making money to men who were already engaged in lawless pursuits. When the depression reduced the demand for their wares and repeal put them out of business, many turned to kidnaping and other criminal activities.

2

The 1920's are usually thought of as a period of prosperity, but a short depression occurred at the very beginning. A "buyers' strike" at home, resulting from resistance to high war-time prices, and a sharp reduction of purchases from abroad in 1920 and 1921 caused numerous bankruptcies and large-scale unemployment. Farmers were especially unfortunate. To produce the food required by our own armies and those of the Allies, many had mortgaged their farms to buy more land. After the war, European nations began again to raise their own food, and if they needed additional supplies they purchased them elsewhere than in the United States because our prices were too high.

The depression began to lift in 1923, and it was the automobile industry in Michigan that led the swing to prosperity. Although the government during the war had ordered a reduction of the number of cars produced for civilians, it had purchased thousands of automobiles and trucks for the army. Besides, plants were expanded to turn out airplanes, engines, cannon, and other materials for war. After restrictions were removed, a great demand for cars came from those who had made money during the war, and young men, who for the first time in their lives had had an opportunity to drive cars in the army, now wanted their own. The changeover to peacetime manufacture was not diffcult, and the automobile plants were soon ready to meet the new demand.

Keen competition and intelligent planning produced cars of a moderate price as well as luxury models. Between 1920 and 1925 the annual output of automobiles doubled. In numbers, the Ford Model T led all the rest. Ford, whose factory was in Highland Park, had built a plant on the River Rouge to produce Eagle boats and other military equipment. After the war he constructed the huge Rouge factory and concentrated his manufacturing in Dearborn.

The Model T was inexpensive and durable. The only color was black. Other manufacturers produced cars with a more attractive appearance, and, seeing his sales decline, Ford in 1927 discontinued the Model T after fifteen million had been sold. The next year the Model A, built to compete with Chevrolet and Plymouth, made its appearance.

Improvements in automobiles during the 1920's included closed bodies, balloon tires, four-wheel hydraulic brakes, and shatter-proof glass. Production continued to increase until 1929 when 5,621,045 automobiles were built, most of them in Michigan.

The manufacture of automobiles promoted prosperity not only because it provided work for many men at relatively high wages but also because it stimulated other industries. Steel, glass and rubber in huge quantities were needed to build cars and equip them with tires. Numerous shops were set up to produce accessories. The increased demand for gasoline caused the growth of the oil industry. Better roads were constructed at the demand of manufacturers and car owners alike; houses were built in the suburbs for persons who could drive to work; tourists in large numbers sought out new and more distant resorts; and gasoline stations and service garages gave work and income to thousands of men.

3

Because Michigan was the leader in the manufacture of automobiles, it was to be expected that airplanes also would be made. Skilled machinists, production experts, engine factories, and investors willing to risk their money in new ventures were ready at hand. A few planes were constructed before World War I, but real production was begun to meet the needs of the Allies and of our own government. Airplane engines, airplanes, and parts were turned out in large numbers, and Detroit became the center for the manufacture of the famous Liberty engine.[1]

The war hastened the development of airplanes and increased the demand for them. Pilots and technicians trained during the war became designers and promoters of the new industry.

The Stout Metal Airplane Company was organized in 1922 by William B. Stout and a group of Detroit investors. Stout was a genius with original ideas in design. His first product, an eight-passenger all-metal plane powered by a Liberty engine, was used by commercial airlines and by the United States postal service. In 1924 the factory was moved from Detroit to the Ford Airport at Dearborn. There Stout developed a trimotor plane. The Ford Motor Company purchased the corporation in 1925 and continued to manufacture the big aluminum planes.

In 1925 the Stinson Aircraft Corporation was organized by Eddie Stinson. A flier since 1911, during the war he had been a flight instructor. In his plant at Northville he built fine passenger planes for airlines. The plant was moved to Wayne in 1929, and the next year it became a division of the Cord Corporation.

Planes were manufactured also by the Buhl Aircraft Company in Detroit and Marysville, from 1925 until 1932, and by the Verville Aircraft Company, 1927 until 1932, in Detroit. The latter was organized by Alfred Verville, a flier who had been in service at McCook Field during the war. Extensive experiments for the improvement of engines for airplanes were carried on by the Packard Motor Company. In 1922, the peak year for the aircraft industry, 248 planes were built in Michigan. Production ceased during the depression of the 1930's, and the industry did not become important in the state afterward. Probably the reason was that airplanes could not be turned out by the mass-production methods in which Michigan excelled.

Interest in lighter-than-air machines led to the organization of the Aircraft Development Corporation of Detroit in 1922. Assisted by a subsidy from the Navy, the company built on Grosse Ile the ZMC-2, an all-metal dirigible. This aluminum ship, after having made successful test flights, was accepted for use by the Navy.

To accommodate the increasing number of airplanes, county and city airports were built during the 1920's for the convenience of individual owners and commercial airlines. At first the traffic was light. Although

[1] During the war, Major General George Owen Squier, a native of Dryden, Michigan, as chief of the Signal Corps, was commander of the United States Air Force.

some passengers and freight were carried in 1919 and 1920, and Detroit was connected with Cleveland by air for a while in 1922, the first entensive lines were initiated by the Stout Air Services in 1926. With Detroit as the center, planes flew to Grand Rapids, Cleveland, and Chicago. In 1927 the Thompson Aeronautical Corporation began operating lines from Detroit to other Michigan cities, to Cleveland, and to Chicago. In spite of these developments, travel by air during the 1920's was still an adventure undertaken by only a few persons.

The first military air base in Michigan was established in 1917 near Mount Clemens. Named Selfridge Field in honor of Lieutenant Thomas E. Selfridge, it was used in training pilots for war service. Later it became the base for the 1st Pursuit Group of the United States Air Corps.

4

The wireless telephone, like the air plane, was greatly improved during the war. Shortly afterward, broadcasting stations were established, and receiving sets for home use could be purchased or they could easily be made by anyone handy with tools. All that he needed were a simple tuning coil (insulated wire wrapped around a cardboard tube would do), a movable bit of copper to slide along the coil where the insulation had been removed, a small condenser, a fragment of galena crystal, and a thin copper wire "catwhisker" adjusted to a sensitive spot on the crystal. A pair of earphones completed his equipment. Radio station WWJ, owned by the *Detroit News*, was the pioneer in public broadcasting. Beginning on August 31, 1920, WWJ sent out regularly scheduled programs. At first they were short and were broadcast usually in the evening. Newspaper announcements informed set owners when to tune in. For a time, the performers were amateurs or persons appearing in local theaters. No one was paid, and none of the programs was sponsored by an advertiser.

Becoming tired of using headsets, people purchased radios with vacuum tubes and loudspeakers so that a number of persons could listen. Owners of radios invited friends and neighbors to come and hear the programs, and sometimes in schools and auditoriums crowds sat through a whole evening listening to music that came mysteriously through the air.

Additional stations were set up in Detroit and other Michigan cities. So great was the interest in radio that advertisers were glad to pay for the privilege of having their products mentioned on the airwaves.

When stations became more numerous and programs more varied, the manufacture and sale of radios increased enormously. In 1921, $10,000,000 were spent in the United States for sets and parts. Making radios became an important industry in Michigan.

5

Mining continued to be the principal occupation in the Upper Peninsula, but the output of copper fell far below the peaks reached during the war. Because of depressed business conditions, copper production fell to 92,262,000 pounds in 1921, only about one third of the record in 1916. There was an increase afterward, but the annual tonnage was less than that of the prewar years. Operating the deep mines was so expensive that only the richest deposits could be worked profitably. A new source of copper was found in the great heaps of tailings, refuse from the treatment of the crushed rock accumulated for many years. Recently discovered processes made possible the extraction from this waste of a great deal of the red metal.

In 1929, only six companies were operating mines: Calumet and Hecla, Copper Range, Mohawk, Seneca, Isle Royale, and Quincy. Production reached 186,402,000 pounds, but because of new methods and improved machinery, fewer employes were needed and company payrolls were reduced. The outlook for the copper country was not favorable.

Production of iron ore during the 1920's was greater than it had been during the previous decade, even though the demands of the World War had provided an artificial stimulus. The quantity shipped in 1920 was the greatest in the history of Michigan mining, 18,993,000 tons. After a sharp drop in 1921 to 4,971,000 tons, there was a quick recovery, and the annual average for the ten years was about fifteen million tons. Production in the three iron ranges followed the general trend, but the Gogebic Range shipped more than either of the other two. On the other hand, while the Gogebic and the Menominee ranges turned out their largest quantity of ore in 1920, the Marquette Range reached the highest point in its history in 1929 with 5,410,000 tons.

Although the mining companies were aware of the dangers of underground work and took precautions to protect the miners, disasters sometimes occurred. The worst one in the long history of mining in Michigan happened in the Barnes-Hecker mine near Ishpeming.

On the morning of November 3, 1926, miners in the lower levels heard a rumble as if from a heavy blast. The solid walls of the drifts trembled from the shock. Knowing that danger threatened, the men ran for the shaft. Four who reached it tried to escape by ladders. Frantically they climbed in the darkness. Below they could hear the swirling water rising higher and higher. Nearly exhausted, one man reached the surface, his boots wet from the flood that was reaching to pull him down. The other three were engulfed by the rusty-red tide that rose too fast for them.

The cause of the disaster was the cracking of a lake bottom and the emptying of the water into the mine. Fifty-one miners perished. The company removed the machinery from the shaft head and sealed the mine, leaving the tall steel derrick as a gaunt monument to the men who had died underground.

6

The production of petroleum gave Michigan a new industry during the 1920's. Traces of oil had been noticed during the territorial period. As early as 1834 settlers discovered oil and gas near Howell, but it was not until 1893 that some gas wells had been drilled and were producing there. Men drilling for salt in the Saginaw Bay region during the 1860's discovered oil, but no attempt to get it out of the ground was made for many years. Exploration for oil was begun in the Port Huron district in 1886, and it was here that the commercial production of oil in Michigan began. By 1891, twenty-two wells had been drilled. The output, however, was small, and by 1920 all had been abandoned.

In the Saginaw region, exploration in 1912 failed to strike the underground pool. Drilling was suspended for some years; then, in 1925, new wells began producing. They were near the city of Saginaw on land that had been laid out into building lots. Each owner sank a well—nearly three hundred of them. Because too many wells were drilled, the pressure of the gas was lowered, and little oil was forced to the surface. It has been estimated that 75 per cent of the oil remained in the pool and will never be recovered. Other wells opened in the southeastern part of Saginaw County in 1934 produced a large volume of oil.

The Muskegon field began production in 1927 and reached the peak, 18,570 barrels a day, two years later. Here again, as in the first Saginaw field, town-lot drilling reduced the pressure so that by 1936 the production had fallen to 280 barrels a day.

Mount Pleasant, in Isabella County, is the center of the greatest Michigan oil-producing area, which includes wells in Midland and

Clare counties. The Discovery Well of the Mount Pleasant field began to produce in 1928. During the 1930's wells were drilled in Mecosta, Gratiot, and Montcalm counties. The West Branch field in Ogemaw County, discovered in 1933, is also important.

In 1935 Michigan stood eighth in rank among the oil-producing states, with an output of 15,776,237 barrels. Oil continues to be an important product of the state. During the two-year period 1945–1946, production was 32,922,680 barrels, and in 1948 and 1949, 33,388,379. Explorations for new oil-bearing regions pierce new pools. In 1948 the Pentwater field in Oceana County and the Eden field in Mason

Oil at Midland

County were discovered. There were, in 1950, 3,818 producing oil wells. To some extent, at least, the oil industry has replaced lumbering in a number of the counties in the cutover lands. Gas produced in some of these fields is piped to numerous cities, where it is used for cooking and heating in homes and for fuel by industries.

To protect the owners of oil-bearing land, the people of the state, and the oil men themselves, the Legislature in a series of laws placed complete regulation of the oil industry in the hands of the Conservation Department. No well may be drilled without a permit, and operations must be carried on according to definite rules. These rules were made to promote the development of the oil industry so that maximum production will be achieved. A tax is collected by the state on all oil that comes out of the ground in Michigan. Owners who lease their lands to oil companies receive as a royalty one eighth of the value of the oil and gas produced.

As a large landowner, Michigan, in the interest of the people, collects royalties and other income from oil found on public land. Even land in private hands which was bought from the state since 1907 is treated as if it were publicly owned if oil is discovered, for the state retains mineral rights to all land which it sells.

To give everyone an equal opportunity, leases to drill on state land are sold at public auction to the highest bidder. The state receives income from rental of the land and also from the royalty as owner. In this way all the people benefit from the production of oil. The oil companies and the persons who lease land for drilling also profit, for strict regulation prevents waste and permits a greater quantity of oil to be taken from the ground.

7

Farmers in Michigan during the 1920's were not very prosperous. Low prices of farm produce, following the collapse of the great wartime demand, kept their incomes down. Besides, prices of manufactured goods which they bought were high as the result of the protective tariff. Even so, because diversified farming was typical in the state, the farmers were not so badly off as those in states where a single staple crop such as corn, wheat, or cotton was grown.

Although general farming was the rule in Michigan, specialties were grown in certain areas. Near the cities, dairying, the raising of poultry, and the growing of fruit and vegetables increased in importance. Hay and grains were valuable cash crops. The Thumb and the Saginaw River Valley produced beans and sugar beets; fruit was the principal product of the region along the Lake Michigan shore from Grand Traverse Bay southward; mint, celery, and onions were grown in the muck lands of the southwestern part of the state; and in the upper part of the Lower Peninsula, the crops were potatoes, cattle, and hay. The Upper Peninsula was essentially a livestock country with dairying the most important agricultural activity. Hay covered three fourths of the farmland and produced half the total value of crops. In addition, oats, wheat, barley, rye, buckwheat, beans, peas, potatoes, and sugar beets were grown.

A study made by the Michigan Agricultural Experiment Station in 1928 of forty-nine farms in Kalamazoo County showed the returns which a farmer received for his labor and management. The average size of the farms was 155 acres, and the average cash investment in each was $12,000. Grains, hay, potatoes, and fruit were the principal products. The cash crops were wheat and potatoes. According to the survey, the average annual cash income was $473. Besides, the farmer had a house and the food from the farm which he and his family consumed. Even so, considering the long hours of work, the cash investment, and the responsibilities of management, the returns were very small.

As a result of the economic conditions of the 1920's, the number of farms in the state declined 13½ per cent. This was greater than that in any other state in the Old Northwest except Ohio. Altogether, the decrease in the area under cultivation was two million acres. Part of the loss can be accounted for by land laid off into subdivisions, especially in Wayne and Oakland counties. A large reduction in the number of farms, however, occurred in the north-central part of the Lower Peninsula where families were starved out because of the poor soil. Many farms were taken by the state for nonpayment of taxes. Another reason for the smaller number of farms was the increase in size from an average of 100 acres in 1920 to 132 in 1930. The use of machinery made farming on a larger scale more economical.

Farmers received many benefits from the state and national governments. Even during the early years of its existence, Michigan Agricultural College[2] carried on experiments to discover better methods of farming and published the results in bulletins. This service was greatly increased after 1914 when Congress passed the Smith-Lever Act. Under its provisions appropriations of United States funds and state funds of an equal amount were used by state agricultural colleges to provide practical demonstrations in farm practices and in home economics. The Extension Service of the Agricultural College had charge of these activities.

In carrying out the program, county agricultural agents and home demonstration agents, going into the fields and into farm homes, helped by personal instruction to improve farming and housekeeping. Boys' and girls' 4-H Clubs were established with leaders to direct the groups in carrying on worth-while projects such as taking care of farm animals, canning, and making clothing. These activities were performed by co-operation of the members of a group.

Additional encouragement and financial support were given by Congress in 1917 to the preparation of country children for successful

[2] In 1921 Michigan Agricultural College added a curriculum in applied science and in 1924 one in liberal arts. In 1925 the name was changed to Michigan State College of Agriculture and Applied Science. It is generally known as Michigan State College.

living on farms by passage of the Smith-Hughes Act. Grants of money from the United States Treasury were offered for the support of vocational education in states which accepted the terms of the act and appropriated an equal sum of money. The Michigan Legislature, which was in session when the act was passed, at once agreed to co-operate and established a State Board of Control for Vocational Education. Under the state law of 1917, rural agricultural school districts might be organized, financial assistance was granted for teaching agricultural subjects, and money was provided to help pay for transportation of pupils to the schools. In 1928 the Future Farmers of America were organized in the schools in order to encourage pupils to put into practice the lessons learned in classes. This was a great benefit to farmers and their children.

The Smith-Hughes Act made provision also for teaching trades and homemaking. Some city schools had had courses in sewing, cooking, and shopwork before 1900, and such vocational work increased gradually. It was after 1917, however, that such courses became more numerous and were greatly improved. High-school pupils in cities and towns were given better opportunities than before to prepare themselves for successful living as adult members of their communities.

8

The growth of manufacturing in Michigan and the increasing use of tractors and farm machinery had important effects on the distribution of population within the state. The movement from rural to urban areas continued during the 1920's so that by 1930 fewer than one third (31.8 per cent) lived in the country.

The decline of copper mining reduced the population of Keweenaw, Ontonagon, and Houghton counties. The last suffered most, losing nearly 20,000 inhabitants during the 1920's. There was a small loss in the iron-producing regions also, except in Dickinson County, which gained 10,000.

The population of the state as a whole increased from 3,668,412 in 1920 to 4,842,325 in 1930. After World War I, immigrants from Europe poured into the United States, and many of them went to Michigan. In 1930, 849,297 foreign-born persons were inhabitants of the state. The Census of 1930 showed that the number of Canadians, Poles, English, Italians, and Scots increased during the 1920's; all other nationality groups decreased. The foreign-born were not evenly distributed. Certain areas contained large settlements of them. For example, in Gogebic County 28.3 per cent of the population was foreign-born; in Keweenaw County, 26.6 per cent; and in Wayne and Iron counties, 25.9 per cent.

Communities of foreign-born persons were numerous, the greatest number and variety being in the Detroit area. In large or small groups they ranged alphabetically from Albanians to Ukranians. The largest nationality groups in the state were Italians, Poles, Hungarians, Swedes, Dutch, Czechoslovaks, Yugoslavs, English, Scots, and Canadians. The last were most numerous of all, but they and the other English-speaking peoples were distributed throughout the population.

Next to the Canadians, the most numerous were the Poles. The greatest concentration of these people was in Hamtramck, a city completely surrounded by Detroit. Growing rapidly because of the expanding automobile industry, Hamtramck had a population of 46,615 in 1920, although it was still a village. When it became a city in 1922, it had 50,000 residents. About half were from Poland, but the majority had become American citizens. Their colorful weddings and other celebrations brought from the Old World still give Hamtramck a character all its own. Other eastern Europeans—Russians, Ukranians, and Czechoslovaks—were numerous in the city.

National groups lived in all the industrial cities and in agricultural and mining regions as well. In Posen Township, Presque Isle County, the inhabitants were predominantly Polish, descendants of men who had worked in the lumber camps. After the timber had been cut, the men bought the land and farmed it. In the village of Posen and in the surrounding countryside the customs of Poland were maintained.

In the Upper Peninsula the dominant elements were Swedes, Norwegians, Italians, Cornishmen, and Finns. Entering the region first as miners and lumberjacks, many later became farmers. This is particularly true of the Finns. Their settlements and farms can easily be recognized by the ever-present *sauna,* the small building in which they take steam baths. The Finns were pioneers in organizing co-operative stores, dairies, and sales agencies.

It is worthy of note that all the various nationality groups, many of them bitterly hostile to each other in Europe, live peaceably together here. Most of them become citizens and they are loyal to their adopted country.

The Census of 1930 revealed the phenomenal growth of the Negro population in Michigan. In 1900, there were only 15,816 Negroes in the state. The number increased to 60,082 in 1920, and to 169,453 in 1930. This great influx was the result of several factors. During World

War I, immigration from Europe ceased, and the industries of the state needed workmen. Negroes were recruited in the southern states and brought to Michigan by the trainload. Others came to join friends and relatives. During the 1920's, restrictions placed on immigration from abroad and the rapid development of manufacturing in the state provided opportunities for additional Negro workmen. Although they settled in all the industrial cities, most of them gravitated to Detroit. In 1930, it had a colored population of 120,000.

Living conditions for Negroes were deplorable. Because their earnings were usually small and because they were not permitted to live where they pleased, they were forced into the worst sections of cities. These became overcrowded, unhealthful slums.

9

Politics in Michigan during the 1920's followed the traditional course—Republicans were elected to all offices, with one exception. In 1922 former Governor Woodbridge N. Ferris defeated Senator Charles E. Townsend, who was running for re-election. Ferris ran on a platform of anti-Newberryism, charging that Townsend, by voting to retain Truman H. Newberry in the Senate, endorsed the use of huge campaign funds. Ferris's reputation for integrity and his personal popularity won the seat for him. He had the distinction of being the first Democrat elected to the United States Senate from Michigan since the formation of the Republican party in 1854.

When Senator Ferris died in 1928, Governor Fred W. Green appointed as his successor Arthur H. Vandenberg, a Grand Rapids newspaper editor. Senator Vandenberg was elected in the fall of 1928, and he remained in office until his death in 1951.

Governors during the decade were Alex J. Groesbeck, 1921–1927, and Fred W. Green, 1927–1931. Groesbeck was elected three times, an honor previously accorded to only two men—John S. Barry and Fred M. Warner. In his campaign Groesbeck promised to work for the reorganization of the state government to make it function more efficiently.

Other governors had urged the necessity of improving the administrative structure, which had become unmanageable. There were eight elective officers—governor, lieutenant governor, secretary of state, treasurer, auditor general, attorney general, superintendent of public instruction, and highway commissioner—and ninety-eight other officers and boards, most of them appointed by the governor with the consent of the Senate. Although the governor, theoretically, had supervisory power over all of them, practically, he could not possibly watch over the large combination of officers, boards, and commissions.

In 1919 the Legislature appointed the Community Council Commission to study the situation and make recommendations. The report, submitted in 1921, contained the following proposals: that only the governor, the lieutenant governor, and the auditor general be elected; that the other principal officers—secretary of state, treasurer, attorney general, superintendent of public instruction, and highway commissioner—be appointed by the governor and removable by him; that there should be a budget director appointed by the governor; that all state agencies having to do with parts of the same general problem or work be gathered into a few departments, each under an officer appointed by the governor. The purpose of these recommendations was to give the governor authority and responsibility similar to the powers vested in the President of the United States.

The Commission also advocated increasing the term of office of the governor to four years, so that he would have time to formulate and carry out his policies. Some of the recommendations, such as giving the governor a four-year term and the power to appoint the principal state officers, would have required amendments to the constitution.

Following the leadership of Governor Groesbeck rather than the proposals of the Commission, the Legislature centralized control over the administration by establishing the State Administrative Board. The governor was chairman, and the other members were the secretary of state, the treasurer, the auditor general, the attorney general, the superintendent of public instruction, and the highway commissioner. The lieutenant governor was later given a place on the Board. Its power to prepare the budget, to pass on all proposed expenditures of state offices, and to direct a central accounting system and a general purchasing department made it a strong organ of control. The authority of the governor was increased by giving him the power to veto decisions of the Board. Later the law was amended to permit a vote of five members to override a veto. This change reduced the power of the governor, making it difficult for him to carry out his policies.

The Legislature followed the advice of the Commission to a certain extent, materially reducing the confusion of boards by establishing five new departments: Welfare, Labor and Industry, Agriculture, Safety, and Conservation. In each of them were united several services formerly independent. The number of boards and officers was reduced from ninety-eight to sixty-five.

Groesbeck was an energetic executive. By bringing pressure to bear, he induced the Legislature to make a fair reapportionment of seats in the House and the Senate, a duty required by the constitution, but one which some members opposed because it would mean larger representation for the more populous southern counties. The governor repeatedly urged the necessity of rebuilding the main roads of the state, advocating the use of concrete instead of gravel. During his administrations more than two thousand miles of trunk highways were improved with the assistance of funds from the United States Government.

The governor believed that transportation for automobiles from one peninsula to the other should be better than it was. At the time, a driver could cross only on the railroad car ferry, and the fare was high. When the railroad company refused to operate ferries for automobiles on the ground that there would not be enough business to make them worth while, Groesbeck got the Legislature to provide for state-owned ships operated by the Highway Department. Today five state-owned automobile ferries shuttle back and forth between Mackinaw City and St. Ignace, carrying thousands of cars and passengers.

Governor Groesbeck had little opposition in the Legislature from the Democrats. In fact, in 1925 there were none in either house. A hostile faction developed in his own party, however, and when he ran in the primary in 1926, trying for a fourth term, he was overwhelmingly defeated by Fred W. Green. Green defeated the Democratic candidate, William A. Comstock, in that year and again in 1928. Governor Green was a furniture manufacturer and a veteran of the Spanish-American War. He was especially interested in promoting the conservation of the state's natural resources.

10

Following World War I and until 1929, there was great optimism about the future. Industry prospered, and during the middle years there was plenty of work. Prices rose higher and higher, and although skilled employes, especially in the automobile industry, had good hourly rates of pay, their annual incomes were not so high as one might suppose. Most of the companies operated with a full force for only seven to nine months of the year. An ever increasing number of labor-saving machines made possible during that length of time the production of as many cars as could be sold. The workmen were then laid off while new models were being prepared. Prosperity in the nation was spotty.

Farmers, coal miners, Michigan copper miners, and textile workers had little share in it.

There was a great real-estate boom. In Detroit new subdivisions were added rapidly. Farms were bought on credit and divided into lots. The lots were sold for ten dollars down and ten dollars a month. Streets and sidewalks were laid out, and the city spent a great deal of money running water mains to outlying districts. In 1917 the area of Detroit was 82.55 square miles. By 1930 it had increased to 140. The population figure rose from 993,739 in 1920 to 1,568,662 in 1930; but it was estimated that the subdivided acreage by that time was extensive enough to provide housing for ten million people.

Promoters were able to sell almost anything. They organized companies to construct a bridge and a tunnel connecting Detroit with Ontario. Either would have been sufficient. The Ambassador Bridge was opened to traffic in 1929 and the Detroit-Windsor Tunnel in 1930. Both became bankrupt and went into receivership.

The cost of living increased so that in many cases both husband and wife had to work to pay expenses. A large part of the seeming prosperity was based on credit buying. Urged on by shrewd salesmen, people bought as much as they could pay for in monthly installments while they were working. A long layoff usually meant that the goods would be repossessed, and too many repossessions meant reduction of orders to the manufacturers, with further layoffs.

The tendency during this period was toward larger and larger financial and industrial organizations. Great holding companies were put together, especially in the field of public utilities, with highly inflated capitalization.

In the automobile field, the Big Three—General Motors, Chrysler, and Ford—dominated the industry. Except for Ford, they owed money to the great financial institutions, as did the smaller independent companies, and the banks had a voice in management. In some cases, at least, the investment was managed for speculation and income rather than for production. Not only the automobile industry, but the so-called heavy industries in general were subject to this policy. Manufacturers of agricultural implements, cement, iron, and steel reduced prices only slightly when demand decreased, but they laid off many employes. This practice reduced the amount of money which would have been spent for consumers' goods and caused further reductions of output and more layoffs.

Too much money was going to too few people to keep the wheels of industry turning normally. The Brookings Institute found that, in

1929, 1 per cent of the people were receiving 23 per cent of the national income. They could not possibly spend it for consumers' goods, and so they invested it in plant expansion, speculation, or otherwise. To support a system of mass production, there must be mass consumption; and the incomes of the majority of the people must be large enough to permit them to buy the goods produced.

There were other conditions also which helped set the stage for the great depression of 1929. The wealthy were not paying their fair share of taxes. Secretary of the Treasury Andrew Mellon, one of the wealthiest men in the country, insisted on reducing income taxes in the higher brackets. He asserted that rich men would not pay at the existing rates. He himself did what others were doing. He organized individual corporations for himself and other members of the family, who sold stock to each other at a loss for income tax report purposes. It was entirely legal, but scarcely ethical for the Secretary of the Treasury, whose duty it was to recommend to Congress means for plugging loopholes in the laws.

Senator James Couzens of Michigan led a bitter attack on Mellon, charging that corporations in which he was interested had received special favors in the form of huge refunds on their tax payments. Mellon retaliated by suing Couzens and the other former Ford stockholders for additional taxes on the money they had received for their stock. Because Ford shares were not listed in the stock market and there were no sales, no one knew what they were worth. When Ford purchased the stock, an internal revenue agent had been asked to set the taxable value. On the basis of his decisions, Couzens paid more than $7,000,000 in income tax. Now Mellon charged that he owed an additional $9,000,000. Couzens and the others fought the suit and won.

Senator Couzens had promised that if the Treasury Department lost the suit, he would give the amount sued for to charity. To keep his pledge he gave $10,000,000 "to promote the health, welfare, happiness and development of the children of Michigan primarily, and elsewhere in the world." The fund was to be used to aid established agencies and to support experiments in better care of children.[3]

During the depression much of the money was spent to relieve the unusual needs of those years. A great deal of it was allotted to a child-health program, paying the cost of sending health nurses, physicians, and dentists into rural districts, especially in the thinly settled

[3] Other large philanthropic agencies in Michigan besides the Children's Fund are: the Kresge Foundation, the Charles S. Mott Foundation, the Horace H. and Mary A. Rackham Fund, the W. K. Kellogg Foundation, and the Ford Foundation.

northern counties of the Lower Peninsula, and the Children's Clinic in Marquette was financed by money from the Children's Fund.

Senator Couzens contributed to other causes also. He gave $640,000 to build a nurses' home and school for Harper Hospital in Detroit, and he built Couzens Hall, the nurses' home, for the University of Michigan Hospital. In 1927, when a maniac blew up the consolidated school at Bath, Clinton County, killing thirty-eight pupils, Senator Couzens paid for a new building, and money from the Children's Fund was used to help care for the injured.

Tariff duties played their part in weakening the economic fabric of the United States. The Fordney-McCumber Tariff of 1922 set the highest rates in the history of the country. Representative Joseph Fordney of Saginaw, who sponsored the bill in the House, was a Michigan Republican of the old school. High tariffs were part of the traditional creed of the GOP, and they were greatly desired by manufacturers who disliked foreign competition and who contributed to the Republican campaigns. The automobile industry, however, was able to do very well without government protection.

The Fordney-McCumber Tariff caused a reduction of imports and, as a matter of necessity, of exports as well; and the Hawley-Smoot Tariff of 1930 almost completely stopped foreign trade. Because foreign nations raised their rates on American goods, automobile manufacturers and others set up factories abroad, further increasing unemployment at home.

The tariff helped increase the financial difficulties of the farmers. During the war many of them had bought land at high prices, mortgaging their farms to do it. After the war, when the demand for foodstuffs decreased and prices fell, farmers produced more to try to earn enough to pay expenses. Tariff duties made prices of manufactured goods high for farmers, and, because Europeans could not sell here, they could not buy farm produce. Bills passed to aid the farmer were vetoed by Presidents Coolidge and Hoover. Finally the Agricultural Marketing Act was passed in 1929, and an attempt was made to buy up surpluses. It failed because farmers produced more to obtain greater benefits; there were still great surpluses. President Hoover advanced no practical means of reducing them, and as long as they existed and increased each year, the farmer received low prices for his crops.

In 1928 there was much unemployment. Many manufacturers solved the problem of overproduction, or underconsumption, as some termed it, by laying off their employes.

Huge amounts of money were being used for speculation in the stock market. Prices of stocks were bid up beyond any reasonable level. Finally, on October 29, 1929, the crash came, and millions of dollars of paper profits were wiped out.

People who had money hoarded it. Unemployment increased. In spite of mounting bankruptcies, layoffs, foreclosures of mortgages on homes and farms, bank failures, and decreasing tax collections, President Hoover and his advisers refused to admit that the economic system was breaking down. He urged employers to continue production at the normal level, saying that recovery would be rapid. A few lines of a popular song of the day reflected his confidence:

> Mr. Herbert Hoover says the clouds will soon roll by.
> So let's have another cup of coffee
> And let's have another piece of pie.

But prosperity was not just around the corner, as some persons believed, and many of the unemployed were unable to buy a cup of coffee, to say nothing of a piece of pie. In 1930 nearly one fifth of Michigan's industrial workers were without jobs. During the decade of the 1920's the economic wheel had made a complete revolution from depression through prosperity to another depression.

SPORTS Michigan is well known for its competitive teams and athletes. *Above left:* Ski jumping at Iron Mountain. *Above right:* The giant football stadium of the University of Michigan, seating capacity, 97,000. *Center right:* Durocher safe at home in 1934 World Series between the Detroit Tigers and St. Louis Cardinals. Mickey Cochrane was the Detroit catcher.

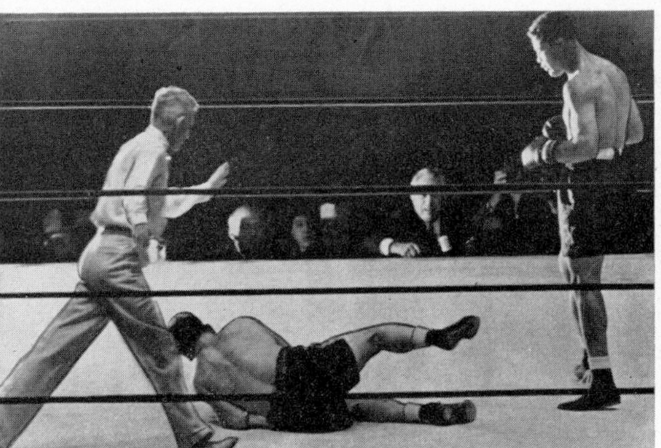

Above left: Detroit's Joe Louis standing over Bob Pastor in the eleventh round of their fight in 1937. *Above right:* Spinnakers bulging, boats in the race to Mackinac Island head north, 1953.

COMMERCIAL FISHING Catching fish for market has always been an important industry in Michigan. *Right:* A fishing hamlet at Au Sable in 1872. *Center left:* Taking fish from a pound net. *Center right:* Fishing nets drying at Lake Charlevoix.

Left: Seven tons of walleyed pike caught in Saginaw Bay in 1935. *Below:* Women fileting herring taken from Saginaw Bay.

AUTOMOBILES (I) Michigan has always been a leader in the automotive industry. *Above left:* Charles B. King at the tiller of his first automobile in 1896. *Top right:* The first gasoline powered Oldsmobile, 1896. *Left:* Henry Ford in his first car, 1896. *Bottom left:* Roy D. Chapin, one of the founders of Hudson Motors, and its president from 1910 to 1936. *Bottom right:* The famous single cylinder Cadillac, one of the first cars manufactured by the Cadillac Motor Company.

AUTOMOBILES (II) The automobile brought many changes in the industrial and social life of Michiganians. *Top:* A 1905 Michigan law required the motorist to pull to the side of the road and stop if approaching horses appeared to be frightened. *Above:* Automobiles served many purposes. Here a saw is driven by power from an automobile engine. *Right:* A fleet of U.S. mail trucks in Detroit. *Below:* A 1926 Chrysler roadster.

AUTOMOTIVE INDUSTRY Many changes have taken place in the industry during the last fifty years. On this page are some examples of this change. The moving assembly line was introduced at the Ford plant in 1913. *Top left:* The assembly line. *Top right:* Hand-operated chain hoists were used on production lines of the Dodge plant for several years after it was opened in 1914.

Center: Assembly line at the Plymouth plant, 1954. *Bottom left:* Mack Avenue shop where Ford's early cars were assembled. *Bottom right:* Ford's present River Rouge plant.

INDUSTRY IN MICHIGAN (I) Michigan's industries, which are many and varied, supply products used throughout the world. The Consumers Power Company supplies electricity for eastern and central Michigan. *Left:* An air view of the Weadock plant at the mouth of the Saginaw River near Bay City. *Center left:* The Peninsular Paper Company on the Huron River in Ypsilanti.

Center right: Air view of the Calcite plant, Michigan Limestone Division, U.S. Steel Company, at Rogers City. *Below left:* Diamond Crystal Salt Company, St. Clair. *Below right:* Buckets carried on an endless cable are used to load gypsum on lake freighters standing in deep water offshore at Alabaster.

INDUSTRY IN MICHIGAN (II) Industrial techniques have changed considerably in the last 100 years. *Top left:* A crude water wheel, used in the nineteenth century near Harbor Springs in the manufacture of brick. *Top right:* Coopers at work at the R. G. Peters salt and lumber plant near Manistee late in the nineteenth century.

Furniture making is one of Michigan's leading industries. Fine workmanship is shown at *center left* in the final operation of applying brass nails to a Victorian love seat at the John Widdicomb Company, Grand Rapids. *Center right:* The final hand trimming and fitting line at the same company.

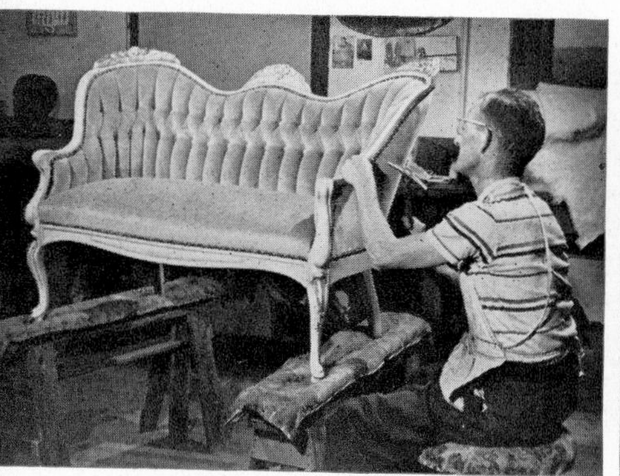

Large-scale production of petroleum in Michigan began in 1925. *Below left:* Freeman Redding Oil Field at Clare. *Below right:* An oil refinery at Alma.

TOURIST INDUSTRY North, east, south or west, Michigan is truly a water wonderland. The state's tourist industry, ranking with manufacturing and agriculture as a leading revenue producer, is a vital factor in its general economy. *Top left:* Tahquamenon Falls in the Upper Peninsula. *Top right:* Trout fishing at Bond Falls. *Center:* Vacationers on Lake Huron. *Bottom left:* Sailing in Otsego County. *Bottom right:* Bathing at St. Clair Metropolitan Beach.

— 28 —

Depression and New Deal

THE DEPRESSION of the early 1930's was world-wide. In the United States the energies of the government were occupied by efforts to provide relief for the suffering, recovery of economic strength, and reform of abuses that had developed during a long period of time. Except for the good-neighbor policy toward the nations of Latin America, which resulted in friendly co-operation in the Western Hemisphere, the government of the United States took little interest in international affairs. Completely occupied by its own troubles, it sought safety and protection of its democratic system within a high wall of isolationism.

In Europe democracy seemed to be doomed. Economic difficulties and internal dissension had permitted dictators to seize power in a number of nations. Stalin, Mussolini, Hitler, and Franco were the strong men of the Continent, and it looked as if Communism or Fascism might spread throughout the world. France was feeble because of internal strife, and Great Britain wanted only peace so that she could repair her fallen fortunes. When war threatened, Neville Chamberlain, the Prime Minister, felt obliged to appease Adolf Hitler. Japan began her attempt to dominate Asia by occupying Manchuria and invading China. As an added threat to the western democracies, Japan leagued herself with Hitler and Mussolini. Riots, civil wars, invasions of weak nations, and bloody purges of political opponents by dictators made many persons believe that civilization itself was doomed.

2

President Hoover was deeply troubled by the economic plight of the country. He hoped that conditions would improve without governmental intervention, for he was convinced that the use of emergency powers would destroy local initiative and even result in the creation of a superstate. Believing that an expanded program of public works might be useful, he recommended the expenditure of $650,000,000 during the fiscal year 1931–1932. The greatest single project was construction of the Hoover Dam, or Boulder Dam, on the Colorado River.

Democrats and progressive Republicans, who gained control of Congress in the election of 1930, urged that direct relief be provided by the national government, but the administration for a time remained firm in its conviction that local agencies must take care of families in need of assistance. Finally, the President realized that aid at least for business, industry, banking, and agriculture was essential.

At Hoover's recommendation Congress established the Reconstruction Finance Corporation in January, 1932, authorized to lend money to banks, commercial enterprises, railroads, and insurance companies. In July the law was amended to permit loans to farmers' co-operatives, to cities for construction of self-liquidating projects, and to states which were unable otherwise to finance relief. A system of home-loan banks was also provided to lend money to insurance companies and other organizations holding mortgages on homes. Although these measures gave some relief, the depression continued to deepen, and emergency expenditures unbalanced the national budget before the end of Hoover's administration.

Because of its highly specialized industrial structure Michigan suffered sooner and more severely than most of the other states. Automobile production fell off from five million units in 1929 to two million in 1933. In 1930, 20 per cent of the state's nonagricultural workers were unemployed; in 1931, 29 per cent; in 1932, 43 per cent; and in 1933, nearly 50 per cent. More than half a million people were dependent on public funds for their daily bread. The situation was most critical in the industrial cities, but eventually rural districts had relief problems as well. In 1932, more than $30,000,000 were spent to relieve distress, $24,000,000 of this sum provided by local taxes.

By this time, however, many people were unable to pay taxes on their property. Delinquencies in the state averaged about one third, in some cities as much as one half. To meet this crisis, the State Legislature in a special session in the spring of 1932 raised the bonding limit of cities so that they might borrow money to provide relief. The Legislature also allocated to the counties a large share of the automobile weight tax. In addition, the state borrowed from the RFC to acquire further funds. By May, 1933, Michigan had received over $21,000,000 from this source.

In Detroit at this time, Frank Murphy was mayor. A veteran of World War I, from 1923 to 1930 he had served as a judge of the Recorder's Court in Detroit. In September, 1930, a special election was held to vote on the question of recalling Mayor Charles Bowles. He was recalled, and Murphy was elected to succeed him.

In Detroit thousands were out of work and without money to buy the necessities of life. They were so nearly desperate that they were likely to follow anyone who offered remedies, no matter how radical. Mayor Murphy was determined that no one should starve, and so he spent money for food for the hungry and opened an abandoned warehouse as a barracks for homeless men. Believing also that critics of the political and economic system had the right to express their ideas, the mayor permitted outdoor mass meetings in the eastern half of Grand Circus Park. There speakers held forth day and night.

The mayor was sharply criticized by many citizens who believed that he was wasting the city's money by feeding idlers, and that he was encouraging the spread of Communism by permitting radicals to talk. Communists did take advantage of the discontent and suffering to stir up trouble.

3

In 1932 the Democrats nominated Franklin D. Roosevelt, governor of New York, to run against Herbert Hoover for the presidency. One of Roosevelt's most vigorous supporters was the Reverend Charles E. Coughlin, the radio priest of Royal Oak.

After the depression set in, Father Coughlin began to speak on political and economic as well as religious subjects. Advocating reforms and attacking Communism, he gained a wide following. He violently attacked President Hoover, bankers, and industrialists. Blaming them for the conditions which existed, he advised his hearers that the alternatives were Roosevelt or ruin.

On election day the people of Michigan, for the first time since 1852, gave a majority to a Democrat for President. Franklin D. Roosevelt received 131,000 more votes than Herbert Hoover. William A. Comstock, the Democratic candidate for governor, received 15,972 more votes than Roosevelt and 190,000 more than his opponent, Governor Wilber M. Brucker, who had been elected in 1930. The only Republican official chosen in 1932 was Frank D. Fitzgerald, secretary of state, the incumbent. The Democrats had a small majority in the Legislature, and they elected a majority of representatives to Congress.

The results of the election relieved much of the tension. Ballots instead of bullets had brought new men and another party to office. There was a feeling of satisfaction in having elected new administrations for state and nation. People looked forward to better days ahead.

Governor William A. Comstock was inaugurated on January 2, 1933. Although he had been elected by distressed citizens who expected reform measures to be adopted, he was himself a conservative Democrat. After being graduated from the University of Michigan in 1899, he engaged in electric-railway construction and operation until 1922. Thereafter, he was a banker and a real-estate broker.

Comstock had long been active in Democratic party affairs. From 1920 to 1924 he was state chairman of the party, and from 1924 to 1928 he was a member of the national committee. He was also a liberal contributor to the party treasury. During the lean years, when running on the Democratic ticket for office was a hopeless venture, Comstock had permitted his name to be placed on the ballot simply to give the loyal party members someone to vote for. And so in 1932 the leaders of the party favored his nomination when at last there was a chance to win the election.

The office of governor in 1933 was no sinecure. Economic conditions were becoming more and more desperate. Positive action for relief, recovery, and reform would have to be attempted immediately, but there were sharp differences of opinion as to what form such action should take.

4

A very serious problem was the condition of the banks in Detroit and in the rest of the state. In Michigan from December, 1929, to

December, 1932, as a result of failures and mergers, the number of banks was reduced by about 25 per cent, and deposits declined 32 per cent. Nearly two hundred banks had failed. In Detroit by the end of 1931, because of closings or mergers, there were only six banks. Four were independent. Each of the two others was the leading unit in a powerful group which consisted of banks and trust companies in Wayne County and in other parts of the state.

The first, the Guardian Detroit Union group, was organized in 1929. The Guardian National Bank of Commerce and the Union Guardian Trust Company were the largest units in this group. The second, the Detroit Bankers' Company, was organized on January 8, 1930. The most important units in this group were the First National Bank in Detroit and the Detroit Trust Company.

It was believed that membership in a group would strengthen individual banks by putting at their disposal the resources of the other banks. In the early 1930's, however, none of them was strong. They were carrying mortgages on property appraised at boom-time prices, they held as collateral stocks and bonds for loans greater than the current value of the security, and they possessed other commercial paper which was of dubious worth. Besides, depositors were becoming worried about the condition of banks and were withdrawing their money, placing the cash in safe-deposit boxes or in the United States Postal Savings system.

The weakest unit in the Guardian group was the Union Guardian Trust Company. Too large a percentage of its assets were mortgages and bonds currently of little value. Needing cash to remain in business, the Guardian Trust Company during 1932 borrowed $15,000,000 from the Reconstruction Finance Corporation. This amount of money helped only temporarily, and in January, 1933, the Guardian group asked for $50,000,000 more. When the RFC examiners were unable to find enough collateral to justify such a loan, the RFC promised to provide a part of the amount if large depositors would guarantee the remainder. Edsel Ford was a director of both the Union Guardian Trust Company and of the Guardian group, and the Ford Motor Company had large deposits in the Guardian banks and in the First National Bank in Detroit. Officers of General Motors and Chrysler, also large depositors, agreed to contribute to a local fund if Ford would do the same. In spite of personal appeals by President Hoover and others, Henry Ford refused.

James Couzens, senior senator from Michigan, was a member of the Senate Committee on Banking and Currency. President Hoover called him to the White House and urged him to use his influence and wealth to help save the Detroit banks. The senator declared that if the banks were too weak to remain open, they should be permitted to fail, and he threatened to "scream from the housetops" if a loan were granted on insufficient security.

On Sunday, February 12, bankers from New York, Chicago, and Detroit, United States Government officials, and heads of automobile manufacturing companies gathered in Detroit and tried to find a way to save the Union Guardian Trust Company. Monday, February 13, was a legal holiday because Lincoln's Birthday had fallen on Sunday, and the banks were closed. Meetings of the bankers continued until late that night. No solution for the problem of meeting the immediate needs of the Union Guardian Trust Company having been found, they agreed that it could not open for business on Tuesday. It was feared that as soon as word of its failure was spread about, there would be runs on other banks, which also would have to close.

To prevent such a ruinous consequence, Governor Comstock was called into conference and asked to close all the banks in the state. Having been convinced that only so drastic a remedy would prevent a complete collapse of the banking structure, he issued a proclamation February 14, before banking hours began, continuing the banking holiday until February 23.[1]

When people heard the news on the radio that morning, they were at first incredulous, then stunned. Those who were accustomed to paying bills by check had little cash on hand, and checks were of no use. Perhaps they should have been prepared for some such event, for the banks in Nevada, Iowa, and Louisiana had been temporarily closed.

The State Legislature by concurrent resolution legalized the governor's proclamation and authorized him to extend the holiday and to restrict withdrawals from the banks when they reopened. On February 21, the governor issued another proclamation, extending the holiday but permitting the banks to open for paying out limited sums of money and to accept, for safekeeping, deposits which might be withdrawn at will. Even before the proclamation, most of the banks had allowed depositors to have small amounts to meet current expenses.

Other states followed Michigan's lead in closing the banks or in restricting their business, and on March 5 President Roosevelt declared a national bank holiday until March 9, when he extended the holiday indefinitely. On that day Congress passed an emergency act which gave

[1] Most Upper Peninsula banks, which are in the Minneapolis Federal Reserve District, remained open. Lower Peninsula banks are in the Chicago District.

the Comptroller of the Currency power to examine all national banks and to open those which appeared to be sound. For the others he was directed to appoint conservators to preserve the assets and to permit the banks to release a percentage of their deposits. The Michigan Legislature passed an act on March 21 permitting the banking commissioner to take over state banks and open them for limited operation or close them under receivership.

At the end of the bank holiday the four independent banks in Detroit reopened. The First National and the Guardian National did not. A federal conservator was placed in charge of each, loans were obtained from the RFC, and good assets were sold to the new National Bank of Detroit, which was financed half by General Motors and half by the RFC. The two closed national banks had more than 800,000 depositors, most of them with small amounts which they needed for living expenses.

In order to permit the paying of these creditors in full, the large depositors generously waived their right to immediate payment of a portion of the amount which they would have received. As a result, all accounts in the First National Bank in Detroit of $300 or less were paid in full, and in the Guardian National Bank of Commerce all those up to $1,000. The Comptroller of the Currency declared that this self-denial by the large depositors represented "one of the most outstanding public-spirited actions coming before this office during the several years of the emergency."[2] As a result of careful management by the conservators and improving business conditions, all the debts of these banks were eventually paid with interest.

In the summer of 1933 the Manufacturers' National Bank of Detroit was opened by the Fords. The purchase by this bank of the good assets of the closed Highland Park State Bank and the Dearborn State Bank made possible payments to the depositors of those institutions.

As an aftermath of the bank crisis, thirty-four bank officers were indicted by a federal grand jury. Several of them were convicted and fined for making false reports to the Federal Reserve Bank. None of the bank officials was charged with having used his position for personal profit at the expense of the depositors.

The condition of banking throughout the state was similar to that in Detroit. Some banks opened after the holiday; others were forced to close. Of the latter, the stronger ones paid all or part of their debts. In 1937 the Legislature passed a comprehensive banking act which

[2] J. F. T. O'Connor, *The Banking Crisis and Recovery Under the Roosevelt Administration* (Chicago: Callaghan and Company, 1938) p. 49.

was intended to strengthen banks and protect depositors. State banks had earlier been made eligible to join the Federal Deposit Insurance Corporation if they could meet the requirements of the national law, thus guaranteeing to depositors a maximum of $5,000 in deposits. The amount was later increased to $10,000. By such measures, confidence in the banks was restored.

5

Another serious problem that faced the governor and the Legislature was how to raise enough money to prevent the state from going bankrupt. Funds were required to pay indebtedness previously incurred, to defray the cost of operating the state agencies, and to help relieve distress.

During the twentieth century, Michigan, like most of the other states, began to spend large sums of money for the benefit of its citizens. There was a great increase in state and local expenditures, especially for hospitals, health and sanitation, highways, conservation of natural resources, and education. In order to provide these benefits, higher taxes were necessary. Between 1914 and 1930, property taxes increased 500 per cent.

The debt of the state was increased by three bond issues: in 1917, $5,000,000 as a war loan; in 1919, $50,000,000 to build highways; and in 1921, $30,000,000 to pay a bonus to Michigan veterans of World War I. Although the bonds were promptly retired as they came due, the debt of the state in 1932 was still more than $60,000,000. This figure, however, was dwarfed by the total outstanding obligations of cities, counties, townships, and school districts in the same year: $721,724,000. This, plus the state indebtedness, made the per capita debt $157 in 1932. In 1902 it had been $14.

The mere increase in debt and expenditure was not necessarily bad. The people themselves had demanded that the state provide better and more numerous services, and if the job was done efficiently the people benefited by the expenditures. The difficulty arose when unemployment and fear for the future dried up the usual sources of taxes.

In Michigan the state and local governments depended to a large extent on returns from the general property tax for the money to meet their expenses. With the deepening of the depression, farmers, homeowners in cities and villages, and corporations had difficulty in paying their taxes. Some of them found it impossible. In 1931, $60,000,000 worth of taxes were delinquent. Assessments were reduced, but tax collections continued to fall off. The United States Census Bureau in 1933 estimated that the delinquency ratio for property taxes was higher in Michigan than in any other state.

According to the law in effect at the time, real estate on which taxes were not paid was subject to sale twenty-six months after the delinquency. If the property was not purchased by an individual or redeemed by the owner, the state bid it in.

During the early months of 1933, farmers throughout the Middle West were in a state of revolt against the courts, which ordered their farms sold for delinquent taxes or for unpaid mortgages. In some cases they threatened violence to judges and sheriffs, or they bought property offered at forced sale for ridiculously low prices.

Some Michigan farmers followed their example. Late in January, about one hundred and fifty farmers near Howard City in Montcalm County picketed a sheriff's sale of farm machinery and furniture for unpaid taxes. Warning others to refrain from bidding, they offered only a few cents for each item. A grand piano was sold for four cents, a hay loader for eleven. The total proceeds of the sale were $2.40, and the purchasers returned the items to the owner.

A few days later a similar sale took place near Stanton in the same county, and at Manistee a crowd of three hundred farmers from Manistee and Benzie counties gathered in front of the courthouse to protest against mortgage foreclosures and delinquent tax sales. When the sheriff agreed to postpone a sale which had been advertised, the crowd disbanded.

In Gratiot County irate farmers abused the receiver of a bank who was selling a farm on which the mortgage had been foreclosed. They bid $3.85 for the property and compelled the receiver to deliver the mortgage. Such actions by usually law-abiding farmers emphasized the seriousness of the situation in Michigan.

The Legislature tried to meet the crisis and save embarrassed property owners from loss. It canceled interest and penalties on taxes delinquent for certain years, postponed tax sales, and provided finally for the payment of delinquent taxes over a period of ten years. As a result, no annual tax sale was held from 1932 to 1938. In the latter year, however, a sale was held in which about a million pieces of real estate were offered. At that time, nearly three million acres were acquired by the state.

A new policy which recognized the basic difference in the soil of southern Michigan from that above the Saginaw Bay–Muskegon line was adopted. In general, land below the line was to be sold to individuals for agricultural use; land above the line was to be retained and placed under the administration of the Conservation Department to be reforested, and numerous areas were to be developed for recreational activities. Under this policy land unsuited for cultivation is not sold to unwary individuals. The forests are being replaced, and there are more and better facilities for outdoor living. These are productive uses. To mention only one benefit, the tourist business of Michigan for many years has been a great source of wealth.

As a result of the demands of property owners, an amendment to the constitution was adopted in 1932 which set a limit of fifteen mills (one and one half cents) on a dollar of assessed valuation as the maximum tax rate which might be levied by state and local governments on property. This amendment, however, did not apply to home-rule cities and villages.

In order to make more money available to local units of government, the Legislature in 1933 gave up the state tax on real estate, and in its place enacted the sales-tax law by which all retail dealers collect a 3 cent tax and turn the proceeds into the state treasury. This tax was very unpopular. Some persons blamed the governor for it, and a salesman might say, "That will cost you a dollar, and three cents for Comstock."

A rumor even became general that the governor was using some of the money to build himself a luxurious mansion. At first he ignored the story, but finally so many people apparently believed it that he offered a cash reward to anyone who could prove it was true. That put an end to the rumor, but people continued to dislike the tax. The sales tax is very productive, and it has become a permanent feature of the money-raising program of Michigan.

The repeal of the prohibition amendments, both state and national, which was completed in 1933, was expected to provide additional revenue to the state treasury and to the Treasury of the United States through taxation of beer, wine, and liquor. Other benefits which advocates of repeal had emphasized were the end of bootlegging with its attendant evils, jobs for the unemployed in breweries and distilleries, and use of some of the surplus grain.

In the fall election of 1932, Michigan voters repealed the state prohibition amendment. Both Congress and the Legislature in the spring of 1933 legalized the manufacture of beer and light wines. A joint resolution passed by Congress on February 20, 1933, proposed a Twenty-first Amendment to the Constitution to repeal the Eighteenth. Each state was required to call a convention to consider the resolution. In Michigan a convention elected by the people met on April 10 and voted ninety-nine to one to ratify the amendment. During the year, other state conventions voted favorably, and in December, 1933, the Twenty-first Amendment was proclaimed in effect, repealing the Eighteenth. Michigan established a Liquor Control Commission to regulate the business, and provided state liquor stores and specially designated dealers who were required to purchase their stocks from the state.

6

Franklin D. Roosevelt was inaugurated on March 4, 1933. The confident tone of his address, which was carried by radio to millions of listeners, gave his fellow countrymen hope for the future. Knowing well that more than words were required, the President had assembled a number of advisors, many of them college professors, who were called by the newspapers the Brain Trust. They rejected the idea that the depression would pass if it were simply permitted to take its course. To them the nation was faced by a grave emergency, and strong measures were necessary to meet it.

Sixteen years earlier the nation had successfully met the emergency of World War I. Congress had given extraordinary powers to President Wilson, and the people had followed his leadership enthusiastically. Production had been increased, armies had been trained, and aid to the Allies had turned the tide to victory.

In 1933, the emergency was more serious. The enemy was not a distant foreign ruler, but hunger and unemployment within the country itself. Machinery for the production and distribution of goods was adequate, but the wheels were idle. The farms of the country had not been devastated, but the cost of raising crops was greater than the selling price. Instead of unity and confidence, there were suspicion and anxiety. Those who had money were afraid to invest it, and those who had none feared that their families would starve. Radical cures for the depression were being offered by Senator Huey Long and others, including Communists. Unless rational means were soon found to improve conditions, hopeless people would follow dangerous leaders.

President Roosevelt had been Assistant Secretary of the Navy in President Wilson's administration. Now he called Congress into special session on March 9 and adopted Wilson's tactics. Appearing before the members of the two houses, he asked that a law on a certain subject be passed. Usually a bill had already been drafted by the Brain Trust.

Frightened by the crisis, Congress at first complied with his requests. The bank law, for example. went through in a single day. Others required more time, but the President kept pressure on Congress by his fireside radio talks to the people and by withholding appointments desired by senators and representatives until after they had passed the laws which he believed necessary to provide relief, recovery, and reform. By such methods he put through Congress in one hundred days a remarkable program of legislation. The alphabetical agencies established then and in succeeding years had far-reaching effects in Michigan.

One of the most pressing needs in the spring of 1933 was to provide relief for the unemployed. A group that particularly needed assistance was the 100,000 or more youths who were roaming from place to place seeking work.[3] To help them, an early act of Congress established the Civilian Conservation Corps. Young men, seventeen to twenty-eight years of age, who had no jobs were enrolled and sent to camps in the country to work at various conservation projects. They were paid $30 a month, $25 of which was allotted to their families. The camps were directed by army reserve officers called to active duty for a limited time. Many of these men, who themselves could not find employment, were glad for the opportunity to serve in this capacity.

There were also other beneficial results. Adequate food and healthful outdoor life greatly improved the physique and the morale of these young men, and courses of study in various subjects were offered so that they might advance their education. The CCC program was continued until 1942, when it was terminated by an act of Congress.

There were 103 CCC camps in Michigan at the height of the program, and during the ten years of its operation thousands of young men engaged in many useful activities. Only a few of the most important can be mentioned. By fighting forest fires, constructing trails and roads through the woods, and planting seedlings, they helped save timber and increase the reforested area. These young men made more land available for recreation by preparing numerous picnic and camp grounds, by building bridges and shelters, and by running roads through state parks. They also cleared streams of obstructions and planted millions of small fish in lakes and streams. The CCC program was bene-

[3] Senator James Couzens had earlier introduced a bill to take care of these youths in army camps. When another senator protested that the expense would be too great, Couzens angrily replied that Congress had appropriated millions for the protection of migratory birds, but it could find no money to help migratory boys.

ficial to the young men in the camps and to all the people of Michigan.

In addition to the CCC program, relief for the unemployed and their dependents was an immediate need. At the request of President Roosevelt, Congress on March 22 passed an act establishing the Federal Emergency Relief Administration. This agency was to make cash allocations to the states, which would use the money to provide either work relief or a dole.

The Michigan Legislature in the spring of 1933 set up the State

Civilian Conservation Corps Camp

Emergency Welfare Commission, and in July Governor Comstock appointed the commissioners whose duty it was to direct the administration of relief in the state. The law provided for an administrator in each county.

The Commission had charge also of the Civil Works Administration program in Michigan, which employed about 170,000 workers on public projects (October, 1933, to May, 1934) with the purpose of bolstering the morale of the unemployed and increasing the purchasing power of people in the communities.

During July, August, and September, 1933, there were 640,000 people on relief in Michigan; and during the first fiscal year, 1933–1934, the State Emergency Welfare Commission spent nearly $43,000,000. Of this total $29,000,000 was supplied by the United States, $11,000,000 by the state, and $2,500,000 by local government units .

On July 7, 1933, Governor Comstock signed the Old Age Assistance Act, which provided a maximum of $30 a month for needy persons over seventy who had been residents of Michigan for at least ten years. In 1935 Congress made money available to the states to assist them in carrying on this program, setting the age at sixty-five and the number of years' residence at five. In 1937 the Michigan Legislature passed a new act in conformity with the law of Congress. The national government also granted funds for the aid of widowed mothers, crippled children, and the blind.

By 1935 it was evident that unemployment was not a temporary condition. During 1934, for example, from October through December, the number in Michigan on relief reached the record high of 815,000. Some parts of the state suffered severely. In Wayne County during the depression the number of people on relief fluctuated from 6 to 29 per cent, in the cutover counties from 24 to 48 per cent, in the mining counties from 26 to 63 per cent, and in the agricultural counties from 7 to 10 per cent.

Before a family was given assistance by a welfare agency, it had to prove that it had exhausted its resources. Usually the last "luxury" with which it was willing to part was its automobile. Will Rogers once quipped that Americans were the only people who ever rode to the poorhouse in their own cars.

Because the FERA and the CWA had been considered temporary expedients and the purpose had been to aid individuals and communities in putting as much money as possible into quick circulation, there had not been careful advance planning of projects. Consequently, much criticism, some of it deserved, was leveled at these agencies.

In 1935, to provide a long-range program which would produce permanent benefits to communities and require the expenditure of large sums for tools and building supplies—"pump priming," it was called—the Works Progress Administration was established. All employable persons without work were to be hired by the WPA, and the states were made responsible for assisting the unemployables.

Besides giving jobs to laborers and skilled craftsmen in various trades, the government made employment opportunities for white-collar workers. Projects were provided for artists, musicians, actors, writers, architects, teachers, and others. The National Youth Administration paid students in schools and colleges for doing necessary part-time work, and other young people were given vocational guidance and training.

The WPA program in Michigan and elsewhere was highly praised and bitterly condemned. Those who found good in it emphasized the improvement in morale of the men and women who were permitted to earn the money they received; the streets, roads, parks, public buildings, and other tangible results of the program; the lift to the economic system as a result of money put into circulation in numerous communities; and the aid to industry through the purchase of materials, tools, and machinery.

The critics of the program asserted that the unemployed could have been saved from starvation more cheaply if they had sat at home and waited for the letter carrier to bring them their welfare checks; that the money spent for materials, tools, and machinery was insufficient to increase appreciably the production of industry; that WPA labor was inefficient and lazy; and that the buildings and other products of the WPA cost the taxpayer more than they were worth.

Some of the complaints were certainly justified, but the critics usually ignored the human benefits of the program. Abner E. Larned, state WPA administrator, emphasized this feature in summarizing the results after the WPA was discontinued in April, 1943. He spoke of the improved morale of the workers, and he asserted that "Over and above the material benefits that have accrued to the state, benefits that will serve the state long after all of us are gone, are the human services that WPA has rendered."

The peak load of WPA employment, he declared, was reached in August, 1938, when 201,631 were on the payroll. During the seven years of the program's existence, 500,000 different persons worked on various projects. Counting four to a family, "This indicates," he said, "that WPA has been the sole means of support, for a time at least, of about 2,000,000 Michigan persons." Larned stated that "WPA faced an unemployment crisis without parallel anywhere else in the nation. The program served as a bridge to carry Michigan from these dire depression conditions in the early 30's when no jobs were to be had to the present, when employment opportunities are abundant."

Larned reported that in Michigan the WPA spent $530,389,595. Of this total a little more than one fourth was contributed by local sponsors: cities, counties, or other units of government. The United States Government provided about three fourths of the funds.

In spending this money, the WPA constructed roads, bridges, sidewalks, hospitals, libraries, schools, auditoriums, police posts, firehouses, and armories. Permanent buildings of masonry replaced wooden structures at Camp Custer, and in Lansing the WPA built a million-dollar water-conditioning plant.

The WPA served 16,000,000 hot lunches to school children, using surplus food which the government had purchased from farmers. Needy jobless women were paid for making garments for distribution to impoverished families and to public institutions. Unemployed musicians, sculptors, painters, writers, handicraft workers, and teachers were given employment by WPA so that their talents, training, and skills were made useful to their communities.

Larned pointed out that the program provided training for men and women to fit them for employment in industry, offering practical courses in aircraft mechanics and maintenance, in automotive mechanics, in machine shop and sheet-metal work, and in welding. Of the 25,000 trained, 82 per cent found jobs as a result of their newly acquired skills.

7

One purpose of the New Deal was to wipe out slum districts in cities and to aid in providing decent housing for low-income families. To furnish means to accomplish this purpose, the Federal Housing Administration, established in 1934 to encourage private building, could lend money for public housing. Several Michigan cities applied for funds.

Although many persons knew that living conditions in the slums were deplorable, the majority were ignorant of the need for improvement. Some resented the intervention of the government in local affairs; others called the program a beginning of Communism.

Thomas P. Danahey, president of the Detroit Real Estate Board, in 1935 appeared before the Common Council and branded the projected housing program as un-American. Later, he became president of the Detroit Housing Commission. Explaining his new point of view, Danahey admitted that his original stand was the result of ignorance. "I had an opportunity to see how the other half lives, and I got the shock of my life," he declared.

The slum area of Detroit he called the "Dead City." Within it were 300,000 persons living in 75,000 housing units unfit for human habitation. Stressing the need for public housing, Danahey called attention to the danger of permitting existing conditions to continue. Fire protection, he said, cost eight and one half times the average amount; juvenile delinquency was 10 per cent greater than elsewhere; and the number of tuberculosis and pneumonia cases was far above the city average. These evils affected the whole community, and taxpayers had to foot the bill. Danahey believed that it would be cheaper as well as more humane to provide healthful habitations.

Some progress was made in Detroit under the law of 1934, but not much. In 1938 only two housing developments, each accommodating about 750 families, were occupied. If all the unfit housing were to be replaced, one hundred such projects would be required.

Tenants for public housing were selected with care. Preference was given to those in the worst slum quarters who were unable to pay for decent privately owned apartments or houses. If their incomes rose above a fixed figure, they were required to move and give room to a low-income family.

There were slums and substandard houses in other Michigan cities than Detroit. Although the number there was much greater, few cities had a lower percentage of unsuitable houses. According to the 1940 Census, in twelve of the smaller cities one fifth or more of the houses were "in need of major repairs," the lowest classification. In one of the cities, one half the houses were in that category. Local surveys of the situation, such as those made in Flint and Kalamazoo, showed a real shortage of residence property with little being done to improve the condition.

The recession of 1937 spurred the government to provide additional funds to aid recovery. A new organization was established to speed the public housing program, and new projects were begun in Detroit.

8

All the economic activities of the state were adversely affected by the depression. For several years factories were closed or they were operating at partial capacity. Better conditions began in 1934. Farming at first scarcely provided a livelihood. In Michigan farmers profited by the repeal of the general property tax and the substitution of the sales tax. Various enactments of the New Deal program, which reduced crop surpluses and saved their farms from forced sales, also improved their condition. Farmers and their wives gained new conveniences, too. Either directly or indirectly through the activities of the Rural Electrification Administration, a New Deal agency, electricity was used on four times as many Michigan farms in 1940 as in 1930.

Copper production fell off sharply from 169,382,000 pounds in 1930 to less than half that annual quantity during the remainder of the decade. The effects of the decline were disastrous to the people of the copper country. In 1934 more than a third of the families in Houghton County were on relief, and in Keweenaw County, nearly two thirds.

Iron mining also felt the heavy hand of the depression. Shipments of ore decreased from 11 million tons in 1930 to 1 million tons in 1932. There was a sixfold increase, however, in 1933, and, before the end of the decade production was up to the normal of more than 12 million tons.

A notable event in this period was the closing of the Chapin Mine at Iron Mountain in 1934. Opened in 1879, when the town was laid out, it had produced continuously since 1880, except in 1932 and 1933. World-famous both for the quantity and the quality of its ore, the Chapin Mine surpassed all others in Michigan with its total production of more than 26 million tons. As a sort of memorial, the huge Cornish pump which was used to drain the mine before electric pumps were introduced still stands on a hill in Iron Mountain. (See Headpiece.)

Economic conditions in general began to improve in 1934, and the upturn continued until the summer of 1937 when a recession set in. Merchants stopped buying because they had piled up large inventories, and reduced spending by the government decreased the purchasing power of individuals. A quick return to pump priming helped recovery, which came in the summer of 1938. Thereafter, threatening conditions in Europe gave manufacturers orders for war materials, thus speeding re-employment.

The depression had a marked effect on the population of Michigan. During the early years of the 1930's, some families left the state and returned to their former homes. As employment increased during later years many came back, and the population in 1940 was 5,356,106, a rise of 400,000 over the 1930 figure.

The distribution of people within the state was affected also. Because of unemployment, many moved from the cities to the villages or the farms from which they had come. They were refugees from the depression, waiting for conditions to improve, rather than permanent settlers in the country. The number that left the cities was large enough to raise the ratio of rural to urban population. In 1930 nearly 32 per cent of the people of Michigan lived in rural areas. In 1940, more than 34 per cent lived there, and it is certain that during the worst years of the depression the difference was even greater.

During these gloomy depression years there were some cheering events. Among them were championships in professional sports. The Detroit Tigers in 1934 were winners of the American League baseball pennant. The next year they won the pennant again, and they defeated the Chicago Cubs in the World Series. In professional football, the Detroit Lions gained the National League world's crown, and in hockey the Red Wings took the Stanley Cup. Detroit was hailed as the "City of Champions" and all Michigan was proud of the triumphs. In addition, during 1935 and 1936, Joe Louis, the Brown Bomber, was battling his way to the top of the heavyweight boxing division by an impressive string of knockout victories. In 1937 he became the world's heavyweight champion, and he retained the title until 1949.

9

The election of 1934 returned the Republicans to power in Michigan. Frank D. Fitzgerald defeated Arthur J. Lacy for governor, the Republicans controlled the senate and had half the members of the house. Senator Vandenberg was re-elected, and a majority of the representatives in Congress were Republicans.

Governor Fitzgerald was an experienced and skillful politician. From 1919 to 1923 he had served as deputy secretary of state, and from 1923 to 1931 as business manager of the State Highway Department. He had been also secretary of the Republican State Central Committee. In 1930 he had been elected secretary of state, and in 1932, when the voters returned him to office, he was the only Republican administrator.

Governor Fitzgerald realized that many state employes must be specialists trained to perform the manifold duties which the government had assumed, and that competent persons were not being appointed under the existing spoils system. Consequently, he named a commission to study the problem of writing a law which would give Michigan the benefits of the merit system. Professor James K. Pollock of the Political Science Department of the University of Michigan was chairman.

The governor advocated sweeping changes which he believed would improve the government of the state. The most important was the proposal of a constitutional amendment that would provide for the appointment of all administrative officers except the governor, the lieutenant governor, and the auditor general. As had happened in 1921, when a similar suggestion had been made, no action was taken.

In 1936 Frank Murphy resigned his office as High Commissioner of the Philippine Islands (he had been Governor General from 1933 to 1935, before the Tydings-McDuffie Act[4] went into effect) and returned to Michigan at the request of the President to run for governor. Roosevelt, running against Alfred M. Landon, governor of Kansas, carried every state except Maine and Vermont. Michigan gave him a plurality of 300,000 votes, and Murphy defeated Fitzgerald by 50,000.[5]

In this election, Senator James Couzens supported Roosevelt. He was defeated in the Republican senatorial primary by ex-Governor Wilber M. Brucker, who in the election was beaten by Prentiss M. Brown, a Democratic member of Congress. Couzens, desperately ill when he appeared in Detroit on the platform with Roosevelt during the campaign, died on October 23, 1936. After the election Governor Fitzgerald appointed Brown to fill Couzens' unexpired term.

Governor Murphy accepted the recommendations of Governor Fitzgerald's merit system commission and used his influence to get a law passed. Two years later, when the Republicans were in control, the Legislature "amended" the act in such a way as to make it nearly useless. Professor Pollock protested vigorously against this action. Others joined in the demand for a real merit system, and in the fall of 1940 the people ratified an amendment to the constitution fixing the merit system firmly into the structure of the state government to make it secure against tinkering by the Legislature.

Other important acts besides civil service reform passed during Murphy's administration were a secret primary law, a revision of the state banking laws, a liberalized law for old age assistance, and an unemployment compensation law.

10

Governor Murphy's greatest problem was how to deal with the sit-down strikes in the plants of automobile companies. Three days before he took the oath of office, UAW-CIO workers had sat down in the Chevrolet and Fisher Body plants of General Motors and refused to leave until the corporation recognized the union as the bargaining

[4] This act promised the Filipinos full independence after a ten-year period of supervision. They elected Manuel Quezon President in 1935. The office of High Commissioner replaced that of Governor General.

[5] Father Charles E. Coughlin was a violent critic of President Roosevelt in this campaign. Calling him "liar" and "double crosser," Father Coughlin exhorted the members of his Union for Social Justice to vote for William Lemke of North Dakota. In 1938, the radio priest added an anti-Semitic crusade to his attacks on Communism and the New Deal.

agent for the men. The sit-down strike was a new technique, used first in the United States by workers in the rubber plants in Akron, Ohio. Previously, when workmen walked out of a factory, the management refused to discuss grievances with them unless they returned to work. If police or troops kept the strikers away from the factory, new employes were hired and the men lost not only the strike but also their jobs. The sit-down was intended to give the workmen job security.

For three years the United States government had expressly recognized the right of workingmen to organize and to bargain collectively with their employers through representatives of their own choice. First, the National Industrial Recovery Act in 1933 had granted that right, and employers had signed codes which contained a clause to that effect. All the automobile companies except Ford accepted the automobile code.[6] Some employers gave only lip service to Section 7a, which provided for collective bargaining. They set up company unions which they controlled, and which, of course, defeated the purpose of the law.

The NRA had practically collapsed, because of its own complexity, the hostile attitude of employers, and the opposition of consumers who blamed the scheme for higher prices, when the Supreme Court in May, 1935, declared it unconstitutional. Almost immediately Congress passed the National Labor Relations Act, also called the Wagner Act, which required employers to bargain with unions selected by the employes, and established the National Labor Relations Board to administer the act. Many corporations ignored the NLRB on the advice of their lawyers, who assured them that the Supreme Court would declare the law unconstitutional.

In Michigan, labor unions had had little influence in the mass-production industries, such as automobiles and steel. Because most of the employes in the automobile factories were unskilled, they were not eligible to join the craft unions; and if one or more of the latter called a strike, it did little more than inconvenience the management.

Recognizing the need for mass organization of workmen in the automobile and other similar industries, some labor leaders at the 1935 convention of the AFL presented a resolution to provide for industrial organization, that is, a union to take in all employes of an industry regardless of their kind of work. When the resolution was rejected, John L. Lewis, head of the United Mine Workers, and others formed the

[6] Except for the requirement that employes be permitted to organize and bargain with their employers, the codes were similar to those which Herbert Hoover as Secretary of Commerce had encouraged various industries to adopt.

Committee for Industrial Organization. The unions under this plan were a part of the AFL until September, 1936, when they were suspended by President William Green and his board of directors. They then joined Lewis' group, which in 1938 was renamed the Congress of Industrial Organizations.

In Michigan the most important of the industrial unions was the United Auto Workers. At first under the leadership of Homer Martin, then somewhat later of the more practical labor leaders, Walter P. Reuther and Richard T. Frankensteen, it grew rapidly. By December, 1936, it was ready to fight for higher wages, better working conditions, and job security.

The test of strength first was made in Flint, where in December, 1936, the UAW-CIO took over Fisher Body and the Chevrolet plants and held them pending negotiations for contracts recognizing the union and providing certain benefits to the workers. Rumors that some departments were going to be moved to other cities and a feeling of resentment against the labor policies of General Motors precipitated the strike. At first only small groups sat down. Their idleness stopped work in other departments which depended on a steady flow of materials, and soon others joined the original strikers. Union leaders took charge after the strike became widespread.

Corporation officers asserted that they would not negotiate as long as the men were in the buildings. The men barricaded themselves in the factories and with fire hoses and steel auto parts fought off attempts by police to dislodge them. Injunctions requiring the strikers to leave the plants were ignored. The sit-down was a lawless tactic, but the workmen believed it was the only way to protect their jobs.

Walter P. Reuther was the leader of the strikers. A tool and die maker who had worked for the Briggs Body Corporation, General Motors, and Ford, he had taken night courses at Detroit's Wayne University. For two years Reuther traveled in Europe and Asia, working his way and studying labor conditions in various countries. Returning to Michigan in 1935, he engaged in union organization activities and became director of the General Motors Division of the UAW-CIO.

When Governor Murphy was inaugurated, the strike at Flint was already in progress. General Motors called upon him at once to send troops to evict the men from the plants. Murphy's policy, however, was to remain neutral and simply to maintain order. He did send National Guard companies to Flint, but they made no attempt to clear the plants. Persons who believed that the government should protect the rights of owners of private property, even at the possible cost of bloodshed, denounced the governor. Murphy, however, refused to change his policy. He called the officials of General Motors and the CIO into conference, and the strike was settled on February 11, when General Motors agreed to recognize the UAW-CIO as the bargaining agent for its members.

This was the first successful campaign of the UAW-CIO. From Flint the leaders moved to Detroit, where a sit-down strike soon induced the Chrysler Corporation, the second of the Big Three automobile manufacturers, to recognize the union. Now Ford alone of this group was unorganized.[7]

II

Ford remained opposed to recognizing the UAW-CIO or any other union. Men who had joined the union were discharged. Charges were filed against Ford by the UAW-CIO with the NLRB, and hearings were held. Even after the constitutionality of the NLRB was upheld by a decision of the United States Supreme Court on April 12, 1937, Ford carried appeals against the orders of the NLRB to the federal courts.

In May, 1937, the UAW inaugurated its effort to organize the Ford Motor Company. The campaign began with a violent incident on May 26, 1937, in which Frankensteen, Reuther, and several other union officers were beaten on the Miller Road overpass to the River Rouge plant.

The contest with Ford went on until 1941. On February 10, 1941, the United States Supreme Court refused to review the case against the NLRB which Ford had appealed to it. On February 18 compliance notices were posted in the Rouge plants, and union men were reinstated. Ford paid thousands of dollars in back wages to employes who had been discharged for union activities.

Ford still discharged men for union activity, and refused to permit the holding of an election to determine whether the employes wanted the UAW-CIO to act for them. On April 2, 1941, the eight-man grievance committee of the UAW-CIO was discharged. Immediately the UAW-CIO struck and picketed the plant. Ford appealed to Governor

[7] The CIO was not uniformly successful in organizing workmen. In June, 1937, Mayor Daniel A. Knaggs of Monroe swore in two hundred special deputies and dispersed CIO pickets at the Republic Steel Company plant. He took this action after a straw vote showed that a majority of the employes wanted to work.

Murray D. Van Wagoner[8] and to President Roosevelt for troops. Both ignored the request. On April 11, Governor Van Wagoner brought UAW-CIO and Ford officials together for a conference. The latter agreed to an election, and the former agreed to end the strike.

In the election supervised by the NLRB on May 21, 1941, 70 per cent of the men voted for the UAW-CIO as their bargaining agent. Ford officials met with the union officers to negotiate a contract, which was announced on June 21. Ford now gave the union all it asked, and more. He agreed to the closed shop and the check-off, features which no other automobile company had included in its contract. The employes had what they had been demanding for years: better pay, job security through seniority rights, a union to present their grievances to management, and a uniformed police force instead of the secret service department.

There was much talk to the effect that the labor upheavals had injured Detroit and Michigan by causing industries to move to other states. Mayor Edward Jeffries denied that this was so, and finally, on March 26, 1940, Harvey Campbell, secretary of the Detroit Board of Commerce, supported him in a news release. "Actually, as we look back on it," Campbell said, "it becomes apparent that Mayor Jeffries is essentially right in criticizing those who should have known better. . . . The recapitulation shows that, while it is true that 35 industries moved part or all of their operations from Detroit between 1937 and 1939, this loss was much more than offset by the expansion of other factories and the opening of new businesses." Statistics proved that 226 new businesses opened and $150,000,000 were spent for expansion between 1937 and 1939. Campbell expressed the belief that labor and management were learning how to live together in peace.

12

In 1938 former Governor Frank D. Fitzgerald was nominated by the Republicans and Governor Frank Murphy by the Democrats. Issues in the campaign were the spending program of the Murphy administration, the so-called Little New Deal for Michigan which the Governor had sponsored, and his handling of the sit-down strikes. Conservative Democrats were so hostile to Murphy that they even nominated their own candidate, who, however, withdrew his name before the election. Former Governor William A. Comstock, a Democrat, opposed Murphy, but Chase S. Osborn, a Republican, supported him. In a letter he

[8] Van Wagoner was elected governor in November, 1940.

declared: "I have been much more in sympathy with the sit-down strikers than with the sit-down employers."

Fitzgerald and the rest of the Republican ticket were elected, including Luren D. Dickinson as lieutenant governor. He was seventy-nine years old, and he had already served six terms in that office. A majority of the senators and representatives also were Republicans. President Roosevelt called Frank Murphy to Washington in 1939 to serve as Attorney General of the United States.

Governor Fitzgerald died on March 16, 1939, and Lieutenant Governor Dickinson was sworn in as his successor. He was the oldest governor in the United States. For many years Dickinson had been an active leader of the Anti-Saloon League and a vocal opponent of wrongdoing. In his inaugural address he condemned in vigorous terms social conditions in Michigan and throughout the nation. In spite of his frequent outbursts, which attracted amused attention outside the state, the Governor did nothing to remedy the evils he talked about. Laws passed during Governor Dickinson's administration included the one already mentioned (page 422), which almost nullified the new merit system, and a law requiring teachers in schools and colleges to take an oath of allegiance to the government.

By the end of the decade the New Deal program had run its course. Bitterly attacked by its enemies and warmly supported by its friends and beneficiaries, it had accomplished much that was good. Banks throughout the nation were sound, and depositors were protected; investors were safeguarded against unscrupulous stock promoters; workingmen had gained security in their jobs, unemployment insurance, minimum wages, and maximum hours; child labor had been abolished; farm prices had been stabilized, some of the surplus crops were used for school lunches, and soil conservation practices had been adopted; slum clearance had begun, and encouragement had been given to both public and private housing. For the first time in the history of the nation the government had acted vigorously to improve the condition of the underprivileged.

Accompanying the benefits were some evils. Union leaders could not or would not control their men, and industry was plagued by numerous strikes. The national debt was increased to a figure that was believed by many to be dangerous. In some localities relief of the unemployed was used for political advantage, and money was wasted on unnecessary projects. Government regulation of many activities previously exempt aroused hostility and led to charges that there was danger of a dictatorship in the United States.

During the second half of the decade, the government of the United States was compelled to give much of its attention to foreign affairs. The dictators in Europe and the military clique in Japan threatened the peace of the world. In the United States the people were strongly opposed to actions that might lead to war. Congress passed several neutrality acts intended to prevent incidents similar to those which had helped to involve the nation in World War I. In 1937, when President Roosevelt proposed that aggressor nations, such as Japan, which had just invaded China, should be "quarantined" by peace-loving countries, there was a great clamor against any sort of intervention.

Hitler's annexation of Austria in 1938 and his seizure of all Czechoslovakia in 1939 caused some change of opinion. The President began to talk of offering France and Great Britain assistance "short of war." Congress voted a billion dollars for naval construction, and after Hitler's sudden invasion of Poland on September 1, 1939, Congress relaxed restrictions on shipments of arms and war materials to his enemies. The people generally approved this action, but there were very many who insisted that the only safe policy for the United States was complete isolation. In Congress, Michigan senators and representatives usually divided on party lines: the Democrats supported the policies of the administration, and the Republicans voted for isolation. Senator Arthur H. Vandenberg was one of the sponsors of a bill in 1939 to require a referendum before war could be declared.

So ended the decade of the thirties. Begun in depression and occupied during most of the years with experiments to accomplish relief, recovery, and reform, it ended with returning prosperity based on war in Europe and in Asia. Whether the United States should take the profits and avoid the calamities of the conflict was the bitter issue of the next two years.

— 29 —

Armorer to the United Nations

DURING THE last decade of the first half of the twentieth century, the world was racked by the most destructive war ever known. Jolted out of its isolationism by the sneak attack on Pearl Harbor, December 7, 1941, the United States turned all its attention to destroying Hitler and Mussolini in Europe and the Japanese war lords in Asia. Besides providing materials for our own armed services, it was necessary to produce prodigiously for our Allies. The people of every state contributed their share, but Michigan led all the rest in production for war.

World War II, which was begun without the traditional declaration, ended without the customary general peace conference. Peace, in fact, was an illusion. Instigated by the ruthless Communist government of Russia, wars broke out in widely separated areas and threatened to sweep over the whole globe in another general conflagration.

Even in the nations of the West, where there was no fighting, Soviet agents enlisted the aid of local malcontents to disrupt the political and economic systems. This internal meddling and the ever-present danger of renewed aggression by Russia were called the "cold war."

2

Nineteen hundred and forty was an election year. As usual the Republican National Convention met first. When the delegates assembled in Philadelphia on June 24, their attention was divided between the desperate situation in Europe and conditions at home.

Abroad, disasters had befallen the western nations. In April, Adolf Hitler had occupied Denmark and Norway. Then, unleashing his land and air forces in a blitzkrieg against the other countries of western Europe, he had conquered the Netherlands, Belgium, and France by June 22. A British expeditionary force had been compelled to flee the Continent after suffering heavy losses, and fleets of Nazi planes rained destruction on England. Only Sweden, Portugal, and Spain were unoccupied by German armies. The first was too weak to resist whatever demands Hitler might make, and the others were ruled by Fascist dictators.

Democratic government in Europe had been destroyed. In Great Britain alone, under the dauntless leadership of Winston Churchill, the people fought to preserve their liberty.

Many Americans believed, with President Roosevelt, that the United States should give Britain as much help as possible. Others feared that aid to Britain would take us into the war. They wanted the nation to remain aloof from European quarrels.

The Republican delegates rejected Thomas E. Dewey of New York, a native of Owosso, Michigan; Senator Robert A. Taft of Ohio; and Senator Arthur H. Vandenberg of Michigan—all isolationists. They nominated Wendell L. Willkie, a former Democrat and a utilities executive who had fought the Tennessee Valley Authority and other New Deal agencies. He, however, endorsed most of Roosevelt's foreign policy.

Breaking with the two-term-limit tradition, the Democrats renominated President Roosevelt. Both nominees promised to keep the nation out of war.

Father Charles E. Coughlin had continued to attack President Roosevelt, and his radio addresses were violently anti-Semitic and anti-British. When he offered his support to Willkie, the Republican candidate curtly rejected it. On September 20, 1940, the Radio Priest suddenly announced that he was giving up broadcasting, explaining cnly that "powerful men" had forced the decision on him. He continued, however, to publish *Social Justice,* for which he claimed 600,000 subscribers.[1]

Beginning in 1939, Father Coughlin had a friend and ally in the Reverend Gerald L. K. Smith, a Protestant preacher. Formerly a follower of Huey Long, Smith settled in Detroit after having stumped the country denouncing labor unions and Communism. He gained the support of some Michigan manufacturers, and became a potent influence among the southerners who were flocking to Detroit to work in the factories. Like Father Coughlin, he was a violent isolationist.

In November, 1940, President Roosevelt was re-elected, but Michigan gave its electoral votes to Wendell L. Willkie, and Arthur H. Vandenberg was returned to his seat in the Senate. In the state election, Murray D. Van Wagoner, a Democrat who had been highway commissioner since 1933, defeated Governor Luren D. Dickinson. For the fifth successive time Democrats and Republicans alternated in winning the governorship.

Other Democrats elected were Frank Murphy (a name candidate, not a relative of the former governor), lieutenant governor; and Theodore I. Fry, treasurer. Harry F. Kelly, chosen secretary of state; Herbert J. Rushton, attorney general; and Vernon J. Brown, auditor general, were Republicans. Of the other two officers on the Administrative Board, Eugene B. Elliott, superintendent of public instruction, was a Republican; and G. Donald Kennedy, highway commissioner, was a Democrat. With a divided cabinet and a Republican majority in the Legislature, Governor Van Wagoner could expect a hectic two years in office.

3

The war caused great anxiety in the United States. Japan continued to extend its sway in Asia; in Europe, Great Britain's position became increasingly desperate. To assist her in staving off defeat and to protect the Americas, President Roosevelt gave her fifty overage destroyers in return for the right to construct air and naval bases on British possessions in the western Atlantic. In September, 1940, at the request of the President, Congress passed the Selective Service

[1] *Social Justice* was barred from the mails by the Postmaster General in April, 1942, because it contained, he asserted, "a systematic and unscrupulous attack on the war effort of the nation. . . ."

Act, requiring all men between the ages of twenty-one and thirty-five to register. This was the first peacetime draft in the history of the nation.

Senator Vandenberg strongly opposed both actions. In letters to his constituents he expressed the opinion that the nation was headed for bankruptcy, and that free citizens of the United States were being made into regimented subjects of a dictatorial government. Sufficient soldiers, he believed, could be obtained by calling for volunteers. Vandenberg also opposed the Lend-Lease Act, which was passed in March, 1941. Senator Prentiss M. Brown, who usually supported the President, opposed the Selective Service Act, but he voted for Lend-Lease.

At this time several Michigan men held important positions in the national government by appointment of the President. In January, 1940, Attorney General Frank Murphy was named a justice of the Supreme Court to fill the vacancy caused by the death of Justice Pierce Butler. The promotion cut short a vigorous crusade against wrong-doing which Murphy had waged against prominent lawbreakers. Although he had been in office only thirteen months, he had sent Tom Pendergast, Democratic boss of Kansas City, to jail for income tax evasion; Earl Browder, Communist leader, for passport fraud; and United States Judge Martin T. Manton, for accepting bribes. In Louisiana he had exposed political racketeers, and he was investigating politicians in Chicago and Jersey City. On the Supreme Court bench, Justice Murphy was a champion for human rights.

A Michigan man whose name rarely appeared in the news was one of the most powerful persons in Washington. Harold D. Smith, Director of the Budget, had been appointed by the President in 1939 on the recommendation of Attorney General Murphy. Although Smith was a Republican, Governor Murphy had made him budget director in Lansing, where he had distinguished himself as an administrator.

Harold D. Smith was not a politician. After completing his college education in Kansas as an electrical engineer, he had turned to public administration and earned a master's degree in that field at the University of Michigan in 1925. Smith became head of the Michigan Municipal League in 1928, after having worked in the Detroit Bureau of Governmental Research and in the League of Kansas Municipalities. From 1934 to 1937 he was director of the Bureau of Government of the University of Michigan, and in 1937 he became budget director of the state.

In Washington, Smith was business manager for the President. Part of his job was to co-ordinate the work of the numerous governmental agencies. Besides, all legislative recommendations from executive departments had to be approved by the Budget Bureau before being introduced in Congress. Likewise, all bills passed by Congress were sent to the Bureau for analysis and for recommendation that they be signed or vetoed. In almost every case, the recommendation was followed. Because of the nature of his duties and his close relationship with the President, Smith was called the most important person in the national administration.

Another Michigan man who distinguished himself in Washington was William S. Knudsen. Appointed director of industrial production on the National Defense Advisory Commission, he resigned from the presidency of General Motors Corporation in September, 1940.

An immigrant from Denmark, Knudsen had worked his way to a top production position in the Ford Motor Company. In 1922 he became a vice-president of General Motors in charge of the Chevrolet Division, and in 1937 he was made president of General Motors. Noted for his ability to increase production, Knudsen overcame shortages of skilled men, machine tools, and materials to multiply the output of equipment for national defense. Later he continued the good work with the Office of Production Management and with the War Department. So that he would have sufficient rank to overrule all except the highest military officers, he was made a lieutenant general.

A former Michigan man, Frank Knox, was appointed Secretary of the Navy in June, 1940. At that time he was publisher of the *Chicago Daily News*. Before going to Chicago, he had owned the *Sault Sainte Marie Evening News*, he had managed Chase S. Osborn's campaign for governor in 1910, and he had been leader of the progressive movement in Michigan for Theodore Roosevelt. Knox built the greatest navy in the world, and he successfully directed it during the war until his death on April 28, 1944.

4

In Michigan the conversion to war production was rapid. By government order, the automobile companies began in August, 1941, to reduce the number of cars assembled so that they could turn out more weapons. After Pearl Harbor, December 7, 1941, the effort was accelerated, and the last cars for civilian use were completed on February 10, 1942. Civilian truck assembly continued until May 31.

Motor vehicle manufacturers made machine guns, airplane engines, tanks, airplane propellers, automatic pilots, torpedoes for submarines and for airplanes, diesel engines, cannon, shells, and dozens of other things. Instead of competing against each other, corporations co-operated, and total production was far beyond that of peacetime. As a reward for excellence in quality and quantity, the Army and the Navy conferred numerous "E" flags on individual plants, and the workmen proudly wore "E" buttons. Because of the manpower shortage, thousands of women worked in factories.

Although production was largely concentrated in the southeastern part of the state, plants elsewhere turned out a variety of goods for war. Iron Mountain made gliders, Grand Rapids made helicopter parts, and Kalamazoo made amphibious tanks. Bay City was noted for the production of subchasers, mine sweepers, landing boats, destroyer escorts, and other war craft.

Existing corporations increased their plant areas, and the government constructed new factories. One was the huge Willow Run airplane plant near Ypsilanti. Built at a cost of $100,000,000, the plant was operated by the Ford Motor Company, and the first B-24 four-engine Liberator bomber came off the line on September 10, 1942. When the factory was at peak production, eighteen of the huge planes were completed each day. More than 8,500 were made before the plant shut down on June 30, 1945.

Another government-owned plant was the giant tank arsenal north of Detroit, which was operated by the Chrysler Corporation. During nearly five years it turned out more than 25,000 tanks—General Grants General Shermans, General Pershings—sometimes at the rate of a thousand a month. Hudson Motor Company operated the Naval Ordnance Plant in Macomb County, manufacturing antiaircraft guns. General Motors divisions ran three government plants. In a huge factory at Grand Blanc, Fisher Body built medium tanks; in a foundry at Flint, Buick produced castings; and in a foundry at Saginaw, Chevrolet also made castings. Packard Motor Company made Rolls-Royce airplane engines.

The demands of war increased iron ore production, which rose to 16,000,000 tons in 1942. It declined gradually to 11,000,000 in 1945. The output of copper reached the peak of 93,528,000 pounds in 1943. This production was possible only because the government set a premium price on Lake copper in recognition of the higher cost of mining in that region.

The great quantity of iron ore and copper taxed the capacity of the ore-carrying fleet and of the locks at Sault Sainte Marie. In 1943 the new MacArthur Lock,[2] built to replace the old Weitzel Lock, was ready for use. The four American locks and the Canadian lock were busy day and night. Because of the strategic importance of the canal, Sault Sainte Marie during the war was the most heavily guarded place in the nation. Thousands of soldiers manned antiaircraft guns, searchlights, radar installations, and machine guns. Barrage balloons swayed restlessly above the locks, tugging at their moorings, and fighter planes on nearby fields were ready to take to the air if enemy bombers were reported.

5

The great war production program in Michigan attracted men and women from all parts of the country. As a result, the population increased rapidly in spite of the 613,542 men who left for service in the armed forces. The high mark was reached in 1942, when there were 5,530,982 people in the state. Other states in the Old Northwest lost population, except Indiana, which made a slight gain.

The rise in population occurred largely in the southeastern counties. Macomb had an increase of 32 per cent; Washtenaw, 21 per cent; and Oakland, 17 per cent. The greatest growth was in the Detroit–Willow Run and the Muskegon regions.

Northern counties suffered losses in population. In Kalkaska and Baraga the decrease was 31 per cent; in Crawford, 29 per cent; in Keweenaw, 27 per cent; in Mackinac, 25 per cent; and in Emmet, 24 per cent. Others lost a smaller proportion.

After the war the population of the state continued to grow, and in 1950 it was 6,371,766. The trend toward the cities continued. According to a new Census Bureau formula, which classified thickly settled regions as urban, even if they were not incorporated, the urban percentage in 1950 was 70.5.

In spite of the smaller rural population, the farmers of Michigan raised larger and larger crops. Increased use of machines reduced the need of hired men, and the demands of war provided markets for all they could grow. Farmers were prosperous, for even after the war government price supports prevented a return to the low incomes of the 1920's. In 1948 and 1949 the production of field crops was the largest in the history of the state.

[2] Senator Prentiss M. Brown and Representative Fred M. Bradley of Rogers City introduced the bills which provided for construction of the new lock. They wanted it named for Chase S. Osborn.

During the war years the colored population of Michigan increased enormously. In 1940 there were 216,463 Negroes in the State; in 1950, 452,000. Plenty of work and high wages were the principal attractions. Besides, Negroes were accepted as members of unions in the CIO. Because few of them had had opportunities to learn trades, they had never before enjoyed the protection of union membership.

The great increase in population in certain areas caused discomfort and suffering because of insufficient housing. By 1943, with the aid of government funds, five permanent low-rent housing developments had been built in Detroit. Two were in cleared slum districts, and three were on previously unoccupied sites. Temporary war housing was provided for 5,183 families by the United States Government.

Willow Village, a large temporary war housing development, was erected by the government near Ypsilanti for single men and women and for the families of married workers in the Willow Run bomber plant. In Muskegon two emergency housing developments were built, quarters for 550 families were erected in Saginaw, and for 1,700 in Pontiac.

All these attempts to provide living quarters were helpful, but thousands of persons had to crowd into unsatisfactory dwellings. Conditions for Negroes, who were forced to occupy the least desirable accommodations, were deplorable. Although some efforts were made to care for their needs, as in the Sojourner Truth Development in Detroit, the number benefited was too small to relieve the congestion.

The situation in Detroit was critical. Thousands of colored people, some recently from the South, had to live in slum areas, most of them east of Woodward Avenue. Earning more money than they were accustomed to, they went outside their own areas to spend it, and some aroused the ire of race-conscious white men.

Transgression by Negroes of the unwritten rules of discrimination had previously caused some trouble in Detroit. The most serious incident had been the attack in 1925 on the family of Dr. Ossian Sweet, who had bought a house in a white neighborhood. Terrified by the mob which was attempting to break in, someone in the house fired and killed one of the attackers. The Sweets were arrested, and Henry Sweet, brother of the doctor, was charged with murder. Defended in court by Clarence Darrow, the famous criminal lawyer of Chicago, he was acquitted.

During the early 1940's the danger of racial clashes increased. White workers from the South became numerous in Detroit, and they were quick to resent any evidence of Negro "impudence." Membership of

Negroes in unions offended them, and rabble-rousers like Gerald L. K. Smith increased their hostility. In 1941 a strike in the Ford Motor Company factory resulted from tension between white men and Negroes; and on February 28, 1942, a mob attacked Negroes moving into the Sojourner Truth housing development, alleging that it was in a white neighborhood. In June, 1943, a strike occurred in the Packard Motor Company plant because three Negroes were given promotion.

6

All of these incidents were the result of prejudices which were heightened by war tension, frayed nerves, inadequate recreational facilities, and crowded living conditions. Many white workers who had come to Detroit found housing little better than some in the Negro quarters. If they had children, few landlords were willing to rent to them.

Because of the existing circumstances, some of the authorities in Detroit feared that interracial clashes might occur, but no one took any effective steps to prevent them. As a matter of fact, they were completely unprepared to cope with the murderous rioting which broke out on Sunday night, June 20, 1943.

The trouble began on the bridge leading from East Jefferson Avenue to Belle Isle, a large park in the Detroit River. Nearly a hundred thousand people were on the island, of whom probably 90 per cent were colored. During the evening several complaints of insult and injury were made to the police. The first large-scale fighting began at 10:30 P.M. at the Jefferson Avenue end of the bridge. Sailors from the nearby naval armory and other white men fought with Negroes leaving the island. Police reserves were dispatched to the scene. They dispersed the mob, which was said to consist of five thousand colored and white people.

Rumors of the riot spread through the city. In a crowded Negro night club on the East Side, the master of ceremonies announced that white men had killed a colored woman and her baby on Belle Isle. Many of the patrons hurried away to spread the story, which was not true. Elsewhere the rumor ran that Negroes had attacked and killed a white woman on the bridge. That story also was false, but some believed it.

Clashes occurred in various parts of the city, most of them on the East Side. By midnight Negroes were attacking white workers on Vernor Highway, and on Warren and Forest avenues, who were driving to and from factories. Police were stationed at the intersection of these streets with Hastings and St. Antoine in what was called "Paradise Valley," the heart of the Negro district. They tried to arrest or drive off the frenzied Negroes, but attacks on streetcars and automobiles continued. Wounded victims of the riots were pouring into Receiving Hospital. On the West Side, where colored and white people lived in the same neighborhoods, no trouble was reported.

About three o'clock on the morning of Monday, June 21, gangs of Negroes in Paradise Valley began to loot stores and damage buildings owned by white persons. This action resulted from the belief that the merchants and landlords for years had overcharged and cheated them. Police sent to stop the looting were attacked.

While the looting was in progress on the East Side, at Woodward Avenue and Charlotte white mobs attacked Negroes leaving all-night movie theaters. Police broke up the mobs.

Colonel A. M. Krech, United States Army, commanding the Detroit area, informed Mayor Edward J. Jeffries that military police stationed in River Rouge Park could be in Detroit in fifty minutes after the governor asked national authorities for their assistance. Because the rioting appeared to be diminishing, at 6:30 A.M., June 21, Police Commissioner John H. Witherspoon informed the mayor that his men had the situation in hand.

New outbreaks occurred, however, and at Mayor Jeffries' telephoned request, Governor Harry F. Kelly left the Governors' Conference in Columbus, Ohio, and flew to Detroit. When he arrived at 11 o'clock, ready to ask for United States troops, Colonel Krech informed him that they could not be sent unless the governor declared martial law. Governor Kelly refused to take that step. He believed that the State Troops and the State Police, which he had ordered to be ready to move into Detroit, would be able to quell the rioters.

At this time gangs of white youths were overturning Negroes' automobiles, attacking the occupants, and setting the cars afire. They entered streetcars, dragged Negroes outside, and beat them. Police broke up the gangs with tear gas and made some arrests. Looting by Negroes on the East Side continued.

During the afternoon of June 21, while hate-crazed Negroes and whites fought and killed each other on the East Side, a drama of good interracial relations was staged west of Woodward Avenue. In Briggs Stadium, the home field of the Detroit Tigers, the championship baseball game of the city high-school league was played between Pershing and Chadsey schools. Colored and white boys and girls in the stands cheered their teams without regard for racial differences.

In late afternoon, several thousand people jammed the Woodward and Davenport-Mack intersection. Sixteen automobiles driven by Negroes were overturned and burned on Woodward in that neighborhood. Other crowds in the downtown area roamed through Cadillac Square, surged around the City Hall and along Washington Boulevard, chasing and attacking the few Negroes who appeared. Police dispersed the mobs with tear gas. Breaking up temporarily, they assembled again and continued their search for victims.

Early in the evening Mayor Jeffries made an appeal by radio for an end of rioting. Governor Kelly proclaimed "modified martial law" in effect in Wayne, Oakland, and Macomb counties. Declaring that the existing emergency made necessary the assistance of the state's armed forces to put down lawlessness, he ordered Michigan State Troops[3] and State Police to Detroit. He set a 10 o'clock curfew, forbade the sale of liquor, and ordered places of amusement to close at 9 P.M.

The mob on Woodward Avenue reassembled near Vernor Highway. Expecting that an advance into the Negro section might be attempted, police set up barricades at Brush, the second north-and-south street east of Woodward. When the mob began moving east on Vernor Highway at about 8:30 P.M., the police held them temporarily at John R., the first street east of Woodward. Fear-crazed Negroes in a building on the corner of John R. and Vernor Highway began shooting into the mob. Police stormed the building and arrested dozens of Negroes.

At the corner of Vernor and Brush a pitched battle took place between police in the street and Negroes in a hotel. After one policeman had been seriously wounded, his comrades hurled gas bombs through the windows, subdued their assailants, and arrested them.

By this time 150 State Police had joined the city policemen. Even so, Mayor Jeffries and Police Superintendent Louis L. Berg agreed that the civil authorities were unable to control the mobs. At the urging of the mayor, Governor Kelly made an official request for United States troops to Brigadier General William E. Gunther of the Sixth Service Command, who had flown from Chicago earlier in the day.

At about 10 P.M. the 701st Military Police Battalion reached Fort Street and Woodward Avenue. Marching north on Woodward Avenue, the soldiers dispersed the mobs, and before 11:30 they had restored order without firing a shot. If they had been asked for twelve hours earlier, much bloodshed would have been avoided.

[3] After the Michigan National Guard was ordered into federal service in 1940, the State Troops were organized to serve as a home guard. Because they had no means of transportation, they did not reach Detroit until Tuesday morning, June 22. The principal duty of the State Troops was to patrol bridges and tunnels, especially those at Port Huron and Detroit.

In response to a telephone request by the governor, President Roosevelt ordered additional troops to Detroit. They arrived on Tuesday morning, June 22, a total of four thousand men. Camps were established in parks, on school grounds, and on the lawn of the Public Library. Setting out from these camps, trucks and jeeps carrying soldiers in full battle gear patrolled the streets of the city. There was little violence on Tuesday, and none thereafter, but Negroes were fearful of new outbreaks.

On Wednesday, June 23, R. J. Thomas, president of the UAW-CIO, offered a program to prevent the recurrence of racial clashes. He asked for increased park and recreational facilities, additional housing for Negroes, an end of discrimination against Negroes in employment, and the appointment by Mayor Jeffries of a special biracial commission to make further recommendations for eliminating friction between white people and Negroes. This program was supported by the newspapers and by many civic leaders.

After calm had settled upon the city again and the troops had been withdrawn, Detroiters had time to consider the cost of the riots. Thirty-four persons—twenty-five Negroes and nine white men—had been killed, and more than a thousand had been wounded. More than eighteen hundred rioters had been arrested, and property to the value of $2,000,000 had been destroyed. These were ugly facts which made a deep impression on the people of Detroit. Some of the recommendations of R. J. Thomas were adopted as long-term plans. For the immediate future, tolerance, understanding, and good will were all important.

The interracial committee appointed by Mayor Jeffries, following Thomas's recommendation, worked quietly and effectively to improve conditions. Through pressure on city agencies and by a program of education, they accomplished a great deal. It is notable that no further racial outbreaks occurred in Detroit.

7

More than a year before the attack on Pearl Harbor, the President had called Michigan's National Guard into federal service. On October 15, 1940, the 32nd Division, composed of men from Michigan and Wisconsin, was ordered to mobilize. The 125th and 126th Infantry Regiments, the 107th Medical Regiment, the 107th Engineer Regiment, and the divisional aviation units were sent to Camp Beauregard, Louisiana, for intensive training.

In February, 1941, the 210th Antiaircraft Regiment was ordered to Fort Sheridan, Illinois, and in April the 182nd, the 119th, and the 177th Field Artillery regiments went to Fort Knox, Kentucky.

The 32nd Division, which had earned the name "Red Arrow" for its swift thrusts through the German positions in France during the First World War, this time was selected to fight in the Southwest Pacific. Having completed training, the division embarked in trans-

World War II—32nd Division in New Guinea

ports at San Francisco in April, 1942, and landed in South Australia. The next move was to Brisbane, on the east coast. New Guinea, north of Australia, was its battle destination.

The Japanese had taken the north shore of the eastern peninsula of New Guinea and were threatening Port Moresby, on the south shore facing Australia. If they should capture it, they would have a convenient base for the invasion of Australia. This threat had to be removed at all costs, for the Allies needed the great island continent as a base of operations for driving the Japanese out of the Western Pacific.

Beginning in September, 1942, the 32nd made contact with the enemy in New Guinea, fighting its way through steaming jungles and across the high and rugged Owen Stanley Mountains. After having helped to destroy the enemy in desperate jungle battles, the 32nd returned to Australia for a rest in April, 1943. General Douglas MacArthur commended the division for its magnificent conduct in battle.

The division was back in New Guinea in September, 1943. After the Japanese had been completely annihilated, the 32nd joined the United Nations' forces for the conquest of the Philippines. Landing first on Leyte in November, 1944, the division took part in liberating that island. Transported then to Luzon, the 32nd fought out the war in the mountainous northern part of the island. The division pushed the Japanese back step by step along the Villa Verde trail, so steep and rugged that armored bulldozers had to be used to make it into a road that could carry supplies. The 32nd was still in action when V-J Day was proclaimed.

After the war, the 32nd became the Wisconsin National Guard Division, and the new 46th Infantry Division was organized as Michigan's own National Guard unit. It had four times the strength of the prewar organization in the state.

During the war a total of 613,542 Michigan men served in the armed forces of the nation. More than two thirds passed through the draft boards composed of volunteers from the communities in which they sat. Working without salary, they performed invaluable services to their fellow citizens and to the nation. Although the law gave the boards little leeway in some cases, in others they had the power to defer men because they were working at jobs necessary for war production, because they were in college preparing for important war-related positions, because they were needed on the farms to increase food production, or because drafting them at the moment would cause hardship at home.

Besides the draft boards, there were many other civilian agencies which used the services of volunteers. Some served on rationing boards, others as civilian-defense workers, and still others made dressings and performed other tasks for the Red Cross. The United Service Organizations, engaged in providing entertainment and comforts for men on leave, gave opportunities to young and old to contribute according to their talents. Some served as hosts or hostesses, others baked cookies or worked in the canteens, and many girls were dancing partners for the boys at evening parties.

Thousands of persons cultivated Victory Gardens, sold war bonds and stamps, and helped collect scrap metal and waste paper. Boys and girls worked at these jobs too, and they gathered tons of milkweed pods. Floss from the pods was used to fill life jackets, which formerly had been stuffed with kapok. With the supply of kapok from Java cut off, the floss of the native weed was a valuable product. In Michigan, during the fall of 1943, boys and girls collected enough pods to produce 150,000 pounds of the processed floss.

Never in a previous war did so many women do so much. Besides serving in the civilian capacities mentioned above and working in factories, hundreds served as auxiliaries to the armed forces as WACS, WAVES, SPARS, and Women Marines. All volunteers, they helped the war effort by performing jobs from which men were released for combat duty.

Unusual precautions were adopted to protect war production centers from possible enemy air raids. Huge sirens screamed signals for practice drills, and night blackouts were ordered from time to time in order to judge if they would be effective in case of a raid. Fortunately, no hostile planes appeared, but two Japanese bombs landed in the state.

Fantastic as the idea may appear, the Japanese released thousands of balloons carrying bombs which they expected would land in the United States. Equipped with instruments to keep them in the prevailing west-to-east air currents, some of the balloons crossed the Pacific and actually dropped their bombs. One was found ten miles northwest of Detroit, where it had burned itself out harmlessly in an open field. The other, discovered near Grand Rapids, caused no damage either. It is believed that some of the forest fires in the northern part of the state may have been caused by balloon bombs. News that the bombs had fallen was not divulged until after V-J Day.

8

Higher education was indispensable for carrying on the war. Soldiers, sailors, marines, and airmen had to know much more than how to handle their weapons. Recognizing the necessity for an expansion of educational facilities, the United States Government sent thousands of officers and enlisted men to school. In Michigan every college and university participated in the huge war-training program. All of them accelerated their schedules, making earlier graduation possible by almost continuous terms throughout the year. All of them also put increased emphasis on scientific and technical courses. A great many sent their instructors to industrial cities to give intensive engineering courses to men employed in war work. Professors and their assistants carried on essential research in university laboratories, helping to develop the atom bomb and other new weapons.

College campuses swarmed with men in uniform as civilian students were drafted into the armed forces. Nearly every college had an Army Specialized Training group or a Navy V-5 or V-12 group. The larger ones had a great many. Michigan State College had AST units in engineering and one in area and language. Men in the latter were trained for special duties with the armies of occupation. In addition, Michigan State College trained more than five thousand Air Force Cadets.

At the University of Michigan there were the Judge Advocate General's School, the Army Japanese Language School, two Civil Affairs Training schools, the Reserve Officers' Naval Architecture Group, Navy V-12 students, and numerous AST groups. The total number of men in uniform trained during the war exceeded thirteen thousand.

After the war, veterans flocked to colleges and universities. Larger enrollments had followed every previous war, but the increase this time was much greater because of the financial aid provided for veterans by Congress.[4] Faculties, classrooms, laboratories, and dormitories were overburdened with the great influx. Quonset huts and other temporary housing had to be provided, especially for those who were married. Older than the traditional college student and matured by their war experience, the veterans were eager to complete their studies. As a rule they made better scholastic records than they had before leaving to serve in the armed forces.

President Truman announced the surrender of Japan on August 14, 1945. The war was over. Throughout the nation there was an immediate outburst of rejoicing. The people of Michigan relaxed in spontaneous celebrations. In every village and city, men, women, and children hastened to the downtown areas, cheering, laughing, shouting, jostling their way good-naturedly along crowded streets and sidewalks. Automobiles were engulfed in the seas of humanity. Traffic was completely deranged. These celebrations provided relief from the strains and worries and uncertainties of the long war years.

In Detroit it was estimated that half a million persons jammed downtown streets. One hundred thousand swarmed to Campau Square in the heart of Grand Rapids. In Battle Creek hundreds of convalescent soldiers from Percy Jones Hospital, many of them on crutches or in wheel chairs, joined the celebrating civilians. The Capitol grounds and surrounding streets in Lansing overflowed with noisy, happy people.

[4] In 1940 the enrollment in colleges and universities in Michigan was 57,752. In 1950, it was 122,801.

9

Even though co-operation in most activities was the rule during the war, partisan politics was as lively as ever. No one was surprised that there was little co-operation between Governor Murray D. Van Wagoner and the Republican Legislature in 1941. The two houses largely ignored his recommendations. On his part, he vetoed thirty-three of the bills sent to him for approval.

When the Republican leaders discovered that they could not muster the two thirds majority necessary to override his vetoes, they decided in July, 1941, to take a recess instead of adjourning. Convening again in October, they opened negotiations with the governor to find ground for a compromise. He agreed to permit the overriding of eleven appropriation vetoes, but he insisted that his policy-making vetoes stand, and they did.

Of the 382 laws passed, 116 had been given immediate effect by a two-thirds vote. In October the Legislature attempted to give immediate effect to fifty-five important acts. The state supreme court, however, held that the maneuver was unconstitutional; and so two thirds of the laws did not become effective until ninety days after the adjournment of the Legislature in October, more than a year after the beginning of the session.

Special sessions of the Legislature called by the governor in 1942 passed laws necessary for wartime. Appropriations were made to support civilian-defense measures, such as protection from air raids, emergency protection of state property, increasing the State Troops, and providing additional funds for the State Police.

In the 1942 election, Harry F. Kelly, a Republican who was secretary of state, defeated Governor Van Wagoner. All the executive offices in the state government were won by Republicans, and the party had a strong majority in the Legislature. A proposal that a constitutional convention be called was rejected by the voters.

The Reverend Gerald L. K. Smith entered the 1942 Republican senatorial primary, promising automobile tires for everybody. Because tires were rationed, this was attractive bait to the unthinking. He received 100,000 votes, insufficient to win the nomination. Undismayed by defeat, Smith organized the America First party. In the fall of 1943, after his candidates for city offices ran poorly in the Detroit election, he moved to Chicago.

The winner in the 1942 Republican senatorial primary was Judge Homer Ferguson of Detroit. He had attracted the attention of the voters by indicting more than two hundred persons in Wayne County while sitting as a grand juror, from 1939 to 1942, investigating vice and corruption. Among those convicted were former Mayor Richard W. Reading of Detroit, former Prosecutor Duncan C. McCrea, and former Sheriff Thomas C. Wilcox of Wayne County.

Judge Ferguson campaigned as a champion of clean government and as a friend of the farmer. The second point gave him an advantage over Senator Prentiss M. Brown, who was running for re-election. In September, while the campaign was in progress, Brown had made a powerful speech in the Senate against the farm lobbyists who were demanding higher prices for produce. Asserting that prices guaranteed to the farmer were fair, he predicted that the increase would upset the administration's efforts to maintain a balance between wages and prices. Editors and columnists praised the speech and denounced the lobbyists as selfish. Public opinion was aroused, and the lobby dropped its demand, but farmers felt that Senator Brown was unsympathetic to them. He was defeated in the election.

As a senator, Ferguson opposed New Deal legislation. He served as a member of the special Senate Committee Investigating the National Defense Program, generally known as the Truman Committee from its chairman, Senator Harry S. Truman. Later, as chairman of the investigating subcommittee of the Executive Expenditures Committee in the Eightieth Congress, he carried on most of the headline-making inquiries.

In January, 1943, President Roosevelt asked ex-Senator Brown to serve as director of the Office of Price Administration. After declining twice, Brown reluctantly accepted the appointment, promising to remain until the appropriation for the agency had been passed by Congress. His predecessor, Leon Henderson, had resigned in December because of illness, brought on in part by the bitter abuse that had been heaped upon him. The new director had the thankless task of trying to hold prices down and give everyone a fair share of gasoline, meat, shoes, coffee, sugar, butter, and other necessities.

Prices of meat, coffee, butter, and potatoes were rolled back in the interest of the consumer, and government subsidies were given to farmers, packers, and coffee dealers so that they could still make a profit. Ceiling prices were established, and President Roosevelt on April 8, 1943, ordered the OPA to "hold the line."

Director Brown was opposed from all directions. Ranchers in the West refused to sell their cattle at ceiling prices; merchants fought grade labeling and sold inferior goods at the ceiling price set for higher-quality products; consumers were bewildered by the numerous regulations and angered by the shortages of commodities; and Congress enacted laws which crippled the OPA program. Nevertheless, the price line was maintained. After the appropriation had been made and after the red-and-blue-point rationing system had been worked out, Brown resigned in October, 1943, and returned to Michigan to practice law. His successor was Chester Bowles.

10

Arthur H. Vandenberg, the senior senator from Michigan, was an influential leader of the isolationists in Congress. Although he had voted for the declaration of war and supported the President's war program, he was suspicious of Stalin's motives, and he opposed permanent co-operation in world affairs.

The senator was one of the leading Republicans invited by the national chairman to attend the 1943 Postwar Advisory Conference. Meeting at Mackinac Island in September, the group prepared resolutions which were intended as a platform for the party in the 1944 election. Senator Vandenberg was chairman of the Foreign Policy Committee.

A resolution which he drew up, providing for postwar co-operation by the United States with other nations, was considered too restrained by the more internationally minded members. Revising it, as they believed, to meet the needs of the times, they produced the statement which was finally agreed upon. The Republican party, it declared, was for "responsible participation by the United States in postwar co-operative organization among sovereign nations to prevent military aggression and to attain permanent peace with organized justice in a free world." This was an advanced stand for the Republicans. Senator Vandenberg supported it although it went beyond his position at the time.

Gradually, however, he came to recognize the necessity in the world of the 1940's and afterward for wholehearted international co-operation. His speech in the Senate on January 10, 1945, was a public announcement of his changed attitude. Urging a fair peace arrangement after our enemies had been defeated, he expressed the hope that the United Nations would stand together in peace as they had in war, and he advocated full co-operation of the United States in world affairs.

This speech won him recognition as leader of the Republicans on foreign policy, and President Roosevelt gratefully acknowledged his influence by consulting him on foreign affairs. Thus began the practice of the bipartisan development of foreign policies. Vandenberg's co-operation with the administration was of inestimable value, for it assured other nations that the United States Government, whether it was controlled by Democrats or Republicans, would continue after the war to participate actively in world affairs.

From this time onward Senator Vandenberg became a statesman of world-wide influence and reputation. President Roosevelt appointed him a delegate to the United Nations Conference on International Organization at San Francisco, where he had an important part in framing the charter of the United Nations. As a result of his influence, the charter was ratified by the Senate on July 28, 1945, by the overwhelming vote of 89 to 2.

Michigan showed that she was proud of her senior senator by returning him to his seat in the election of 1946 by a majority of 567,647 votes. Republicans had a majority in the Eightieth Congress, and Vandenberg was president pro tempore of the Senate and chairman of the powerful Foreign Relations Committee. Both were extremely important positions, the first more so than usual, because there was no Vice-President.[5]

In 1947 Vandenberg led the Senate in support of the President's Truman Doctrine, which promised "to support free peoples who are resisting attempted subjugation by armed minorities and by outside pressures." Congress expressed its approval by voting millions of dollars to strengthen Greece and Turkey against Communist threats.

Vandenberg also supported the Marshall Plan, suggested by Secretary of State George C. Marshall, by which the United States would advance money to help European nations help themselves through long-range programs of economic development.

In 1948, on motion by Vandenberg, the Senate invited the nations of western Europe to combine for mutual protection against any agressor. Twelve accepted the invitation, and Secretary of State Dean Acheson negotiated the North Atlantic Defense Treaty, which included the United States and Canada in the defense organization. Ratification by the Senate served notice on any would-be aggressor that the United States was ready to take the side of an intended victim.

In the preconvention presidential campaign of 1948, Vandenberg was the preferred candidate of the internationalists in the Republican party. Although he insisted that he did not want to run, men like

[5] President Roosevelt died on April 12, 1945, and Vice-President Harry S. Truman took the oath as President.

Senator Henry Cabot Lodge, Jr., of Massachusetts and Governor James H. Duff of Pennsylvania worked for his nomination. At the convention, Arthur E. Summerfield, national committeeman of Michigan, and Governor Kim Sigler held the Michigan delegation for Vandenberg until it was obvious that he could not be nominated. Vandenberg got what he wanted, the opportunity to write the foreign-policy plank for the party platform.

Governor Thomas E. Dewey of New York was nominated. He lost, but in Michigan, his native state, he defeated President Truman by 35,000 votes. Senator Homer Ferguson was re-elected by a majority of nearly 45,000 votes over his Democratic opponent, Frank E. Hook.

Senator Vandenberg became ill in 1949 and was frequently absent from his seat. Nevertheless he continued his fight to maintain bipartisanship in foreign policy and to keep the United States active in defending other nations against threatened Communist aggression. Sometimes he returned to the Senate against the advice of his physician. Finally he was confined to his bed, but he remained optimistic to the end. Only six weeks before his death, President Truman sent him a telegram expressing hope for his recovery, saying, "The country needs you." Senator Vandenberg replied: "I have abiding faith in the future of our good old U.S.A."[6] He died on April 18, 1951.

II

Two problems which faced the Michigan Legislature in 1943 were reapportionment and corruption. The first was the result of the movement toward the cities, increasing the population of the counties in the southeastern part of the state and decreasing it elsewhere. In spite of the constitutional provision which requires the Legislature to reapportion the seats in both houses after each national census, no change had been made since 1925.

The subsequent shift of population produced unfair representation. For example, in the Cheboygan District a member of the House represented 19,471 people; in the Ontonagon District one member represented 24,719; and in the Fourth District of Wayne County, one member represented 164,176. Having the advantage of overrepresentation, the counties with shrinking population were anxious to keep it.

Under pressure from Governor Harry F. Kelly, in 1943 the House reapportioned the seats, improving considerably the previous condition.

[6] Arthur H. Vandenberg, Jr., *The Private Papers of Senator Vandenberg* (Boston: Houghton Mifflin Company, 1952), pp. 577, 579.

Nearly half the districts were affected. Some counties which previously had had their own representative were combined with one or more counties and given only one representative for the group. The Upper Peninsula lost two seats, and counties in the Lower Peninsula lost ten. Of the twelve, six were given to Wayne County and six were distributed among Oakland, Genesee, Ingham, Macomb, and Washtenaw counties. The Senate ignored the constitutional requirement, refusing to reapportion, even though senatorial districts were as much out of balance as were those of the House.

The problem of corruption in the Legislature was attacked by a grand jury and the courts. In 1943 there was talk in Lansing that lobbyists were purchasing the votes of legislators. Attorney General Herbert J. Rushton petitioned the Ingham County Circuit Court for an inquiry into the charges of bribery. Judge Leland W. Carr was named grand juror to make the investigation, and Kim Sigler was appointed special prosecutor.

A key figure in the proceedings was Charles F. Hemans, a lobbyist-briber who turned state's evidence. In a little black book he had a record of payments which he had made to legislators from bankers, loan-company officers, race-track promoters, slot-machine owners, and others who wanted special favors. Sigler, the dramatic, crusading prosecutor, obtained the conviction of twenty defendants in 1944.

The investigation continued. Senator Warren G. Hooper of Albion was to testify before the grand juror on January 12, 1945, about the use of money to influence legislation on horse racing. On January 11 his bullet-riddled body was found in his burning car beside a lonely road. Three men were sent to prison for conspiring to have him murdered, but the killer was never found.

In September, 1945, Judge Carr was appointed to the State Supreme Court, and his place as grand juror was taken by Judge Louis E. Coash. In the spring of 1946, Judge Coash discharged Sigler and appointed Richard B. Foster special prosecutor. Three bankers and sixteen legislators were indicted, but they were not tried because Hemans suddenly refused to testify. Then he fled the state. Arrested by federal authorities, he was tried and convicted of crossing the state line to avoid serving as a witness. After a term in federal prison, he pleaded guilty to a charge of bribery in Michigan.

Hemans still refused to give testimony, and the bank cases were dropped. Although of the 125 men indicted by the grand juror only forty-six were convicted, the political careers of many legislators were ruined, and the reputations of some businessmen were tarnished. The fate of those caught in the grand-jury net was a grim warning to others who might in the future be tempted to buy special privileges or to sell their votes.

In 1944 President Franklin D. Roosevelt ran for a fourth term. Because the war was still being fought, many persons who otherwise would have been against him favored his re-election. In Michigan he defeated Governor Thomas E. Dewey of New York by 22,476 votes. Governor Harry F. Kelly was re-elected, the first incumbent in fourteen years to succeed himself in the office of chief executive. The Republicans won all the state offices and a majority of seats in both houses of the Legislature and in Congress.

In 1946, Kim Sigler, the colorful prosecutor of the legislators and businessmen who had been indicted by the grand juror, won the Republican nomination for governor. Formerly a Democrat himself, he defeated former Governor Murray D. Van Wagoner by 350,000 votes.

At the same election the voters added two amendments to the constitution. One provided a bonus for returning veterans. The other required that one third of the proceeds from the sales tax be diverted to local governments and to school districts. The amendment in addition directed that each year a large portion of the sales tax collected by the state during the previous year also be distributed to the schools. By this means, residents of cities, villages, and school districts threw the burden of supporting their schools upon the state instead of assuming a larger responsibility themselves.

Governor Sigler laid before the Legislature a number of recommendations for improving the government of the state. He asked for constitutional amendments to increase to four years the terms of the governor and the principal administrative officers, to empower the governor to appoint the attorney general and the secretary of state, and to give the legislature the authority to fix salaries.

Even though the governor called the legislators into special sessions, these recommendations were rejected. The Legislature did, however, enact part of his program. It consolidated some state agencies, and it established the Department of Administration which he had demanded as a means of centralizing management of state affairs in the hands of the governor.

The Department of Administration began to function in August, 1948. Headed by the controller, who is appointed by the governor, the Department supervises and regulates all state administrative activities. It prepares and administers the budget, controls purchasing, and watches over the uniform accounting system. By co-ordinating the work of numerous agencies, it can increase their efficiency and promote economy. The Department of Administration gives the governor the means for managing state affairs.

Governor Sigler's wrangles with the Legislature split his party, and his extensive travels during his term made many persons believe that he was neglecting the business of the state. When he ran for re-election in 1948, G. Mennen Williams, the Democratic candidate, defeated him by 163,854 votes, while Governor Dewey won a majority over President Truman in the state.

12

Governor Williams was thirty-seven years old. After being graduated from Princeton and the University of Michigan Law School with honors, he had entered government service as a career. He was assistant attorney general of Michigan in 1938, and in 1939 he became executive assistant to United States Attorney General Frank Murphy. From 1942 until 1946 Williams served as an air combat intelligence officer in the Navy, rising from lieutenant (j.g.) to lieutenant commander. In 1946 and 1947 he was deputy director of the office of Price Administration in Michigan, and during the next two years he was a member of the State Liquor Control Commission. Williams was a liberal. He was supported by New Dealers in general and by labor organizations.

Besides the governor, in 1948 only two other Democrats were elected to office—John W. Connolly, lieutenant governor; and Stephen J. Roth, attorney general. The Legislature was controlled by the Republicans.

The people approved an amendment which empowered the Legislature to fix the salaries of legislators and of state officers. They voted down, however, a proposal on the ballot for calling a convention to revise the constitution.

Governor Williams and the Legislature spent a great deal of time sparring for political advantage. The legislators rejected the governor's request for a fair employment practices law, state-subsidized housing, stricter control over public utilities, repeal of restrictive labor legislation, and a corporation profits tax.

Constructive enactments of the Legislature included laws protecting lakes and streams from pollution, increasing unemployment and workmen's compensation, raising payments for old age assistance and for aid to dependent children, and reviving the Straits of Mackinac Bridge

Authority. Both the governor and the Legislature claimed credit for these acts.

Governor Williams did not wait until 1950 to begin campaigning for re-election. During his whole term he traveled tirelessly throughout the state, carrying his program to the people. No town was too distant, and no audience too small. He was always ready to make a speech, to crown a queen, or to call the figures for a square dance. His friendly smile won him many votes. Even the legislators who opposed his policies were willing to follow his lead as dancing master.

Early on the morning of May 5, 1949, both houses of the Legislature were waiting for the report of a conference committee so that they could vote and adjourn. In session since 10 o'clock of the previous morning, they were sleepy and quarrelsome. At 3:30 A.M., Governor Williams appeared in the House. Throwing off his coat, he invited everyone to dance. Weary legislators, Republicans and Democrats alike, lined up with lady visitors, and the governor put them through the figures of a square dance. Music was provided by the Senate Republican floor leader at the piano, an unusual example of legislative-executive harmony.

The Republicans chose former Governor Harry F. Kelly to oppose Williams in 1950. When the votes were counted, Kelly had a majority of 6,108. While the Democrats were considering asking for a recount, the official tally was made. Williams led Kelly by 1,154 votes. The Republicans demanded a recount. As the days passed, Williams' majority steadily increased. After more than three fourths of the precincts had been counted, Kelly conceded the victory to Williams.

G. Mennen Williams was the first Democrat after Woodbridge N. Ferris to win two terms as governor. His victory was a personal triumph, for the other Democrats on the state ticket were defeated. Again Republicans dominated the Legislature, and the governor knew that his program would find little favor there.

13

As the war drew to a close, the word "reconversion" was frequently used in the newspapers and in conversation. Everyone wanted to return to peacetime conditions as soon as possible. After V-J Day there was an overwhelming demand that soldiers and sailors be returned home and that restrictions on the national economy be removed. Consumers were anxious to buy all sorts of goods, and manufacturers were eager to supply the market quickly.

The automobile industry was particularly desirous to begin production. Since February, 1942, not a single car had been made for civilian use, and dealers had long lists of impatient customers. Reconversion was not easy. Plants had to be cleared of machinery used to manufacture war equipment, new machines had to be set up, and materials had to be procured. Shortages of everything were serious.

Besides, there were labor troubles. Strikes occurred in numerous industries, further restricting the output of essential parts for cars. The longest and most serious for Michigan was the strike of the UAW-CIO against General Motors. Beginning on November 21, 1945, it was not settled until March 13, 1946. Officials of General Motors steadfastly refused to grant wage demands which they believed to be unreasonable. Finally the corporation and the union leaders compromised on an increase of 18½ cents an hour and liberal vacation allowances. Chrysler and Ford avoided strikes by giving their men higher wages.

The situation at Ford's attracted widespread interest because Henry Ford II had recently succeeded his grandfather as president of the company. Unlike his father, Edsel, Henry II had had a college education. Attending Yale from 1936 to 1940, he had majored in sociology. Then he went to work in the Ford factory. When the war began, Henry II entered the Navy as an ensign and served until his father died in 1943.

Released from the Navy, Henry II was made vice-president of the Ford Motor Company in charge of sales and promotion. His grandfather resumed the office of president which he had conferred on Edsel some years earlier. The founder of the company, however, was becoming too old to direct the business, and so in 1944 Henry II was made executive vice-president. On September 1, 1945, he was promoted to president.

Immediately he began to reorganize the company. One of his first actions was the dismissal of Harry Bennett, director of administration, who for many years had been Henry Ford's aide and strong-arm man. Promotions were made within the organization and able men were brought in from outside. Henry II also began disposing of experimental farms and other properties which had little or nothing to do with the making of automobiles.

The dethronement of Bennett was in keeping with Henry II's publicly expressed interest in improving human relations in industry. He was not an easy mark, however. Before the union leaders presented their demands in November, he issued a statement charging that the union had not kept its part of the contract with the Ford Motor Company. The new president demanded that the union accept full responsibility for performance in return for any advantages which might be given.

Although Walter P. Reuther, first vice-president of the UAW-CIO, replied angrily to the charge, he agreed to negotiate. Instead of the 30 per cent increase in wages which he demanded, Ford granted 15 per cent, and Reuther promised that there would be no strikes.

Automobile production in 1945, because of the shortages of materials and the difficulties of reconversion, was only 70,000 passenger cars. The next year, however, the number rose to 2,149,000. The General Motors strike, strikes against the suppliers of parts, and shortages of materials kept the output far below the total of 3,779,682 in 1941, the last year of production before the war. The demand was still much greater than the supply of cars.

A new automobile manufacturing company was organized in 1945. One of the founders was Joseph W. Frazer, chairman of the Graham-Paige Corporation, which had built cars until 1940. The other founder was Henry J. Kaiser, a West Coast industrialist. During the war he built ships for the government.

After the production of planes was halted in the Willow Run bomber plant, the Kaiser-Frazer Company took it over. Two cars named for the founders, the Kaiser and the Frazer, were manufactured.

In 1946 there was a dual celebration in Detroit. One was the Automobile Golden Jubilee, which marked the fiftieth anniversary of the first appearance of automobiles on the streets. The other commemorated the sesquicentennial of Detroit as an American town.

For the first, leaders of the industry assembled in Detroit and chose fourteen of the pioneers whose names would be inscribed in the Automotive Hall of Fame. Among them were Charles B. King and Henry Ford, who had built and driven their cars in Detroit in 1896. Both were present at the Jubilee, which continued from May 29 until June 11. The most spectacular event was the Motor City Cavalcade, which included magnificent floats and 245 early automobiles. Chugging along over the asphalt pavement of Woodward Avenue, which had been sprayed with gold paint for the occasion, the old cars received most of the attention of the thousands of spectators.

The principal feature of the sesquicentennial observance was a colorful pageant entitled "Song of Our City—the Saga of Detroit." Elaborately staged in Olympia, the pageant consisted of tableaux, scenes, ballets, and choruses depicting the history of Detroit from the day of its founding by Cadillac until it had become a great industrial city.

The production of automobiles increased year by year. In 1947 it was more than three and a half million; in 1948, nearly four million; and in 1949, more than five million. Besides cars, more than a million trucks were built each year.

New labor-management contracts were due to be negotiated in 1949. Philip Murray, president of the CIO and of the United Steel Workers of America, demanded that the United States Steel Corporation raise wages and pay for pensions and insurance for their workmen. When the corporation refused and Murray threatened to call a strike, President Truman asked for a sixty-day truce and appointed a factfinding board to recommend a settlement. The board rejected the wage demand as unjustified, but approved the idea of a contribution by the corporation to a pension and insurance fund. It expressed the opinion that industry should provide for the depreciation of the human machine just as it had always done for its buildings and machinery.

The steel industry was slow to accept the recommendation; but when Walter P. Reuther, president of the UAW-CIO, reminded Henry Ford II that it was time to make a new contract, it was signed within ten days. Included in it was a plan by which men who had worked for thirty years might retire at the age of sixty-five with a pension of $100 a month, including social security annuities. Medical and hospital benefits were given also. Other manufacturing companies gradually adopted the policy. American workmen could look forward with less anxiety to their years of retirement.

Walter P. Reuther had been elected president of the UAW-CIO in 1946. After the end of the war, as first vice-president, he had led a faction in the union which opposed Communists who were trying to take control. In 1947, he moved swiftly against the radical group and forced out all its leaders. On April 20, 1948, he was severely wounded by shots fired through the window of his home. Although the would-be killer was never apprehended, it was believed that he was a Communist or in the pay of the party.

Prosperity in the automotive industry continued, especially for the Big Three—General Motors, Chrysler, and Ford. Some of the smaller manufacturers found it difficult to meet the wage increases and other benefits which had been given to the workmen. During 1950 production reached a new high point with an output of 6,673,000 passenger cars and 1,337,154 trucks. In spite of high wages and high taxes, profits in 1950 were also the highest in the history of the industry.

The Korean War, which began on June 25, 1950, made necessary the sending of American troops, along with those of others of the

United Nations, to drive out the North Korean aggressors. With Soviet Russia obviously aiding the North Koreans, many feared that a third world war might be precipitated. As a result production in every field was increased to meet the threat.

Production of iron ore after the war fell to 8,477,425 tons in 1946, then rallied to an average of about 11,000,000 tons a year. A gradual working out of high-grade ore, and increasing costs of bringing it up from mines which go deeper and deeper, caused the mining companies to turn to the vast deposits of low-grade ore in the Upper Peninsula.

Research engineers of the Cleveland-Cliffs Company discovered an ingenious method of separating the particles of metal from the rock which contains it. The low-grade ore will be dug from open pits, which are less expensive to operate than mines with deep shafts. Using the process which has been perfected, the iron will be recovered and prepared for the blast furnaces. Since it is estimated that there are two billion tons of low-grade ore in the Upper Peninsula, iron mining will continue to be an important Michigan industry.

The future of copper mining is not so certain. After the war, Calumet and Hecla was the principal producer. The output of Michigan mines in 1946 was 43,326,000 pounds, less than half the total in 1943. Because the price of copper fell in 1949, Calumet and Hecla shut down its mines.

Calumet and Hecla and the Copper Range Company own great areas of land in the Upper Peninsula. Exploration by their geologists has shown large deposits of low-content copper. If future demand for the metal raises the price sufficiently, those deposits will be exploited.

At present a great new copper mining development is under way in the Ontonagon region. Aided by a Reconstruction Finance Corporation loan of $57,000,000, the White Pine Copper Company, a subsidiary of the Copper Range Company, is preparing to attack the world's largest known deposit of the metal. Before starting to mine, the company will build a railroad and a town complete with churches, schools, and stores. About 1,500 men will be employed. The mine is expected to yield 70,000,000 pounds of copper a year, and it is estimated that operations can continue for half a century. If this prediction comes true, Michigan will continue to be an important producer of copper.

14

Each decade of the period 1920 to 1950 can be pretty well characterized by a short phrase. In the 1920's it was "prosperity and speculation"; in the 1930's, "depression and recovery"; in the 1940's, "hot war and cold war."

During the middle years of the twenties prosperity was general, except among farmers. The manufacture of automobiles increased enormously. The production of petroleum had its beginning, and the industry expanded until by 1950 there were 3,818 oil wells, most of them in the cutover area of the Lower Peninsula.

The population of the state increased, and the trend toward urban districts continued. In 1950, only about 30 per cent of the people lived in the country. Because of restrictions on immigration, the number of foreign-born decreased, but that loss was more than made up by the number of Negroes who settled in the state.

A significant development in education was the improvement of vocational training in the public schools. This was made possible by the aid of federal funds under the Smith-Hughes Act of 1917. Another improvement was the consolidating of small school districts into larger ones. By combining their resources, they provide modern buildings with adequate equipment for broader education. They are able, also, to engage more competent teachers. In 1950 three thousand buses were used to carry nearly two hundred thousand pupils to school.

The number of students attending colleges and universities in Michigan more than quadrupled. In 1920 the enrollment was 30,000; in 1950, 122,000. Among the reasons for the increase were more-widespread prosperity, a realization of the need for higher education, and the financial support given by Congress to veterans who wanted to attend college.

The Republicans had complete political control of the state in the 1920's. During more than half the decade Alex J. Groesbeck was governor. His three terms were notable for the beginning of an extensive concrete-road building program, for reapportionment of seats in the Legislature, and for the organization of the Administrative Board as a centralizing agency of state government.

The stock market crash in October, 1929, put an end to wild speculation which had absorbed a great share of the nation's credit. There followed a gradual economic decline which became the depression of the 1930's. Among the causes were unbridled speculation, a high protective tariff, easy credit, and faulty distribution of the national income. Mass production could not be sustained because too large a share of the proceeds was taken by too few persons.

As a highly industrialized state, Michigan suffered quickly and severely from the depression. The chronic distress of the farmers contributed to the gravity of the situation. Factories shut down, the unemployed searched in vain for work, and farms were sold for delinquent taxes or because the owners could not meet payments on mortgages. The closing of all the banks in Michigan on February 14, 1933, set the pattern for other states and for the nation as well.

Because of the great decline in property values, the Legislature in 1933 replaced the state property tax by a tax on retail sales. The people of Michigan by referendum and by a convention repealed their own prohibition amendment and helped to repeal the Eighteenth Amendment to the Constitution of the United States.

In 1932, for the first time since 1852, Michigan gave all its electoral votes to a Democrat for President. Besides giving a majority to Franklin D. Roosevelt, the voters elected William A. Comstock, a Democrat, governor. He was conservative, but Frank Murphy, also a Democrat, who was governor from 1937 to 1939, was a liberal and a New Dealer.

To the dismay of conservatives, Murphy, as mayor of Detroit, permitted radicals to hold public meetings, and he spent public funds for relief of the jobless. As governor, he refused to order the National Guard to drive sit-down strikers from automobile factories. During his career, he held more high offices in the government of the state and of the United States than any other native of Michigan.

Michigan industrialists in general were hostile to unions of workingmen. During the 1930's, however, encouraged by acts of Congress, unions developed rapidly in Michigan. The CIO became powerful enough to win recognition for itself and to improve conditions for factory workers.

Slum clearance and public housing programs were initiated in the 1930's. Considerable progress was made, especially in Detroit.

World War II dominated the decade of the 1940's. Although the United States remained neutral, at least in name, until the attack on Pearl Harbor, industrial plants expanded their capacity to produce weapons for the nations of western Europe. Preparations by our own government for national defense immensely increased production. Michigan led all the states in turning out materials for war.

Senator Arthur H. Vandenberg became the leading Republican exponent of bipartisan collaboration in formulating foreign policy. Although he was urged by powerful leaders of his party to run for President in 1948, he made no attempt to win the nomination. Senator Vandenberg helped draw up the Charter of the United Nations, and he participated in the first session of the organization. To the end of his life, he maintained that collective security, founded on co-operation among nations, was the only means of preventing another world war. The cold war of threats, sabotage, internal upheavals, and plots against western nations carried on by the Soviet government of Russia emphasized the wisdom of Senator Vandenberg's stand. Thus far united action has prevented war. If war comes, united action should provide strength enough to destroy the power that desires to enslave the world.

30

The Fabulous Fifties

THE 1950's were notable for more remarkable changes than any other similar period in history. In the Western world, especially in the United States, economic conditions improved immensely. Americans had more of everything—more houses, with a television aerial on nearly every roof, more money, more leisure, more cars, and more churches. Automation in factories and offices relieved men and women of much of the drudgery of labor, and frozen foods were a boon to busy housewives.

Scientific developments were amazing. In medicine the Salk vaccine promised to eliminate the scourge of polio, new drugs to alleviate mental illness were discovered, and isotopes were successfully used in combating cancer. Atomic reactors were constructed to generate electric current, and nuclear-powered submarines proved the practicality of adapting atomic energy to maritime transportation. Jet-propelled aircraft cut in half the time distance between cities, and space capsules carrying complex electronic devices were put into orbit around the earth.

Some evidences of better international relations occurred in the decade of the 1950's. The United Nations, although sometimes racked by violent dissension in the Assembly and by crippling vetoes in the Security Council, continued to provide a useful means of communication and achieved some important results. In 1957-1958, the International Geophysical Year, nations of the world cooperated in the greatest scientific program ever devised to study all sorts of physical phenomena. In Europe, former enemies joined in the Iron and Steel Community and the Common Market to improve economic conditions and to reduce bitter competition which might lead to war.

Another sort of cooperation, begun in the late 1940's, became routine. The United States Government provided funds for rehabilitating its former enemies, Japan and West Germany, assisting them to attain a prosperity they had never known before. Besides, billions of dollars were poured into nations whose people were in distress. One purpose was to aid in the improvement of their economic systems so that they could help themselves; the other was to align them with the West and to prevent their falling under the influence of the Soviet government.

The cold war, continued from the 1940's by Josef Stalin and his successor, Nikita Khrushchev, cast a pall over much of the world. In poverty-stricken nations, Soviet propaganda was potent. To counteract it, vast expenditures were made by nations of the West, sometimes with satisfying results. A few rulers, sensing a splendid opportunity, accepted generous gratuities from both sides.

The Soviet government made great technological strides, aided by some defectors from Germany, the United States, and Great Britain. Many Americans became panic-stricken in 1950 when Senator Joseph R. McCarthy of Wisconsin made the sensational charge that Communists in government service were shaping the policy of the United States. For five years, his virulent attacks on individuals and organizations resulted in Senate investigations, witch hunts, and widespread reluctance to speak the truth for fear of being persecuted as a dangerous person. Finally sanity returned, men began to talk back, and in December, 1954, the Senate passed a resolution condemning McCarthy's conduct. Although this action halted his campaign of vilification, a sense of insecurity persisted for a time.

This feeling was revived when on October 5, 1957, the Russians launched the first earth satellite and repeated the performance in November. Surprise, shock, and chagrin were mingled in the reaction of Americans. Recognizing the propaganda value to Russia of proclaiming to the world the technical proficiency of the Soviet system, they castigated their own government for its tardiness in scientific achievement. To some degree their pride was salved when Explorer I was blasted into orbit on January 31, 1958.

In addition to primacy in orbiting satellites, the Russians claimed to have intercontinental ballistic missiles capable of striking any city in the United States. Our intermediate missiles, based at strategic points around the world for unleashing against the Soviet Union, gave some feeling of satisfaction, but our ICBM program was behind schedule.

The cold war was punctuated by the sudden unprovoked attack of Communist North Koreans against South Korea on June 25, 1950. Trained and supplied by the Russians, the northerners expected quickly to overwhelm their feeble neighbor. South Korea, as a ward of the United Nations, appealed for assistance. President Harry S. Truman, acting for the world organization, immediately threw American soldiers into the conflict. Other nations sent troops, but the United States provided the major strength and suffered the heaviest losses, especially after the Red Chinese began the war anew when the North Koreans had been defeated. An uneasy truce was arranged in 1953, and the fighting ceased. This war disclosed a new source of danger, the unscrupulous Communist government of China, which was growing in power and in ability to coerce weak nations in Asia.

Although Khrushchev alternated between vows to destroy the United States and suggestions that the proper sphere for competition was not war but economic development, the Red Chinese made constant threats against the security of the Western world. Throughout the decade the United States was the leader of the West in the unrelenting contest with the Communist nations.

In the United States the decade was marked by great prosperity and a serious recession. Economic well-being reached new heights, based to a great extent on production for defense. Wages, salaries, and dividends increased so that, it was estimated, 51 per cent of the families in the nation had incomes of more than $5,000 a year. High purchasing power made possible the sale of 7,950,000 automobiles in 1955. Children remained in school longer than before, and college enrollments rose. With more money to spend, families moved from cities to new suburban areas.

An adverse economic reaction occurred in 1957 and continued through 1958 and 1959. When overproduction caused shutdowns and slowdowns in factories, unemployment insurance helped relieve distress, but recovery was slow. It was significant that in spite of greater output up to 1957, employment declined. Automation, temporarily at least, was throwing men out of work both in factories and offices.

In the United States there was internal strife which had international repercussions. An opinion of the Supreme Court in 1954 held that segregated schools were illegal and the Court ordered that integration of white and colored pupils be effected "with all deliberate speed." Southerners resented this intrusion into their domain and asserted the right to retain their traditional social system. In some states public schools were closed, and in Little Rock, Arkansas, by order of the governor, soldiers of the National Guard prevented colored children from entering white schools. To enforce the order of the Court, President Dwight D. Eisenhower sent federal troops to Little Rock. Gradually, and with great deliberation, some Negroes were admitted to white schools in several states, but the problem was not solved during the 1950's.

Trouble occurred also because of orders to end segregation in hotels, restaurants, buses, parks, and other public facilities. Southerners were responsible for most of the offenses, but Northerners were not without blame in the matter of segregation, especially in preventing Negroes from purchasing houses wherever they wanted to live. This strife over the rights of a minority caused embarrassment to the United States Government in its endeavors to induce the colored peoples of Asia and Africa to align themselves with the West instead of with the Communist nations.

In spite of having more money and more goods than ever, Americans were not content. During this decade of sudden change and fearsome threats, many suffered from feelings of anxiety and confusion. This condition resulted partly from multiplication of the means of communication. More persons than in previous periods not only read and heard of catastrophes at home and abroad, but they also saw disturbing scenes on television. Having a great deal to lose, they had a sense of insecurity, wondering how long peace and prosperity would continue.

The people of Michigan, of course, were affected by all the national and international developments. For example, there were 4,900 casualties from Michigan in the Korean War. The recession of 1957–1958 reduced the production of automobiles, increased unemployment, and laid a heavy burden on welfare funds, because of the importance to the economy of the state of the automobile industry. On account of the movement to suburban areas, some cities lost population and found their revenues from taxation decreasing.

Michigan suffered from some severe disasters during this decade. On February 8, 1951, a fire broke out in the State Office Building in

Lansing. Burning for several days, it nearly destroyed the two top stories. The remainder of the seven-story building was severely damaged by smoke and water. An irremedial loss was the destruction of many state records. Besides appropriating funds for repairing the building and constructing another, the Legislature provided for a fireproof records and archives center.

Unlike many other states, Michigan fortunately had been spared recurring destruction by violent forces of nature. During the 1950's, however, tornadoes plagued many areas in the southern part of the lower peninsula. The first struck Port Huron on May 21, 1953. This was a sort of prelude. On June 8, six tornadoes whirled across the state causing numerous fatalities and great property damage. Four persons were killed near Erie, four at Tawas City, and one at Brown City. The severest loss was at Flint, where 200 homes were destroyed and 116 persons were killed, 28 of them children. Nearly 1,000 were hurt and the loss in property was $10,000,000.

Governor G. Mennen Williams dispatched state police and members of the National Guard to the devastated area, and he hastened to the scene, where he took command in person. The American Red Cross set up two shelters to feed and house the homeless. Hospitals in Flint were crowded with injured. In the National Guard armory, which served as a temporary morgue, hundreds of persons searched for missing relatives. To aid the sufferers, funds were contributed by the Red Cross, the United States Government, General Motors Corporation, and the UAW-CIO. Most of the houses destroyed had been occupied by families of workers in Flint factories.

After the area had been cleared of debris, rebuilding began. Much of the work was done by volunteers who contributed their varied skills without compensation. Forty-five hundred men, it was estimated, cooperated in this reconstruction project, laboring for the most part during weekends. Women also helped, especially with painting and decorating, and children carried water for the thirsty workers. "Operation Tornado," as it was called, was a magnificent example of community service.

Some persons in Michigan and elsewhere blamed atomic explosions for causing the numerous tornadoes in various parts of the country. The chief of the scientific division of the United States Weather Bureau denied the connection. In proof he pointed out that more destructive tornadoes had occurred before atomic experiments were conducted, and he asserted that an ordinary thunderstorm expends energy five to ten times as great as that of an atom bomb.

Three years later, the state was again lashed by tornadoes. On the evening of April 3, 1956, three roared across the counties of Kent, Ottawa, Allegan, Barry, Manistee, Benzie, Leelanau, and Grand Traverse. Most of the damage was done in the Grand Rapids area where Standale, Hudsonville, Leonard Heights, and Comstock Park were in the direct path of one. Standale suffered the greatest destruction, its business district being nearly wiped out. In rural areas houses and barns were smashed and many animals were killed. Eighteen persons died, and property damage was estimated at $6,000,000.

State police, National Guardsmen, local police, the Red Cross, and Civil Defense volunteers were mobilized to assist the injured and the homeless. Especial commendation was given to the Civil Defense personnel who were in action for the first time. Previous training enabled them to move quickly to the sites where aid was necessary with ambulances and station wagons to remove the injured and the homeless. Leaders assigned volunteers with special skills to the repairing of damaged houses on which they worked without compensation. The orderliness of the operation illustrated what trained civilians could do in case of an attack by enemy bombs.

Six weeks later, on May 13, twenty tornadoes whipped the state in places far apart—Menominee in the Upper Peninsula; Allen Park and Lincoln Park, both suburbs of Detroit; and Flint, to name the most damaged localities. Although property damage was great and many were injured, only six persons were killed.

The centennial of the Soo Canal was observed by a summer-long program of activities at Sault Sainte Marie in 1955. Every evening a pageant called the Centurama was presented, and there were parades and displays of fireworks. In Pullar Stadium the International Exposition featured exhibits relating to marine transportation. Three early residences were opened as museums; the Indian Agency, built in 1827 and occupied by Henry R. Schoolcraft, Indian agent, and later by Charles T. Harvey, general agent in charge of operations for the company which built the first locks; the John Johnston home, erected in 1795; and the house of Father Frederick Baraga. Local ladies in century-old costumes served as guides. Security restrictions were relaxed so that visitors might have a close view of the four great locks as they look today.

A great achievement was the building of the Mackinac Bridge under the direction of the Mackinac Bridge Authority appointed by Governor G. Mennen Williams in 1950. Prentiss M. Brown, formerly United States Senator, was chairman of the Authority; and David B. Steinman was the designer and consulting engineer. Erected at a cost of $100,000,000, the bridge links the two peninsulas of Michigan, connecting Mackinaw City with St. Ignace. A picture appears between pages 494 and 495.

Many difficulties had to be overcome. Envisioned years ago as a desirable project, engineers and geologists had reported that the underwater rock formation was not solid enough to support the tremendous weight of a bridge. Only in 1951, after the conditions had again been thoroughly investigated, did experts present conclusive proof of the feasibility of proceeding. The problem of raising funds for construction was solved when the Legislature gave the Authority permission to issue revenue bonds.

Beginning work in 1954, contractors laid the foundations 206 feet below the lake level and raised on them the main towers to a height of 552 feet above the water. They completed the work in 1957. The total length of the suspension bridge, including anchorages, is 8,614 feet, the longest in the world. The center suspension span, 3,800 feet, is the second longest. With the approaches, the bridge is 5 miles long. Required to be high enough to permit passage of the largest lake vessels, the height at the center is 148 feet. A roadway 48 feet wide provides space for four lanes of traffic. The bridge was opened in November, 1957, and official dedication ceremonies were held in June, 1958. Tolls are collected to provide revenue to retire the bonds. During the first full year of operation, income was over $5,000,000, more than enough to meet the annual interest charge of $4,200,000.

This magnificent bridge, beautiful as well as useful, is the fulfillment of a long-time desire to unite the two peninsulas with a convenient connection. Previously, five state-owned ferries shuttled back and forth across the straits carrying automobiles, buses, and trucks. It was a pleasant fifty-minute trip in fair weather, but when tourist travel was heavy and during the hunting season, cars waited in line for two or three hours or more. Besides, during the winter, ice sometimes blocked the passage. Cars cross the bridge in ten minutes.

2

The population of Michigan increased from 6,371,766 in 1950 to 7,823,194 in 1960, a gain of nearly 23 per cent, greater than that of any of the other states of the Old Northwest. During the first half of the decade the rate of rise was rapid, exceeded only by that of California and Florida. Then a decline began. A research study indicated that in

1957–1958 a loss of approximately 90,000 occurred in migration to other states, and it was estimated that 100,000 probably left in 1958–1959. The cause was the reduction in manpower needs of the automobile and associated industries, especially during the 1957–1958 recession. Nevertheless, natural increase by births in the decade was sufficient to offset loses by death and migration and to show an increase in 1960.

In previous decades, the trend had been from rural regions to the cities, especially the larger ones. To almost everyone's surprise, the Census of 1960 proved that the larger cities lost rather than gained population. The movement out of the cities was not to farms but to fringe areas outside the city limits. Reasons were the great increase in births, overcrowded schools, insufficient parking places, and high taxes levied to pay for extending utilities and constructing schools.

High wages and easy home financing made possible the building of houses in areas where the owners were liable for only county and township taxes. Many city services were lacking. Often there were no paved streets, inadequate water mains, little fire or police protection, and no public lighting. Schools were seldom adequate. Shopping, however, was more convenient because supermarkets and even large centers were established to accommodate the people in the growing communities. In addition, the stores attracted many residents of the cities and thus were in part responsible for the decay of downtown retail business sections. Some observers viewed with dismay this exodus of middle-class families, declaring that cities were losing their most stable and intelligent element. Although they earned their living in the cities, they lived outside and accepted no responsibility for the deterioration which they had helped to create.

Unfortunately for those who withdrew from cities to escape high taxes, fringe settlements frequently developed into cities, at least in size. Some of them incorporated and accepted the duties of heavily populated areas. Even if they did not incorporate, the inhabitants had to pay for necessary services. Taxes were increased to provide for health, safety, and school facilities. Unless the new community had industries within its limits, the cost was likely to be excessive. A study of urbanized townships in the Flint area showed that government costs multiplied twenty times after the population density grew. One of the disadvantages which suburbanites had tried to escape had overtaken them.

Residents of the old cities also were unhappy. Not only was their pride injured, but also their pocketbooks. Because payments to the cities by the state from receipts of the sales tax, the intangibles tax, the gasoline tax, and the weight tax were based on a head count, income was cut drastically in some cases. Detroit, for example, lost 179,424 inhabitants, or 9 per cent of its 1950 population, resulting in an annual reduction of $2,000,000 in revenue from the state.

The 1960 Census showed that the population of Saginaw, Jackson, Pontiac, Monroe, Battle Creek, Muskegon, and Port Huron was smaller than in 1950. Flint gained enough residents to promote it to second place ahead of Grand Rapids, which had added only 798 persons in ten years.[1] A few other old cities, including Lansing, Ann Arbor, and Midland showed appreciable gains—17, 34, and 93 per cent respectively. Two new cities which had developed from fringe settlements, Livonia in Wayne County and Oak Park in Oakland, had phenomenal growth. The former nearly quadrupled its 1950 population and the latter had a sevenfold increase. The older cities, seeing their revenue from property taxes and state aid declining, discharged employees, reduced services, and considered taxing the wages and salaries of all persons working within their corporate limits to obtain needed revenue.

Increases in county population, especially in the southern part of the Lower Peninsula, emphasized the exodus from the cities. For example, Wayne County, outside Detroit, grew by 69 per cent, Oakland by 74 per cent, and Macomb by 119 per cent. Washtenaw, Monroe, and Livingston counties also showed large growth. Some experts asserted that the only solution to the problem of providing services on an equitable basis in the heavily populated regions is to combine the numerous municipal governments into a few authorities having jurisdiction over wide areas.

In the Upper Peninsula the total population increased, but eight counties had fewer residents than in 1950. Houghton County alone lost four thousand people.

3

Education during the 1950's was a topic of lively interest. Increased enrollment in schools and colleges required more tax money for buildings and teachers. Critics charged, as they had in earlier years, that educators by adding all sorts of unnecessary subjects had raised the cost of education and had softened the curriculum so that pupils completing high school had no sound basis of knowledge. Especially after

[1] After the Census was taken, Grand Rapids annexed territory with sufficient inhabitants to raise it again to second place. Some other cities increased their population by annexing fringe areas. By this means Kalamazoo's population rose from 57,704 in 1950 to 82,089 in 1960.

the Russians had fired their first two satellites late in 1957, chagrin over Soviet superiority in space navigation caused Americans to turn in wrath against the schools, which were blamed for the unreadiness of the nation. More thorough training in mathematics and the sciences was demanded. Crash programs were adopted, and accelerated courses for gifted students were arranged.

One result of the insistence on improvement in schools and colleges was the enactment by Congress of the National Defense Education Act in 1958. Under this law, funds were granted to assist schools to strengthen their programs in science, mathematics, and foreign languages. Funds also were provided for loans to needy undergraduates by colleges and universities, and fellowships were made available for graduate students.

During the decade a new teaching aid was developed. Instruction by television provided by universities or by commercial stations was broadcast for children in schoolrooms and even for college students. By this means, one exceptionally able teacher could reach a great number of pupils.

An experiment to extend such instruction over a huge area was conducted during the years 1958-1960. Classroom courses for elementary and secondary classes were transmitted from Purdue University to a DC-7 flying at twenty thousand feet over north-central Indiana. The plane in turn rebroadcast the programs, which could be received by schools in a section of Michigan, in the other states of the Old Northwest, and in a part of Kentucky. So successful was the experiment that the sponsors planned to have the system operating in 1961.

Enrollment in elementary schools increased from 696,289 pupils in 1950 to 1,032,980 in 1960, and in high schools from 372,582 in 1950 to 592,184 in 1960. The number of school districts in 1950 was 4,800. The state superintendent of public instruction and others interested in improving the schools advocated drastically reducing the number of districts by consolidation. During the 1950's, districts were combined until at the end of the decade there were only 2,100. Nevertheless, there were still 1,300 one-room schools and 1,700 districts without high schools. The usual practice for these districts was to pay tuition for their pupils in high schools in neighboring cities. Some cities, especially if their buildings were crowded, rejected pupils from outside districts. Further consolidation appeared to be necessary to provide additional secondary schools.

Thirty-one four-year colleges and universities and sixteen community colleges offered higher education to students of Michigan, of other states, and in fact of the world; for during the 1950's the number of foreign students increased greatly. In the University of Michigan, for example, twice as many were enrolled in 1959 as in 1949. Many were sent by their own governments; others came on scholarships provided by the United States Government, by American foundations, and by universities. The college and university population grew from 95,000 in 1950 to 158,000 in 1960. One study indicated that by 1965 the enrollment will be 210,000.

Of the thirty-one colleges and universities, nine were supported by the state. One of them, Wayne State University, was added during the decade. Previously a part of the Detroit school system, it was made a state institution, governed by an elected board, by the Legislature in 1956.

In addition, the University of Michigan opened two branches and Michigan State University, one. In 1956, Flint College of the University of Michigan was established to meet the need of the area for a four-year college. The first two years were being offered by Flint Junior College. In a building erected for the purpose by Charles Stewart Mott, junior and senior courses are given in literature, science, and the arts, in business administration, and in education. Graduates receive University of Michigan degrees.

The other branch is the Dearborn Center of the University. Situated on a campus of 210 acres donated by the Ford Motor Company, it includes the estate of Henry Ford and his former home, Fairlane. A gift of $6,500,000 accompanied the property. Four buildings were erected, and classes began in September, 1959. Only students who have completed two years of college study and who want to major in engineering or business administration are admitted. Following a cooperative program, they spend part of their time in classes and part in business or industry. Besides intending at this center to prepare additional specialists needed by an expanding economy, University authorities hoped that it and the one at Flint would help provide educational facilities for the increasing number of young men and women preparing to enter college.

In 1955, its centennial year, Michigan State College became Michigan State University by act of the Legislature. Four years later it opened its Oakland branch near Rochester on a 1,400 acre campus, the gift of Mr. and Mrs. Alfred G. Wilson, together with $2,000,000 for the first academic building. Students may major in arts and sciences, education, engineering, or business administration. Regardless of the field of study, special emphasis is given to providing a broad background of liberal arts. This branch is expected to serve students largely from Oakland and Macomb counties.

Besides Michigan State, three other colleges were designated universities by the Legislature: Western Michigan University at Kalamazoo, Eastern Michigan University at Ypsilanti, and Central Michigan University at Mount Pleasant. First established as normal schools for the training of teachers, they had gradually developed additional departments and for many years they had been in reality regional colleges.

Two new institutions were projected near the end of the decade. One, called Grand Valley State College, was intended to serve the counties of Kent, Ottawa, Muskegon, Allegan, Newaygo, Montcalm, Barry, and Ionia. The planners petitioned the Legislature for financial assistance. To become a state-supported institution, they were told that they would have to raise $1,000,000 and obtain a campus site. In 1960 it appeared that these requirements would be met. The other institution has been named Delta College. To be situated in Frankenlust Township, Bay County, it will be of special service to young men and women of Midland, Bay, and Saginaw counties.

An unusual educational institution is the National Music Camp at Interlochen. Built on the site of a ghost town fifteen miles south of Traverse City, it is the largest operation of the kind in the United States. The camp, founded in 1928 by Joseph E. Maddy of the University of Michigan, has grown until in recent years it has been occupied during the summer by 2,500 persons, faculty, staff, and students. There are more than 300 buildings on a tract of 1,000 acres. As the name implies, the camp is situated between two lakes which are useful for recreation.

The purpose of the camp is to train boys and girls in junior, intermediate, and high school divisions in music, dramatics, ballet, modern dance, and art. These activities are geared to performance in numerous public concerts, recitals, dance programs, dramatic presentations, radio broadcasts, telecasts, and exhibits. By affiliation with the University of Michigan, the camp is able to offer a program of courses taught by members of the faculty of the School of Music, the School of Education, and the College of Architecture and Design.

Beginning in the fall of 1961, the Interlochen Arts Academy, a secondary school in which music and the arts will be emphasized, will operate from September until June. A co-educational boarding school, it will provide exceptional opportunity for pupils of high school age who have superior talents in art, music, dramatics, or creative writing.

4

Michigan is really a "Water Wonderland." This slogan, appearing on all automobile license plates issued by the state, advertises one of its most interesting features. Washed by waters of all the Great Lakes except Ontario, spangled with 11,000 inland lakes, and traversed by numerous rivers, Michigan has many attractions for tourists. Swimming, fishing, boating, skin diving, and water skiing are available in every part of the state.

Parks, recreation areas, and improved camp sites on streams or lake shores are used by the ten million vacationers who annually visit Michigan. Hunting and fishing are popular sports. During recent years shooting preserves have been established by individuals or groups to which hunters are admitted on payment of a fee. The game consists principally of pheasants and wild ducks.

Winter sports have become increasingly popular during the past decade. Eighty-three centers offer skiing, tobogganing, and skating. In the southern area, snow-making machines prolong the season. Winter carnivals attract famous athletes and thousands of spectators. Winter and summer, Michigan has many outdoor features to attract her own residents and visitors. In fact, tourism is the third largest business activity in the state, ranking after manufacturing and agriculture in annual financial returns.

The historical marker program begun by the state Historical Commission in 1955 provides an interesting and instructive feature for travelers. Set up beside highways and in roadside parks, these markers contain concise and accurate information about historic events which occurred on the spot or in the neighborhood. On some of the markers, a map shows the developments in an area, such as the one near Bessemer which marks the sites of mines in the Gogebic Iron Range, and another in Ypsilanti with routes of all the old interurban car lines delineated.

Some of the markers were purchased by organizations, but nost of them were paid for out of an appropriation by the Legislature. The texts on all of them were prepared under supervision of the Commission. Cooperation by the Highway Department and Conservation Department made possible the placing and maintenance of the markers. Over 130 have been erected, and more will be provided when additional funds become available.

5

A five-year road-building program, begun in 1957, by the fall of 1960 had put Michigan in first place in the construction of interstate highways. These freeways, paid for in part with federal funds, are linking together Michigan's principal cities and making connections with other states. When the program began, there were only 101 miles of such roads; in the fall of 1960, there were 537. Completion of Interstate 94 from Detroit to Stevensville on Lake Michigan, the longest toll-free interstate highway in the nation, provided 203 miles of clear driving without a traffic light or a vehicular grade crossing.

Work was progressing on the extension of Interstate 75, linking Detroit with Sault Sainte Marie, two-lane sections of U.S. 23 were being replaced by divided highways, and U.S. 16 between Detroit and Muskegon was nearly completed as a freeway. Besides, in Detroit the Edsel Ford and the John C. Lodge expressways were open for their full length and the Walter P. Chrysler Expressway was under construction. Only Los Angeles, with a much larger area, has more miles of freeways than Detroit.

Another project of the Highway Department was the building of a bridge between Houghton and Hancock in the Upper Peninsula. Replacing a totally inadequate structure which carried railroad trains and motor traffic across the Keweenaw Waterway, the Portage Lake Lift Bridge was dedicated in June, 1960. The over-all length is 1,310 feet with a center span 250 feet long which can be raised 100 feet to permit the passage of lake steamers. The bridge has two decks—the lower one for trains and the upper for automobiles and pedestrians. Secretary of the Army, Wilbur M. Brucker, a former governor of Michigan, was principal speaker at the dedication. The International Bridge Authority, created by the Michigan legislature in 1935, began work in September, 1960, on a $20,000,000 bridge across the St. Mary's River, linking the American and Canadian Soos.

Construction of freeways and the improvement of old roads have helped to better the safety record of drivers in Michigan. In addition, the setting of definite speed limits outside towns by an act of 1956—sixty-five miles an hour in daylight and fifty-five miles at night—strict enforcement of traffic laws, and suspension or cancellation of drivers' licenses for frequent violations, have had a marked effect.

Another factor was the requirement of instruction for youths before they were licensed to drive. A law passed by the legislature in 1956 provided for driver education in the high schools of the state. This law, the first of its kind in the United States, was intended to produce skilled drivers. Pupils are required to study safe driving for thirty hours in a classroom and to take six hours of instruction in an automobile. In order to obtain a driver's license, all persons under eighteen must pass the approved driver education course.

Even though there were numerous fatal accidents, the results of all these efforts were notable. In the fall of 1958, the National Safety Council commended Michigan for reducing the number of traffic deaths from 2,016 in 1955 to 1,537 in 1957. At about the same time the American Automobile Association presented to Governor G. Mennen Williams a bronze plaque naming Michigan as the safest state for pedestrians in 1957. The next year Michigan tied with Connecticut for first place in pedestrian safety. In 1958 the death toll from traffic accidents was reduced to 1,352. Unfortunately, it rose in 1960 to 1,575, the highest since 1956.

The opening of the St. Lawrence Waterway in 1959 was hailed as an event of great significance for Michigan, whose ports now have direct access to the harbors of the world. Too little time has elapsed to discover the full effect of this situation. One statistic, however, is of interest. Detroit is closer to Liverpool by water, than over the combined land and water route by way of New York. Besides, no transfer from freight cars to ships is necessary. The economy of direct water connection is evident.

Thus far, Detroit and Muskegon have benefited most by the opening of the seaway. Bay City also has profited by the water route. In 1959 the *Henry B. Wilson*, a 438-foot guided missile destroyer, was launched there in the yards of the Defoe Shipbuilding Company. The first of four such ships ordered by the Navy, it could be built in Michigan only because the new seaway made possible the delivery of the vessel to the Atlantic coast.

6

The economy of Michigan reached high and low points during the decade. Closely geared to the manufacture of automobiles, it flourished or languished according to the condition of that industry. At the beginning, the record production of 6,673,000 cars brought prosperity to the state. Because of restrictions on materials made necessary by the Korean War, the number declined in 1951 and 1952, in the latter year to 4,321,000. The all-time peak was reached in 1955 when 7,950,000 automobiles were driven off the assembly lines. Profits also reached a record level, General Motors reporting more than a billion dollars, the first time any American corporation had earned so much. It was suggested that the perfect national symbol of the prosperous year 1955 was an automobile with a colorful body embellished with sparkling chrome.

Nearly six million cars were made in 1956 and more than six million in 1957. A nationwide recession in 1958 reduced production in that year to 4,247,000. Another factor in the smaller output was the importation of small foreign automobiles in increasing numbers. In 1958 they represented 12 per cent of the cars sold in the United States, and in 1959 it was estimated that more than a million were in use.

American manufacturers were slow to catch the implication of the small car invasion, brushing it off as a passing fad. One company, however, American Motors, under the aggressive leadership of George Romney, had been very successful in marketing its compact cars. In 1958, 200,000 of them were sold. Finally, the Big Three began preparing to meet the competition, and in the spring of 1959 the Ford Motor Company announced that it would have a compact car in production later in the year. The other two companies followed suit, and sales of all cars in 1959 increased to 5,600,000. However, profits on the cheaper cars were lower, and the state treasury received smaller revenues from the weight tax and the sales tax.

Employment in Michigan reached its peak in 1955 when 2,616,000 persons were working. Afterwards, it declined and in August of 1958, during the recession, 16½ per cent of the labor force was unemployed. The average for the year was 13½ per cent. Even in 1959, when production of automobiles increased, unemployment was 11 per cent, nearly twice that of the nation at large.

There were several reasons for this condition. One was automation in the factories. Year after year, because of the introduction of laborsaving machinery, fewer men were required to produce the cars. For example, in 1953, 900,000 workers, 500,000 in Michigan, turned out 6,117,000; in 1960, 800,000, about 300,000 of them in Michigan, made 6,694,000. After every shutdown to tool up for a new annual model, fewer men were called back to work.

Another reason, suggested by the figures above, was the gradual reduction of the number of automobiles made in Michigan. Eighteen other states had plants making parts or assembling the finished product. Decentralization was an economy measure to reduce the cost of transportation. California was second in output, Missouri third, and

Wisconsin fourth. Even though most of the parts were made in Michigan and shipped to the other factories, many jobs were lost. The consolidation of smaller producers, Packard and Studebaker, and Hudson and Nash, the latter building cars in Wisconsin, and the demise of the Kaiser-Frazer Company in 1955 left Michigan with a large pool of highly skilled workmen without jobs.

A third cause of unemployment was too great a dependence on a single industry. Not only the principal centers—Lansing, Hamtramck, Detroit, Dearborn, Pontiac, and Flint—were affected by a slackening national demand for automobiles, but many other towns and cities as well. Small factories in numerous communities throughout the state were engaged in supplying parts, tools, and accessories for the big manufacturers. Economists warned that the condition would continue unless greater diversification was provided. The situation was made worse by a major shift in defense procurement from wheeled vehicles with piston-driven engines to jet aircraft, long-range missiles, and electronics.

Charges, largely political, were made in 1957 that heavy taxes and an unfavorable climate for industry were driving manufacturers from the state. As a matter of fact, there was really no large exodus of industry during the decade. Statistics gathered in 1959 showed more establishments than in 1953.[2] Besides, the automobile companies, public utilities, and other industries were spending great sums of money for expansion of their operations. An economist asserted that in 1957 state and local taxes were $181 per capita, placing Michigan in twelfth position among the states. Calculation on another basis, however, showed that taxes amounted to only $83.54 per $1,000 of personal income, ranking Michigan thirty-first.

The need for additional and diversified industries was widely recognized. The Michigan Economic Development Commission, established in 1947, worked toward this end. Besides, a group composed of more than two hundred leaders of business, industry, labor, and other segments of the state's economy, appointed in 1959 by Governor Williams, set out to disseminate information about the rich resources of Michigan. Called Industrial Ambassadors, it hoped to attract new manufacturing plants.

During the 1950's, relations between management and labor were fairly stable. Walter Reuther, president of the UAW-CIO, in 1955 demanded a guaranteed annual wage to stabilize the earnings of work-

[2] The industries that moved away employed more persons than those which began operating.

ingmen. Following his usual tactic, he first approached one of the Big Three, the Ford Motor Company, making the guaranteed annual wage a part of the union's program in negotiating a new labor contract. The company rejected the idea. Finally, a compromise was arrived at by which the company agreed to pay a supplement to state unemployment compensation for a maximum of twenty-six weeks, the legal duration of payments. By this plan, an employee who was laid off would be paid from 60 to 65 per cent of his regular wages. After winning this concession, Reuther obtained similar terms from General Motors and Chrysler.

When the time to negotiate a new contract in 1958 approached, the Big Three let it be known that they would not easily be coerced. The implication was that they would stand together; if one were closed by a strike to influence negotiations, the others would shut down. Not wanting to cause widespread unemployment, Reuther made moderate proposals, and contracts were speedily signed.

Ever since 1936, when the CIO was expelled from the American Federation of Labor, there had been speculation about a possible recombination. It was believed that such a move would greatly strengthen organized labor. However, basic differences, for instance, craft unions as differentiated from industrial unions, caused difficulties. Besides, personality conflicts of leaders appeared to make unification impossible. Nevertheless, in 1955 the two merged. George Meany, president of the AFL, became president of the new AFL-CIO, and Walter Reuther, president of the UAW, executive vice-president. The new union had fifteen million members.

At first this great combination of labor power frightened industrial leaders. They soon learned, however, that not much had changed. Bickering between craft and industrial unions, especially over jurisdictional rights, and internal tensions among the leaders dissipated much of the potential strength. After only two years, James R. Hoffa and his Teamsters Union were expelled on the grounds of corrupt practices. By this action, the AFL-CIO lost nearly a million and a half members and their dues. Hoffa, although harassed by government probes and lawsuits, worked assiduously to strengthen the Teamsters at the expense of the AFL-CIO by organizing the unorganized and seeking alliances with other individual unions.

Although greater diversification in economic pursuits is needed, especially some increase in other than heavy industry, a great variety of products are manufactured in Michigan. According to government figures, of a total of 453 types of industry, 369 are represented. The state led in the number of employees engaged in making mobile homes, internal combustion engines, metalworking machinery, stokers, hardware, steel springs, breakfast cereals, salt, alkalines and chlorine, public building fixtures, professional furniture, and soda fountain and bar equipment. It was first in production of transportation equipment, second in pulp and paper products, third in machinery except electrical, sixth in chemicals and drugs, and ninth in food products.

Even though a change in emphasis of defense work has cost Michigan some employment, the United States Government is spending nearly a billion dollars a year in the state for special products: wheel and track vehicles, electronic computers for intercontinental ballistic missiles and intermediate range missiles, rocket parts, gasoline engines, guided-missile destroyers, high-speed cameras, rocket engines for space vehicles, and jet engines. Besides, plants containing special machines and tools are maintained in readiness for speedy resumption of operation in case of national emergency.

8

Because Michigan is famous for manufacturing, the importance of its farms is frequently overlooked. As a matter of fact, it is one of the leading agricultural states. Its great variety of soils makes possible the growing of many sorts of crops. Michigan is first in the production of red tart cherries, thanks principally to the broad fruit belt along the shore of Lake Michigan. In the general classification "fruit," the state recently has been fourth in the value of the crop, surpassed only by California, Florida, and New York, and has also been fourth in the value of vegetables harvested. For years it has been first in the quantity of navy beans raised, and it is near the top in the production of honey. Another very important activity is dairy farming. Its products are the largest single source of income for Michigan farmers.

Changes in agriculture occurred during the 1950's. One was a decrease in the number of farms and an increase in the average size. The principal reason was greater mechanization, which is better adapted to larger areas. The number of acres cultivated has declined as a result of conservation practices and the growth of suburban settlements. Besides, less land and fewer farmers are necessary to produce needed crops. It has been estimated that a century ago one farm worker produced food for four and a half persons. Today he produces enough for twenty.

The trend toward fewer and larger farms worked by a greater number of machines has been notable in growing sugar beets. In 1949, this crop was raised in thirty-seven counties; ten years later, in only twenty-six. From the earliest days the Saginaw Bay and the Thumb area were most important in beet culture, and during the 1950's production became concentrated there. In fact, four counties, Tuscola, Saginaw, Huron, and Bay provided 81 per cent of beets grown in the state. Although there have been great fluctuations in annual output, in the later years of the decade it surpassed a million tons. The sugar manufactured in five refineries in the region is an important product.

One crop, formerly grown in the same area, has been discontinued. From about 1890 until 1954, chicory was raised almost exclusively in Michigan. Although the plantings were small, it was a specialty crop which returned a good profit. Marketed largely in the Gulf and the South Atlantic states for use as an additive to coffee, the annual value was about a million dollars. As the result of a tariff reduction in 1951, foreign chicory began to replace the native product, and cultivation of the root was abandoned in 1955.

A problem which disturbs agricultural experts and farmers alike is the high cost of farming in Michigan. The price of land has risen, a large area is necessary for efficient operation, and machinery is expensive. Surveys show that $50,000 is the minimum amount needed simply to get started. How can a young man who wants to own and operate a farm obtain such a sum of money, and where will he find reserve capital to carry him over a bad season? One expert has suggested that he may have to incorporate and sell stock just as industrialists did when individuals were unable to provide sufficient capital for establishing a factory.

9

Although Michigan long since lost its position as the leading lumber producer, it still has 19,000,000 acres of forest, more than half the land area of the state. Of these, 3,750,000 are in 23 state forests, and 2,500,000 in 5 national forests. Two-thirds of the land is privately owned. Reforestation is carried on and selective logging is practiced both by governmental agencies and by some commercial owners. Preventive measures and prompt action by the Department of Conservation have greatly reduced losses by forest fires. For example, in 1930, 290,000 acres were destroyed; in 1960, only 2,978.

Principal forest products are lumber, veneer, and pulpwood. During the past sixty years the output of lumber fell from 2,800,000,000 board feet to under 400,000,000. During the depression in 1932, the low point of 160,000,000 board feet was reached. Production rose to 615,000,000 in 1948, and then gradually declined. A notable increase has occurred in the number and output of pulp mills. Most of the product is used by Michigan paper mills. The principal stock is provided by aspen, at one time considered useless. Trees are cut also for the manufacture of veneer. Some is used for fine plywood; the remainder for fruit baskets and berry crates. Besides, charcoal is made for use in outdoor grills, and a great variety of other products are turned out: shingles, laths, rustic furniture, woodenware, utility poles, piling, fence posts, fuel, clothespins, and ice cream sticks.

Christmas trees are a special forest product. In recent years the annual cut has been nearly 2,000,000, and Michigan is second only to Montana among the states in commercial sales. Although wild trees formerly supplied the market, today nearly 50 per cent are grown on plantations. Because they are given careful attention and shaped by pruning from time to time, these trees are more attractive and bring higher prices. Preferences for species vary with individuals, but Scotch pines are in greatest demand. The sale of Christmas trees in Michigan produces $7,000,000 annually.

10

During the 1950's changes occurred in mining. Iron ore was being taken from twenty-eight mines in the Marquette, Menominee, and Gogebic ranges in 1959. An annual average output of eleven million long tons gave Michigan second place in the nation. Because the expense of operating deep mines which produce high-grade ore was heavy, some years ago companies began experimenting with low-grade ores which are close to the surface and almost unlimited in quantity. The experiments were successful. Taconite and jaspilite are ground to powder and the iron is separated from the rock, a process called beneficiation. The iron is compressed into pellets 65 per cent pure, excellent material for blast furnaces. This development was necessary if Michigan iron was to compete successfully with high-grade foreign ores cheaply available to American steel mills through the St. Lawrence Waterway. Three beneficiation plants were operating in the Upper Peninsula.

Michigan is still an important copper producer, standing fifth among the states. In 1959, nine mines were operating and two companies were reclaiming copper from tailings of older mines. During the first half of the decade the annual output fell below 50,000,000 pounds. Then the White Pine Mine began to produce, and during the next five years the average was 114,000,000. White Pine, taking a low-grade copper sulphide from shallow workings, furnished more than two-thirds of the output. The Copper Range Company, which owns White Pine, has discovered two additional deposits in the vicinity which are believed to be sufficient for forty years of mining. Exploration goes on. Geologists express the opinion that many other rich deposits in the Upper Peninsula are yet to be found.

Petroleum production was lagging until the discovery of new fields near the end of the decade in Calhoun, Hillsdale, and Jackson counties resulted in the drilling of numerous wells. Oil from the Scipio, Pulaski, and Albion fields added more than 2,000,000 barrels to the annual output. The number of wells was 4,300 in 41 of the 83 counties of the state. Besides oil, wells also produce large quantities of natural gas, important for use by industry and for home heating.

Salt has been an important product for a century, and since 1880 Michigan has held first position among the states as the source of supply of this mineral. During the 1950's, the output was 4,000,000 to 5,000,000 tons a year. More than half of it is used in the manufacture of soda ash, bromine, chlorine, and other chemicals. The seemingly inexhaustible deposits of salt continue to attract chemical companies to the state.

In addition to the minerals which have been mentioned, Michigan is first in the production of peat and gypsum, second in sand and gravel, and fourth in cement.

II

The political history of Michigan during the 1950's might best be described as monotonous, but politics was far from being dull. The re-election of Governor G. Mennen Williams each biennium and the choosing at the same time of a majority of Republicans for the Legislature was certainly repetitious. So also was the near deadlock between the executive and the legislative branches. Republicans charged that organized labor controlled the Democratic party; Democrats replied that the automobile manufacturers dominated the Republican organization.

Neither allegation was entirely true. The UAW-CIO was very active in support of Governor Williams. In addition, other Democrats and liberals were usually in accord with his social betterment program. One powerful labor union, however, the Teamsters, led by James R. Hoffa, was bitterly hostile to the governor. In 1948 he had induced the

Democrats to name the union's attorney as national committeeman, and he entered Victor Bucknell in the gubernatorial primary. Aroused by Hoffa's attempt to control the party, August Scholle, president of the Michigan CIO, and Frank X. Martel, president of the Detroit and Wayne County AFL, joined forces and helped nominate Williams. Rebuffed by the Democrats, Hoffa thereafter supported Republican candidates in national and state elections.

Domination of the Republican party by the Big Three automobile makers was true to a certain extent. They contributed funds, and some individuals related to General Motors Corporation and the Ford Motor Company became active party leaders. The most prominent and successful was Arthur E. Summerfield, wealthy Flint Chevrolet dealer. First as chairman of the Genesee County organization and later as national committeeman, he dominated the party in Michigan. At the National Convention in 1952, he delivered the state delegation to General Dwight D. Eisenhower and was named national chairman of the Republican party. His capable management of the campaign earned him the appointment as postmaster general.[3]

Another significant element of Republican party strength lies in some of the areas out-state. Conservative and fearful of labor unions and city dwellers, it provides a solid core of opposition to new ideas, especially if they will, if enacted into law, increase the cost of government. As is the case in many other states, the agricultural areas are over-represented because they had a legislative majority in earlier years and have refused to relinquish it.

In spite of the constitutional requirement that the Legislature reapportion after every national census, no general redistribution of seats was made after 1925 until 1943, when the House of Representatives was reapportioned. Senate districts remained unchanged despite the growing disparity of population in urban and rural areas.

In 1952 an amendment provided for what was called a "balanced" Legislature. The number of representatives was increased from 100 to 110 and senators from 32 to 34. District lines were drawn to give urban inhabitants a greater proportion of representatives. Even so, the number of contituents in a district varies from a low of 30,000 in a rural area to 90,000 in an urban area. The intention of the amendment to make the Senate represent counties rather than persons is evident in the great disparity in the number of constituents in urban and rural regions. For example, the thirty-second district, in the Upper

[3] One automotive executive, George Romney, president of American Motors, took a moderate position. He organized a nonpartisan group, Citizens for Michigan, with the intention of promoting active and intelligent interest in state government.

Peninsula, contains 55,600 inhabitants; the twentieth, an agricultural section in the Thumb, 126,900; and the twelfth, Oakland County, largely urban, 690,200.

G. Mennen Williams won six elections, a record for the state and the nation. He campaigned constantly, meeting thousands of persons in every part of the state and making them feel that he was sincerely interested in their welfare. Mrs. Williams, also, was a tireless campaigner. Besides, the governor was fortunate to have the dedicated service of Neil Staebler, state chairman of the Democratic party from 1950 to 1961. His success in uniting Democrats, liberals, and labor into a combination that could win elections earned national recognition for him.

Governor Williams' opponent in 1952 was Fred M. Alger, Jr., secretary of state, grandson of former Governor, Senator, and Secretary of War, Russell A. Alger.[4] General Eisenhower, the Republican candidate for President, won 1,551,000 of the 2,798,000 votes cast in Michigan, and it was expected that he would carry the candidates of the party for state offices to victory. When the unofficial count gave Williams a plurality of 8,618, Alger asked for a recount in 1,569 precincts. Williams requested that the ballots in 1,908 precincts be recounted. The governor's official plurality was 9,978. All other Democrats were defeated.

Governor Williams easily won the elections of 1954, 1956, and 1958. As was the case in earlier years, these were personal victories, but Neil Staebler's work began to produce broader results. In the fall of 1954 Democrats were elected to every state office, and Patrick V. McNamara, officer of the AFL Plumber's Union and a member of the Detroit Board of Education, was elected United States senator. The Democrats were successful also in the spring election of 1957, providing the governor at last with an administrative board consisting entirely of members of his own party. Besides, Philip A. Hart was elected to the Senate in 1958, giving Michigan two Democratic senators for the first time since 1856, when Lewis Cass and Charles E. Stuart were senators for the state.

Although the Democrats won all offices for which a statewide vote was cast, the Republicans controlled the Legislature because of the existing apportionment. During each of his six terms, Governor Williams put into the budget large items for education, for an expanded mental health program, for additional unemployment compensation, and for other social and humanitarian causes. The Legislature usually slashed the figures deeply; then, because of the governor's wide-

[4] See pages 452-453 for the elections of 1948 and 1950.

spread support, it relented and voted increased funds, but not as much as he wanted. Except for these reluctant concessions, neither lawmakers nor governor would compromise.

The most important issue, taxation, was a constant cause of contention. Since 1933, the sales tax had been the principal producer of revenue. Comparatively little, however, could be used for general expenses because by an amendment to the constitution in 1946, more than two-thirds of the receipts had to be paid to school districts and units of local government. The amount was raised in 1954 to five-sixths. Because some other revenues, for instance, weight taxes on automobiles and the tax on gasoline, were earmarked for the Highway Department, the Legislature had difficulty finding sufficient funds for the normal operation of the government. Rapid growth of population during the 1950's increased the gravity of the situation.[5]

The tax structure of Michigan is an amorphous conglomeration which includes numerous nuisance taxes voted in desperation whenever there was need for additional funds. Whether by intention or by lack of planning, the burden is inequitably distributed. A group of economists who studied the problem, reported that persons with an income of less than $2,000 were paying 20 per cent in state and local taxes, while those with incomes of more than $10,000 were paying only 7 per cent.

Governor Williams throughout his tenure of office urged the adoption of a corporation profits tax. The Legislature rejected his proposal and increased the rates on consumers' goods—gasoline, liquor, beer, and cigarettes. Later, the governor advocated a personal income tax. Instead, the Legislature in 1959 levied a 1 per cent "use tax." This was obviously a subterfuge to increase the sales tax, which was limited by the Constitution to 3 per cent. When the matter came before the state Supreme Court, it declared the "use tax" unconstitutional.

An intelligent attempt to work out a balanced system of taxation was made by a Citizens Advisory Committee consisting of executives in industry, leaders of farm organizations, and officers of labor unions. They selected Harvey E. Brazer, a University of Michigan economist, to conduct a study. Assisted by a staff of university professors, he drew up a plan which included taxes on corporation profits and on personal incomes. The Citizens Advisory Committee accepted it, but because it resembled Governor Williams' proposals, the Legislature in 1959 rejected it.

During the legislative session of 1959, which was not adjourned until

[5] Michigan's financial troubles were not unique. A news service survey in 1959 discovered that twenty-eight other states were trying to raise additional revenue.

December 19, bitterness against the governor and his tax program reached new heights and depths. An incident resulting from the controversy embarrassed some Republican lawmakers and industrialists. The text of a telegram sent to Republican senators by Joseph H. Creighton, lobbyist for the Michigan Manufacturers Association, was divulged to a reporter and published in the newspapers. It read: "You have him over the barrel for the first time in ten years. Keep him there 'til he screams 'uncle'. God bless each of you."

Opponents of Governor Williams charged that he was turning Michigan into a welfare state, that he had raised taxes so high that industry was leaving, and that he was bankrupting the state by exorbitant expenditures. His adherents cited statistics published by the United States Census Bureau showing that in 1957 Michigan was thirty-fourth among the states in per capita spending for welfare; they pointed out survey figures which proved that more industries were moving to Michigan than were leaving and that large corporations in the state were spending millions of dollars for expansion; and they called attention to the fact that only the Legislature can levy taxes and that the governor may spend only as much as the Legislature appropriates.

It was no secret that Governor Williams was hoping for an office in the national government in 1961. Much of the misrepresentation was apparently intended to upset his plans. When the deadlock over taxes caused a deficit of $95,000,000, lack of funds to pay state employees, and inability to meet current bills, the news was broadcast across the nation that Michigan was bankrupt. The charge was false. Michigan's credit was good, but the constitution permitted borrowing no more than $250,000. Persons who did not know the facts accepted the allegation as truth. The governor's opponents injured his political reputation; they also damaged the reputation of their state.

Because additional income was necessary, the Legislature in 1960 placed on the ballot a proposed amendment to the constitution to permit levying a 4 per cent sales tax. Besides, it raised the rates on gasoline, beer, liquor, cigarettes, intangibles, and business activities. It also laid a tax of 4 per cent on motel rentals.

Many persons believed that the constitution of 1908 should be replaced by a new one, or at least revised because of changed conditions. When the Legislature rejected requests to put on the 1960 ballot a proposal to facilitate the calling of a constitutional convention, the League of Women Voters, the Junior Chamber of Commerce, and Citizens for Michigan circulated petitions and gave the people an opportunity to vote on the question.

On March 3, 1960, Governor Williams announced that he would not run for re-election in November. Republicans were jubilant. It was generally believed that he hoped to be nominated for Vice President or to be appointed to a Cabinet position. Three months later he announced his support of Senator John F. Kennedy for nomination as President, and he campaigned vigorously for him. When John F. Kennedy was elected to the Presidency, he appointed Williams Assistant Secretary of State for African Affairs, and the former governor and Mrs. Williams visited Africa to study its problems at first hand.

The Republican nominee for governor was Paul D. Bagwell, a professor of Michigan State University, who had been defeated by Williams in 1958. Considered too liberal by some of the leaders of the party, they had opposed his nomination, even though he had come closer to defeating Governor Williams than had any other Republican since 1952. Bagwell favored calling a constitutional convention and the sales tax amendment.

Lieutenant Governor John B. Swainson was nominated by the Democrats. He opposed the sales tax amendment and the proposal to call a convention. Governor Williams campaigned for the state ticket of his party, but he spoke in favor of calling a constitutional convention.

Senator John F. Kennedy received a plurality in the election of 1960, the first Democratic nominee to carry Michigan since 1944. Swainson defeated Bagwell in the contest for governor; the Democratic nominees for lieutenant governor and for the administrative offices were elected; Justice Theodore Souris, who had been appointed to the Supreme Court by Governor Williams, retained his position; and Senator McNamara was returned to his seat.

In the Legislature, however, the Republicans again had majorities—two in the House and ten in the Senate. Since practically all the former members had been re-elected, the only change in Lansing was a new chief executive. Some expressed the opinion that Swainson's experience in the Legislature before he became lieutenant governor would improve relations between governor and lawmakers. Others doubted that the Republican majority would cooperate with any Democrat in the governor's chair.

The relative position of the parties in the national House of Representatives was unchanged—eleven Republicans and eleven Democrats. Michigan's increase in population during the 1950's entitled her to an additional representative in Congress. If the governor and the Legislature do not agree on redistricting the state, he will be elected at large.

Both of the proposed amendments to the constitution were approved by the voters. One put the question of calling a convention on the April, 1961, ballot and set a new rule for determining the result. The significant change provides that a simple majority of those voting yes on the question will decide that a convention will be held. Previously, a favorable majority of all votes cast in the election was required. Under that rule, failure to vote on the question was actually a negative vote.

The other amendment authorized the Legislature to levy a 4 per cent sales tax. Called into special session by Governor Williams, both houses passed a tax law, and he signed it. Although it was expected to produce $50,000,000 of additional revenue during the second half of the fiscal year, it would not solve the financial problem. A deficit estimated at $50,000,000 would remain. Michigan's tax structure was still in need of revision. It may be effected by the constitutional convention which a majority in the April, 1961, election decided should meet in the fall. The future of Michigan will be in the hands of the delegates and of the people who will vote for or against ratification of a new constitution.

— 31 —

Michigan, Past and Present

THE EVENTS which have been recorded in this book are a part of history. The present and the future remain. Today, Michigan is a better place to live in than it was three hundred years ago, or even fifty years ago. Few who know the facts will want a return of "the good old days."

Today is better than yesterday because men and women have labored and studied and used their intelligence to improve conditions. In the field of health, for example, persistent research and application of knowledge have eradicated the old scourges: cholera, diphtheria, smallpox, and malaria.

A century ago, nearly everyone in the rural district had the ague, as they called it. Alternately shaken by chills and parched with fever, the sufferers could do little except wait for cool weather in the fall to relieve their suffering. Some died; others recovered. No governmental agency did anything about it.

Years later it was learned that a type of mosquito transmitted the disease. The mosquitoes were destroyed, and there was no more malaria in Michigan. In this case and in others, group action has been largely responsible for better health conditions. City, county, state, and national health departments co-operate to discover and check diseases in localities and throughout the nation.

Private agencies also play important parts. The W. K. Kellogg Foundation, for example, organized in 1930 to promote the health, education, and welfare of mankind in general, and of children in particular, has done a great deal in a number of Michigan counties. Co-operating with school authorities, health officers, physicians, and dentists, the Foundation has assisted in working out practical solutions for community problems in health and education.

Emphasis on community co-operation has been especially strong during the last fifty years, and results show the benefits of such programs. In 1950 the State Health Department reported that the past half century has been the healthiest on record. While the population almost tripled, the general death rate fell 36 per cent. Infant mortality dropped 84 per cent. A larger number of better-trained physicians and nurses, more numerous hospitals, and alert health departments deserve credit for the improvement. No one doubts that continued research and co-operation will produce further advances in the future.

Many persons today fondly recall the "little red schoolhouse" which they attended. Seen through the romantic haze of intervening years, it appears to have been a very pleasant place. As a matter of fact, few men and women want their children to go to such a school. The cast-iron stove roasted the nearest pupils and permitted those farthest away to shiver from the cold. The open water bucket with a dipper floating on top would not be tolerated today, and the harassed teacher, trying to instruct pupils of all grades and ages, does not meet modern standards.

Today in many rural areas, teachers who are specialists in their subjects conduct classes in large, well-equipped consolidated schools. Buses carry the pupils to school and home again. Besides reading, writing, and arithmetic, there are numerous other subjects geared to the interests and the abilities of the pupils. Facilities for education have improved enormously.

In addition to primary and high schools, in recent years sixteen Michigan cities have established community colleges. Graduates of high schools in those cities may take two years of college work without leaving home. Courses which prepare students for various occupations are offered, as well as academic subjects. Community colleges receive financial support from the state.

Nine state-supported colleges and universities and twenty private institutions provide higher education for 152,294 young men and women. Most of the students are from Michigan, but a large proportion come from other states and from foreign countries. The number entering has been increasing each year, and the trend is still upward.

Great changes in agriculture have occurred during the past century. Michigan State University and the state and national departments of agriculture have helped the farmer produce bigger crops and better livestock. Machinery has taken much of the drudgery out of farming, and farmers now have the benefit of electric light and power. Today, the farmer's family is not isolated. The automobile, the telephone, radio, and television keep him in touch with people and events not only in the state but throughout the world.

Industry, too, has changed. Machines, to a great extent, have replaced tools, and the necessity for great capital investments has resulted in the organization of large manufacturing companies. Today, instead of the small shops formerly owned and operated by one person with a few employes, there are great corporations owned by thousands of stockholders and managed by men hired by a board of directors. Mass production by huge factories has made goods that were formerly luxuries available to nearly everyone.

To keep mass-production industries operating, mass consumption is necessary. In other words, persons who earn wages must receive enough money so that they can purchase the goods which are manufactured. Before the 1930's, that was not the case. According to a report of the National Bureau of Economic Research, in 1929 5 per cent of the population had 34 per cent of the wealth. During the 1930's and the 1940's, by the use of income taxes and other devices, the ratio was changed so that in 1950 the 5 per cent had only 18 per cent of the wealth. This redistribution has made it possible for more persons to purchase more goods, thereby keeping the wheels of production turning.

One reason for the changed ratio has been the increase in the wages of workingmen. To match the strength of great corporations, powerful labor unions were organized. With the assistance of favorable legislation, they won for their members higher wages and better working conditions. Workingmen today have a forty-hour week, unemployment compensation, and retirement pensions. Production has increased, and in spite of higher wages and higher taxes, profits have been greater than ever before.

The development of great corporations and powerful labor unions has given rise to certain problems. Industries tend to become monopolies if they are not regulated by government; unions, also, may become monopolistic if they are permitted to extend their influence unchecked. Besides, some managers and labor leaders prefer a fight to calm negotiations. In most industries, on the other hand, management and employes have learned to work together for their common benefit.

A great improvement has been the changed attitude toward the unfortunate. In earlier days, old men and women in Michigan without means of support were auctioned off to whoever offered to keep them at the lowest price. Today, aged persons receive old-age pensions, not as charity, but because they are needy neighbors. Special care is provided for blind and crippled children to help them become useful members of the community. All of these developments, and others of a similar nature, are the result of an aroused social consciousness.

Many of the laws which make provision for those who cannot help themselves were passed during the terrible depression of the early 1930's. That experience taught compassion, and the people found a leader who understood their needs. Senator Arthur H. Vandenberg once said of President Franklin D. Roosevelt: ". . . history will accord him credit for making America *social-minded*.[1] . . . And it was high time this phenomenon should come to pass because our best defense of democracy—in a sodden, saddened world of dictators—is to make democracy consciously and intimately advantageous to our whole people." With this goal in mind, slum clearance, public housing, and social security become necessary features of our democratic system.

A great advance has been made in the public attitude toward the use of natural resources. Formerly, few objected to reckless destruction of the forests for the enrichment of a few. Cutover lands in Michigan were abandoned or sold to unwary persons for farms. During the past half century, the state has intervened to prevent such practices. Under control by the Conservation Department, thousands of acres have been reforested, logging is carried on in a scientific manner so that young trees are permitted to grow, and numerous public parks and recreation areas have been established. Hunting, fishing, and camping are encouraged. Besides, the Conservation Department stopped the wasteful drilling of oil wells, and the state receives an income from oil produced in Michigan. These arrangements are for the general welfare.

During the past half century, roads and the means of transportation have been improved amazingly, and Michigan took the lead in both fields. It will be recalled that the first mile of concrete road in the world was laid in Wayne County, and the state has constructed a modern highway system. Automobiles, buses, and trucks, most of them made in Michigan, carry passengers and freight rapidly and economically.

In addition to the economic advantages of motor vehicles, there have been social advantages, also. Ease of travel has brought the people of the state closer together. Besides, Michiganians travel through other states, thereby learning to know their fellow countrymen, and thousands of persons come to Michigan every year on business or for vacation

[1] Vandenberg added here: "Of course, history will have some *other* things to say which I charitably pass in the spirit of the moment." Speech at the Gridiron Club Meeting in April, 1940. Arthur H. Vandenberg, Jr., *The Private Papers of Senator Vandenberg* (Boston: Houghton Mifflin Company, 1952), p. 166.

trips. Automobiles are helping to draw Americans into a closer bond of fellowship.

Unfortunately, with the benefits have come some evils. For example, automobiles give criminals a means of quick escape from the scenes of their crimes. Besides, automobiles have become a major cause of death. In 1950, 1,680 persons were killed by automobiles in Michigan, a larger number than those who died of pneumonia or tuberculosis. In 1955 the death toll reached 2,016. Afterwards, by education and by stricter control of traffic, deaths were reduced to 1,575 in 1960. There is still need for greater care by both drivers and pedestrians.

One who looks back to conditions only a century ago can see that changes for the better have occurred in almost every field of human endeavor. Technological advances during the past fifty years have been almost incredible. Persons who in their lifetime have seen the emergence of automobiles, airplanes, motion pictures, radio, television, and the use of atomic energy may believe that nothing further can be discovered. If they do, they are as shortsighted as the head of the Patent Bureau, who, it is said, resigned in 1833 because he thought there would be no more important inventions.

Young people, certainly, are not going to be satisfied with the world their elders have made. They will accept as a challenge the task of building soundly on the foundations which exist. The American system is not perfect, but it is better than it ever was before and, for Americans, it is the best in the world. The present level has been reached by democratic methods, and the same methods can be used to make further advances.

The future holds great promise for young persons of all ages. They may well adopt for their motto an inscription in the National Archives Building in Washington: "What is past is prolog." What has happened up to now is marvelous, but it is only the starting point for greater and better things.

MICHIGAN CHRONOLOGY

1608 Champlain founded Quebec
1609 Champlain fought Iroquois near Lake Champlain
Henry Hudson sailed up Hudson River
1615 Fr. Le Caron, Recollect, in Huronia
Champlain and Brulé to Lake Nipissing, to Huronia, and across Lake Ontario
1622 Etienne Brulé to Lake Superior and Upper Peninsula
1634 Jean Nicolet to Lake Michigan and Wisconsin
1635 Death of Champlain at Quebec
1641 Frs. Isaac Jogues and Charles Raymbault to Sault
1649 Iroquois destroyed missions in Huronia
1654 Groseilliers to Lake Superior
1658 Groseilliers and Radisson to Lake Superior and Hudson Bay
1660 Fr. Ménard to Upper Peninsula and Wisconsin; wintered at L'Anse
1663 Jean Talon intendant, 1663–1668 and 1670–1672
1665 Fr. Allouez to La Pointe, Wis., and later to St. Joseph, Mich.
1666 Gen. de Tracy's successful expedition against the Iroquois
1667 Peace with the Iroquois
1668 Fr. Marquette founded mission at Sault Sainte Marie
1669 Frs. Allouez and Dablon at Green Bay
1670 Frs. Dollier de Casson and De Galinée passed through the Detroit River
Hudson's Bay Company founded
1671 St. Lusson at the Sault claimed land for Louis XIV
Fr. Marquette founded mission at St. Ignace
1672 Frontenac governor to 1682
1673 Jolliet and Marquette descended the Mississippi River
1675 Death of Marquette near Ludington
1679 La Salle built Fort Miami at mouth of St. Joseph River
1682 La Salle descended Mississippi River to the Gulf
1686 Duluth built Fort St. Joseph (Port Huron)
1689 King William's War to 1697
Frontenac again governor to 1698
St. Joseph mission founded (Niles)

1690 Fort de Buade built (St. Ignace)
1691 Fort St. Joseph built (Niles)
1694 Cadillac commandant at St. Ignace (Fort de Buade or Michilimackinac)
1696 Louis XIV ordered evacuation of the western posts
1698 Cadillac left Fort de Buade
1701 July 24, Cadillac founded Detroit
1702–1713 Queen Anne's War (War of Spanish Succession)
1711 Cadillac governor of Louisiana to 1717
1712 Foxes besieged Detroit
1713 Peace of Utrecht; Acadia ceded to Britain
1713–1734 French expeditions against Foxes
1715 New Fort Michilimackinac (Mackinaw City)
1720–1763 New Fort St. Joseph (Niles)
1744–1748 King George's War (War of Austrian Succession)
1748 Ohio Company given land grant on Ohio River
Treaty of Aix-la-Chapelle
1749 Expedition of Céleron de Blainville
1749–1753 Forts Presque Isle (Erie, Pa.), Le Boeuf (Waterford, Pa.), Machault (Venango, now Franklin, Pa.) built by French
1752 Langlade's raid on Pickawillany (Piqua, Ohio)
1753–1754 George Washington's mission to Fort Le Boeuf
1754 Washington surrendered Ft. Necessity; French and Indian War to 1760
1755 Braddock's defeat
Acadians deported; some to Detroit
1756–1763 Seven Years' War in Europe
1756 Montcalm took Oswego
1757 Montcalm took Fort William Henry
Pitt, the elder, became war minister; chose Amherst and Wolfe as commanders in America
1758 British took Louisbourg, Ft. Frontenac, and Ft. Duquesne
1759 British took Ft. Niagara, Ft. Ticonderoga, Crown Point, and Quebec
1760 Capitulation of Gov. Vaudreuil at Montreal
Major Robert Rogers received the surrender of Detroit from Belestre, last French commandant
1763 Treaty of Paris; French territory east of the Mississippi River ceded to Great Britain
Pontiac's War; Proclamation of October 7, 1763

1764 Bradstreet made treaty with Indians at Detroit
1766 Sir William Johnson held a council with Indians at Oswego; Pontiac made peace
1774 The Quebec Act
1775 Henry Hamilton to Detroit as lieutenant governor
1777 Raids from Detroit into Kentucky
1778 George Rogers Clark captured Kaskaskia and Cahokia
Daniel Boone and Simon Kenton prisoners of Indians at Detroit
Attack on Boonesboro, Ky., from Detroit
Hamilton took Vincennes
1779 Clark took Vincennes
Hamilton sent a prisoner to Virginia
Fort Lernoult built (Detroit)
Fort on Mackinac Island built
1780 Raids from Detroit into Kentucky
1781 Spanish flag raised over Ft. St. Joseph (Niles)
1782 Raids from Detroit into Kentucky
Battle of Blue Licks
Moravian-Indian town built at Mount Clemens; abandoned 1786
1783 Treaty of Paris between Great Britain and the United States
1785 Land Ordinance passed by Congress
1787 May 25 to September 17, Constitution drawn up at Philadelphia by the Convention
July 13, Northwest Ordinance passed by Congress of Confederation in New York
Michigan still under British rule; Detroit in the District of Hesse
1788 First courts held in Detroit; Judge William Dummer Powell
Marietta, Ohio, founded
1790 Defeat of Harmar by Indians in Ohio
1791 Province of Upper Canada established; Detroit in Kent County (British)
St. Clair defeated in Ohio by Indians
1792 First election in Detroit to assembly at Niagara-on-the-Lake (Ontario)
1794 Wayne's victory over the Indians and British Militia from Detroit at Fallen Timbers on the Maumee, Aug. 20
1795 Wayne's treaty with the Indians at Greenville, Ohio
1796 British abandoned fur posts on the Lakes
July 11, Captain Moses Porter raised the American flag over Ft. Lernoult at Detroit
Lt. Col. J. F. Hamtramck took command July 13
Gen. Anthony Wayne arrived August 13
Winthrop Sargent, acting governor of the N.W. Territory, established Wayne County, August 15
Mackinac occupied Sept. 1

1798 Solomon Sibley elected Representative to N.W. Territory Legislature at Cincinnati
1799 Jacob Visger and François Chabert elected as additional representatives
1800 Act of Congress, May 8, divided Michigan between N.W. Territory and Indiana Territory
Second election of representatives
1802 Detroit incorporated; first post office
1803 January, Michigan became part of Indiana Territory
1804 U.S. Land Office established in Detroit
1805 Detroit completely destroyed by fire
Michigan Territory organized; Detroit the capital
1807 Gov. William Hull's treaty with the Indians
1808 American Fur Company founded by John Jacob Astor
1809 Illinois Territory established; Fr. Gabriel Richard's printing press in Detroit
1812–1814 War with Great Britain
Hull surrendered Detroit, August 16, 1812
Perry's victory on Lake Erie, September 10, 1813
Battle of the Thames, October 5, 1813
Lewis Cass governor of Michigan Territory, 1813-1831
1815 British built fort on Drummond Island
Edward Tiffin's adverse report on Michigan
1816 Rev. John Monteith to Detroit; Indiana a state
1817 Catholepistemiad incorporated
The *Detroit Gazette*
Rush-Bagot Agreement
1818 Illinois a state; Wisconsin attached to Michigan
Walk-in-the-Water to Detroit from Buffalo
1819 Michigan sent a delegate to Congress
Treaty of Saginaw
1820 Governor Cass's exploring expedition; Treaty of Sault Sainte Marie
1821 Treaty of Chicago
1822 Fort Brady at Sault Sainte Marie; Fort Saginaw
1823 Michigan granted legislative council
1825 Erie Canal completed
All county officers, except judges, elected
1828 First Capitol, in Detroit, occupied
1830 Gen. John T. Mason territorial secretary
1831 Cass resigned to become Secretary of War
Stevens T. Mason acting governor
George B. Porter governor to 1834
1832 Black Hawk War
Cholera epidemic
Legislative Council petitioned Congress for an enabling act

1833 Treaty of Chicago
1834 Petition for enabling act rejected
Cholera epidemic
Land west of Lake Michigan to the Missouri River attached to Michigan
1835 The Toledo War
Constitution written and ratified
"State" government inaugurated
Stevens T. Mason governor
1836 Wisconsin Territory organized
First Convention of Assent at Ann Arbor, September 4; dissented
Second, the "Frost-bitten Convention," at Ann Arbor, December 14; assented
Erie and Kalamazoo Railroad began operating
Treaty of Washington
1837 Michigan admitted to the Union by act of Congress, January 26, 1837
Dr. Douglass Houghton first state geologist
Rev. John D. Pierce first superintendent of public instruction
1837–1838 Rebellion of 1837, or the Patriot War (Canada)
1841 Douglass Houghton's report on copper and iron in the Upper Peninsula
University of Michigan opened in Ann Arbor
Fort Wayne authorized; completed, 1851 (Detroit)
1842 Treaty of La Pointe; all Upper Peninsula cleared of Indian title
Detroit had first free, tax-supported school
1844 William A. Burt, surveyor, discovered iron ore on site of Negaunee
Fort Wilkins built at Copper Harbor
1847 Frankenmuth founded; beginning of German settlement in Saginaw Valley
1847–1887 Michigan first in the production of copper
1847 Holland founded by party from the Netherlands led by Rev. Albertus C. Van Raalte
1848 New Capitol at Lansing first occupied
King James Strang began Mormon settlement on Big Beaver Island
Lewis Cass Democratic candidate for President
1850 New state constitution
1851 First academic degree granted to a woman in Michigan
1852 State Normal School opened at Ypsilanti, the first teacher training school west of Albany
Michigan Central Railroad and Michigan Southern Railroad reached Chicago
First Ladies' Library Association in Michigan began in Kalamazoo

1854 First statewide convention of the Republican Party at Jackson
1855 Soo Ship Canal and locks opened to traffic
1856 Abraham Lincoln spoke at political rally in Kalamazoo, August 27
State received 3,000,000 acres of public land for grants to railroads
1857 Michigan Agricultural College, first agricultural college in the United States; now Michigan State University
First railroad in the Upper Peninsula, Marquette to Ishpeming
1860 Salt produced at Saginaw
1864 Bessemer steel produced at Wyandotte
1871 Holland and Manistee swept by fire
Forest fires destroyed timber in a wide swath from Lake Michigan to Lake Huron
1873 Portage Lake canals through Keweenaw Peninsula completed
1874 The Kalamazoo case decided in favor of high schools
1877 Ore shipped from Menominee Iron Range
1879 New state Capitol at Lansing occupied
Jo Labadie a leader in the Knights of Labor in Detroit
1881 Weitzel Lock built at Sault Sainte Marie by United States Government
1881 Michigan gave Soo Canal and locks to the United States Government
Railroad car ferry service begun between the two peninsulas
Destructive forest fires in the Thumb
1884 Ore shipped from Gogebic Iron Range
1885 Railroad to Lake Superior at Ashland, Wisconsin, encouraged increased production in Gogebic Iron Range
Lumber mill strike in the Saginaw Valley
Ten-hour law for workmen
Law limiting child labor
1886 Michigan College of Mines opened at Houghton
1888 Peak of lumber output in Michigan: more than four billion board feet
Montana takes from Michigan first position in production of copper
1889 Jo Labadie first president of the Michigan Federation of Labor
1890–1900 Michigan first in the production of iron ore
1890–1906 Henry B. Brown, Justice, United States Supreme Court
1891 The Australian ballot required by law
Grand Trunk Railroad tunnel between Port Huron, Michigan, and Sarnia, Ontario
1892 Car ferries of Ann Arbor Railroad connected Frankfort, Michigan, with Kewaunee, Wisconsin
1894 Strike of miners in Ironwood

1895 Central Michigan College of Education opened at Mount Pleasant
1896 First automobiles in Detroit: Charles B. King, March 6; Henry Ford, June 4
The Poe Lock at the Soo completed
1899 Northern Michigan College of Education opened at Marquette
Oldsmobile plant in Detroit; moved to Lansing in 1902
1901 Cadillac Motor Company organized
1903 Ford Motor Company organized
Packard Motor Company in Detroit
Buick Motor Company began making cars in Flint
1905 Western Michigan College of Education opened at Kalamazoo
State Highway Department organized
1908 General Motors Company organized by William C. Durant
Michigan's third constitution approved by voters
1909 First mile of concrete road built
Hudson Motor Company organized
1911 Chevrolet Motor Company organized; moved from Detroit to Flint in 1913
1912 Workmen's Compensation Act
1913 Strike of copper miners
1914 Dodge Brothers began producing automobiles
1916 Michigan prohibition amendment adopted
1918 State woman suffrage amendment adopted
1919 Fifty-million-dollar bond issue to build roads
1920 August, WWJ, *Detroit News* radio station, pioneer in United States, broadcasting regular programs
1922 Airplane line to Cleveland
1925 Large-scale production of petroleum began
Seats in State Senate and House reapportioned
Chrysler Motor Corporation organized
1929 Ambassador Bridge opened
1930 Tunnel between Detroit and Windsor, Ont., opened
1932 Forty-three per cent of workingmen in Michigan cities unemployed
State prohibition amendment repealed
1933 February 14, Michigan banking holiday began
Repeal of national prohibition amendment
Old age assistance act passed
Sales tax supplanted property tax as a source of revenue for the state
1936 UAW-CIO organized
1937 Sit-down strikes in Flint and in other cities
1938 Blue Water Bridge connecting Port Huron and Sarnia, Ont., opened
1940–1949 Frank Murphy, Justice, United States Supreme Court

1940 Merit system (civil service) amendment
32nd Division began intensive war training

1942–1943 32nd Division in New Guinea

1943 Race riots in Detroit
Postwar Advisory Conference of Republican leaders on Mackinac Island
Reapportionment of seats in State House of Representatives; no action in Senate
Beginning of grand jury investigation of corruption in the Legislature

1944 Gov. Thomas E. Dewey of New York, a native of Michigan, nominated by the Republicans for President

1944–1945 32nd Division in the Philippines

1945 Senator Arthur H. Vandenberg helped frame charter of the United Nations

1948 G. Mennen Williams elected governor. Served six terms

1950 Automobile manufacturers reached peak production of 6,673,000 cars. Profits also highest in history of the industry

1952 Constitutional amendment regarding reapportionment adopted

1953 June 8, tornadoes lashed state; 116 killed in Flint

1955 Celebration of centennial of Soo Canal
Record production of automobiles: 7,950,000

1956 April 3, tornadoes struck again; 18 killed in Grand Rapids area

1957 November, Mackinac Bridge opened to traffic

1959 Production of field crops highest in the history of state

1960 Houghton-Hancock Bridge completed
Four per cent sales tax amendment adopted
Preliminary amendment for calling constitutional convention adopted

GOVERNORS OF THE STATE OF MICHIGAN

Stevens Thomson Mason	Democrat	1835–1839
William Woodbridge	Whig	1840–1841
James Wright Gordon (Lt. Gov.)	Whig	1841
John S. Barry	Democrat	1842–1845
Alpheus Felch	Democrat	1846–1847
William L. Greenly (Lt. Gov.)	Democrat	1847
Epaphroditus Ransom	Democrat	1848–1849
John S. Barry	Democrat	1850–1851
Robert McClelland	Democrat	1852–1853
Andrew Parsons (Lt. Gov.)	Democrat	1853–1854
Kinsley S. Bingham	Republican	1855–1858
Moses Wisner	Republican	1859–1860
Austin Blair	Republican	1861–1864
Henry H. Crapo	Republican	1865–1868
Henry P. Baldwin	Republican	1869–1872
John J. Bagley	Republican	1873–1876
Charles M. Croswell	Republican	1877–1880
David H. Jerome	Republican	1881–1882
Josiah W. Begole	Fusion	1883–1884
Russell A. Alger	Republican	1885–1886
Cyrus G. Luce	Republican	1887–1890
Edwin B. Winans	Democrat	1891–1892
John T. Rich	Republican	1893–1896
Hazen S. Pingree	Republican	1897–1900
Aaron T. Bliss	Republican	1901–1904
Fred M. Warner	Republican	1905–1910
Chase S. Osborn	Republican	1911–1912
Woodbridge N. Ferris	Democrat	1913–1916
Albert E. Sleeper	Republican	1917–1920
Alexander J. Groesbeck	Republican	1921–1926
Fred W. Green	Republican	1927–1930
Wilber M. Brucker	Republican	1931–1932
William A. Comstock	Democrat	1933–1934

Frank D. Fitzgerald	Republican	1935–1936
Frank Murphy	Democrat	1937–1938
Frank D. Fitzgerald	Republican	1939
Luren D. Dickinson (Lt. Gov.)	Republican	1939–1940
Murray D. Van Wagoner	Democrat	1941–1942
Harry F. Kelly	Republican	1943–1946
Kim Sigler	Republican	1947–1948
G. Mennen Williams	Democrat	1949–1960
John B. Swainson	Democrat	1961–

A SELECTED LIST OF BOOKS ON MICHIGAN HISTORY

GENERAL HISTORIES

COOLEY, THOMAS M., *Michigan: A History of Governments*. Boston, 1892.
DUNBAR, WILLIS F., *Michigan Through the Centuries*. New York, 1955.
FULLER, GEORGE N., *Michigan, A Centennial History of the State and Its People*. Chicago, 1939.
Michigan, A Guide to the Wolverine State. New York, 1941.
MOORE, CHARLES, *History of Michigan*. Chicago, 1915.
QUAIFE, M. M. and GLAZER, SIDNEY, *Michigan: From Primitive Wilderness to Industrial Commonwealth*. New York, 1948.
UTLEY, HENRY M. and CUTCHEON, BYRON M., *Michigan as a Province, Territory, and State*. New York, 1906.

AUTOMOBILE INDUSTRY

COHN, DAVID, *Combustion on Wheels*. Boston, 1944.
EPSTEIN, RALPH, *The Automobile Industry*. Chicago, 1928.
LEWIS, EUGENE W., *Motor Memories, A Saga of Whirling Gears*. Detroit, 1947.
NEVINS, ALLAN, *Ford, Expansion and Challenge*. New York, 1957.
———, *Ford: The Times, the Man, the Company*. New York, 1954.
POUND, ARTHUR, *The Turning Wheel: The Story of General Motors*. New York, 1934.
RAE, JOHN B., *American Automobile Manufacturers*. Philadelphia, 1959.

EARLY HISTORY

GOODRICH, CALVIN, *The First Michigan Frontier*. Ann Arbor, 1940.
KELLOGG, LOUISE P. (ed.), *Early Narratives of the Northwest, 1634–99*. New York, 1917.
———, *The French Regime in Wisconsin and the Northwest*. Madison, 1925.
———, *The British Regime in Wisconsin and the Northwest*. Madison, 1935.
OGG, FREDERIC A., *The Old Northwest*. New Haven, 1919.

PARKMAN, FRANCIS, *La Salle and the Discovery of the Great West*. Boston, 1869.

PARKMAN, FRANCIS, *A Half Century of Conflict*. Boston, 1892.

———, *Montcalm and Wolfe*. Boston, 1884.

———, *Conspiracy of Pontiac*. Boston, 1851.

PECKHAM, HOWARD, *Pontiac and the Indian Uprising*. Princeton, 1947.

RUSSELL, NELSON V., *The British Regime in Michigan and the Old Northwest, 1760–1796*. Northfield, Minn., 1939.

EDUCATION

KNAUSS, JAMES O., *The First Fifty Years: Western Michigan College, 1903–1953*. Kalamazoo, 1953.

KUHN, MADISON, *Michigan State: The First Hundred Years*. East Lansing, 1955.

MOORE, VIVIAN LYON, *The First Hundred Years of Hillsdale College*. Ann Arbor, 1944.

MULDER, ARNOLD, *The Kalamazoo College Story*. Kalamazoo, 1958.

PUTNAM, DANIEL, *A History of the Michigan State Normal School*. Ypsilanti, 1899.

ROSALITA, SISTER MARY, *Education in Detroit Prior to 1850*. Lansing, 1928.

SAGENDORPH, KENT, *Michigan, The Story of the University*. New York, 1948.

SHAW, WILFRED B., *History of the University of Michigan*. New York, 1920.

STENENGA, PRESTON J., *Anchor of Hope*. Grand Rapids, 1954.

INDIANS

DENSMORE, FRANCES, *Chippewa Customs*. Washington, 1929.

GREENMAN, EMERSON F., *The Indians of Michigan*. Lansing, 1961.

HINDSDALE, WILBERT B., *Archaeological Atlas of Michigan*. Ann Arbor, 1931.

———, *The First People of Michigan*. Ann Arbor, 1930.

KINIETZ, W. VERNON, *The Indians of the Western Great Lakes, 1615–1760*. Ann Arbor, 1940.

QUIMBY, GEORGE I., *Indian Life in the Upper Great Lakes: 11,000 B.C. to A.D. 1800*. Chicago, 1960.

LUMBERING

BECK, EARL, *Songs of the Michigan Lumberjacks*. Ann Arbor, 1941.

HOLBROOK, STEWART H., *Holy Old Mackinaw*. New York, 1938.

MAYBEE, ROLLAND H., *Michigan's White Pine Era: 1840–1900*. Lansing, 1960.

WADSWORTH, WALLACE C., *Paul Bunyan and His Great Blue Ox*. New York, 1926.

MINING

BENEDICT, C. HARRY, *Red Metal*. Ann Arbor, 1952.
GATES, WILLIAM B., *Michigan Copper and Boston Dollars*. Cambridge, 1951.
HATCHER, HARLAN, *A Century of Iron and Men*. Indianapolis, 1950.
HAVIGHURST, WALTER, *Vein of Iron: The Pickands Mather Story*. Cleveland, 1958.
HOLBROOK, STEWART H., *Iron Brew*. New York, 1939.
MURDOCH, ANGUS, *Boom Copper*. New York, 1943.

POLITICS

DILLA, HARRIETTE, *Politics of Michigan, 1865–1878*. New York, 1912.
DORR, HAROLD M., *The Michigan Constitutional Conventions of 1835–1836*. Ann Arbor, 1940.
HARRIS, WILMER C., *Public Life of Zachariah Chandler, 1856–1875*. Chicago, 1917.
LIVINGSTON, WILLIAM, *A History of the Republican Party*. Detroit, 1900.
LOVETT, WILLIAM P., *Detroit Rules Itself*. Boston, 1930.
MILLSPAUGH, ARTHUR, *Party Organization and Machinery in Michigan Since 1890*. Baltimore, 1917.
PINGREE, HAZEN S., *Facts and Opinions*. Detroit, 1895.
SARASOHN, STEPHEN R. and VERA H., *Political Party Patterns in Michigan*. Detroit, 1957.
STOCKING, WILLIAM, *Under the Oaks*, Detroit, 1904.
STREETER, FLOYD, *Political Parties in Michigan, 1837–1860*. Lansing, 1918.

REGIONAL HISTORY

BOND, BEVERLY W., JR., *The Civilization of the Old Northwest, 1788–1812*. New York., 1934.
BULEY, R. CARLYLE, *The Old Northwest, 1815–40*. Indianapolis, 1950.
FOWLE, OTTO, *Sault Ste. Marie and Its Great Waterway*. New York, 1925.
HATCHER, HARLAN, *Lake Erie*. New York, 1945.
HEDRICK, ULYSSES P., *The Land of the Crooked Tree*. New York, 1948.
JAMISON, JAMES K., *This Ontonagon Country*. Ontonagon, 1939.
LANDON, FRED, *Lake Huron*. New York, 1944.
NUTE, GRACE L., *Lake Superior*. New York, 1944.
POWERS, PERRY F., *History of Northern Michigan*. Chicago, 1912.
QUAIFE, MILO M., *Lake Michigan*. New York, 1944.
SAWYER, ALVAH L., *A History of the Upper Peninsula of Michigan*. Chicago, 1911.
WOOD, EDWIN O., *Historic Mackinac*. New York, 1918.

RELIGION

MARQUIS, THOMAS G., *The Jesuit Missions*. Toronto, 1916.
PARÉ, GEORGE, *The Catholic Church in Detroit*. Detroit, 1951.
PILCHER, ELIJAH, *Protestantism in Michigan*. Detroit, 1878.
PITEZEL, JOHN H., *Lights and Shades of Missionary Life*. Cincinnati, 1859.

SPECIAL SUBJECTS

ARMSTRONG, LOUISE V., *We Too Are the People*. New York, 1938.
BALD, F. CLEVER, *Detroit's First American Decade*. Ann Arbor, 1948.
BINGAY, MALCOLM, *Detroit Is My Own Home Town*. Indianapolis, 1946.
BURTON, CLARENCE M., *The City of Detroit, Michigan, 1701–1922*. Chicago, 1922.
CARSON, GERALD, *Cornflake Crusade*. New York, 1957.
CATLIN, GEORGE B., *The Story of Detroit*. Detroit, 1923.
DUNBAR, WILLIS F., *Kalamazoo and How It Grew*. Kalamazoo, 1959.
FARMER, SILAS, *History of Detroit and Michigan*. Detroit, 1884.
FULLER, GEORGE N., *Economic and Social Beginnings of Michigan, 1805–1837*. Lansing, 1916.
GILPIN, ALEC R., *The War of 1812 in the Old Northwest*. East Lansing, 1958.
HAMIL, FRED C., *Michigan in the War of 1812*. Lansing, 1960.
HAVIGHURST, WALTER, *The Long Ships Passing*. New York, 1942.
HYMA, ALBERT, *Albertus C. Van Raalte and His Dutch Settlements in the United States*. Grand Rapids, 1947.
IVEY, PAUL, *The Pere Marquette Railroad Company*. Lansing, 1919.
JOHNSON, IDA A., *The Michigan Fur Trade*. Lansing, 1919.
KARPINSKI, LOUIS C., *Bibliography of the Printed Maps of Michigan, 1804–1880*. Lansing, 1931.
MARTIN, HELEN M., *They Need Not Vanish, A Discussion of the Natural Resources of Michigan*. Lansing, 1942.
MASON, PHILIP P., (ed.), *Schoolcraft's Expedition to Lake Itasca*. East Lansing, 1958.
MILLER, RAYMOND C., *Kilowatts at Work, A History of the Detroit Edison Company*. Detroit, 1957.
MULDER, ARNOLD, *Americans from Holland*. New York, 1947.
OSBORN, CHASE S. and STELLANOVA, *Schoolcraft, Longfellow, and Hiawatha*. Lancaster, Pa., 1942.
PETERSEN, EUGENE T., *Conservation of Michigan's Natural Resources*. Lansing, 1960.
PIETERS, ALEIDA J., *A Dutch Settlement in Michigan*. Grand Rapids, 1923.
QUAIFE, MILO M., *The Capture of Old Vincennes*. Indianapolis, 1927.
———, *The Kingdom of St. James*. New Haven, 1930.

Russell, John A., *The Germanic Influence in the Making of Michigan.* Detroit, 1927.

Williams, Frederick D., *Michigan Soldiers in the Civil War.* Lansing, 1960.

Williams, Mentor L. (ed.), *Schoolcraft's Narrative Journal of Travels.* East Lansing, 1953.

Wood, William C. H., *War with the United States.* Toronto, 1915.

Woodford, Frank B., *Father Abraham's Children: Michigan Episodes in the Civil War.* Detroit, 1961.

BIOGRAPHIES

Babst, Earl D. and Vander Velde, Lewis G. (eds.), *Michigan and the Cleveland Era.* Ann Arbor, 1948.

Barnard, Harry, *Independent Man: The Life of Senator James Couzens.* New York, 1958.

Campbell, Murray, and Hatton, Harrison, *Herbert H. Dow.* New York, 1951.

Ford, R. Clyde, and Hoyt, Charles O., *John D. Pierce.* Ypsilanti, 1905.

Haviland, Laura, A *Woman's Life Work.* Grand Rapids, 1887.

Hemans, Lawton T., *Life and Times of Stevens T. Mason.* Lansing, 1930.

Jamison, James K., *By Cross and Anchor: The Story of Frederick Baraga on Lake Superior.* Paterson, N. J., 1946.

Laut, Agnes C., *Cadillac.* New York, 1931.

Lewis, Martin D., *Lumberman from Flint: The Michigan Career of Henry H. Crapo, 1855–1869.* Detroit, 1958.

Lodge, John C., *I Remember Detroit.* Detroit, 1949.

McCarty, Dwight G., *The Territorial Governors of the Old Northwest.* Iowa City, 1910.

McLaughlin, Andrew C., *Lewis Cass.* Boston, 1891.

McNaughton, Frank, *Mennen Williams of Michigan.* New York, 1960.

Marquis, Samuel S., *Henry Ford, An Interpretation.* Boston, 1923.

Nute, Grace L., *Caesars of the Wilderness.* New York, 1943.

Osborn, Chase S., *The Iron Hunter.* New York, 1919.

Powell, Horace B., *The Original Has This Signature—W. K. Kellogg.* New York, 1956.

Quaife, Milo M. (ed.), *Alexander Henry's Travels and Adventures in Canada and the Indian Territories between 1760 and 1776.* Chicago, 1921.

Raymond, Ethel, *Tecumseh.* Toronto, 1915.

Richards, William C., *The Last Billionaire, Henry Ford.* New York, 1948.

Rintala, Edsel K., *Douglass Houghton,* Detroit, 1954.

Sagendorph, Kent, *Stevens Thomson Mason.* New York, 1947.

SIMONDS, WILLIAM ADAMS, *Edison, His Life, His Work, His Genius.* New York, 1934.

———, *Henry Ford, Motor Genius.* New York, 1929.

SMITH, SHIRLEY W., *James B. Angell: An American Influence.* Ann Arbor, 1954.

———, *Harry Burns Hutchins and the University of Michigan.* Ann Arbor, 1951.

SWARD, KEITH, *The Legend of Henry Ford.* New York, 1948.

VANDENBERG, ARTHUR H., JR., *The Private Papers of Senator Vandenberg.* Boston, 1952.

WILLIAMS, R. D., *The Honorable Peter White.* Cleveland, 1907.

WOODFORD, FRANK B., *Lewis Cass.* New Brunswick, N. J., 1950.

———, *Mr. Jefferson's Disciple: A Life of Judge Woodward.* East Lansing, 1953.

WOODFORD, FRANK B., and HYMA, ALBERT, *Frontier Ambassador: Gabriel Richard.* Detroit, 1958.

Acknowledgments and Picture Credits

The Michigan Historical Commission and the author both wish to express their deep appreciation for the assistance received in their search for, and acquisition of, the pictures used in *Michigan in Four Centuries.* The co-operation given by the Michigan institutions and individuals listed below went far beyond the ordinary courtesies extended to requests for help of this kind.

Public and private depositories: Alcona County Historical Society, Allegan County Historical Society, Automobile Manufacturers Assoc., Burton Historical Collection of the Detroit Public Library, Chrysler Corp., Detroit *Free Press,* Detroit Historical Museum, Detroit *News,* Detroit Planning Commission, East Mich. Tourist Council, Ford Motor Co. Archives, Ford Museum, Grand Rapids Public Library, Grand Rapids Public Museum, Holland Museum, Mich. Conservation Dept., Mich. Highway Dept., Mich. Historical Commission, Mich. State Library, Mich. Tourist Council, Monroe County Historical Society, Muskegon County Historical Society, Oldsmobile Corp., Presque Isle Historical Society, University of Mich. Historical Collections, University of Mich. News Service, University of Mich. Transportation Library, John Widdicomb Co. of Grand Rapids.

Chambers of Commerce: Adrian, Albion, Battle Creek, Alma, Bellaire, Corunna, Ellsworth, Fremont, Grand Marais, Drummond Island, Harbor Springs, Harrisville, Holland, Hillsdale, Jackson, Ludington, Menominee, Munising, Muskegon, Olivet, Pontiac, Port Huron, Quincy, Saginaw, Sault Sainte Marie, Sturgis, Tawas, Thompsonville, Traverse City, Union Pier, Vassar, Wakefield, Ypsilanti, Zeeland, Greenville.

Individuals who were especially helpful: Mrs. Ruth Abrams, Grand Rapids Public Library; Charles Bohler, Charles Floyd, and Norman Smith, Mich. Conservation Dept.; Murphy Cutler, William Langham, Mich. Highway Dept.; E. C. Corwin, John Widdicomb Co.; Frank Davis, East Mich. Tourist Assoc.; Frank DuMond, director, Grand Rapids Public Museum; Chester Ellison; Dr. Lawrence Frost, Monroe County Hist. Society; Guy Gage, Harbor Springs; John Grey, Mich. Tourist Council; Mrs. Nellie Hansen, Alcona County Hist. Society; Ellen Hathaway; Virgil Haynes, Harbor Springs; David Lewis, Ford Motor Co. News Dept.; Mrs. Esther Loughin, Mich. State Library; Leo Natanson, Transportation Library; Miss Margot Pearsoll, Detroit Historical Museum; Curran Russell, Manistee; Wynn Sears, Ford Motor Co. Archives; Mrs. Elleine H. Stones, chief, Burton Historical Collection; F. F. Williams, Lansing.

The following list shows the source from which each picture in this book was gathered. Credit is recorded picture by picture (left to right, top to bottom) and line by line (lines separated by dashes):*

Mining—Iron (I): Detroit *News*; Detroit *News*—Detroit *Free Press*—F.A.—Mich. State Library.

Mining—Iron (II): M.H. Comm.—M.H. Comm.; Detroit *News*—B.H.C.

Mining—Copper: Detroit *News*—G.R.L.; T.C.—Detroit *News*; Detroit *News*.

Forts in Michigan: M.H.C.—M.H.C.—M.H. Comm.—Conservation Dept.

Lumbering (I): B.H.C.; C. Russell Coll.—C. Russell Coll.; Guy Gage Coll.—W. J. Brinen Lumber Co.; G.R.L.

Lumbering (II): G.R.L.—G.R.L.; C. Russell Coll.—G.R.L.—Conservation Dept.; Grand Rapids Public Museum.

Lumbering (III): C. Russell Coll.—C. Russell Coll.; C. Russell Coll. —Conservation Dept.; T.C.—B.H.C.

Salt Mining: All pictures C. Russell Coll.

Education: M.H.C.; M.H.C.—G.R.L.—M.H.C.; M.H.C.

Lake Transportation (I): M.H. Comm.—Transportation Library—B.H.C.; M.H.C.—C. Russell Coll.

Lake Transportation (II): Transportation Library—Detroit *Free Press* —B.H.C.; Highway Dept.

Civil War: M.H. Comm.; M.H.C.—M.H.C.; M.H.C.

Railroads and Interurbans: G.R.L.—Guy Gage Coll.; G.R.L.—Transportation Library; M.H.C.

Politics and Government: Chester Ellison; M.H.C.—Shiawassee *News* —T.C.

City and Town Life: M.H.C.—Mich. State Library—Holland Museum —G.R.L.; Guy Gage Coll.

Soo Canal: M.H.C.—T.C.—Highway Dept.—Highway Dept.

Agriculture (I): Conservation Dept.—M.H. Comm.—C. Russell Coll. —F. F. Williams Coll.—Mich. Dept. of Agriculture.

Agriculture (II): All pictures Mich. Dept. of Agriculture.

Agriculture (III): Mich. Dept. of Agriculture; Shiawassee *News*—Highway Dept.—Alma C. of C.; Saginaw C. of C.

Conservation: All pictures Mich. Conservation Dept.

Bridges and Ferries: G.R.L.; John Longyear Coll. at M.H.C.—F.A.; G.R.L.—Transportation Library.

Travel: M.H.C.; B.H.C.—Transportation Library—M.H. Comm.—M.H. Comm.

Highway Development: Highway Dept.; Highway Dept.—F.A.—F.A.; F.A.

* The following abbreviations are used: Automobile Manufacturers Association: A.M.A.; Michigan Historical Commission: M.H. Comm.; Michigan Historical Collections: M.H.C.; Burton Historical Collection: B.H.C.; Grand Rapids Library: G.R.L.; Tourist Council: T.C.; Ford Motor Co. Archives: F.A.; Collection: Coll.; Chamber of Commerce: C. of C.

Entertainment: G.R.L.—M.H.C.; Detroit *Free Press*—Virgil D. Haynes, Harbor Springs C. of C.; A.M.A.

Sports: Detroit *News;* Univ. of Mich. News Service—Detroit *Free Press* —Detroit *News;* Detroit *Free Press.*

Commercial Fishing: B.H.C.—Mich. Conservation Dept.; T.C.—Conservation Dept.; Mich. Conservation Dept.

Automobiles (I): A.M.A.; A.M.A.—F.A.—A.M.A.; M.H. Comm.

Automobiles (II): A.M.A.—F.A.—A.M.A.—Chrysler Motor Co.

Automotive Industry: F.A.; Dodge Motor Co.—Chrysler Motor Co.—F.A.; F.A.

Industry in Michigan (I): Saginaw C. of C.—Ypsilanti Board of Commerce; Abrams Photo Co.—Port Huron C. of C.; T.C.

Industry in Michigan (II): Guy Gage Coll.; C. Russell Coll.—John Widdicomb Co.; John Widdicomb Co.—Mich. Conservation Dept.; T.C.

Tourist Industry: All pictures Mich. Tourist Council.

INDEX